Environmental Law and Policy

THIRD EDITION

Elaine L. Hughes
Alastair R. Lucas
William A. Tilleman

2003
EMOND MONTGOMERY PUBLICATIONS LIMITED
TORONTO, CANADA

Printed in Canada.

Edited, designed, and typeset by WordsWorth Communications, Toronto.

We acknowledge the financial support of the Government of Canada through the Book Publishing Industry Development Program (BPIDP) for our publishing activities.

National Library of Canada Cataloguing in Publication

Environmental law and policy / [edited by] Elaine L. Hughes, Alastair R. Lucas, William A. Tilleman. — 3rd ed.

Accompanied by an online index.
ISBN 1-55239-120-5

1. Environmental law—Canada. I. Hughes, Elaine L. (Elaine Lois), 1959-
II. Lucas, Alastair R. III. Tilleman, William A.

KE3619.E585 2003   344.71′046   C2003-904403-3
KF3775.ZA2E585 2003

Preface

In preparing the third edition, the editors continue to be convinced that environmental law and policy is one of the most important areas of law to be studied today. With the heightened national and international concern over the environment has come a need for more, and better, education in relation to environmental matters in all sectors. Students and teachers of law and related disciplines share this concern. In this context, the editors have attempted to develop a set of basic environmental law and policy materials that would be useful to students and teachers alike.

Environmental law and policy is a vast subject area. Our approach, therefore, was to continue to try to identify the major directions that the law has taken, and survey these in the materials. In the process, we have attempted to provide learning materials in relation to as many of the major issues in environmental law as feasible in a work of this length. We have attempted to retain a national focus and to include perspectives from each region of Canada where possible. In planning the book—originally and in the subsequent editions—we attempted to use materials that were applicable in all regions, or that served as useful illustrations of an approach common to several jurisdictions. We have tried to provide a sampling of statutes, regulations, guidelines, cases, government policy, and academic writings in the area. We have also tried to illustrate the links between environmental law and the many social and legal issues to which it relates, including science, politics, the economy, and some basic ethical and philosophical concerns. An important objective was to ensure that the materials can accommodate a variety of perspectives and teaching approaches. If we have been able to provide some fundamental knowledge of the major legal initiatives, and a base for future learning in more specialized areas of environmental law, we will have accomplished our goal.

In the third edition, we have attempted to respond to the suggestions of teachers and students who have used the book during the past decade, and to our own critiques as users of the book. We have also been sensitive to changing concerns and emerging issues and perspectives. All of the second edition chapters have been updated. Of course, as with many subjects, the Web now provides a ready source of continuous updates to the material; however, the fluid nature of Web site citations has meant that we have retained traditional citations by which materials can be located whenever possible. An online index to this edition can be found on the Web at http://www.emp.on.ca/elp3/index.html.

Without the assistance of some of the most knowledgeable experts and academics across the country, this project would have once again been impossible. As fellow educators, all our contributors have wrestled with the need for good teaching materials in an area that is changing rapidly and regularly, where the issues seem to proliferate instead of stabilize. While we have done our best to ensure that the materials are current and that we have not omitted any major developments, we hope that readers of this edition, as with those of the first two editions, will pass on their comments and suggestions to us.

A grant from the Rocky Mountain Mineral Law Foundation once again supported critical third-edition research and editorial assistance. For this support, we are deeply grateful. We also express our sincere appreciation to the following individuals, who worked beyond the call of duty to assist us in our third-edition editorial duties: Omolara Oladipo, LLM (research assistance); Kim Cordeiro (manuscript preparation); the staff of the faculties of law at both the University of Alberta and the University of Calgary; and our family members, who have continued to encourage and support our work.

Elaine L. Hughes
Alastair R. Lucas
William A. Tilleman

March 2003

Author Biographies

Bowden, Marie Ann

Professor Bowden received her BA (Hons.) from Mount Allison University in 1976, her LLB from Queen's University in 1979, and her LLM from Osgoode Hall Law School in 1981. She has been with the University of Saskatchewan, Faculty of Law, since 1981. Her major teaching subjects are environmental law, property law, legal writing and research, and municipal law. She has a number of publications to her credit, including works on environmental impact assessment, property law, water law, and the regulation of intensive livestock operations.

Castrilli, Joseph F.

Joseph F. Castrilli practises in the areas of environmental and natural resources law. He graduated from the Faculty of Law, Queen's University, in 1984, was called to the Ontario bar in 1986 and the British Columbia bar in 1998. He obtained an LLM in environmental and natural resources law in 1997 from the Northwestern School of Law of Lewis and Clark College in Portland, Oregon. He has appeared as counsel before various federal and provincial administrative tribunals and courts on matters such as air, water, solid, and hazardous waste management; land-use planning; contaminated lands; environmental assessment; pesticides; and toxic substances. He has acted as consultant, adviser, or counsel to the Office of the Auditor General of Canada, the Commissioner of Environment and Sustainable Development, the North American Commission for Environmental Cooperation, the International Joint Commission, the federal Department of the Environment, the Law Reform Commission of Canada, the Office of the Environmental Commissioner of Ontario, and the Niagara Escarpment Commission on various environmental issues. He also is a former research director with the Canadian Environmental Law Association. He has written extensively in the areas of environmental and natural resources law and his articles have appeared in numerous law journals, texts, and professional publications. He has been a special lecturer in environmental law at the faculties of law, Queen's University and the University of Toronto, a lecturer in environmental law at Osgoode Hall Law School, York University, and a visiting professor and an instructor in environmental policy at the School of Public Administration, Queen's University. He has been an instructor in public law (administrative law and Charter remedies) and civil litigation in the Law Society of Upper Canada—Bar Admission Course. He also has been a member of the environmental law section executive of the Canadian Bar Association (Ontario) as well as a member of the Ontario Environmental Assessment Board Advisory Committee.

Charles, William

William Charles is a professor emeritus and a former dean of the Faculty of Law at the Dalhousie Law School. He currently serves on several provincial administrative boards and in the past has been chair of the Environmental Assessment Board of Nova Scotia and chair of the Law Reform Commission.

Charles received his LLB from Dalhousie University in 1958 and subsequently acquired his LLM from Harvard University in 1960 and from Michigan in 1971. He was awarded an honorary LLD from Dalhousie in 2001. He is a member of the Nova Scotia bar and was appointed a QC in 1983.

A teacher of law for some 34 years, Professor Charles retired from full-time teaching in 1994 and part-time teaching in 1997. His main areas of teaching included legislation, torts, environmental law, and remedies. Much of his research and writing has been in the area of tort law and includes a short text on the *Assessment of Damages in Personal Injury Cases* (Carswell, 1990). He has contributed material to other legal publications including *Water Law in Canada: The Atlantic Provinces*, G.V. LaForest and Associates (1973), *Studies in Canadian Tort Law*, L. Klar, ed. (1977), co-authoring *Evidence and the Charter of Rights and Freedoms* (Butterworths, 1989), as well as periodical articles.

His most recent activities have involved judicial court reform in Nova Scotia, the Caribbean, and Ethiopia.

Duncan, Linda F.

Linda Duncan is an international consultant on environmental law and compliance. She is currently advising the government of Bangladesh in the development and implementation of their environmental law and compliance system. Previously held positions include: head, Law and Enforcement Cooperation, North American Commission for Environmental Cooperation; assistant deputy minister, Renewable Resources, Yukon; assistant professor and coordinator of the Dalhousie Marine Environmental Law Program (MELP), Dalhousie Law School; senior legal adviser to the CIDA-sponsored Environment Development in Indonesia Project (EMDI); chief of enforcement, Environmental Protection, Environment Canada; founding executive director, Alberta Environmental Law Centre; and counsel and environmental law consultant in environmental, resources, and aboriginal matters. She has written extensively in the area of environmental enforcement and compliance.

Elgie, Stewart A.G.

Stewart Elgie has worked as an environmental lawyer and professor since 1988. He received his LLM from Harvard University in 1988 and his LLB from the University of Western Ontario in 1986. In 2001, he received the Law Society of Upper Canada medal for exceptional contributions to law.

He is currently an associate professor at the University of Ottawa, Faculty of Law (2003), and has worked as law professor, specializing in environmental and natural resources law, at Osgoode Hall Law School (part time, 1997-2002), the University of British Columbia (part time, 1993-1996), and the University of Alberta (full time, 1990-1992). He has published numerous articles in academic and non-academic journals on a variety of environmental policy and law subjects.

From 2001 to 2003, Elgie was the executive director of the Canadian Boreal Trust, a non-profit organization dedicated to conserving Canada's northern boreal ecosystems. Prior to that, from 1992 to 2001, he was the founder and managing lawyer of the Sierra Legal Defence Fund (SLDF), a national non-profit environmental law organization. In that role, he served as counsel on a number of precedent-setting public interest environmental cases across Canada—including four successful appearances before the Supreme Court of Canada on major environmental/constitutional cases.

Since 1996, Elgie has served as a member of Canada's National Advisory Committee on the North American Agreement for Environmental Cooperation (the NAFTA Side Agreement), which he chaired from 1996 to 2001. He also has served as a member of the federal government's Endangered Species Legislative Task Force, and has spearheaded the national campaign for federal endangered species legislation.

Prior to founding SLDF, he worked as an environmental lawyer in Alaska, including litigating against Exxon over the *Valdez* oil spill.

Giroux, Lorne

LLL (Laval) 1968, LLM (Harvard) 1970, Docteur en droit (Laval) 1976. Professeur titulaire, Université Laval, depuis 1980; professeur grege, Université Laval, 1970-1975. Membre du Barreau du Quebec. Sujets d'enseignment : droit de l'aménagement du territoire, droit municipal. Publications : *Aspects juridiques du règlement de zonage au Québec*, PUL, Quebec, 1979; « Les pouvoirs des corporations municipales locales en matière d'aménagement », dans M. Poirier, ed., *Droit québécois de l'aménagement du territoire*, Éditions Revue de droit, Université de Sherbrooke, Sherbrooke, 1983, 71; "Property Rights, Municipal Corporations and Judicial Review" (1984) vol. 25 *Cahiers de droit* 617.

Halley, Paule

Paule Halley holds an LLB (Université Laval), an LLM (Université Laval), and an LLD (Université du Québec à Montréal). She is an associate professor with the Université Laval, Faculty of Law, and a member of the Québec Bar Association. In 2002, she was appointed Canada Research Chair in Environmental Law. She teaches environmental law and criminal law and has written numerous articles on a variety of environmental law and policy topics. She is author of *Le droit pénal de l'environnement* (Yvon Blais, 2001), *La loi fédérale sur les pêches et son régime pénal de protection environnementale* (1992), *Le droit, l'environnement et la déréglementation* (1997), and is currently a member of the advisory board of the Kativik Environmental Advisory Committee (Nunavik), the Institut québécois des hautes études internationales, le Groupe d'études inuites et circumpolaires, and the Centre québécois du droit de l'environnement.

Hughes, Elaine L.

Elaine Hughes received her BSc (Zoology) from the University of Alberta in 1980, her LLB from the same institution in 1984, and an LLM in environmental law from the University of British Columbia in 1988.

Hughes is a professor with the Faculty of Law at the University of Alberta, and an inactive member of the Law Society of Alberta. She teaches environmental, international environmental, animal welfare, and natural resources law, and has published numerous articles in the areas of domestic and international environmental law. She currently is a member of the advisory board of the Environmental Research and Studies Centre at the University of Alberta, acts as co-chair of the environmental law subsection of the Canadian Association of Law Teachers, and is a member of the board of the Canadian Council on International Law.

Kwasniak, Arlene J.

Arlene J. Kwasniak has practised law in Edmonton, Alberta since 1981. She was with the Environmental Law Centre from 1991 to 2002. Since 2002 she has been in private practice focusing on environmental, conservation, and natural resources law. Kwasniak also teaches environmental law at the Faculty of Law, University of Calgary. She has published books and articles, has served on numerous advisory committees and boards, and has given many talks in the areas of environmental, conservation, and natural resources law and policy. Her books include *Public Rangeland Law and Policy* (1991), *A Conservation Easement Guide to Alberta* (1997), *Reconciling Political and Ecosystem Borders: A Legal Map* (1998), and *Alberta Wetlands: A Law and Policy Guide* (2001).

Kwasniak holds a BSc from Eastern Michigan University, an MA in philosophy from Wayne State University, an LLB from the University of Alberta, and a LLM in environmental and natural resources law from Lewis and Clark, Northwestern School of Law.

Lucas, Alastair

Alastair Lucas is professor of law and chair of natural resources law at the Faculty of Law, and adjunct professor of environmental science at the University of Calgary. He is also director of the University of Calgary—Latin American Energy Organization Energy and Environmental Law Project. Recent publications include *Human Rights in Natural Resource Development: Public Participation in the Sustainable Development of Mining and Energy Resources* (with Donald Zillman and George Pring) (Oxford University Press, 2002). He is co-editor of Butterworths' *Canadian Environmental Law* and author of various articles on energy, environment, and natural resources law. He is a special legal advisor to the North American Commission for Environmental Cooperation.

Mickelson, Karin

Karin Mickelson holds an AB (Duke University), an LLB (University of British Columbia), and an LLM (Columbia University). She is an associate professor at the Faculty of Law, University of British Columbia, and has taught courses on international environmental law, public international law, environmental law, real property, and legal theory. Her current research focuses on the impact of developing countries on the evolution of international environmental law.

Muldoon, Paul

Paul Muldoon has an MA from McMaster University and an LLM from McGill University. He completed his undergraduate law degree at the University of Ottawa and his undergraduate arts degree at Wilfrid Laurier University.

Muldoon is the executive director of the Canadian Environmental Law Association (CELA). Founded in 1970, CELA is a legal aid clinic in the province of Ontario that undertakes environmental litigation and law reform activities. Prior to joining CELA in early 1994, he practised law representing environmental and other public interest groups on a variety of matters.

He has written articles and books on a number of topics, including environmental rights, toxic water pollution, biotechnology, and international environmental law. Muldoon is author of the *Law of Intervention* and co-author of *The Environmental Bill of Rights: A Practical Guide* (Emond Montgomery, 1995) and has sat on various advisory boards, such as the science advisory board to the International Joint Commission.

Rees, William E.

William Rees has taught at the University of British Columbia since 1969-1970 and is currently professor and director of the university's School of Community and Regional Planning. His teaching and research emphasize the public policy and planning implications of global environmental trends and the necessary ecological conditions for sustainable socioeconomic development. Much of his work is in the realm of ecological economics and human ecology. He is best known for his invention of "ecological footprint analysis," a quantitative tool that estimates humanity's ecological impact on the ecosphere in terms of appropriated ecosystem (land and water) area. This research has helped to reopen the issue of human carrying capacity as a consideration in the sustainable development debate. Rees has been invited to lecture on his work across Canada, as well as in Australia, Austria, China, Germany, Great Britain, Japan, Mexico, the Netherlands, Norway, Indonesia, Italy, Korea, Japan, the former Soviet Union, Spain, Sweden, and the United States. He was awarded a UBC Killam Research Prize (1996) in acknowledgment of his research achievements.

Rounthwaite, Ian

Ian Rounthwaite has a BA (University of Toronto, 1974), an LLB (University of Windsor, 1977), and an LLM (University of Michigan, 1979). He is currently a professor at the University of Calgary, Faculty of Law. Prior to joining the Calgary faculty in 1981, he taught as an assistant professor at the University of Saskatchewan (1979-1981), a sessional lecturer at the University of Windsor (1979), and a teaching fellow at that same institution (1977-1978). He is a member of the Law Society of Alberta. His teaching subjects include property law, environmental law, and environmental ethics.

Saunders, J. Owen

Owen Saunders is executive director of the Canadian Institute of Resources Law and adjunct professor in the Faculty of Law at the University of Calgary, where he teaches public international law. Professor Saunders studied economics at St. Francis Xavier University and Queen's University, and holds law degrees from Dalhousie University and the University of London (London School of Economics and Political Science). His research interests have included international environmental law, law and economics, trade law, and constitutional law. He has written numerous articles on the legal aspects of natural resources management, and has acted as an adviser to federal, provincial, and foreign governments, as well as international organizations, on resources management and environmental issues.

Tilleman, William A., QC

William A. Tilleman is an adjunct professor of law, the first and only chair of the Alberta Environmental Appeal Board (1993-2004), and a member of the board of governors, University of Calgary. Tilleman studied advanced negotiation at Harvard Law School and holds a BComm (University of Calgary), an LLB (University of Alberta), a JD (Brigham Young University), and an LLM and JSD from Columbia University. He is qualified to practise law in Canada and the United States, and has represented industry and government at the federal and provincial level on environmental matters. Current work includes counsel for the Nunavut Impact Review Board and Nunavut Water Board. Books include *Environmental Law and Policy* (Emond Montgomery, 3d ed., co-editor) and *Dictionary of Environmental Law and Science* (Emond Montgomery, 1994).

Tollefson, Chris

Chris Tollefson is an associate professor at the University of Victoria, Faculty of Law, and founding executive director of the UVic Environmental Law Centre. He has published on a wide variety of environmental, natural resource, citizen participation, and trade/environment-related topics. His books include *The Wealth of Forests: Markets, Regulation and Sustainable Forestry* (1998) and *Cleanair.ca: A Citizen's Action Guide* (2000). He is the past chair of the Sierra Legal Defence Fund and is currently a member of the National Advisory Committee to the Canadian governmental signatories to the North American Agreement on Environmental Cooperation.

Valiante, Marcia

Marcia Valiante is a professor at the Faculty of Law, University of Windsor, teaching in the areas of environmental law, international environmental law, land-use planning law, and property law. She has BSc and BA degrees from the University of New Hampshire, an LLB from Osgoode Hall Law School, and an LLM from Queen's University, and is a member of the Law Society of Upper Canada. She has practised law and works with a number of community groups on local environmental issues. Her research interests include public participation in environmental decision making, environmental assessment and planning, and Great Lakes environmental issues.

VanderZwaag, David

David VanderZwaag is a professor at Dalhousie Law School and the School for Resource and Environmental Studies, and a member of the Environmental Law Commission, World Conservation Union. Teaching in the areas of torts, environmental law, and international environmental law, he has been past director of Dalhousie's Marine and Environmental Law Program and a co-director of an interdisciplinary graduate program in marine affairs. He has published over 50 articles relating to marine and environmental management. His book publications include *Canada and Marine Environmental Protection: Charting a Legal Course Towards Sustainable Development* (Kluwer Law International, 1995), *Canadian Ocean Law and Policy* (editor) (Butterworths, 1992), and *The Challenge of Arctic Shipping: Science, Environmental Assessment and Human Values* (co-editor) (McGill–Queen's University Press, 1990). He is regional editor for the Atlantic provinces of *Canadian Environmental Law*, 2d ed. VanderZwaag holds graduate degrees from Princeton Theological Seminary (MDiv), the University of Arkansas School of Law (JD), Dalhousie Law School (LLM), and the University of Wales (PhD).

Acknowledgments

This book, like others of its nature, contains extracts from published materials. We have attempted to request permission from and to acknowledge in the text all sources of such material. We wish to make specific reference here to the authors, publishers, journals, and institutions that have been generous in giving their permission to reproduce works in this text. If we have inadvertently overlooked any acknowledgment, we offer our sincere apologies and undertake to rectify the omission in any further editions.

Aboriginal Self-Government: The Government of Canada's Approach to Implementation of the Inherent Right and the Negotiation of Self-Government (Ottawa: Minister of Indian Affairs and Northern Development, 1995).

T. Alcoze, "Our Common Future: Native Land Use and Sustainable Development," in The Guelph Seminars on Sustainable Development (Guelph, ON: University of Guelph, 1990).

R. Anand and I.G. Scott, QC, "Financing Public Participation in Environmental Decision Making" (1982) vol. 60 *Canadian Bar Review* 81.

D.S. Ardia, "Does the Emperor Have No Clothes? Enforcement of International Laws Protecting the Marine Environment" (1998) *Michigan Journal of International Law* 497. Reprinted with permission.

G.M. Bankobeza et al., "Environmental Law" (2001) vol. 35, no. 2 *International Lawyer* 659. © ABA Publishing. Reprinted by permission.

B.J. Barton, R.T. Franson, and A.R. Thompson, *A Contract Model for Pollution Control* (Vancouver: Westwater Research Centre, 1984), c. V.

J. Benedickson, *Environmental Law* (Toronto: Irwin Law, 2002).

T.A. Berwick, "Responsibility and Liability for Environmental Damage: A Roadmap for International Environmental Regimes" (1998) vol. 10 *Georgetown International Environmental Law Review* 257. Reprinted with permission of the publisher, Georgetown International Environmental Law Review © 1998.

P.W. Birnie and A.E. Boyle, *International Law and the Environment*, 2d ed. (Oxford: Oxford University Press, 2002).

R.D. Bullard, "Anatomy of Environmental Racism and the Environmental Justice Movement," in R.D. Bullard, ed., *Confronting Environmental Racism: Voices from the Grassroots* (Boston: South End Press, 1993), 15.

L.K. Caldwell, "Introduction: Implementing an Ecological Systems Approach to Basinwide Management," in L.K. Caldwell, ed., *Perspectives on Ecosystem Management for the Great Lakes—A Reader* (Albany, NY: State University of New York Press, 1988).

J. Cameron, "Future Directions in International Environmental Law: Precaution, Integration and Non-State Actors" (1996) vol. 19 *Dalhousie Law Journal* 122.

Canadian Council of Ministers of the Environment, A Canada-Wide Accord on Environmental Harmonization (available online at http://www.ccme.ca/assets/pdf/accord_harmonization_e.pdf.

Canadian Council of Ministers of the Environment, Inspections and Enforcement Sub-Agreement (Winnipeg: CCME, May 2001) (available online at http://www.ccme.ca/assets/pdf/insp_enfsubagr_e.pdf).

Canadian Environmental Law Association and Ontario College of Family Physicians, "Environmental Standard Setting and Children's Health" (Toronto: CELA and OCFP Environmental Health Committee—Children's Health Project, 2000).

J.E. Carroll, *Environmental Diplomacy—An Examination and a Prospective of Canadian–US Transboundary Relations* (Ann Arbor, MI: University of Michigan Press, 1983). © The University of Michigan Press. Reproduced by permission.

L.W. Cole, "Foreword: A Jeremiad on Environmental Justice and the Law" (1995) vol. 14 *Stanford Environmental Law Journal* ix. Copyright 1995, Board of Trustees of the Leland Stanford Junior University. Reprinted with permission.

Compliance and Enforcement Policy for the Canadian Environmental Protection Act, 1999 (Ottawa: Environment Canada, 2001) (available on the Web at http://www.ec.gc.ca/CEPARegistry/documents/policies/candepolicy/toc.cfm).

G. Cormick et al., *Building Consensus for a Sustainable Future: Putting Principles into Practice* (Ottawa: National Round Table on the Environment and Economy, 1996).

A. D'Amato and K. Engel, eds. *International Environmental Law Anthology* (Cincinnati: Anderson, 1996). © 1996 Anderson Publishing Company. Reprinted with permission.

E.F. Dukes and K. Firehock, *Collaboration: A Guide for Environmental Advocates* (Charlottesville, VA: University of Virginia, Wilderness Society, and National Audubon Society, 2001).

L.F. Duncan, "Effective Environmental Enforcement: The Missing Link to Sustainable Development" (LLM thesis, Dalhousie University, Dalhousie Law School, 1999), at 13-18 (edited).

L.F. Duncan, *Enforcing Environmental Law: A Guide to Private Prosecution* (Edmonton: Environmental Law Centre, 1990). Reprinted with permission.

S.A.G. Elgie, "Injunctions, Ancient Forests and Irreparable Harm: A Comment on Western Canada Wilderness Committee v. A.G. British Columbia" (1991) vol. 25 *UBC Law Review* 387.

D.P. Emond, "The Greening of Environmental Law" (1991) vol. 36 *McGill Law Journal* 742. Reprinted with permission.

Environmental Commissioner of Ontario, *Having Regard: Annual Report 2000-2001* (Toronto: ECO, 2001). Reprinted with permission.

Executive Resource Group for the Ontario Ministry of the Environment, *Managing the Environment: A Review of Best Practices*, vol. 1 (Ontario: Ministry of the Environment, 2001). © Queen's Printer for Ontario, 2001. Reproduced with permission.

B.C. Field and N.D. Olewiler, *Environmental Economics*, 1st Canadian ed. (Toronto: McGraw-Hill Ryerson, 1995). © 1995 McGraw-Hill Ryerson Limited. Reproduced with permission

Fisheries Act, Habitat Protection and Pollution Prevention Provisions, Compliance and Enforcement Policy (Ottawa: Government of Canada, July 2001).

M.A.H. Franson, R.T. Franson, and A.R. Lucas, *Environmental Standards* (Edmonton: Environment Council of Alberta, 1982).

C. Giagnocavo and H. Goldstein, "Law Reform or World Re-form: The Problem of Environmental Rights" (1990) vol. 35 *McGill Law Journal* 345. Reprinted with permission.

D. Gibson, "Constitutional Entrenchment of Environmental Rights," in N. Duple, ed., *Le droit à la qualité de l'environnement* (Montreal: Quebec Amerique, 1988), 275. Reprinted with permission.

N. Gunningham and P. Grabosky, with D. Sinclair, *Smart Regulation: Designing Environmental Policy* (Oxford: Oxford University Press, 1998). Reprinted by permission of Oxford University Press.

G. Hardin, "The Tragedy of the Commons" (1968) vol. 162 *Science* 1243. Reprinted with permission.

K. Harrison, "Is Cooperation the Answer? Canadian Environmental Enforcement in Comparative Context" (Spring 1995) vol. 14, no. 2 *Journal of Policy Analysis and Management* 221. © John Wiley & Sons, Inc. 1995. This material is used by permission of John Wiley & Sons, Inc.

R.L. Heilbroner, *Understanding Microeconomics*, 2d ed. (Englewood Cliffs, NJ: Prentice-Hall, 1972).

E.L. Hughes, "Fishwives and Other Tails: Ecofeminism and Environmental Law" (1995) vol. 8, no. 2 *Canadian Journal of Women and the Law* 502. © 1995 University of Toronto Press Incorporated. Reprinted by permission.

E.L. Hughes and D. Iyalomhe, "Substantive Environmental Rights in Canada" (1998-99) vol. 30, no. 2 *Ottawa Law Review* 229.

International Law Association, Helsinki Rules on the Uses of the Waters of International Rivers (August 1966), report of the 52nd Conference.

International Law Association, Montreal Rules on Water Pollution in an International Drainage Basin (August 1982), report of the 60th Conference.

R. Kapashesit and M. Klippenstein, "Aboriginal Group Rights and Environmental Protection" (1991) vol. 36 *McGill Law Journal* 925. Reprinted with permission.

R.A. Kelly and D.K. Alper, *Transforming British Columbia's War in the Woods: An Assessment of the Vancouver Island Regional Negotiation Process of the Commission on Resources and Environment* (Victoria: University of Victoria Institute for Dispute Resolution, 1995). Reprinted with permission.

M. Kheel, "License To Kill: An Ecofeminist Critique of Hunters' Discourse," in C. Adams and J. Donovan, eds., *Animals and Women: Feminist Theoretical Explorations* (Durham, NC: Duke University Press, 1995). Reprinted with permission.

J.P. Kimmel Jr., "Disclosing the Environmental Impact of Human Activities: How a Federal Pollution Control Program Based on Individual Decision Making and Consumer Demand Might Accomplish the Environmental Goals of the 1970s in the 1990s" (1989) vol. 138 *University of Pennsylvania Law Review* 505. Reprinted with permission.

Y. King, "The Ecology of Feminism and the Feminism of Ecology," in J. Plant, ed., *Healing the Wounds: The Promise of Ecofeminism* (Toronto: Between the Lines, 1989). Reprinted with permission.

J.L. Knetsch, "Economics, Losses, Fairness and Resource-Use Conflicts," in M. Ross and J.O. Saunders, eds., *Growing Demands on a Shrinking Heritage: Managing Resource-Use Conflicts* (Calgary: Canadian Institute of Resources Law, 1992). Reprinted with permission.

P.L. Lallas, "The Role of Process and Participation in the Development of Effective International Environmental Agreements: A Study of the Global Treaty on Persistent Organic Pollutants (POPs)" (2000/2002) vol. 19 *UCLA Journal of Environmental Law and Policy* 83.

A.R. Lucas, "The New Environmental Law," in R. Watts and D. Brown, eds., *Canada: The State of Federation: 1989* (Kingston, ON: Queen's University, Institute for Intergovernmental Affairs, 1990).

A.R. Lucas, "Voluntary Initiatives for Greenhouse Gas Reduction" (2000) vol. 10 *Journal of Environmental Law and Practice* 89.

C. McCool, "Costs in Public Interest Litigation: A Comment on Professor Tollefson's Article, When the 'Public Interest' Loses: The Liability of Public Interest Litigants for Adverse Cost Awards" (1996) vol. 30 *UBC Law Review* 309.

D.G. McFetridge, "The Economic Approach to Environmental Issues," in G.B. Doern ed., *The Environmental Imperative: Market Approaches to the Greening of Canada* (Toronto: C.D. Howe Institute, 1990), 84. Reprinted with permission.

E. McWhinney, "The New International Environmental Protection Law: The Enforcement Role of the International Court of Justice," in Canadian Bar Association Committee Report, *Sustainable Development in Canada: Options for Law Reform* (Ottawa: Canadian Bar Association, 1990), 303. Reproduced with permission from the Canadian Bar Association.

J.A. Mintz, "Two Cheers for Global POPs: A Summary and Assessment of the Stockholm Convention on Persistent Organic Pollutants" (2001) vol. 14 *Georgetown International Environmental Law Review* 319. Reprinted with permission of the publisher, Georgetown International Environmental Law Review © 2002.

J. Moffet, "Judicial Review and Environmental Policy: Lessons for Canada from the United States" (1994) vol. 37 *Canadian Public Administration* 140.

J. Moffet, B. Davis, and B. Mausberg, "Supporting Negotiated Environmental Agreements with Statutory and Regulatory Provisions: An Overview for Ontario" (Toronto: Environmental Defence Canada, 2002). Reprinted with permission.

P. Muldoon and B. Rutherford, "Environment and the Constitution: Submission to the House of Commons Standing Committee on Environment" (Toronto: Canadian Environmental Law Association and Pollution Probe, 1991), appendix E (edited).

O. Nadon, "Civil Liability Underlying Environmental Risk-Related Activities in Quebec" (1998), 24 CELR (NS). Reprinted with permission.

National Wildlife Federation and Canadian Institute for Environmental Law and Policy, *A Prescription for Healthy Great Lakes: Report of the Program for Zero Discharge* (Toronto: CIELAP and NWF, 1991).

A.M. Polinsky, *An Introduction to Law and Economics*, 2d ed. (Toronto: Little, Brown & Co., 1989). Reprinted with the permission of Aspen Law & Business.

S. Prentice, "Taking Sides: What's Wrong with Eco-Feminism?" (Spring 1988) *Women and Environments* 9.

P. Renaud, "The Environmental Assessment Process and Public Participation in Québec: Concrete Elements for Sustainable Development" (1996) vol. 27 *Revue Générale de Droit* 375. Reproduced with permission.

J.B. Ruhl, "Thinking of Environmental Law as a Complex Adaptive System: How To Clean Up the Environment by Making a Mess of Environmental Law" (1997) vol. 34 *Houston Law Review* 933. Reprinted with permission.

A. Scott, "Economic Incentives: The Problem of Getting Started," in Canadian Society of Environmental Biologists, Alberta Chapter, *Economy & Ecology, The Economics of Environmental Protection* (symposium held February 19-20, 1985, University of Alberta, Edmonton), 75.

J. Sherman, M. Gismondi, and M. Richardson, "Not Directly Affected: Using the Law To Close the Door on Environmentalists" (1996) vol. 31, no. 1 *Journal of Canadian Studies* 102.

P. Singer, "Not for Humans Only: The Place of Nonhumans in Environmental Issues," in K.E. Goodpaster and K.M. Syre, eds., *Ethics and Problems of the 21st Century* (Notre Dame, IN: University of Notre Dame Press, 1979).

D.W. St. Pierre, "The Tradition from Property to People: The Road to the Recognition of Rights for Non-Human Animals" (1998) vol. 9, no. 2 *Hastings Women's Law Journal* 255. © 1998 by University of California, Hastings College of the Law. Reprinted from Hastings Women's Law Journal.

Standing Committee on Environment and Sustainable Development, *Enforcing Canada's Pollution Control Laws: The Public Interest Must Come First!* (Ottawa: House of Commons Standing Committee on Environment and Sustainable Development, 1998).

B. Stevens and A. Rose, "A Dynamic Analysis of the Marketable Permits Approach to Global Warming Policy: A Comparison of Spatial and Temporal Flexibility" (2002) vol. 94, no. 1 *Journal of Environmental Economics and Management* 45. Reprinted with permission.

C.D. Stone, "Should Trees Have Standing?—Toward Legal Rights for Natural Objects" (1972) vol. 45 *University of Southern California Law Review* 450. Reprinted with permission.

J. Swaigen and R. Woods, "A Substantive Right to Environmental Quality," in J. Swaigen, ed., *Environmental Rights in Canada* (Toronto: Butterworths and CELRF, 1981), 195. Reprinted with permission of the Canadian Institute for Environmental Law and Policy, www.cielap.org/.

M. Swenarchuk, *Civilizing Globalization: Trade and Environment, Thirteen Years On*, Canadian Environmental Law Association, report no. 399, March 2001 (available online at CELA, http://www.cela.ca/).

A. Szekely, "Transboundary Issues in North America," in First North American Conference on Environmental Law, Proceedings, CIELAP, ELI, FUNDEA, Tepotzotlan, Mexico (1992), 79, at 79 (English translation).

M.F. Teisl, B. Roe, and R.L. Hicks, "Can Eco-Labels Tune a Market? Evidence from Dolphin-Safe Labeling" (2002) vol. 43, no. 3 *Journal of Environmental Economics and Management* 339. Reprinted with permission.

C. Tollefson, "Strategic Lawsuits and Environmental Politics: Daishowa Inc. v. Friends of the Lubicon" (1996) vol. 31, no. 1 *Journal of Canadian Studies* 119.

C. Tollefson, "When the 'Public Interest' Loses: The Liability of Public Interest Litigants for Adverse Costs Awards" (1995) vol. 29 *UBC Law Review* 303.

"Undermining the Law: Addressing the Crisis in Compliance with Environmental Mining Laws in BC" (Vancouver: West Coast Environmental Law and Environmental Mining Council of BC, 2001).

M. Valiente, "Legal Foundations of Canadian Environmental Policy," in D. Van Nijnatten and R. Boardman, *Canadian Environmental Policy: Context and Cases*, 2d ed. (Don Mills, ON: Oxford University Press, 2002), 3. Copyright © Oxford University Press Canada 2002. Reprinted by permission.

T.S. Veeman, "The Application of Economic Analysis to Public Land and Resource Management: An Overview," in T.J. Cottrell, ed., *Role of Economics in Integrated Resource Management*, Proceedings held October 16-18, 1985 (Hinton, AB: Alberta Forestry, Land and Wildlife, 1985), 17.

Voluntary Measures To Ensure Environmental Compliance: A Review and Analysis of North American Initiatives (Montreal: Commission for Environmental Cooperation (CEC), 1998), at 25 (reprinted in (Fall 1998) *North American Environmental Law and Policy*).

K. Webb, "Pollution Control in Canada: The Regulatory Approach in the 1980s," *Study Paper, Administrative Law Series* (Ottawa: Law Reform Commission of Canada, 1988).

J. Woodward and T. Syed, "The Importance of Aboriginal Rights and Perspectives for Species Protection and Habitat Conservation," paper presented at the National Conference on Aboriginal Law and Governance, Pacific Business and Law Institute, Vancouver, BC, June 21, 2000, at 4-14 to 4-23. Reprinted with permission.

World Commission on Environment and Development, *Mandate for Change: Key Issues, Strategy and Workplan* (Geneva: WCED, 1985).

Contents

Online Index
(available at http://www.emp.on.ca/elp3/index.html)

Detailed Contents

Online Index
(available at http://www.emp.on.ca/elp3/index.html)

Table of Cases

A page number in boldface type indicates that the text of the case or a portion thereof is reproduced. A page number in lightface type indicates that the text is merely quoted briefly, referred to, or mentioned. Cases within excerpts are not listed.

Foreword

The year 2003 marks the 10th anniversary of *Environmental Law and Policy* and the 35th anniversary of the introduction of teaching environmental law in Canadian law schools. Early environmental law courses in Canada were characterized by a number of features: (1) teaching materials that were made up of cases (mostly tort cases), statutory excerpts, and articles that came from scientific rather than law journals; (2) persistent comment from faculty members who believed that environmental law had no place in a law school curriculum (after all, they argued, it was already well covered in the torts class under the heading "nuisance"); and finally, (3) an irrepressible enthusiasm among faculty and students that the law could be enlisted in support of the environment. From this somewhat inauspicious beginning in the late 1960s environmental law began to grow in popularity and sophistication. When I last taught the course nine years ago, more than 70 students were enrolled (compared with 18 in 1974) and we were using a new "casebook" that successfully integrated the writings and ideas of the leading environmental scholars and practitioners from across Canada. That casebook was the first edition of *Environmental Law and Policy*.

The third edition of this casebook continues to build on the strengths of the first two editions. Contrary to what one might have assumed from an authorial team of strong environmentalists, the book and the courses it supports are well balanced. There is, of course, a pro-environment bias, but it is tempered by a clear understanding of how complex environmental issues are and, as a result, how illusory simple solutions are. In fact, environmental regulation and compliance is extraordinarily complex. The book is also well balanced in its use of secondary materials and references, drawing as it does from a broad range of academic, governmental, and NGO sources. The book defines environmental law in very broad terms, from both a substantive and a process perspective, and it now includes topics such as endangered places and species, topics that were seldom part of those early courses.

In my view, the two most important aspects of this edition are its accessibility to students and its provocative and stimulating approach to the subject. Its accessibility flows from the clear, non-technical writing and the authors' capacity to present complicated ideas in a well-organized, straightforward manner. The book challenges students and readers to imagine emerging trends in domestic and international law and how those new developments might be used to secure a better environmental future.

This is a book that will make teaching environmental law and policy stimulating and enjoyable for both instructor and student. Professors Hughes, Lucas, and Tilleman have assembled a veritable who's who of Canadian environmental law teachers and lawyers as contributing authors and have overseen the development of a book that is an important contribution to both faculty and students. The third edition of this book is a clear signal that *Environmental Law and Policy* can take its place beside the best law teaching resources in Canada today.

D. Paul Emond

July 2003

CHAPTER ONE

The Environment: Ecological and Ethical Dimensions

Karin Mickelson and William Rees

I. INTRODUCTION

A. "Environmental" Law: Social Myth or Ecological Reality?

How any society relates to the rest of reality is profoundly affected by an elaborate set of accepted "facts," unquestioned assumptions, and entrenched beliefs about the world that are derived from the historical and cultural experience of its people. It is our culture's "story" about reality that provides the "context in which life [can] function in a meaningful manner and profoundly affects how [we] act in the world."[1] In short, every culture expresses a world view or paradigm that shapes its social relationships, its political institutions, and the nature of its economic enterprise.

We raise this assumption at the outset to emphasize that there can be as many world views as there are cultures and that each world view only more or less coincides with reality. Thus, our most sacred beliefs, however well sustained by the evidence to date, may simply be wrong. The important point is that while we think that we act from factual *knowledge*, much individual action and government policy is undertaken on the basis of unsubstantiated *belief*. We will argue below that much of contemporary environmental law derives from erroneous perception and as such remains ecologically naive. Indeed, much of our world view may be little more than social myth, a collection of "shared illusions."[2]

---

1   T. Berry, *The Dream of the Earth* (San Francisco: Sierra Club Books, 1988), 123.

2   See S. Beer, "I Said, You Are Gods" (1981) vol. 15, no. 3 *Teilhard Review* 1, at 5-8.

B. Sustainable Development as a Context for Change

The need to revisit the historic underpinnings of "environmental law" arises in the context of society's current efforts to shift to a more sustainable development path.[3] This potentially revolutionary quest was stimulated by the publication of *Our Common Future*, the 1987 report of the World Commission on Environment and Development ("the Brundtland commission").[4]

The Brundtland commission defined sustainable development as "development that meets the needs of the present without compromising the ability of future generations to meet their own needs"[5] but was curiously ambiguous in elaborating on its own definition. Emphasizing the role of poverty in the ecological degradation of less-developed countries (with less emphasis on the role of wealth and consumption in the North), the commission equated sustainable development with "more rapid economic growth in both industrial and developing countries" on grounds that "economic growth and diversification ... will help developing countries mitigate the strains on the rural environment."[6] Consistent with this interpretation, the commission observed that "a five to tenfold increase in world industrial output can be anticipated by the time world population stabilizes some time in the next century."[7] This reflection of the prevailing expansionist world view guaranteed an enthusiastic reception for the commission's report in corporate boardrooms and by conservative governments everywhere.

At the same time, in recognition of the additional stress that such growth implies for the environment, the commission cast sustainable development in terms of more material- and energy-efficient resource use, new ecologically benign technologies, and "a production system that respects the obligation to preserve the ecological base for development,"[8] while guaranteeing "the sustainability of ecosystems upon which the global economy depends."[9] Such environmental caveats seemed sufficient to capture the imagination of mainstream environmentalism and ensured nearly universal acceptance of the

---

3   Portions of this chapter are revised or abstracted from W.E. Rees, *Defining "Sustainable Development,"* CHS Research Bulletin (Vancouver: UBC Centre for Human Settlements, 1989); "Sustainable Development and the Biosphere: Concepts and Principles" (1990) *Teilhard Studies* 23 ("Rees 1990a"); "The Ecology of Sustainable Development" (1990) vol. 20, no. 1 *The Ecologist* 18 ("Rees 1990b"); "Economics, Ecology, and the Limits of Conventional Analysis" (1991) *Journal of the Air Waste Management Association* 40/41; *Understanding Sustainable Development: Natural Capital and the New World Order* (Vancouver: UBC School of Community and Regional Planning, 1992) (unpublished manuscript). Dr. Rees's work on ecological footprint analysis was supported, in part, by a grant to UBC from the Canadian Tri-Council Eco-Research Program.

4   World Commission on Environment and Development, *Our Common Future* (Oxford: Oxford University Press, 1987).

5   Ibid., at 43.

6   Ibid., at 89.

7   Ibid., at 213. While this may seem like an extraordinary rate of expansion, it implies an average annual growth rate in the vicinity of only 3.5-4.5 percent over the next 50 years. Growth in this range has already produced a near fivefold increase in world economic output since World War II.

8   Ibid., at 89.

9   Ibid., at 67.

commission's report. In their initial enthusiasm, hardly anyone seemed to notice the commission's failure to analyze either the structural roots of poverty in our present economic system or whether the prescribed scale of material growth is biophysically possible under any conceivable production system.

The (perhaps politically expedient) ambivalence of *Our Common Future* ensured subsequent vigorous debate over what the commission really meant or should have said. Consequently, there are now numerous competing and divergent conceptions of sustainable development. Not surprisingly, many authors of all political stripes stress the need for "fundamental" changes in humankind–environment relationships. In fact, however, most prescriptions from the academic mainstream and the bureaucratic establishment would require little more than modest adjustments to the status quo.[10]

In contrast, this chapter interprets "fundamental" much more literally. We argue that sustainable development will require significant change in social attitudes and expectations and in the structure of the industrial economy. Many scientists believe that global pollution and accelerating rates of resource depletion represent serious threats to critical life-support functions of the ecosphere. These negative trends cannot be corrected through improvements in material efficiency and traditional "end-of-pipe" waste treatment alone. Stabilizing and reversing global ecological decline may require that we reassess and reject many of the values and beliefs that have long prevailed in the industrial states of the northern hemisphere and that we restructure many of the sociopolitical institutions that sustain them.

In this context, our starting premise is that the present legal and institutional framework governing industrial society's relationship with the ecosphere may well be unequal to the challenge of sustainability. If our dominant social paradigm is fundamentally flawed, incremental changes and marginal improvements to existing legal instruments (such as improved enforcement and higher fines) are unlikely to contribute significantly to sustainable development. Any major shift in societal values and beliefs will require parallel changes in institutional mechanisms for governance. In short, rather than make adjustments to existing humankind–environment relationships, environmental law for sustainable development must reflect and enforce changes in the nature of those relationships themselves.

C. Our Prevailing Cultural Myth

The scientific or "Cartesian" world view that presently dominates western society is characterized by a mechanical view of the universe as "a vast machine, wound up by God to tick forever."[11] Descartes perceived reality as divided into the independent realms of mind and matter, and from the perspective of mind, he saw the external material world

---

10   See Canadian Council of Resource and Environment Ministers (CCREM), *Report of the National Task Force on Environment and Economy* (Ottawa: CCREM, 1987) for a well-known Canadian example.

11   M. Berman, *The Reenchantment of the World* (New York: Bantam, 1984), 21.

"as a machine and nothing but a machine." To Descartes, there was no purpose, life, or spirituality in matter.[12]

Descartes extended his mechanistic view to include living organisms: "I do not recognize any difference between the machines made by craftsmen and the various bodies that nature alone composes."[13] From this perspective, he even saw human thought as an iterative mechanical process by which the mind confronts the world as separate object. Descartes's separation of the observer from the observed and his reductionist approach provided the methodological framework for all subsequent scientific enquiry and helped formalize the notion of objective knowledge.

However, it was Sir Isaac Newton who first succeeded in "validating" the Cartesian view of the universe. His *Principia* (1687) revealed the seemingly universal laws of mass and motion, which describe the universe as a mechanical machine of unlimited dimensions behaving according to strict mathematical rules. For the first time, humankind had a body of science that satisfied Descartes's vision of mechanical predictability and seemingly gave humans the ability to manipulate nature indefinitely toward their own ends. By the end of the 17th century, the founders of the scientific world view had abolished the ancient organic perception of the earth as a living entity.

Scientific materialism provided the foundation of industrial culture and explains why our prevailing cultural myth presumes human dominance over the rest of the natural world. To be sure, postmodern philosophers have rejected the strict determinism of "normal" (Cartesian) science, and the complex systems theory is beginning to undermine our confidence that nature is knowable and can be bent predictably to serve human purposes (discussed below). However, at the beginning of the 21st century, industrial society still operates primarily from the foundation of belief that "nothing in nature can resist the human will." In effect, human beings "through technological advance [will seek] to simulate and redesign to our liking all biological processes, so that we may achieve ever more control over the conditions of life."[14] The arrogant anthropocentrism of the dominant world view permeates every aspect of modern life, including the structure of our economic system, the legal/institutional framework erected to support it, and the mechanisms by which we regulate our relationship with external reality, the ecosphere.

II. ECOLOGICAL PRINCIPLES

A. Purpose and Introduction

This section introduces readers to the basic ecological principles that should govern the relationship between humankind and the rest of the biophysical environment. Ironically, these ecological principles do not at present play a significant role in the governance of

---

12   F. Capra, *The Turning Point: Science, Society, and the Rising Culture* (New York: Simon and Schuster, 1982), 60.

13   Descartes, cited in Capra, ibid., at 61.

14   W. Leiss, "Instrumental Rationality, the Domination of Nature and Why We Do Not Need an Environmental Ethic," in P.P. Hanson, ed., *Environmental Ethics: Philosophical and Policy Perspectives* (Burnaby, BC: Institute for the Humanities, Simon Fraser University Publications, 1986), 178.

human ecological relationships. De facto, human ecology—the actual physical nature of human use of, and impact on, the earth—has been shaped more by economic forces, social policy considerations, and political expediency than it has by the science of humankind–environment interaction. Not surprisingly, the present structure of environmental law reflects society's prevailing sociopolitical bias. The problem is that the dominant world view in northern industrial democracies long since abandoned any reference to the biological, chemical, and physical laws that govern material and energy flows through the human economy in the real world.

B. Economics as Human Ecology?

For present purposes, ecology might be defined as the scientific study of the flows of energy and material resources through ecosystems, and of the competitive and cooperative mechanisms that organisms have evolved for the allocation of these resources among different species. Similarly, economics is commonly defined as the scientific study of the efficient allocation of scarce resources among competing uses in human society. Thus, ecology and economics share not only the same semantic roots, but also much of the same substantive focus. Logically, it could be argued that economics is really human ecology.

Or rather, it should be. The problem is that significant theoretical differences have evolved between the modern forms of these sister disciplines. Ecological theory has firm roots in real-world biology, chemistry, and the thermodynamics laws that are the universal regulators of all energy and material transformations in the organic world. By contrast, the dominant economic theory had deserted its classical organic roots by the end of the 19th century. Neoclassical economics (currently enjoying a remarkably uncritical renaissance the world over) is firmly rooted in the methods and concepts of Newtonian analytic mechanics.

We are therefore confronted with a double irony in coping with problems of human economies and environment. Ecologists, who possess appropriate theory, have historically all but ignored humankind. Meanwhile, mainstream economists who study humankind resource linkages exclusively, do so from the ecologically irrelevant realm of analytic mechanics. We explore this crucial dichotomy below.

C. Economy as Mechanism

The neoclassical (neoliberal) economic paradigm upon which so much economic policy in the industrial north is based ignores the biophysical basis of life. Inspired by Newtonian physics, neoclassical economics was conceived as a sister science, "the mechanics of utility and self-interest."[15] As a result, the economic process is abstracted from nature and viewed as an independent and "self-sustaining circular flow between production and consumption," in which "complete reversibility is the general rule, just as in mechanics."[16]

---

15   W. Jevons, *The Theory of Political Economy*, 2d ed. (London: Macmillan, 1879).

16   N. Georgescu-Roegen, "Energy and Economic Myths" (1975) vol. 41, no. 3 *Southern Economic Journal* 347, at 348.

Indeed, prevailing economic theory "lacks any [physical] representation of the materials, energy sources, physical structures, and time dependent processes basic to an ecological approach."[17] It produces analytic models based on reductionist and deterministic assumptions about resources, people, firms, and technology that bear little relationship to their counterparts in the real world.

A major tenet of the neoclassical school is the belief that resources are more the product of human ingenuity than they are of nature. According to economic theory, rising market prices for scarce materials encourage conservation on the one hand and stimulate technological substitution on the other. It is part of the conventional wisdom of mainstream economists that these factors have been more than sufficient to overcome emerging resource scarcities.[18] Standard neoclassical texts therefore conclude that "exhaustible resources do not pose a fundamental problem."[19]

Neither do we perceive pollution as a serious ecological constraint on the human enterprise. Environmental degradation is accepted as a necessary "tradeoff" against economic growth and the appropriate level of environmental quality is seen largely as a matter of public choice. People are free to degrade their environments in exchange for jobs or income with no significant additional penalty. At best, the damage costs of pollution are considered to be mere "externalities" resulting from market imperfections that can eventually be efficiently "internalized" through improved technology, "getting the prices right" (for example, ecological fiscal reform), and better regulation.

In summary, the neoclassical perspective sees the natural environment as little more than a static backdrop to human affairs. Thus, unburdened by any sense of significant environment–economy connectedness, the political mainstream readily associates "sustainable development" with sustained economic growth. Environmental concerns are acknowledged but as only one of many sets of competing values and interests. The presumption seems to be that within a broadly utilitarian framework, society will ultimately arrive at a politically "practical" interpretation of sustainable development through the usual power brokering, negotiation, and compromise. Certainly ecological absolutes have no seat at the bargaining table.

D. In Contrast, Ecological Reality

For all its political and institutional sophistication, the human economy is fundamentally directed toward a problem encountered by all other species—the dependence for life on materials from elsewhere in the biosphere.[20]

17   P. Christenson, "Increasing Returns and Ecological Sustainability," in R. Costanza, ed., *Ecological Economics: The Science and Management of Sustainability* (New York: Columbia University Press, 1991).

18   P.A. Victor, *Indicators of Sustainable Development: Some Lessons from Capital Theory*, a background paper prepared for a workshop on Indicators of Sustainable Development (Ottawa: Canadian Environmental Advisory Council, 1990), 14.

19   P. Dasgupta and D. Heal, *Economic Theory and Exhaustible Resources* (London: Cambridge University Press, 1979), 205.

20   D. Rapport, "The Interface of Economics and Ecology," in A.-M. Jansson, ed., *Integration of Economy and Ecology—An Outlook for the Eighties* (Stockholm: Askö Laboratories, University of Stockholm, 1984).

In contrast to the mechanical vision, the ecological world view holds that for all our technological wizardry and purported mastery over the natural environment, humankind is still very much a product and part of nature. Indeed, at a very basic level there is little to distinguish humankind from the millions of other species with which we share the planet. Like all other organisms, we survive and grow by extracting energy and materials from the ecosystems of which we are a part. Like all other organisms, we "consume" these resources before returning them in altered form to the ecosphere. From this perspective, far from existing in splendid isolation, the human economy is and always has been an inextricably integrated, completely contained, and wholly dependent subset of the ecosphere.

There are, of course, important differences of degree and kind between humans and other organisms. Unlike other species' populations, the human populations of many countries and of the world as a whole have been expanding at an accelerating rate for many decades. This in itself imposes ever-mounting demands on the productive capacity of the ecosystems that sustain us. In addition, technological "progress" has permanently altered the chemistry of human ecology. Human-dominated ecosystems must cope not only with the natural metabolites of our bodies but also with thousands of industrial metabolites, the synthetic by-products of economic activity. While the former are readily assimilated and recycled, there is often no assimilative capacity for the latter. Indeed, many synthetic chemicals are dangerously toxic. It is the combination of the expanding energy and material demand of the human economy and the consequent inevitable increase in pollution that provides the starting point for the analysis of all population–environment linkages.

1. Obligate Dependence

From a strictly anthropocentric perspective, the ecosphere provides three types of critical functions that sustain the economic activities of humankind.[21] First, the ecosphere is the source of all material resources. Some resources such as air, water, and food we consume directly. Others serve as raw material inputs to the production of economic goods and services. There are several categories of resources:

- Non-renewable resources, such as petroleum, of which there are finite stocks that will eventually be depleted by any level of use.
- Renewable resources, including plants and animals—living things—that are capable of regeneration and therefore may be in continuous supply despite moderate consumption by human beings.
- Replenishable resources, including clean air, water, and soil, various components of which (oxygen, essential nutrients) are the products of the biological processes of photosynthesis, nitrogen fixation, decomposition, etc., involved in biogeochemical recycling.
- Continuing resources including alternative energy sources such as solar radiation, wind, and tides. While limited in local availability or rate of supply, these resources

---

21   For a fuller discussion, see M. Jacobs, *The Green Economy* (London: Pluto Press, 1991).

are essentially inexhaustible. (In contrast, both renewable and replenishable resources are potentially exhaustible from overexploitation.)

The second function of the ecosphere is waste assimilation. As noted, "waste" includes the organic excretia and dead bodies of plants and animals, as well as industrial metabolites and eventually all discarded manufactured products themselves. Natural organic matter and nutrients can be "processed" and recycled repeatedly through the ecosphere—indeed, this is essential to systems continuity. Industrial metabolites and products are more problematic. Some human-made synthetics are non-reactive (biologically inert) and relatively harmless. However, many others are toxic or otherwise harmful to life. Because of bioaccumulation, the environment may be said to have a near-zero tolerance for highly active compounds such as chemical carcinogens and radionuclides. Waste in every category may be perceived as pollution in certain circumstances.

Third, the ecosphere provides certain services that benefit humankind. These include amenities such as opportunities for outdoor recreation and sheer aesthetic enjoyment. More important however, biophysical systems perform certain life-support functions essential to life as we know it. Maintaining atmospheric composition, stabilizing climate, regenerating the ozone layer, and the carbon sink functions of vegetation and soils are examples of vital ecosphere functions. While difficult to quantify and price, it should be clear that many such services of nature have great positive economic value. A recent study of the economics of just 17 ecosystem services in 16 ecological regions estimated their value at US$16-54 trillion per year (averaging $33 trillion) compared to a total gross global product of US$18 trillion.[22]

2. The New Science: A World of Chaos

In just the last three or four decades the world has seen what is, in effect, the consolidation of a second scientific revolution. The seeds were planted with the development of Einsteinian relativity and quantum mechanics, but have flowered with new mathematical tools and the astonishing number-crunching capacity of modern computers. Our artificially stinted linear-mechanical paradigm is beginning to give way to a view of nature that, while still deterministic at the material level, is relentlessly non-linear. Such terms as "complexity theory," "deterministic chaos," "non-linear dynamics," "autopoiesis," and "Prigoginian self-organization" capture the flavour of the paradigm shift fairly well. This new science of complex systems has serious implications for the assumptions regarding prediction and standards of proof that underlie environmental law.

An explosion of theoretical and empirical literature reinforces the idea that the interaction of the simple laws of physics and chemistry can produce systems behaviour of extraordinary complexity and richness. Conversely, systems of inordinate complexity are able to generate patterns of beautiful simplicity. Perhaps most important in the present context, is recognition that the interplay of even strictly deterministic rules can quickly generate patterns of systems behaviour that are inherently unpredictable even if we

---

22   R. Costanza et al., "The Value of the World's Ecosystem Services and Natural Capital" (1997) 387 *Nature* 253.

possess near-perfect knowledge of the initial state of the experimental system. To the extent that such counter-intuitive behaviour is characteristic of real-world ecosystems, economic systems, and social systems, it requires a serious reevaluation of dominant decision models and the prevailing approach to development and environment.

Two classes of phenomena are particularly relevant to this issue. The first is the apparent chaos that can emerge from even the simplest dynamic system. In simplest terms, a dynamic system is one governed by strict rules such that the state of the system at any point in time unambiguously determines the future state of the system. In theory, then, if we know how the system is behaving now, we can predict what it will look like at any point in the future. In a model system, this requires simply performing an iterative sequence of calculations. The outcome of any calculation in the sequence both determines the next state of the system and provides the starting values for the subsequent iteration (that is, the system's behaviour is governed by internal feedback).

This seems the very essence of predictable order, of Newtonian mechanism in fact: determine the rules governing the behaviour of the system, insert the starting values, and the future will unfold without any surprises. However, when we apply such models to many real world phenomena, the state of the model after just a few iterations bears no evident relationship to reality. The problem usually lies in small errors of measurement. The internal dynamics of the system are such that these errors are fed back and amplified with each iteration. Given sufficient time, any inaccuracy will derail the model. Better measurement does not help, at least not for long. The tiniest, unavoidable, measurement error can render even a perfect model useless as a predictive tool.

The general problem is called "sensitive dependence on initial conditions"[23] and the behaviour it produces in both mathematical models and real systems—even simple ones—is called chaos. Chaotic behaviour has always existed, but generally went unnoticed in our dedication to normal (Cartesian) science. If actually encountered, it was ignored because the math was too difficult. Now that computers are up to the task, "the dreadful truth has become inescapable: Chaos is everywhere. It is just as common as the nice simple behavior so valued by traditional physics."[24] Chaos explains why even the best computer models cannot predict the weather next week.

The second phenomenon is the unexpected, dramatic (or even catastrophic) change that can occur in previously stable systems under stress. To understand this behaviour we must recognize that key variables of complex systems, such as ecosystems, may range considerably within broad domains of stability. Within these domains, all points tend to converge toward a centre of gravity called an "attractor."[25] Traditional dynamic models used in forecasting are characterized by a single equilibrium (a point attractor) or a repeating cycle of values (a periodic attractor). Chaotic systems, by contrast, trace a complex, often elegant, highly organized pattern of individually unpredictable paths—

---

23 Sometimes called the butterfly effect—the flap of a butterfly's wing in New Guinea sets off a tornado in Texas the following week.

24 J. Cohen and I. Stewart, *The Collapse of Chaos* (New York: Penguin Books, 1994), 190.

25 Kay refers to the stable domain and its attractor as "thermodynamic branch" and "optimum operating point," respectively: J. Kay, "A Nonequilibrium Thermodynamic Framework for Discussing Ecosystem Integrity" (1991) vol. 15, no. 4 *Environmental Management* 483.

a "strange attractor"—within the stable domain as internal feedback continually changes the system's dynamics. In any iteration, the system will retain its familiar character and behaviour as long as key variables remain under the influence of their customary attractors.

Now, although it may not initially be obvious, dynamic systems may have several attractors separated from each other by a system of unstable "ridges" or bifurcations (picture a terrain of watersheds each isolated from the others by irregular hills and ridges). "Catastrophe" occurs when a key systems variable, perhaps driven by some persistent change in an important control variable, is displaced far from its usual attractor. If the variable reaches a bifurcation, it may be captured by an adjacent attractor instead of returning to its accustomed domain. Suddenly, the quality of the system changes dramatically. Indeed, catastrophe is characterized by large discontinuous changes in systems characteristics and behaviour resulting from incrementally small changes in key variables. A last, marginal change in temperature or pressure and the whole system flips into a new stability domain controlled by a different attractor. There is no guarantee that the system will ever return to its former state. For example, Kay has been "unable to find a single example of an ecosystem flipping back after undergoing such a dramatic reorganization."[26]

Various real world systems as different as commercial fisheries, malaria control, acid-sensitive lakes, the gulf stream, global climate, and the economy seem to be prone to catastrophic behaviour and there is reason to believe it is characteristic of most complex dynamic systems. This is worrisome because the situation is actually more complicated than described above. First, neither the existence nor the nature of multiple attractor(s), simple or chaotic, is knowable before the fact. Second, the very act of exploiting or otherwise manipulating the system changes its internal dynamics and shifts the location of both its attractor(s) and the bifurcations between them. Indeed, some existing attractors may disappear and new ones may emerge spontaneously. Third, the customary attractor may shrink even as systems variability increases under stress (that is, the system becomes less resilient, more brittle). All these changes enhance the probability of catastrophic bifurcation. In other words: (1) any persistent incremental stress may increase the probability of dramatic qualitative and quantitative changes in the future state of the system, and (2) both the nature and magnitude of these changes are inherently unpredictable.

We ignore these findings at considerable risk to future global society. Humans have become the driving force of global ecological change, and there is every reason to believe that ours is a world of multiple strange attractors.

3. The Environmental Crisis: Human Ecological Dysfunction

A continuous, adequate, and reliable supply of the three ecosphere functions described earlier is a necessary precondition for civilized human existence. The functional integrity of the ecosphere is not something that can be indefinitely bargained away or "traded off" against other economic benefits. Unfortunately, it is the cumulative impact of precisely

---

26   Ibid., at 487.

such tradeoffs in the form of thousands of individually insignificant decisions that is driving the increasingly global environmental crisis. Growing human populations and rising material expectations are resulting in consumption rates that exceed the productivity of renewable and replenishable resources. Soil erosion, fisheries depletion, deforestation, species extinction, falling water tables, and similar trends are the inevitable result on every continent. At the same time, pollution (including hormone mimicry and the toxic contamination of the human food web), caused mainly by the "production" and industrial transformation of non-renewable resources into biological and chemically active contaminants, has also reached global proportions, filling available sinks to overflowing. Overconsumption and pollution both contribute to the erosion of biophysical life-support functions.

These observations suggest that it is the present form of human population–environment linkages and the overwhelming scale of the human enterprise that pose the greatest ecological threats to continued human existence. The global ecological crisis is not as much a problem with the ecosphere as it is of human ecological dysfunction. The uncertainties associated with this insight are heightened by our increasing understanding of complex systems behaviour. As the economy expands, there is a finite possibility that for all the *apparent* success of technology in freeing us from the whims of nature, we could actually be "on the verge of extinction, blissfully unaware that a mathematical fiction in the space of the possible is about to become reality. And the really nasty feature is that may take only the tiniest of changes to trigger the switch."[27]

4. More Bad News: The Economy as Consumption

Another part of the problem is our failure to understand the ecological basis of the economic process. Contrary to the assumptions of neoclassical mechanics, the ecologically relevant flows through the material economy are not circular money flows but unidirectional energy and matter flows. This is because the ultimate regulator of the economy is not mechanics but rather thermodynamics. Thermodynamic principles govern the flows of energy and matter in nature and are therefore essential to understanding the connectedness of the economy (human ecology) to the rest of the ecosphere.

Of particular relevance is the second law of thermodynamics (the entropy law): in every material transformation, available energy and matter are continuously and irreversibly degraded to the unavailable state.[28] This law dictates that the material economy necessarily contributes to a constant increase in global net entropy (disorder) through the continuous irreversible dissipation of energy/matter.[29] The economic process "feeds" on

---

27   Cohen and Stewart, supra note 24, at 212.

28   See Georgescu-Roegen, supra note 16, and "The Steady State and Ecological Salvation: A Thermodynamic Analysis" (1977) vol. 27, no. 4 *Bioscience* 266.

29   For example, a new automobile represents only a fraction of the energy and material that has been permanently dissipated as pollution in the manufacturing process (typically 25 metric tonnes per tonne of finished vehicle). Similarly, modern energy-subsidized agriculture may consume several fossil calories for every calorie of food energy produced.

available energy and material resources first produced by nature and returns them to the ecosphere as useless waste. These energy/material flows in the economy are unidirectional and irreversible.[30] Without reference to this entropic flow throughout "it is virtually impossible to relate the economy to the environment," yet the concept is "virtually absent from economics today."[31]

Perhaps the most ecologically relevant insight from the application of thermodynamics to economics is the recognition that all stages of economic "production" *require* consumption. This unacknowledged reality lies at the heart of the so-called environmental crisis. The economy is dependent upon low entropy energy and matter produced elsewhere in the ecosphere and upon finite waste sinks. Since the scale of our material economies is increasing and the ecosystems upon which they depend are not, consumption everywhere has begun to exceed sustainable rates of biological production. Meanwhile, the attendant pollution undermines the remaining productive capacity of the ecosphere. Much of today's wealth is, therefore, an illusion, derived from the irreversible conversion of productive "natural capital" into perishable manufactured capital on the one hand and the harmful dissipation of available energy and material on the other.[32]

From the ecological perspective, our confidence in markets and technological innovation to solve the ecological crisis is also misplaced. While rising prices may stimulate the search for substitutes in the case of non-renewable commodities, such as copper, they are silent on the status of ecologically essential materials and processes—the "free" goods of nature for which there are no markets.[33] Pricing, costs, and profits, the primary scarcity indicators offered by the neoclassical school, fail utterly when the assumptions upon which they are based do not obtain.[34] Thus, while human survival ultimately depends on the integrity of the ecosphere, we cannot depend on market mechanics to sound the alarm or to stimulate a technological fix. The industrialized world is currently basking in the apparent "triumph of capitalism" and the prospect of an invigorated global economy through vastly expanded markets. However, as indicated by accelerating global change, even current rates of consumption and pollution may well be permanently eroding the very basis of life.

It should now be apparent why ecological economics would see "public choice" respecting environmental quality as seriously constrained by ecological limits. World economic activity has increased fivefold since World War II and now produces effects at the level of the ecosphere itself. Persistent deterioration of key environmental variables is no mere "externality" but rather the symptom of systemic human ecological dysfunction. The real-world connectedness of the economy and the ecosphere has resulted in global

---

30   Material recycling may seem to contradict this principle. However, recycling always involves the dissipation of additional energy and matter.

31   H. Daly, "Sustainable Development: From Concept and Theory Towards Operational Principles," in *Steady-State Economics*, 2d ed. (Washington, DC: Island Press, 1991), 1.

32   Rees, 1990a and 1990b, supra note 3.

33   The ozone layer is a compelling example. It went from worthless to priceless as soon as its function was realized.

34   See Victor, supra note 18.

ecological trends that, if forced beyond unseen limits or bifurcations, may not be reversible. Indeed, Rees has recently argued that unsustainability is an inevitable "emergent property" of the interaction of techno-industrial society, as presently configured, and the ecosphere.[35] Sustainable development requires a radical transformation of our perception of the ecological basis for economic activity and a corresponding shift in cultural values. Maintenance of the ecosphere's life-support functions is an absolute condition for long-term economic sustainability. This severely limits social choice in the search for a politically "practical" approach to future development.

5. Some Good News: The Self-Producing Ecosphere

Fortunately, the ecosphere has the capacity to recover from human abuse—*ecosystems are inherently self-producing and self-sustaining*. The ecosphere therefore appears to defy the entropy law: it "is in many respects self-generating—its productivity and stability determined largely through its internal interactions."[36]

The organizational property that enables living systems to produce themselves is known as autopoiesis.[37] Economies also have some of the proporties of autopoiesis, but there is a difference. While economies are contained by and feed off their host ecosystems, ecosystems are able to access an extraplanetary source of free energy, the sun. Indeed, photosynthesis is the engine of ecostemic autopoiesis, enabling the stuff of ecosystems to be constantly transformed and recycled. In thermodynamic terms, photosynthesis is the most important productive process on Earth and the ultimate source of all biological capital (renewable resources) used by the human economy.[38]

Autopoiesis is a property of living things and of the coevolution of the complex, interdependent relationships (energy, material, and information flows) linking the ecosphere's major components. The structural integrity of these relationships is essential not only to the functioning of the system, *but also for the production and maintenance of the participating components themselves*. By destroying ecological integrity, overharvesting and pollution may ultimately undermine the ability of the ecosphere to produce the type of environment necessary for civilized existence.

---

35 W.E. Rees, "Globalization and Sustainability: Conflict or Convergence?" (2002) vol. 22, no. 4 *Bulletin of Science, Technology and Society* 249.

36 D. Perry et al., "Bootstrapping in Ecosystems" (1989) vol. 39, no. 4 *Bioscience* 230-37, at 230.

37 H. Maturana and F. Varela, *The Tree of Knowledge* (Boston: New Science Library, 1988), 43.

38 Photosynthesis is, of course, subject to the laws of thermodynamics. The process merely captures a minute fraction of the solar energy dissipating from the sun. However, in terms of the earth-as-system, it is this photosynthetic energy that maintains the ecosphere as a continuously differentiating self-organizing system suspended far above thermodynamic equilibrium.

E. Maintaining Natural Capital: A Necessary Condition for Sustainability

> Sustainable development, as a goal, rejects policies and practices that support current living standards by depleting the productive base, including natural resources, and that leave future generations with poorer prospects and greater risks than our own.[39]

Global change and awareness of the need to protect the integrity of the ecosphere has recently forced economists to begin treating biophysical resources and processes as unique forms of productive capital. The implications of this convergence of ecological and economic thinking are being explored through various interpretations of a "constant capital stock" criterion for sustainability.[40] In essence, this criterion requires that each generation leave the next an undiminished stock of productive assets. There are two interpretations of the constant capital stock idea:[41]

1. each generation should inherit an aggregate stock of manufactured and natural assets no less than the stock inherited by the previous generation. This corresponds to Daly's conditions for "weak sustainability";
2. each generation should inherit a stock of natural assets *alone* no less than the stock of such assets inherited by the previous generation.[42] This is a version of "strong sustainability" as defined by Daly.[43]

The first interpretation reflects the neoclassical assumption that human-made and natural assets are substitutes and that biological assets (for example, forests) can rationally be liquidated through "development" as long as subsequent investment in manufactured capital (for example, machinery) provides an endowment of equivalent dollar value to the next generation.[44]

---

39 R. Repetto, *World Enough and Time: Successful Strategies for Resource Management* (New Haven, CT: Yale University Press, 1986), 15.

40 See H. Daly, supra note 31; J. Pezzey, *Economic Analysis of Sustainable Growth and Sustainable Development*, Environment Department Working Paper no. 15, (Washington, DC: World Bank, 1989); R. Costanza and H. Daly, *Natural Capital and Sustainable Development* (paper prepared for the CEARC Workshop on Natural Capital, Vancouver, BC, March 15-16, 1990); D. Pearce, A. Markandya, and E. Barbier, *Blueprint for a Green Economy* (London: Earthscan, 1989); D. Pearce, E. Barbier, and A. Markandya, *Sustainable Development: Economics and Environment in the Third World* (Hants, UK: Edward Elgar, 1990).

41 As adapted from Pearce et al. 1989, supra note 40. Both interpretations assume that existing stocks are adequate. If populations are growing or material standards increasing, the stock of productive capital will have to be increased to satisfy the sustainability criterion.

42 "Natural assets" encompasses not only material resources (for example, petroleum, the ozone layer, forests, soils) but also process resources (for example, waste assimilation, photosynthesis, soils formation). It also includes renewable as well as exhaustible resources. For ecological reasons, our primary interest is in maintaining physical stocks of biological resources. (Note that the depletion of non-renewables could be compensated by investment in renewable assets.)

43 Daly, supra note 31.

44 "Equivalent endowment" would be defined in terms of monetary value, wealth-generating potential, jobs, and similar economic criteria. (It is worth noting that humankind has regrettably failed to achieve even the modest objectives of "weak sustainability" in much of the world.)

The second interpretation better reflects the ecological principles favoured here. In particular, maintaining stocks of biophysical capital recognizes the multifunctionality of ecological resources, "including their role as life support systems"[45]—that is, autopoiesis. In this respect, "strong sustainability" recognizes that manufactured and natural capital "are really not substitutes but complements in most production functions."[46] (Indeed, since manufactured capital is made from natural capital, the latter is a *prerequisite* for the former.)

Conventional economic analysis does suggest a theoretical means to identify the appropriate (optimal) level of natural capital and therefore the optimal scale of the economy. Development of the "environment" should proceed only to the point at which the marginal costs associated with natural capital depletion (particularly reduced ecological services) just equal the marginal benefits (in the form of jobs and income from commodity production).[47] Beyond this point, growth of the material economy is "anti-economic growth" that ultimately "makes us poorer rather than richer."[48] However, there is a problem. It is relatively easy to estimate the economic benefits associated with natural capital depletion. However, scientific uncertainty and poor data make it virtually impossible to cost out (quantify and price) the resulting loss of ecological services.

In *Sustainable Development: Economics and Environment in the Third World*, Pearce et al. observe that conserving natural capital may seem particularly relevant to developing countries in which socioeconomic stability is immediately and directly threatened by deforestation, desertification, soil erosion, falling water tables, and the like.[49] In these circumstances there can be little doubt that existing stocks of natural capital are well below bioeconomic optima and must actually be enhanced for long-term survival, let alone sustainability.

However, they also note that further reductions of natural capital may impose significant risks on society "even in countries where it might appear we can afford to [reduce stocks]." These risks reside in our imperfect knowledge of ecological functions, the fact that loss of such functions may be irreversible, and our inability to substitute for those functions once lost. In short, because of the unique and essential services provided by ecological capital, we cannot risk its depletion.[50] "In the face of uncertainty and irreversibility, conserving what there is could be a sound risk-averse strategy."[51]

---

45   Pearce et al. 1990, supra note 40, at 7.

46   Daly, supra note 31, at 22.

47   Marginal and cost–benefit analyses may be conceptually elegant but are fraught with serious theoretical problems and data limitations that limit their practical value. See L. Lave and H. Gruenspecht, "Increasing the Efficiency and Effectiveness of Environmental Decisions: Benefit–Cost Analysis and Effluent Fees—A Critical Review" (1991) vol. 41 *Journal of the Air Waste Management Association* 680, and Rees 1991a, supra note 3.

48   H. Daly, "Boundless Bull" (Summer 1990) *Gannett Center Journal* 113.

49   Pearce et al. 1990, supra note 40.

50   For example, the present unaccounted economic value of the world's remaining forests in terms of climate regulation, global heat distribution, the stabilization of water regimes, and as carbon sinks may well exceed their market value as wood fibre.

51   Pearce et al. 1990, supra note 40, at 7.

F. Implications for Environmental Law

If the arguments outlined above are basically correct, such global trends as ozone depletion, atmospheric pollution and accompanying climatic change, soil erosion, and deforestation indicate that the present world population at current average material standards
using existing technologies, already exceeds the long-term carrying capacity of the earth.
The only way to stabilize the relationship between humankind and the ecosphere is to
reorder the economy from its emphasis on the accumulation of financial and manufactured capital to the rehabilitation of natural capital and its essential life-support functions.
Sustainable development means that for the first time since the beginning of the industrial revolution, the environment must be treated as the independent variable and the
economy the dependent one in the development equation. Environmental law must rise to
the corresponding challenge of ensuring the restoration of essential natural capital and of
protecting the common rights of all to the ecological services essential for civilized
existence.

Unfortunately, current developmental trends such as trade agreements that create an
increasingly competitive global economic environment tend to mitigate against economy–
ecology reconciliation. For example, the exercise of property rights such as timber
licences to capture private economic benefits currently recognized in the marketplace
(for wood and woodfibre) inevitably destroys the ecological public or "open access"
benefits and services (such as the flood damage avoidance and climate stabilization
values) associated with forest capital. These latter benefits may even be of equivalent or
greater economic value but currently go unpriced and are unprotected by law. In the case
of global trade, commodity price competition in the absence of legally enforceable
ecological constraints may reduce the economic surpluses necessary for adequate rein-
vestment in maintenance of productive natural capital assets (forests, agricultural soils,
fishery stocks, etc.). In effect, this forces resource owners to liquidate stocks to survive
economically (or simply to invest the proceeds in some alternative) and in the process to
destroy the essential ecological processes and functions upon which life as we know it
depends.

The domestic and international legal problems associated with issues of this kind
extend beyond the bounds of environmental law as currently conceived. In addition, any
such fundamental shift to sustainable development must occur in a just and equitable
manner and on a global scale.

III. ON ENVIRONMENTAL RACISM AND "ECO-APARTHEID"

Environmental justice is about social transformation directed toward meeting human need
and enhancing the quality of life—economic equality, health care, shelter, human rights,
species preservation, and democracy—using resources sustainably. ... Environmental problems therefore remain inseparable from other social injustices such as poverty, racism,
sexism, unemployment, urban deterioration, and the diminishing quality of life resulting
from corporate activity.[52]

---

52   R. Hofrichter, *Toxic Struggles: The Theory and Practice of Environmental Justice* (Gabriola Island, BC:
New Society Publishers, 1993), 3.

It is well known that the relatively impoverished have always suffered the greatest consequences of local environmental decay. Certainly since the beginning of the industrial revolution, the urban poor, particularly racial and ethnic minorities, have borne the greatest ecological costs of economic activity and growth. Robert Bullard[53] emphasizes that the correlation between chronic exposure to ecological hazards and race is much stronger than that between exposure and poverty.

There is little question that the "environmental racism" implicit in Bullard's assertion constitutes one of the most pressing moral and legal conundrums associated with achieving sustainability.[54] Rees and Westra argue that the problem is increasingly a global one—that unnecessary consumption by the wealthy is now visiting violence and even death on the poor and otherwise marginalized, particularly in developing countries—and that it is time for the international community to address the problem.[55]

Toward this end, consider the five basic principles originally proposed by Bullard as the basis of a *national* legal framework for environmental justice:[56]

- The right to protection—no individual should need to fear exposure to extreme personal risk from human-induced environmental degradation.
- A strategy of prevention—prevention (the elimination of risk before harm occurs) should be the preferred strategy of governments.
- Shift the burden of proof—environmental justice requires that entities applying for operating permits or undertaking activities potentially damaging to public health and property of others be required to prove the safety of their operations.
- Obviate proof of intent—the law should allow differential impact (on the poor or minorities), as shown by statistical analysis, to infer discrimination "because proving intentional or purposeful discrimination [in court] is next to impossible."[57] Do actions that continue to manifest gross negligence with regard to the poor or minority races not constitute de facto eco-injustice (or eco-racism)?
- Redress existing inequities—targets should be set and resources made available to compensate individuals and mitigate damages where environmental and related health problems are greatest.

Since eco-justice for all is also a desirable goal of international development, these principles could help frame international law governing relationships among countries

53   R. Bullard, "Decision Making," in L. Westra and P. Wenz, eds., *Faces of Environmental Racism: Confronting Issues of Global Justice* (Lanham, MD: Rowman and Littlefield, 1995). (Reprinted from (1994) vol. 36, no. 4 *Environment* 39.)

54   L. Westra, "Institutionalized Environmental Violence and Human Rights," in D. Pimentel, L. Westra, and R. Noss, eds., *Ecological Integrity: Integrating Environment, Conservation and Health* (Washington, DC: Island Press, 2000), 279; L. Westra and P. Wenz, "The Faces of Environmental Racism: The Global Equity Issues," in Westra and Wenz, supra note 53.

55   W.E. Rees and L. Westra, "When Consumption Does Violence: Can There Be Sustainability and Environmental Justice in a Resource-Limited World?" in J. Agyeman, ed., *Just Sustainabilities: Development in an Unequal World* (London: Earthscan, 2002).

56   Bullard, supra note 53.

57   Ibid., at 18.

and controlling the behaviour of transnational corporations. The latter are increasingly being granted the rights of persons in international treaties such as NAFTA.[58] It is time these corporations were also required to assume moral responsibility for their actions.

The formal logic of common law throws additional useful light on the subject. In Canada, for example, the most important common law tort action today, both in terms of number of claims made and its theoretical importance, is the negligence cause of action (see the discussion in chapter 3). Negligence law focuses on compensation for losses caused by unintentional but unreasonable conduct that harms legally protected interests. Unreasonable conduct is taken to mean the omission to do something that a reasonable person guided by those considerations that ordinarily regulate human affairs would do, or doing something that a prudent, reasonable person would not do.

Here is clear recognition that fault may be found even in the case of unintended harm if the latter results from careless or unreasonable conduct. Moreover, a negligence action may be launched in Canada in the event of environmental assault. The plaintiff must establish on balance five key elements of the tort—legal duty, breach of the standard of care, cause in fact, proximate cause, and damage to the plaintiff. How might this work in the international arena? There is no doubt that eco-violence—from oil spills to human-induced floods or increasingly wild storm events—damages the plaintiff. The causal links between careless consumption/disposal and eco-violence are also becoming better established. In this light, failure to act responsibly on the part of liable or offending nations would seem to breach a reasonable standard of care. What is missing in international law is acknowledgment of the offence and the capacity to create and enforce a legal duty to act.[59]

Section 219 of Canada's *Criminal Code*, RSC 1985, c. C-46, as amended, clearly dictates that lack of intent to harm is no defence if damage results from knowing acts performed with careless disregard for others: "Everyone is criminally negligent who (a) in doing anything, or (b) in omitting to do anything that it is his duty to do, shows wanton or reckless disregard for the lives or safety of other persons" (where "duty" means a duty imposed by law). Every person who causes the death of another person through criminal negligence is guilty of an indictable offence and liable to imprisonment for life. Significantly, s. 222(5)(b) of the Code states that "a person commits homicide when, directly or indirectly, by any means, he causes the death of a human being, by being negligent."

There is no *prima facie* moral reason why the behavioural standards imposed by international law should not be as rigorous as those required by domestic law. For example, if human-induced climate change can be shown to be a cause of death and destruction, then are not countries like Canada and the United States guilty of "wanton or reckless disregard for the lives or safety of other persons" if they fail to act decisively to reduce their profligate fossil fuel consumption and carbon dioxide emissions, particularly

---

58   This often occurs at the expense of national sovereignty, democracy, local desires, and, possibly, eco-justice. For example, in August 2000, a NAFTA tribunal ordered Mexico to pay California-based Metalclad Corporation US $16.7 million as compensation for a Mexican municipality's refusal to allow the company to run a hazardous waste dump in the community.

59   Note, however, that there is no such reluctance to act in the creation of treaties pertaining to trade such as NAFTA or GATT/WTO or when alleged breaches of such treaties occur.

given the proliferation of options for conservation and the increasing availability of alternative energy? (These countries have among the world's highest levels of CO_2 emissions per capita).

The overall point here is that if the world is to achieve global sustainability it will require an unprecedented level of international cooperation both to acknowledge the existence of such problems and to create the international institutional and legal regime necessary to ensure the environmental safety and security of all persons. In particular, no resident of the global village should be exposed to environmental hazards as the result of the negligent behaviour of other persons, corporations, or governments, even if the causative act occurs in another nation.

IV. ENVIRONMENTAL ETHICS

A. Introduction: The Relevance of Ethical Considerations

However radical they may appear, the advances in ecological economics noted above remain relentlessly anthropocentric in tone. Even the new science is generally interpreted as saying that we should protect "the environment" to protect ourselves. This section carries the debate even further, to a consideration of the ethical dimensions of human-kind–ecosphere relationships. Such ethical considerations are highly relevant to the study of environmental law. It is true that in a discipline deeply influenced by positivism, any inquiry into the moral underpinnings of a field of law tends to be regarded with no small degree of suspicion. Nevertheless, an awareness of the ethical dimensions of environmental law is essential to an understanding of the field itself, its evolution into its present form, and its possible future development.

We proceed on the assumption, noted above, that law generally, and environmental law in particular, embodies certain presuppositions regarding "nature" or "the environment." Traditionally, the environment has been regarded as a set of resources available for human consumption and exploitation; to the extent that law has dealt with "environmental" issues, it has tended to do so with a view to safeguarding human interests in these resources. Environmental degradation or pollution are usually understood, if not defined, in terms of harm to humans or impairment of human interests; thus, even the assimilative capacity of ecosystems is treated as yet another resource for the benefit of humans. Consider the following definition of "pollution" from the British Columbia *Waste Management Act*: "the presence in the environment of substances or contaminants that substantially alter or impair the *usefulness* of the environment."[60] While "environment" is defined as "the air, land, water and all other external conditions or influences under which humans, animals and plants live or are developed" and it might therefore be argued that "usefulness" must be understood broadly to include usefulness to all species, there is no doubt that environmental protection is understood in instrumental terms, as serving some purpose other than simply protecting ecosystems for their own sake. This position is not at all atypical; indeed, it can be said to characterize most current environmental law and policy.

---

60   RSBC 1996, c. 482, s. 1(1).

There has long been an undercurrent of philosophical and legal opinion that has looked beyond these assumptions, and attempted to construct alternative ways of conceptualizing the relationship between humans and the natural world. In the concluding paragraph to *Silent Spring*, the work widely credited with launching the modern environmental movement in North America, Rachel Carson asserted, "the 'control of nature' is a phrase conceived in arrogance, born of the Neanderthal age of biology and philosophy, when it was supposed that nature exists for the convenience of man."[61] Over the last 40 years, this type of thinking has become widespread, challenging the legal system and its participants to confront the ethical dimensions of the broader legal framework within which we make decisions that affect the ecosphere. The fundamental implication is that environmental law does in fact make assumptions about the ethical status (or lack of status) of the environment; a decision to treat the ecosphere as a collection of resources for human use and enjoyment is not ethically value-neutral.

In this section, we present a range of alternative ethical perspectives on the environment. We do not attempt to provide a comprehensive account of environmental ethics, but to highlight some of the most significant points of debate. We then proceed to consider some of the ways in which legal scholars have attempted to evaluate and rethink the ethical dimensions of existing environmental law and policy.

B. Approaches to Environmental Ethics

1. Introduction and Overview

The field of "environmental ethics" has become vast and complicated over the course of its development,[62] with various points of consensus and controversy. Of the latter, one of the most significant is whether environmental ethics ought to be utilitarian and instrumental (that is, derived from or contributing to human interests) or in contrast, ought to flow from a recognition of nature's possessing "inherent" or "intrinsic" value, which ought to be respected (even at the cost of sacrificing certain human interests).

One environmental philosopher, John Rodman, identifies four "currents of thought" in modern environmentalism: resource conservationism, wilderness preservationism, moral

---

61   (Boston: Houghton Mifflin, 1962), 297.

62   There are a number of journals devoted exclusively to the subject, such as *Environmental Ethics*, *Environmental Values*, *Ethics and the Environment*, and *The Trumpeter: Journal of Ecosophy*. This is in addition to articles dealing with various aspects of environmental ethics published in other journals, as well as a growing number of anthologies and treatises. See, for example, J.R. Des Jardins, *Environmental Ethics: An Introduction to Environmental Philosophy*, 2d ed. (Belmont, CA: Wadsworth Publishing, 1997); R.F. Nash, *The Rights of Nature* (Madison, WI: University of Wisconsin Press, 1989); A. Light and H. Rolston III, eds., *Environmental Ethics: An Anthology* (Oxford: Blackwell Publishers, 2003); C. Palmer, *Environmental Ethics* (Santa Barbara, CA: ABC-CLIO, 1997); C. Pierce and D. VanDeVeer, eds., *People, Penguins and Plastic Trees*, 2d ed. (Belmont, CA: Wadsworth Publishing, 1995); L. Pojman, ed., *Environmental Ethics: Readings in Theory and Application*, 2d ed. (Belmont, CA: Wadsworth Publishing, 1998); A. Wellington, A. Greenbaum, and W. Cragg, eds., *Canadian Issues in Environmental Ethics* (Peterborough, ON: Broadview Press, 1997). A useful concise survey of the field is C. Palmer, "An Overview of Environmental Ethics," in Light and Rolston, *Environment Ethics*, at 15.

extensionism, and ecological sensibility.[63] The first two schools of thought, characteristic of the early environmental movement, are still very much a part of the current environmental debate. Resource conservationism is primarily concerned with the development of "wise" resource utilization practices that take into account the interests of society as a whole and also incorporate notions of sustainability.[64] Wilderness preservationism focuses on the value of nature as sanctuary; wilderness is valued because of its beauty and inspirational qualities. Historically, these two have occupied opposing camps; however, both view nature in essentially instrumental terms. Thus, Rodman characterizes the differences between them as "a family quarrel between advocates of two different forms of human use—economic and religio-esthetic."[65]

While these two schools of thought have clear ethical dimensions, such as the problem of how to take into account the interests of future generations, they tend to leave the existing ethical framework essentially untouched. Human interests remain the touchstone.[66] The last two categories identified by Rodman, however, by positing some notion of inherent or intrinsic value in nature, pose significant challenges to traditional ethical and legal thinking about the natural world; these two perspectives will be the focus for the remainder of this section.

2. Extending the Boundaries

The "extensionist" approach calls for the extension of ethical or moral consideration to entities that, according to conventional thought, lie outside the boundaries of the moral community. This can be seen as resulting from the growing realization that these entities are "like us" in some morally relevant way: sentient, capable of feeling pain, and/or alive. This is the type of approach pioneered in the literature on animal rights.[67] The most significant point of controversy in extensionism is that of "moral eligibility": whether everything ought to be included in humankind's moral community and, if not, where the ethical "cutoff line" should be drawn.[68] Aldo Leopold's famous "land ethic" represents

---

63 J. Rodman, "Four Forms of Ecological Consciousness Reconsidered," in D. Scherer and T. Attig, eds., *Ethics and the Environment* (Englewood Cliffs, NJ: Prentice Hall, 1983), 82.

64 Ibid., at 82.

65 Ibid., at 85.

66 Rodman acknowledges that some of the historical figures he places in the "preservationist" category do have some sense of the value of nature apart from human interests; as such, his categorization may be an oversimplification. For the purposes of the present discussion, however, it has the merit of providing an analytical framework for a very complex field. The less anthropocentric aspects of wilderness preservationism are dealt with in the following discussion of extensionism and ecological sensibility.

67 The animal rights or animal liberation literature is quite extensive in its own right. A classic articulation of the arguments can be found in P. Singer, *Animal Liberation* (New York: Avon Books, 1975). For a treatment from a legal perspective, see D. Hoch, "Environmental Ethics and Nonhuman Interests: A Challenge to Anthropocentric License" (1987/88) vol. 23, no. 2 *Gonzaga Law Review* 331. Over the years, there has been considerable debate about the connection between animal liberation and environmental ethics. For a fairly recent entry in the debate, see D. Jamieson, "Animal Liberation Is an Environmental Ethic" (1998) vol. 7, no. 1 *Environmental Values* 41. See also the discussion in chapter 11.

68 See the discussion in R.F. Nash, supra note 62, at 3-12.

the view that moral boundaries have to extend beyond living beings to reflect the interconnectedness of ecosystems:

> All ethics so far evolved rest upon a single premise: that the individual is a member of a community of interdependant parts. ... The land ethic simply enlarges the boundaries of the community to include soils, waters, plants and animals, or collectively: the land. ... [A] land ethic changes the role of *Homo sapiens* from conqueror of the land-community to plain member and citizen of it. It implies respect for his fellow-members, and also respect for the community as such.[69]

An excellent example of extensionist thought is found in the work of Christopher Stone, discussed below, under the heading "Environmental Ethics: Implications for Law."

3. "Re-visioning" the Framework

The extensionist approach stretches the boundaries of the existing ethical framework. In contrast, the approach that Rodman labels "ecological sensibility" calls for a "re-visioning" of the framework. Re-visionists agree with many of the criticisms of existing structures raised by the extensionists; however, they perceive the inadequacies as going to the heart of those structures, and are thus highly skeptical about their capacity to accommodate radically different ways of thinking about the environment. They seek new alternatives, focusing on the need for the realization that we are all part of one community both ecologically and morally. Rather than demanding that we merely extend to "others" the same consideration we expect for our "selves," many writers in this camp call for a radical reconceptualization of the understanding of "self" to encompass notions of interconnectedness and interdependence. The writers seek not so much reform as revolution; they question all the assumptions that form the unexamined subtext of our individual and collective world views.

Deep ecology is one perspective that deliberately sets itself apart from more traditional approaches to environmentalism. The term "deep ecology" was first used by the Norwegian philosopher Arne Naess in 1972 to describe a way of relating to the natural world that would stand in stark contrast to the anthropocentric bias of "shallow ecology," a term under which Naess lumped most of the environmental and conservation movement.[70] As its name suggests, deep ecology goes beyond "surface" criticism to question the fundamental assumptions of the dominant world view of western/modern/industrialized society.[71]

---

69   A. Leopold, "The Land Ethic," in Light and Rolston, supra note 62, 38, at 39.

70   A. Naess, "The Shallow and the Deep, Long-Range Ecology Movements: A Summary" (1973) vol. 16 *Inquiry* 95.

71   For a general overview of deep ecology, see B. Devall and G. Sessions, *Deep Ecology, Living as if Nature Mattered* (Salt Lake City, UT: Peregrine Smith, 1985) and A. Naess, *Ecology, Community and Lifestyle: Outline of an Ecosophy*, trans. and ed. D. Rothenberg (Cambridge: Cambridge University Press, 1989). See also B. Devall, *Simple in Means, Rich in Ends: Practicing Deep Ecology* (Salt Lake City, UT: Peregrine Smith, 1988); A. Drengson and Y. Inoue, eds., *The Deep Ecology Movement: An Introductory Anthology* (Berkeley, CA: North Atlantic Books, 1995). For a recent concise survey by one of the leading figures in the movement, see B. Devall, "The Deep, Long-Range Ecology Movement 1960-2000—A Review" (2001) vol. 6 *Ethics and the Environment* 18.

From a deep ecology perspective, the dominant world view can be said to incorporate two elements: first, and most important, anthropocentrism, or the view of human beings as separate from and exercising dominion over the natural world, and second, the faith in "progress," growth, and the endless possibility of technological advancement. This world view views the relationship between humanity and nature as a hierarchy, with humanity firmly on top; it is therefore not surprising that the environment is not taken into account in any balance of interests test unless doing so would benefit humans. At the same time, faith in progress and technology lend support to the conviction that any environmental problems are byproducts of temporary technological shortcomings, and can be overcome by the application of new and better scientific techniques.

The two basic elements of the dominant world view are reflected in individual and collective consumption patterns, characterized by a failure to distinguish between "vital" or basic needs and "peripheral" wants or desires. Humans are reduced to selfish consumers, and the environment, in the final analysis, is simply that which is consumed. The corresponding attitude toward nature is encapsulated in the question: how can "it" best be exploited to fulfill our so-called needs?

As an alternative, deep ecology proposes an ethic grounded in two norms: self-realization and biocentric equality.[72] The notion of "self-realization," while couched in familiar language, involves a concept of "selfhood" radically different from that which is currently the norm. It incorporates a sense of "organic wholeness"[73] or connectedness to a reality outside the boundaries of individual experience; in fact, the deep ecologist would question the "reality" of boundaries and argue that we are all part of an all-encompassing "self." Biocentric equality is the premise that "all things in the biosphere have an equal right to live and blossom and to reach their own individual form of unfolding and self-realization within the larger self-realization ... all organisms and entities in the ecosphere, as parts of the interrelated whole, are equal in intrinsic worth."[74] Thus, deep ecology calls for a holistic world view that takes into account the interconnectedness of all components of the planetary ecosystem.

Obviously, these norms have far-reaching implications. The proposed shift from anthropocentrism to biocentrism, for example, would require an abandonment of utilitarian rationales for environmental protection in favour of approaches that recognize the "intrinsic value" of nature and natural objects. Within such a "life-centered" world view, we would have to come to view ourselves, individually and collectively, as part of nature rather than separate from and above it. At the individual level, a shift to biocentrism would require an acceptance of responsibility for one's own impact on the environment and of the need to minimize that impact through voluntary limitations on personal behaviour and fundamental changes in consumption patterns. At the societal level, such a shift would have obvious implications for cherished notions of development and progress; it would certainly require that we relinquish the myth of "endless progress," and would ultimately involve the redefinition of these terms in ecologically sustainable and ethically justifiable ways.

---

72   See B. Devall and G. Sessions, supra note 71, at 66-69.

73   Ibid., at 67.

74   Ibid.

While deep ecologists are careful to save their most scathing criticism for "modern," "western," "industrialized" society, much of their analysis tends to generalize about humanity in terms of its impact on nature. By contrast, other perspectives on environmental ethics extend the analysis of domination and hierarchy to deal with the manner in which these perceived "natural" orderings are reproduced in human societies and relationships.

Social ecologists, for example, are reluctant to treat "human" domination of nature as conceptually monolithic; instead, their analysis of domination extends to a consideration of the ways in which the hierarchy of humans over nature is reproduced and reinforced by the various forms of social hierarchy. Murray Bookchin, perhaps the best known among social ecologists, sums up their basic position as follows: "Social ecology has made the understanding of hierarchy—its rise, scope, and impact—the centerpiece of its message of a liberating, rational, and ecological society."[75] Bookchin and other social ecologists are suspicious of analyses of the environmental crisis that do not consider the players involved and their varying degrees of responsibility, and thus end up lumping together the powerful and the powerless. The latter, from this perspective, are more the victims of environmental degradation than its perpetrators.[76]

Along the same lines as social ecologists, ecofeminists have taken issue with the extent to which environmental problems are characterized by deep ecologists as being caused by "anthropocentrism." Instead, they speak of "androcentrism" and question the extent to which "human" domination of nature translates into "male" domination of nature.[77] The ecofeminist perspective further extends the analysis of domination and hierarchy by postulating that the domination of nature by humans, of the poor by the rich, and of women by men are three facets of the same problem and are interconnected at the conceptual level.[78]

---

75   M. Bookchin, *Remaking Society: Pathways to a Green Future* (Boston: South End Press, 1990), 61. See also M. Bookchin, *The Philosophy of Social Ecology*, 2d ed. (Montreal: Black Rose, 1995); J. Biehl and M. Bookchin, *The Politics of Social Ecology* (Montreal: Black Rose, 1998); J. Biehl, ed., *The Murray Bookchin Reader* (Montreal: Black Rose, 1999). A recent anthology that includes critical evaluations of social ecology is A. Light, ed., *Social Ecology After Bookchin* (New York: Guilford Press, 1998).

76   Moreover, social ecologists are unwilling to name "rationality" per se as one of the sources of environmental problems. Bookchin states this position in no uncertain terms: "To sidestep the social basis of our ecological problems, to obscure it with primitivistic cobwebs spun by self-indulgent mystics and anti-rationalists, is to literally turn back the clock of ecological thinking to an atavistic level of trite sentiment that can be used for utterly reactionary purposes." *Remaking Society*, supra note 75, at 43.

77   Anthologies that provide good introductions to ecofeminism are I. Diamond and G.F. Orenstein, eds., *Reweaving the World: the Emergence of Ecofeminism* (San Francisco: Sierra Club Books, 1990); J. Plant, ed., *Healing the Wounds: The Promise of Ecofeminism* (Toronto: Between the Lines, 1989); K.J. Warren, ed., *Ecological Feminism* (London: Routledge, 1994). A recent work that examines the connection of ecofeminism to environmental politics is C.J. Cuomo, *Feminism and Communities: An Ethic of Flourishing* (London: Routledge, 1998).

78   See J. Plant, "Searching for Common Ground: Ecofeminism and Bioregionalism," in I. Diamond and G.F. Orenstein, supra note 77, at 155.

It may be slightly misleading to classify ecofeminism as one environmental perspective, rather than a variety of related perspectives sensitive to this conceptual connection.[79] The point of agreement among them is that overcoming the "ideology of domination" requires an analysis sensitive to both feminist and ecological concerns; to ignore or downplay one form of hierarchy is to lose sight of the fact that the various forms reinforce each other and in many cases are difficult to separate.[80]

Like deep ecologists, many ecofeminists seek to reconceptualize notions of "selfhood," and have a sense of the importance of grounding ethics in the basic fact that "we are all part of one another."[81] In practical terms, ecofeminists seek to develop strategies for resistance to hierarchy and creation of alternatives to current environmentally destructive practices. For this reason, ecofeminism offers empowering visions of the role of individuals in bringing about potential change; as one ecofeminist puts it, "ecofeminism is concerned not only with preserving our planet, but with teaching us how to respect all cycles of life, how to celebrate all forms of diversity, and how to enrich the quality of our own lives and the lives that touch ours."[82]

The three perspectives outlined above grow out of the western tradition, and are to varying degrees reactions against it. They express, in secular philosophical terms, concepts that are sometimes articulated in religious or spiritual terms. The notion that there is a spiritual dimension underlying human–nature relations is not a new one, but it is one that is gaining momentum as various religious groups come to realize the magnitude of environmental problems.[83]

In particular, there has been strong interest in non-western religious and cultural traditions that may be said to embody possibly more harmonious or at least less destructive ways of relating to the natural world.[84] Jainism is one example; best known for the concept of avoidance of causing harm, Jainism extends this consideration to the natural

79   Scholars located the roots of this connection in different eras. Some ecofeminist writers trace such conceptual connections to the Scientific Revolution; others take the analysis further back. See, for example, C. Merchant, *The Death of Nature: Women, Ecology and the Scientific Revolution* (San Francisco: Harper & Row, 1980). Ecofeminists also differ in the emphasis placed on the "bond" between women and nature. Some argue that this connection is "natural" and common to almost all cultural traditions; hence, its use (or misuse) by patriarchy should not be a reason to abandon or deny it. Others express concern about taking for granted some of the assumptions that have been utilized as justifications to subjugate and control both women and the natural world. For a discussion of this and other aspects of ecofeminism from a social ecologist perspective, see J. Biehl, *Finding Our Way: Rethinking Ecofeminist Politics* (Montreal: Black Rose Books, 1991).

80   See K.J. Warren, "The Power and the Promise of Ecological Feminism" (1990) vol. 12, no. 2 *Environmental Ethics* 125.

81   J. Plant, supra note 78, at 156.

82   A.E. Simon, "Ecofeminism: Information and Activism" (1991) vol. 13, no. 1 *Women's Rights Law Reporter* 35, at 35.

83   See H.G. Coward and D.C. Maguire, *Visions of a New Earth: Religious Perspectives on Population, Consumption, and Ecology* (Albany, NY: SUNY Press, 2000).

84   There have, of course, also been a number of attempts to develop or rediscover this type of perspective from within the Judaeo–Christian–Islamic tradition of revealed monotheistic religion. See the chapter on "The Greening of Religion," in Nash, supra note 62, at 87.

world. An ancient Jain aphorism states: "All life is bound together by mutual support and interdependence." Jain ethics, which include avoiding waste and non-acquisitiveness, place prime importance on non-violence in thought, speech, and action.[85] The focus is not merely on the avoidance of causing harm to other forms of life, but on attempting to incorporate respect for life into one's everyday activities. These ethics are given practical application, and are reflected in the rule that Jains are to have either limited or no involvement in "industries which require raw materials from the plant and animal kingdoms or those which poison the air, earth, rivers and sea with harmful effluents."[86]

The sort of attitude toward the natural world manifested in this type of ethical framework is obviously quite different from that which characterizes modern industrial society. In particular, it is less hierarchical and it seems to downplay the importance of "progress" and accumulation. Such an attitude is certainly not unique to Jainism. One writer, who engages in a comparison of values regarding law and environment among the Hopi Indians and in the modern United States, points out that the Hopi value stability, balance, and harmony over growth, expansion, and progress.[87] These values seem to be common to many land-based and indigenous peoples.[88]

Marie Wilson, a spokesperson for the Gitskan Wet'suwet'en Tribal Council in northwestern British Columbia, articulates some of these same perspectives from a Gitskan perspective:

> I believe all people started out connected to the land. People like the Gitskan copied nature because they were surrounded by it, not protected from it as we are. They saw the cycle of life, from the very smallest to the very largest, all connected, and saw that the system itself punished any breaking of the cycle. ... The people saw and understood the checks and balances that were exhibited by the cycle and chose to base their fundamental truths and authority and responsibility on something that has worked for millions of years. They fitted themselves to the cycle of life.[89]

Yet, without taking anything away from contemporary indigenous philosophies or world views, we should note that even for pre-agricultural humans, learning to "[fit] themselves to the cycle of life" in new habitats may have been a hard lesson. The recent paleoecological, anthropological, and archeological literature tells a convincing story of the extinctions of large mammals and birds that accompanied first contact and settlement

---

85   "A Five Point Plan for Jain Ecology" (1991) vol. 18, no. 1 *Jain Digest* 22.

86   Ibid.

87   R. Ragsdale, "Law and Environment in Modern America and Among the Hopi Indians: A Comparison of Values" (1986) vol. 10, no. 2 *Harvard Environmental Law Review* 417, at 456.

88   For a useful, concise discussion, see L.A. Whitt, M. Roberts, W. Norman and V. Grieves, "Indigenous Perspectives," in D. Jamieson, ed., *A Companion to Environmental Philosophy* (Oxford: Blackwell Publishers, 2001), 3. See also: J.A. Grim, ed., *Indigenous Traditions and Ecology: The Interbeing of Cosmology and Community* (Cambridge, MA: Harvard University Press, 2001).

89   M. Wilson, "Wings of the Eagle," in J. Plant and C. Plant, eds., *Turtle Talk* (Philadelphia: New Society Publishers, 1990), 76, at 79.

of their habitats by human beings.[90] It may have been centuries before various groups of prehistoric hunter–gatherers came to live in more or less stable dynamic equilibrium—or steady state—within their self-altered ecosystems. (This is a lesson that modern humans may be forced to relearn). The main point is that once people have settled into their ecosystems and perhaps developed a sense of engaged consciousness with nature, it is not they who set the agenda and then attempt to incorporate non-human interests. Instead, "law" is dictated at least in part by the realities of the physical surroundings of the community. Law is not imposed by humans on nature; if anything, the reverse is true. This is a radically different twist on the phrase "law of the land."

While some writers have raised the possibility of turning toward the traditional wisdom of indigenous peoples in order to find solutions to current environmental problems,[91] the threat of "cultural appropriation" is very real.[92] Moreover, indigenous views of a "proper" relationship to the environment may not necessarily coincide with environmentalist concerns. Wilson warns:

> At the risk of sounding scornful or derogatory, I have to say that the Indian attitude toward the natural world is different from the environmentalists'. I have had the awful feeling that when we are finished dealing with the courts and our land claims, we will then have to battle the environmentalists and they will not understand why. I feel quite sick at this prospect because the environmentalists want these beautiful places kept in a state of perfection: to not touch them, rather to keep them pure. So that we can leave our jobs and for two weeks we can venture into the wilderness and enjoy this ship in a bottle. In a way this is like denying that life is happening constantly in these wild places, that change is always occurring. Human life must be there too. Humans have requirements and they are going to have to use some of the life in these places. I do believe that life does not need humans but, rather, humans do need the rest of life. We are very small within the structure.[93]

There is a real need to balance interest in indigenous perspectives against respect for the uniqueness of the cultural context in which those perspectives evolved. There are no "ready-made" answers, no set of solutions that we will be able to adopt wholesale from other cultures. While we may have to fashion our own solutions, the existence of alternative models reminds us of basic truths that seem to have dropped from sight: there is

---

90   J. Diamond, *The Third Chimpanzee* (New York: HarperCollins, 1992); T.F. Flannery, *The Future Eaters: An Ecological History of the Australasian Lands and Peoples* (Chatsworth, NSW: Reed Books, 1994).

91   See, for example, A.L. Booth and H.M. Jacobs, "Ties That Bind: Native American Beliefs as a Foundation for Environmental Consciousness" (1990) vol. 12, no. 1 *Environmental Ethics* 27. Booth and Jacobs also prepared *Environmental Consciousness: Native American Worldviews and Sustainable Natural Resource Management: An Annotated Bibliography* (Chicago: Council of Planning Librarians, 1988).

92   Booth and Jacobs, supra note 91, at 42-43, acknowledge that there is "a delicate line between respectful learning and intellectual plundering," but are confident that "[a]n open hearted and respectful investigation of Native American cultures, particularly when members of these cultures voluntarily share with us their understandings and perceptions, can help us discover new directions in which to travel to realize our own potentials."

93   Wilson, supra note 89, at 82-83.

nothing predestined about the path we have chosen, there is more than one way of relating sustainably to the ecosphere, and there are certainly alternatives to growthbound definitions of "development."

It is an awareness of this choice that informs bioregionalism, a perspective that attempts to find practical applications for ethical thinking about the environment.[94] In some ways it could be characterized as a synthesis of some of the ideas developed in the environmental ethics literature with the sense of place common to land-based cultures. Bioregionalists seek "to become dwellers in the land ... to come to know the earth fully and honestly, the crucial and perhaps only and all-encompassing task is to understand *place*, the immediate specific place where we live."[95] The bioregionalist perspective incorporates the analysis of hierarchy and domination and attempts to visualize alternative means of social organization that would lead to a more balanced relationship with nature and the natural world; in so doing, they may point the way toward real alternatives.

C. Environmental Ethics: Implications for Law

The preceding discussion has examined a number of perspectives that critique existing assumptions about the environment and propose alternatives. What are the implications for environmental law and policy?

Law and legal academics were affected by the increased awareness of environmental concerns in the early 1970s. As the philosophical debates about the ethical status (or non-status) of the environment grew more heated, corresponding debates among legal scholars increased. Two articles written at that time by legal academics are still considered important landmarks in the literature dealing with the extension of some form of ethical consideration to nature.

An early treatment of the subject, now a classic in the legal literature dealing with the environment, is the 1972 article "Should Trees Have Standing? Towards Legal Rights for Natural Objects," by Christopher Stone.[96] Stone, a law professor at the University of Southern California, proposed that legal consideration in the form of rights be extended "to forests, oceans, rivers and other so-called 'natural objects' in the environment— indeed to the natural environment as a whole."[97] This notion that the environment could

---

94   See, for example, K. Sale, *Dwellers in the Land* (San Francisco: Sierra Club Books, 1985); V. Andruss et al., eds., *Home! A Bioregional Reader* (Gabriola Island, BC: New Society, 1990).

95   Sale, supra note 94, at 42.

96   (1972) vol. 45, no. 2 *Southern California Law Review* 450. Reprinted as *Should Trees Have Standing?— Towards Legal Rights for Natural Objects* (Los Altos, CA: William Kaufman, 1974). All page references are to the law review version.

97   Ibid., at 456.

have "rights" was greeted with considerable skepticism by the legal community, despite the fact that Stone was careful to fit his proposals within the existing legal framework, thus leaving its underlying assumptions more or less untouched.[98]

Stone was interested in what he termed the "interplay between law and the development of social awareness."[99] As a legal philosopher, he was intrigued by the ways in which law reflects societal understandings of ethical problems:

> Societies, like human beings, progress through different stages of sensitiveness, and ... in our progress through these stages the law ... has a role to play, dramatizing and summoning into the open the changes that are taking place within us.[100]

Stone's work in this area was motivated at least in part by longstanding theoretical interests; it is worth noting, however, that his decision to write and publish the "Standing" piece was a direct response to a concrete set of circumstances. The US Forest Service had granted a permit to Walt Disney Enterprises to develop Mineral King Valley, a wilderness area in the Sierra Nevada Mountains.[101] The Sierra Club brought suit for an injunction, arguing that the project would adversely affect the area's aesthetic and ecological balance. The Federal District Court granted a preliminary injunction; the Court of Appeals for the Ninth Circuit reversed, on the grounds that Sierra Club had no "standing" to bring the question to the courts.

The case revolved around the question of standing: whether the Sierra Club was the proper party, whether it had a legally protectable and tangible interest at stake in the litigation. The irony of the situation was obvious to Stone; clearly, the entity that had a tangible interest at stake in the litigation was the valley itself. Thus, the basic thrust of his argument developed in response to the Mineral King situation: why, after all, should the valley itself not be granted some form of legal recognition? Here the Sierra Club was merely using whatever legal tactics it could in order to stop the development project. What was required was a way of conceptualizing these types of situations which would eliminate the need for such legal gymnastics; Stone set out to develop such a conceptual framework.

Not at all unaware of the controversial nature of his proposals, Stone begins his argument with a discussion of "the unthinkable":

---

98   In fact, toward the end of the article, Stone does discuss the need for a fundamental transformation in our attitude toward the environment. (Ibid., at 499-501.) This perspective is developed in his more recent book, C.D. Stone, *Earth and Other Ethics: The Case for Moral Pluralism* (New York: Harper & Row, 1987). Today, 30 years after the publication of the original article, one suspects that many if not most lawyers would still find his ideas not so much revolutionary as bizarre. This is either a tribute to Stone's farsightedness or a commentary on the slowness of change within the legal system; probably both. See also chapter 11.

99   Garrett Hardin, foreword to *Should Trees Have Standing?* 1974, supra note 96, ix, at xii (quoting conversation with Stone).

100 Ibid, at xii-xiii.

101 The development was to consist of a $35 million complex of motels and recreational facilities.

Throughout legal history, each successive extension of rights to some new entity has been, thereetofore, a bit unthinkable. We are inclined to suppose the rightlessness of rightless "things" to be a decree of nature, not a legal convention acting in support of some status quo. It is thus that we defer considering the choices involved in all their moral, social, and economic dimensions.[102]

Thus, the idea of extending rights to any entity "is bound to sound odd or frightening or laughable ... partly because until the rightless thing receives its rights, we cannot see it as anything but a *thing* for the use of 'us'—those who are holding rights at the time."[103]

Stone goes on to describe the "rightlessness" of natural objects at common law.[104] He uses the example of pollution of a stream to illustrate how a common law understanding of "environmental harm" focuses exclusively on the interests of any humans involved. The stream itself would be "rightless" in the sense that

- it would not have standing to initiate proceedings;
- only damage to the interests of humans would be taken into account in determining the granting of legal relief; the notion of "damage to the stream" would be meaningless unless it were put in the context of damage to human interests; and
- if there were a favourable judgment, it would be based on what it would take to compensate the human litigant, and would run to his or her benefit.

The third aspect of the stream's "rightlessness" would be particularly important from an environmental standpoint, given that the amount needed to compensate the plaintiff would probably be far less than that needed to remedy the damage to the stream and it would almost certainly be insufficient to force the polluter to stop polluting.[105]

Stone shows that bringing the environment into the existing framework can have considerable instrumental value. For example, Stone argues that the legal recognition of injuries should extend to taking into account the full cost to the environment; that is, make the quantum of damages correspond to the full extent of injury to the natural object in question.[106] From a wholly anthropocentric perspective, this would be one way— perhaps the only way—of taking the full costs of pollution into account; the natural object could be viewed as "the guardian of unborn generations as well as of otherwise unrepresented but distantly injured contemporary humans."[107]

However, Stone maintains that he is going beyond anthropocentricity in advocating the consideration of injuries that are presently not taken into account. These costs, such as those relating to the loss of commercially valueless species or the disappearance of wilderness areas, are not economically measurable, and thus could not be assessed in the

---

102   Stone, supra note 96, at 453.

103   Ibid., at 455.

104   Ibid., at 459-63.

105   Ibid., at 462.

106   Ibid., at 473-79.

107   Ibid., at 475.

form of damages.[108] Moreover, Stone recognizes the limitations of "homocentricity," and toward the end of his article discusses the need for a "radical new conception of man's relationship to the rest of nature."[109] He asks:

> What is it within us that gives us this need not just to satisfy basic biological wants, but to extend our wills over things, to objectify them, to make them ours, to manipulate them, to keep them at a psychic distance? Can it all be explained on "rational" bases? Should we not be suspect of such needs within us, cautious as to why we wish to gratify them?[110]

The actual proposals embodied in Stone's 1972 piece were overtaken by liberalization of standing requirements and statutory developments in US environmental law.[111] Nevertheless, the piece remains notable for its attempt to incorporate alternative ways of thinking about the environment into law.

A 1973 article by Laurence Tribe, "Ways Not To Think About Plastic Trees: New Foundations for Environmental Law," is another early but significant piece in the legal literature on the environment.[112] Tribe goes further than Stone in attempting to move beyond anthropocentricity; his position can be seen as falling somewhere between a straight extensionist and a re-visionist approach.

Analyzing the theoretical underpinnings of the then newly emerging field of environmental law, Tribe describes the "basic platform" of the field as one of "analytic sophistication in the service of human need."[113] Tribe gives an overview of the supposed obstacles to "good" environmental policy, and finds none of them so troublesome as the basic problem of "ideological boundaries": the tradition within which environmental planners operate, one that "regards the satisfaction of individual human wants as the only defensible measure of the good" and "perceives the only legitimate task of reason to be that of consistently identifying and then serving individual appetite, preference, or desire."[114]

Tribe recognizes that environmentalists often make arguments on the basis of human interest out of a perfectly understandable desire to conform to the "demands of legal doctrine and the exigencies of political reality."[115] However, he regards this as self-defeating and proposes an alternative approach, which would recognize value in nature quite apart from its instrumental value in the satisfaction of human desires and would ground environmental policy in a sense of obligation towards the natural world. He expresses the following concern:

---

108 Ibid. In order to address the third aspect of "rightlessness," the problem of the potential beneficiary of the judgment, Stone advocates making the environment a beneficiary in its own right, through setting up a mechanism such as a trust fund, to be administered by the guardian in the interests of the natural object. Ibid., at 480-81.

109 Ibid., at 495.

110 Ibid., at 465-56.

111 See "Preface," in C.D. Stone, *Earth and Other Ethics*, supra note 98, at 3.

112 (1974) vol. 83, no. 7 *Yale Law Journal* 1315-48.

113 Ibid., at 1317.

114 Ibid., at 1325.

115 Ibid., at 1330.

What the environmentalist may not perceive is that, by couching his claims in terms of human self-interest—by articulating environmental goals wholly in terms of human needs and preferences—he may be helping to legitimate a system of discourse which so structures human thought and feeling as to erode, over the long run, the very sense of obligation which provided the initial impetus for his own protective efforts.[116]

Furthermore, Tribe points out, if environmental concerns are couched in terms of human interests, there will be few obstacles to throwing those interests into the balance along with more conventional human values such as those associated with resource development:

[O]nce obligation has been transformed into a mere matter of personal preference, the tendency is inevitable to compare the value of wilderness with the value of strip mined coal in terms of self-interest. From there, it is but a short step to an even more blatantly reductionist approach: In order to insure that the comparison is "rational," the two values will almost certainly be translated into smoothly exchangeable units of satisfaction, such as dollars. While certain discontinuities may still be recognized—destruction of *all* wilderness areas may not be deemed worth even an infinite supply of coal—they will tend to be gradually eroded by the pressure toward analytic conformity.[117]

As theoretical grounding for an alternative approach, Tribe proposes a "synthesis of immanence with transcendence": an approach that would combine respect for what is, with an appreciation for the ongoing process of change in nature and of humanity as a part of nature. He describes this approach in the following terms:

Such a synthesis requires the sanctification neither of the present nor of progress but of *evolving processes of interaction and change*—processes of action and choice that are valued for themselves, for the conceptions of being that they embody, at the same time that they are valued as means to the progressive evolution of the conceptions, experiences, and ends that characterize the human community in nature at any given point in its history.[118]

However, when Tribe attempts to address concrete proposals for incorporating such a synthesis into environmental law and policy, he retreats to extensionism. He falls back on vague notions of granting "rights" to natural objects and suggestions that environmental legislation incorporate language referring to obligations toward nature.[119] Tribe appears to be groping toward a radically different approach, but in the end relies on standard legal language and mechanisms without really explaining how they could be adapted to new ways of thinking; he thus fails to demonstrate how a "synthesis of immanence and transcendence" would translate into actual law and policy.[120]

Both Stone and Tribe view law as being adaptable to changing perceptions of the ethical status of the environment. Thus, after going through his analysis of the treatment

---

116 Ibid., at 1330-31.

117 Ibid., at 1331-32.

118 Ibid., at 1338.

119 Ibid., at 1341.

120 D.P. Emond points this out in "Co-operation in Nature: A New Foundation for Environmental Law" (1984) vol. 22, no. 2 *Osgoode Hall Law Journal* 323-48, at 325-26.

of the environment within the then existing legal framework, Stone offers a concrete set of proposals to address its inadequacies. He argues that an extension of legal consideration to natural objects can be accomplished in such a way as to fit within the existing legal traditions. With regard to the question of standing, for example, he suggests that we handle the legal problems of natural objects through the appointment of a guardian—that is, in the same way as we handle those of human beings who are legally incompetent.[121] Similarly, Tribe visualizes reforms in environmental law and policy in order to reflect his proposed "new foundation"; for example, he proposes that environmental impact statements incorporate "explicit references to obligations felt towards nature."[122]

However, the approach pioneered in the legal literature by Stone and Tribe has certainly not been uncontroversial. It has been subjected to a great deal of criticism from (at least) two sides: from writers who do not see the point of moving "beyond anthropocentrism" and from those who reject all variations on anthropocentric models, accusing Stone and Tribe of perpetuating the very bias they are supposedly trying to overcome.

A representative critic of the first school is P.S. Elder,[123] whose basic point is that Stone and the deep ecologists, whom he lumps together, "do not take us anywhere in solving environmental disputes, that conventional ethics and law do not already go."[124] He argues that natural objects lack the characteristics upon which persons' claims to moral considerateness are based: "awareness, self-consciousness, the ability to formulate goals, act to attain them and to appreciate their attainment."[125] Elder continues:

> It is, therefore, a distortion of our concepts to claim that plants or non-living natural objects can "want" to survive or remain undisturbed. There is "nobody home" who could care, or who could suffer. And if they do not care, why should we?[126]

---

121 Stone, supra note 96, at 464-73. The guardian would presumably be an environmental group, of which, as Stone points out, there are an increasing number with the requisite expertise and resources to enable them to function in this manner. The passage of time and corresponding mushrooming of environmental groups would only seem to strengthen Stone's argument on this point. Stone anticipates what is possibly the most significant objection to his proposal: that it would be difficult if not impossible for the guardian to judge the needs of the natural object in its charge. He counters by arguing that in fact we judge the interests of "abstract" entities such as corporations all the time, and if anything it would probably be easier to determine or judge the needs of a natural object, where certain criteria of "wellness" are beyond dispute. Ibid., at 471.

122 Tribe, supra note 112, at 1341.

123 P.S. Elder, "Legal Rights for Nature: The Wrong Answer to the Right(s) Question" (1984) vol. 22, no. 2 *Osgoode Hall Law Journal* 285, at 285. Elder's attitude toward this type of enterprise is summed up at the outset:

> I reject [Stone's] claim that non-animal and perhaps non-living objects ought to have legal standing. The only stone which could be of moral concern and hence deserving of legal rights, is one like Christopher. This may tell today's "deep ecologist" that "anthropocentric" thinkers such as myself are "shallow"; but epithets do not replace analysis.

124 Ibid.

125 Ibid., at 288.

126 Ibid.

Elder goes on to critique what he sees as the implicit—and unavoidable—anthropocentrism of both Stone's proposals and the deep ecology perspective. In a nutshell, he is critical of any approach that presumes that humans can "speak for the environment." Given that we cannot avoid anthropocentricity, he seems to be saying, let us at least be upfront about it, and let us not "distort" our existing legal framework.

Attacking from the other direction, John Livingston points out that the power to "confer" rights implies control, and the conferral of rights is highly problematic when examined from the perspective of concern about human domination of the natural world.[127] Livingston claims that advocates of rights for the environment have to address the "ultimate question ... whether *all* of non-human nature ought to move into the control of the human relationship."[128] He elaborates:

> Taken to its extreme, the result of the extension of rights would be to "humanize," or domesticate the entire planet. All life would be a human farm.[129]

Livingston's attitude toward environmental rights is essentially a reflection of his general skepticism as to whether modification of existing legal provisions can in fact deal with the "real" problem: "the *a priori* assumption that all non-human life is dedicated to human service."[130] He continues, "The law cannot deal with this obstacle because it is neither a moral nor a statutory issue. It is a cultural predisposition."[131] Livingston does, however, find some "residual merit" in the debate over environmental rights, "if only for having shown that environmental despoliation, degradation and the barbarous interspecies behaviour of humankind may have no remedies within the Western cultural tradition."[132] He concludes:

> The need is not to invest endless time, energy and creativity in futile attempts to rationalize rights for non-humans within the existing belief structure, but rather to systematically address, with every intellectual tool at our disposal, the pathological species-chauvinist belief structure itself.[133]

More recently, a similar cynicism about law was expressed in "Law Reform or World Re-form: The Problem of Environmental Rights."[134] The authors, Cynthia Giagnocavo and Howard Goldstein, launch an attack on "neo-rights" theory, and particularly on Stone and Tribe. Arguing from a deep ecology perspective, they reject legal reforms as mere tinkering at the margins:

---

127 J. Livingston, "Rightness or Rights?" (1984) vol. 22, no. 2 *Osgoode Hall Law Journal* 309-21, at 309.

128 Ibid., at 320.

129 Ibid.

130 Ibid., at 314.

131 Ibid.

132 Ibid.

133 Ibid., at 321.

134 C. Giagnocavo and H. Goldstein, "Law Reform or World Re-form: The Problem of Environmental Rights" (1990) vol. 35, no. 2 *McGill Law Journal* 345-86.

The legally trained will ask of deep ecology, "What are you offering lawyers?"; lawyers need to feel that there is something for them to do. Our response is that deep ecology offers "lawyers," as lawyers, precious little. Conservative jurisprudence, which sees law as being both the most appropriate and most effective instrument of social change, is in need of rethinking. Ecological disasters such as oil spills and the depletion of the ozone layer provide ample evidence of how inadequate the legal framework is for dealing with deep-rooted cultural problems like our destruction of the planet.[135]

The authors go on to argue that legal reform is not only useless, but potentially dangerous in that it diverts attention from the need for real change: "Environmental rights might at best save a forest here or a river there, but in enriching and legitimating the very institution which contributes to the reification of trees and water as 'property,' they may be harming the world more than healing it."[136] They conclude that the changes required for a real and lasting solution to our environmental problems "can only be brought about by a re-writing of our metaphysic."[137]

In contrast, Elaine Hughes, in a piece entitled "Fishwives and Other Tails: Ecofeminism and Environmental Law,"[138] takes a very different approach. Hughes acknowledges the potential danger of co-opting ecofeminism by attempting to incorporate its insights into a critique and reconstruction of environmental law. However, she notes, fundamental changes are required in order to address environmental problems, and ecofeminism offers "a rich source of ideas about how one might 're-vision' the entire framework of environmental law."[139] Furthermore, "a transition must begin somewhere."[140] Hughes does not trivialize the dangers of co-option, [141] but seems to conclude that a failure to engage with the law has its own dangers.

Hughes sets out to analyze pollution control legislation, of which the most common type is the regulatory statute aimed at controlling the level of pollutant discharge into the ambient environment. She specifically focuses on water pollution provisions in the federal *Fisheries Act*. Having set out the basic model for such legislation, Hughes evaluates it from a radical feminist perspective:

[T]he entire approach is based upon setting up a hierarchy of degradation of (violence against) nature. We do not seek to protect nature from all harm, because of its inherent value. Instead, we seek to regulate how much harm is done, stopping short only when we might harm our own self-interest. As a result, some damage is simply allowed, such as

---

135 Ibid., at 347.

136 Ibid., at 384-85.

137 Ibid., at 386.

138 (1995) vol. 8, no. 2 *Canadian Journal of Women and the Law* 502-30.

139 Ibid., at 511.

140 Ibid.

141 In fact, she is quite upfront about the personal nature of her engagement with this issue, and the need to think critically about her own position as an environmental lawyer. Ibid., at 510-11. For a commentary on the dangers of legal co-option in the context of the environmental justice movement, see L.W. Cole, "Foreword: A Jeremiad on Environmental Justice and the Law" (1995) vol. 14, no. 1 *Stanford Environmental Law Journal* ix-xviii.

pollution caused by an unregulated substance, or any pollution that falls within the regulatory standards or the permit terms and conditions. Other harm is deemed to be unacceptable, but in practice is condoned; pollution in contravention of the statute or permit is
illegal, but the response is usually to allow such conduct to continue under the auspices of a
compliance agreement. Even when formal sanctions, such as criminal prosecution, are
used, the response is unlikely to require the polluter's activities to cease permanently.
Instead, the best result expected from the application of formal sanctions is statutory
compliance; the offender is reduced to an acceptable level of environmental harm.[142]

Hughes notes that there are parallels between this treatment of nature in environmental regulation and the legal approaches to violence against and degradation of women.
She draws the comparison to the regulation of pornography, noting that the definition of
what is "obscene" is to a large extent based on "the degree of societal harm that may
flow from exposure to the material,"[143] rather than on the "actual harm done to the
women who must pose for the camera."[144] She concludes that "our laws regulate, rather
than prohibit, this environmental damage, just as they engage in the social regulation
(not prohibition) of the degree of violence against women."[145]

Starting from the premise that the challenge is one of replacing a system based on
domination with a system based on equality, Hughes notes that "ecofeminism itself
suggests a number of different principles upon which human relationships with the
environment could be based."[146] She proceeds to explore these principles of "kinship,
interconnection, cyclic patterns, use of emotion, and responsibility,"[147] before turning to
a consideration of how they might be built into a "re-visioned" *Fisheries Act*:

> My approach has been to try to imagine a law in which nature is of central importance. ... I
> have tried to put fish into a social position of substantive equality, where their interests are
> accorded no less importance than human interests (while recognizing that their well-being
> is in our best interests). While there is a danger of anthropomorphism here, I have tried to
> avoid this by framing the law on the basis of human responsibility to nature, not by looking
> at nature's "rights." In other words, I have tried to draft a model law in which we are
> required to realize that fish do count, and which makes people both individually and
> collectively responsible for behaviour that treats fish as a "lesser other."[148]

Hughes' version of the *Fisheries Act* takes up less than four pages of text, but it
provides a fascinating example of an attempt to envision a fundamentally different
framework that is nonetheless recognizable from the perspective of traditional legal

---

142 Hughes, supra note 138, at 514.

143 Ibid., at 515.

144 Ibid.

145 Ibid., at 516.

146 Ibid., at 517.

147 Ibid., at 526.

148 Ibid., at 525.

approaches to environmental regulation.[149] Her approach exemplifies an attitude toward the potential role of law in environmental protection that avoids, on the one hand, the polar extremes of naive optimism about the capacity of the legal system as it presently exists to address environmental problems and, on the other hand, unrelieved cynicism about the capacity of law to do anything at all. However, as Hughes acknowledges, the most significant obstacles standing in the way of implementing an approach such as she proposes is "the political and cultural acceptability of the underlying notion that nature should be treated with equality and respect."[150] She notes, "Unless our dominant cultural attitude toward nature changes, there can be no political will to even examine ecofeminist proposals."[151]

Thus, Hughes seems to leave us with the same question as the other scholars who have tackled the interface between environmental ethics and environmental law: can any species of legal mechanism or legal reform address problems the roots of which lie deep within our "cultural myths"?

V. CONCLUSION

[The] extension of ethics, so far studied only by philosophers, is actually a process in ecological evolution. Its sequences may be described in ecological as well as in philosophical terms. An ethic, ecologically, is a limitation on freedom of action in the struggle for existence. An ethic, philosophically, is a differentiation of social from antisocial conduct. These are two definitions of one thing.[152]

This chapter provides an overview of our evolving understanding of the relationship between humans and the ecosphere. The first section contrasts prevailing economic rationality with basic ecological principles and reveals that mechanistic utilitarian economic models no longer adequately reflect biophysical reality. The second section, on environmental ethics, shows that current environmental law shares much with economic theory; in particular, the underlying premises of both treat the ecosphere merely as a collection of resources for human use and enjoyment.

The way that any culture relates to "the environment," as revealed by its economic activities and institutional structures such as environmental law, is invariably a reflection of that culture's dominant world view. Any world view can only be a partial representation of reality and, as such, must constantly evolve as knowledge improves and circumstances require. The point to emphasize is that environmental law derives not from nature

---

149 Hughes points out that her attempt to incorporate ecofeminist principles led her to build on many of the same policies that "reform environmentalism has been working towards for years." She mentions participatory democracy, risk-aversiveness, environmental reclamation, and accountability. However, she insists, "Where ecofeminism takes the proposal beyond reform environmentalism is: first, in the requirement that decision-makers take into account the real dangers that lie in our current tendency to treat nature as 'something apart,' rather than our home; and second, in the notion that *no* level of harm is acceptable." Ibid., at 526 (emphasis in original).

150 Ibid., at 530.

151 Ibid.

152 Leopold, supra note 69, at 38.

but rather from human perceptions of nature. Existing environmental law in Canada clearly reflects the currently dominant scientific and ethical perspective of industrial cultures everywhere, but there is nothing "natural," preordained, or inevitable about that perspective. On the contrary, it is only one of an indeterminate number of possible alternatives.

On an infinite planet, it might matter little how far human perceptions of nature departed from the "true" nature of external reality. However, as the scale of the human enterprise approaches that of the ecosphere, it is essential that the internal structure and "variety," and the behaviour of our management models mirror, or at least acknowledge, the corresponding characteristics of the natural world. We argue that accelerating global change provides sufficient evidence to seriously question the validity of our prevailing ethical, economic, and scientific assumptions about human–environment relationships.

Consider a precedent: for most of human evolution a geocentric "the-world-is-flat" perception of the universe was an adequate first approximation of reality. In fact, most people even today could live their entire lives without penalty as if the world were flat and the centre of all creation. It only became necessary to incorporate a heliocentric round earth into the European world view with the expansion of trade and navigation that accompanied the Scientific Revolution. Sometimes dramatic shifts in the perception of reality will be stiffly resisted by established interests and painfully slow to triumph— only in 1992 did the Catholic Church admit its error in persecuting Galileo for his confirmation of Copernican reality over 300 years before.

Traditional and land-based cultures live in immediate contact with their natural surroundings, often very aware of the limitations and the fragility of the ecosystems that sustain them. They have developed practices, sometimes over a period of millennia, that enable them to survive and thrive as part of nature. These practices represent an understanding of, and adaptation to, the particular environment in which a culture has evolved, if only long after having significantly altered the habitat and even driven easily hunted mammals and birds to extinction. The perceived role of humanity may vary considerably among present-day versions of this traditional world view, from that of "one creature among many" to that of steward of the whole, but what many of these perspectives have in common is a recognition of the limitations of both human knowledge of and human power over the natural world.

This is a realization that we too are having to confront, as the limitations of our scientific, economic, and legal models become increasingly apparent. If mechanistic science and derivative economic models see humanity as separate from and dominant over natural process, late 20th-century science argues for holism and greater humility in recognition of the ever-evolving and forever partial nature of human understanding. With the convergence of ethics and ecology, we are being forced to confront our dependence on our natural surroundings and on natural processes; the ethical dimensions of this dependence are only beginning to be explored.

Whether the origins are philosophical or scientific, new or ancient, ways of thinking about the natural world and our place within it have profound implications for law. The message of accelerating global change seems to be that it is time to move beyond a "flat earth" approach to environmental law and policy. The challenge is a significant one. While law is not completely rigid and can to some extent be adapted to meet changing social values and needs, it tends to follow rather than to lead those changes. Thus, those skeptical about the possibility of using law to alter our environmental practices have a point. However, they lose sight of one important consideration: law may not create new realities, but it can mediate the debate between those who are satisfied with the status quo and those who are striving to visualize alternatives and put them into practice. In that sense, it has an important—indeed, a crucial—role to play.

QUESTIONS

1. Complexity theory, particularly in relation to ecosystem behaviour, shows the world to be a far less predictable place than linear mechanistic science, upon which most environmental law is premised. For example, environmental impact assessment generally assumes linear change and predictable outcomes. In light of continued human dependence on ecosystem integrity, in the future how should our emerging understanding of complex systems characterized by lags, thresholds and other forms of discontinuous behaviour affect the structuring of legal responses to environmental protection?

2. Following the prevailing reductionist and mechanistic interpretation of nature, traditional property law assumes that the environment can be divided up into marketable commodities and harvested for private profit. At present, there is growing support for the privatization of "natural capital" stocks (for example, fish stocks and forests) on the assumption that private ownership will better ensure resource conservation. However, market and related economic conditions may encourage stock liquidation. This is problematic because we now recognize that these same stocks provide a wide range of common pool life-support functions in addition to being marketable goods. This means that the exploitation for private gain of a particular stock (for example, a forest for lumber) may destroy a greater value of biophysical services upon which all life depends (for example, carbon sink, biodiversity, and climate stabilization functions). How, in your opinion, should the common or public values associated with privately owned resource stocks be treated by society and in law?

3. Should human interests be the determinative factor in decision making regarding environmental protection or resource exploitation? Do you agree with Stone that granting "rights" to the environment, or to particular natural objects, could offer a useful tool for balancing human and non-human interests? What are the conceptual and practical difficulties with Stone's proposal? What are the advantages of his proposal, both from an anthropocentric and from a non-anthropocentric perspective? Does Hughes's proposal, based on the notion of human responsibility toward nature, represent a better alternative?

4. Many now argue that far-reaching changes in societal values are going to be necessary in order to address the environmental problems that we currently face. Consider the following statement:

> When most people see a large automobile and think first of the air pollution it causes, rather than the social status it conveys, environmental ethics will have arrived. In a fragile biosphere, the ultimate fate of humanity may depend on whether we can cultivate deeper sources of fulfillment, founded on a widespread ethic of limiting consumption and finding non-material enrichment. An ethic becomes widespread enough to restrain antisocial behaviour effectively, moreover, only when it is encoded in culture, in society's collective memory,

experience, and wisdom. (Alan Durning, "Asking How Much Is Enough," in *State of the World 1991: A Worldwatch Institute Report on Progress Toward a Sustainable Society* (New York and London: W.W. Norton, 1991), 153, at 165-66.)

In your opinion, what role, if any, does law have to play in developing, promoting, or "encoding" such an ethic? How could it best do so?

5. What is our moral obligation to future generations? See J. Gaba, "Environmental Ethics and Our Moral Relationship to Future Generations: Future Rights and Present Virtue" (1999) vol. 24 *Columbia Journal of Environmental Law* 249.

6. To what extent should questions of eco-justice and transboundary environmental impacts influence private consumption decisions? Could such considerations be incorporated into domestic laws?

FURTHER READINGS

C. Palmer, "An Overview of Environmental Ethics," in A. Light and H. Rolston III, eds., *Environmental Ethics: An Anthology* (Oxford: Blackwell, 2003), chapter 15.

W.E. Rees, "Globalization and Sustainability: Conflict or Convergence?" (2002) vol. 22, no. 4 *Bulletin of Science, Technology and Society* 249.

World Commission on Environment and Development, *Our Common Future* (Oxford: Oxford University Press, 1987).

CHAPTER TWO

Jurisdictional Issues

Marie-Ann Bowden

I. INTRODUCTION

P. Muldoon and B. Rutherford
**"Environment and the Constitution: Submission to the House of
Commons Standing Committee on Environment"**
(Toronto: Canadian Environmental Law Association and Pollution
Probe, 1991), appendix E (edited)

Division of Powers

The *Constitution Act, 1867* sets out the division of powers between the federal and the provincial governments. The list of powers is meant to be exhaustive and the federal and provincial governments are to be supreme within their own sphere.

Provincial Jurisdiction

The provinces have jurisdiction to regulate with respect to pollution matters by virtue of their primary jurisdiction over "Property and Civil Rights in the Province" (s. 92(13)) and "Generally all matters of a merely local or private nature in the Province" (s. 92(16)). It can be said that property and civil rights are the provincial equivalent of the federal peace, order and good government. Given that a good deal of pollution arises in the context of land use and land use planning, pollution regulation appears to be of a local and regional nature. Provinces do not, however, have the right to regulate out of province companies. Other sources of provincial jurisdiction are found in their control and ownership of their land, mines and minerals (s. 109) and non-renewable natural resources, forestry and electrical energy (s. 92A).

Federal Jurisdiction

The federal power to legislate over environmental matters is clear where such matters have interprovincial and international effects; however, it is unclear that the power to legislate national environmental standards would survive a jurisdictional challenge.

Parliament's jurisdiction to regulate the environment comes from a number of different heads of power. It is questionable that any one head of power gives Parliament the jurisdiction that it needs to play a strong role in providing national standards and policy. Especially in areas where land pollution, land use and resource conservation are involved, the federal government would undoubtedly be challenged for stepping into provincial jurisdiction.

The significant federal powers involved can be characterized into two groups: functional and conceptual. The functional powers are as follows:

• "Navigation and Shipping" (s. 91(10))
• "Sea Coast and Inland Fisheries" (s. 91(12))
• "Canals, Harbours, Rivers and Lake Improvements" (s. 108)
• "Federal Works and Undertakings" (s. 91(29) and 92(10))

While "Agriculture" (s. 95) might be added to this list, and although it is framed as a concurrent power, that is shared with the provinces, it has essentially been emptied of meaning by judicial pronouncement. It is difficult to see it as a true concurrent power.

It is clear that the above exclusive powers allow Parliament to legislate over specific activities which necessarily involve matters of environmental quality.

The conceptual powers, however, arguably provide Parliament with general authority to legislate over broadly defined activities which by analogy or implication include matters of environmental quality. They are as follows:

• "Criminal Law" (s. 91(27))
• "Peace, Order and Good Government" (s. 91)
• "Taxation" (s. 91(3))
• "Trade and Commerce" (s. 91(2))
• "Public Debt and Property" (the Spending Power, s. 91(1A)).

II. FEDERAL–PROVINCIAL CONFLICTS

A. Functional Powers

Fowler v. R
[1980] 2 SCR 213

[The appellant operated a logging business in coastal British Columbia. As part of the operation, logs were removed from the forest by dragging them across a small stream causing the deposit of debris in the stream bed. The stream, which flowed into the coastal salt waters of the province, at times contained fish and was used for spawning and rearing of salmon. No evidence established that the deposit of the debris in any way affected the fish or the fry. The appellant was charged pursuant to s. 33(3) of the *Fisheries Act*, RSC 1970, c. F-14, as amended.]

MARTLAND J: The sole issue which is to be determined in this appeal is that which is raised in the constitutional question propounded in the order of the Chief Justice of this Court: "Is Section 33(3) of the *Fisheries Act*, RSC 1970, c. F-14, within the legislative competence of the Parliament of Canada?"

Section 33 of the *Fisheries Act* appears under the heading "Injury to Fishing Grounds and Pollution of Waters" and contains, *inter alia*, the following subsections:

33(1) No one shall throw overboard ballast, coal ashes, stones, or other prejudicial or deleterious substances in any river, harbour or roadstead, or in any water where fishing is carried on, or leave or deposit or cause to be thrown, left or deposited, upon the shore, beach or bank of any water or upon the beach between high and low water mark, remains or offal of fish, or of marine animals, or leave decayed or decaying fish in any net or other fishing apparatus; such remains or offal may be buried ashore, above high water mark.

. . .

(3) No person engaging in logging, lumbering, land clearing or other operations, shall knowingly permit to be put, any slash, stumps, or other debris into any water frequented by fish or that flows into such water, or on the ice over either such water, or at a place from which it is likely to be carried into either such water.

. . .

(11) For the purposes of this section and sections 33.1 and 33.2, "deleterious substance" means

(a) any substance that, if added to any water, would degrade or alter or form part of a process of degradation or alteration of the quality of that water so that it is rendered or is likely to be rendered deleterious to fish or fish habitat or to the use by man of fish that frequent that water, or

(b) any water that contains a substance in such quantity or concentration, or that has been so treated, processed or changed, by heat or other means, from a natural state that it would, if added to any other water, degrade or alter or form part of a process of degradation or alteration of the quality of that water so that it is rendered or is likely to be rendered deleterious to fish or fish habitat or to the use by man of fish that frequent the water … .

The respondent contends that subs. (3) of s. 33 is valid legislation because of the legislative authority of Parliament in respect of "Sea Coast and Inland Fisheries" under s. 91(12) of the *British North America Act* [now *Constitution Act, 1867*]. The appellant submits that subs. (3) falls within provincial legislative powers, relying upon ss. 92(5), 92(10), 92(13) and 92(16) of the Act.

. . .

The legislation in question here does not deal directly with fisheries, as such, within the meaning of those definitions. Rather, it seeks to control certain kinds of operations not strictly on the basis that they have deleterious effects on fish but, rather, on the basis that they might have such effects. *Prima facie*, subs. 33(3) regulates property and civil rights within a province. Dealing, as it does, with such rights and not dealing specifically with "fisheries," in order to support the legislation it must be established that it provides for matters necessarily incidental to effective legislation on the subject-matter of sea coast and inland fisheries.

The criteria for establishing liability under subs. 33(3) are indeed wide. Logging, lumbering, land clearing and other operations are covered. The substances which are proscribed are slash, stumps and other debris. The amount of the substance which is deposited is not relevant. The legislation extends to cover not only water frequented by fish but also water that flows into such water, ice over any such water and any place from which slash, stumps and other debris are likely to be carried into such water.

Subsection 33(3) makes no attempt to link the proscribed conduct to actual or potential harm to fisheries. It is a blanket prohibition of certain types of activity, subject to provincial jurisdiction, which does not delimit the elements of the offence so as to link the prohibition to any likely harm to fisheries. Furthermore, there was no evidence before the Court to indicate that the full range of activities caught by the subsection do, in fact, cause harm to fisheries. In my opinion, the prohibition in its broad terms is not necessarily incidental to the federal power to legislate in respect of sea coast and inland fisheries and is *ultra vires* of the federal Parliament.

Appeal allowed.

Northwest Falling Contractors v. R
[1980] 2 SCR 292

[Three thousand gallons of diesel fuel stored on the appellant's property were spilled into the tidal waters of British Columbia. The appellant was charged with violating s. 33(2) of the *Fisheries Act*, RSC 1970, c. F-14, as amended.]

MARTLAND J: The main issue which is to be determined in this appeal is as to whether it was within the legislative competence of the Parliament of Canada to enact subs. 33(2) of the *Fisheries Act*, RSC 1970, c. F-14, as amended [now s. 36(3), RSC 1985, c. F-14].

Subsection (2) is one of a number of provisions appearing in the section which comes under the heading "Injury to Fishing Grounds and Pollution of Waters." The following are the relevant subsections of s. 33:

33(2) Subject to subsection (4), no person shall deposit or permit the deposit of a deleterious substance of any type in water frequented by fish or in any place under any conditions where such deleterious substance or any other deleterious substance that results from the deposit of such deleterious substance may enter any such water.

[Other subsections of s. 33 are reproduced in *Fowler v. R*, supra.]

. . .

The appellant's main argument was that the legislation under attack is really an attempt by Parliament to legislate generally on the subject matter of pollution and thus to invade the area of provincial legislative power over property and civil rights. He points to the very broad definition of "water frequented by fish" in subs. 33(11) which refers to "Canadian fisheries waters" which, under s. 2, includes "all waters in the territorial sea of Canada and all internal waters of Canada." He also refers to the broad scope of the definition of "deleterious substance." When these definitions are applied to subs. 33(2) it is said that the subsection is really concerned with the pollution of Canadian waters.

The charges laid in this case do not, however, effectively bring into question the validity of the extension of the reach of the subsection to waters that would not, in fact, be fisheries waters "or to substances other than those defined in paragraph (a) of subsection 33(11)." The charges relate to diesel fuel spilled into tidal waters. The task of the Court in determining the constitutional validity of subs. 33(2) is to ascertain the true nature and character of the legislation. It is necessary to decide whether the subsection is aimed at the protection and preservation of fisheries. In my opinion it is.

Basically, it is concerned with the deposit of deleterious substances in water frequented by fish, or in a place where the deleterious substance may enter such water. The definition of a deleterious substance is related to the substance being deleterious to fish. In essence, the subsection seeks to protect fisheries by preventing substances deleterious to fish entering into waters frequented by fish. This is a proper concern of legislation under the heading of "Sea Coast and Inland Fisheries."

The situation in this case is different from that which was considered in *Dan Fowler v. Her Majesty the Queen*, a judgment of this Court recently delivered. That case involved the constitutional validity of subs. 33(3) of the *Fisheries Act* and it was held to be *ultra vires* of Parliament to enact. Unlike subs. (2), subs. (3) contains no reference to deleterious substances. It is not restricted by its own terms to activities that are harmful to fish or fish habitat. The basis of the judgment in the *Fowler* case is set out in the following passage:

> Subsection 33(3) makes no attempt to link the proscribed conduct to actual or potential harm to fisheries. It is a blanket prohibition of certain types of activity, subject to provincial jurisdiction, which does not delimit the elements of the offence so as to link the prohibition to any likely harm to fisheries.

In my opinion, subs. 33(2) was *intra vires* of the Parliament of Canada to enact. The definition of "deleterious substance" ensures that the scope of subs. 33(2) is restricted to a prohibition of deposits that threaten fish, fish habitat or the use of fish by man.

Appeal dismissed.

NOTES AND PROBLEMS

1. Although the cases included in this section address alleged federal intrusions into provincial jurisdiction, provincial environmental legislation has not been immune from

constitutional challenge. For example, in *Re Canadian National Railway Co. et al. and Director Under the Environmental Protection Act et al.* and two other appeals (1991), 80 DLR (4th) 269 (Ont. Div. Ct.), the constitutionality of a control order issued by the Director under the *Environmental Protection Act*, RSO 1980, c. 141 (EPA), was challenged. The appellants maintained that the land, which was the subject of the order, lay within the boundaries of a federally controlled harbour and thus lay within the exclusive jurisdiction of the federal government relating to federal public lands (s. 91(1A)) and navigation and shipping (s. 91(10)). To the extent that the order interfered with these functional powers of the federal government, it was, in the appellants' opinion, *ultra vires*. The Divisional Court disagreed.

Legislation addressing pollution control is not the exclusive domain of either level of government and in this case the legislation in question was properly grounded in provincial property and civil rights (s. 92(13)). There was no attempt to regulate either use of land for navigation and shipping or any other essential aspect of that federal power. Federal lands are not to be classed as enclaves immune from provincial regulation. Finally, the doctrine of paramountcy was not applicable as there was no actual conflict established between the Act or the order and any federal legislation.

2. The result was different however in *R v. Kupchanko*, [2002] BCJ no. 148 (CA), where an order under the *Wildlife Act*, RSBC 1996, c. 488, prohibited entering a wildlife management area "with a conveyance of any description which [was] powered by a motor which exceeds a rating of ten horsepower." Kupchanko had operated his higher-rated boat on a river within a designated area and was thus charged. He challenged the constitutional validity of the order, and was successful. Although the province could validly regulate to ensure environmental protection goals, insofar as this order affected navigation, a matter exclusively within federal jurisdiction, it was *ultra vires*. As a result, the order was read down so as not to apply to conveyances operating on navigable rivers.

3. In *R v. Canadian Pacific Ltd.* (1995), 17 CELR (NS) 129 (SCC) Canadian Pacific (CP) was charged with unlawfully discharging a contaminant (smoke) into the natural environment and causing adverse effects pursuant to s. 13(1)(a) of the EPA. CP's controlled burns to clear weeds and brush from its right of way had adversely affected adjoining residential properties.

At trial CP was able to establish due diligence and was acquitted. This was overturned upon appeal. CP then appealed to the Ontario Court of Appeal and ultimately to the Supreme Court of Canada challenging the legislation on two constitutional grounds: first, that the section of the EPA was vague and uncertain and thus in violation of s. 7 of the *Canadian Charter of Rights and Freedoms* and, second, that interjurisdictional immunity applied in relation to the section because CP is a federally regulated undertaking.

The court succinctly determined that the legislation applied to the appellant's maintenance along the right of way. With regard to the s. 7 arguments, the court, although divided in its reasons, unanimously upheld s. 13(1)(s) finding that it was not "unconstitutionally vague or overbroad." The court strengthened the cause for statutory protection of the environment by stating:

> Section 13(1) is sufficiently precise to provide for a meaningful legal debate, when the provision is considered in light of the purpose and subject matter of the EPA, the nature of the provision as a regulatory offence, the societal value of environmental protection, related

provisions of the EPA, and general interpretive principles. Section 13(1)(a) is also proportionate and not overbroad. The objective of environmental protection is itself broad, and the legislature is justified in choosing broad, flexible language to give effect to this objective.

B. Conceptual Powers

R v. Crown Zellerbach Ltd. et al.
[1988] 1 SCR 401

[Crown Zellerbach, a logging operator, was charged with contravening s. 4(1) of the *Ocean Dumping Control Act*, SC 1974-75-76, c. 55 (now part 7, division 3 of the *Canadian Environmental Protection Act, 1999*, SC 1999, c. 33 [CEPA 1999]), which prohibited the dumping of any substance into the sea without obtaining and complying with a permit. The "sea" as defined by the Act included the internal waters of Canada other than fresh waters. Although the respondent had a permit to dump under the legislation, it did not cover Beaver Cove, the area in question. The navigable waters of the cove were within the province of British Columbia and, through Johnstone Strait, were connected to the Pacific Ocean. There was no evidence that the dumping of the woodwaste by the respondent in any way interfered with either navigation or marine life.

Both at trial and the Court of Appeal it was held that s. 4(1) was *ultra vires* the federal government.]

LE DAIN J: ... As the constitutional question indicates, the issue raised by the appeal is the constitutionality of the application of s. 4(1) of the Act to the dumping of waste in waters, other than fresh waters, within a province. The respondent concedes, as it must, that Parliament has jurisdiction to regulate dumping in waters lying outside the territorial limits of any province. It also concedes that Parliament has jurisdiction to regulate the dumping of substances in provincial waters to prevent pollution of those waters that is harmful to fisheries, if the federal legislation meets the tests laid down in the *Fowler* and *Northwest Falling* cases. It further concedes, in view of the opinion expressed in this Court in *Interprovincial Co-operatives Ltd. v. The Queen*, [1976] 1 SCR 477, that Parliament has jurisdiction to regulate the dumping in provincial waters of substances that can be shown to cause pollution in extra-provincial waters. What the respondent challenges is federal jurisdiction to control the dumping in provincial waters of substances that are not shown to have a pollutant effect in extra-provincial waters. The respondent contends that on the admitted facts that is precisely the present case. The respondent submits that in so far as s. 4(1) of the Act can only be read as purporting to apply to such dumping it is *ultra vires* and, alternatively, that it should be read, if possible, so as not to apply to such dumping. In either case the appeal must fail. ...

In this Court the Attorney General of Canada [principally submitted] that the control of dumping in provincial marine waters, for the reasons indicated in the Act, was part of a single matter of national concern or dimension which fell within the federal peace, order and good government power. He characterized this matter as the prevention of ocean or marine pollution. His reliance on the specific heads of federal jurisdiction with respect to navigation and shipping and seacoast and inland fisheries, as well as others of a maritime nature, was rather as indicating, in his submission, the scope that should be assigned to federal jurisdiction under the peace, order and good government power to regulate the dumping of substances for the prevention of marine pollution. The Attorney General of Canada made it plain that he was not relying in this Court on ancillary or necessarily incidental power. His contention was that the control of dumping in provincial marine waters was an integral part of a single matter of national concern. Nor did he rely in this Court on the peace, order and good government power as a basis of federal jurisdiction to enact the *Ocean Dumping Control Act* in implementation of the *Convention on the Prevention of Marine Pollution by Dumping of Wastes and other Matter*. He referred to the Convention and its Annexes and indicating the mischief to which the act is directed as supporting his characterization of the matter in relation to which the Act was enacted. ...

Before considering the relationship of the subject-matter of the Act to the possible bases of federal legislative jurisdiction something more should be said about the characterization of that subject-matter, according to the respective contentions of the parties. As I have indicated, the appellant contends that the Act is directed to the control or regulation of marine pollution, the subject-matter of the *Convention on the Prevention of Marine Pollution by Dumping of Wastes and other Matter*. The respondent, on the other hand, contends that by its terms the Act is directed at dumping which need not necessarily have a pollutant effect. It prohibits the dumping of *any* substance, including a substance not specified in Schedule I or Schedule II, except in accordance with the terms and conditions of a permit. In my opinion, despite this apparent scope, the Act, viewed as a whole, may be properly characterized as directed to the control or regulation of marine pollution, in so far as that may be relevant to the question of legislative jurisdiction. The chosen, and perhaps only effective, regulatory model makes it necessary, in order to prevent marine pollution, to prohibit the dumping of any substance without a permit. Its purpose is to require a permit so that the regulatory authority may determine before the proposed dumping has occurred whether it may be permitted upon certain terms and conditions, having regard to the factors or concerns specified in ss. 9 and 10 of the Act and Schedule III.

· · ·

I agree with Schmidt Prov. Ct. J and the British Columbia Court of Appeal that federal legislative jurisdiction with respect to seacoast and inland fisheries is not sufficient by itself to support the constitutional validity of s. 4(1) of the Act because that section, viewed in the context of the Act as a whole, fails to meet the test laid down in *Fowler* and *Northwest Falling*. While the effect on fisheries of marine pollution caused by the dumping of waste is clearly one of the concerns of the Act it is not the only effect of such pollution with which the Act is concerned. A basis for federal legislative jurisdiction to control marine pollution generally in provincial waters cannot be found in any of the specified heads of federal jurisdiction in s. 91 of the *Constitution Act, 1867*, whether taken individually or collectively.

It is necessary then to consider the national dimensions or national concern doctrine (as it is now generally referred to) of the federal peace, order and good government power as a possible basis for the constitutional validity of s. 4(1) of the Act, as applied to the control of dumping in provincial marine waters.

...

From this survey of the opinion expressed in this Court concerning the national concern doctrine of the federal peace, order and good government power I draw the following conclusions as to what now appears to be firmly established:

1. The national concern doctrine is separate and distinct from the national emergency doctrine of the peace, order and good government power, which is chiefly distinguishable by the fact that it provides a constitutional basis for what is necessarily legislation of a temporary nature;

2. The national concern doctrine applies to both new matters which did not exist at Confederation and to matters which, although originally matters of a local or private nature in a province, have since, in the absence of national emergency, become matters of national concern;

3. For a matter to qualify as a matter of national concern in either sense it must have a singleness, distinctiveness and indivisibility that clearly distinguishes it from matters of provincial concern and a scale of impact on provincial jurisdiction that is reconcilable with the fundamental distribution of legislative power under the Constitution;

4. In determining whether a matter has attained the required degree of singleness, distinctiveness and indivisibility that clearly distinguishes it from matters of provincial concern it is relevant to consider what would be the effect on extra-provincial interests of a provincial failure to deal effectively with the control or regulation of the intra-provincial aspects of the matter.

This last factor, generally referred to as the "provincial inability" test and noted with apparent approval in this Court in *Labatt*, *Schneider* and *Wetmore*, was suggested, as Professor Hogg acknowledges, by Professor Gibson in his article, "Measuring 'National Dimensions'" (1976), 7 *Man. LJ* 15, as the most satisfactory rationale of the cases in which the national concern doctrine of the peace, order and good government power has been applied as a basis of federal jurisdiction. As expounded by Professor Gibson, the test would appear to involve a limited or qualified application of federal jurisdiction. As put by Professor Gibson at p. 34-35:

> By this approach, a national dimension would exist whenever a significant aspect of a problem is beyond provincial reach because it falls within the jurisdiction of another province or of the federal Parliament. It is important to emphasize however that the *entire* problem would not fall within federal competence in such circumstances. Only that aspect of the problem that is beyond provincial control would do so. Since the "PO & GG" clause bestows only residual powers, the existence of a national dimension justifies no more federal legislation than is necessary to fill the gap in provincial powers. For example, federal jurisdiction to legislate for pollution of interprovincial waterways or to control "pollution price-wars" would (in the absence of other independent sources of federal competence) extend only to measures to reduce the risk that citizens of one province would be harmed by the non-co-operation of another province or provinces.

To similar effect he said in his conclusion at p. 36:

> Having regard to the residual nature of the power, it is the writer's thesis that 'national dimensions' are possessed by only those aspects of legislative problems which are beyond the ability of the provincial legislatures to deal because they involve either federal competence or that of another province. Where it would be possible to deal fully with the problem by co-operative action of two or more legislatures, the 'national dimension' concerns only the risk of non-co-operation, and justifies only federal legislation addressed to that risk.

This would appear to contemplate a concurrent or overlapping federal jurisdiction which, I must observe, is in conflict with what was emphasized by Beetz J in the *Anti-Inflation Act* reference—that where a matter falls within the national concern doctrine of the peace, order and good government power, as distinct from the emergency doctrine, Parliament has an exclusive jurisdiction of a plenary nature to legislate in relation to that matter, including its intra-provincial aspects.

As expressed by Professor Hogg in the first and second editions of his *Constitutional Law of Canada*, the "provincial inability" test would appear to be adopted simply as a reason for finding that a particular matter is one of national concern falling within the peace, order and good government power: that provincial failure to deal effectively with the intra-provincial aspects of the matter could have an adverse effect on extra-provincial interests. In this sense, the "provincial inability" test is one of the indicia for determining whether a matter has that character of singleness or indivisibility required to bring it within the national concern doctrine. It is because of the interrelatedness of the intra-provincial and extra-provincial aspects of the matter that it requires a single or uniform legislative treatment. The "provincial inability" test must not, however, go so far as to provide a rationale for the general notion, hitherto rejected in the cases, that there must be a plenary jurisdiction in one order of government or the other to deal with any legislative problem. In the context of the national concern doctrine of the peace, order and good government power, its utility lies, in my opinion, in assisting in the determination whether a matter has the requisite singleness or indivisibility from a functional as well as a conceptual point of view.

· · ·

Marine pollution, because of its predominantly extra-provincial as well as international character and implications, is clearly a matter of concern to Canada as a whole. The question is whether the control of pollution by the dumping of substances in marine waters, including provincial marine waters, is a single, indivisible matter, distinct from the control of pollution by the dumping of substances in other provincial waters. The *Ocean Dumping Control Act* reflects a distinction between the pollution of salt water and the pollution of fresh water. The question, as I conceive it, is whether that distinction is sufficient to make the control of marine pollution by the dumping of substances a single, indivisible matter falling within the national concern doctrine of the peace, order and good government power.

Marine pollution by the dumping of substances is clearly treated by the *Convention on the Prevention of Marine Pollution by Dumping of Wastes and other Matter* as a distinct and separate form of water pollution having its own characteristics and scientific considerations. ... The limitation of the undertaking in the Convention, presumably for reasons of state policy, to the control of dumping in the territorial sea and the open sea cannot, in my opinion, obscure the obviously close relationship, which is emphasized in the UN Report, between pollution in coastal waters, including the internal marine waters of a state, and pollution in the territorial sea. Moreover, there is much force, in my opinion, in the appellant's contention that the difficulty of ascertaining by visual observation the boundary between the territorial sea and the internal marine waters of a state creates an unacceptable degree of uncertainty for the application of regulatory and penal provisions. This, and not simply the possibility or likelihood of the movement of pollutants across that line, is what constitutes the essential indivisibility of the matter of marine pollution by the dumping of substances.

There remains the question whether the pollution of marine waters by the dumping of substances is sufficiently distinguishable from the pollution of fresh waters by such dumping to meet the requirement of singleness or indivisibility. In many cases the pollution of fresh waters will have a pollutant effect in the marine waters into which they flow, and this is noted by the UN Report, but that report, as I have suggested, emphasizes that marine pollution, because of the differences in the composition and action of marine waters and fresh waters, has its own characteristics and scientific considerations that distinguish it from fresh water pollution. Moreover, the distinction between salt water and fresh water as limiting the application of the *Ocean Dumping Control Act* meets the consideration emphasized by a majority of this Court in the *Anti-Inflation Act* reference—that in order for a matter to qualify as one of national concern falling within the federal peace, order and good government power it must have ascertainable and reasonable limits, in so far as its impact on provincial jurisdiction is concerned.

For these reasons I am of the opinion that s. 4(1) of the *Ocean Dumping Control Act* is constitutionally valid as enacted. ...

LA FOREST J (dissenting): The issue raised in this appeal involves the extent to which the federal Parliament may constitutionally prohibit the disposal of substances not shown to have a pollutant effect in marine waters beyond the coast but within the limits of a province.

. . .

I start with the proposition that what is sought to be regulated in the present case is an activity wholly within the province, taking place on provincially owned land. Only local works and undertakings are involved, and there is no evidence that the substance made subject to the prohibition in s. 4(1) is either deleterious in any way or has any impact beyond the limits of the province. It is not difficult, on this basis, to conclude that the matter is one that falls within provincial legislative power unless it can somehow be established that it falls within Parliament's general power to legislate for the peace, order and good government of Canada. ...

There are several applications of the peace, order and good government power that may have relevance to the control of ocean pollution. One is its application in times of emergency. The federal Parliament clearly has power to deal with a grave emergency without regard to the ordinary division of legislative power under the

Constitution. The most obvious manifestation of this power is in times of war or civil insurrection, but it has in recent years also been applied in peacetime to justify the control of rampant inflation; see: *Re: Anti-Inflation Act, supra*. But while there can be no doubt that the control of ocean pollution poses a serious problem, no one has argued that it has reached such grave proportions as to require the displacement of the ordinary division of legislative power under the Constitution.

A second manner in which the power to legislate respecting peace, order and good government may be invoked in the present context is to control that area of the sea lying beyond the limits of the provinces. The federal government may not only regulate the territorial sea and other areas over which Canada exercises sovereignty, either under its power to legislate respecting its public property, or under the general power respecting peace, order and good government under s. 91 (*Reference re Off-shore Mineral Rights of British Columbia*, [1967] SCR 792) or under s. 4 of the *Constitution Act, 1871* (UK), 34 & 35 Vict. c. 28. I have no doubt that it may also, as an aspect of its international sovereignty, exercise legislative jurisdiction for the control of pollution beyond its borders; see: *Reference re Newfoundland Continental Shelf*, [1984] 1 SCR 86.

In legislating under its general power for the control of pollution in areas of the ocean falling outside provincial jurisdiction, the federal Parliament is not confined to regulating activities taking place within those areas. It may take steps to prevent activities in a province, such as dumping substances in provincial waters that pollute or have the potential to pollute the sea outside the province. Indeed, the exercise of such jurisdiction, it would seem to me, is not limited to coastal and internal waters but extends to the control of deposits in fresh water that have the effect of polluting outside a province. Reference may be made here to *Interprovincial Co-operatives Ltd. v. The Queen*, [1976] 1 SCR 477, where a majority of this Court upheld the view that the federal Parliament had exclusive legislative jurisdiction to deal with a problem that resulted from the depositing of a pollutant in a river in one province that had injurious effects in another province. This is but an application of the doctrine of national dimensions triggering the operation of the peace, order and good government clause.

It should require no demonstration that water moves in hydrologic cycles and that effective pollution control requires regulating pollution at its source. That source may, in fact, be situated outside the waters themselves. It is significant that the provision of the *Fisheries Act* upheld by this Court in *Northwest Falling Contractors Ltd. v. The Queen, supra*, as a valid means of protecting the fisheries not only prohibited the depositing of a deleterious substance in water, but *in any place* where it might enter waters frequented by fish. Given the way substances seep into the ground and the movement of surface and ground waters into rivers and ultimately into the sea, this can potentially cover a very large area. Indeed, since the pollution of the ocean in an important measure results from aerial pollution rather than from substances deposited in waters, similar regulations could be made in respect of substances that so pollute the air as to cause damage to the ocean or generally outside the provinces. ...

The power above described can be complemented by provisions made pursuant to the criminal law power. Thus specific provisions prohibiting the deposit of particular substances could be devised in a manner similar to the prohibitions in the *Food and Drugs Act*, RSC 1970, c. F-27. The combination of the criminal law power with its power to control pollution that has extra-provincial dimensions gives the federal Parliament very wide scope to control ocean pollution. ...

In fact, as I see it, the potential breadth of federal power to control pollution by use of its general power is so great that, even without resort to the specific argument made by the appellant, the constitutional challenge in the end may be the development of judicial strategies to confine its ambit. It must be remembered that the peace, order and good government clause may comprise not only prohibitions, like criminal law, but regulation. Regulation to control pollution, which is incidentally only part of the even larger global problem of managing the environment, could arguably include not only emission standards but the control of the substances used in manufacture, as well as the techniques of production generally, in so far as these may have an impact on pollution. This has profound implications for the federal-provincial balance mandated by the Constitution. The challenge for the courts, as in the past, will be to allow the federal Parliament sufficient scope to acquit itself of its duties to deal with national and international problems while respecting the scheme of federalism provided by the Constitution.

                                        . . .

All physical activities have some environmental impact. Possible legislative responses to such activities cover a large number of the enumerated legislative powers, federal and provincial. To allocate the broad subject-matter of environmental control to the federal government under its general power would effectively gut provincial legislative jurisdiction. As I mentioned before, environment protection, of course, encompasses far more than environmental pollution, which is what we are principally concerned with here. To take an example from the present context, woodwaste in some circumstances undoubtedly pollutes the environment, but the very depletion of forests itself affects the ecological balance and, as such, constitutes an environmental problem. But environmental pollution alone is itself all-pervasive. It is a by-product of everything we do. In man's relationship with his environment, waste is unavoidable. ... In Canada, both federal and provincial levels of government have extensive powers to deal with these matters. Both have enacted comprehensive and specific schemes for the control of pollution and the protection of the environment. Some environmental pollution problems are of more direct concern to the federal government, some to the provincial government. But a vast number are interrelated, and all levels of government actively co-operate to deal with problems of mutual concern. ...

To allocate environmental pollution exclusively to the federal Parliament would, it seems to me, involve sacrificing the principles of federalism enshrined in the Constitution. ...

It is true, of course, that we are not invited to create a general environmental pollution power but one restricted to ocean pollution. But it seems to me that the same considerations apply. I shall, however, attempt to look at it in terms of the qualities or attributes that are said to mark the subjects that have been held to fall within the peace, order and good government clause as being matters of national concern. Such

a subject, it has been said, must be marked by a singleness, distinctiveness and indivisibility that clearly distinguishes it from matters of provincial concern. In my view,
ocean pollution fails to meet this test for a variety of reasons. In addition to those
applicable to environmental pollution generally, the following specific difficulties
may be noted. First of all, marine waters are not wholly bounded by the coast; in
many areas, they extend upstream into rivers for many miles. The application of the
Act appears to be restricted to waters beyond the mouths of rivers (and so intrude less
on provincial powers), but this is not entirely clear, and if it is so restricted, it is not
clear whether this distinction is based on convenience or constitutional imperative.
Apart from this, the line between salt and fresh water cannot be demarcated clearly; it
is different at different depths of water, changes with the season and shifts constantly;
see: UN Report, at p. 12. In any event, it is not so much the waters, whether fresh or
salt, with which we are concerned, but their pollution. And the pollution of marine
water is contributed to by the vast amounts of effluents that are poured or seep into
fresh waters everywhere (id., at p. 13). There is a constant intermixture of waters;
fresh waters flow into the sea and marine waters penetrate deeply inland at high tide
only to return to the sea laden with pollutants collected during their incursion inland.
Nor is the pollution of the ocean confined to pollution emanating from substances
deposited in water. In important respects, the pollution of the sea results from emissions in the air, which are then transported over many miles and deposited into the
sea. ... I cannot, therefore, see ocean pollution as a sufficiently discrete subject upon
which to found the kind of legislative power sought here. It is an attempt to create a
federal pollution control power on unclear geographical grounds and limited to part
only of the cause of ocean pollution. Such a power then simply amounts to a trun-
cated federal pollution control power only partially effective to meet its supposed
necessary purpose, unless of course one is willing to extend it to pollution emanating
from fresh water and the air, when for reasons already given such an extension could
completely swallow up provincial power, no link being necessary to establish the
federal purpose.

    This leads me to another factor considered in identifying a subject as falling within
the general federal power as a matter of national domain: its impact on provincial
legislative power. Here, it must be remembered that in its supposed application within
the province the provision virtually prevents a province from dealing with certain of
its own public property without federal consent. A wide variety of activities along the
coast or in the adjoining sea involves the deposit of some substance in the sea. In fact,
where large cities like Vancouver are situated by the sea, this has substantial relevance to recreational, industrial and municipal concerns of all kinds. ... These are
matters of immediate concern to the province. They necessarily affect activities over
which the provinces have exercised some kind of jurisdiction over the years. Whether
or not the "newness" of the subject is a necessary criterion for inventing new areas of
jurisdiction under the peace, order and good government clause, it is certainly a relevant consideration if it means removing from the provinces areas of jurisdiction
which they previously exercised. ...

    A further relevant matter, it is said, is the effect on extra-provincial interests of a
provincial failure to deal effectively with the control of intra-provincial aspects of the
matter. I have some difficulty following all the implications of this, but taking it at

face value, we are dealing here with a situation where, as we saw earlier, Parliament has extensive powers to deal with conditions that lead to ocean pollution wherever they occur. The difficulty with the impugned provision is that it seeks to deal with activities that cannot be demonstrated either to pollute or to have a reasonable potential of polluting the ocean. The prohibition applies to an inert substance regarding which there is no proof that it either moves or pollutes. The prohibition in fact would apply to the moving of rock from one area of provincial property to another. I cannot accept that the federal Parliament has such wide legislative power over local matters having local import taking place on provincially owned property ... here the provision simply overreaches. In its terms, it encompasses activities—depositing innocuous substances into provincial waters by local undertakings on provincial lands—that fall within the exclusive legislative jurisdiction of the province.

Finally, it was argued that the provision might be read down to apply to federal waters only, but I do not think this is possible ... I would dismiss the appeal with costs and reply to the constitutional question in the affirmative.

Friends of the Oldman River Society v. Canada
(Minister of Transport and Minister of Fisheries and Oceans)
(1992), 132 NR 321 (SCC)

[In response to an application by the province of Alberta to construct a dam on the Oldman River, the federal minister of transport issued an approval pursuant to s. 5 of the *Navigable Waters Protection Act*, RSC 1985, c. N-22. In reviewing the application, the minister considered the effect of the project on marine navigation and attached appropriate conditions relating thereto, but he did not subject the application to an environmental assessment as provided in the Environmental Assessment and Review Process Guidelines Order, SOR/84-467. Friends of the Oldman River Society applied for an order in the nature of *certiorari* to quash the approval as well as *mandamus* to require the minister of transport and the minister of fisheries and oceans to comply with the guidelines order.]

LA FOREST J: The protection of the environment has become one of the major challenges of our time. To respond to this challenge, governments and international organizations have been engaged in the creation of a wide variety of legislative schemes and administrative structures. In Canada, both the federal and provincial governments have established Departments of the Environment, which have been in place for about twenty years. More recently, however, it was realized that a department of the environment was one among many other departments, many of which pursued policies that came into conflict with its goals. Accordingly at the federal level steps were taken to give a central role to that department, and to expand the role of other government departments and agencies so as to ensure that they took account of environmental concerns in taking decisions that could have an environmental impact.

To that end, s. 6 of the *Department of the Environment Act*, RSC 1985, c. E-10, empowered the Minister for the purposes of carrying out his duties relating to environmental quality, by order, with the approval of the Governor-in-Council, to establish guidelines for use by federal departments, agencies and regulatory bodies in carrying out their duties, functions and powers. Pursuant to this provision the *Environmental Assessment and Review Process Guidelines Order* ("*Guidelines Order*") was established and approved in June 1984; SOR/84-467. In general terms, these guidelines require all federal departments and agencies that have a decision-making authority for any proposal, i.e., any initiative, undertaking or activity that may have an environmental effect on an area of federal responsibility, to initially screen such proposal to determine whether it may give rise to any potentially adverse environmental effects. If a proposal could have a significant adverse effect on the environment, provision is made for public review by an environmental assessment panel whose members must be unbiased, free of political influence and possessed of special knowledge and experience relevant to the technical, environmental and social effects of the proposal.

The present case raises the constitutional and statutory validity of the *Guidelines Order* as well as its nature and applicability.

[See chapter 6 for a discussion of the issues directly related to environmental assessment.]

. . .

Constitutional Question

[Is the guidelines order so broad as to offend ss. 92 and 92A of the *Constitution Act, 1867* and therefore constitutionally inapplicable to the Oldman River Dam owned by Alberta?]

The constitutional question asks whether the *Guidelines Order* is so broad as to offend ss. 92 and 92A of the *Constitution Act, 1867*. However, no argument was made with respect to s. 92A for the apparent reason that the Oldman River Dam project does not, in the appellant's view, fall within the ambit of that provision. The process of judicial review of legislation which is impugned as *ultra vires* Parliament was recently elaborated on in *Whitbread v. Walley* ... and does not bear repetition here, save to remark that if the *Guidelines Order* is found to be legislation that is in pith and substance in relation to matters within Parliament's exclusive jurisdiction, that is the end of the matter. It would be immaterial that it also affects matters of property and civil rights (at p. 1286). The analysis proceeds first by identifying whether in pith and substance the legislation falls within a matter assigned to one or more of the heads of legislative power.

While various expressions have been used to describe what is meant by the "pith and substance" of a legislative provision, in *Whitbread v. Walley* I expressed a preference for the description "the dominant or most important characteristic of the challenged law." Naturally, the parties have advanced quite different features of the *Guidelines Order* as representing its most important characteristic. For Alberta, it is the manner in which it is said to encroach on provincial rights, although no specific matter has been identified other than general references to the environment. Alberta argues that Parliament has no plenary jurisdiction over the environment, it being a matter of legislative jurisdiction shared by both levels of government, and that the *Guidelines Order* has crossed the line which circumscribes Parliament's authority over the environment. The appellant Ministers argue that in pith and substance the *Guidelines Order* is merely a process to facilitate federal decision-making on matters that fall within Parliament's jurisdiction—a proposition with which the respondent substantially agrees.

The substance of Alberta's argument is that the *Guidelines Order* purports to give the Government of Canada general authority over the environment in such a way as to trench on the province's exclusive legislative domain. Alberta argues that the *Guidelines Order* attempts to regulate the environmental effects of matters largely within the control of the province and, consequently, cannot constitutionally be a concern of Parliament. In particular, it is said that Parliament is incompetent to deal with the environmental effects of provincial works such as the Oldman River Dam.

I agree that the *Constitution Act, 1867* has not assigned the matter of "environment" *sui generis* to either the provinces or Parliament. The environment, as understood in its generic sense, encompasses the physical, economic and social environment touching several of the heads of power assigned to the respective levels of government. Professor Gibson put it succinctly several years ago in his article "Constitutional Jurisdiction over Environmental Management in Canada" (1973), 23 *UTLJ* 54, at p. 85:

> "environmental management" does not, under the existing situation, constitute a homogeneous constitutional unit. Instead, it cuts across many different areas of constitutional responsibility, some federal and some provincial. And it is no less obvious that "environmental management" could never be treated as a constitutional unit under one order of government in any constitution that claimed to be federal, because no system in which one government was so powerful would be federal.

. . .

It must be recognized that the environment is not an independent matter of legislation under the *Constitution Act, 1867* and that it is a constitutionally abstruse matter which does not comfortably fit within the existing division of powers without considerable overlap and uncertainty. A variety of analytical constructs have been developed to grapple with the problem, although no single method will be suitable in every instance. ...

In my view the solution to this case can more readily be found by looking first at the catalogue of powers in the *Constitution Act, 1867* and considering how they may be employed to meet or avoid environmental concerns. When viewed in this manner it will be seen that in exercising their respective legislative powers, both levels of government may affect the environment, either by acting or not acting. This can best be understood by looking at specific powers.

[The judgment proceeds to examine the example of exclusive federal jurisdiction over interprovincial railways, as well as navigation and shipping.]

. . .

Environment impact assessment is, in its simplest form, a planning tool that is now generally regarded as an integral component of sound decision-making. Its fundamental purpose is summarized by R. Cotton and D.P. Emond in "Environmental Impact Assessment," in J. Swaigen, ed., *Environmental Rights in Canada* (1981), 245, at p. 247:

> The basic concepts behind environmental assessment are simply stated: (1) early identification and evaluation of all potential environmental consequences of a proposed undertaking; (2) decision making that both guarantees the adequacy of this process and reconciles, to the greatest extent possible, the proponent's development desires with environmental protection and preservation.

As a planning tool it has both an information-gathering and a decision-making component which provide the decision maker with an objective basis for granting or denying approval for a proposed development. ... In short, environmental impact assessment is simply descriptive of a process of decision-making.

. . .

Because of its auxiliary nature, environmental impact assessment can only affect matters that are "truly in relation to an institution or activity that is otherwise within [federal] legislative jurisdiction"; see: *Singer (Allan) Ltd. v. Quebec (Procureur general)*, [1988] 2 SCR 790 ... . Given the necessary element of proximity that must exist between the impact assessment process and the subject matter of federal jurisdiction involved, this legislation can, in my view, be supported by the particular head of federal power invoked in each instance. In particular, the *Guidelines Order* prescribes a close nexus between the social effects that may be examined and the environmental effects generally. Section 4 requires that the social effects examined at the initial assessment stage be "directly related" to the potential environmental effects of a proposal, as does s. 25 in respect of the terms of reference under which an environmental assessment panel may operate. Moreover, where the *Guidelines Order* has application to a proposal because it affects an area of federal jurisdiction, as opposed to the other three bases for application enumerated in s. 6, the environmental effects to be studied can only be those which may have an impact on the areas of federal responsibility affected.

I should make it clear, however, that the scope of assessment is not confined to the particular head of power under which the Government of Canada has a decision-making responsibility within the meaning of the term "proposal." Such a responsibility, as I stated earlier, is a necessary condition to engage the process, but once the initiating department has thus been given authority to embark on an assessment, that review must consider the environmental effect on all areas of federal jurisdiction. There is no constitutional obstacle preventing Parliament from enacting legislation under several heads of power at the same time ... . In the case of the *Guidelines Order*, Parliament has conferred upon one institution (the "initiating department") the responsibility, in the exercise of its decision-making authority, for assessing the environmental implications on all areas of federal jurisdiction potentially affected. Here, the Minister of Transport, in his capacity of decision maker under the *Navigable Waters Protection Act*, is directed to consider the environmental impact of the dam on such areas of federal responsibility as navigable waters, fisheries, Indians and Indian lands, to name those most obviously relevant in the circumstances here.

. . .

In the end, I am satisfied that the *Guidelines Order* is in pith and substance nothing more than an instrument that regulates the manner in which federal institutions must administer their multifarious duties and functions. Consequently, it is nothing more than an adjunct of the federal legislative powers affected. In any event, it falls within the purely residuary aspect of the "Peace, Order and Good Government" power under s. 91 of the *Constitution Act, 1867*. Any intrusion into provincial matters is merely incidental to the pith and substance of the legislation. It must also be remembered that what is involved is essentially an information gathering process in furtherance of a decision-making function within federal jurisdiction, and the recommendations made at the conclusion of the information gathering stage are not binding on the decision maker. ...

For the foregoing reasons I find that the *Guidelines Order* is *intra vires* Parliament and would thus answer the constitutional question in the negative.

NOTE

Ultimately the federal environmental impact assessment of the Oldman River Dam was completed. Unfortunately, the project was virtually complete by the time the recommendations of the Environmental Assessment Panel were made public. Interestingly, the panel concluded that "[t]he environmental, social and economic costs of the project are not balanced by corresponding benefits and finds that, as presently configured, the project is unacceptable." The panel did recognize the realities of the situation, however, and therefore their first recommendation suggested that the minister "decommission the dam by opening the low level diversion tunnels to allow unimpeded flow of the river." In the event that the recommendation was not accepted by the minister, further recommendations regarding conditions for approval were included in the report (Oldman River Dam: Report of the Environmental Assessment Panel (Hull, QC: FEARO, 1992)).

R v. Hydro-Québec
(1997), 217 NR 241 (SCC)

[Hydro-Québec was charged with breaching a 1989 interim order restricting the emission of polychlorinated biphenyls (PCBs). The interim order was made by the minister of the environment under the authority of ss. 34 and 35 of the *Canadian Environmental Protection Act*, RSC 1985, c. 16 (4th Supp.) (now *Canadian Environmental Protection Act, 1999*, SC 1999, c. 33 [CEPA 1999]), which provided for the regulation of toxic substances. Hydro-Québec sought to have these sections and the interim order declared *ultra vires* the federal government.]

LA FOREST J (L'Heureux-Dubé, Gonthier, Cory, and McLachlin JJ): This Court has in recent years been increasingly called upon to consider the interplay between federal and provincial legislative powers as they relate to environmental protection. Whether viewed positively as strategies for maintaining a clean environment, or negatively as measures to combat the evils of pollution, there can be no doubt that these measures relate to a public purpose of superordinate importance, and one in which all levels of government and numerous organs of the international community have been increasingly engaged. In the opening passage of this Court's reasons in what is perhaps the leading case, *Friends of the Oldman Society v. Canada (Minister of Transport)*, [1992] 1 SCR 3, at pp. 16-17, the matter is succinctly put this way:

> The protection of the environment has become one of the major challenges of our time. To respond to this challenge, governments and international organizations have been engaged in the creation of a wide variety of legislative schemes and administrative structures.

The all-important duty of Parliament and the provincial legislatures to make full use of the legislative powers respectively assigned to them in protecting the environment has inevitably placed upon the courts the burden of progressively defining the extent to which these powers may be used to that end. In performing this task, it is incumbent on the courts to secure the basic balance between the two levels of government envisioned by the Constitution. However, in doing so, they must be mindful that the Constitution must be interpreted in a manner that is fully responsive to emerging realities and to the nature of the subject matter sought to be regulated. Given the pervasive and diffuse nature of the environment, this reality poses particular difficulties in this context.

This latest case in which this Court is required to define the nature of legislative powers over the environment is of major significance. The narrow issue raised is the extent to and manner in which the federal Parliament may control the amount of and conditions under which Chlorobiphenyls (PCBs)—substances well known to pose great dangers to humans and the environment generally—may enter into the environment. However, the attack on the federal power to secure this end is not really aimed at the specific provisions respecting PCBs. Rather, it puts into question the constitutional validity of its enabling statutory provisions. What is really at stake is whether Part II ("Toxic Substances") of the *Canadian Environmental Protection Act*, RSC 1985, c. 16 (4th Supp.), which empowers the federal Ministers of Health and of the Environment to determine what substances are toxic and to prohibit the introduction of such substances into the environment except in accordance with specified terms and conditions, falls within the constitutional power of Parliament.

· · ·

In considering how the question of the constitutional validity of a legislative enactment relating to the environment should be approached, this Court in *Oldman River, supra*, made it clear that the environment is not, as such, a subject matter of legislation under the *Constitution Act, 1867*. As it was put there, "the *Constitution Act, 1867* has not assigned the matter of 'environment' *sui generis* to either the provinces or Parliament" ... . Rather, it is a diffuse subject that cuts across many different areas of constitutional responsibility, some federal, some provincial ... . Thus Parliament or a provincial legislature can, in advancing the scheme or purpose of a statute, enact provisions minimizing or preventing the detrimental impact that statute may have on the environment, prohibit pollution, and the like. In assessing the constitutional validity of a provision relating to the environment, therefore, what must first be done is to look at the catalogue of legislative powers listed in the *Constitution Act, 1867* to see if the provision falls within one or more of the powers assigned to the body (whether Parliament or a provincial legislature) that enacted the legislation ... . If the provision in essence, in pith and substance, falls within the parameters of any such power, then it is constitutionally valid.

· · ·

I have gone on at this length to demonstrate the simple proposition that the validity of a legislative provision (including one relating to environmental protection) must be tested against the specific characteristics of the head of power under which it is proposed to justify it. For each constitutional head of power has its own particular characteristics and raises concerns peculiar to itself in assessing it in the balance of Canadian federalism. This may seem obvious, perhaps even trite, but it is all too easy (see: *Fowler v. The Queen*, [1980] 2 SCR 213) to overlook the characteristics of a particular power and overshoot the mark or, again, in assessing the applicability of one head of power to give effect to concerns appropriate to another head of power when this is neither appropriate not consistent with the law laid down by this Court respecting the ambit and contours of that other power.

· · ·

What appears from the analysis in *RJR-MacDonald* [[1995] 3 SCR 199] is that as early as 1903, the Privy Council ... had made it clear that the power conferred on Parliament by s. 91(27) is "the criminal law in its *widest sense*" (emphasis added). Consistently with this approach, the Privy Council in *Proprietary Articles Trade Association v. Attorney-General for Canada*, [1931] AC 310 (hereafter *PATA*), at p. 324, defined the criminal law power as including any prohibited act with penal consequences. As it put it, at p. 324: "The criminal quality of an act cannot be discerned ... by reference to any standard but one: Is the act prohibited with penal consequences?" This approach has been consistently followed ever since and, as *RJR-MacDonald* relates, it has been applied by the courts in a wide variety of settings. Accordingly, it is entirely within the discretion of Parliament to determine what evil it wishes by penal prohibition to suppress and what threatened interest it thereby wishes to safeguard, to adopt the terminology of Rand J in the *Margarine Reference* ... .

Contrary to the respondent's submission, under s. 91(27) of the *Constitution Act, 1867*, it is also within the discretion of Parliament to determine the extent of blameworthiness that it wishes to attach to a criminal prohibition. So it may determine the nature of the mental element pertaining to different crimes, such as a defence of due diligence like that which appears in s. 125(1) of the Act in issue. This flows from the fact that Parliament has been accorded plenary power to make criminal law in the widest sense. This power is, of course, subject to the "fundamental justice" requirements of s. 7 of the *Canadian Charter of Rights and Freedoms*, which may dictate a higher level of *mens rea* for serious or "true" crimes; cf. *R v. Wholesale Travel Group Inc.*, [1991] 3 SCR 154, and *R v. Rube*, [1992] 3 SCR 159 ... but that is not an issue here.

The *Charter* apart, only one qualification has been attached to Parliament's plenary power over criminal law. The power cannot be employed colourably. Like other legislative powers, it cannot, as Estey J put it in *Scowby v. Glendinning*, [1986] 2 SCR 226, at p. 237, "permit Parliament, simply by legislating in the proper form, to colourably invade areas of exclusively provincial legislative competence." To determine whether such an attempt is being made, it is, of course, appropriate to enquire into Parliament's purpose in enacting the legislation. As Estey J noted in *Scowby*, at p. 237, since the *Margarine Reference*, it has been "accepted that some legitimate public purpose must underlie the prohibition." Estey J then cited Rand J's words in the *Margarine Reference* (at p. 49) as follows:

> A crime is an act which the law, with appropriate penal sanctions, forbids; but as prohibitions are not enacted in a vacuum, we can properly look for some evil or injurious or undesirable effect upon the public against which the law is directed. That effect may be in relation to social, economic or political interests; and the legislature has had in mind to suppress the evil or to safeguard the interest threatened.

> . . .

In the *Margarine Reference, supra*, at p. 50, Rand J helpfully set forth the more usual purposes of a criminal prohibition in the following passage:

> Is the prohibition ... enacted with a view to a public purpose which can support it as being in relation to criminal law? *Public peace, order, security, health, morality: these are the ordinary though not exclusive ends served by that law.* ... [Emphasis added by the court.]

As the final clause in the passage just cited indicates, the listed purposes by no means exhaust the purposes that may legitimately support valid criminal legislation. ... His concern in the *Margarine Reference*, as he indicates in the *Lord's Day* case (at p. 509), was that "in a federal system distinctions must be made arising from the true object, purpose, nature or character of each particular enactment." In short, in a case like the present, all one is concerned with is colourability. Otherwise, one would, in effect, be reviving the discarded notion that there is a "domain" of criminal law, something Rand J, like Lord Atkin before him, was not prepared to do. All of this is, of course, consistent with the view, most recently reiterated in *RJR-MacDonald*, at pp. 259-261, that criminal law is not frozen in time.

During the argument in the present case, however, one sensed, at times, a tendency, even by the appellant and the supporting interveners, to seek justification solely for the purpose of the protection of health specifically identified by Rand J. Now I have no doubt that that purpose obviously will support a considerable measure of environmental legislation, as perhaps also the ground of security. But I entertain no doubt that the protection of a clean environment is a public purpose within Rand J's formulation in the *Margarine Reference*, ... sufficient to support a criminal prohibition. It is surely an "interest threatened" which Parliament can legitimately "safeguard," or to put it another way, pollution is an "evil" that Parliament can legitimately seek to suppress. Indeed, as I indicated at the outset of these reasons, it is a public purpose of superordinate importance; it constitutes one of the major challenges of our time. It would be surprising indeed if Parliament could not exercise its plenary power over criminal law to protect this interest and to suppress the evils associated with it by appropriate penal prohibitions.

This approach is entirely consistent with the recent pronouncement of this Court in *Ontario v. Canadian Pacific Ltd.*, [1995] 2 SCR 1031, where Gonthier J, speaking for the majority, had this to say, at para. 55:

> It is clear that over the past two decades, citizens have become acutely aware of the importance of environmental protection, and of the fact that penal consequences may flow from conduct which harms the environment. ... Everyone is aware that individually and collectively, we are responsible for preserving the natural environment. I would agree with the Law Reform Commission of Canada, *Crimes Against the Environment*, *supra*, which concluded at p. 8 that:
>
>> ... a fundamental and widely shared value is indeed seriously contravened by some environmental pollution, a value which we will refer to as the right to a safe environment.

To some extent, this right and value appears to be new and emerging, but in part because it is an extension of existing and very traditional rights and values already protected by criminal law, its presence and shape even now are largely discernible. Among the new strands of this fundamental value are, it may be argued, those such as *quality of life*, and *stewardship* of the natural environment. At the same time, traditional values as well have simply expanded and evolved to include the environment now as an area and interest of direct and primary concern. Among these values fundamental to the purposes and protections of criminal law are the *sanctity of life*, the *inviolability and integrity of persons*, and the *protection of human life and health*. It is increasingly understood that certain forms and degrees of environmental pollution can directly or indirectly, sooner or later, seriously harm or endanger human life and human health.

. . .

What the foregoing underlines is what I referred to at the outset, that the protection of the environment is a major challenge of our time. It is an international problem, one that requires action by governments at all levels. And, as is stated in the preamble to the Act under review, "Canada must be able to fulfil its international obligations in respect of the environment." I am confident that Canada can fulfil its international obligations, in so far as the toxic substances sought to be prohibited from entering into the environment under the Act are concerned, by use of the criminal law power. The purpose of the criminal law is to underline and protect our fundamental values. While many environmental issues could be criminally sanctioned in terms of protection of human life or health, I cannot accept that the criminal law is limited to that because "certain forms and degrees of environmental pollution can directly or indirectly, sooner or later, seriously harm or endanger human life and human health," as the paper approvingly cited by Gonthier J in *Ontario v. Canadian Pacific*, *supra*, observes. But the stage at which this may be discovered is not easy to discern, and I agree with that paper that the stewardship of the environment is a fundamental

value of our society and that Parliament may use its criminal law power to underline that value. The criminal law must be able to keep pace with and protect our
emerging values.

. . .

Without attempting to regurgitate the whole of s. 34, I shall simply give some
flavour of the nature of the prohibitions created by the regulations made thereunder.
Generally, s. 34 includes regulations providing for or imposing requirements respecting the quantity or concentration of a substance listed in Schedule I that may be released into the environment either alone or in combination with others from any
source, the places where such substances may be released, the manufacturing or
processing activities in the course of which the substance may be released, the manner and conditions of release, and so on. In short, s. 34 precisely defines situations
where the use of a substance in the List of Toxic Substances in Schedule I is prohibited, and these prohibitions are made subject to penal consequences. This is similar to
the techniques Parliament has employed in providing for and imposing highly detailed requirements and standards in relation to food and drugs, which control their
import, sale, manufacturing, labelling, packaging, processing and storing (see: *Food
and Drugs Act*, RSC 1985, c. F-27). These techniques have, in a number of cases
including several in this Court, been upheld as valid criminal law ... . Other statutes
providing for extensive control of hazardous products that are justifiable in whole or
in part under the criminal law power include the *Hazardous Products Act*, RSC 1985,
c. H-3 ... and the *Explosives Act*, RSC 1985, c. E-17.

What Parliament is doing in s. 34 is making provision for carefully tailoring the
prohibited action to specified substances used or dealt with in specific circumstances.
This type of tailoring is obviously necessary in defining the scope of a criminal prohibition, and is, of course, within Parliament's power. As Laskin J noted in
Morgentaler v. The Queen, [1976] 1 SCR 616, at p. 627: "I need cite no authority for
the proposition that Parliament may determine what is not criminal as well as what
is." More recently, Stevenson J in *R v. Furtney*, [1991] 3 SCR 89, at pp. 106-7, speaking of decriminalization of lotteries in certain circumstances, had this to say:

> It constitutes a definition of the crime, defining the reach of the offence, a constitution-
> ally permissive exercise of the criminal law power, reducing the area subject to criminal
> law prohibition where certain conditions exist. I cannot characterize it as an invasion of
> provincial power any more than the appellants were themselves able to do.

. . .

In *Crown Zellerbach*, I expressed concern with the possibility of allocating legislative power respecting environmental pollution exclusively to Parliament. I would
be equally concerned with an interpretation of the Constitution that effectively allocated to the provinces, under general powers such as property and civil rights, control
over the environment in a manner that prevented Parliament from exercising the leadership role expected of it by the international community and its role in protecting the basic
values of Canadians regarding the environment through the instrumentality of the criminal law power. Great sensitivity is required in this area since, as Professor Lederman
has rightly observed, environmental pollution "is no limited subject or theme, [it] is a
sweeping subject or theme virtually all-pervasive in its legislative implication" ... .

Turning then to s. 35, I mentioned that it is ancillary to s. 34. It deals with emergency situations. The provision, it seems to me, indicates even more clearly a criminal purpose, and throws further light on the intention of s. 34 and of the Act generally. It can only be brought into play when the Ministers believe a substance is not specified in the List in Schedule I or is listed but is not subjected to control under s. 34. In such a case, they may make an interim order in respect of the substance if they believe "immediate action is required to deal with a significant danger to the environment or to human life and health."

[The majority of the court held that the legislation fell "wholly within Parliament's power to enact laws under s. 91(27) of the *Constitution Act, 1867*," and that it was "not necessary to consider" whether it could be upheld using peace, order, and good government (POGG).]

LAMER CJC and IACOBUCCI J (Sopinka and Major JJ) (dissenting): ... [W]e believe the pith and substance of Part II of the Act lies in the wholesale regulation by federal agents of any and all substances which may harm any aspect of the environment or which may present a danger to human life or health. That is, the impugned provisions are in pith and substance aimed at protecting the environment and human life and health from any and all harmful substances by regulating these substances. It remains to be seen whether this can be justified under any of the heads of power listed in s. 91 of the *Constitution Act, 1867*. In that connection, we will begin by considering s. 91(27), the criminal law power.

· · ·

Parliament has been given broad and exclusive power to legislate in relation to criminal law by virtue of s. 91(27) ... . This power has traditionally been construed generously. As La Forest J noted in *RJR-MacDonald*, at p. 240, "[i]n developing a definition of the criminal law, this Court has been careful not to freeze the definition in time or confine it to a fixed domain of activity."

Nevertheless, the criminal law power has always been made subject to two requirements: laws purporting to be upheld under s. 91(27) must contain prohibitions backed by penalties; and they must be directed at a "legitimate public purpose."

· · ·

The next step is therefore to examine the impugned provisions and determine whether they meet these criteria. In our view, they fall short. While the protection of the environment is a legitimate public purpose which could support the enactment of criminal legislation, we believe the impugned provisions of the Act are more an attempt to regulate environmental pollution than to prohibit or proscribe it. As such, they extend beyond the purview of criminal law and cannot be justified under s. 91(27).

· · ·

Ascertaining whether a particular statute is prohibitive or regulatory in nature is often more of an art than a science. As Cory J acknowledged in *Knox Contracting*, ... what constitutes criminal law is often "easier to recognize than define" (p. 347). Some guidelines have, however, emerged from previous jurisprudence.

The fact that a statute contains a prohibition and a penalty does not necessarily mean that statute is criminal in nature. Regulatory statutes commonly prohibit violations of their provisions or regulations promulgated under them and provide penal sanctions to be applied if violations do, in fact, occur. Any regulatory statute that lacked such prohibitions and penalties would be meaningless. However, as La Forest J himself recognized ... the penalties that are provided in a regulatory context serve a "pragmatic" or "instrumental" purpose and do not transform the legislation into criminal law ... . In environmental law, as in competition law or income tax law, compliance cannot always be ensured by the usual regulatory enforcement techniques, such as periodic or unannounced inspections. Hence, in order to ensure that legal standards are being met, a strong deterrent, the threat of penal sanctions, is necessary. La Forest J relied on this rationale in concluding that the penal sanctions contained in the *Competition Act* (in *Thomson Newspapers*) and the *Income Tax Act* (in *McKinlay Transport*) did not affect the characterization of those statutes as regulatory in nature for purposes of s. 8 of the *Canadian Charter of Rights and Freedoms*.

At the same time, however, a criminal law does not have to consist solely of blanket prohibitions. It may, as La Forest J noted in *RJR-MacDonald, supra*, at p. 263-64, "validly contain exemptions for certain conduct without losing its status as criminal law." ... These exemptions may have the effect of establishing "regulatory" schemes which confer a measure of discretionary authority without changing the character of the law, as was the case in *RJR-MacDonald, supra*.

Determining when a piece of legislation has crossed the line from criminal to regulatory involves, in our view, considering the nature and extent of the regulation it creates, as well as the context within which it purports to apply. A scheme which is fundamentally regulatory, for example, will not be saved by calling it an "exemption." As Professor Hogg suggests, ... "the more elaborate [a] regulatory scheme, the more likely it is that the Court will classify the dispensation or exemption as being regulatory rather than criminal." At the same time, the subject matter of the impugned law may indicate the appropriate approach to take in characterizing the law as criminal or regulatory.

· · ·

In this case, there *is* no offence until an administrative agency "intervenes." Sections 34 and 35 do not define an offence at all: which, if any, substances will be placed on the List of Toxic Substances, as well as the norms of conduct regarding these substances, are to be defined on an on-going basis by the Ministers of Health and the Environment. It would be an odd crime whose definition was made entirely dependent on the discretion of the Executive. This further suggests that the Act's true nature is regulatory, not criminal, and that the offences created by s. 113 are regulatory offences, not "true crimes": see: *R v. Wholesale Travel Group Inc.*, [1991] 3 SCR 154, *per* Cory J. Our colleague, La Forest J, would hold that the scheme of the impugned act is an effective means of avoiding unnecessarily broad prohibitions and carefully targeting specific toxic substances. The regulatory mechanism allows the schemes to be changed flexibly as the need arises. Of course, simply because a scheme is effective and flexible does not mean it is *intra vires* the federal Parliament.

This is particularly true in light of the striking breadth of the impugned provisions. The 24 listed heads of authority in s. 34 allow for the regulation of every conceivable aspect of toxic substances; in fact, in case anything was left out, s. 34(1)(x) provides for regulations concerning "any other matter necessary to carry out the purposes of this Part." It is highly unlikely, in our opinion, that Parliament intended to leave the criminalization of such a sweeping area of behaviour to the discretion of the Ministers of Health and the Environment.

· · ·

For all of the above reasons, we are unable to uphold the impugned provisions of the Act under the federal criminal law power. That being said, we wish to add that none of this should be read as foredooming future attempts by Parliament to create an effective national—or, indeed, international—strategy for the protection of environment. We agree with La Forest J that achieving such a strategy is a public purpose of extreme importance and one of the major challenges of our time. There are, in this regard, many measures open to Parliament which will not offend the division of powers set out by the Constitution, notably the creation of environmental crimes. Nothing, in our view, prevents Parliament from outlawing certain kinds of behaviour on the basis that they are harmful to the environment. But such legislation must actually seek to *outlaw* this behaviour, not merely regulate it.

· · ·

The impugned provisions are not justified under s. 91(27) of the *Constitution Act, 1867*. We will now consider the appellant's second argument, namely that the provisions may be upheld under the peace, order and good government power.

· · ·

The test for singleness, distinctiveness and indivisibility is a demanding one. Because of the high potential risk to the Constitution's division of powers presented by the broad notion of "national concern," it is crucial that one be able to specify precisely what it is over which the law purports to claim jurisdiction. Otherwise, "national concern" could rapidly expand to absorb all areas of provincial authority. As Le Dain J noted in *Crown Zellerbach, supra*, at p. 433, once a subject matter is qualified of national concern, "Parliament has an exclusive jurisdiction of a plenary nature to legislate in relation to that matter, including its intra-provincial aspects."

· · ·

The definition of "toxic substances" in s. 11, combined with the definition of "substance" found in s. 3, is an all-encompassing definition with no clear limits. Many human activities could involve the use of materials falling within the meaning of "toxic substances" as defined by the impugned legislation. As noted earlier, the definition of "substance" includes "organic or inorganic matter, whether animate or inanimate." Paragraphs (a) through (g) of the definition in s. 3(1) do little to narrow this initial broad scope. Paragraph (g), which refers to "any animate matters ... contained in effluents, emissions or wastes that result from any work, undertaking or activity" could, on its plain wording, conceivably include any effluent containing human or animal waste, garbage containing food remnants, or similar items commonly dealt with by municipal waste disposal services.

· · ·

The majority of this Court in *Crown Zellerbach, supra*, at pp. 436-37, found marine pollution to constitute a single, distinct, and indivisible subject-matter, on the basis that the *Ocean Dumping Control Act*, SC 1974-75-76, c. 55, distinguished between the pollution of salt water and the pollution of fresh water, both types of waters having different compositions and characteristics. In Part II of the *Canadian Environmental Protection Act*, there is no analogous clear distinction between types of toxic substances, either on the basis of degree of persistence and diffusion into the environment and the severity of their harmful effect or on the basis of their extraprovincial aspects. The lack of any distinctions similar to those in the legislation upheld in *Crown Zellerbach* means that the Act has a regulatory scope which can encroach widely upon several provincial heads of power, notably, s. 92(13) "property and civil rights," s. 92(16) "matters of a merely local or private nature," and s. 92(10) "local works and undertakings." In our view, this failure to circumscribe the ambit of the Act demonstrates that the enabling provisions lack the necessary singleness, distinctiveness and indivisibility.

Another criterion that can be used to determine whether the subject matter sought to be regulated can be sufficiently distinguished from matters of provincial interest is to consider whether the failure of one province to enact effective regulation would have adverse effects on interests exterior to the province. This indicator has also been named the "provincial inability" test (see: *Crown Zellerbach, supra,* at pp. 432-34). If the impugned provisions of the Act were indeed restricted to chemical substances, like PCBs, whose effects are diffuse, persistent and serious, then a *prima facie* case could be made out as to the grave consequences of any one province failing to regulate effectively their emissions into the environment. However, the s. 11(a) threshold of "immediate or long-term harmful effect on the environment" also encompasses substances whose effects may only be temporary or local. Therefore, the notion of "toxic substances" as defined in the Act is inherently divisible. Those substances whose harmful effects are only temporary and localized would appear to be well within provincial ability to regulate. To the extent that Part II of the Act includes the regulation of "toxic substances" that may only affect the particular province within which they originate, the appellant bears a heavy burden to demonstrate that provinces themselves would be incapable of regulating such toxic emissions. It has not discharged this burden before this Court.

· · ·

These reasons confirm that the subject matter does not fulfill the characteristics of singleness, distinctiveness and indivisibility required to qualify as a national concern matter.

[The dissent also held that the legislation could not be upheld under the trade and commerce power as some interveners had argued, and declared the provisions *ultra vires*.]

PROBLEM

Examine the provisions of the federal *Species at Risk Act*, reproduced in chapter 12. What federal powers did the draftspersons have in mind to justify the legislative scheme?

C. Harmonization

Canadian Council of Ministers of the Environment
A Canada-wide Accord on Environmental Harmonization
http://www.ccme.ca/assets/pdf/accord_harmonization_e.pdf

Vision

Governments working in partnership to achieve the highest level of environmental quality for all Canadians.

Purpose of the Accord

To provide a framework and mechanisms to achieve the vision and to guide the development of sub-agreements pursuant to the Accord.

The Objectives of Harmonization

The objectives of harmonization are to:

- enhance environmental protection;
- promote sustainable development; and
- achieve greater effectiveness, efficiency, accountability, predictability and clarity of environmental management for issues of Canada-wide interest, by:
  1. using a cooperative approach, to develop and implement consistent environmental measures in all jurisdictions, including policies, standards, objectives, legislation and regulations;
  2. delineating the respective roles and responsibilities of the Federal, Provincial and Territorial governments within an environmental management partnership by ensuring that specific roles and responsibilities will generally be undertaken by one order of government only;
  3. reviewing and adjusting Canada's environmental management regimes to accommodate environmental needs, innovation, expertise and capacities, and addressing gaps and weaknesses in environmental management; and
  4. preventing overlapping activities and inter-jurisdictional disputes.

Principles

Governments agree that their environmental management activities will reflect the following:

1. those who generate pollution and waste should bear the cost of prevention, containment, cleanup or abatement (polluter pays principle);

2. where there are threats of serious or irreversible environmental damage, lack of full scientific certainty shall not be used as a reason for postponing cost-effective measures to prevent environmental degradation (precautionary principle);
3. pollution prevention is the preferred approach to environmental protection;
4. environmental measures should be performance-based, results-oriented and science-based;
5. openness, transparency, accountability and the effective participation of stakeholders and the public in environmental decision-making is necessary for an effective environmental management regime;
6. working cooperatively with Aboriginal people and their structures of governance is necessary for an effective environmental management regime;
7. Canada-wide approaches on how to meet the objectives of this Accord will allow for flexible implementation required to reflect variations in ecosystems and local, regional, provincial and territorial conditions;
8. decisions pursuant to the Accord will be consensus-based and driven by the commitment to achieve the highest level of environmental quality within the context of sustainable development;
9. nothing in this Accord alters the legislative or other authority of the governments or the rights of any of them with respect to the exercise of their legislative or other authorities under the Constitution of Canada;
10. legislation, regulations, policies and existing agreements should accommodate the implementation of this Accord;
11. the environmental measures established and implemented in accordance with this Accord will not prevent a government from introducing more stringent environmental measures to reflect specific circumstances or to protect environments or environmental values located within its jurisdiction;
12. this Accord and sub-agreements do not affect aboriginal or treaty rights;
13. all Canadians should be confident that their environment is respected by neighbouring Canadian jurisdictions.

Sub-Agreements

1. The governments will enter into multi-lateral sub-agreements to implement the commitments set out in this Accord. These sub-agreements will be related to specific components of environmental management or environmental issues to be addressed on a Canada-wide partnership basis.
2. These sub-agreements or their implementation agreements will delineate specific roles and responsibilities to provide a one-window approach to the implementation of environmental measures; in the case of environmental assessment that means a single assessment and a single review process which may involve more than one jurisdiction.
3. Roles and responsibilities will be undertaken by the order of the government best situated to effectively discharge them. In assessing which government is best situated, governments will give consideration to applicable criteria, such as:

- scale, scope and nature of environmental issue
- equipment and infrastructure to support obligations
- physical proximity
- efficiency and effectiveness
- human and financial resources to deliver obligations
- scientific and technical expertise
- ability to address client or local needs
- interprovincial/interterritorial/international considerations.

4. Pursuant to this Accord, governments may also enter into regional or bilateral implementation agreements on regional or local issues, for specific ecosystems, for the purposes of providing for necessary variations in the implementation of environmental measures, or for facilitating cooperation in matters not specifically covered under this general multi-lateral Accord.

5. In undertaking a role under a sub-agreement, a government will assume results-oriented and measurable obligations for the discharge of that role, and commit to regular public reporting to demonstrate that its obligations have been met.

6. When a government has accepted obligations and is discharging a role, the other order of government shall not act in that role for the period of time as determined by the relevant sub-agreement.

7. In instances where a government is unable to fulfil its obligations under this Accord, the concerned governments shall develop an alternative plan to ensure that no gaps are created within the environmental management regime. As a general guideline, these plans will be completed within six months.

8. In areas where governments have been unable to reach consensus on a Canada-wide approach, each government is free to act within its existing authority and will advise the other governments accordingly.

9. When a sub-agreement or implementation agreement assigns specific roles or responsibilities to one order of government, the other order of government will review and seek to amend as necessary their legislation, regulations, policies and existing agreements to provide for the implementation of that sub-agreement.

10. Nothing in this Accord will prevent a government from taking action within its authority to respond to environmental emergencies consistent with existing emergency response agreements.

Administration

1. It is the intention of Ministers to conclude sub-agreements on all areas of environmental management that would benefit from Canada-wide coordinated action.

2. Through the Canadian Council of Ministers of the Environment (CCME), ministers will set priorities and establish workplans for addressing issues of Canada-wide significance pursuant to this Accord. Any government may bring forward issues for consideration by the Council of Ministers.

3. Ministers will review progress under the Accord and will provide regular public reports on meeting obligations under the Accord.
4. The resource implications of any adjustments to government programming resulting from this Accord and its sub-agreements will be examined and addressed.
5. This Accord and its sub-agreements may be amended from time to time with the consent of the governments.
6. This Accord comes into force as of January 29, 1998. A government may withdraw from this Accord six months after giving notice.
7. The Council of Ministers in consultation with the public will review this Accord 2 years after the date of its coming into force to evaluate its effectiveness and determine its future.
8. Each government will make the Accord and Canada-wide sub-agreements available to the public.

NOTES AND PROBLEMS

1. What is the Canadian Council of Ministers of the Environment (CCME)? What is its mandate and to whom is it accountable? See the CCME Web site, http://www.ccme.ca.

2. The Canada-wide Accord on Environmental Harmonization did not receive universal support. In particular, the House of Commons Standing Committee on Environment and Sustainable Development, which held hearings prior to the signing of the Accord to survey the diverse opinions of business, labour, industry, aboriginal, and environmental groups, was highly critical of the initiative. The consequent committee report disputed the underlying justification for the agreement of the duplication and overlap of responsibility, and questioned the environmental benefits associated with devolving responsibility for environmental management from the federal government to the provinces. The committee recommendations bluntly suggested a delay of the ratification of the Accord until its specific concerns could be addressed and full public consultation completed. In spite of the committee's opinion, the Accord was signed in January 1998. See House of Commons Standing Committee on Environment and Sustainable Development, *Report on the Harmonization Initiative of the Canadian Council of Ministers of the Environment* (Ottawa: The Committee, December 1997).

3. The challenges to the Accord continued in court when the Canadian Environmental Law Association (CELA) sought a declaration that the agreements were of no force and effect because the then minister of the environment had exceeded her authority in signing them or had fettered her discretion by agreeing not to act with respect to matters within her statutory authority. Although the Federal Court of Appeal held that the matter was justiciable, it found that the minister was within her authority to enter such agreements by virtue of s. 7 of the *Department of Environment Act*, RSC 1985, c. E-10 and ss. 6, 98, and 99 of the *Canadian Environmental Protection Act*, RSC 1985, c. 16 (4th Supp.) (CEPA 1985). With regard to the issue of fettering her discretion, the court held that the argument was premature as there was insufficient factual basis on which to make a determination; whether fettering might occur was dependent upon the content of the

future sub agreements. See *Canadian Environmental Law Association v. Canada (Minister of Environment)* (1999), 30 CELR (NS) 59 (FCTD).

4. Is the Accord a *de facto* amendment of the constitution, albeit not a *de jure* change? Over time, could this practice become a constitutional convention?

5. On problems with the transparency and enforceability of interdepartmental and intergovernmental agreements generally, see F. Gertler, "Lost in (Intergovernmental) Space: Cooperative Federalism in Environmental Protection," in S. Kennett, ed., *Law and Process in Environmental Management* (Calgary: CIRL, 1993), chapter 4.

III. EMERGING JURISDICTIONS

A. Municipalities

114957 Canada Ltée (Spraytech, Société d'arrosage) v. Hudson (Town)
[2001] 2 SCR 241

L'HEUREUX-DUBÉ J: The context of this appeal includes the realization that our common future, that of every Canadian community, depends on a healthy environment. In the words of the Superior Court judge: "Twenty years ago, there was very little concern over the effect of chemicals such as pesticides on the population. Today, we are more conscious of what type of an ... environment we wish to live in, and what quality of life we wish to expose our children [to]" ((1993), 19 MPLR (2d) 224, at p. 230). This Court has recognized that "[e]veryone is aware that individually and collectively, we are responsible for preserving the natural environment ... environmental protection [has] emerged as a fundamental value in Canadian society" ... .

Regardless of whether pesticides are in fact an environmental threat, the Court is asked to decide the legal question of whether the Town of Hudson, Quebec, acted within its authority in enacting a by-law regulating and restricting pesticide use.

The case arises in an era in which matters of governance are often examined through the lens of the principle of subsidiarity. This is the proposition that law-making and implementation are often best achieved at a level of government that is not only effective, but also closest to the citizens affected and thus most responsive to their needs, to local distinctiveness, and to population diversity. La Forest J wrote for the majority in *R v. Hydro-Québec*, [1997] 3 SCR 213, at para. 127, that "the protection of the environment is a major challenge of our time. It is an international problem, one that requires action by *governments at all levels*" (emphasis added). His reasons in that case also quoted with approval a passage from *Our Common Future*, the report produced in 1987 by the United Nations' World Commission on the Environment and Development. The so-called "Brundtland Commission" recommended that "local governments [should be] empowered to exceed, but not to lower, national norms" (p. 220).

There are now at least 37 Quebec municipalities with by-laws restricting pesticides: J. Swaigen, "The *Hudson* Case: Municipal Powers to Regulate Pesticides Confirmed by Quebec Courts" (2000), 34 CELR (NS) 162, at p. 174. Nevertheless, each level of government must be respectful of the division of powers that is the hallmark of our federal system; there is a fine line between laws that legitimately complement each other and those that invade another government's protected legislative sphere. Ours is a legal inquiry informed by the environmental policy context, not the reverse.

· · ·

There are two issues raised by this appeal:

1. Did the Town have the statutory authority to enact By-law 270?
2. Even if the Town had authority to enact it, was By-law 270 rendered inoperative because of a conflict with federal or provincial legislation?

· · ·

In *R v. Sharma*, [1993] 1 SCR 650, at p. 668, this Court recognized "the principle that, as statutory bodies, municipalities 'may exercise only those powers expressly conferred by statute, those powers necessarily or fairly implied by the expressed power in the statute, and those indispensable powers essential and not merely convenient to the effectuation of the purposes of the corporation' (Makuch, *Canadian Municipal and Planning Law* (1983), at p. 115)." Included in this authority are "general welfare" powers, conferred by provisions in provincial enabling legislation, on which municipalities can draw. As I.M. Rogers points out, "the legislature cannot possibly foresee all the powers that are necessary to the statutory equipment of its creatures. ... Undoubtedly the inclusion of 'general welfare' provisions was intended to circumvent, to some extent, the effect of the doctrine of *ultra vires* which puts the municipalities in the position of having to point to an express grant of authority to justify each corporate act."

· · ·

While enabling provisions that allow municipalities to regulate for the "general welfare" within their territory authorize the enactment of by-laws genuinely aimed at furthering goals such as public health and safety, it is important to keep in mind that such open-ended provisions do not confer an unlimited power. Rather, courts faced with an impugned by-law enacted under an "omnibus" provision such as s. 410 [of the Quebec *Cities and Towns Act (CTA)*] must be vigilant in scrutinizing the true purpose of the by-law. In this way, a municipality will not be permitted to invoke the implicit power granted under a "general welfare" provision as a basis for enacting by-laws that are in fact related to ulterior objectives, whether mischievous or not.

· · ·

[S]ince there is no specific provision in the provincial enabling legislation referring to pesticides, the by-law must fall within the purview of s. 410(1) *CTA*. The party challenging a by-law's validity bears the burden of proving that it is *ultra vires*.

· · ·

Recent commentary suggests an emerging consensus that courts must respect the responsibility of elected municipal bodies to serve the people who elected them and exercise caution to avoid substituting their views of what is best for the citizens for those of municipal councils. *Barring clear demonstration that a municipal decision was beyond its powers, courts should not so hold.* In cases where powers are not expressly conferred but may be implied, courts must be prepared to adopt the "be-nevolent construction" which this Court referred to in *Greenbaum*, and confer the powers by reasonable implication. Whatever rules of construction are applied, they must not be used to usurp the legitimate role of municipal bodies as community representatives. [Emphasis added by the court.]

· · ·

In *Shell*, ... Sopinka J for the majority quoted the following with approval from Rogers ... :

In approaching a problem of construing a municipal enactment a court should endeavour firstly to interpret it so that the powers sought to be exercised are in consonance with the purposes of the corporation. The provision at hand should be construed with reference to the object of the municipality: to render services to a group of persons in a locality with a view to advancing their health, welfare, safety and good government.

· · ·

The Town's By-law 270 responded to concerns of its residents about alleged health risks caused by non-essential uses of pesticides within Town limits. Unlike *Shell*, in which the Court felt bound by the municipal enactments' "detailed recital of ... purposes" ... , the by-law at issue requires what Sopinka J called the reading in of an implicit purpose. Based on the distinction between essential and non-essential uses of pesticides, it is reasonable to conclude that the Town by-law's purpose is to minimize the use of allegedly harmful pesticides in order to promote the health of its inhabitants. This purpose falls squarely within the "health" component of s. 410(1).

· · ·

Kennedy J correctly found (at pp. 230-31) that the Town Council, "faced with a situation involving health and the environment," "was addressing a need of their community." In this manner, the municipality is attempting to fulfill its role as what the Ontario Court of Appeal has called a "trustee of the environment" (*Scarborough v. R.E.F. Homes Ltd.* (1979), 9 MPLR 255, at p. 257).

· · ·

To conclude this section on statutory authority, I note that reading s. 410(1) to permit the Town to regulate pesticide use is consistent with principles of international law and policy. My reasons for the Court in *Baker v. Canada (Minister of Citizenship and Immigration)*, [1999] 2 SCR 817, at para. 70, observed that "the values reflected in international human rights law may help inform the contextual approach to statutory interpretation and judicial review." As stated in *Driedger on the Construction of Statutes* ... :

[T]he legislature is presumed to respect the values and principles enshrined in international law, both customary and conventional. These constitute a part of the legal context in which legislation is enacted and read. *In so far as possible, therefore, interpretations that reflect these values and principles are preferred.* [Emphasis added by the court.]

The interpretation of By-law 270 contained in these reasons respects international law's "precautionary principle," which is defined as follows at para. 7 of the *Bergen Ministerial Declaration on Sustainable Development* (1990):

In order to achieve sustainable development, policies must be based on the precautionary principle. Environmental measures must anticipate, prevent and attack the causes
of environmental degradation. Where there are threats of serious or irreversible damage, lack of full scientific certainty should not be used as a reason for postponing measures to prevent environmental degradation.

Canada "advocated inclusion of the precautionary principle" during the Bergen
Conference negotiations (D. VanderZwaag, CEPA Issue Elaboration Paper No. 18,
CEPA and the Precautionary Principle/Approach (1995), at p. 8). The principle is
codified in several items of domestic legislation ... .

Scholars have documented the precautionary principle's inclusion "in virtually
every recently adopted treaty and policy document related to the protection and preservation of the environment" (D. Freestone and E. Hey, "Origins and Development
of the Precautionary Principle," in D. Freestone and E. Hey, eds., *The Precautionary
Principle and International Law* (1996), at p. 41.) As a result, there may be "currently sufficient state practice to allow a good argument that the precautionary principle is a principle of customary international law" (J. Cameron and J. Abouchar, "The
Status of the Precautionary Principle in International Law," in *ibid.* at p. 52). ... In
the context of the precautionary principles' tenets, the Town's concerns about pesticides fit well under their rubric of preventive action.

                                              • • •

This Court stated in *Hydro-Québec, supra,* at para. 112, that *Oldman River* ...
"made it clear that the environment is not, as such, a subject matter of legislation
under the *Constitution Act, 1867.* As it was put there, 'the *Constitution Act, 1867* has
not assigned the matter of 'environment' *sui generis* to either the provinces or Parliament' (p. 63). Rather, it is a diffuse subject that cuts across many different areas of
constitutional responsibility, some federal, some provincial (pp. 63-64)." As there is
bijurisdictional responsibility for pesticide regulation, the appellants allege conflicts
between By-law 270 and both federal and provincial legislation. These contentions
will be examined in turn.

                                              • • •

The appellants argue that ss. 4(1), 4(3) and 6(1)(j) of the [federal] *Pest Control
Products Act* ("*PCPA*"), and s. 45 of the *Pest Control Products Regulations* allowed
them to make use of the particular pesticide products they employed in their business
practices. They allege a conflict between these legislative provisions and By-law 270.
In *Multiple Access Ltd. v. McCutcheon,* [1982] 2 SCR 161, at p. 187, Dickson J (as he
then was) for the majority of the Court reviewed the "express contradiction test" of
conflict between federal and provincial legislation. At p. 191, he explained that "there
would seem to be no good reasons to speak of paramountcy and preclusion except
where there is actual conflict in operation as where one enactment says 'yes' and the
other says 'no'; 'the same citizens are being told to do inconsistent things'; compliance with one is defiance of the other." ... By-law 270, as a product of provincial
enabling legislation, is subject to this test.

Federal legislation relating to pesticides extends to the regulation and authorization of their import, export, sale, manufacture, registration, packaging and labelling.

The *PCPA* regulates which pesticides can be registered for manufacture and/or use in Canada. This legislation is permissive, rather than exhaustive, and there is no operational conflict with By-law 270. No one is placed in an impossible situation by the legal imperative of complying with both regulatory regimes. Analogies to motor vehicles or cigarettes that have been approved federally, but the use of which can nevertheless be restricted municipally, well illustrate this conclusion. There is, moreover, no concern in this case that application of By-law 270 displaces or frustrates "the legislative purpose of Parliament."

. . .

Multiple Access also applies to the inquiry into whether there is a conflict between the by-law and provincial legislation, except for cases (unlike this one) in which the relevant provincial legislation specifies a different test. The *Multiple Access* test, namely "impossibility of dual compliance," see: P.W. Hogg, *Constitutional Law of Canada* (loose-leaf ed.), vol. 1, at p. 16-13, was foreshadowed for provincial-municipal conflicts in *dicta* contained in this Court's decision in *Arcade Amusements* ... . There, Beetz J wrote that "otherwise valid provincial statutes which are *directly contrary* to federal statutes are rendered inoperative by that conflict. Only the same type of conflict with provincial statutes can make by-laws inoperative.

. . .

The court summarized the applicable standard as follows: "A true and outright conflict can only be said to arise when one enactment compels what the other forbids." See also: *Law Society of Upper Canada v. Barrie (City)* (2000), 46 OR (3d) 620 (SCJ), at pp. 629-30: "Compliance with the provincial Act does not necessitate defiance of the municipal By-law; dual compliance is certainly possible"; *Huot v. St-Jérôme (Ville de)*, JE 93-1052 (Sup. Ct.), at p. 19:

> [TRANSLATION] A finding that a municipal by-law is inconsistent with a provincial statute (or a provincial statute with a federal statute) requires, first, that they both deal with similar subject matters and, second, that obeying one necessarily means disobeying the other.

As a general principle, the mere existence of provincial (or federal) legislation in a given field does not oust municipal prerogatives to regulate the subject matter. As stated by the Quebec Court of Appeal in an informative environmental decision, *St-Michel-Archange (Municipalité de) v. 2419-6388 Québec Inc.*, [1992] RJQ 875 (CA), at pp. 888-91:

> [TRANSLATION] According to proponents of the unitary theory, although the provincial legislature has not said so clearly, it has nonetheless established a provincial scheme for managing waste disposal sites. It has therefore reserved exclusive jurisdiction in this matter for itself, and taken the right to pass by-laws concerning local waste management away from municipalities. The *Environment Quality Act* therefore operated to remove those powers from municipal authorities.
>
> According to proponents of the pluralist theory, the provincial legislature very definitely did not intend to abolish the municipality's power to regulate; rather, it intended merely to better circumscribe that power, to ensure complementarity with the municipal management scheme. ...

The pluralist theory accordingly concedes that the intention is to give priority to provincial statutory and regulatory provisions. However, it does not believe that it can be deduced from this that any complementary municipal provision in relation to planning and development that affects the quality of the environment is automatically invalid. ...

A thorough analysis of the provisions cited *supra* and a review of the environmental policy as a whole as it was apparently intended by the legislature leads to the conclusion that it is indeed the pluralist theory, or at least a pluralist theory, that the legislature seems to have taken as the basis for the statutory scheme.

In this case, there is no barrier to dual compliance with By-law 270 and the [provincial] *Pesticides Act*, nor any plausible evidence that the legislature intended to preclude municipal regulation of pesticide use. The *Pesticides Act* establishes a permit and licensing system for vendors and commercial applicators of pesticides and thus complements the federal legislation's focus on the products themselves. Along with By-law 270, these laws establish a tri-level regulatory regime.

. . .

I have found that By-law 270 was validly enacted under s. 410(1) *CTA*. Moreover, the by-law does not render dual compliance with its dictates and either federal or provincial legislation impossible. For these reasons, I would dismiss the appeal with costs.

NOTE

Can you think of other areas for local environmental initiative that may be justified according to the reasoning in *Spraytech*? See *Ben Gardiner Farms Inc. v. West Perth (Township)* (2001), 42 CELR (NS) 3 (Ont. Div. Ct.), wherein a zoning bylaw that prohibited more than a specified number of livestock units on farm operations was upheld.

B. Aboriginal Jurisdictions

Aboriginal Self-Government: The Government of Canada's Approach to Implementation of the Inherent Right and the Negotiation of Self-Government
(Ottawa: Minister of Indian Affairs and Northern Development, 1995)

The Inherent Right of Self-Government Is a Section 35 Right

The Government of Canada recognizes the inherent right of self-government as an existing Aboriginal right under section 35 of the *Constitution Act, 1982*. It recognizes, as well, that the inherent right may find expression in treaties, and in the context of the Crown's relationship with treaty First Nations. Recognition of the inherent right is based on the view that the Aboriginal peoples of Canada have the right to govern themselves in relation to matters that are internal to their communities, integral to their unique cultures, identities, traditions, languages and institutions, and with respect to their special relationship to their land and their resources.

The Government acknowledges that the inherent rights of self-government may be enforceable through the courts and that there are different views about the nature, scope and content of the inherent right. However, litigation over the inherent right would be lengthy, costly and would tend to foster conflict. In any case, the courts are likely to provide general guidance to the parties involved, leaving it to them to work out detailed arrangements.

For these reasons, the Government is convinced that litigation should be a last resort. Negotiations among governments and Aboriginal peoples are clearly preferable as the most practical and effective way to implement the inherent right of self-government.

Within the Canadian Constitutional Framework

Aboriginal governments and institutions exercising the inherent right of self-government will operate within the framework of the Canadian Constitution. Aboriginal jurisdictions and authorities should, therefore, work in harmony with jurisdictions that are exercised by other governments. It is in the interest of both Aboriginal and non-Aboriginal governments to develop co-operative arrangements that will ensure the harmonious relationship of law which is indispensable to the proper functioning of the federation.

In light of the wide array of Aboriginal jurisdictions or authorities that may be the subject of negotiations, provincial governments are necessary parties to negotiations and agreements where subject matters being negotiated normally fall within provincial jurisdiction or may have impacts beyond the Aboriginal group or Aboriginal lands in question. Territorial governments should be party to any negotiations and related agreements on implementing self-government north of the sixtieth parallel.

. . .

Different Circumstances

Given the vastly different circumstances of Aboriginal peoples throughout Canada, implementation of the inherent right cannot be uniform across the country or result in a "one-size-fits-all" form of self-government. The Government proposes to negotiate self-government arrangements that are tailored to meet the unique needs of Aboriginal groups and are responsive to their particular political, economic, legal, historical, cultural and social circumstances.

Scope of Negotiations

Under the federal approach, the central objective of negotiations will be to reach agreements on self-government as opposed to legal definitions of the inherent right. The Government realizes that Aboriginal governments and institutions will require the jurisdiction or authority to act in a number of areas in order to give practical

effect to the inherent right to self-government. Broadly stated, the Government views
the scope of Aboriginal jurisdiction or authority as likely extending to matters that
are internal to the group, integral to its distinct Aboriginal culture, and essential to its
operation as a government or institution. Under this approach, the range of matters
that the federal government would see as subjects for negotiation could include all,
some, or parts of the following: ...

- property rights, including succession and estates
- land management, including: zoning; service fees; land tenure and access; and
  expropriation of Aboriginal land by Aboriginal governments for their own
  public purposes
- natural resources management
- agriculture
- hunting, fishing and trapping on Aboriginal lands ...

In some of these areas, detailed arrangements will be required to ensure harmonization of laws, while in others, a more general recognition of Aboriginal jurisdiction
or authority may be sufficient.

There are a number of other areas that may go beyond matters that are integral to
Aboriginal culture or that are strictly internal to an Aboriginal group. To the extent
that the federal government has jurisdiction in these areas, it is prepared to negotiate
some measure of Aboriginal jurisdiction or authority. In these areas, laws and regulations tend to have impacts that go beyond individual communities. Therefore, primary law-making authority would remain with the federal or provincial governments,
as the case may be, and their laws would prevail in the event of a conflict with Aboriginal laws. Subject matters would include: ...

- environmental protection, assessment and pollution prevention
- fisheries co-management
- migratory birds co-management ...

There are a number of subject matters where there are no compelling reasons for
Aboriginal governments or institutions to exercise law-making authority. These subject
matters cannot be characterized as either integral to Aboriginal cultures, or internal to
Aboriginal groups. ... In these areas, it is essential that the federal government retain
its law-making authority. Subject matters in this category would include: ...

- management and regulation of the national economy ...
- protection of the health and safety of all Canadians ...

Mechanisms for Implementation

The Government anticipates that agreements on self-government will be given effect
through a variety of mechanisms including treaties, legislation, contracts and non-
binding memoranda of understanding.

...

Application of Laws

As a right which is exercised within the framework of the Canadian Constitution, the inherent right will not lead to the automatic exclusion of federal and provincial laws, many of which will continue to apply to Aboriginal peoples or will co-exist alongside validly enacted Aboriginal laws.

To minimize the possibility of conflicts between Aboriginal laws and federal or provincial laws, the Government believes that all agreements, including treaties, should establish rules of priority by which such conflicts can be resolved. The Government takes the position that negotiated rules of priority may provide for the paramountcy of Aboriginal laws, but may not deviate from the basic principle that those federal and provincial laws of overriding national or provincial importance will prevail over conflicting Aboriginal laws. Prior to the conclusion of self-government agreements, federal and provincial laws would continue to apply to the extent that they do currently.

Haida Nation v. BC and Weyerhaeuser
(2002), 44 CELR (NS) 1 (BCCA)

LAMBERT JA: The principal issue in this appeal is about whether there is an obligation on the Crown and on third parties to consult with an aboriginal people who have specifically claimed aboriginal title or aboriginal rights, about potential infringements, before the aboriginal title or rights have been determined by a Court of competent jurisdiction.

. . .

The Haida people, as petitioners, say that there is a legal obligation on the Crown and on Weyerhaeuser to consult them before authorizing logging operations on the Queen Charlotte Islands, known to the Haida people as Haida Gwaii, and over which the Haida people have claimed to hold aboriginal title.

The Crown and Weyerhaeuser say that there is no obligation on the Crown or on Weyerhaeuser to consult the Haida people about logging on the Queen Charlotte Islands until the Haida people have obtained a judgment of a court of competent jurisdiction declaring the aboriginal title and rights of the Haida people over Haida Gwaii and demonstrating that the logging operations would be a *prima facie* infringement of that aboriginal title or those aboriginal rights.

The issue is an important one. If the Crown can ignore or override aboriginal title or aboriginal rights until such time as the title or rights are confirmed by treaty or by judgment of a competent court, then by placing impediments on the treaty process the Crown can force every claimant of aboriginal title or rights into court and on to judgment before conceding that any effective recognition should be given to the claimed aboriginal title or rights, even on an interim basis.

. . .

The Roots of the Obligation To Consult

In my opinion, the roots of the obligation to consult lie in the trust-like relationship which exists between the Crown and the aboriginal people of Canada. That trust-like relationship was reflected in the Royal proclamation of 1763:

> And whereas it is just and reasonable, and essential to our Interest, and the Security of our Colonies, that the several Nations or Tribes of Indians *with whom We are connected, and who live under our Protection*, should not be molested or disturbed in the Possession of such Parts of Our Dominions and Territories as, not having been ceded to or purchased by Us, are reserved to them, or any of them, as their Hunting Grounds (my emphasis).

The trust-like relationship is now usually expressed as a fiduciary duty owed by both the federal and Provincial Crown to the aboriginal people. Whenever that fiduciary duty arises, and to the extent of its operation, it is a duty of utmost good faith.

In *R v. Sparrow*, Chief Justice Dickson and Mr. Justice La Forest said this at pp.1108-1109, about the roots of the fiduciary duty:

> In *Guerin*, … the Musqueam Band surrendered reserve lands to the Crown for lease to a golf club. The terms obtained by the Crown were much less favourable than those approved by the Band at the surrender meeting. *This Court found that the Crown owed a fiduciary obligation to the Indians with respect to the lands. The sui generis nature of Indian title, and the historic powers and responsibility assumed by the Crown constituted the source of such a fiduciary obligation.* In our opinion, *Guerin*, together with *R v. Taylor and Williams* (1981), 34 OR (2d) 360, ground a general guiding principle for s. 35(1) (my emphasis).

So the trust-like relationship and its concomitant fiduciary duty permeates the whole relationship between the Crown, in both of its sovereignties, federal and provincial, on the one hand, and the aboriginal peoples on the other. One manifestation of the fiduciary duty of the Crown to the aboriginal peoples is that it grounds a general guiding principle for s. 35(1) of the *Constitution Act, 1982*.

It would be contrary to that guiding principle to interpret s. 35(1), which reads in this way:

> 35(1) The existing aboriginal and treaty rights of the aboriginal peoples of Canada are hereby recognized and affirmed.

as if it required that before an aboriginal right could be recognized and affirmed, it first had to be made the subject matter of legal proceedings; then proved to the satisfaction of a judge of competent jurisdiction; and finally made the subject of a declaratory or other order of the court. That is not what s. 35(1) says and it would be contrary to the guiding principles of s. 35(1), as set out in *R v. Sparrow*, to give it that interpretation. Yet that interpretation is what was effectively given to it by the chambers judge in this case and by the chambers judge in *Westbank v. British Columbia*.

The Content of the Duty To Consult

Chief Justice Lamer addressed the question of the content of the duty to consult in *Delgamuukw* at paras. 165 to 169 under the heading "Justification and Aboriginal

Title." Since the complete text of that statement of Chief Justice Lamer's reasons is available I will not set it out in full here. However, para. 168 is of crucial importance to these reasons.

> *Moreover, the other aspects of aboriginal title suggest that the fiduciary duty may be articulated in a manner different than the idea of priority. This point becomes clear from a comparison between aboriginal title and the aboriginal right to fish for food in Sparrow. First, aboriginal title encompasses within it a right to choose to what ends a piece of land can be put.* The aboriginal right to fish for food, by contrast, does not contain within it the same discretionary component. *This aspect of aboriginal title suggests that the fiduciary relationship between the Crown and aboriginal peoples may be satisfied by the involvement of aboriginal peoples in decisions taken with respect to their lands.* **There is always a duty of consultation.** *Whether the aboriginal group has been consulted is relevant to determining whether the infringement of aboriginal title is justified,* in the same way that the Crown's failure to consult an aboriginal group with respect to the terms by which reserve land is leased may breach its fiduciary duty at common law: *Guerin.* **The nature and scope of the duty of consultation will vary with the circumstances.** In occasional cases, when the breach is less serious or relatively minor, it will be no more than a duty to discuss important decisions that will be taken with respect to lands held pursuant to aboriginal title. Of course, even in these rare cases when the minimum acceptable standard is consultation, this consultation must be in good faith, and with the intention of substantially addressing the concerns of the aboriginal peoples whose lands are at issue. **In most cases, it will be significantly deeper than mere consultation.** Some cases may even require the full consent of an aboriginal nation, particularly when provinces enact hunting and fishing regulations in relation to aboriginal lands. (The emphasis and the double emphasis are mine.)

Para. 169 deals with compensation for infringement and with the relationship between advance consultation and subsequent infringement. This is what was said:

> Second, *aboriginal title,* unlike the aboriginal right to fish for food, *has an inescapably economic aspect,* particularly when one takes into account the modern uses to which lands held pursuant to aboriginal title can be put. *The economic aspect of aboriginal title suggests that compensation is relevant to the question of justification as well, a possibility suggested in Sparrow and which I repeated in Gladstone. Indeed, compensation for breaches of fiduciary duty are a well-established part of the landscape of aboriginal rights: Guerin.* **In keeping with the duty of honour and good faith on the Crown, fair compensation will ordinarily be required when aboriginal title is infringed.** *The amount of compensation payable will vary with the nature of the particular aboriginal title affected and with the nature and severity of the infringement* **and the extent to which aboriginal interests were accommodated.** Since the issue of damages was severed from the principal action, we received no submissions on the appropriate legal principles that would be relevant to determining the appropriate level of compensation of infringements of aboriginal title. In the circumstances, it is best that we leave those difficult questions to another day. (The emphasis and double emphasis are mine.)

I regard the reference to "the extent to which aboriginal interests were accommodated" in relation to the determination of compensation for an infringement as being a significant indication that Chief Justice Lamer regarded the accommodation process as a process which preceded the infringement which itself will occur before the aboriginal title is declared by a court of competent jurisdiction in proceedings alleging both the title and the infringement.

. . .

The Remedy

Both the Crown Provincial and Weyerhaeuser had an obligation to consult the Haida people in 1999 and 2000 about accommodating the aboriginal title and aboriginal rights of the Haida people when consideration was being given to the renewal of Tree Farm Licence 39 and Block 6. That obligation extended to both the cultural interests and the economic interests of the Haida people. ...

In this case, the obligation to consult and to seek an accommodation arose from these circumstances:

> a) The Provincial Crown had fiduciary obligations of utmost good faith to the Haida people with respect to the Haida claims to aboriginal title and aboriginal rights;
>
> b) The Provincial Crown and Weyerhaeuser were aware of the Haida claims to aboriginal title and aboriginal rights over all or at least some significant part of the area covered by TFL 39 and Block 6, through evidence supplied to them by the Haida people and through further evidence available to them on reasonable inquiry, an inquiry which they were obliged to make; and
>
> c) The claims of the Haida people to aboriginal title and aboriginal rights were supported by a good *prima facie* case in relation to all or some significant part of the area covered by TFL 39 and Block 6.

. . .

The strength of the Haida case gives content to the obligation to consult and the obligation to seek an accommodation. I am not saying that if there is something less than a good *prima facie* case then there is no obligation to consult. I do not have to deal with such a case on this appeal. But certainly the scope of the consultation and the strength of the obligation to seek an accommodation will be proportional to the potential soundness of the claim for aboriginal title and aboriginal rights.

In my opinion, the obligations to consult and seek an accommodation with the Haida people were enforceable, legal and equitable duties at the relevant times in 1999 and 2000 of the Crown Provincial, MacMillan Bloedel, and its successor, Weyerhaeuser. The chambers judge has found as a fact that the Haida people were not consulted when the replacement of TFL 39 and its transfer to Weyerhaeuser occurred, and that the Haida people objected to the replacement and to the transfer. No accommodation with the Haida people was sought by the Crown, by MacMillan Bloedel, or by Weyerhaeuser. In my opinion, the Crown Provincial and Weyerhaeuser were in breach of these enforceable, legal and equitable duties to the Haida people.

NOTES AND PROBLEMS

1. For a broad discussion of the implementation of the principle of aboriginal self-government, see Canada, Royal Commission on Aboriginal Peoples, *Report of the Royal Commission on Aboriginal Peoples* (Ottawa: Canada Communication Group, 1996), vol. 2, part 1, chapter 3.

2. One week before the *Haida* case was set for hearing, the decision in *Taku River Tlingit First Nation v. Ringstad* (2002), 43 CELR (NS) 169 (BCCA) was handed down. The court held that there was an obligation on the Crown to consult with aboriginal people who had claimed aboriginal title and rights. The Crown position that the duty only arose once a court of competent jurisdiction had endorsed the existence and scope of the aboriginal interest was not accepted by the majority. Undoubtedly, one or both of these cases will be worthy of Supreme Court of Canada consideration.

FURTHER READINGS

K. Harrison, *Passing the Buck: Federalism and Canadian Environmental Policy* (Vancouver: UBC Press, 1996).

J.O. Saunders, ed., *Managing Natural Resources in a Federal State* (Scarborough, ON: Carswell, 1986).

M. Valiente, "Legal Foundations of Canadian Environmental Policy: Underlining Our Values in a Shifting Landscape," in D. VanNijnatten and R. Boardman, eds., *Canadian Environmental Policy: Context and Cases*, 2d ed. (Don Mills, ON: Oxford University Press, 2002), chapter 1.

CHAPTER THREE

Common Law and Environmental Protection: Legal Realities and Judicial Challenges*

William Charles and David VanderZwaag

I. INTRODUCTION

Private litigation is not an ideal route to secure environmental protection for numerous reasons. Private litigation, relying on the happenstance of a motivated and financially able plaintiff, cannot replace the need for long-term planning processes. The costs of litigation may be prohibitive because of attorney fees and the financial drain of securing witnesses. Private lawsuits tend to be reactive and adversarial with traditional legal requirements, such as the need for a property interest, often favouring defendants.

Nevertheless, private litigation may have a critical role to play in environmental protection. Litigation may be the only way to air legitimate grievances where governmental officials have refused to act or polluters have failed to listen. The profile of an environmental issue might be elevated through a lawsuit, and a court offers a decision-making forum less prone to political pressures.

Just how active judges should be in policy making will remain a controversial issue. A call for conservative approaches might be based on the notion that elected officials are the more proper vehicle for social policy decisions. However, common law doctrines carry inherent value judgments that are open to creative jurisprudential evolutions based on changing societal perspectives.

Longstanding common law actions of negligence, nuisance, strict liability, riparian rights, and trespass to the person have been developed and used to protect individual rights to physical integrity and property. As yet, however, we have not developed a legal theory that would give us a justiciable right to be free of the harmful effects of toxic

* The authors gratefully acknowledge the assistance of former Dalhousie law students Ian Whan Tong and Susan Taylor, and present research assistant Anastasia Makrigiannis, in the research and production of this chapter.

substances, in spite of our growing awareness of the dangerous realities. Instead, we remain closely tied to the tradition that "English law reduces environmental problems to questions of property." (L.A. Scarman, *English Law—The New Dimension* (London: Stevens & Sons, 1974), at 51.)

This chapter, in a two-part format, illustrates the potential power, but also key limitations, of common law to protect the environment. The following section highlights the basic legal requirements of negligence (including public authority liability), private nuisance, public nuisance, strict liability, riparian rights, trespass to the person, and trespass to land. The final section focuses on judicial challenges in toxic torts where plaintiffs are exposed to toxic agents (chemical, biological, or radiological).

II. OVERVIEW OF COMMON LAW DOCTRINES

A. Negligence

The most important tort action today, both in terms of the number of claims made and its theoretical importance, is the negligence cause of action. Unlike other torts, which protect specific interests from wrongful interference, the negligence action seems to have few limits. In a broad sense, negligence law deals with the compensation of losses caused by unintentional but unreasonable conduct that harmfully affects legally protected interests. Unreasonable conduct has been defined as "the omission to do something which a reasonable [person] guided by those considerations which ordinarily regulate the conduct of human affairs, would do, or doing something which a prudent, reasonable [person] would not do" (per Alderson B in *Blyth v. Birmingham Water Works Co.* (1856), 156 ER 1047, at 1049 (Ex. Ct.)).

A negligence action, in which a defendant is held to the standard of care of a reasonable person, may be effectively used in the area of environmental litigation. To be successful, a plaintiff must establish, on the balance of probabilities, five key elements of the tort. These elements are legal duty, breach of the standard of care, cause in fact, proximate cause, and damage to the plaintiff.

Smith Brothers Excavating Windsor Ltd. v. Camion Equipment & Leasing Inc. (Trustee of)
(1994), 21 CCLT (2d) 113 (Ont. Gen. Div.)

CUSENATO J: In the early hours of April 28, 1987, two storage tanks on the Camion property were vandalized by strangers. ...

The valves on each tank were intentionally opened to permit the escape of the fluids. The larger storage tank contained estimated quantities of methanol in excess of 1,300,000 litres, and it is believed that this total amount was released.

A good quantity of the released methanol escaped the berm area, crossing the Camion property at the southerly property line, and thereafter flowed in a southwest direction in the area of the plaintiffs' property.

This caused not only surface damage, but more importantly, the contaminants seeped into the underground water system.

$\cdots$

The plaintiff has ... raised security as a major issue for the consideration of this court. In this regard the plaintiff suggests the defendants fell far short of the standard of care required to protect such product from interference and escape.[1]

The plaintiffs' counsel suggests that it is due to this failure of the defendants to provide appropriate security whether the escape here is from negligent, or intentional acts of the defendants or strangers, its ultimate result is the harm visited upon the plaintiff.

It is for this failure and resulting harm for which this action is brought and for which the plaintiff suggests the defendants are liable. On this issue of security, Harve Plante testified that at all times there was at least one member of his staff located at the property. In the evenings and after midnight, a dispatcher was present for Camion's trucking business and while not in attendance specifically to guard the tank, there was a people presence. To add to this presence, Camion after 5:00 PM each day or when the business was closed from pedestrian traffic, located 3 German Shepherd dogs in the vicinity of the tanks. These dogs were located in different areas of the yard and were controlled by a 25 foot leash and a 200 foot slide cable. A security company was also retained for weekends and holidays to carry out periodic inspections when the business was closed.

The defendant pleads that even with these precautions to secure the property which it pleads accords with the minimum standard of care required within the industry, vandalism occurred.

The escape of the fluid and the tampering of the tanks as confirmed by Chief Tessier, results from intentional acts by the parties unknown. There is also no argument that it was by individuals with special knowledge of their operation and not children.

Although the examination of Harve Plante confirms [the company] could have retained the services of a full-time security officer, he acknowledges this was not done because of the expense, nor was it a requirement within the industry.

To this end as to licensing requirements or minimum security compliance from Government or regulatory bodies, there is no evidence.

It is with this background that the court is to consider the issue of liability and whether the defendants have met the standard of care required in its storage of methanol and its protection from interference by strangers.

In applying the principles of negligence to the fact situation before the court, we are left with the duty of the defendants to its neighbours and the standard of care required.

Although, hindsight is a useful tool as to what could have been done at least in the area of its obligations, the real question is whether what was done fell below the accepted standard of care imposed within the industry, and constitutes negligence.

---

1   Editors' note: The case sometimes refers to plaintiffs since the legal action was continued by the principal creditor of the original plaintiff who succumbed to bankruptcy. The judgment also uses the terms defendant and defendants with the latter term applicable since Camion Equipment, the owner of the property where the spill occurred, and the lessee of the larger storage tank were both sued.

If liability were to be determined alone based on the principles of negligence, I do not find from the evidence that the plaintiff has established a breach of the duty of care or that this defendant Camion has fallen below the standard of care acceptable within the industry. In the evidence of Fire Chief Tessier, he confirms that he is not aware of any special security that is required or provided for tank farms.

I accept from the evidence that additional security measures could have been implemented and put in place not only for accidental causes but intentional.

That is, not however, the test for liability in negligence since we first commence with a duty and breach of this duty to establish liability. ...

As I have earlier stated, the defendants while they owe a duty of care to their neighbour, the breach of which constitutes negligence, such a breach of duty is not established on the facts before me.

Upon the evidence, the defendants met the standard of care within the industry which as it relates to security for tank farms is minimal. Although greater security could have been provided, if the obligation does not exist and the standard of care as required is met, the failure to provide additional security does not alone constitute negligence.

Aside from the question of security, one additional issue as to negligence has been raised. The issue relates to the actions of the defendants after the spill.

The plaintiffs allege there was delay on the part of the defendants in the clean-up and immediate remediation of the land. ...

On this issue ... it is my conclusion that the defendants immediately after the spill acted without delay. They retained ... a firm of scientific environment engineers to assess the environmental problems. Upon completion of this firm's assessment, they developed an immediate course of action and proceeded in consultation with the Ministry of the Environment. Upon my examination of the defendant's conduct and the steps implemented for remediation, it was not only appropriate, but carried out within reasonable time limits. For these reasons, the plaintiff fails on this ground of negligence.

B. Public Authority Liability

A field of negligence law that is bound to take on increasing importance is the liability of public authorities. The ever expanding role of government officials in regulatory activities may lead to future lawsuits over the adequacy of official conduct in preventing or controlling polluting activities. The doctrine of Crown immunity, which, historically, has provided protection against civil liability, has in recent years been significantly limited both by statutory provisions and judicial decisions. With immunity very much limited, courts have strained to develop an appropriate test for determining governmental civil liability. The Supreme Court of Canada's decision in *Just v. British Columbia*, [1989] 2 SCR 1228 is the seminal authority in Canada and is applied by the Ontario court in the environmental case that follows.

Gauvin v. Ontario (Ministry of Environment)
(1995), 22 CELR (NS) 277 (Ont. Gen. Div.);
aff'd. (1997), 26 CELR (NS) 325 (Ont. Div. Ct.)

CHADWICK J: The action arises from failure of a septic sewage system which is located on the plaintiffs' property. The plaintiffs purchased the property in February 1988 and at the time of the purchase they requested various documents from the vendor, including a certificate of approval for the use of the septic sewage system.

The septic system had been installed on the property in the summer of 1986. The system was installed by the defendant Gerald Ferguson Sand & Gravel Limited, and was subject to the provisions of the *Environmental Protection Act*, RSO 1980, c. 141 and its regulations.

[The court then reviewed the events surrounding the construction of the septic system and its inspection and approval by the Ministry of Environment (MOE). The contractor failed to certify that the system's sand filter bed complied with the regulations, yet the ministry issued a use permit, notwithstanding the irregularities in the paperwork and without additional inspections.]

Mr. Farrell on behalf of MOE contends that the activities of MOE as it related to the approval and inspection of this septic system was purely a policy decision and as such the decision was made in good faith and therefore MOE is immune from civil liability. The plaintiffs contend that the activities of MOE amount to an operational decision and therefore the decision is reviewable by the court to see whether they have met the proper standard of care.

Reference has been made by both counsel to the decision in *Just v. The Queen in Right of British Columbia* (1989), 64 DLR (4th) 689 (SCC). In that case, the plaintiff was injured as a result of a huge rock falling on his car as he was driving on the Whistler highway in British Columbia. The Minister of Highways had a statutory duty to maintain highways and as part of that duty, the ministry established a special crew to inspect cliff faces. At trial the plaintiff's action was dismissed on the ground that the defendant's system of inspection and its implementations were policy matters in respect of which no liability could arise. The plaintiff appealed to the British Columbia Court of Appeal and that appeal was also dismissed. On appeal to the Supreme Court of Canada, the court considered the distinction between operational and policy decisions. The court recognized that it is sometimes difficult to distinguish between policy and operational decisions. At p. 708 he makes the following comment:

> As a general rule, the traditional tort law duty of care will apply to a government agency in the same way that it will apply to an individual. In determining whether a duty of care exists, the first question to be resolved is whether the parties are in a relationship of sufficient proximity to warrant the imposition of such a duty. In the case of a government agency, exemption from this imposition of duty may occur as a result of an explicit

statutory exemption. Alternatively, the exemption may arise as a result of the nature of the decision made by the government agency. That is, a government agency will be exempt from the imposition of a duty of care in situations which arise from its pure policy decisions.

Applying the principles in *Just v. Queen in Right of British Columbia*, I am of the view that the activities of MOE are operational in nature and not policy decisions. In this particular case the key element before any sewage system can be used is the user permit. The use permit is not issued by the MOE until they are satisfied from their inspection that the system has been constructed in accordance with the act and regulations. In addition, they require the contractor to provide a certificate and evidence that the purchase of the required filter sand both in the required quantities and quality. In this case the contractor did not follow the normal requirements, namely sign the certificate and provide evidence that the filter sand was delivered to the site in question. The user permit should not have been issued until the contractor had satisfied the normal ministry requirements.

On the evidence one can conclude that the proper amount of filter sand was not provided as required for this type of septic installation. As such MOE has breached the standard of care required of them.

[The negligent contractor was found jointly and severally liable.]

NOTES

1. Although in each of the foregoing cases the court did not discuss the duty issue in any detail, in many cases, it is a complicated issue that has prompted much judicial comment and analysis. The modern approach to the duty issue has its origins in the two-stage approach outlined in the decisions in *Anns v. Merton London Borough Council*, [1978] AC 728 (HL) and *Kamloops v. Nielsen*, [1984] 2 SCR 2. This approach requires a court in the first stage to question whether the circumstances of the case disclose a reasonably foreseeable harm occurring as a result of the defendant's action and, in addition, to determine whether the relationship of the parties is sufficiently close to meet a proximity requirement. If the foresight and the proximity requirements are satisfied, a court can then declare that a *prima facie* duty to exercise care on the part of the defendant exists. The court then moves on to the second stage, which requires it to consider whether there are policy reasons that would compel the court to refuse to recognize and give effect to the *prima facie* duty to care.

2. In more recent decisions, the Supreme Court has further refined the *Anns/Kamloops* approach. The Supreme Court has suggested, for example, that a proximate relationship can be identified by looking at established categories of cases or analogous ones in which proximity of relationship has been recognized and declared by other courts. Besides previously recognized categories, the Supreme Court has indicated that proximity can be created by a number of factors such as expectations, representations, and reliance, as well as property or other interests. After a consideration of these factors, the court then decides whether it would be fair and just to impose a duty of care in relation to what appears to be a proximate relationship.

The Supreme Court has cautioned that there is no single unifying characteristic of proximity and has noted that in some cases the parties' situation is affected by the provisions of a governing statute. Such statutory provisions, the court has said, are particularly important in cases where the situation before the court does not fall within judicially recognized categories of proximate relationships (for example, *Cooper v. Hobart* (2001), 206 DLR (4th) 193 (SCC)). Yet, even though the requirements of a *prima facie* duty in the form of foresight and proximity appear to have been satisfied, the Supreme Court has declared in more recent cases that a court is still free at the first stage of its analysis to take into account unspecified "broad policy issues" that are relevant to the relationship between the parties.

If all the requirements of the first stage are satisfied, the court then proceeds to the second stage where so-called residual policy considerations are applied. These include the effect of a recognized duty of care on other legal obligations, as well as on the legal system or society as a whole. In cases involving public authority liability, the distinction between policy and operational decisions is applied at this stage as well. If a case involves a novel situation that does not fall within recognized categories but has been deemed by the court to have satisfied the foresight and proximity requirements of the first stage, it is still subject to review at the second stage where "residual policy consid-erations" can be applied.

Such is the analytical process through which a modern Canadian court must now proceed in order to determine the duty issue—a far cry from the rather simplistic "neigh-bour" test of *Donoghue v. Stevenson*, [1932] AC 562 (HL)!

C. Private Nuisance

A private nuisance is usually defined as an unreasonable interference with the use and enjoyment of land that is owned or occupied by another person. Liability may be im-posed, even though the defendant did not intend and was not negligent in causing the interference. If the interference involves a form of physical damage to the land itself or personal injury to occupants, courts have been quick to conclude a finding of nuisance given the substantial gravity of interference. Where the interference involves interference with the plaintiff's enjoyment of the property—for example, by loud noises or noxious odours—courts will weigh various factors in determining whether a nuisance exists. Key factors include duration of the interference, gravity, the neighbourhood (for example industrial/urban versus rural), utility of the defendant's activity, and whether the plaintiff has abnormal sensitivities. The following case introduces two additional common nui-sance issues: the defence of statutory authority and injunctive relief.

Mandrake Management Consultants Ltd. v. Toronto Transit Commission
(1993), 11 CELR (NS) 100 (Ont. CA)

GALLIGAN JA (BROOKE JA concurring): The trial judge found that the defendant's northbound subway trains on the Yonge-University-Spadina line cause noise and vibrations when they are about to enter the east end of St. George station, creating a nuisance to the plaintiffs. In addition to awarding the plaintiffs nominal damages for nuisance until trial, he ordered the defendant to remove a frog which forms an integral part of a double crossover at the entrance to the station. From that judgment the defendant appeals.

. . .

Issues

The three main issues which were addressed by the trial judge and which were debated before this Court are the following:

1. Does the operation of the defendant's Yonge-University-Spadina subway line create a nuisance at law to the plaintiffs?
2. If the answer to that question is yes, is the defendant entitled to rely on the defence of statutory authority?
3. If that issue is resolved in the plaintiffs' favour, are they entitled, in addition to damages, to a mandatory order directing the defendant to alter structurally its subway system in order to eliminate the noise and vibrations?

The trial judge resolved each of those three issues in the plaintiffs' favour. I am unable to do so and would hold against the plaintiffs on each of them.

. . .

Does the Operation of the Defendant's Yonge-University-Spadina Subway Line Cause a Nuisance at Law to the Plaintiffs?

The problem is the reconciliation of the conflict which occurs when competing interests come into contact with one another. The most recent authority on the subject of nuisance is the judgment of the Supreme Court of Canada in *Tock v. St. John's Metropolitan Area Board* (1989), 64 DLR (4th) 620. While there were differences of opinion among the judges who participated in the judgment upon the breadth of the defence of statutory authority, there was no disagreement with that part of the judgment of La Forest J which appears at pp. 639-40:

> The courts have traditionally approached this problem of reconciling conflicting uses of land with an eye to a standard based, in large part, on the formulations of Knight Bruce V-C in *Walter v. Selfe* (1851), 4 De G & Sm. 315, 64 ER 849, and Bramwell B in *Bamford v. Turnley* (1862), 3 B & S 66, 122 ER 27, at 83-4 and at 32-3 respectively. There it was observed that the very existence of organized society depended on a generous application of the principle of "give and take, live and let live." It was therefore appropriate to interpret as actionable nuisances only those inconveniences that materially interfere with ordinary comfort as defined according to the standards held by those of plain and sober tastes. In effect, the law would only intervene to shield persons from interferences to their enjoyment of property that were unreasonable in the light of all the circumstances.
>
> The courts are thus called upon to select among the claims for interference with property and exclude those based on the prompting of excessive "delicacy and fastidiousness"

to employ the terms of Knight Bruce V-C. The courts attempt to circumscribe the ambit of nuisance by looking to the nature of the locality in question and asking whether the ordinary and reasonable resident of that locality would view the disturbance as a substantial interference with the enjoyment of land. Among the criteria employed by the courts in delimiting the ambit of the tort of nuisance are considerations based on the severity of the harm, the character of the neighbourhood, the utility of the defendant's conduct, and the question whether the plaintiff displayed abnormal sensitivity.

That passage leads me to the opinion that, at least in cases such as this which involve only interference with tranquility and amenities, when determining whether or not one person's use of property constitutes a nuisance to another the court ought to weigh the following four factors:

(a) The nature of the locality in question;
(b) The severity of the harm;
(c) The sensitivity of the plaintiff; and
(d) The utility of the defendant's conduct.

. . .

I start by saying that while private rights cannot be trampled upon in the name of the public good, where an essential public service is involved the factor of the utility of the defendant's conduct must not be disregarded. Indeed, I think it must be given substantial weight. An indication of the kind of weight which should be given to this factor where a highway is involved appears in the reasons for judgment delivered by McIntyre J on behalf of the Supreme Court of Canada in *St. Pierre v. Ontario (Minister of Transportation & Communications)* (1987), 39 DLR (4th) 10, at p. 18:

Highways are necessary: they cause disruption. In the balancing process inherent in the law or nuisance, their utility for the public good far outweighs the disruption and injury which is visited upon some adjoining lands.

While it has been argued that *St. Pierre* is distinguishable because it arises out of land compensation proceedings, the views of McIntyre J support my opinion that the utility of essential public services is an important consideration in the balancing process inherent in a nuisance case.

Any unusual sensitivity of one property owner to the use being made of the other must be carefully weighed because one owner's unusual sensitivity must not be allowed to turn the other's reasonable use of its property into one which is unreasonable. While the interference with the personal comfort of people at 15 Bedford Road is significant and at certain times of the day fairly frequent, that discomfort has not prejudicially affected the profitable operation of the plaintiffs' businesses at their business premises. Finally, the plaintiffs' expectations of the quiet and tranquility of a residential area cannot reasonably be fulfilled in the essentially commercial area where 15 Bedford Road is located.

. . .

I have reached the conclusion that the plaintiffs failed to establish that the defendant has caused them nuisance. It is my opinion that their action should have been dismissed on that ground.

The Defence of Statutory Authority

In the event that I am wrong in holding that the defendant's operation of its subway system did not cause actionable nuisance to the plaintiffs, I turn to the defence of statutory authority. The defendant says that it is immune from liability when it causes the sensible personal discomfort which interferes with the plaintiffs' use and enjoyment of their property because it is acting under statutory authority. That the definition and the application of the defence of statutory authority are as difficult as is the definition of nuisance itself is evident from the three sets of reasons for judgment delivered by the Supreme Court of Canada in *Tock*, *supra*.

Before attempting to determine the applicability of the defence in this case, I think it is appropriate to make some general, and perhaps obvious, observations. The defendant is a body created by statute. It performs statutory duties and has imposed upon it statutory responsibilities. Its subway system was conceived, developed and built in different sections over several decades. The system which was in existence in 1984, at the time the plaintiffs' complaints began, was a complex undertaking. Its parts are so interrelated and interdependent that a problem at one place which might seem isolated can cause service irregularities or difficulties in other parts of the system many miles away.

The seminal statutory authority under which the defendant operates is the *Municipality of Metropolitan Toronto Act* (the "Act"). The defendant is also subject to control and regulation by a bewildering array of regulatory authorities, all of which find their genesis in statutes of various kinds. Its subway development projects are the concern of the municipalities affected by them and by the governments which are required to provide financial support for them. Its projects are subjected to scrutiny by authorities with health, safety, urban planning and environmental concerns. Finally, any subway project must be approved by the Ontario Municipal Board (the "OMB").

. . .

What this small bit of background demonstrates to me is that the defendant did not put the tracks, with which we are concerned, where they are solely by the exercise of its own discretion. It did so because ultimately, it was told where and how the tracks were to be located by statutory authorities without whose permission the line and station could not have been built.

[The court then considered the contents of ss. 106 and 107 of the *Municipality of Metropolitan Toronto Act*, SO 1953, c. 73 and continued:]

In my respectful view the decision of the trial judge and the plaintiffs' argument fail to take account of the fact that a certain amount of noise and vibrations is an inevitable consequence of the operation of railways. Moreover, the authorities establish that statutory authority is a defence to an action for nuisance caused by noise and vibrations resulting from the operation of a railway. Section 107(1) of the Act not only grants powers to the defendant but also imposes a positive duty upon it to construct, maintain and operate a transportation system by means, among others, of surface, underground and overhead railways. The Legislature, in authorizing the use of railways as a part of a transportation system, obviously knew that noise and vibrations are an unfortunate but unavoidable side effect of any railway. I do not think a close analysis of the exact words used in s. 107(1) is necessary to avoid the inescapable inference that when the Legislature authorized the construction of railways as part of a transportation system it also authorized the noise and vibrations which necessarily go with them.

[The court then considered three different views of the defence of statutory authority as expressed by members of the Supreme Court in *Tock* and concluded:]

It is my opinion, therefore, that no matter which of the views of the defence of statutory authority expressed in *Tock* will ultimately prevail, in this case the defendant is entitled to the benefit of the defence. It is impossible to operate a railway without causing noise and vibrations. When the Legislature authorized the construction and operation of an underground railway it authorized the causing of noise and vibrations which must of necessity result from its operation. The defendant has taken all reasonable steps to minimize the amount of noise and vibrations which its trains cause.

. . .

The Remedy

Mr. Shibley argued that the trial judge's mandatory order is supported by a long line of unchallenged authority which holds that where a nuisance is proved the plaintiff is entitled to an order preventing the continuation of the nuisance, unless the defendant shows that damages would be an adequate remedy. ... The general rule, to which little exception could be taken, was developed in cases where an occupier of land was restrained from continuing the nuisance when only the occupier who was causing the nuisance would be detrimentally affected by the injunction. No case has been referred to the court, and I have been unable to find any, where the court issued an injunction which might affect the safety and convenience of thousands of members of the public using a system of mass transit. Broad as the language is in some of the cases to which we were referred, I can find nothing in any of them to suggest that the rule mentioned above should be applied in this type of case.

An injunction is a discretionary remedy. In a case such as this one, I would expect that a mandatory injunction requiring the alteration of a complex subway system would be made only after carefully balancing the harm which would occur if the order were not made with the harm which the making of such an order could cause to the public at large.

Because it was given by a highly qualified witness whose credibility was accepted, was unchallenged and not contradicted, it is my opinion that the trial judge ought to have accepted the evidence that the removal of the frog could detrimentally affect provisions for safety and impact prejudicially upon the flexibility which is important to the efficient operation of the system. It seems to me that even a realistic possibility of compromising the safety and convenience of thousands of passengers using the public mass transit system so greatly outweighs the periodic sensible personal discomfort of the occupants of 15 Bedford Road that the latter pales into insignificance.

The remedy ordered by the trial judge is so grossly disproportionate to the harm suffered by the plaintiffs that it cannot be supported.

A public transit system like the Toronto subway is an incredibly complex thing.
This subway was planned after meticulous study and wide consultation. Experts in
the fields of transportation, construction and safety had input into its design, construction and operation. The courts have none of that expertise and should be reluctant indeed to remove a part of that system, particularly when, as in this case, the
suggestion to do so came on its own motion.

· · ·

While I am not prepared to say that there could never be a case where a court
might be entitled to order a change in the structure or operation of a public transit
system, I would think a court would only do so in circumstances where it was responding to the infliction of serious harm to many people and where it was clear that
the order could not possibly compromise the safety or efficiency of the system. This
is not such a case. This mandatory order should not have been made.

NOTES AND QUESTIONS

1. A key issue in nuisance law, not raised in the *Mandrake* case, is whether the cause
of action should be restricted to those having an interest in land. Judicial opinions have
varied. In *Hunter v. Canary Wharf Ltd.*, [1997] 2 All ER 426 (HL), the majority of the
House of Lords held that in order to bring an action for private nuisance, one must have
interest in the land such as ownership, a lease, or an exclusive right of possession.
Therefore, in this case, the spouses of the plaintiffs' children could not recover under
private nuisance as they did not have a sufficient proprietary interest in the land. Yet, in
Devon Lumber Co. v. MacNeill (1987), 45 DLR (4th) 300, the New Brunswick Court of
Appeal held that resident members of a land occupier's family can bring an action in
private nuisance, while in *Sutherland v. Canada (Attorney General)* (2001), 202 DLR
(4th) 310, the British Columbia Supreme Court agreed with the majority decision in
Canary Wharf and refused the claim of non-owner residents.

Giving the right to sue in private nuisance to occupiers who do not have proprietary
interests is supportable on various grounds such as the polluter pays and precautionary
principles becoming prevalent in environmental jurisprudence. The dissenting opinion in
the *Canary Wharf* case noted that the expansion of nuisance actions to include members
of households was also in accord with international human rights norms, such as the right
of a child not to be subjected to unlawful interference with his or her home.

2. The three different views expressed in *Tock* by different groups of Supreme Court
justices as to the defence of statutory authority can be summarized as follows:

   a. Writing for herself and two other members of the court, Wilson J would have
      restricted the defence to two situations: (a) where the statutory provisions in question
      imposed a duty on the defendant and a nuisance was the inevitable result of
      discharging that duty if the defendant was not negligent, and (b) if the legislation,
      although not mandatory, did specify the manner or location of doing the thing
      authorized and a nuisance was inevitable result (again, in the absence of negligence).

However, if the legislation was permissive and merely conferred an authority on a public body and gave it discretion whether to carry out the action or not and how best to do it, then the public body must act in such a way as to avoid creating a nuisance. If a nuisance is created, the public body will be liable regardless of whether there was negligence or not. In other words, the defence of inevitable consequences is not available.

b. LaForest and Dickson JJ would have restricted the applicability of the defence but stopped short of eliminating it. They held that statutory authority protects a public body from actions for nuisance if the disturbances and loss of amenities are the unavoidable consequence of the public body carrying out its statutory mandate. They reasoned that to allow an action for nuisance would, in effect, deny the statutory mandate.

c. Sopinka J held that a public body is immunized from liability if it shows there is no practical possibility of carrying out its mandate without causing a nuisance to others. Justice Sopinka further explained that the burden of proof with respect to the defence of statutory authority is on the party advancing the defence, which is not easy because the courts strain against a conclusion that private rights are intended to be sacrificed to the common good. The defendant must negate that there are alternate methods of carrying out the work. The mere fact that one is considerably less expensive will not avail. If only one method is practically feasible, it must be established that it was practically impossible to avoid the nuisance. It is insufficient for the defendant to negate negligence.

In the more recent public nuisance case of *Ryan v. Victoria (City)*, [1999] 1 SCR 201, the court declared that the appropriate test to use to determine whether the defence of statutory authority was available to the defendant was the traditional rule as restated by Sopinka J in *Tock*.

3. Lower-court decisions in which the *Tock* case has been argued and applied show a clear tendency to limit the availability of the statutory authority defence in private nuisance actions to public authorities and a decided degree of uncertainty as to the bases for that restriction. Judges in different courts have relied on all the tests outlined in *Tock* with a slight majority favouring the Wilson J approach. In several cases, the courts have applied two or all three tests in reaching its decision. The lower-court dilemma is perhaps best demonstrated by the comments of Eberle J in *Bell Canada v. Olympia & York Developments Ltd.* (1992), 13 MPLR (2d) 161, at 180 (Ont. Ct. Gen. Div.):

I can see no good purpose in my attempting to analyze, and possibly to harmonize, such conflicting judgments, and I do not. I say no more than that, in my best interpretation, probably none of the judgments would mandate the acceptance of the defence of statutory authority in the present case. And at the very worst, I believe that only a minority would do so. It is not necessary to say any more on this issue.

Given the prevailing lower-court confusion and tendency to limit the applicability of the defence of statutory authority, there is the distinct possibility that municipal corporations and other public bodies will try to have legislative provisions enacted that will provide the immunity they desire.

4. What is the legal effect on private rights of the issuance of an approval or licence and compliance by a defendant who, nevertheless, still pollutes as a consequence of the approved undertaking? One view is that the effect is similar to statutory authorization. A contrary view holds that the issuance of the approval does not protect the holder from an action by a private citizen for interference with private rights (see *City of Portage La Prairie v. BC Pea Growers Ltd.*, [1966] SCR 150). Courts adopting the latter approach appear to take the position that the purpose of approvals is to ensure that the undertaking is operated in accordance with government-accepted procedures and that they do not operate to authorize a nuisance or to take away private rights. The more recent decision of the Supreme Court of Canada in *Tock* should lend support to this approach because of its limiting effect upon the defence of statutory authority. For one of the few discussions of this issue, see M.D. Faieta et al., *Environmental Harm: Civil Actions and Compensation* (Toronto: Butterworths, 1996), at 257.

5. While the *Mandrake* case shows how courts may resort to "balancing the equities" in determining whether to grant injunctive relief against a nuisance, the questions whether and how to weigh the equities remain controversial. For example, how is the potential loss of hundreds of jobs in a locally important polluting industry to be weighed against hard-to-quantify public health risks and threats to the environment? For a US case where the majority of the New York Court of Appeals refused to issue an injunction against a cement plant critical to the local economy and chose to grant permanent damages instead (leading to a stinging criticism by a strong dissent), see *Boomer v. Atlantic Cement Co.*, 26 NY 2d 219; 257 NE 2d 870 (1970).

6. Normal farming practices may be protected from common law nuisance actions by provincial statutes. The majority of provinces provide protection from nuisance claims only; however, Nova Scotia's "right to farm" legislation is an exception because it may protect farmers from negligence claims too. See *Agricultural Operations Practices Act*, SNB 1986, c. A-5.2 (a revised Act is subject to proclamation); *Agricultural Operation Practices Act*, RSA 2000, c. A-7; *Farm Practices Act*, SNS 2000, c. 3; *Farm Practices Protection Act*, SM 1992, c. F.45; *Act Respecting the Preservation of Agricultural Land and Agricultural Activities*, RSQ 1996, c. P-41.1; *Farm Practices Protection (Right To Farm) Act*, RSBC 1996, c. 131; *Agricultural Operations Act*, SS 1995, c. A-12.1; *Farming and Food Production Protection Act*, SO 1998, c. 1; *Farm Practices Act*, RSPEI 1988, c. F-4.1; and *Farm Practices Protection Act*, SNL 2001, c. F-4.1 (to be proclaimed, not yet in force).

D. Public Nuisance

A public nuisance has been defined as an "action brought to protect the public interest in freedom from damages to health, safety, morality, comfort or convenience" (O.M. Reynolds, "Public Nuisance: A Crime in Tort Law" (1978) vol. 31 *Oklahoma Law Review* 318). This civil action has its roots in the criminal law and more specifically in the common law offence of common nuisance. The civil action of public nuisance developed in the 18th and 19th centuries and was intended to supplement the criminal offence. However, the modern tort of public nuisance does not require an unlawful act as its basic requirement and has grown from its function as an ancillary criminal remedy into an independent common law tort.

Originally designed to deal with obstructions of public highways, rights of way, or navigable waters, this tort has expanded to cover the pollution of beaches and shoreline properties, as well as noise-generating activities and street prostitution.

In order to determine whether a particular activity interferes unreasonably with the public interest, a court must balance, in a general manner, the defendant's right to engage in an activity, without undue restriction, against the public right to have its interests protected. Several factors may be considered by the court such as the trouble or inconvenience caused by the activity, the ease or difficulty involved in taking steps to avoid the risk, the general practice of others, the utility of the activity, and the character of the neighbourhood. "The more harmful and less useful the activity, the more likely it is that it will be termed a (public) nuisance. Where the activity results not in material damage to public property but to questions of public's comfort and sensibilities, the balancing is more difficult" (L.N. Klar, *Tort Law*, 2d ed. (Scarborough, ON: Carswell, 1996), at 527, citing *Chessie v. J.D. Irving Ltd.* (1982), 140 DLR (3d) 501 (NBCA)).

In general, actions in public nuisance must be commenced by the attorney general on the theory that the rights of the public are vested in the Crown. The only exception to this rule occurs in a situation where the public right interference is such that some private right is interfered with at the same time. For example, where an obstruction is so placed on a highway that the owner of the premises abating upon the highway has his or her own private access to and from the property interfered with, that person can be considered to have suffered "special damage." It is clear that in cases where a public nuisance results in personal injury or damage to or interference with the plaintiff's property, the special damages requirement is met. However, where the plaintiff suffers loss of business profits (or economic loss), the issue is more difficult and the answer less clear as to whether this type of loss qualifies as "special damage." Courts have differed in their views whether the plaintiff's loss must be particular or special in kind (as compared to the public loss) or whether a greater degree of damage of the same kind is sufficient. In several cases, Canadian courts have taken a narrow view of special damages. The *Hickey* case that follows is one such case.

Hickey v. Electric Reduction Co. of Canada, Ltd.
(1970), 21 DLR (3d) 368 (Nfld. TD)

FURLONG CJ: For our present purposes then, I am assuming that the plaintiffs' assertion is true in substance, and that is, that the defendant discharged poisonous material into the waters of Placentia Bay, from its plant at Long Harbour, Placentia Bay, polluting the waters of the bay, poisoning fish "and rendering them of no commercial value."

So at the outset, we are put on inquiry to consider whether the facts disclose the creation of a tortious act, that is to say, the creation of a private nuisance, or the commission of a criminal act, which is to say, a public nuisance. The former is a civil wrong, actionable at the suit of an affected person.

The latter has been defined by Sir James Stephen in his *Digest of the Criminal Law*, 9th ed. (1950) (using the term "common nuisance"), in these words at p. 179:

> A common nuisance is an act not warranted by law or an omission to discharge a legal
> duty, which act or omission obstructs or causes inconvenience or damage to the public
> in the exercise of rights common to all His Majesty's subjects.

Salmond, *The Law of Torts*, 15th ed. (1969), expresses it more succinctly at p. 64:

> A public or common nuisance is a criminal offence. It is an act or omission which
> materially affects the reasonable comfort or convenience of life of a class of Her Maj-
> esty's subjects ... .

and he adds:

> A public nuisance falls within the law of torts only in so far as it may in the particular
> case constitute some form of tort also. Thus the obstruction of a highway is a public
> nuisance; but if it causes any special and peculiar damage to an individual, it is also a
> tort actionable at his suit.

What has happened here? The defendants by the discharge of poisonous waste
from its phosphorous plant at Long Harbour, Placentia Bay, destroyed the fish life of
the adjacent waters, and the plaintiffs, as all other fishermen in the area suffered in
their livelihood. I have said "all other fishermen," but the resulting pollution created
a nuisance to all persons—"all Her Majesty's subjects"—to use Stephen's phrase. It
was not a nuisance peculiar to the plaintiffs, nor confined to their use of the waters of
Placentia Bay. It was a nuisance committed against the public.

. . .

Counsel for the plaintiffs, Mr. Robert Wells, argued that when a public nuisance
has been created anyone who suffers special damage, that is direct damage has a right
of action. I am unable to agree to this rather wide application of Salmond's view that
a public nuisance may become a tortious act. I think the right view is that any person
who suffers peculiar damage has a right of action, but where the damage is common
to all persons of the same class, then a personal right of action is not maintainable.
Mr. Wells suggests that the plaintiffs' right to outfit for the fishery and their right to
fish is a particular right and this right having been interfered with they have a cause
of action. This right which they enjoy is a right in common with all Her Majesty's
subjects, an interference with which is the whole test of a public nuisance; a right
which can only be vindicated by the appropriate means, which is an action by the
Attorney-General, either with or without a relator, in the common interest of the public.

NOTES

1. Various cases since *Hickey* have recognized some economic losses as a special
injury allowing private actions for recovery under public nuisance to proceed. For example, in *Gagnier v. Canadian Forest Products Ltd.* (1990), 51 BCLR (2d) 218 (SC), the
British Columbia Supreme Court allowed the claim of a crab fisher to proceed against
defendant operators of pulp mills for economic loss resulting from closure caused by
pollution of a crab fishery. Referring to the *Hickey* decision as too narrow, the court
indicated that economic loses could be recovered under public nuisance if a plaintiff

shows a significant difference in degree of damage from the public generally. The action was later dismissed because of inadequate records of income earned and circumstantial evidence that Mr. Gagnier did not intend to continue fishing for crab. See M.D. Faieto et al., *Environmental Harm*, at 178.

The *Marine Liability Act*, SC 2001, c. 6, s. 88, lists categories of claimants who may seek recovery from the Ship-source Oil Pollution Fund for loss of income associated with oil spills from ships. Claimants include individuals who harvest, hold, or rear fish; marine plant harvesters; owners of fishing vessels who rent vessels to holders of commercial fishing licensees issued in Canada; fish handlers on shore; persons who rent or charter boats for sport fishing; and fish plant workers.

2. Unless spelled out in legislation, the "outer limits" of which types of economic losses are recoverable may remain uncertain with courts deciding on a case-by-case basis whether a reasonable degree of proximity exists between the contamination and the loss. For example, how far along "the chain" of various impacted businesses will recovery be allowed for a coastal oil spill? See E. Gold, D. VanderZwaag, and M. Doelle, "Economic Loss and Environmental Damages: Developments in Claims for Offshore Oil Pollution" (1991) vol. 1 *Journal of Environmental Law and Practice* 129; V.P. Goldberg, "Recovery for Economic Loss Following the Exxon Valdez Oil Spill" (1994) vol. 23 *Journal of Legal Studies* 1; and D. VanderZwaag, *Canada and Marine Environmental Protection: Charting a Legal Course Towards Sustainable Development* (London: Kluwer Law International, 1995), at 176-78.

3. The nuisance standing requirement is increasingly being vanquished by statutes seeking to liberalize traditional limitations on private actions. For example, the *Environmental Rights Act* of the Northwest Territories, SNWT 1990, c. 38, grants every resident the right to protect the environment from the release of contaminants by commencing an action in the Supreme Court. A person commencing an action would not have to establish a pecuniary or property right or interest, nor any greater or different harm than any other person. See also Ontario's *Environmental Bill of Rights, 1993*, SO 1993, c. 28, and the *Yukon Environment Act*, SY 1991, c. 5, discussed in chapter 11. The *Fisheries Act*, RSC 1985, c. F-14, s. 42(3), provides licensed commercial fishers a statutory right of action for losses of income resulting from unlawful deposits of deleterious substances into water frequented by fish.

4. A further area of potential liability opened by the legal door of public nuisance is recovery for environmental or natural resource damage per se. A leading case allowing a government to sue for environmental damages is *Commonwealth of Puerto Rico v. SS Zoe Colocotroni*, 628 F. 2d 652 (1st Cir. 1980), involving oil pollution damage to the coastal and marine environment. There, the US First Circuit Court of Appeals allowed the government of Puerto Rico to sue for reasonable costs of restoring the environment based on Puerto Rican legislation allowing specifically for damages to natural resources. The court left open the question whether the state could sue under common law for damages to the environment.

Although the concept of environmental damages has been controversial because of difficulties in quantification, some treaties and statutes are adopting the concept. For example, the 1992 protocols to the International Civil Liability for Oil Pollution Damage Convention, 1969 and the 1971 International Convention on the Establishment of an

International Fund for Compensation for Oil Pollution Damage allow a form of environmental damages measured by costs of reasonable measures of reinstatement actually
undertaken or to be undertaken (the 1992 protocols and both conventions are reprinted in
International Environment Reporter vol. 21, at 1501 and vol. 21, at 1701). Canada has
adopted recovery for reasonable reinstatement costs associated with oil spills from ships
in the *Marine Liability Act*, SC 2001, c. 6, s. 51(2). Section 84 of Ontario's *Environmental Bill of Rights Act, 1993*, SO 1993, c. 28, allows any resident of Ontario to bring an
action for significant harm to a public resource. Although a damage award is not allowed,
a court may grant injunctive relief and order the parties to negotiate a restoration plan.
Residents in the Northwest Territories may also seek damages for contamination of the
environment that would be payable to the minister responsible for the environment. See
Environmental Rights Act, SNWT 1990, c. 38, s. 6(3)(4). The US *Oil Pollution Act* of
1990, 33 USC §2701 et seq., passed in the wake of the *Exxon Valdez* disaster, allows
recovery for natural resource damages. See J.S. Seevers Jr., "NOAA's New Natural
Resource Damage Assessment Scheme: It's Not About Collecting Money" (1996) vol. 53
Washington & Lee Law Review 1473.

5. Recovery for injuries to public natural resources, besides being based on the action
of public nuisance, might be grounded in other doctrinal sources including the public
trust doctrine, the inherent *parens patriae* jurisdiction of courts to intervene on behalf of
those who cannot care for themselves, and the emerging right to a clean and healthy
environment. See Edward H.P. Brans, *Liability for Damage to Public Natural Resources:
Standing, Damage and Damage Assessment* (The Hague: Kluwer Law International,
2001), at 47-58, and the discussions in chapters 11 and 12.

E. Strict Liability

An example of liability regardless of fault on the part of the defendant is found in cases
where the defendant collects things on his or her land that are likely to do mischief if they
escape. If they do escape, the defendant will be held strictly liable—that is, liable for the
damages resulting from such an escape, even though the defendant may not have been
careless or at fault in allowing the escape. This so-called rule has its origins in the case of
Rylands v. Fletcher (1868), LR 3 HL 330. The essential elements of the tort created by
the decision in this case can be listed as follows: (1) the defendant is in lawful occupation
of property, (2) on which is stored a dangerous agent or thing constituting a non-natural
use of land, (3) escape of the agent or thing from the defendant's property, and (4)
causing damage to the plaintiff. The non-natural use requirement has, traditionally and
historically, been the factor most frequently considered by courts, but they have given it
both a broad and a narrow meaning. Considered broadly, a non-natural use has been held
to be any use that exposes the neighbourhood to special dangers. It has been suggested
that some courts adopt a narrower view of "non-natural" by requiring that the use be not
only hazardous but also unusual or special in the sense that it is not one originally
conducted on land. See L.N. Klar, *Tort Law*, 2d ed., at 456.

In *Cambridge Water Company v. Eastern Counties Leather*, [1994] 1 All ER 53 (HL),
a case involving the pollution of a plaintiff's water supply by chemicals previously
considered "safe" but later coming under government regulation, the House of Lords

continued to embrace the traditional technical distinctions of non-natural use and escape from land but added the additional requirement of foreseeability of damage. There, the trial judge had found the storage of organochlorines in the vicinity of an industrial village to be a natural use of land. When the case reached the House of Lords, Lord Goff expressed the opinion that the storage of substantial quantities of chemicals on industrial premises was to be regarded as an "almost classic case" of non-natural use (at 79). Lord Goff also rejected the US interpretation and application of *Rylands* that imposes strict liability in cases where damage is caused by "ultra-hazardous operations" (at 75). He did so on the basis that the law commission had expressed serious misgivings about the adoption of this test and that this decision should be made by Parliament. Lord Goff concluded that because *Rylands v. Fletcher* was "essentially as an extension of the law of nuisance to cases of isolated escapes from land" and because foreseeability was already an element of nuisance, that the defendant could not be held liable for the unforeseeable damage from escaped chemicals (at 76).

As a result of the House of Lords' decision in *Cambridge Water*, there has been some concern expressed within common law jurisdictions that the *Rylands v. Fletcher* principle is no longer applicable in tort law. The United Kingdom appears to have subsumed it within nuisance, while Australia has abolished the principle and absorbed it into negligence law: *Burnie Port Authority v. General Jones Pty. Ltd.*, [1994] 120 ALR 42. The issue was addressed in the British Columbia Supreme Court in *John Campbell Law Corp. v. Strata Plan* 1350, [2001] BCJ no. 2037 (BCSC), with the court's conclusion that "*Rylands v. Fletcher* is still judicially considered in Canada" (para. 27).

NOTES

1. It should be noted that the strict liability rule of *Rylands v. Fletcher* requires some abnormal non-natural use of land that results in actual damage to the land, goods, or person of the plaintiff, whereas nuisance merely requires a natural or usual but "unreasonable" use of land that can result in mere inconvenience to the occupier. See G.H.L. Fridman, *The Law of Torts in Canada*, vol. 1 (Scarborough, ON: Carswell, 1989), at 177-78.

2. Consider whether the US approach of applying strict liability to abnormally dangerous activities is preferable to the House of Lords' reliance on historical distinctions. Section 520 of the *Restatement (Second) of Torts* provides:

In determining whether an activity is abnormally dangerous, the following factors are to be considered:
   (a) existence of a high degree of risk or some harm to the person, land or chattels of others;
   (b) likelihood that the harm that results from it will be great;
   (c) inability to eliminate the risk by the exercise of reasonable care;
   (d) extent to which the activity is not a matter of common usage;
   (e) inappropriateness of the activity to the place where it is carried on; and
   (f) extent to which its value to the community is out-weighed by its dangerous attributes.

3. A broadening of strict liability application may support the implementation of the principles of precaution, pollution prevention, and polluter pays; the White Paper on Environmental Liability issued in 2000 by the European Commission (EC) recommended

that there be a European Union directive providing for strict liability for damage caused by EC-regulated dangerous activities.

4. Should the House of Lords' approach in *Cambridge Water* of allowing a lack of reasonable foreseeability of damage to negate civil liability be followed? Professor Bruce Pardy has argued that foreseeability should not be a relevant consideration in strict liability because pursuant to the precautionary principle, "environmental risk should be expected and assumed." Further, the compensatory function of tort law suggests that between two "innocent" parties, the one who causes damage should pay. See B. Pardy, "Applying the Precautionary Principle to Private Persons: Should It Affect Civil and Criminal Liability?" (2002) vol. 43 *Les Cahiers de Droit* 63.

5. While various defences may be raised to civil actions, such as act of God, contributory negligence of the plaintiff, consent, and statutory authority (the main defence in nuisance actions), the intervening act of third parties defence has raised considerable uncertainty in the strict liability field. In 1913, the Privy Council, in the case of *Rickards v. Lothian*, [1913] AC 263, held that the deliberate acts of a third party causing the escape from the defendant's land of damaging objects would constitute an intervening act and thus act as a defence in a *Rylands v. Fletcher* context. This would seem to conflict with the decision of Cusinato J in the *Smith Bros. Excavating* case, above, where the court held that it was no defence that the escape of methanol fluid was due to the malicious acts of vandals. The court appeared to draw a distinction between nuisance and a *Rylands v. Fletcher* situation involving abnormal use of land, holding that in the latter situation the highest standard of care was required. In the *Smith* situation, the court concluded that the defendants had failed to prove that they used every effort to avoid the escape and that they had secured their property by imposing all known and available security. The action failed only because the plaintiffs were unable to prove damages. By contrast, in a nuisance situation the court suggested that it would be unlikely that liability would be imposed if the defendant showed that the nuisance resulted from a natural use or operation of the land and had done nothing knowingly to create the nuisance and had pursued activities with reasonable care.

The rejection of the traditional defence of malicious acts of third parties may be the result of the court considering a *Rylands v. Fletcher* situation as an extension of nuisance, to be governed by similar legal principles. One legal commentator has suggested that "in the context of a dangerous activity, the degree of anticipation required of the defendant ought to be significantly higher than in the case of ordinary activities" (L.N. Klar, *Tort Law*, 2d ed., at 466). On this reasoning, the defence would not be available unless the defendant could meet the higher standard of care.

F. Riparian Rights

Riparian rights—rights held by the owner of land bordering a river, lake, or stream—are often argued by plaintiffs in environmental cases because of the potential for a high environmental standard to be imposed. The most important riparian rights, for environmental purposes, are those that pertain to both the natural quantity and the natural quality of water flow.

The extent to which courts may dilute such strict rights is subject to some uncertainty. A "domestic use" or "ordinary use" exception is quite clear where a riparian owner may use water for domestic purposes such as drinking, stock watering, and washing, without incurring liability to a lower riparian. See G. LaForest, *Water Law in Canada—The Atlantic Provinces* (Ottawa: Department of Regional Economic Expansion, 1972), at 224. Other secondary uses, such as waste disposal, may also be argued and actions may lie only if the use is "unreasonable," a standard that is subject to case-by-case interpretation.

The case of *Gauthier v. Naneff*, [1971] 14 DLR (3d) 513 (Ont. HC), demonstrates a strict judicial approach toward environmental protection. There, plaintiff riparian landowners sought an injunction against the holding of a speedboat regatta on Lake Ramsay in Sudbury and argued outboard motorboats would negatively effect the purity and potability of the water. The court, noting the need to interpret the word "unreasonable" in the light of present-day knowledge of and concern for pollution problems, indicated that every riparian proprietor has an entitlement to water quality without sensible alteration. The court refused to consider the economic arguments of the defendants, such as the goal of raising money for charities, and granted an injunction.

Other courts have been willing to consider social and economic interests, particularly at the stage of deciding whether to grant an injunction for riparian interferences. For example, in *Lockwood v. Brentwood Park Investments Ltd.* (1970), 10 DLR (3d) 143 (NSCA), the court, while willing to find a violation of riparian rights by the defendant apartment complex developers, who diverted brook waters with resultant loss of amenities to the downstream plaintiff, refused to grant an injunction stopping further diversions. The court questioned whether the traditional strict approach to riparian rights developed in England should be applied in present urban situations with their population pressures.

Riparian rights have also been stated to extend to lands abutting the sea or other tidal waters. See G. LaForest, *Water Law in Canada*, at 200. For example, in *Corkum v. Nash* (1991), 87 DLR (4th) 127 (CA), the court granted the owner of property abutting on the high-water mark of a salt water harbour an injunction requiring defendants to remove wharves on the shore that interfered with the owner's riparian right of access. In Alberta, one court allowed costs on a solicitor–client basis where the Department of Environment refused to act on a ministerial order that sought to avoid infringing personal property rights and riparian rights when the applicant had successfully challenged a government decision to release effluent into an intermittent creek. *Stelter v. Alberta (Director, Air & Water Approvals Division, Environmental Protection)* (April 22, 1999), Carswell Alta. 402; file no. 9903-010515 (QB, Dea J).

G. Trespass to the Person in the Form of Battery

The general tort of trespass to the person covers three more specific subtorts called battery, assault, and false or wrongful imprisonment. The subtort of battery is the most relevant weapon to be used in the environmental context but even this tort has limited use because of the need to prove intention.

Battery is defined as the deliberate application of force to the person of another that results in harm to that person or offensive contact. The wrong that the law seeks to prevent by awarding damage compensation is the violation of a person's bodily integrity.

Although actual intention may be difficult to prove in environmental cases, the doctrine of substantial certainty may assist a plaintiff. An act is intentional in law when the defendant can be said to desire the consequences that flow from the act or can be said to have been substantially certain that such consequences would occur.

The case of *Macdonald v. Sebastian* (1988), 81 NSR 2d 189 (TD), demonstrates the applicability of battery in the environmental context. Three plaintiffs, a mother and her two children, were exposed to unacceptable levels of arsenic in the water supply of their leased premises owned by the defendant. Since the defendant, a medical doctor, had knowledge of the high arsenic levels and obvious damages to the health and safety of tenants, the court was willing to find a deliberate act of battery. Punitive damages in the amount of $7,000 per plaintiff were awarded in addition to $1,000 in general damages for each plaintiff.

H. Trespass to Land

Trespass to land involves an intended but unjustifiable interference with another person's possession of land. No physical damage to the property need occur. Interference with the legal right of possession is sufficient.

The tort consists of an act of direct physical entrance upon land in the possession of another, or remaining upon such land after being told to leave, or placing or projecting any object upon the land. In each case, the act must be done without lawful justification. The two key elements of the tort are intention and direct entry. The latter requirement particularly has caused problems for plaintiffs in cases involving the spraying of insecticides and other toxic chemicals where wind drift causes the chemicals to depart from their intended target and to be deposited upon the plaintiff's property (see L.N. Klar, *Tort Law*, 2d ed., at 88). Similarly, oil jettisoned into the water by the defendant and carried into the plaintiff's foreshore was found not to constitute a trespass because the interference with the plaintiff's land was not the direct result of the defendant's act, *Southport Corp. v. Esso Petroleum Co.* (1954), 2 QB 182, reversed on other grounds (1955), 3 All ER 864 (HL). Such an approach clearly poses a problem for a plaintiff whose land has been affected by toxic chemicals that are dumped upon the defendant's land and are carried by percolating groundwater to the plaintiff's land. There would seem to be considerable weight to the argument that in these circumstances where the interference was "set in motion by the defendants assisted only by natural and inevitable forces," they ought to be treated as sufficiently direct to constitute a trespass (L.N. Klar, *Tort Law*, 2d ed., at 89).

What constitutes a physical entry upon land may be a legal issue. It is doubtful whether vibrations constitute physical entry and certain smells do not (*Phillips v. California Standard Co.* (1960), 31 WWR 331 (Alta. TD). Some US courts grappling with the problem have insisted upon the entry of something tangible having appreciable mass and visible to the naked eye. This approach would not allow for the recognition of industrial dust or noxious fumes. (See W.P. Keeton et al., eds., *Prosser and Keeton on Law of Torts*, 5th ed. (St. Paul, MN: West Publishing, 1984), at 71.) However, other US court decisions have found a trespass to land in the entry of invisible gases and microscopic particles where they do harm or cause a substantial interference. See, for example, *Martin v. Reynolds Metals*, 342 P. 2d 790 (Or. 1959), where the court noted that by requiring a substantial interference, the doctrine of trespass to land would tend to merge with the doctrine of nuisance. (See also *Bradley v. American Smelting and Refining*, 709 P. 2d 782 (Wash. 1985).)

III. CHALLENGES AND JUDICIAL STRUGGLES IN TOXIC TORTS

Toxic torts, a term commonly used to describe civil lawsuits brought by plaintiffs to address exposure to toxic agents (chemical, biological, or radiological), tend to fall into three major categories, each with jurisprudential challenges. First, plaintiffs may try to prevent a threatened exposure to toxic agents, such as preventing the spraying of herbicides on a nearby property, by arguing a defendant's activity if allowed would be tortious (wrongful) and, therefore, an injunction should be imposed prohibiting or restricting the activity. Scientific uncertainties regarding toxic substances often abound, with limited and sometimes conflicting studies making conclusions on genetic or biological effects difficult.

Various challenges are raised for the judiciary. Should traditional burden and standards of proof be followed with plaintiffs having to establish all the elements of causes of action, including causation, on a balance of probabilities? In light of the precautionary principle evolving under international environmental law, where decision makers are urged to err on the side of caution in situations of scientific uncertainty, should the burden of proof be shifted to defendants? What type and level of risk should form the basis for judicial and injunctive action? What should be the role of courts in an age of specialized regulatory agencies?

A second category of cases involve plaintiffs suffering a present injury, such as a serious disease like cancer, where establishing a causal link to a defendant's tortious activity is often a central obstacle. Two types of situations are prevalent. In the "indeterminate plaintiff" scenario, the plaintiff finds it difficult to prove causation because of limitations in scientific evidence and the reality that non-tortious causes such as lifestyle and genetic predisposition may also explain an illness. Epidemiological studies of increase of disease among a given population usually do not rule out the possibility that a particular plaintiff's disease was caused by factors other than defendant's activity (for example, natural causes). Extrapolating the results of toxic tests on animal subjects to humans also carries uncertainties. In the "indeterminate defendant" situation, the plaintiff is able to establish an illness linked to a tortious activity, such as the negligent manufacture of a chemical or drug, but is unable to identify a specific defendant. Long latency periods for disease may make it difficult to point the legal finger at a particular defendant, especially where numerous defendants may have been involved in the manufacture and distribution of a particular toxic agent. Generic marketing further complicates the "indeterminate defendant" situation.

Again courts are faced with various jurisprudential challenges. Should the traditional common law "but for" test for establishing causation—that is, the plaintiff must establish on the balance of probabilities that but for the defendant's tortious activity, injury would not have occurred—be rejected? If so, what should replace the test?

A third category of cases involves plaintiffs exposed to a toxic agent or agents but who have no "present injury" in the traditional sense of a manifest physical or personal injury. Various types of "damage" may nevertheless be claimed including recovery for an enhanced risk of future disease, money to monitor health or ecological impacts, compensation for the fear of getting cancer (or other serious disease), and a reduction in property value linked to public perceptions of risk. Again, judicial challenges are raised such as the potential to open litigation floodgates unless some strict legal limits are imposed.

A. Prevention of Threatened Exposure to Toxic Agents

Palmer v. Nova Scotia Forest Industries
(1983), 2 DLR (4th) 397 (NSTD)

NUNN J: This is an application by the named plaintiffs in their individual capacities and as representatives of others for an injunction restraining the defendant, a company engaged in the forest industry in Nova Scotia, from spraying certain areas in the Province of Nova Scotia with phenoxy herbicides.

. . .

The subject of dioxins and chlorophenols has been widely disputed in many countries of the world both politically and before regulatory agencies. To my knowledge this is the first occasion where the dispute has reached the courts in Canada.

. . .

In the present case the allegation is that these offending chemicals, if they get to the plaintiffs' land, will interfere with the health of the plaintiffs thereby interfering with their enjoyment of their lands. Clearly such an interference, if proved, would fall within the essence of nuisance. As a serious risk of health, if proved, there is no doubt that such an interference would be substantial. In other words, the grounds for the cause of action in nuisance exist here provided that the plaintiffs prove the defendant will actually cause it, i.e., that the chemicals will come to the plaintiffs' lands and that it will actually create a risk to their health. With this, I will deal later.

. . .

Again there is no doubt in my mind that, if it is proved that the defendant permits any of these substances on the plaintiffs' lands, it would constitute a trespass and be actionable.

. . .

The complete burden of proof, of course, rests upon the plaintiffs throughout for all issues asserted by them. If the spraying had actually occurred, they would have to prove by a preponderance of probabilities the essential elements of either or all of the alleged causes of action as I have set them out. However, the spraying has not occurred and this application is for a *quia timet* injunction. This can be translated as "which he fears." In other words, a plaintiff does not have to wait until actual damage occurs. Where such damage is apprehended, an application for a *quia timet* injunction is an appropriate avenue to obtain a remedy which will prevent the occurrence of the harm.

[The court noted that a *quia timet* injunction requires a "strong case of probability."]

· · ·

The plaintiffs must, however, prove the essential elements of a regular injunction, namely, irreparable harm and that damages are not an adequate remedy as they are also essential elements of the *quia timet* injunction.

Finally, any injunction is a discretionary remedy and sufficient grounds must be established to warrant the exercise by the court of its discretion.

I am satisfied that a serious risk to health, if proved, would constitute irreparable harm and that damages would not be an adequate remedy. Further, recognizing the great width and elasticity of equitable principles, I would have no hesitation in deciding that such a situation would be one of the strongest which would warrant the exercise of the court's discretion to restrain the activity which would create the risk.

This matter thus reduces itself now to the single question. Have the plaintiffs offered sufficient proof that there is a serious risk of health and that such serious risk of health will occur if the spraying of the substances here is permitted to take place?

· · ·

Because of the nature of the issues in dispute, the witnesses produced and the testimony given, the enormous publicity attached to the trial and the public interest involved, the evidence went far beyond the particular substances involved and related to all the phenoxy herbicides and their derivatives. The whole trial took on the aura of a scientific inquiry as to whether the world should be exposed to dioxins. Scientists from all over North America, as well as from Sweden were called and testified. Scientific reports and studies from scientists the world over were filed as part of the evidence. In order to give both sides full opportunity to present their cases fully, it was necessary to grant this latitude although both parties were aware that the final decision would have to relate to the particular facts between the parties before the court.

As to the wider issues relating to the dioxin issue, it hardly seems necessary to state that a court of law is no forum for the determination of matters of science. Those are for science to determine, as facts, following the traditionally accepted methods of scientific inquiry. A substance neither does nor does not create a risk to health by court decree and it would be foolhardy for a court to enter such an inquiry. If science itself is not certain, a court cannot resolve the conflict and make the thing certain.

Essentially a court is engaged in the resolution of private disputes between parties and in the process follows certain time-honoured and well-established procedures and applies equally well-established principles of law, varying and altering them to adjust to an ever-changing society. Part of the process is the determination of facts and another part the application of the law to those facts, once determined, and designing the remedy. As to the occurrence of events, the court is concerned with "probability" and not with "possibility."

· · ·

As to Canada and the United Kingdom, both have registered 2,4-D and 2,4,5-T for forestry use with a maximum TCDD [dioxin] level of 0.1 parts per million. Registration for use in Canada for 2,4-D was in 1947 and 2,4,5-T in 1952. In both jurisdictions reviews are made periodically after reviews of the literature and independent study by highly trained and competent scientists. The evidence indicates this to be an ongoing process. In both countries registration for use is still in effect and neither jurisdiction has accepted that there are valid studies which would cause them to cancel the registration.

· · ·

I do not mention regulatory agencies of other countries but there are some countries, notably Sweden, where 2,4,5-T is either restricted or prohibited. However, I have no evidence before me indicating that any such restriction or prohibition is the result of a scientific inquiry. All seem to be political decisions made for whatever reason. Even in the United States no such inquiry has been made and completed. Those decisions, therefore, are of no help to me.

To some extent this case takes on the nature of an appeal from the decision of the regulatory agency and any such approach through the courts ought to be discouraged in its infancy. Opponents to a particular chemical ought to direct their activities towards the regulatory agencies or, indeed, to government itself where broad areas of social policy are involved. It is not for the courts to become a regulatory agency of this type. It has neither the training nor the staff to perform this function. Suffice it to say that this decision will relate to, and be limited to, the dispute between these parties.

· · ·

Having accepted Mr. Ross' testimony and accepting the evidence of Donald Freer and ex. D-70 that the defendant's supply of 2,4,5-T is formulated with a TCDD content of "non-detectable" at 0.01 parts per million, it is obvious that the amount of TCDD to be sprayed in Nova Scotia by the defendant is infinitesimally small. ... It is, therefore, in the light of this concentration of TCDD that I must consider whether the plaintiffs have met the burden of proof.

· · ·

A great deal of the evidence submitted related to animal studies where TCDD was reported to have caused various effects indicating it to be, among other things, foetotoxic, teratagenic, carcinogenic and to cause immunological deficiencies, enzymatic changes, liver problems and the like. Also it is alleged to bioaccumulate and be persistent both in soil and in tissue. I do not pretend to have included all of its effects, but those are the most major. I was asked to make findings of fact in all of these areas, but I decline to do so. Nothing would be added to the body of scientific fact by any such determination by this court. That TCDD has had all of these effects is undoubtedly true in the experiments described, but, in every case, the effect must be related to dose. In the animal studies the doses are extremely high and, in all cases, many, many thousands of times greater than any dose which could be received in Nova Scotia.

· · ·

This brings me to the next suggestion by the plaintiffs which is that cancer, as a disease, has a long incubation period and the effects of dioxin cannot be known until time passes, approximately 40 years, so that it can be determined whether dioxin is indeed carcinogenic in humans. This again is not my function. I am to determine only if there is a probability of risk to health. To this point in time there is not sufficient acceptable evidence despite 35 years of use. One of the plaintiffs' witnesses, Dr. Daum, suggested that the only approach is to wait that period without permitting any further use. I cannot accept that. She is working from the premise that any substance should be proved absolutely safe before use but, as commendable as that may be, it is not practical nor is it in conformity with currently accepted determinations for use of many substances. I doubt very much if any substance can be proved absolutely safe.

If all substances which are carcinogenic or otherwise toxic were removed from use, we would have no air to breathe or potable water and many common everyday products, necessary to our life, would be removed. The key to the use of all these is dosage. Where it can be determined that there is a safe dosage, according to acceptable scientific standards, then a substance can be used. Our regulatory agencies and scientists around the world are daily involved in this very area.

As well, virtually all chemicals are toxic, but those in use generally are safe if used below the toxic levels, i.e., if the dose received is below the safety levels. Scientists also determine a "no observable effect level." That is a level of intake of any particular substance where no effect is observed. It is, in most cases, far below the safe level, at least several orders of magnitude (each order being a multiple of 10) lower.

In these determinations effect on humans is assessed by extrapolation from animal studies. This is a well-known and widely accepted approach and some of the evidence here was based on this method.

I am satisfied that the overwhelming currently accepted view of responsible scientists is that there is little evidence that, for humans either 2,4-D or 2,4,5-T is mutagenic or carcinogenic and that TCDD is not an effective carcinogen, and further, that there are no-effect levels and safe levels for humans and wildlife for each of these substances.

. . .

Having reached this point it is appropriate to add that the evidence of risk assessments clearly indicates that any risk here in Nova Scotia, if, indeed, there is a risk at all, is infinitesimally small and many, many times less than one in a million which level, apparently, is regarded as a safe and acceptable risk by most of the world's regulatory agencies. Putting this in perspective, as indicated by Dr. Wilson in his evidence, the risk of cancer to a smoker is 1 in 800 and for a non-smoker continuously in the same room with smokers it is 1 in 100,000, while the risk to a person drinking two litres of water per day from a stream immediately after being sprayed (which will not happen with buffer zones) is 1 in 100,000 million or 100,000 times less than 1 in a million, which itself is regarded as a *de minimus* risk.

. . .

I am unable to accept that the plaintiffs have proved any strong probability or a sufficient degree of probability of risk to health to warrant the granting of the remedy sought, a *quia timet* injunction.

. . .

There is, accordingly, no nuisance, real or probable. As to trespass, none has been proved as probable to occur. Possibilities do not constitute proof. Similarly, there has been no basis established for the application of the rule in *Rylands v. Fletcher*, as neither the danger of the substance nor the likelihood of its escape to the plaintiffs' lands has been proved.

NOTES AND QUESTIONS

1. A serious health risk, if proved, would have been considered a substantial interference with the use and enjoyment of land and thus a private nuisance, according to Nunn J. Why require a serious health risk as opposed to some health risk? Consider other ways to define a health risk. What about a reasonable medical concern or a reasonable ecological concern? Is a "serious health risk" the only type of an irreparable injury for which a *quia timet* injunction would be appropriate?

2. Nunn J indicated that there may be safe doses of dioxins and no observable effect levels (NOELs). Consider the following statement from T. Schrecker, *The Pitfalls of Standards* (Hamilton, ON: Canadian Centre for Occupational Health and Safety, 1986), at 4:

> [W]e usually do not know (and indeed, may well never know) whether NOELs emerging from experiments conducted with a specific substance represent a genuine absence of effect or merely reflect a failure to detect effects which might still be highly important when extrapolated to a large exposed human population. The use of safety/uncertainty factors takes this consideration into account. However, to reiterate the point made earlier, their use assumes the existence of biological thresholds. In the absence of this assumption, the choice of an uncertainty factor represents a normative decision about acceptable risk.

3. Read carefully Nunn J's discussion of human health risks. Should courts treat voluntary risks differently from involuntary risks? Should judges consider the possibility of multiple exposures to chemical substances and the potential for synergistic effects? Nunn J touched upon the potential of reversing the burden of proof with the defendant having to show that a substance is absolutely safe before allowance of use. Is he correct that such a reversed burden would not be practical? Consider alternative standards to absolute safety, such as those outlined in D. VanderZwaag, *Canada and Marine Environmental Protection: Charting a Legal Course Towards Sustainable Development* (London: Kluwer Law International, 1995), at 407-8:

> The precautionary principle, while still evolving in its legal development, but suggesting the need to grant the benefit of doubt to environmental protection rather than high risk activities, may be the creative normative wedge to rethink common law doctrines such as nuisance and injunctive requirements. Something less than a serious health risk, for example, reasonable medical or ecological concern, might be considered to amount to a nuisance. The burden of proof regarding a reasonable concern might be shifted from plaintiffs to defendants who would have to show the lack of a reasonable medical or ecological concern before being allowed to undertake industrial or development activities. One may also envision a change in the injunctive standard of proof from a strong probability to something less, such as a reasonable possibility. [Footnotes omitted.]

4. An additional issue raised in the *Palmer* case was whether a group of plaintiffs could maintain a representative action (on behalf of other persons living near the spray sites) under Nova Scotia's Civil Procedure Rules. Nunn J found that the key legal

requirements of numerous persons and common interest (in this case, risk to health) were met. Six provinces—British Columbia, Manitoba, Newfoundland and Labrador, Ontario, Quebec, and Saskatchewan—have enacted detailed class action legislation. See *Class Proceedings Act*, RSBC 1996, c. 50; *Class Proceedings Act*, SM 2002, c. 14; *Class Actions Act*, SNL 2001, c. C-18.1; *Class Proceedings Act, 1992*, SO 1992, c. 6; *Code of Civil Procedure*, RSQ c. C-25, book IX; and *Class Actions Act*, SS 2001, c. C-12.01.

In *Hollick v. Metropolitan Toronto (Municipality)*, [2001] SCJ no. 67; 42 CELR (NS) 26, the Supreme Court of Canada noted three advantages of class actions: serving judicial economy by avoiding a multiplicity of individual suits; distributing litigation costs among class members and thereby improving access to justice; and ensuring that wrongdoers modify their behavior to fully account for public harm. While noting that class action legislation should be interpreted liberally to give effect to the benefits, the court found that the appellant Hollick was not able to show that the class action was the preferable means of resolving common issues involving 30,000 persons experiencing air and noise pollution from a landfill. The presence of a small claims trust fund, established by the respondent to compensate individual claimants up to $5,000 on a no-fault basis for "offsite impacts," was a decisive factor in the court's finding that judicial redress through a class action was not preferable in the particular case.

5. For a critical review of the *Palmer* decision and consideration of most of the questions above, see B.H. Wildsmith, "Of Herbicides and Humankind: Palmer's Common Law Lessons" (1986) vol. 24 *Osgoode Hall Law Journal* 161. He notes that in a matter of weeks after the Nova Scotia decision, the major supplier of 2,4,5-T products, Dow Chemical in Midland, Michigan, announced it would no longer market products containing 2,4,5-T and the US Environmental Protection Agency totally banned the use of 2,4,5-T for any purpose in the United States (ibid., at 163).

6. In *Hoffman v. Monsanto Canada Inc.*, 2002 SKQB 190, a group of organic farmers is seeking an injunction to prevent the defendant from marketing genetically modified wheat, alleging that genetic pollution of normal wheat is all but inevitable and will cause irreparable harm to the farmers' organic enterprises. What causes of action are available? What obstacles to success do you foresee?

B. Proving Causation of Present Injury

1. Addressing the Indeterminate Plaintiff Challenge

Jones v. Mobil Oil Canada Ltd.
(1999), 248 AR 1 (QB)

ROMAINE J: Mr. Jones alleges that his cattle were exposed to or ingested harmful chemicals and that Mobil is at fault because it failed to erect adequate fencing, because it, or its agents, spilled harmful fluids and polluted the ground, the groundwater and surface water and because it conducted its operations so that Mr. Jones' cattle had access to these pollutants. Mobil denies that its operations were the cause of any ill health or failure of Mr. Jones' cattle.

. . .

I find that Mobil was in breach of its duty to erect effective fencing, given the notice it had of the problem and that it had erected more effective fencing at a reasonable cost at other locations in the area. I also find that Mobil was in breach of its duty by failing to provide any fencing for some of its facilities in the earlier years of the period in question.

[Nuisance was also found.]

Causative Link

Has Mr. Jones established a causative link between the actions or failure to act of Mobil that constitute negligence or nuisance and the failure of his herd?

Mr. Jones must prove on a balance of probabilities that Mobil's negligence or the nuisance for which it is liable caused or materially contributed to the failure of his herd. As long as Mobil's actions or failure to act are part of the cause of the failure, Mobil may be liable even if there were other contributing causes. If the other contributing causes are tortious, there may be contribution from other tortfeasors. If the other contributing causes are Mr. Jones' own negligence, there may be issues of contributory negligence. If the other contributing causes are non-tortious, there is no apportionment between such non-tortious and tortious causes.

The onus of proving that Mobil's negligence or nuisance materially contributed to the failure of his herd is on Mr. Jones. However, as established by the Supreme Court of Canada in *Snell v. Farrell* (1990), 72 DLR (4th) 289 ... causation need not be determined with scientific precision, and it is essentially a question of fact that can be answered by the application of ordinary common sense. As pointed out by Sopinka, J in [that case], although the burden of proof remains on the plaintiff throughout the trial, in the absence of evidence to the contrary put forward by the defendant, an inference of causation may be drawn, even in the absence of positive or scientific proof of causation. If some evidence has been adduced by the defendant, that evidence must be weighed against the evidence put forward by the plaintiff. In weighing such evidence, it is necessary to have regard to what evidence it was in the power of one side to have produced and in the power of the other to have contradicted. Sopinka, J also addresses the issue of expert testimony ... . He comments that it is not essential that experts provide a firm opinion supporting the plaintiff's case, as medical experts ordinarily determine causation in terms of certainties, while a lesser standard is demanded by the law. Sopinka, J adopted the reasoning of an American court in *Sentilles v. Inter-Caribbean Shipping Corp.*, 361 US 107 (1959) to the effect that neither the lack of medical unanimity nor the fact that other potential causes of the condition existed and were not conclusively negated necessarily impairs a court's power to draw an inference in favour of the plaintiff. Nor does the particular form of words used by the medical expert as led in his evidence. Again, the inference can be founded on common sense, after taking into consideration the medical evidence.

. . .

The Supreme Court continued its analysis of the principles of causation in *Athey v. Leonati et al.* (1996), 140 DLR (4th) 235, and confirmed that causation is not to be applied too rigidly. It is now clear that it is not necessary for a plaintiff to establish that the negligence of the defendant is the sole cause of the injury. As stated by Major J at page 239 of *Athey* (*supra*), as long as a defendant is part of a cause of the damage, such defendant is liable, even if there exist other preconditions to the injury, as long as the actions or inactions of the defendant caused or materially contributed to the damage. A defendant is not excused from liability merely because other causal factors for which the defendant is not responsible exist.

In his summary of applicable principles on page 245 of the decision, Sopinka J identified three scenarios relevant to the determination of causation. The third scenario is where the tortious act of the defendant alone could have caused the injury, or the pre-existing condition alone could have caused it. In this case, the trial judge must determine on a balance of probabilities whether the defendant's negligence materially contributed to the injury.

In this case, there is evidence from Mr. Jones that his cattle had access to oilfield contaminants and hydrocarbons at various times and at various locations from 1982 to 1992. Members of the herd suffered a variety of symptoms, including reproductive failure and problems and failure to thrive. Mr. Jones had testing done from time to time on seriously ill and dead animals and soil and water which gave rise to circumstantial evidence of exposure to and consumption of drill site material and the possibility of contamination, although the veterinary experts could not give positive diagnoses of poisoning. There is no real issue that Mr. Jones' herd was exposed from time to time to noxious substances, either because of inadequate fencing or because of the contamination to soil and water caused by the buried flare pit at the 1 of 29 site. There is some direct evidence of ingestion of contaminants by particular animals both in Mr. Jones uncontradicted testimony of observations at the 9 of 30 site during and after the workovers, and in testing done on dead animals. In addition, there is evidence of the proclivity of cattle to consume these contaminants when they are accessible to them.

There was evidence from Mobil's expert, Dr. Edwards, about the difficulty of making a diagnosis of oilfield poisoning and of the frustration this creates for ranchers. For the most part, Mr. Jones' complaints are not of severe poisoning with the dramatic symptoms that would alert a rancher or a local veterinarian to the possibility of a problem, but of the less severe symptoms of loss of appetite, failure to thrive and long-term reproductive difficulty. Dr. Schipper's investigation and report did not support a diagnosis of contamination, but neither did it rule this out. Dr. Oehme's opinion is that the available documentation supports the exposure of Mr. Jones' cattle to oilfield contaminants, and confirms that consumption of such contaminants may produce many of the clinical signs and symptoms reported.

Mr. Jones does not have to prove conclusively that exposure to contaminants or ingestion of them led to the symptoms suffered by the herd: the test is the balance of probabilities. There must be more than conjecture for an inference to be drawn in the absence of exact proof. Such inference must be reasonable. However, the inability of the experts to give a firm diagnosis, or to agree on a diagnosis, is not fatal to such an inference. All the evidence must be considered in considering whether such an inference is reasonable.

· · ·

Despite the evidence of selenium deficiency in the Jones herd, I am satisfied that it can be reasonably inferred that the chronic poor performance of his cattle was caused by or materially contributed to by exposure to and ingestion of oil and gas contaminants. The strongest alternate theory put forward by Mobil was the theory that selenium deficiency caused the damage, but given the good state of Mr. Jones herd when the exposure to toxic substances had been removed, even though the herd was at that time selenium deficient, given the well documented incidents of exposure to toxic substances in the period when the damage was suffered, and given the opportunities of each party to bring forward evidence and to establish their case, I find that it is more likely than not that Mobil's negligence and its responsibility in nuisance caused the damage to Mr. Jones' herd.

NOTES AND QUESTIONS

1. The material contribution approach as an alternative to the traditional "but for" test for causation continues to be rather elusive. In *Athey v. Leonati*, [1996] 3 SCR 458, at 466, Major J provided only minimal guidance suggesting a "contributing factor is material if it falls outside the *de minimis* range." For a critique of the unanswered questions left by the material contribution test—exactly when it should be applied, what standard is set, and how it differs from the "but for" test—see G. Demeyere, "The 'Material Contribution' Test: An Immaterial Contribution to Tort Law: A Comment on Briglio v. Faulkner" (2000) vol. 34 *UBC Law Review* 317.

2. What factors might be considered in determining material contribution? The *Restatement Second of Torts* in s. 433 lists the following considerations to be weighed in determining whether negligent conduct was a substantial factor in producing harm: (a) the number of other factors that contribute in producing the harm and the extent of the effect that they have in producing it; (b) whether the actor's conduct has created a force or series of forces that are in continuous and active operation up to the time of the harm, or has created a situation harmless unless acted upon by other forces for which the actor is not responsible; and (c) lapse of time. Various authors have suggested that the material contribution and substantial factor approach are synonymous and have noted the tendency for factual causation to be blurred with the question of remoteness of damage. See B. Pardy, "Risk, Cause, and Toxic Torts: A Theory for Standard of Proof" (1989) vol. 10 Adv. Q. 277, at 286.

3. The case of *Allen v. United States*, 588 F. Supp. 247 (D. Utah 1984), involving plaintiffs suffering from various forms of cancer arguably linked to the negligent failure of the US government to warn communities of radiation fallout from open air nuclear testing in the 1950s and 1960s, provides a practical example of the application of the substantial factor approach in the toxic tort causation context. Factual connections weighed by the court in allowing some of the cancer claims included geographical proximity of plaintiff to the Nevada test site; consistency in the type of cancer associated with radiation exposure; time and extent of exposure to fallout; radiation sensitivity factors, such as age; and a latency period consistent with radiation etiology. Although the case was reversed on the grounds of governmental immunity for a discretionary function, 816 F. 2d 1417 (10th Cir. 1987), the case still offers useful precedent.

4. Lord Wilberforce in *McGhee v. National Coal Board*, [1973] 3 All ER 1008 (HL), suggested that where a defendant's negligence has materially increased the risk of injury and the injury occurs within the scope of the risk, the defendant should bear the burden of disproving causation. While such a material increase of risk and/or reverse onus approach was rejected by the Supreme Court of Canada in *Snell v. Farrell*, the approach has been suggested by legislative reformers. See L. Collins, "Material Contribution to Risk and Causation in Toxic Torts" (2001) vol. 11 *Journal of Environmental Law and Practice* 107, at 122.

5. The common sense approach embraced in *Snell v. Farrell* and applied in the *Jones* case does not ensure that plaintiffs will succeed where both potential tortious and non-tortious causes are in controversy. For example, in *Guimond Estate v. Fiberglass Canada Inc.* (1999), 221 NBR (2d) 118 (CA), the court refused to infer causation where health problems of a builder of fiberglass boats might be attributable to exposure to styrene fumes emitted from resins and gelcoats manufactured by the defendant, Fiberglass Canada, but also might be attributable to psychological problems associated with stress from a downturn in the economy and the inability of doctors to diagnose the builder's medical condition.

2. Addressing the Indeterminate Defendant Challenge

Sindell v. Abbott Laboratories
607 P. 2d 924 (Cal. 1980)

MOSK J: This case involves a complex problem both timely and significant: may a plaintiff, injured as the result of a drug administered to her mother during pregnancy, who knows the type of drug involved but cannot identify the manufacturer of the precise product, hold liable for her injuries a maker of a drug produced from an identical formula?

Plaintiff Judith Sindell brought an action against eleven drug companies ... on behalf of herself and other women similarly situated. The complaint alleges as follows:

Between 1941 and 1971, defendants were engaged in the business of manufacturing, promoting, and marketing diethylstilbesterol (DES), a drug which is a synthetic compound of the female hormone estrogen. The drug was administered to plaintiff's mother and the mothers of the class she represents, for the purpose of preventing miscarriage. In 1947, the Food and Drug Administration authorized the marketing of DES as a miscarriage preventative, but only on an experimental basis, with a requirement that the drug contain a warning label to that effect.

. . .

During the period defendants marketed DES, they knew or should have known that it was a carcinogenic substance, that there was a grave danger after varying periods of latency it would cause cancerous and precancerous growths in the daughters of the mothers who took it, and that it was ineffective to prevent miscarriage. Nevertheless, defendants continued to advertise and market the drug as a miscarriage preventative. They failed to test DES for efficacy and safety; the tests performed by others, upon which they relied, indicated that it was not safe or effective. In violation of the authorization of the Food and Drug Administration, defendants marketed DES on an unlimited basis rather than as an experimental drug, and they failed to warn of its potential danger.

Because of defendants' advertised assurances that DES was safe and effective to prevent miscarriage, plaintiff was exposed to the drug prior to her birth. She became aware of the danger from such exposure within one year of the time she filed her complaint. As a result of the DES ingested by her mother, plaintiff developed a malignant bladder tumor which was removed by surgery. She suffers from adenosis and must constantly be monitored by biopsy or colposcopy to insure early warning of further malignancy.

The first cause of action alleges that defendants were jointly and individually negligent in that they manufactured, marketed and promoted DES as a safe and efficacious drug to prevent miscarriage, without adequate testing or warning, and without monitoring or reporting its effects.

A separate cause of action alleges that defendants are jointly liable regardless of which particular brand of DES was ingested by plaintiff's mother because defendants collaborated in marketing, promoting and testing the drug, relied upon each other's tests, and adhered to an industry-wide safety standard. DES was produced from a common and mutually agreed upon formula as a fungible drug interchangeable with other brands of the same product; defendants knew or should have known that it was customary for doctors to prescribe the drug by its generic rather than its brand name and that pharmacists filled prescriptions from whatever brand of the drug happened to be in stock. ... Each cause of action alleges that defendants are jointly liable because they acted in concert, on the basis of express and implied agreements, and in reliance upon and ratification and exploitation of each other's testing and marketing methods.

. . .

We begin with the proposition that, as a general rule, the imposition of liability depends upon a showing by the plaintiff that his or her injuries were caused by the act of the defendant or by an instrumentality under the defendant's control. ... But we approach the issue of causation from a different perspective: we hold it to be reasonable in the present context to measure the likelihood that any of the defendants supplied the product which allegedly injured plaintiff by the percentage which the DES sold by each of them for the purpose of preventing miscarriage bears to the entire production of the drug sold by all for that purpose. Plaintiff asserts in her briefs that Eli Lilly and Company and five or six other companies produced 90 percent of the DES marketed. If at trial this is established to be the fact, then there is a corresponding likelihood that this comparative handful of producers manufactured the DES which caused plaintiff's injuries, and only a 10 percent likelihood that the offending producer would escape liability.

If plaintiff joins in the action the manufacturers of a substantial share of the DES which her mother might have taken, the injustice of shifting the burden of proof to defendants to demonstrate that they could not have made the substance which injured plaintiff is significantly diminished. While 75 to 80 percent of the market is suggested as the requirement by the Fordham Comment (at p. 996), we hold only that a substantial percentage is required.

The presence in the action of a substantial share of the appropriate market also provides a ready means to apportion damages among the defendants. Each defendant will be held liable for the proportion of the judgment represented by its share of that market unless it demonstrates that it could not have made the product which caused plaintiff's injuries. In the present case, as we have seen, one DES manufacturer was dismissed from the action upon filing a declaration that it had not manufactured DES until after plaintiff was born. Once plaintiff has met her burden of joining the required defendants, they in turn may cross-complain against other DES manufacturers, not joined in the action, which they can allege might have supplied the injury-causing product.

Under this approach, each manufacturer's liability would approximate its responsibility for the injuries caused by its own products. Some minor discrepancy in the correlation between market share and liability is inevitable; therefore, a defendant may be held liable for a somewhat different percentage of the damage than its share of the appropriate market would justify. It is probably impossible, with the passage of time, to determine market share with mathematical exactitude. But just as a jury cannot be expected to determine the precise relationship between fault and liability in applying the doctrine of comparative fault ... or partial indemnity ... , the difficulty of apportioning damages among the defendant producers in exact relation to their market share does not seriously militate against the rule we adopt.

NOTES

1. The *Sindell* case left numerous issues unresolved, including what constitutes a substantial share of the market; what is the appropriate scope of market analysis (local, county, state/provincial, national); whether a plaintiff's overall recovery should be limited to the percentage of market share represented by defendants sued; and how far market share liability should be extended outside the generic drug context. In *Brown v. Superior Ct.*, 44 Cal. 3d 1049; 751 P. 2d 470 (1988), the California Supreme Court clarified that a plaintiff's recovery should be limited by the proportion of the market share represented by defendants impleaded.

2. Courts in the United States have adopted numerous varieties of market share liability. See D.M. Schultz, "Market Share Liability in DES Cases: The Unwarranted Erosion of Causation in Fact" (1991) vol. 40 *DePaul Law Review* 771, at 785.

3. A version of market share liability has been adopted by British Columbia in the *Tobacco Damages and Health Care Costs Recovery Act*, SBC 2000, c. 30. Under s. 3 of the Act, the government may take a direct action against tobacco manufacturers to recover health care costs on an aggregate basis for insured persons suffering from disease caused by exposure to tobacco. In order for the government to recover such costs, it must prove on the standard of a balance of probabilities that, first, a breach of duty was committed by the defendant, second, the type of tobacco product can cause or contribute to disease, and third, during the period of the breach of duty, the type of tobacco product that the defendant either promoted or manufactured was sold in British Columbia. If these elements are successfully proven, the court then presumes that the group exposed to this type of tobacco product would not have been exposed but for the manufacturer's breach of duty, and the exposure to the tobacco product caused or contributed to the

disease or the risk of disease of a segment of British Columbia's population. Each defendant will be held liable for a proportion of the costs equivalent to its market share of the product, which will be calculated by the court based on the formula provided under s. 1(6) of the Act. See E. Edinger, "The Tobacco Damages and Health Care Costs Recovery Act" (2001) vol. 35 *Canadian Business Law Journal* 95. Similar legislation in Newfoundland has received royal assent; however, the Act has yet to be proclaimed; see *Tobacco Health Care Costs Recovery Act*, SNL 2001, c. T-4.2.

4. Market share liability is not the only approach available for addressing the indeterminate defendant challenge. Other approaches include concert of action theory (acting pursuant to a common design to harm the plaintiff), enterprise liability (adhering to an inadequate industry standard through industry-wide cooperation), and alternative liability (involving tortious conduct of two or more actors with harm caused to the plaintiff by only one of them and uncertainty as to which one caused the harm). The latter approach was applied by the Supreme Court of Canada in *Cook v. Lewis*, [1951] SCR 830, where two hunters negligently fired simultaneously—injuring the plaintiff—but the plaintiff could not prove which hunter fired the injuring shot. The court decided that the defendants in such a situation should bear the burden of proving that they did not harm the plaintiff. For a discussion on the various approaches, see K.J. Owen, "Industry-Wide Liability: Protecting Plaintiffs and Defendants" (1992) vol. 44 *Baylor Law Review* 45 and J. Pizzirusso, "Increased Risk, Fear of Disease and Medical Monitoring: Are Novel Damage Claims Enough To Overcome Causation Difficulties in Toxic Torts?" (2000) vol. 7 *Environmental Law* 183.

5. Causation innovations have also occurred outside indeterminate defendant and plaintiff situations. For example, in *Hollis v. Dow Corning Corp.*, [1995] 4 SCR 634, the Supreme Court of Canada further developed its pragmatic approach to causation in upholding the plaintiff's claim against the defendant company for negligent failure to warn of the risks of silicone breast implants. The majority of the court adopted a subjective standard for causation in the context of a manufacturer's failure to warn. That is, in order to establish a causal link between the negligent failure to warn and the plaintiff's injury, the plaintiff would merely have to show that she would not have undergone the surgery if properly warned. The rejected objective test would have focused on whether a reasonable woman in the plaintiff's circumstances would have consented to the surgery despite the risk. See V. Black and D. Klimchuk, "Torts—Negligent Failure To Warn—Learned Intermediary Rule—Causation—Appellate Court Powers: Hollis v. Dow Corning Corp." (1996) vol. 75 *Canadian Bar Review* 355.

C. Broadening the Concept of Present Injury

1. Recovery for Enhanced Risk of Future Injury

Ayers v. Jackson TP
525 A. 2d 287 (NJ 1987)

STEIN J: The litigation involves claims for damages sustained because plaintiffs' well water was contaminated by toxic pollutants leaching into the Cohansey Aquifer from a landfill established and operated by Jackson Township. After an extensive trial, the jury found that the township had created a "nuisance" and a "dangerous condition" by virtue of its operation of the landfill.

. . .

A toxicologist summarized the known hazardous characteristics of the chemical substances. He testified that of the twelve identified chemicals, four were known carcinogens. Other potential toxic effects identified by the toxicologist included liver and kidney damage, mutations and alterations in genetic material, damage to blood and reproductive systems, neurological damage and skin irritations.

. . .

No claims were asserted by plaintiffs seeking recovery for specific illnesses caused by their exposure to chemicals. Rather, they claim damages for the enhanced risk of future illness attributable to such exposure. They also seek to recover the expenses of annual medical examinations to monitor their physical health and detect symptoms of disease at the earliest possible opportunity.

. . .

Except for a handful of cases involving traumatic torts causing presently discernible injuries in addition to an enhanced risk of future injuries, courts have generally been reluctant to recognize claims for potential but unrealized injury unless the proof that the injury will occur is substantial.

. . .

Among the recent toxic tort cases rejecting liability for damages based on enhanced risk is *Anderson v. W.R. Grace & Co.*, 628 F. Supp. 1219 (D. Mass. 1986). ... The Court in *Anderson* explained that its reluctance to recognize the enhanced risk claims was based on two policy considerations. Its first concern was that recognition of the cause of action would create a flood of speculative lawsuits. *Id.* at 1232. In addition, the court stated:

> A further reason for denying plaintiffs' damages for the increased risk of future harm in this action is the inevitable inequity which would result if recovery were allowed. "To award damages based on a mere mathematical probability would significantly undercompensate those who actually do develop cancer and would be a windfall to those who do not."

The majority of courts that have considered the enhanced risk issue have agreed with the disposition of the District Court in *Anderson*.

. . .

Other courts have acknowledged the propriety of the enhanced risk cause of action, but have emphasized the requirement that proof of future injury be reasonably certain. ... Additionally, several courts have permitted recovery for increased risk of disease, but only where the plaintiff exhibited some present manifestation of disease. ... We observe that the overwhelming weight of the scholarship on this issue favours a right of recovery for tortious conduct that causes a significantly enhanced risk of injury.

. . .

For the most part, the commentators concede the inadequacy of common-law remedies for toxic-tort victims. Instead, they recommend statutory or administrative mechanisms that would permit compensation to be awarded on the basis of exposure and significant risk of disease, without the necessity of proving the existence of present injury.

Our disposition of this difficult and important issue requires that we choose between two alternatives, each having a potential for imposing unfair and undesirable consequences on the affected interests. A holding that recognizes a cause of action for unquantified enhanced risk claims exposes the tort system, and the public it serves, to the task of litigating vast numbers of claims for compensation based on threats of injuries that may never occur. It imposes on judges and juries the burden of assessing damages for the risk of potential disease, without clear guidelines to determine what level of compensation may be appropriate. It would undoubtedly increase already escalating insurance rates. It is clear that the recognition of an "enhanced risk" cause of action, particularly when the risk is unquantified, would generate substantial litigation that would be difficult to manage and resolve.

Our dissenting colleague, arguing in favor of recognizing a cause of action based on an unquantified claim of enhanced risk, points out that "courts have not allowed the difficulty of quantifying injury to prevent them from offering compensation for assault, trespass, emotional distress, invasion of privacy or damage to reputation."

. . .

It may be that this dilemma could be mitigated by a legislative remedy that eases the burden of proving causation in toxic-tort cases where there has been a statistically significant incidence of disease among the exposed population. Other proposals for legislative intervention contemplate a funded source of compensation for persons significantly endangered by exposure to toxic chemicals. We invite the legislature's attention to this perplexing and serious problem.

[The court dismissed the claims on the basis of unquantified enhanced risk of disease, while noting "we need not and do not decide whether a claim on the basis of enhanced risk of disease that is supported by testimony demonstrating that the onset of the disease is reasonably probable ... could be maintained."]

2. Medical Surveillance Expenses

Ayers v. Jackson TP
525 A. 2d 287 (NJ 1987)

The claim for medical surveillance expenses stands on a different footing from the claim based on enhanced risk. It seeks to recover the cost of periodic medical examinations intended to monitor plaintiffs' health and facilitate early diagnosis and treatment of disease caused by plaintiffs' exposure to toxic chemicals.

. . .

It is inequitable for an individual, wrongfully exposed to dangerous toxic chemicals but unable to prove that disease is likely, to have to pay his own expenses when medical intervention is clearly reasonable and necessary. In other contexts, we have intervened to provide compensation for medical expenses even where the underlying disease was not compensable.

. . .

We find a helpful analogy in *Reserve Mining Co. v. EPA*, 514 F. 2d 492 (8th Cir. 1975), where the issue was whether to grant injunctive relief compelling defendant to cease discharging wastes from its iron ore processing plant into the air of Silver Bay, Minnesota, and the waters of Lake Superior. The court concluded that "[i]n assessing probabilities in this case, it cannot be said that the probability of harm is more likely than not," at 520. Moreover, the court said, "the level of probability does not readily convert into a prediction of consequences." The best that could be said was that the existence of the contaminant in the air and water gave "a reasonable medical concern for the public health." The public's exposure to the contaminant in the air and water created "some health risk." The court ruled that "the existence of this risk to the [affected] public justifies ... requiring abatement of the health hazard on reasonable terms as a precautionary and preventative measure to protect the public health." The critical holding for our purposes is that the public health interest may justify judicial intervention even when the risk of disease is problematic.

Our conclusion regarding the compensability of medical surveillance expenses is not dissimilar to the result in the *Reserve Mining* case. The likelihood of disease is but one element in determining the reasonableness of medical intervention for the plaintiffs in this case. Other critical factors are the significance and extent of their exposure to chemicals, the toxicity of the chemicals, the seriousness of the diseases for which individuals are at risk, and the value of early diagnosis. Even if the likelihood that these plaintiffs would contact cancer were only slightly higher than the national average, medical intervention may be completely appropriate in view of the attendant circumstances. A physician treating a Legler-area child who drank contaminated well water for several years could hardly be faulted for concluding that that child should be examined annually to assure early detection of symptoms of disease.

Accordingly, we hold that the cost of medical surveillance is a compensable item of damages where the proofs demonstrate, through reliable expert testimony predicated upon the significance and extent of exposure to chemicals, the toxicity of the chemicals, the seriousness of the diseases for which individuals are at risk, the relative increase in the chance of onset of disease in those exposed, and the value of early diagnosis, that such surveillance to monitor the effect of exposure to toxic chemicals is reasonable and necessary. In our view, this holding is thoroughly consistent with our rejection of plaintiffs' claim for damages based on their enhanced risk of injury. That claim seeks damages for the impairment of plaintiffs' health, without proof of its likelihood, extent, or monetary value. In contrast, the medical surveillance claim seeks reimbursement for the specific dollar costs of periodic examinations that are medically necessary notwithstanding the fact that the extent of plaintiffs' impaired health is unquantified.

NOTES AND QUESTIONS

1. How appropriate would medical surveillance damages be in jurisdictions that have socialized medical arrangements?

2. As in the litigation in the aftermath of the Three Mile Island nuclear incident in the United States, courts have also established public health funds to finance studies on the long-term health effects of a polluting activity and to support public education programs. See A. Taylor, "Public Health Funds: The Next Step in the Evolution of Tort Law" (1994) vol. 21 *Boston College Environmental Affairs Law* 753.

3. Would a broader concept of ecological surveillance expenses be more appropriate so that funds might be used to support scientific investigations of long-term environmental impacts of chemical exposures caused by tortious behaviour? A statutory move in such a direction may be seen in CEPA 1999, where discretion was granted to courts to direct offenders to pay an amount for the purposes of conducting research into the ecological use and disposal of a substance in respect of which an offence was committed. See SC 1999, c. 33, s. 291(1)(n).

4. The *Ayers* case also discussed the potential statute of limitations problem for toxic tort victims. The traditional view was that statutes of limitations (requiring legal actions to be brought within a time period designated by statute) began to run at the time of the defendant's tortious act or the date of the toxic exposure. Because of the long latency period typical of illnesses caused by chemical pollutants, victims often discover their injury and the existence of a cause of action a considerable time after the expiration of the statute of limitations. Consider the merits of a liberal "discovery rule" such as that of New Jersey, which delays until the victim discovers both the injury and the facts suggesting that a third party may be responsible (525 A. 2d 287, at 299).

3. Recovery for the Fear of Contracting a Serious Disease (Cancer)

Potter v. Firestone Tire & Rubber Co.
863 P. 2d. 795 (Cal. 1993)

BAXTER J: This is a toxic exposure case brought by four landowners living adjacent to a landfill. As a result of defendant Firestone's practice of disposing of its toxic wastes at the landfill, the landowners were subjected to prolonged exposure to certain carcinogens. While none of the landowners currently suffers from any cancerous or precancerous condition, each faces an enhanced but unquantified risk of developing cancer in the future due to the exposure.

. . .

"Fear of cancer" is a term generally used to describe a present anxiety over developing cancer in the future. Claims for fear of cancer have been increasingly asserted in toxic tort cases as more and more substances have been linked with cancer. Typically a person's likelihood of developing cancer as a result of a toxic exposure is difficult to predict because many forms of cancer are characterized by long latency periods (anywhere from 20 to 30 years), and presentation is dependent upon the interrelation of myriad factors.

The availability of damages for fear of cancer as a result of exposure to carcinogens or other toxins in negligence actions is a relatively novel issue for California courts. Other jurisdictions, however, have considered such claims and the appropriate limits on recovery. Factors deemed important to the compensability of such fear have included proof of a discernible physical injury ... proof of a physical impact or physical invasion ... or objective proof of mental distress.

We must now consider whether, pursuant to California precedent, emotional distress engendered by the fear of developing cancer in the future as a result of a toxic exposure is a recoverable item of damages in a negligence action.

Parasitic Recovery: Immune System Impairment and/or Cellular Damage as Physical Injury

. . .

No California cases address whether impairment of the immune system response and cellular damage constitute "physical injury" sufficient to allow recovery for parasitic emotional distress damages. Courts in other jurisdictions that have considered this issue recently have come to differing conclusions. ... [Here] the statement of decision by the trial court does not include an express finding that plaintiffs' exposure to the contaminated well water resulted in physical injury, cellular damage or immune system impairment.

. . .

Nonparasitic Fear of Cancer Recovery

We next determine whether the absence of a present physical injury precludes recovery for emotional distress engendered by fear of cancer. Firestone argues that California should not recognize a duty to avoid negligently causing emotional distress to another, but, if such a duty is recognized, recovery should be permitted in the absence of physical injury only on proof that the plaintiff's emotional distress or fear is caused by knowledge that future physical injury or illness is more likely than not to occur as a direct result of the defendant's conduct.

. . .

We cannot say that it would never be reasonable for a person who has ingested toxic substances to harbour a genuine and serious fear of cancer where reliable medical or scientific opinion indicates that such ingestion has significantly increased his or her risk of cancer, but not to a probable likelihood. Indeed, we would be very hard pressed to find that, as a matter of law, a plaintiff faced with a 20 percent or 30 percent chance of developing cancer cannot genuinely, seriously and reasonably fear the prospect of cancer. Nonetheless, we conclude, for the public policy reasons identified below, that emotional distress caused by the fear of a cancer that is not probable should generally not be compensable in a negligence action.

As a starting point in our analysis, we recognize the indisputable fact that all of us are exposed to carcinogens every day. As one commentator has observed, "[i]t is difficult to go a week without news of toxic exposure. Virtually everyone in society is conscious of the fact that the air they breathe, water, food and drugs they ingest, land on which they live, or products to which they are exposed are potential health hazards. Although few are exposed to all, few also can escape exposure to any." ...

Thus, all of us are potential fear of cancer plaintiffs, provided we are sufficiently aware of and worried about the possibility of developing cancer from exposure to or ingestion of a carcinogenic substance. The enormity of the class of potential plaintiffs cannot be overstated, indeed, a single class action may easily involve hundreds, if not thousands, of fear of cancer claims. ...

With this consideration in mind, we believe the tremendous societal cost of otherwise allowing emotional distress compensation to a potentially unrestricted plaintiff class demonstrates the necessity of imposing some limit on the class.

· · ·

A second policy concern that weighs in favor of a more likely than not threshold is the unduly detrimental impact that unrestricted fear liability would have in the health care field. As *amicus curiae* California Medical Association points out, access to prescription drugs is likely to be impeded by allowing recovery of fear of cancer damages in negligence cases without the imposition of a heightened threshold. To wit, thousands of drugs having no known harmful effects are currently being prescribed and utilized. New data about potentially harmful effects may not develop for years. If and when negative data are discovered and made public, however, one can expect numerous lawsuits to be filed by patients who currently have no physical injury or illness but who nonetheless fear the risk of adverse effects from the drugs they used. Unless meaningful restrictions are placed on this potential plaintiff class, the threat of numerous large adverse monetary awards, coupled with the added cost of insuring against such liability (assuming insurance would be available), could diminish the availability of new beneficial prescription drugs or increase their price beyond the reach of those who need them most.

· · ·

A third policy concern to consider is that allowing recovery to all victims who have a fear of cancer may work to the detriment of those who sustain actual physical injury and those who ultimately develop cancer as a result of toxic exposure. That is, to allow compensation to all plaintiffs with objectively reasonable cancer fears, even where the threatened cancer is not probable, raises the very significant concern that defendants and their insurers will be unable to ensure adequate compensation for those victims who actually develop cancer or other physical injuries.

· · ·

A fourth reason supporting the imposition of a more likely than not limitation is to establish a sufficiently definite and predictable threshold for recovery to permit consistent application from case to case.

· · ·

To summarize, we hold with respect to negligent infliction of emotional distress claims arising out of exposure to carcinogens and/or other toxic substances: Unless an express exception to this general rule is recognized: in the absence of a present physical injury or illness, damages for fear of cancer may be recovered only if the plaintiff pleads and proves that (1) as a result of the defendant's negligent breach of a duty owed to the plaintiff, the plaintiff is exposed to a toxic substance which threatens cancer; *and* (2) the plaintiff's fear stems from a knowledge, corroborated by reliable medical or scientific opinion, that it is more likely than not that the plaintiff will develop the cancer in the future due to the toxic exposure.

· · ·

When a defendant acts with oppression, fraud or malice, no reason, policy or otherwise, justifies application of the more likely than not threshold. Any burden or consequence to society from imposing liability is offset by the deterrent impact of holding morally blameworthy defendants fully responsible for the damages they cause, including damage in the form of emotional distress suffered by victims of the misconduct who reasonably fear future cancer.

NOTES

1. George J, in a dissenting opinion, noted that the majority of jurisdictions and legal commentators recognize that a "more likely than not" threshold standard is *not* applicable to *present* injury of serious emotional distress claims. Rather, a plaintiff's likelihood of actually developing the feared disease is simply one factor in assessing the reasonableness of his or her claim (863 P. 2d 795, at 833).

2. In the *Potter* case, the Supreme Court of California also recognized medical monitoring costs as a compensable item of damages and addressed the plaintiffs' claim of intentional infliction of emotional distress as well. To recover on the intentional infliction claim, plaintiffs would have to show that the defendant's "extreme and outrageous conduct was directed at plaintiffs or undertaken with knowledge of their presence and consumption of groundwater, and with knowledge of a substantial certainty that they would suffer severe emotional injury upon discovery of the facts" (863 P. 2d 795, at 800).

3. Should a showing of severe mental distress be enough in an intentional infliction of mental suffering claim? In Canada there is precedent suggesting plaintiffs must establish some "recognizable physical or psychopathological harm" or "a visible and provable illness." See Wilson J in *Frame v. Smith*, [1987] 2 SCR 99, at 128, and A.M. Linden and L.N. Klar, *Canadian Tort Law: Cases, Notes & Materials*, 10th ed. (Toronto: Butterworths, 1994), at 65-66, note 1.

4. Public Perception of Risk/Fear and Reduced Property Value

Adkins v. Thomas Solvent Co.
487 NW 2d 715 (Mich. 1992)

BOYLE J: The question before us is whether a claim for relief may be maintained by plaintiffs who claim the right to damages in nuisance for property depreciation caused by environmental contamination of ground water despite testimony by both plaintiffs' and defendants' experts that their properties were not and would never be subject to ground water contamination emanating from the defendants' property.

· · ·

The crux of the plaintiffs' complaint is that publicity concerning the contamination of ground water in the area (although concededly not their ground water) caused diminution in the value of the plaintiffs' property. This theory cannot form the basis for recovery because negative publicity resulting in unfounded fear about dangers in the vicinity of the property does not constitute a significant interference with the use and enjoyment of land.

· · ·

However, on the present state of the record, plaintiffs do not contend that the condition created by the defendant causes them fear or anxiety. Thus, not only have these plaintiffs not alleged significant interference with their use and enjoyment of property, they do not here posit any interference at all.

Plaintiffs correctly observe that property depreciation is a traditional element of damages in a nuisance action. ... We are not persuaded, however, and the dissent has not cited authority to the contrary, that an allegation of property depreciation alone sets forth a cognizable claim in private nuisance of significant interference with the use and enjoyment of a person's property. Diminution in property values caused by negative publicity is, on these facts, *damnum absque injuria*—a loss without an injury in the legal sense.

· · ·

If any property owner in the vicinity of the numerous hazardous waste sites that have been identified can advance a claim seeking damages when unfounded public fears of exposure cause property depreciation, the ultimate effect might be a reordering of a polluter's resources for the benefit of persons who have suffered no cognizable harm at the expense of those claimants who have been subjected to a substantial and unreasonable interference in the use and enjoyment of property.

LEVIN J (dissenting): Plaintiffs should, in our opinion, be allowed to recover damages in nuisance on proofs introduced at a trial tending to show that the defendants actually contaminated soil and ground water in the neighbourhood of plaintiffs' homes with toxic chemicals and industrial wastes, that the market perception of the value of plaintiffs' homes was actually adversely affected by the contamination of the neighbourhood, and thus that plaintiffs' loss was causally related to defendants' conduct.

· · ·

The majority of jurisdictions addressing the question hold that when property owners are awarded damages in compensation for diminution of property value attributable to easements for power lines, gas or oil pipe lines, or related structures, the elements and measure of compensation include potential purchasers' fear or apprehension of danger. Most of these authorities hold that because such fears in fact materially affect property values, they should be included in the calculus of damage.

NOTES

1. The future of damages for "stigmatized" property in Canada remains uncertain. In *Tridan Developments Ltd. v. Shell Canada Products Ltd.* (2002), 57 OR (3d) 503, the Ontario Court of Appeal reversed a lower court's granting of $350,000 for the loss of property value due to stigma associated with the contamination of Tridan's land due to a gas leakage from Shell's service station. The case, however, provides a limited precedent since the court concluded on the facts that no stigma loss was present since the contaminated site was required to be remediated (at a cost of $550,000) to pristine condition. The

court did not discuss in detail the legal parameters of stigma damage and did not foreclose such a head of damage, at least where a site was not cleaned to a pristine state.

2. For commentary supporting recognition of stigma damages and suggesting four elements that a plaintiff property owner would have to prove, see J. Hierlmeier, "The Enigma of Stigma: A New Environmental Contamination Challenge Facing Canada's Judiciary" (2002) vol. 11 *Dalhousie Journal of Legal Studies* 179. The four elements are (1) a stigma exists, (2) the diminution in property value is not speculative, (3) cleanup costs are inadequate to fully compensate the owner, and (4) the fear of stigma is not unreasonable.

FURTHER READINGS

B. Bilson, *The Canadian Law of Nuisance* (Toronto: Butterworths, 1991).

R. Cotton and R. Mansell, "Civil Liability for Environmental Damage," chapter 18 in R. Cotton and A.R. Lucas, eds., *Canadian Environmental Law*, 2d ed. (Toronto: Butterworths, 1991) (looseleaf, vol. 1).

M.D. Faieta, H.B. Kohn, R. Kligman, and J. Swaigen, *Environmental Harm: Civil Actions and Compensation* (Toronto: Butterworths, 1996).

E.J. Swanson and E.L. Hughes, *The Price of Pollution: Environmental Litigation in Canada* (Edmonton: Environmental Law Centre, 1990).

CHAPTER FOUR

Environmental Law in Quebec

Lorne Giroux and Paule Halley

I. INTRODUCTION

Chapter 3 raises the question whether the common law and private litigation can still prove to be efficient legal tools for environmental protection. The question derives mainly from the development of a large body of environmental legislation and regulation, whereby the state has assumed a larger share of the task of preventing or reducing environmental degradation.

In Quebec, this same question can be asked about the civil law. The development of a regulatory regime based on the *Environment Quality Act*, RSQ, c. Q-2 (EQA) brings into sharper focus the inadequacies and shortcomings of using private civil law remedies. As will be seen in the following pages, the theoretical basis for private litigation is different in Quebec; yet, there are great similarities between the common law and the civil law with respect to the issues, the problems, and the outcome. This chapter begins with an explanation of the theoretical foundations of the civil law as applied to the area of private environmental litigation. The chapter highlights the debate over the concept of fault and administrative approvals and also considers recent developments in the law of agricultural activities. The subsequent sections explore the recurring problem of causation and look at a more promising procedural development: the class action. The final section provides an overview of two interrelated areas of law that have developed to address public participation: the public right to participate in the enforcement of the EQA and public participation in the context of environmental assessment.

II. THE LEGAL CONTEXT

The province of Quebec is under a dual legal system. Since the *Quebec Act* of 1774 (UK), the rights of the citizens of Quebec "to hold and enjoy their Property and Possessions, together with all Customs and Usage relative thereto, and all other their Civil Rights" (s. 8) has been held to apply to private law: the law as between subject and subject—that is, involving the rights of one subject against another. See O'Connor, "Property and Civil Rights in the Province" (1940) vol. 18 *Canadian Bar Review* 311, at 337.

At the time of the *Quebec Act*, Quebec private law was governed by the Coutume de Paris (Custom of Paris) but was later codified in the *Civil Code of Lower Canada* (CCLC), which came into force on August 1, 1866. On January 1, 1994, the *Civil Code of Lower Canada* was replaced by the *Civil Code of Quebec* (CCQ), enacted by SQ 1991, c. 64.

On the other hand, starting with the British conquest, public law in Quebec—that is, the law as between the subject and the institutions of government—has been the domain of British law. Even today, in such areas as constitutional and administrative law, should Quebec statutory law be silent on any given question, resort has to be had to common law principles (R. Dussault and L. Borgeat, *Administrative Law Treatise*, vol. 1 (Scarborough, ON: Carswell, 1985), at 18-21).

III. THE CIVIL LAW AND THE ENVIRONMENT

This duality covers the field of environmental law as well. In Quebec, as with most other provinces, there is a regulatory regime in place whereby the state has assumed a large part of the responsibilities of protecting the environment. However, the civil law of Quebec is also the theatre of private environmental litigation based on the maxim "*Sic utere tuo ut alienum non laedas.*"

While the issues dealt with in litigation and the practical results reached by the civil law in private environmental disputes present many similarities with those of the common law, the theoretical underpinnings are somewhat different. For instance, the civil law does not recognize the difference between private and public nuisance. As will be seen in the following article, the civil law concepts of "abus de droit" (abuse of right) and "troubles de voisinage" (neighbourhood annoyances) can be said to be analogous to the concept of private nuisance in the common law.

O. Nadon
**"Civil Liability Underlying Environmental Risk-Related Activities
in Quebec"**
(1998), 24 CELR (NS) 141-44, 145-47, and 153-63*

Introduction

The *Civil Code of Lower Canada* ("CCLC") came into force in Quebec on August 1, 1866. Based on French Law and the Napoleonic Code, it then came under various influences, namely, common law. Since its initial recognition, civil law has changed considerably and jurisprudence thereunder has evolved. When last reformed on January 1, 1994, the *Civil Code of Quebec* ("CCQ") superseded the CCLC. Consequently, in several respects, the difference between contractual liability and extra-contractual liability was eliminated. For instance, a person may be bound to pay bodily

---

*   Updated and abridged English version of "*La responsabilité du pollueur et l'évolution de la notion de faute,*" in Quebec Bar, Continuing Education Department, *Développements récents du droit de l'environnement* (1996) (Cowansville, QC: Yvon Blais Publications, 1996) (footnotes abridged).

injury, moral or material, in matters of contractual as well as extra-contractual liability. With respect to contractual liability, art. 1458 CCQ does not refer to fault but to the *"failure in the duty to honour ... undertakings."* As for extra-contractual liability, the second paragraph of art. 1457 CCQ qualifies fault as the *"failure in the duty to abide by the rules of conduct"* (the French version only mentions "fault" whereas the English version makes no mention thereof). The concept of fault, whether or not specifically mentioned, will apply in a greater number of fields and more broadly. However, in other cases, it will be sidestepped. In fact, liability may be incurred under circumstances not falling under contractual or extra-contractual spheres. Thus, the reform codified the abusive exercise of rights somewhat clarifying the uncertainty surrounding this concept, the target of various jurisprudential trends since 1896 (with *Drysdale v. Dugas* (1896), 26 SCR 20) and moves us toward a liability where the concept of fault has no place. In environmental risk-related activities, it will have some impact. The purpose of this article is not to discuss statutory liability under the *Environment Quality Act*, RSQ, c. Q-2, but to rather discuss some aspects of extra-contractual liability closely affecting the environment under the CCQ. In particular, we will examine the general principles of art. 1457 CCQ and those of presumed fault under art. 1465 CCQ with respect to the person having custody and control over a thing.

Lastly, we will see the principles of the abusive exercise of rights whether or not related to property. We will analyse the distinctions between the abusive exercise of rights and neighbourhood annoyances. From this perspective, we will see that there does not have to be a fault to give rise to liability and the obligation to repair damages.

1. The General Framework of the Proven Fault

Article 1457 CCQ constitutes the codification of the general principle of extra-contractual civil liability. For liability to exist a fault must be committed, the victim must sustain damages and there must be causation or a causal link between the two. These fundamental items must be proven by different means and degrees of evidence.

1.1 The Concept of Fault

Where did this important concept that has led some writers to state that in Quebec there is no civil liability if there is no fault, originate? The Supreme Court of Canada ruled along these lines in the *Lapierre* case [[1985] 1 SCR 241; to be more specific, Nadon notes that the SCC "set aside the theory of risk in Quebec because it would serve to set aside the classic view of civil liability by creating an objective fault"]. According to Judge Jean-Louis Baudouin, it is *"categorical imperative"* albeit a *"flexible and adjustable tool."* [See *La responsabilité civile*, 4th ed. (Cowansville, QC: Yvon Blais Publications, 1994), at 79.]

In our western culture, fault dates back to the beginning of mankind. Some religions attribute the first fault, original sin, to Adam and Eve. They did what their Creator had forbidden and a serious sanction ensued. As you can see, the concept of fault is well anchored, the law inheriting the principles disseminated by some religions.

However, in our modern society, we should no longer have to refer *solely* to the concept of fault to incur civil liability especially where environmental protection is involved. As environmental damage has a social dimension, horizons must be broadened. Even art. 1457 CCQ, which reads as follows, gives us a way out of this quagmire.

> 1457. Every person has a duty to abide by the rules of conduct, which lie upon him, according to the *circumstances*, *usage* or law, so as not to cause injury to another.
>
> Where he is endowed with reason and fails in this duty, he is responsible for any injury he causes to another person and is liable to reparation for the injury, whether it be bodily, moral or material in nature.
>
> He is also liable, in certain cases, to reparation for injury caused to another by the *act* or *fault* of another person or by the *act of things* in his custody. [Our emphasis.]

Jean-Louis Baudouin [*supra*, at 81-82] summarizes the definitions emanating from doctrine and jurisprudence and details the broadening of art. 1457 CCQ as follows:

> Most definitions revolve around two governing ideas: failure in a pre-existing duty and the breach of a standard of conduct.
>
> *failure in a duty*: For some, a person who fails to abide by the rules of conduct imposed by the legislator is at fault. Where no *specific standard on behaviour* was provided for, fault exists when, intentionally or by a simple imprudent act, the person transgresses the general duty not to injure others. ...
>
> *breach of a standard of behaviour*: A person whose conduct is contrary to what is expected from a reasonable person under similar circumstances is at fault. *Article 1457 CCQ however gives a new indication by specifying that this standard of conduct may result from usage or law. The word usage must be understood herein in a broad sense and not in a technical sense.* [Our emphasis and translation.]

Sometimes, the concept of fault is easily identifiable while other times there is room for interpretation by the courts. In recent years however there has been progress in appreciating the concept of fault. Jean-Louis Baudouin [*supra*, at 32] underscores this moreover:

> There has been progressive transformation of the concept of civil fault in jurisprudence. For some years now, the courts have been *less stringent with respect to standards required to ascertain civil misconduct.* [Our emphasis and translation.]

In fact, we note this "broadening of horizons" referred to above. This evolution is somewhat predictable. The power relationships have changed. For instance, the old maxim *"The King Can Do No Wrong"* no longer has a place in our democratic free society. Contrary to what prevailed, this political view of society has raised our concerns about the social impact of environmental damage and the agent at fault may now be the State, the Crown and Crown Corporations. [See M. Bélanger, *La responsabilité de l'etat et de ses sociétés en environnement* (Cowansville, QC: Yvon Blais Publications, 1994).] In fact, art. 1376 CCQ has codified this tendency:

> 1376. The rules set forth in this Book apply to the State and its bodies, and to all other legal persons established in the public interest, subject to any other rules of law which may be applicable to them.

1.2 Temporal Fault

When is the fault appreciated? Is it when the fault is committed or when the damage occurs? This question relates to prescription from the viewpoint of the damage. In fact, arts. 2925 and 2926 CCQ read as follows:

> 2925. An action to enforce a personal right or movable real right is prescribed by three years, if the prescriptive period is not otherwise established.
> 2926. Where the right of action arises from moral, corporal or material damage appearing progressively or tardily, the period runs from the day the damage appears for the first time.

It is not too difficult to appreciate the damage when it occurs shortly after the fault is committed as behavioural standards do not change very quickly. But what happens if an act giving rise to the liability takes place 30 years before the damage occurs? Do the rules of interpretation apply according to past or current standards? What if the act giving rise to the liability could not be equated to a fault 30 years ago but, today, it has become socially unacceptable behaviour or a legal obligation established by regulatory standards? The answer is clear and leaves no room for conflicting interpretation: *the fault is appreciated when it is committed.* Any other approach would give the concept of fault a *retroactive nature.*

Consider the example of underground tanks that contained petroleum products. In Quebec, an estimated 40,000 of these tanks have long been abandoned, a large number buried 30 or 40 years ago. With time, the surfaces of the tanks have deteriorated, corrosion has set in and, in 1997, we often discover that hydrocarbons have leaked from cracks and spread into the environment sometimes over wide distances through the ground water table. When the tanks were buried and then abandoned because they were no longer used, no legislative norm or standard existed with respect to their installation let alone their removal. Trade practices at the time, or socially acceptable behaviour, left the tanks in the ground without any protective measures. Only much later, in 1991, did the *Petroleum Products Regulation* [RRQ, c. U-1.1, r. 1] fix the standards for removing these underground tanks after two years of non-use.

In this particular example, *no fault could be attributed* to the owner, the operator or the person having the care of these tanks when they were installed or when they ceased to be used. What about the victim who sustained material damages of thousands perhaps millions of dollars? The traditional concept of fault affords no relief to this victim who alone must bear the consequences of past activities while he sustains damages today and cannot claim them. Herein, the three-year prescription period is inconsequential as there was no fault.

1.3 The Causal Link

Proof of causation or the causal link between the damages sustained and the fault committed is fundamental in civil liability. Moreover, even if the concept of fault is eliminated as a fundamental element of liability and replaced by another concept, risk for instance, the causal link would still be paramount. This element is germane. In environmental matters, it is often a serious problem of evidence: how do you prove the causal link between chronic exposure to a carcinogenic substance if the latency period is 15 or 20 years before the symptoms of the disease or illness manifest themselves? How do you determine liability in the event of damages where no fault was committed and where the event is associated with a risk-related activity?

It is interesting to note that the concepts, even if different, are closely akin to each other. In some cases, we presume the causal link: if the occurrence of an act increases the chances of sustaining damage, in other words, presents a risk, while in other cases, we talk of fault which encompasses an obvious danger which subsequently arises. If the concept of fault is replaced by the concept of risk, the result is the same. Liability can exist even if no fault is committed. In environmental matters, the concept of risk is much more conducive to liability than the concept of fault. In fact, when dealing in risk-related activities involving handling, storing or manufacturing toxic substances, extreme care is the rule and regulation for these types of activities expressly do prevent the occurrence of injurious acts. Why must the fault in pursuing these activities be sought when damage occurs? What if there is no fault, but damage occurs nonetheless? Here, the *occurrence of the risk* is the *causa causans* of the damage.

2. *Presumed Fault of the Person Entrusted with the Custody of a Thing*

We have seen that under certain circumstances, a presumption of causal link exists between the fault and the damages. Consider the circumstances where the fault is the subject of the presumption. This is provided under art. 1465 CCQ with respect to the liability of a person entrusted with the custody of a thing.

The third paragraph of art. 1457 CCQ reads as follows:

> He is also liable, in certain cases, to reparation for injury caused to another by the act or fault of another person or *by the act of things in his custody.* [Our emphasis.]

This paragraph is in keeping with the section limiting general extra-contractual liability based on the concept of fault discussed in part 1. It also sets out the principles of art. 1465 CCQ which creates a presumption of fault on the part of a person entrusted with the custody of a thing in cases where the *autonomous act* of the thing causes damage. In this event, for the victim to benefit from the prescription of this article against the custodian, the damage must have been caused by the autonomous act of the thing under the custody of the person and *without human intervention on the thing.* The victim does not have to prove fault, that is to say, the exact cause of the accident, because it is presumed. This is an especially useful presumption for the person benefiting from it because the technical proof of the defectiveness of an extremely sophisticated apparatus or the complex demonstration of a scientific phenomenon associated with a toxic substance is not within everyone's grasp and experts may contradict one another in some cases. Article 1465 CCQ reads as follows:

> 1465. *A Person entrusted* with the custody of a thing is liable to reparation for injury resulting from the *autonomous act* of the thing, unless he proves that he is not at fault. [Our emphasis.]

Within the framework of this section, it is no longer the act by a person which will make the behaviour wrong but the status of the person, namely that of custodian, which will incur his liability and oblige him to repair the injury caused by the thing "unless the custodian proves that he did not commit any fault."

If the person's behaviour is not at fault, this situation being covered by the general framework of art. 1457 CCQ, then the custodian's burden of proving that he did not commit any fault does not pertain to his general behaviour as a person but rather the way he exercised the custody over a thing [*Montreal v. Watt and Scott*, [1922] AC 555]. In other words, the custodian will have to prove that all the aspects of his custody were flawless.

This interpretation gives more meaning to art. 1465 CCQ. In fact, as a thing cannot be blamed for committing a fault, which defies common sense, the other aspects under this section must be considered. As it is the *autonomous act* of the thing that must cause the damage to trigger the presumption mechanism, that is to say, *without any human intervention*, it is obvious that the custodian cannot be blamed for the poor handling—wrongful act—of the thing, which would dismiss the application of art. 1465 CCQ, given human intervention. Likewise, a person entrusted with the custody could not avoid liability by showing that his intervention was prudent and diligent, that is to say, without fault which would lead us to a paradox, or even a contradiction, since no human intervention should be taken into consideration. *In fact, at the time of the damage, the thing must have had an inherent activity, not inert.*

Closer examination of the aspects of art. 1465 CCQ will help us to grasp the nuances.

2.1 The Person Entrusted with the Custody of a Thing

What does this mean? The concept of custody is found in certain circumstances. The terms developed by jurisprudence [*Calestagne* (1939), 77 SC 82; *Russo*, [1986] RRA 36; *Héroux Machine Parts*, [1967] BR 349; *Cohen*, [1967] SCR 469] are "power of control, direction and supervision," "right of control, supervision and command," or "right of direction, effective supervision and control." The following definition summarizes the concept [Baudoin, *supra*, at 407]:

> Within the broad sense, custody is the relationship between the person in charge and the object, a relation based on a power to supervise, control and direct enabling the former to *avert* damage which may be caused by the autonomous act of the latter. [Our emphasis and translation.]

Based on this definition, all these facets must be present. Not all types of custody fall under the scope of art. 1465 CCQ and each case must be considered individually. Thus, an owner, while meeting all the requirements of a person entrusted with the custody of a thing may in fact not pay any attention to, or supervise, this object for reasons having nothing to do with negligence or carelessness. He could, for instance, entrust the custody of a thing to an experienced third party and therefore release himself from the physical custody. He would no longer have possession of or control over the thing.

Similarly, the simple holder of a thing would not have custody within the meaning of art. 1465 CCQ if he does not have control over it. A tenant who does not exercise any control over a thing and does not assume supervision would be in the same position.

These examples clearly show that the concept of custody and control is not easily discernable. We cannot rely on appearances. Legal custody is insufficient: real and physical custody matters. [See *Salaison Rive-sud Inc. v. Kordatzakis*, [1987] RRA 679 (SC).]

On the other hand, in each situation, certain presumptions must not parallel art. 1465 CCQ.

2.2 Temporal Custody

As we asked ourselves when the fault should be appreciated, we must also ask ourselves when custody and control apply before liability is incurred. Is it when the *autonomous act of the thing* occurs either by leakage, infiltration or migration of contaminants or a fall, for instance? This question must be answered affirmatively otherwise the applicable conditions entailing the application of art. 1465 CCQ are no longer met. Furthermore, the last paragraph of art. 1457 CCQ clearly mentions: "by the act of things in his custody." The use of the present tense clearly decides when custody must take place to trigger the framework of art. 1465 CCQ.

However, in certain cases, custody and control may be exercised for several years while in other cases, these aspects would have ended well before the injurious act.

When does custody cease? Could a person who abandoned a product by burying it so that he no longer has to take care of it cease to have custody and control? And what if the property on which the thing in question was abandoned is sold to a third party then to another who knows nothing about if and, after 50 years, discovers that the ground and underground water are contaminated? It seems obvious that a person cannot have the custody and control of a thing when he is unaware of its presence.

2.3 Rebuttable Liability

The principles of art. 1465 CCQ apply as follows: the victim proves that he sustained damage, that the damage originated from the autonomous act of a thing and that the defendant had the physical custody of the thing when the damage occurred. The victim does not have to prove the custodian's fault or the exact cause of the accident but that it is linked to the autonomous act of the object, substance or thing. The person entrusted with the custody is then presumed to have committed a fault. He is not presumed liable as such but will be if he cannot show that his custody was earmarked by all necessary precautions under the circumstances—in a nutshell, he did everything to prevent an incident which he should have foreseen (*Sault Ste. Marie*). Of course, the more the custodian has control of a dangerous product or one with risks, the greater his burden of proof is.

While he does not have to prove "*superior force*" ("force majeure" in French) or the act of a third party to rebut the presumption against him, the custodian may certainly do so if he cannot show any absence of fault in the custody of the thing; this would be more prudent, even necessary. [See Minister of Justice, Comments on art. 1465 CCQ, who "judges this burden too heavy for the custodian."] Some distinctions are necessary. In fact, a *superior force* would certainly exonerate the custodian who could not foresee this event and thus avoid it. But the *superior force* is a rare event. Moreover, in the case of the act of a third party, if the custodian did not take precautions to avoid harmful intervention by a third party during the custody, he might fail and be found liable. [*Cadorette v. Caron*, [1964] BR 523 (Que.).] This defence is in fact codified under art. 1470 CCQ where a definition of *superior force* is also given. This article reads as follows:

> Art. 1470 A person may free himself from his liability for injury caused to another by proving that the injury results from superior force, unless he has undertaken to make reparation for it. A superior force is an unforeseeable and irresistible event, including external causes with the same characteristics.

3. The Abusive Exercise of a Right and Neighbourhood Annoyances

Concepts attached to the abusive exercise of a right whether linked to property or not are certainly likely to most often apply in environmental civil liability matters. Industrial activities and the legal and regulatory obligations governing these activities have characteristics most often found under this framework. Moreover, it is hereunder that the so-called theory of no-fault liability was born in Quebec.

It all started in 1896 with the *Drysdale* case [(1896), 26 SCR 20, at 27]:

> He has the right to have a stable on his land but he does not have the right to spread (*emit*) odours into the living rooms and dining rooms of respondent or to pollute the atmosphere so as to seriously hinder it ... . And he exercises his right to have a stable only if he pays for the serious damages which he causes to his neighbours. *These are the consequences he should have foreseen when he chose the site of his establishment.* [Our emphasis and translation.]

The Honourable Justice Taschereau does not link the liability to the concept of fault but clearly to the *inherent risk* in carrying on a certain trade, in this case, a stable. For this reason, we prefer to qualify this framework as "liability based on the concept of risk" rather than "no-fault liability" which is less negative in relation to the traditional framework of civil liability and, at the same time, serves to clearly show that we are venturing into a special and somewhat different framework. [See, for example, *Bolduc v. Bell Mobilité Cellulaire* (1994), 17 CELR (NS) 102; *Lessard v. Bernard*, [1996] RDI 210 (CS Qué.).]

Before closely examining this framework, we wish to specify that, although the abusive exercise of a right and neighbourhood annoyances seem to fall under the same principles, they do differ. In fact, liability created by neighbourhood annoyances is but an application of an abusive exercise of a right under certain circumstances.

3.1 The Abusive Exercise of a Right

In the 1994 reform, the *Civil Code of Quebec* first codified the concept of abusive exercise of the right in art. 7:

> 7. No right may be exercised with the intent of injuring another or in an excessive and unreasonable manner which is contrary to the requirements of good faith.

While the wording of this article is brief, its scope is broad. We can retain the following aspects with respect to the exercise of a right:

- it cannot be exercised with the intent of injuring another, or
- in an excessive and unreasonable manner;
- which is contrary to the requirements of good faith.

These elements are first and foremost linked to the exercise of a *right*. The word right has a very broad scope. It may be a right to sue, a right to carry on an activity, a right of usage over a thing or any other defined right.

> This section sanctions the theory of the abusive exercise of a right acknowledged by doctrine as well as by jurisprudence and specifies the scope. Like Article 6, it inserts in the Code *a rule resting on the respect of the principles of justice and moral and social values in the exercise of rights* by indicating the two cornerstones of the abusive exercise of a right: the intent to injure or the excessive and unreasonable act.
>
> If, in its application, the theory of the abusive exercise of a right often draws upon the principles and concepts of civil liability namely those of fault and damage, *it remains however separate*. Because *the abusive exercise is neither a simple error nor negligence*: it arises when a right, *the licitness of which is not challenged, the normal exercise of which is completely legal*, is implemented contrary to the requirements of good faith. The abuse exists because this exercise, by seeking to injure, does not respect the realm of the exercise of the rights of others or because the manner was excessive and unreasonable, *it upsets the balance between the rights of one and the rights of others*. [Our emphasis and translation.]

These comments [Minister of Justice, Comments on art. 7 CCQ, (Quebec City: Publications du Québec, 1993)] complement the scope to be given to this legislative provision. It outlines the cases of application of risk-related environmental activities. Thus, despite the fact that a plant holds all necessary authorization permits and certificates, respects all legal and regulatory requirements and pursues its activities with all requisite care and attention, liability may be incurred if an incident occurs and causes damages to several victims. This liability will then be based on the concept of risk because the activities will have "upset the balance between the rights of one and the rights of other." [*Cadorette, supra* and *Drysdale, supra.*] In a recent decision of the Superior Court, Honourable Justice Nicole Duval-Hesler stated [*St-Eustache v. 149644 Canada Inc.* (1996-03-28), JE 96-954; aff'd. (1996-06-27), JE 96-1552]:

> Quebec recognizes three main categories of the abusive exercise of rights: the malicious exercise of a right (marked by bad faith and the intention to cause injury); the abnormal, tactless or incorrect exercise of a right (marked by abnormal use or the absence of ordinary precautions); and lastly, the anti-social exercise of a right (detrimental to others, even without the intention to cause injury or the absence of fault).
>
> The application of the theory of the abusive exercise of the right of ownership or occupancy raises highly genuine questions:
>
> 1. does the granting of municipal or other permits constitute a valid defence? The answer is no: according to jurisprudence an administrative authorization is not a "freehand whereby the operator can exceed the normal measure of inconveniences";

2. can there be an abusive exercise of a right even when all the legal requirements and provisions have been observed and the most modern techniques have been adhered to? The answer is yes: one must dwell more on the "abnormal or excessive nature of the inconveniences causes" than on "the defendant's fault";

3. is the installation's past history a determining factor? The answer to this third question contains subtleties: "the past history of the installation is not a grounds of defence in itself" but the knowledge of the situation by the plaintiff before purchasing it could act as a factor "to mitigate the damages because of the foreseeability of the inconveniences"... .

Finally, we add that the Quebec legislator has now codified the abusive exercise of a right under the combined regime of Articles 6, 7 and 976 CC. The criteria maintained by the legislator includes the good faith of the holder of the right and the neighbour's acceptance of normal neighbourhood annoyances given the nature of the status of their merits or local practice. This criteria is largely consistent with criteria maintained by the Ontario Court of Appeal in the aforementioned Mandrake case.

What we used to refer to as the theory of the abusive exercise of a right, now codified in art. 7 CCQ, has over the years, in our opinion, through the development of jurisprudence, the diversification of situations giving rise to liability and the open-mindedness essential to the evolution of law and its capacity to adapt to social changes, become liability based on the concept of risk and not on fault.

3.2 Neighbourhood Annoyances

The *Civil Code of Quebec* codified the evolution of jurisprudence in matters of abusive exercise of a right and neighbourhood annoyances in art. 976 CCQ which reads as follows:

976. Neighbours shall suffer the normal neighbourhood annoyances that are not beyond the limit of tolerance they owe each other, according to the nature or location of their land or local custom.

The Civil Code Revision Office's comments on this article are as follows:

This article wants to specify the legal obligation of good neighbourliness, already set out in Article 1057 CC by imposing, over and above the obligation of diligence, the obligation not to cause "intolerable discomfort" *regardless of the measures undertaken to eliminate it.*

This obligation has long been recognized in Quebec law either under the authority of an abusive exercise of a right or under the *word nuisance based on common law.* Recently, it has been more rightly appreciated as a *special legal obligation separate from that of Article 1057 CC and the concept of fault upon which it is based.*

This provision imposes on *everyone* and *not just on owners,* the obligation not to injure his neighbour. This obligation exists even in the absence of fault and *notwithstanding administrative authorization.* [Our emphasis and translation.]

During the 1994 reform of the *Civil Code of Quebec,* the legislator did away with old concepts that no longer corresponded to today's reality. The aforementioned comments with respect to the scope of art. 976 CCQ confirm the legislator's clear intention to acknowledge liability based on the concept of risk, separate from *the general liability under art. 1457 CCQ and the concept of fault upon which it is based.* We also want to add that the justice minister's comments on art. 976 CCQ mention that art. 976 CCQ was adopted for the purpose of modernizing traditional rules to further take environmental laws, the value of the water, and quality of life into consideration.

The courts, no doubt heartened by the new *Civil Code of Quebec* and the minister's accompanying comments, reaffirmed the case law trend started by the *Drysdale* case in the last century in two recent judgments.

In *Bolduc v. Bell Mobilité Cellulair [supra]*, the court fully applied principles set out in *Katz v. Reitz*, [1973] CA 230 (Que.) and which the court of appeal had acknowledged in *CECM v. Lambert*, [1984] CA 179 (Que.) at 180.

In *Maheux v. Boutin* [[1996] RRA 265, and cases cited therein], the court stated as follows:

> Pursuant to Article 7 CCQ no right may be exercised with the intention of injuring another or in an excessive and unreasonable manner contrary to the requirements of good faith. Lastly, Article 976 CCQ obliges neighbours to suffer the normal neighbourhood annoyances that are not beyond the limit of tolerance they owe one another. The legislator provides that *any breach in the respect of these rights (property and private life) is subject to the payment of bodily* damages, moral or material (Article 1607 CCQ) [Our emphasis and translation.]

It is pointless to have recourse to the concept of fault here. The legislative framework of the abusive exercise of a right, under art. 7 CCQ, and neighbourhood annoyances, under art. 976 CCQ, do not force it to find the persons responsible for the damages sustained by the victim. It is, in fact, a special framework separate from the one based on the concept of fault.

In operating a risk-related activity likely to contaminate or pollute the ambient surroundings in the immediate neighbourhood, but also over a large distance, it does not suffice to respect the laws and regulations or the conditions of a certificate of authorization to be released from any civil liability. Nor does it suffice to take all necessary precautions to avoid injurious acts. In fact, the person who foresees the occurrence of undesirable events can only think about what is foreseeable. *Thus, what is unforeseeable will fall under the framework of liability based on the concept of risk.*

Conclusion

As environmental law takes on importance and becomes part of numerous aspects of human life and most industrial activities, we realize that environmental statutory law is not alone in protecting individuals, ambient milieus and the environment. As we prepare to leave this century where civil law has so evolved, we see the reaffirmation of an environmental civil liability where old principles walk in hand with new approaches. This evolution in law encourages the person who exercises a risk-related activity to really change his or her view of the environment. In this progressive movement, reserves and fears are normal but, in time, will dissipate.

IV. THE CIVIL CODE, THE CONCEPT OF FAULT, AND THE GRANTING OF ADMINISTRATIVE APPROVALS

In practice, a review of the cases shows that in litigation based on the theory of "troubles de voisinage" judges are not as concerned with finding fault, whether proven or presumed, as much as with establishing whether the environmental prejudice or inconvenience suffered exceeds that which should be normal in the circumstances. In *Gourdeau v. Letellier de St-Just* (CA Québec, #200-09-003473-011, 30 April 2002, JE no. 2002-856), the Court of Appeal recently confirmed that liability under art. 976 CCQ is not determined on the basis of proven or presumed fault, but rather whether the limit of tolerance that neighbours owe each other has been exceeded. The position of the majority of the court is clear (para. 43): "The proposal based on measurement of the inconvenience suffered, as opposed to demonstration of a fault, is more consistent with the modern legislative trend stressing the environment and quality of life"(our translation).

In this case, the 25-foot-high party walls complied with municipal bylaws but since 1941 they had deprived the views and balconies of certain apartments built on the neighbouring lot of air and light. The court concluded that the means adopted to protect privacy greatly exceeded normal and acceptable measures (par. 47): "In terms of the sought after goal, the height of the walls was disproportionate and excessive, and their configuration was totally unacceptable. The neighbours' right is to have access to their property and to enjoy, not a right to a view, but the benefits of air and light" (our translation).

The recourses based on the theories of "abus de droit" and "troubles de voisinage" have been met with a variety of defences.

Priority of establishment is not in itself a valid defence because there can be no vested rights to a nuisance. But to mitigate damages, the courts can rely on the fact that the plaintiff was aware of the existing situation prior to acquiring his or her property.

The defendant cannot escape liability by establishing that his or her activity has been authorized by governmental authority as evidenced by the issuance of the necessary permits, *if* it is conducted in a manner that exceeds the normal measure of inconvenience that should be acceptable in the circumstances. Most of the existing cases deal with authorizations, such as municipal permits, that allow only the establishment of the activity. It is likely that specific environmental approvals, especially those setting allowable effluent levels, will prove to be a more difficult defence for the courts to deal with in the future.

That question came before the Quebec Court of Appeal in *Gestion Serge Lafrenière v. Calvé*, [1999] RJQ 1313. That case involved a request for an interlocutory injunction by a riparian owner of Lake Heney, in the Outaouais Region, seeking the closure of a fish farming operation whose phosphorus-rich final effluent was discharged in a stream flowing into the lake. Scientific evidence showed rapid eutrophication of the lake on a scale likely to cause irreparable harm.

Among the issues tackled by the Court of Appeal in *Gestion Serge Lafrenière* was whether ss. 976, 981, and 982 CCQ have precedence over the EQA. These sections read as follows:

> 976. Neighbours shall suffer the normal neighbourhood annoyances that are not beyond the limit of tolerance they owe each other, according to the nature or location of their land or local customs.

...

981. A riparian owner may, for his needs, make use of a lake, the headwaters of a watercourse or any other watercourse bordering or crossing his land. As the water leaves his land, he shall direct it, not substantially changed in quality or quantity, into its regular course.

No riparian owner may by his use of the water prevent other riparian owners from exercising the same right.

982. Unless it is contrary to the general interest, a person having a right to use a spring, lake, sheet of water, underground stream or any running water may, to prevent the water from being polluted or used up, require the destruction or modification of any works by which the water is being polluted or dried up.

The petitioner, president of the "Association pour la protection du lac Heney," submitted the argument that even if the respondent was operating its fish farm in accordance with a valid certificate of approval issued under the authority of the EQA, the CCQ, especially s. 982 and its provision of the private right of a neighbour to a clean environment, should have precedence. Therefore, such private right could be enforced by the court notwithstanding a valid authorization granted under the statute.

In a carefully reasoned opinion, Gendreau J, writing for a unanimous bench, rejected the petitioner's logic as too absolute, because it would deprive the holder of a certificate of authorization of any legal protection with respect to the effluents covered by such authorization. Thus, in principle, the operation of the statute should have precedence over private law rules as expressed in the CCQ.

However, according to the court, there could arise situations whereby an activity likely to have an impact on environmental quality is authorized without there being any specific limits established by law, by regulation, or in the certificate of authorization itself as to the level of contaminants that can be discharged in the environment during the course of such activity. In such an instance, private law rules could then be invoked as a backup to impose limits on an environmental authorization granted by public authority (at 1326-27):

> À mon avis, l'application de la *Loi sur la qualité de l'environnement* devrait habituellement avoir préséance sur les règles du droit privé. Toutefois, il pourrait se trouver des situations où, comme ici, une activité est autorisée sans que, pour autant, les limites sur les rejets dans l'environnement ne soient fixées par la loi, les règlements ou le certificat d'autorisation. Un voisin ne pourrait-il pas alors se prévaloir des règles du droit civil relatives au bon voisinage pour forcer l'exploitant à prendre les mesures raisonnables en vue de réduire les inconvénients causés par son exploitation? Les dispositions du droit privé seraient alors supplétives et apporteraient un tempérament à une autorisation d'usage du territoire délivrée par l'autorité publique. On peut certainement imaginer d'autres situations de même nature.

As will be seen later, in a situation such as that arising in *Gestion Serge Lafrenière,* the plaintiff can also try to obtain redress by attacking the validity of the certificate of authorization relied upon by the defendant whose activity the plaintiff complains is causing him or her environmental harm.

V. THE SPECIAL CASE OF AGRICULTURAL ACTIVITIES

Agricultural activities carried out in agricultural zones established under the *Act Respecting the Preservation of Agricultural Land and Agricultural Activities*, RSQ, c. P-41.1 (APALAA), enjoy specific statutory protection from civil proceedings for damages or to obtain injunctions for dust, odour, or noise arising from the conduct of such activities. Quebec's "right to farm" legislation not only reinstates the defence of prior occupation (s. 100) but grants what amounts to total immunity from civil recourse as long as there is compliance with regulatory standards. The Quebec statute goes so far as to exclude dust, odour, and noise produced by agricultural activities from the standard of "troubles de voisinage" embodied in s. 976 CCQ.

**Act Respecting the Preservation of Agricultural Land and
Agricultural Activities
RSQ, c. P-41.1, s. 79**

79.17. *Liability for dust, noise or odours.* In an agricultural zone, no person shall incur liability toward a third person by reason of dust, noise or odours resulting from agricultural activities, or shall be prevented by a third person from exercising such agricultural activities, if they are exercised, subject to section 100,

(1) in accordance with the regulatory standards adopted under the *Environment Quality Act* (chapter Q-2) that relate to dust and noise or, as regards odours, in accordance with the standards aimed at reducing the inconvenience caused by odours resulting from agricultural activities, originating from the exercise of the powers provided for in subparagraph 4 of the second paragraph of section 113 of the *Act respecting land use planning and development* (chapter A-19.1);

(2) in accordance with the provisions of the *Environment Quality Act* (RSQ, chapter Q-2) as regards any matter not covered by regulatory standards.

79.18. *Burden of proof.* Where a plaintiff or an applicant in an action or proceedings brought against a person exercising agricultural activities in an agricultural zone

(1) claims damages to compensate for the dust, noise or odours resulting from the activities, or

(2) applies for an injunction to prevent or modify the exercise of the activities, it is incumbent upon the plaintiff or applicant, to establish liability, to prove that the person exercising the agricultural activities has contravened the applicable regulatory standards or the *Environment Quality Act* (chapter Q-2), as the case may be.

79.19. *Limit of tolerance.* In an agricultural zone, the inconvenience caused by dust, noise or odours resulting from agricultural activities does not exceed the limit of tolerance neighbours owe each other, insofar as the activities are exercised, subject to section 100,

(1) in accordance with the regulatory standards adopted under the *Environment Quality Act* (chapter Q-2) that relate to dust and noise or, as regards odours, in accordance with the standards aimed at reducing the inconvenience caused by odours resulting from agricultural activities, originating from the exercise of the

powers provided for in subparagraph 4 of the second paragraph of section 113 of the *Act respecting land use planning and development* (chapter A-19.1) ;

(2) in accordance with the provisions of the *Environment Quality Act* as regards any matter not covered by regulatory standards.

79.19.1. *Interpretation.* Nothing in this division shall be interpreted as enabling a person who carries on an agricultural activity to avoid liability for a gross or intentional fault committed in carrying on that activity.

79.19.2. *Presumption.* The agricultural activities of a breeding unit that are carried on in accordance with subdivisions 1.1 and 1.2 of Division I of this chapter are, for the purposes of sections 79.17 to 79.19, deemed to be carried on in compliance with the standards aimed at reducing the inconvenience caused by odours resulting from agricultural activities, originating from the exercise of the powers provided for in subparagraph 4 of the second paragraph of section 113 of the *Act respecting land use planning and development* (chapter A-19.1).

The drafting of s. 79.19 of the statute, which closely follows the wording of s. 976 of the CCQ, shows the underlying purpose of those provisions. As seen earlier, s. 976 CCQ allows the courts to grant relief to victims of pollution who suffer inconveniences exceeding the limit of what is tolerable, taking into account the nature and location of their land and the local customs. Relief is available, even when the activities of the defendant are conducted in accordance with regulatory standards, upon a finding that they cause nuisances of an abnormal and exorbitant character. For example, see *Messier v. Agromex,* [1996] RRA 1029, at 1030-31 (CS), where the defendant was held liable for pollution of well water resulting from the spreading of manure, even though such activity had been done in accordance with all applicable regulations.

In the case of inconveniences resulting from dust, odours, and noise generated by agricultural activities conducted in an agricultural zone as established under the APALAA, the legislative intent is clearly to exclude both recourses in damages and via injunction by a deeming provision to the effect that those activities do not exceed the limits of tolerance set by s. 976 CCQ. The only condition required of the farmer to benefit from such immunity is that these activities be exercised in compliance with the statutory and regulatory standards set out in ss. 79.17 and 79.19 APALAA.

The scope of the immunity purported to be granted by these provisions can be best appreciated if one takes into account the following facts:

1. There are no provincial regulations under EQA setting standards for dust, odours, and noise generated by agricultural activities in an agricultural zone.
2. The control of odours from such activities, and especially from hog farming, is left to be dealt with under local land-use regulations by the setting of minimum separation distances between agricultural uses and other uses.
3. A complex statutory scheme has been established under land-use planning legislation whose only purpose is to severely restrict the powers of local municipalities to exercise their zoning powers in agricultural zones and to set minimum separation distances. (See L. Giroux, "Le droit environmental et le secteur agricole (prise 2):

la Loi agricole de 2001," in *Développements récents en droit de l'environnement—2002*, Barreau du Québec, Formation permanente, vol. 175 (Cowansville, QC: Yvon Blais Publications, 2002), at 265-363).

4. Specific rights to expand animal breeding activities (especially hog farming) in an agricultural zone are granted by ss. 79.2.4-79.2.7 APALAA. An expansion carried out according to these rights is exempt from the provisions of local zoning bylaws dealing with agricultural uses and setting separation distance requirements. Furthermore, even if such an expansion has the effect of aggravating the adverse environmental impacts to neighbours resulting from an increase in breeding activities, those activities are nonetheless deemed to be conducted in compliance with the municipal standards from which they are exempt (s. 79.19.2 APALAA).

5. Nothing in these provisions requires that, in order to benefit from the statutory immunity, agricultural practices in an agricultural zone be conducted according to "normal farming practices," as is the case with "right to farm" legislation elsewhere in Canada. The only limit to such immunity is when there is "gross or intentional fault in carrying on that activity" under s. 79.19.1 APALAA.

Given the scope of the definition of "agricultural activities" in the Quebec statute (s. 1(0.1)), which extends to "activities relating to the storage, packaging, processing and sale of farm products" carried out by a producer on his or her farm "with respect to farm products from his [or her] operation or, secondarily, from the operation of other producers," Quebec's "right to farm" provisions are undoubtedly the most generous in the country for farming interests. For a critical review, see L. Giroux, "Où s'en va le droit québécois l'environnement?" in *Développements récents en droit de l'environnement (1997)*, Barreau du Québec, Formation permanente, vol. 90 (Cowansville, QC: Yvon Blais Publications, 1997), 381, at 440-49.

VI. CAUSATION

The problem of causation with respect to environmental litigation is as acute in the civil law as it is in the common law.

Current judicial thinking on causation in Quebec civil law is summarized in the following observations by Gonthier J of the Supreme Court of Canada in *Laferrière v. Lawson*, [1991] 1 SCR 541, at 608-9:

> By way of summary, I would make the following brief, general observations:
>
> - The rules of civil responsibility require proof of fault, causation and damage.
> - Both acts and omissions may amount to fault and both may be analyzed similarly with regard to causation.
> - Causation in law is not identical to scientific causation.
> - Causation in law must be established on the balance of probabilities, taking into account all the evidence: factual, statistical and that which the judge is entitled to presume.
> - In some cases, where a fault presents a clear danger and where such a danger materializes, it may be reasonable to presume a causal link, unless there is a demonstration or indication to the contrary.

- Statistical evidence may be helpful as indicative but is not determinative. In particular, where statistical evidence does not indicate causation on the balance of probabilities, causation in law may nonetheless exist where evidence in the case supports such a finding.
- Even where statistical and factual evidence do not support a finding of causation on the balance of probabilities with respect to particular damage (e.g. death or sickness), such evidence may still justify a finding of causation with respect to lesser damage (e.g. slightly shorter life, greater pain).
- The evidence must be carefully analyzed to determine the exact nature of the fault or breach of duty and its consequences as well as the particular character of the damage, which has been suffered, as experienced by the victim.
- If after consideration of these factors a judge is not satisfied that the fault has, on his or her assessment of the balance of probabilities, caused any real damage, then recovery should be denied.

In civil liability matters, certain presumptions may facilitate the victim's proof. The Supreme Court of Canada acknowledged a presumption when the rules of conduct are codified or regulated. In *Morin v. Blais*, [1977] 1 SCR 570, the court noted, at 579-80:

> The mere breach of a regulation does not give rise to the offender's civil liability if it does not cause injury to anyone. However, many ... provisions lay down elementary standard of care and make them binding regulations at the same time. Breach of such regulations constitutes civil fault. In cases where such fault is immediately followed by an accident which the standard was expressly designated to prevent, it is reasonable to presume that there is a causal link between the fault and the accident, unless there is a demonstration or a strong indication to the contrary.

In *CSR St-François v. PCO Services Ltée*, [1991] RRA 185 (Qué. CA), the defendant had sprayed the pesticide "methoxychlor 25 E" on the lawn, shrubs, and trees of an industrial property and some of the maple trees on the plaintiff school board's adjoining lot had also been sprayed. One month later, the plaintiff's maple trees started to turn red and eventually lost their foliage and died.

Although it could not furnish scientific proof of the exact nature and toxicity of the product, the school board relied on a presumption of fact (*res ipsa loquitur*) to argue that the burden of proof had been reversed and now rested on the defendant to establish that it was not at fault.

The Quebec Court of Appeal, in confirming the judgment at trial, held that no evidentiary burden could be imposed on the defendant nor could a presumption of fault be inferred unless the plaintiff could first establish a causal relationship between the spraying of the pesticide and the withering of the trees. The defendant's expert witness had given two possible causes for the environmental damage to the trees: insufficient dilution of the pesticide prior to spraying, an explanation excluded by the evidence, or the possibility of a microclimate phenomenon due to the location of the trees. Since the second explanation was possible in the circumstances of the case, the Court of Appeal confirmed the trial judge's finding that the plaintiff school board had not established a causal relationship between the environmental damage and the actions of the defendant.

Perhaps the most spectacular example of proof or causation difficulties in private environmental litigation lies with the case of *Berthiaume v. Val Royal Lasalle Ltée*,

[1992] RJQ 76 (Que. SC). *Berthiaume* was a consolidation of six civil suits in damages arising from the installation of urea formaldehyde foam insulation (UFFI) in private residences. Plaintiffs sued both the UFFI installation contractors and the manufacturers for alleged impairment to their health resulting from toxic vapours and microscopic dust given off by the foam insulation. They claimed pecuniary compensation for property damage caused by noxious odours and other material damage caused by the product itself and by its faulty installation in the walls of their houses. They also claimed damages for the resulting loss in property value. Some of the claimants also sued the Canada Mortgage and Housing Corporation (CMHC) for having recommended and subsidized the use of the product. In one of the cases, the Quebec government was also included as a defendant because it provided subsidies to promote UFFI home insulation in an energy-saving program. Some of the defendant installation contractors also called in warranty both the UFFI manufacturers and their own insurers. The foam had been installed in the plaintiffs' homes from March 1977 to September 1980. UFFI was finally banned in Canada in 1981.

The trial lasted six years and five months, with 460 days of hearing. The transcript of the evidence (114,000 pages) and of the arguments occupied 809 volumes. There were 1,820 exhibits, and 122 witnesses gave testimony. Hurtubise J took the case under advisement on February 20, 1990 and rendered a 1,099-page judgment on December 13, 1991.

A number of issues was discussed, not only about the chemical composition, properties, and toxicity of UFFI and its effect on the plaintiffs' health, but also about Canadian product certification and standard-setting processes. A good part of the judgment is devoted to the liability of insurers and the scope of "pollution clauses" in insurance contracts.

In the end, the plaintiffs failed because the trial judge held that they had not established a causal relationship between the alleged injury and the use of the products. The judge found that some of the plaintiffs did suffer symptoms as alleged, but these symptoms were relatively light in character and non-specific in their nature. They could thus have resulted from a variety of causes.

While the average levels of formaldehyde (given off by UFFI) was slightly higher in UFFI-insulated homes, there were other factors that could have been of influence, such as the age of the house, the nature of the walls, and the existence of other sources of formaldehyde within the house. Furthermore, existing instruments able to measure such levels were "fragile," making it impossible to trace a "dosage response" curve between formaldehyde levels and the seriousness of the symptoms. As for as the risk of cancer, the trial judge held that on the preponderance of evidence, the plaintiffs had not established the existence of such a risk, but that the weight of the evidence pointed in fact to the opposite. The claims for material damages and loss of property value were also dismissed.

The trial judge expressly stated that, with the rejection of risk theory in the *Lapierre* case, liability rested on the need to establish fault, prejudice, and causation on the balance of probabilities. On causation, the Superior Court relied on both *Laferrière v. Lawson*, as well as *Snell v. Farrell*, as establishing the evidentiary standard to be met by plaintiffs.

On appeal, the appellants abandoned any challenge to the trial judge's principal finding of fact that no personal injury nor material damage had been established. They claimed general damages for odours coming from the release of formaldehyde from UFFI and compensation for fear and anxiety resulting from the installation of the product in their homes. They also claimed for the cost of removal of the foam insulation from their houses and for the loss of property values once the insulation was removed.

The Court of Appeal rejected all those claims. Since the appellants had failed to prove the materiality of any health risk, they could not avoid having to prove causation by simply saying that the respondent installors had deprived them of a chance to avoid future health problems likely to cause a depreciation of their homes. The rules of civil liability did not allow them to rely on the concept of loss of opportunity in such a way. Furthermore, by putting forward such an argument based on future health problems, the appellants, in fact, were asking for a re-evaluation of the whole of the findings of fact upon which rested the fundamental conclusion of the judgment at trial. Since the appellants could not demonstrate manifest or overriding error on the part of the trial judge, the Court of Appeal refused to make such a re-evaluation. As for the claim for foul odours, the court found that it had not been proved. See *Berthiaume v. Réno-Dépôt Inc.*, [1995] RJQ 2796; (1997), 21 CELR (NS) 188 (CA).

VII. CLASS ACTIONS

Since 1979, the *Code of Civil Procedure*, RSQ, c. C-25 (CCP), has authorized class actions in Quebec (arts. 999-1051). Unlike other Canadian legislation authorizing class actions, the conditions set out in the CCP do not include the requirement that the class action be the best means of settling the matter in dispute. The conditions required for class actions are provided for in art. 1003 CCP:

> 1003. The court authorizes the bringing of the class action and ascribes the status of representative to the member it designates if of opinion that:
>
> (a) the recourses of the members raise identical, similar or related questions of law or fact;
>
> (b) the facts alleged seem to justify the conclusions sought;
>
> (c) the composition of the group makes the application of article 59 or 67 difficult or impracticable; and
>
> (d) the member to whom the court intends to ascribe the status of representative is in a position to represent the members adequately.

The usefulness of the class action in environmental litigation received a big boost with the decision of the Court of Appeal in *Comité d'environnement de la Baie Inc. v. Société d'électrolyse et de chimie Alcan*, [1990] RJQ 655; (1992), 6 CELR (NS) 150 (Que. CA), leave to appeal refused [1990] 2 SCR xi. In that case, the court was sitting on appeal from a Superior Court judgment refusing to grant authorization to institute a class action (art. 1002 CCP) on the ground that the requirements of the Code had not been met (art. 1003 CCP).

The case arose out of the defendant's operations at its docking facilities for the unloading of mineral ore required in its aluminum smelting process. It was argued that dust from the fallout of these mineral substances caused damages to the houses of the 2,400 members of the group, making maintenance and cleaning more costly and depriving the owners of the enjoyment of their property.

In the Superior Court, Alcan had argued successfully that, in particular, the causes of action of the members of the group did not raise "identical, similar or related questions of law or fact" as required by art. 1003(a) of the Code.

The Court of Appeal reversed this decision and granted the authorization. The court held that art. 1003(a) does not require that all or even most of the questions raised be identical, similar, or closely related. It is enough that members of the group raise a number of issues of law or fact that are sufficiently related to justify a class action. Such was the case here with the questions of the standard of care required from the defendant to prevent air pollution, the applicability of the *volenti non fit injuria* principle, and the rules of prescription.

As for the possibility that collective recovery (art. 1031 CCP) would not be feasible or convenient as alleged by the company, the court decided that the provisions of the Code gave the judge, to whom a motion for authorization is presented, some discretion in deciding what questions are to be dealt with collectively and what questions are to be decided individually. A judge does not have to dismiss the motion simply because the applicant has proposed collective recovery while individual recovery would be more expedient (art. 1037 CCP). In the circumstances of the case, the basis of responsibility was the same for all members of the group. The principal differences between the claims would relate to the damages suffered by individual members and, even then, there might be some similar categories of damage. The trial judge might then decide to limit the common questions in an appropriate manner and order individual recovery of the damages.

In rendering the unanimous judgment of the court, Kaufman J extolled the advantages and virtues of the class action in environmental matters (at 661 RJQ):

> The class action recourse seems to me a particularly useful remedy in appropriate cases of environmental damage. Air or water pollution rarely affect just one individual or one piece of property. They often cause harm to many individuals over a large geographic area. The issues involved may be similar in each claim, but they may be complex and expensive to litigate, while the amount involved in each case may be relatively modest. The class action, in these cases, seems an obvious means for dealing with claims for compensation for the harm done when compared to numerous individual law suits, each raising many of the same issues of fact and law.

In *Nadon v. Anjou (Ville d')*, [1994] RJQ 1823; 28 MPLR (2d) 139 (CA), the Court of Appeal again emphasized the particularly well-adapted nature of class actions for litigation raising environmental protection issues. The application was for authorization to institute a class action for damages and an injunction, on behalf of approximately 200,000 people who were allergic to ragweed pollen, against 23 municipalities for contravening the bylaw obliging them to eradicate ragweed from their land by August 1. The Court of Appeal reversed the Superior Court decision and authorized the class action. In this connection, the court stressed that the conditions set out in art. 1003 CCP are interpreted in a non-restrictive manner and that once they have been met there is little discretion left to the court, which does not need to rule on the validity in law of the conclusions of the recourse.

The following are some of the other class actions authorized by the court. In *Association des propriétaires et locataires de St-Ignace-du-Lac Inc. v. Meunier* (December 13, 1990), CS Montréal, no. 500-06-00002-903, JE no. 91-3235, Pinard JP, Annuaire de jurisprudence no. 91-2313, Pinard JP authorized a class action by lake residents for damages and an injunction against the contamination of lake waters caused by the respondent's sawmill activities, which were conducted in such a manner that woodwaste was disposed of in the lake. Class actions have also been authorized for victims of the severe floods of the summer of 1996 in the Saguenay and Lac St-Jean regions. In these actions, the victims are claiming damages against the owners and operators of dams and dikes, whom they hold partially or totally responsible for loss of property and personal injury. They allege that, due to negligence and carelessness on the part of the owners and operators, some of which were agents of the Crown, the floods were not properly controlled. For an outlook on some of the complex issues involved in these actions, see *Arseneault v. Société immobilière du Québec* (November 7, 1997), Chicoutimi no. 150-06-000001-974, JE no. 98-237, Bernard J (Sup. Ct.).

VIII. STATUTORY RIGHTS

As mentioned at the outset, Quebec is not different from the rest of Canada, because Quebec, like other provinces, relies on regulatory legislation as the main component of its environmental protection policy. Quebec's EQA contains the main elements of the basic provincial regulatory model as outlined in chapter 5. However, there are a few differences worth mentioning. The following subsections focus on public participation in the enforcement of the EQA and in the context of environmental assessment.

A. Public Right To Participate in the Enforcement of the EQA

Since 1978, one of the special features of the Quebec statute is the important right given to the public to participate in the enforcement of the environmental regulatory regime. Participation is accomplished by a liberalization of the rules governing standing. Today, the Quebec Superior Court has a unique and progressive statutory power to grant injunctive relief.

Environment Quality Act
RSQ 1977, c. Q-2

Division III.1

The Right to a Healthy Environment and to the Protection of Living Species

19.1. *Environmental rights.* Every person has a right to a healthy environment and to its protection, and to the protection of the living species inhabiting it, to the extent provided for by this Act and the regulations, orders, approvals and authorizations issued under any section of this Act and, as regards odours resulting from agricultural activities, to the extent prescribed by any standard originating from the exercise of the powers provided for in subparagraph 4 of the second, paragraph of section 113 of the *Act respecting land use planning and development* (chapter A-19.1).

19.2. *Recourse.* A judge of the Superior Court may grant an injunction to prohibit any act or operation which interferes or might interfere with the exercise of a right conferred by section 19.1.

19.3. *Natural person.* The application for an injunction contemplated in section 19.2 may be made by any natural person domiciled in Québec frequenting a place or the immediate vicinity of a place in respect of which a contravention is alleged.

Attorney general. It may also be made by the Attorney General and by any municipality in whose territory the contravention is being or about to be committed.

19.4. *Security.* In the case where an interlocutory injunction is applied for, the security contemplated in article 755 of the *Code of Civil Procedure* shall not exceed $500.

19.5. *Service.* Every action or motion made pursuant to this division must be served on the Attorney General.

19.6. *Priority.* Every application for an injunction made under this division shall be heard and decided by preference.

19.7. *Provisions not applicable.* Sections 19.2 to 19.6 do not apply in the case where a depollution project or programme has been duly authorized or approved under this Act, or in the case where a depollution attestation has been issued under this Act, except with regard to any act contrary to the provisions of a certificate of authorization, a depollution programme, a depollution attestation or any applicable regulation.

The Superior Court is empowered to grant an injunction, "to prohibit any act or operation which interferes ... with the exercise" of the right to a healthy environment and to the protection of the living species inhabiting it (s. 19.2 EQA). Recall that these rights, granted by s. 19.1 EQA, fall within certain environmental rights sought by those wishing to strengthen environmental laws in Canada (see chapter 11).

In practice, because of the provisions of ss. 19.13 and 19.7, the scope of this right is limited to cases where there has been a contravention of the Act, of a regulation, or of an order, approval, or authorization issued under the Act. This would include, for example, the right to enjoin a promoter from carrying on an activity or development project undertaken without first submitting it to the environmental assessment process and the governmental approval required by ss. 31.1 to 31.9 of the EQA (*Béchard v. Selenco* (1989), 3 CELR (NS) 307 (Que. CA), at 322).

Under s. 19.7 EQA, the holding of a certificate of approval is a valid defence barring a plaintiff from obtaining an injunction under s. 19.1 or 19.3 unless the plaintiff can establish that the holder of such certificate is acting contrary to its terms and conditions.

In such an instance, the Court of Appeal, in *Gestion Serge Lafrenière v. Calvé*, [1999] RJQ 1313, discussed above, has recognized that the plaintiff in injunction is entitled to seek a declaration that the certificate of approval delivered to the defendant under the statutory scheme is null and void. Such a declaration by the court would lift the obstacle represented by s. 19.7 EQA to the granting of injunctive relief to enforce the plaintiff's right to environmental quality as provided by ss. 19.1 and 19.3 EQA (at 1318):

Dans un tel contexte [plaintiff's request for a declaration of nullity], un citoyen victime de dommage à son environnement par l'action d'un tiers a l'intérêt suffisant pour demander la nullité du permis autorisant cette activité. Cela découle, à mon avis, de la nécessité de procurer un remède judiciaire pour faire respecter le droit à la qualité de l'environnement, une valeur sociale reconnue tant par le législateur que par les tribunaux.

In that case, the Court of Appeal decided that the plaintiff had made a strong case that the certificate of approval delivered by the minister of the environment should be declared null and void. The court said that, in delivering a certificate of approval allowing the plaintiff to increase its phosphorous discharges from its fish farming operation, the minister had acted in an unreasonable manner because he was well aware that the lake into which the effluents flowed was already at risk. In addition, the minister had created an estoppel situation by not respecting his prior commitment to residents that, prior to the issuance of the approval, there would be more studies and research on the effects on the lake of an increase in discharges. The court thus came to the conclusion that the plaintiff was entitled to interlocutory injunctive relief in spite of s. 19.7 EQA.

The duties of the minister of the environment on a request for a certificate of approval are set out under s. 24 EQA, which reads as follows:

> The Minister shall, before giving his approval to an application made under section 22, ascertain that the emission, deposit, issuance or discharge of contaminants into the environment will be in accordance with the act and regulations. He may, for that purpose, require any alteration in the plan or project submitted.

When the environmental impacts of an activity for which a certificate of approval is sought are not the subject of a specific regulation, the minister is allowed a large measure of discretion. He or she has to make sure that the projected activity is not "likely to affect the life, health, safety, welfare or comfort of human beings, or to cause damage to or otherwise impair the quality of the soil, vegetation, wildlife or property" under the terms of s. 20 of the EQA.

In *Gélinas v. Grand-Mère (Ville)*, [2002] RJQ 721, the Superior Court applied the "reasonableness simpliciter" test (*Baker v. Canada*, [1999] 2 SCR 817) as the appropriate standard of review for such ministerial discretion under s. 24. In that instance, the court declared null and void, at the request of a municipality, a certificate of approval granted under s. 22 EQA for a hog farm. The court held that the minister had not acted reasonably in approving the project even if he was appraised of the fact that the pipe carrying liquid manure pumped from the confining building to the holding tank was to be placed immediately above the main water pipe delivering drinking water to the inhabitants of the town.

Returning to statutory recourses, the right to an injunction under the EQA does not preclude access to the common law remedy of injunction (CCP, ss. 751-761), the advantages of using the statutory remedy lie with the fact that not only is standing much easier to achieve (because it is granted to "any natural person domiciled in Quebec, frequenting a place or the immediate vicinity of a place in respect of which a contravention is alleged") but also, in the case of an interlocutory injunction, security for costs that could be required from the applicant cannot exceed $500.

In *Enterprises BCP Ltée v. Bourassa* ((February 27, 1984), CA Montréal, no. 500-90-000995-811, JE no. 84-279, digested in *Canadian Environmental Law*, 2d ed., vol. 1, ref. Q-4.8), the Quebec Court of Appeal tried to define the boundaries of the regulatory regime and the civil law theory of "abus de droit" and "troubles de voisinage" as grounds for injunctive relief. On an appeal from a Superior Court judgment issuing an injunction under s. 19.2 EQA, the Court of Appeal held that

> 1. Under s. 19.1 of the EQA, the court can, upon request, order the cessation of any activity conducted or operated without the certificate of authorization required under s. 22 of the EQA.

2. Under the statutory regime, this judicial stop order can only remain in force until a certificate of authorization has been obtained. The court thus held that the injunction should expire upon (appellant industry's) reception of the certificate.

3. A court can grant injunctive relief based upon both (a) section 19.1 of the EQA (for a contravention to the regulatory regime) and (b) the civil law theory of "*abus de droit*" and "*troubles de voisinage.*" In such a case, that part of the order based on s. 19.1 is subject to the limitations set out in s.19.7, but not the order based on the civil law principles.

4. Thus, an order requiring the cessation of all operations of an industrial plant—because environmental approval has not yet been granted—is limited by the proviso in s. 19.7, to the period until a certificate of authorization is granted (under s. 22). However, those orders with respect to the manner of conducting the industrial operations (shutting off idling truck engines, prohibiting dumping of waste in the open) are not subject to the limitations of s. 19.7.

Hence, *Enterprises BPC Ltée* shows the willingness of the courts to try to integrate traditional civil law concepts and contemporary regulatory legislation in order to fashion a more efficient environmental protection remedy available to private citizens.

The Quebec Court of Appeal has refused to restrict the scope of the statutory recourse granted by ss. 19.1 to 19.7 EQA. In *Nadon v. Anjou*, [1994] RJQ 1823; 28 MPLR (2d) 139 (CA), the appellant had been refused authorization by the Superior Court to institute a class action against the city of Montreal and 22 other municipalities of the Montreal Urban Community (MUC). In her action, the appellant was seeking an injunction under s. 19.1 to compel the respondent municipalities to eradicate ragweed from the lands they owned as mandated by a clean air bylaw enacted by the MUC and approved by the minister of the environment under ss. 124 and 124.2 of the Act.

The Court of Appeal reversed and granted the authorization to institute the class action. The court pointed out that ss. 19.1 to 19.7 had been inserted in the EQA in 1978 to liberalize access to the courts for citizens seeking to enforce the Act and the regulations. The court rejected the argument, on the basis of a strict reading of s. 19.2, that it could not allow for the granting of a mandatory injunction.

An interlocutory injunction can also be granted under these sections, but the Court of Appeal has stated that they do not excuse the petitioner from establishing that the granting of the interlocutory injunction is "necessary in order to avoid serious or irreparable injury … or a factual or legal situation of such a nature as to render the final judgment ineffectual" as required by s. 752 CCP.

Recent decisions have ruled that, in the case of an objective violation of a public interest statute (violation objective d'une loi d'intérêt public) there is an almost irrebuttable presumption that there is serious or irreparable injury (*Constantineau v. Marzalek*, [1996] RDJ 154 (CA); *Québec (PG) v. Entreprises Raymond Denis Inc.*, [1993] RJQ 637 (CA), leave to appeal refused by the Supreme Court on March 23, 1993, [1993] 3 SCR vi). The undertaking of an activity or the conduct of an operation without prior authorization having been obtained when it is required under s. 22, 31.1, 32, 54, or 55 EQA is a typical example of the violation of an objective norm. Furthermore, in the total absence of prior authorization, the court does not have to inquire about the balance of convenience and inconvenience and the interlocutory injunction will then issue. Because of s. 126 EQA, this is the case even against the government or one of its agencies (*Québec (PG) v. Société du Parc industriel du centre du Québec*, [1979] CA 357).

As stated earlier, there is a great similarity between Quebec and the other provinces regarding fundamental problems of environmental law, such as matters of causation. In the area of judicial enforcement of environmental rights, however, Quebec has taken the lead by codifying environmental rights and granting broad standing to residents and special injunction powers to the courts.

QUESTION

Compare the civil law and the common law on matters such as causation and proof of fault. Also, compare the standing rules in Quebec with common law standing rules, and those set out in other Canadian legislation. Which model is better suited to environmental protection?

B. Public Participation and Environmental Assessment

Quebec has had an accessible public participation process for environmental issues since 1978 (LQ, 1978, c. 64), when the Bureau d'audiences publiques sur l'environnement (BAPE) was established. BAPE is a permanent, quasi-judicial agency that is separate from Quebec's Ministry of Environment and operates under its own mandate (ss. 6.3 and 31.3 EQA). Its mission is to inform and consult with the public on environmental issues or projects subject to public consultation. At the request of the minister, BAPE can proceed with inquiries, mediation, and public hearings in the environmental assessment process. It can also undertake special consultations, such as public review of government's policies and programs (for example, hazardous waste, forest protection, waste and water management).

In 1978, Quebec became the first province in Canada to enshrine an environmental impact assessment process in its legislation (ss. 31.1 to 31.9 EQA). The purpose of the environmental impact assessment and review procedure is to ensure that environmental concerns are integrated into project development and implementation planning. At two points during this process, the public has an opportunity to participate. First, BAPE provides the public with information and, second, any citizens who consider that the project should be publicly discussed and assessed can submit a request for public hearings to the minister (s. 31.3 EQA). In the case of hearings, the procedure followed by BAPE is based on public exchange between the board, citizens, agencies, and ministries, and the promoter (*Rules of Procedure Relating to the Conduct of Public Hearings*, RRQ 1981, c. Q-2, r. 19). At the end of the process, BAPE submits its report to the ministry, to be released to the public within 60 days (s. 6.7 EQA). The ministry then submits its own recommendations and the BAPE report to the Cabinet for it to decide on the project's development (s. 31.5 EQA).

P. Renaud
"The Environmental Assessment Process and Public Participation in
Québec: Concrete Elements for Sustainable Development"
(1996) vol. 27 *Revue Générale de Droit* 375, at 383-86 and 389-92

Public Participation (BAPE)

Step 4 [public participation] takes place in two phases, that is, the information period followed by inquiry and mediation or by inquiry and public hearing.

Public Information and Consultation Phase

The Minister mandates the BAPE to make the proponent's impact statement available to the public. To do so, the BAPE opens local consultation centres for a 45-day period for the benefit of citizens directly affected by the project. During this same period, it must also make the statement available for public consultation in its Québec City and Montréal offices, as well as in two university libraries. The impact statement, the summary, and other relevant documents are all tabled at these places.

At the beginning of the public information and consultation phase, BAPE professionals travel to the region targeted by the project to inform all interested parties about the environmental assessment procedure and the role of the BAPE. As a rule, the proponent attends the information sessions organized by the BAPE and may be called upon to answer certain questions regarding the project.

It is important to point out that the public information and consultation phase is not intended to turn into a public debate. However, it is during this period that citizens, groups or municipalities may request a public hearing or mediation process when they consider that a project contains any number of contentious elements. All applications for a public hearing or mediation must be addressed directly to the Minister and must specify the applicant's motives and interests with regard to the project environment. The Minister must then analyze the application and deem whether or not it is "frivolous" (justified). He then mandates the BAPE to conduct one of the following: an inquiry and mediation, or an inquiry and public hearing. This decision is a ministerial prerogative.

If no applications for a public hearing or mediation are submitted to the Minister, the second part of Step 4 is simply omitted. This second part is optional and has no legal substance until one or more applications have been submitted to the Minister.

Inquiry and Mediation

When the Minister of the Environment and Wildlife receives one or more applications for an inquiry and public hearing or mediation, he may, if he deems them not to be frivolous, entrust the BAPE with an inquiry and mediation mandate under subsection 6.3 of the Act. However, in a case where the applicants have submitted a request for an inquiry and public hearing, they maintain their right to this request.

Once the BAPE has received this mandate, to be carried out over a two month period, the BAPE president appoints a commissioner who is responsible for conducting the inquiry and mediation process and submitting a report to the Minister within the prescribed time frame. The inquiry and mediation process is unique to the BAPE and is founded on the principle of transparency. It can thus be qualified as administrative and public and, in this sense, differs from the traditional mediation process.

In December 1995, the BAPE adopted rules of procedure relating to the conduct of environmental mediation. All BAPE commissioners are under oath and bound by the BAPE Code of Ethics, adopted in 1992 and amended in 1995 to include the concept of environmental mediation. This Code stipulates that the Commission of Inquiry and Mediation must "foster public understanding of environment-related projects and shall encourage the public to express their opinions freely." It also stipulates that members shall avoid any situations involving a conflict of interest, act with impartiality, and foster mutual respect among participants. Commissioners also hold all powers conferred upon them by the *Act respecting public inquiry commissions*. For example, persons who refuse to appear before the Commission, produce, documents, or answer questions that may lawfully be put to them can be held in contempt, and the commissioner is entitled to proceed in the same manner as any court or judge in similar circumstances. However, no commissioner has had to exercise this power to date, since all mediation sessions and public hearings held have been conducted in a transparent manner, this principle being agreed to in advance by all participating parties.

Despite these powers, commissioners who act as mediators cannot impose a decision. The commissioner is an impartial third party who helps the dissenting parties identify the points on which they agree and disagree, and seek solutions. The commissioner is present at all mediation sessions.

The BAPE has broken the mediation process down into three phases: information, analysis and consent, and mediation as such.

At the end of the Commission's mandate, the BAPE submits the commissioner's report to the Québec Minister of the Environment and Wildlife, who has 60 days to make it public.

. . .

Inquiry and Public Hearing

Instead of issuing a mandate for inquiry and mediation, or when mediation has proved impossible and the Minister has not deemed the applications frivolous, the Minister can mandate the BAPE to proceed with an inquiry and hold a public hearing. In such a case, the Commission must observe the *Rules of Procedure Relating to the Conduct of Public Hearings* approved by the government.

The BAPE president begins by forming an independent inquiry commission mandated to conduct an inquiry, hold public hearings in two parts, and submit a report to the Minister within the prescribed time frame of four months. All such commissions are mandated to clarify and make information concerning the project comprehensible to the public.

Depending on the scope and complexity of the project undergoing the environmental assessment procedure, commissions are composed of between two and five BAPE members. These commissions are normally chaired by a member of the BAPE and include other members selected for their knowledge or expertise on the elements and issues specific to the project.

Since public participation is the key to the hearing, the public is strongly encouraged to contribute information, express opinions, or suggest improvements to the project; in short, to use their concrete knowledge of the situation to help identify project repercussions and thereby enable Cabinet to reach a more informed decision.

The purpose of the first part of the public hearing is to gather and disseminate as much information on the project as possible to enable participants to better understand the project and its impacts. It is thus the ideal occasion for all those involved to gain a better understanding of the different aspects of the project undergoing environmental assessment.

The current procedure is simple and is based on a direct public exchange between commission members and the public, the proponent, and the organizations and government departments concerned. The Commission ensures that an atmosphere of mutual respect is maintained and that the consultation and inquiry process is fair.

Once this part of the public hearing is completed, individuals, groups or organizations have a minimum of three weeks to prepare their written brief or oral presentation.

During the second part of the public hearing, individuals, groups and organizations are invited to present their opinions on the project. They may voice their support, express their objections, or suggest changes that could make the project more acceptable. In general, the quality of this testimony is impressive and the public participates actively. After the briefs are presented and the oral presentations heard, the Commission hears all other persons, including the applicants and the proponent, who may wish to rectify any project-related matters that have been raised during this part of the hearing.

The second part of the hearing provides the Commission with concrete knowledge of the project environment. It helps to better identify project repercussions and the values of the communities involved, thereby enabling members to consider all pertinent elements in their analysis.

Holding the public hearing in two separate parts, that is, gathering information and allowing the public to express its opinion, is a uniquely Québec-style approach. It enables participants to be better informed so that they can make more relevant comments during the second part of the hearing. This results in superior testimony and more enlightened, productive opinions.

Once the hearing is over, the Commission continues studying the project using the documents tabled at the hearing, including the briefs submitted by the public and the transcripts of the proceedings, and drafts its report. At the end of its mandate, the BAPE submits the Commission's report to the Minister of the Environment and Wildlife, who has 60 days to make it public.

QUESTIONS

1. Compare the public participation process for environmental assessment of the EQA with rules set out in other Canadian legislation. Is it significant that Quebec, as a matter of policy, does not participate in initiatives such as the CCME's harmonization initiatives?

2. Are there, elsewhere in Canada, potential conflicts between common law rules and remedies and statutory regimes established under federal and provincial environmental protection statutes?

FURTHER READINGS

Barreau du Québec, Formation permanente, *Développements récents en droit de l'environnement* (Cowansville, QC: Yvon Blais Publications, 1991 (vol. 19); 1992 (vol. 38); 1994 (vol. 55); 1996 (vol. 77); 1997 (vol. 90); 1998 (vol. 108); 1999 (vol. 124); 2000 (vol. 139); 2002 (vol. 175)).

R. Daigneault and M. Paquet, *L'Environnement au Québec, commentaires* (Montreal: CCH, 1994) (looseleaf).

P. Granda and O. Nadon, "Quebec Regulatory Controls," in R. Cotton and A. Lucas, eds., *Canadian Environmental Law*, 2d ed. (Toronto: Butterworths) (looseleaf).

P. Halley, *Le droit pénal de l'environnement* (Cowansville, QC: Yvon Blais Publications, 2001).

CHAPTER FIVE

Regulatory Legislation*

Alastair R. Lucas

I. INTRODUCTION

Environmental regulatory legislation at the federal and provincial levels has developed only in the last 30 years. Legislative approaches have changed in several stages so that today environmental legislation retains classic approval and regulatory offence provisions at its core, but has evolved to include sophisticated alternatives such as economic instruments, consultation processes, and an array of enforcement and compliance tools. This chapter charts this evolution and, because it is impossible to address the statutes of each jurisdiction in detail, presents a model that incorporates the essential elements of the provincial statutes and an overview of the federal CEPA 1999. Attention is given to the role and the development of environmental standards. The last part of the chapter looks at environmental regulatory offences, which are an essential component of such statutes, using the federal *Fisheries Act* as an example.

A.R. Lucas
"The New Environmental Law"
in R. Watts and D. Brown, eds., *Canada: The State of Federation: 1989*
(Kingston, ON: Queen's University, Institute for
Intergovernmental Affairs, 1990), at 168-71

Waste Control Laws

This first generation of environmental statutes includes the basic air, water and land pollution statutes enacted by Canada, and by the provinces in the early 1970s. One category of these statutes is those that established separate environment departments for the first time. The essential object of these Acts was control of waste that was being deposited on land or discharged into water or air. Regulatory systems were

---

* The author gratefully acknowledges the research assistance of Cheryl Sharvit and Joseph Chan.

established to identify waste sources, to bring these sources under permit, then by means of permit terms or conditions, to control the quality and quantity of waste discharged. Failure to comply with these requirements was made an offence punishable upon summary conviction by modest fines. Waste discharge likely to cause harm to human life or health or to the environment upon which human life depends, was often established as a general offence.

These statutes were clean-up laws, designed to minimize discharge of human and industrial waste into the environment. The underlying assumption was that the natural environment, with its air, water and land components, could, through careful management, be used to dispose of, dilute and cleanse the waste produced by human activity. It was a matter of measuring, then carefully and fairly allocating this environmental assimilative capacity.

It was recognized by governments and their advisors that civil legal actions, designed to resolve disputes between private parties and compensate persons damaged, were an ineffective legal tool for general systematic control of environmentally harmful waste discharge. It was also recognized that existing public health statutes and miscellaneous provisions scattered through natural resource development statutes were not equal to the task of comprehensive environmental control.

Waste control statutes include comprehensive environmental statutes such as the Ontario *Environmental Protection Act*, and the Quebec *Environment Quality Act*, which deal with air, water and land pollution from the base of comprehensive definitions of "pollution," "contaminant," and "environment," and single resource statutes such as the Alberta *Clean Air, Clean Water*, and *Land Surface Conservation and Reclamation Acts*, which covered much of the same ground but established a separate regulatory system for each environmental medium. Federal first generation environmental statutes include the *Clean Air Act*, the *Canada Water Act*, and the *Fisheries Act Pollution Amendments* and *Industry Regulations.* Gaps were filled and Acts were fine-tuned through development of regulations, policies, and procedures during the late 1970s and early 1980s.

These environmental laws were administered by environment departments, that were largely technical agencies, staffed by the scientific and engineering experts necessary to implement the permit schemes and develop "safe" standards for waste discharge. Initially, a great deal of effort was expended simply to bring all waste sources under permit.

A second generation of environmental statutes is now emerging. These laws are a response to overwhelming evidence that the waste control approach, while significant, is only one aspect of an effective environmental protection regime. A central objective of these new laws is control of persistent toxic substances. These materials either accumulate in the environment to produce conditions dangerous to the natural environment, or are simply so toxic and so persistent that even small amounts create serious danger over large periods of time. Such small dose toxicity and slow decomposition characteristics make the established assimilative waste regulation approach unsuitable for dealing effectively with toxic substances.

The new laws thus recognize that environmental protection is a long-term process that must address potential intergenerational effects of environmental damage.

Because new scientific knowledge about the toxicity of particular substances is continually developing, the laws must be flexible and include the means for identification and effective regulation of new contaminants. The approach is preventive, but also anticipatory.

Also reflected in these second generation statutes is the fact that toxic substances respect no boundaries—provincial or international. The second generation environmental laws are consequently outward looking, and international in their development, implementation and administration. Provincial laws must reflect interprovincial and federal-provincial understandings and commitments, and must also, if they are to contribute to the solution of the global problem, reflect current international conditions and Canada's international obligations. Federal laws such as CEPA must clearly implement specific international environmental commitments and must also be consistent with current international thinking about global environmental protection.

Another characteristic of the new environmental statutes is that enforcement provisions are far more sophisticated than the simple offence sections of the clean-up legislation. There is greater flexibility to permit the regulators a choice of appropriate enforcement tools, ranging from expeditious tickets for minor offenses, to serious indictable criminal offenses for actions that endanger life or health, mandatory administrative orders and civil legal actions. Negotiation techniques may be used in appropriate circumstances and provision is made for citizen involvement in regulatory processes, particularly in enforcement.

The serious criminal offenses which carry large fines and even potential imprisonment, have caught the attention of the corporate sector. Interest is particularly keen when these offenses are combined with officer and director liability provisions that may render corporate officials personally liable for environmental offenses and subject to fine or imprisonment even if they merely acquiesced or failed to make appropriate inquiries into activity that resulted in serious environmental harm. The clear message is that environmental offenses are serious crimes, and that nothing short of demonstrating that all reasonable care was taken in the circumstances will excuse corporate employees and even officers and directors. This has provided strong incentives for corporations to review or audit their compliance with environmental requirements, take any necessary corrective action, and prepare and implement environmental protection polices and plans so that environmentally damaging actions can be avoided.

K. Webb
"Pollution Control in Canada: The Regulatory Approach in the 1980s"
Study Paper, Administrative Law Series
(Ottawa: Law Reform Commission of Canada, 1988), at 14-15

Underlying the shift from blanket prohibitions to control regimes was a fundamental shift in approach toward government handling of industrial pollution, a shift from simplistic, difficult-to-enforce commandments to more practical restrictions. While not without its share of problems, this shift represented the first indication of government coming to grips with environmental protection in Canada. Perhaps this new approach was no more clearly evident than in the following remarks of the federal Minister of Fisheries when major *Fisheries Act* pollution provision amendments were tabled in the House of Commons in 1970:

> The sections in question [that is, the existing blanket prohibitions] were all too embrac-
> ing, all too comprehensive ... . What we really need in legislation of this kind is not an
> absolute prohibition on everything thrown into our waters but more precise measure-
> ments of what can be thrown into water and still keep it clear, clean and useful to
> fisheries ... . [B]y defining in the regulations the concentrations of the various chemi-
> cals which can or cannot be tolerated ... we will have a more precise and useful tool in
> legislation ... .

The more "precise and useful" control approach is inherently more interventionist than the simpler prohibition method of earlier years. Government must determine what are acceptable levels of pollutants, which abatement technologies are practica- ble, what industries can afford, and what the public will tolerate. The control ap- proach is also considerably more flexible than the blanket prohibition method in the sense that standards can be established for each industry sector, for particular re- gions, and even for individual operations.

But the increased flexibility is achieved at a cost: increased government involve- ment in business decision making. From a practical standpoint, the shift from prohi- bition to control drove pollution abatement decisions underground into the quiet and less visible regulation and licence-negotiating process of government. Over time, and in response to continued public pressure to do so, aspects of these underground bu- reaucratic processes have since made their way back to the surface, to be more public, but progress has been slow.

NOTES

1. Voluntary agreements for environmental protection based on discretionary statu- tory powers and the exercise of enforcement discretion became a preferred approach to the implementation of environmental legislation in most jurisdictions during the 1990s. This was a consequence of market-based ideology and government cost cutting. Now, however, there is evidence in provinces such as Ontario of a refocusing on statutory requirements and stricter enforcement, and legislative changes to reflect the new focus.

2. D. Paul Emond presents a different analysis of the development of environmental legislation in "The Greening of Environmental Law" (1991) vol. 36 *McGill Law Journal* 742. His focus is on process and emphasizes preventive assessment and consensual decision making. (Environmental impact assessment concepts, legislation, and processes are treated specifically in chapter 6. Consensual approaches to resolution of environmen- tal disputes, particularly mediation and bargaining techniques, are considered in chapter 14.) This emphasis on public participation and consultation may also be seen as an element of an emerging third generation of environmental legislation, namely, laws to promote sustainability or "sustainable development." Sustainability draws much of its inspiration from the definition offered by the UN World Commission on Environment and Development (the Brundtland commission) in 1987 (at 8) of development that

meets the needs of the present without compromising the ability of future generations to meet their own needs.

This definition was expanded in subsequent international instruments, and legal "principles" have emerged, particularly from the work done by the International Law Association's Committee on the Legal Aspects of Sustainable Development. In its fifth report in 2002 (New Delhi Declaration of Principles of International Law Relating to Sustainable Development), seven principles and their definitions were presented: (1) the duty of states to ensure sustainable natural resource development; (2) equity and eradication of poverty; (3) common but differentiated responsibilities of developed and developing countries; (4) a precautionary approach to human health, natural resources, and ecosystems; (5) public participation and access to information and justice; (6) democratic and transparent governance; and (7) integration of economic development, human rights, and social and environmental objectives.

The preamble to CEPA 1999 declares that "the primary purpose of this Act is to contribute to sustainable development through pollution prevention." As discussed below, it also incorporates the precautionary principle, both generally and specifically, in relation to assessment of toxic substances. According to Supreme Court of Canada dicta in *114957 Canada Ltée (Spraytech, Société d'arrosage) v. Hudson (Town)*, [2001] 2 SCR 241, there may be sufficient state practice to allow a good argument that the precautionary principle is a principle of customary international law that must be taken into account in establishing the context for interpretation of Canadian legislation. Other provisions of CEPA 1999 that address these sustainability principles include the parts on pollution prevention and life-cycle management or virtual elimination of toxics, the parts that establish advisory and consultative processes, an environmental protection cause of action, citizen investigation submissions, and an environmental registry.

3. Some recent changes to environmental legislation reflect swings in government policy concerning the enforcement of legislative requirements, as the Environmental Commissioner of Ontario (ECO) explains below.

Environmental Commissioner of Ontario
Having Regard: Annual Report 2000-2001
(Toronto: ECO, 2001), at 77-78

[The Ontario Ministry of the Environment's] use of voluntary agreements for environmental protection increased between 1995 and 2000, as the ministry looked for cost-effective ways to deliver its mandate. In the ECO's 1997 annual report, we noted that ministries were beginning to promote voluntary agreements, and called for these ministries to establish a general legal and policy framework for their use, after broad public consultation. MOE [Ministry of the Environment] did not respond to this recommendation with a legislative or policy framework.

. . .

In 1998, the Ontario government passed Bill 82, which amended environmental protection statutes to strengthen enforcement and investigation powers and penalties. The stronger enforcement and penalty provisions allow provincial officers to issue a broader range of orders, extend provisions that prohibit the illegal disposal of waste and introduce new penalties for polluters, such as increased maximum fines, wider use of jail terms, restitution orders, forfeiture of items seized as a result of an environmental offence, and court-directed forfeiture of collecting unpaid fines. Bill 82 also gave MOE the regulatory authority to introduce administrative monetary penalties (AMPs) for minor environmental infractions.

. . .

In November 2000, the government enacted new legislation, the *Toughest Environmental Penalties Act (TEPA)*, which greatly increased the maximum penalties for major environmental offences.

The Shift Back to Mandatory Abatement

[D]uring the Walkerton Inquiry, an internal MOE memorandum, disclosed as part of the Inquiry evidence, announced a major shift in MOE's internal policy—from voluntary to mandatory abatement. The MOE memo, distributed to all district managers and supervisors in March 2000, called for strict compliance with MOE's Compliance Guideline and announced a movement away from voluntary abatement and towards mandatory abatement. The memorandum put forward a new interpretation of the section of the Compliance Guideline that previously permitted MOE to use voluntary abatement measures in specific situations. The memorandum sets out an expectation that, where even one of the mandatory criteria exists, a control document will be issued and mandatory abatement pursued.

II. PROVINCIAL REGULATORY LEGISLATION

Provincial legislation that regulates discharge of environmental contaminants is by no means uniform. There are, however, enough common elements to suggest a basic legislative model. Typically, a regime for licensing and controlling contaminant discharges is established. Breaches of licensing requirements or terms and conditions of licences are quasi-criminal offences. Another central element is an array of powers to issue mandatory administrative orders in the event of unapproved release of contaminants.

The following is a more complete outline of the basic model:

1. Interpretation (definitions of key application and limitation terms)
2. Statement of purposes
3. Scope of application (whether the Crown is bound and general exclusions)
4. Prohibition against discharge of contaminants without an approval
5. Application procedure provisions and power in a designated official or authority to grant approvals
6. Enforcement order powers
7. Exemption or variance powers
8. Appeals
9. Enabling powers for economic instruments and market-based approaches
10. Offences and penalties
11. Regulation-making powers

NOTES AND QUESTIONS

1. Review your provincial environmental regulatory statute. How many elements of the basic model can you identify? Do any parts or provisions differ fundamentally from the model? If so, in what are the particulars?

2. In each statute, certain key terms delineate the application of the regime and establish standards for environmental harm. For example, "environment" or some version of the term is defined.

- Alberta *Environmental Protection and Enhancement Act*, RSA 2000, c. E-12, s. 1(t):

"environment" means the components of the earth and includes:
   (i) air, land and water,
   (ii) all layers of the atmosphere,
   (iii) all organic and inorganic matter and living organisms, and
   (iv) the interacting natural systems that include components referred to in subclauses (i) to (iii).

- Ontario *Environmental Protection Act*, RSO 1990, c. E.10, s. 1(1): "'natural environment' means the air, land and water, or any combination or part thereof, of the Province of Ontario." This includes private land and is not limited to public land within the province: *Re Rockcliffe Park Realty Ltd. v. Ontario (Director Minister of the Environment)* (1975), 62 DLR (3d) 17 (CA).

Things subject to regulation are also defined. For example:

- Alberta *Environmental Protection and Enhancement Act*, RSA 2000, c. E-12, s. 1(mmm): "substance" means

   (i) any matter that
      (A) is capable of becoming dispersed in the environment, or
      (B) is capable of being transformed in the environment into matter referred to in paragraph (A).
   (ii) any sound, vibration, heat, radiation or other forms of energy, and
   (iii) any combination of things referred to in subclauses (i) and (ii).

- Ontario *Environmental Protection Act*, RSO 1990, c. E.19, s. 1(1):

"contaminant" means any solid, liquid, gas, odour, heat, sound, vibration, radiation or combination of any of them resulting directly or indirectly from human activities that may cause an adverse effect.

- Nova Scotia *Environment Act*, SNS 1994-95, c. 1, s. 3(k):

"contaminant" means, unless otherwise defined in the regulations, a substance that causes or may cause an adverse effect; section (ba): "waste" means a substance that causes or may cause an adverse effect if added to the environment, and includes rubbish, slimes, tailing, fumes, smoke (from mines or factories), other air emissions, or other industrial wastes, effluent, sludge, sewage, garbage, refuse, scrap, litter or other waste products of any kind.

• British Columbia *Waste Management Act*, RSBC 1996, c. 482, s. 1: "waste" includes:

   (a) air contaminants,

   (b) litter,

   (c) effluent,

   (d) refuse,

   (e) biomedical waste,

   (f) special wastes, and

   (g) any other substance designated by the Lieutenant Governor in Council,

whether or not the type of waste referred to in paragraphs (a) to (f) or designated under paragraph (g) has any commercial value or is capable of being used for a useful purpose.

"Special Waste" means:

   (a) a substance that is prescribed as a special waste by the Lieutenant Governor in Council, and

   (b) if the Lieutenant Governor in Council prescribes circumstances in which a substance is special waste, a substance that is present in those circumstances.

Applications may be defined in terms of pollution sources rather than or in addition to contaminants or substances. Thus

• Alberta *Environmental Protection and Enhancement Act*, RSA 2000, c. E-2, s. 1(a):

"activity" means an activity or part of an activity listed in the Schedule of Activities;

• Ontario *Environmental Protection Act*, RSO 1990, c. E.19, s. 1(1): "source of contaminant" means anything that discharges into the natural environment any contaminant. "Source of contaminant" must be a source outside the natural environment and not part of the natural environment itself: *CNR v. Ontario (Director Under the Environmental Protection Act)* (1992), 6 CELR (NS) 211, at 223 (Div. Ct.); aff'd. (1992), 8 CELR (NS) 1, at 5 (Ont. CA).

Standards for environmental harm, in addition to those established by definitions of activities or conditions such as "pollution" or things such as "contaminant" or "waste" may also be defined in terms of effects. For example:

• Alberta *Environmental Protection and Enhancement Act*, RSA 2000, c. E-12, s. 1(b):

"adverse effect" means impairment of or damage to the environment, human health or safety or property.

• Ontario *Environmental Protection Act,* RSO 1990, c. E.19, s. 1(1):

"adverse effect" means one or more of:

   (a) impairment of the quality of the natural environment for any use that can be made of it,

   (b) injury or damage to property or to plant or animal life,

   (c) material discomfort to any person,

   (d) an adverse effect on the health of any person,

   (e) impairment of the safety of any person,

   (f) rendering any property or plant or animal life unfit for human use,

   (g) loss of enjoyment of normal use of property, and

   (h) interference with the normal conduct of business.

• Nova Scotia *Environment Act*, SNS 1994-95, c. 1, s. 3(c):

"adverse effect" means an effect that impairs or damages the environment, including an adverse effect respecting the health of humans or the reasonable enjoyment of life or property.

3. What is the purpose of the definition of "special waste" in addition to the definition of "waste" in the BC *Waste Management Act*?

4. Do purpose sections have any practical use or are they merely elaborate political statements?

5. Is it necessary to include exemption or variance provisions in environmental regulatory statutes?

6. Is it necessary to include appeal provisions in environmental regulatory statutes or will general law rights to judicial review suffice? Judicial review is discussed in chapter 7.

7. In addition to traditional administrative powers to make enforcement orders and quasi-criminal powers to prosecute offences, many modern statutes make use of "administrative monetary penalties" or AMPs, as explained by Benedickson in the following excerpt.

J. Benedickson
Environmental Law
(Toronto: Irwin Law, 2002), at 134-36

Although breaches of regulatory provisions, including environmental legislation, have traditionally been viewed as matters for prosecutorial action, recent statutory enactments have introduced an alternative process in the form of administrative penalty mechanisms, occasionally described as administrative monetary penalties (AMP). AMP provisions should be distinguished from ticketable offences where the manner of initiating the proceedings is modified but the matter remains within the jurisdiction of the courts.

Sanctions resulting from administrative rather than judicial proceedings are generally expected to provide less costly and more expeditious enforcement. They will also possibly be found more convenient from the perspective of offenders who accept the administrative determination of the contravention, a process that does not result in a criminal record. For precisely this reason, however, some observers question whether AMPs will serve as an effective deterrent.

Administrative penalty schemes will ordinarily involve a notification procedure setting out the details of the violation and the financial penalty determined to be applicable. An administrative hearing on the appropriateness of the penalty, or possibly an administrative appeal or review of the entire offence and penalty proceeding, will generally be set out.

Alberta implemented an administrative penalty arrangement in the *AEPEA*, under which the director, if of the opinion that a contravention of designated sections of the Act or regulations has occurred, may impose a penalty as provided for by regulation. Persons who elect to pay the administrative penalty in respect of a contravention are not subject to charges under the *AEPEA* in connection with the contravention. In case of non-payment, the province may recover the amount owing in an action in debt. … In connection with an earlier review of an Alberta AMP, where the level of the penalty assessed was challenged, the Alberta appeal board had remarked:

> The Board believes the amount of the penalty must reflect the regulatory matrix and associated criteria. The Board believes that to achieve the goal of deterrence, the penalty must also be high enough so that those who violate the law without reasonable excuse will not be able to "write off" the penalty as an acceptable trade-off for the harm or potential harm done to Alberta's environment.

Although it had been assumed that AMPs would, apart from administrative reviews, operate more or less without legal challenge, questions have been raised about the availability of a due diligence defence.

III. FEDERAL REGULATORY LEGISLATION: THE TOXICS CONTROL MODEL

A. Overview of CEPA 1999

CEPA 1999, the successor to the original 1988 Act, is the cornerstone federal environmental regulatory statute. For constitutional, as well as historical and federal administrative policy reasons, the Act's structure and elements differ somewhat from the provincial regulatory model. It incorporates several matters that were once the subject of separate legislation, including disposal at sea, control of nutrients, standards for fuels, and emissions from engines.

The Act is also the formal articulation of federal environmental policy on a number of matters. It includes the ideas of the "polluter pays" and pollution prevention and sets out requirements for pollution prevention plans. The precautionary principle is included in the Act's preamble and is used as a specific criterion when interpreting assessments of whether substances are toxic for the purposes of the Act. It also provides context for the interpretation of other sections. The principle, as stated in the preamble, is that a "lack of full scientific certainty shall not be used as a reason for postponing cost effective measures to prevent environmental degradation" where there are threats of serious or irreversible damage. Other principles include "virtual elimination of persistent and bioaccumulative substances," which is embedded in the toxics control part and "preservation of biodiversity," which is implemented in the part on regulation of biotechnology and in the toxics control and pollution prevention requirements.

Equivalency agreements are the main technique for harmonizing CEPA 1999 requirements with those of provincial regulatory legislation. Provisions of CEPA 1999 do not apply in any jurisdiction for which there is an order declaring that the provisions do not apply. Such orders may be made by Cabinet on the recommendation of the minister of the environment, where the minister and a provincial or territorial government agree in writing that the jurisdiction has in force laws that are equivalent to standards and requirements established by CEPA 1999 regulations and has provisions for citizen requests for investigation of alleged offences similar to those in CEPA 1999.

The major difference between CEPA 1999 and the provincial regulatory statutes is the apparent lack in CEPA 1999 of broad contaminant discharge prohibitions supported by a permit or approval system (there is a limited permit system for ocean discharges). CEPA 1999 also contains a part on toxics control, which establishes a basis, but not a complete statutory scheme, for a prohibition and approval system for the regulation and management of toxic substances. This is potentially the regulatory heart of CEPA 1999. A substance is "toxic" (except where the expression "inherently toxic" appears) if:

> 64. [I]t is entering or may enter the environment in a quantity or concentration or under conditions that
>> (a) have or may have an immediate or long-term harmful effect on the environment or its biological diversity;
>> (b) constitute or may constitute a danger to the environment on which life depends; or
>> (c) constitute or may constitute a danger in Canada to human life or health.

"Inherently toxic" is not defined.

> 3(1) "[S]ubstance" means any distinguishable kind of organic or inorganic matter, whether animate or inanimate, and includes
>> (a) any matter that is capable of being dispersed in the environment or of being transformed in the environment into matter that is capable of being so dispersed or that is capable of causing such transformations in the environment,
>> (b) any element or free radical,
>> (c) any combination of elements of a particular molecular identity that occurs in nature or as a result of a chemical reaction, and
>> (d) complex combinations of different molecules that originate in nature or are the result of chemical reactions but that could not practically be formed by simple combining individual constituents, and except for the purposes of sections 66, 80 to 89 and 104 to 115, includes
>> (e) any mixture that is a combination of substances and does not itself produce a substance that is different from the substances that were combined,
>> (f) any manufactured item that is formed into a specific physical shape or design during manufacture and has, for its final use, a function or functions dependent in whole or in part on its shape or design, and
>> (g) any animate matter that is, or any complex mixtures of different molecules that are, contained in effluents, emissions or wastes that result from any work, undertaking or activity.

The toxics provisions then establish a series of process stages. First, information may be gathered on whether a substance is toxic or capable of becoming toxic. Next, substances are assessed to determine if they are toxic. This stage involves a priority substances list of substances for which, once listed, the health and environment ministers must carry out an assessment and determine toxicity. Persons using, manufacturing, supplying, or importing substances on two other lists, the domestic substances list and the non-domestic substances list, are required to supply specified information to the minister of the environment, which is then assessed to determine whether the substance is toxic before allowing import, manufacture, or use.

If a substance is found to be toxic, the final stage is regulation. The governor in council may, on the recommendation of the ministers, decide that the substance should be added to the toxic substances list. The ministers are expressly required in interpreting the results of a screening assessment to apply a "weight of evidence approach and the precautionary principle" (s. 76.1). Where they are satisfied that a substance meets the criteria for virtual elimination, they must propose the implementation of such elimination of the substance. Otherwise, a listed substance may then be made the subject of regulations by the governor in council, which must be done within two years of listing. The regulation of toxics under CEPA 1999 has been characterized as "life-cycle" management, so that the full range of actions in relation to a substance from production or importation to disposal may be regulated.

Regulations with respect to substances on the list of toxic substances may "provid[e] for or impos[e] requirements" respecting a series of matters, including

93(1)(a) the quantity or concentration of the substance that may be released into the environment either alone or in combination with any other substance from any source or type of source;

(b) the places or areas where the substance may be released;

(c) the commercial, manufacturing or processing activity in the course of which the substance may be released;

(d) the manner in which and conditions under which the substance may be released into the environment, either alone or in combination with any other substance; ...

(l) the total, partial or conditional prohibition of the manufacture, use, processing, sale, offering for sale, import or export of the substance or a product containing it; ...

(r) the manner, conditions, places and method of disposal of the substance or a product containing it, including standards for the construction, maintenance and inspection of disposal sites.

B. Virtual Elimination

Where a substance is screened and the ministers propose to recommend that it be added to the list of toxic substances, and they are satisfied that the substance is persistent and bioaccumulative, results primarily from human activity, and is not a naturally occurring radionuclide or inorganic substance, the ministers must propose implementation of virtual elimination under the Act (s. 77(4)). This means "ultimate reduction of the quantity or concentration of the substance in the release below the level of quantification specified by the ministers" (s. 65(1)) in a virtual elimination list. "Level of quantification" means "the lowest concentration that can be accurately measured using sensitive but routine sampling and analytical methods" (s. 65.1), and in specifying this concentration, a variety of factors, including environmental or health risks and other relevant social, economic, or technical matters must be taken into account (s. 65(3)). Implementation of virtual elimination requires preparation and submission to the minister of a plan to accomplish the purpose (s. 79). Though it seems to be contemplated that elimination plan measures may be incorporated in regulations, there does not appear to be a mechanism for direct enforcement of obligations under virtual elimination plans themselves.

The toxics control part of CEPA 1999 provides the legislative power to create a regulatory system for any substance that fits the broad definition of "toxic" on the basis of standards for quantity, concentration, and place of release of substances, and including prohibitions and regulation of substance disposal. Control is then achieved though the wide array of classic and innovative compliance mechanisms that range from prosecutions to economic instruments and market-based approaches. It is unlikely that these powers would support a permit or approval system. Rather, regulation is through the toxicity assessment process itself—toxics are identified, then managed according to generic standards and requirements prescribed by regulation.

C. Pollution Prevention Plans

The minister of the environment has broad powers to publish notices requiring specified persons to prepare and implement pollution prevention plans for substances or groups of substances that are on the schedule I list of toxic substances or that are likely to cause international air or water pollution. Though there is provision for guidelines and model plans, there is no requirement that plans be submitted to or reviewed by Environment Canada. Preparers are merely required to file a declaration within the specified time that a plan has been prepared and is being implemented and to keep a copy of the plan in their files. Marcia Valiente has lamented the wide ministerial discretion and approach and has characterized these as:

> "a middle ground between a completely voluntary system and a comprehensive mandatory system ... [one that] accepts that industry is the central designer of pollution prevention, but [that fits the] design into a minimal administrative framework."

See M. Valiente, "The Legal Foundations of Canadian Environmental Policy," in D. Van Nijnatten and R. Broadman, eds., *Canadian Environmental Policy*, 2d ed. (Toronto: Oxford University Press, 2002), at 1 and 14.

D. International Air and Water Pollution

The ministers of environment and health are authorized to act to prevent, control, or correct international air or water pollution. This includes substances from a Canadian source likely to create or contribute to pollution in a country other than Canada or to violate an international agreement binding on Canada (CEPA 1999, divisions 6 and 7). There are provisions for consultation with other governments, but, subject to reciprocity with the other country, the minister is ultimately required to take action either by requiring pollution prevention plans or by recommending necessary regulations to Cabinet. Release of substances in contravention of the regulations is prohibited and specific ministerial powers are in place to require proponents of activities likely to produce international pollution to submit plans and specifications, and, if necessary, to issue interim remedial and preventive orders.

E. Economic Instruments

The minister of the environment is authorized to establish "guidelines programs and other measures for the development and use of economic instruments and market-based approaches" (s. 332). There are specific powers to enable the federal Cabinet to make regulations concerning deposits and refunds (s. 325) and tradeable units systems (s. 326).

The latter may provide the authority for the establishment of emission-trading systems for greenhouse gas emission reduction in order to meet international climate change agreement obligations. There is also a provision for regulations concerning fees and charges that may encompass emission fees (s. 328).

F. Enforcement and Compliance Techniques

Apart from market-based techniques such as emissions trading and the citizen "application for investigation" process, which is continued from its predecessor statute, CEPA 1999 includes a range of new and innovative enforcement and compliance techniques. "Environmental protection alternative measures" may be adopted under agreement where an offence of a specified category is alleged to have been committed and the attorney general, after consulting the minister of the environment, is satisfied that this would be appropriate with regard to a series of factors, including the nature of the offence; compliance history; protection of the environment, human life and health, and other interests of society; whether the person charged accepts responsibility; and whether there is sufficient evidence to proceed with a prosecution. Agreements may contain appropriate terms and conditions, including reasonable costs of verifying compliance. Upon filing of an agreement, charges will be stayed or adjourned.

Administrative orders called "environmental protection compliance orders" may be issued by enforcement officers for periods up to 180 days where officers have reasonable grounds to believe that any provision of the Act or the regulations has been contravened (ss. 234-241). Orders may prescribe a range of requirements, including the shutdown of any activity, work, or undertaking for a specified period. Persons to whom orders may be issued are those who own or have charge, management, or control of the contaminant substance in question or the property on which it is located, or who cause or contribute to the alleged contravention.

Provisions for injunction applications by the minister are included (s. 311). Persons suffering loss as a result of conduct that contravenes any provision of the Act may also apply for injunctions (s. 39) or bring civil actions (s. 40) to recover compensation. In addition to these conventional remedies, a new environmental protection action is established. This is a citizen suit provision analogous to similar causes of action under US federal environmental statutes. However, there are conditions that apply to such suits. An action may be brought in any court of competent jurisdiction only by an individual who has applied for an investigation under the Act, and only if the minister has either failed to conduct such investigation within a reasonable time or has made an unreasonable response to such investigation. The action must be against a person who committed an offence under the Act that caused significant harm to the environment. Remedies include declaratory or prohibitory orders, orders requiring action to prevent continuation of the offence, and orders requiring the parties to negotiate a mitigation plan. The standard of proof for the offence and the resulting significant harm is specified to be judged on a balance of probabilities. Defences include due diligence, authorized conduct, and officially induced mistake of law. The court may stay proceedings and award costs, though in deciding to award costs, the court may consider any special circumstances, including whether the action is a test case or raises a novel point of law.

QUESTIONS

1. What is the purpose of the complex CEPA 1999 scheme for assessment and re-scheduling of a toxic substance before regulations can be adopted? Why not list toxic substances in schedule I directly?

2. Are the equivalency provisions of CEPA 1999 likely to prevent duplication and potential inconsistency of CEPA 1999 regulations with provincial legislation? What problems do you foresee?

3. To what extent can CEPA 1999 be used to address global environmental issues such as ocean pollution and global warming? What specific questions should be asked?

IV. ENVIRONMENTAL STANDARDS

In approving contaminant discharges under provincial or federal statutes, decisions must be based on standards established by regulation, or by non-binding guidelines. How are these standards or guidelines established? What is their scientific or technical basis? Do they relate to substances discharged, or to the ambient environment into which the substances are discharged? What is the procedure for standard setting?

In the following extract, these questions are discussed in the context of a generalized model for setting environmental standards. To make legal sense of the model it is necessary to consider how or to what extent it applies to the specific structure, scheme, and requirements of each provincial and federal environmental regulatory statute.

M.A.H. Franson, R.T. Franson, and A.R. Lucas
Environmental Standards
(Edmonton: Environment Council of Alberta, 1982), at 23-47

A Model Procedure for Setting Environmental Standards

What Are Standards?

One of the first barriers that must be overcome is terminological. Writers in different fields clearly mean different things when they write about standards, guidelines, and objectives. Some legal writers distinguish between guidelines and standards, for example, on the basis of their legal impact. For them, a standard is a legally enforceable specification of the amount of pollutant that may be discharged or present in the ambient medium. There is a tendency for the popular press to follow this distinction. In contrast, technical writers would not necessarily follow this distinction. For them, an objective might refer to the particular uses that are desired for the water or air. A standard would specify the amount of contaminant that could be discharged, but it might or might not be legally enforceable. The model we will outline in this report is intended to establish a consistent terminology for the purposes of this report. When we come to evaluate the particular practices and standards of each jurisdiction we shall relate our findings to the terminology we have used in this model.

Definition of Terms

"*Objective*" denotes a goal or purpose toward which an environmental control effort is directed. Examples of objectives are as follows: to preserve and enhance the salmon fishery in these waters; to prevent crop damage caused by air pollution; to protect the public health.

"*Criteria*" are compilations or digests of scientific data that are used to decide whether or not a certain quality of air or water is suitable for the chosen objectives. A simple example of a criterion that might be used to judge the suitability of water quality for a certain species of fish might be:

Concentration of Pollutant	Effect
A mg/L	No adverse effects noted
B mg/L	Lowest level at which sublethal effects noted
C mg/L	Lowest level at which mortalities noted
D mg/L	No survival

"*Standard*" denotes a prescribed numerical value or set of values to which concentrations or amounts actually occurring in the ambient medium or the discharge to that medium may be compared, whether legally enforceable or not. Examples of standards are:

Average concentration of Pollutant X in the air shall not exceed Y micrograms per cubic metre during any 24-hour period. (Ambient)

Maximum daily discharge of Pollutant A from Point Source B shall not exceed Z kg. (Effluent)

How Should Standards Be Set?

The traditional, technically-based approach to setting standards is as follows:

1. Identification of uses of the ambient resource to be protected or *objectives* to be met.
2. Formulation of *criteria* through collection and/or generation of scientific information.
3. Formulation of *ambient quality standards* from the criteria.
4. Development of *effluent standards* for discharges into the environment that will produce a quality meeting the ambient standard.
5. Development of *monitoring and other information-gathering programs* that will refine the data inputs to the previous steps and provide feedback on whether the objectives are being met.

Each of these components in the standards-setting process will be examined in the following sections.

Identification of Objectives

The setting of objectives for pollution control and environmental preservation/ restoration is the keystone of any rational standards-setting process.

Scope and Character of Objectives

Traditionally, selection of objectives has taken the form of identifying uses to be protected, implying human purpose. Surely this is an excellent starting point, and one still widely used in practice, but during the 1970's, with increased scientific and public awareness of ecological principles, it came to be recognized that appropriate objectives might include more than just the very readily identifiable human uses such as water supply, water-based recreation, and fishing in the case of water, and respiration and damage-free agriculture in the case of air. A bold expression of the turning away from a purely anthropocentric approach to water quality objectives was the *US Federal Water Pollution Control Act* of 1972 (PL92-500). In the words of Philip T. Cummings, who was Senate majority counsel for this bill, "One of the organizing principles of the 1972 act ... was that the policy of the government is to restore the integrity of the water. That is not dependent on some judgment about its use but about its original character. That is an ecological principle rather than the economic principle of beneficial use."

In practical terms, however, the objectives of the legislation were expressed in a way closely related to human uses. Section 101 (a)(2) stated that "it is the national goal that wherever attainable, an interim goal of water quality which provides for the protection and propagation of fish, shellfish, and wildlife, and provides for recreation in and on the water be achieved by July 1, 1983." This is the so-called "fishable/swimmable" goal.

Objective-Setting Process

Decisions about objectives for air and water resource quality are fundamentally neither technical nor legal decisions. In a democratic society the objectives should express, as accurately as possible, the collective will and perceptions of all people likely to have some interest in the condition of the resource. While ultimately these expressions must be gathered, evaluated, and summarized by the regulatory authority, the opportunity for public input must be systematically provided for. This suggests that the formulation-of-objectives stage is one of the most important points in the standards-setting process for contact between the regulatory agency and the public. ...

Quality Criteria

Criteria consists of the supporting scientific data that enable us to answer questions such as, "Is this water safe to drink?" "Is the air safe to breathe?" "Can this lake support a healthy trout fishery?" Because of the extremely large number of elements and compounds now contained in our air and water resources and the many ways they affect potential uses of the resources, the answers to these questions can be very complex.

Information Needs

In contrast to the formulation of objectives, the formulation of criteria is strictly a scientific matter. It involves gathering of data on the effects of potential pollutants and combinations of pollutants on the uses in question, and in the absence of data, experimentation to generate such information. This is never a small task, and in the case of the more sensitive objectives, can be formidable indeed, for several reasons. First, the number of substances and other quality parameters that can affect sensitive objectives is very large. According to Loucks in the USSR over 400 harmful substances have been defined for drinking water, and over 60 for fish life. Janardan and Schaeffer state that an estimated 60,000 organic compounds are produced and used by various industries in the US. The number of substances is growing rapidly; many new chemicals are synthesized and thus added to our environment each year. Second, the effect of any substance in the air or water is rarely, if ever, expressible in black-and-white terms. That is, if a certain concentration of a substance clearly causes no harm at all, it is unlikely that a marginally higher concentration will clearly cause substantial harm. Rather, the effects of substances are usually more accurately represented by a continuum from states of nearly perfect safety (or perhaps even necessity in the case of certain trace elements), through states that may cause distress to certain sensitive individuals or species, to those causing more widespread and more severe harmful effects at increasing levels. Some pollutants appear to have a "threshold effect." Third, this approach does not take into account the possibility of synergistic and antagonistic effects among pollutants, that is, the possibility that one or several pollutants may either intensify or counteract the effects of one or several others.

Form of Criteria

An idealized criterion for a particular use would therefore identify a very large number of pollutants and combinations of pollutants, assess the risk of adverse effects occurring at a number of potential levels of those pollutants, and identify and evaluate the risk of effects of pollutant interactions. In practice, such criteria would be enormously difficult to generate, and the expense of doing so could not be justified. On a practical level, therefore, we are limited to formulating criteria on the basis of a limited number of parameters of the greatest and/or most obvious concern, gathering the available information on conditions likely to be clearly harmful, clearly safe, and to lie in the "grey area" between, and considering any interactions that may come to light.

Ambient Quality Standards

The third step is the formulation of ambient quality standards, that is, the prescription of the quality of water or air that is deemed necessary to protect the desired objectives, in the light of scientific knowledge supplied by the criteria and of socioeconomic factors affecting the control of pollution. Ambient standards may set upper limits on the mass or concentration of harmful substances, may set lower limits on the presence of desired substances such as dissolved oxygen, or may prescribe a range of desirable value (e.g., for pH). The values may be specified as averages over some given time period, extreme values never to be exceeded, or values that may be exceeded only for specified time periods.

    The setting of ambient standards is not fundamentally a technical decision. Even if one assumes that the criteria provide a very complete technical background for decision, the standards set inevitably reflect value judgments. This is an important point, and one that has often been misunderstood.

Technical Evaluation

This phase of the standard setting will require specialized input not only from scientists but also from economists and experts in various industries. All this is not to say that the evaluation of benefits and costs should be limited to this input from the "experts"—it is well recognized that intangible and nonquantifiable benefits and costs will result from a water quality decision. These are recognized at a later stage of the process.

The output of this technical evaluation stage will be a number of alternative water quality standards, with an evaluation of each in terms of how well it meets the proposed objectives, what risks it poses to the achievement of the objectives, and the benefits and costs that are likely to flow from the achievement of that standard. Each alternative standard will include recommended limits on the parameters relevant to the uses being protected. When these alternatives are being formulated, attention must be paid to two other practical problems ... . First, does the standard, determined largely from laboratory study and the literature, make sense in the real world? For example, is it possible to conceive of a situation in which a body of water would be in regular violation of standards developed, on the basis of good technical data, to protect fish life, and yet be found to support a healthy fish population of the desired type? Second, is the proposed standard measurable by methods currently available for practical field use? A nonmeasurable standard not only cannot be enforced, but actually invites violation and disrespect of the entire regulatory process.

[T]he primary purpose of water quality standards is to maximize the level of protection of beneficial uses, and the second purpose is to minimize the cost of meeting the standards, and the job of the standards-setting body is to balance these conflicting objectives in a way that yields the greatest net social benefits. At this point in the process, the standards-setting agency has in hand (or should) the best information that the physical, biological, and social sciences can provide.

Political Choice Process

Information needs. If the regulatory agency has already done an effective job of securing public input into the setting of objectives, some information about public preferences may already be at hand. However, it may be appropriate to give members of the public and interest groups a further opportunity to consider and comment explicitly on proposed standards, to react to information generated in the technical evaluation, to bring forward new data that may not have been accessible to those performing the technical evaluation, to state preferences concerning hard- or impossible-to-quantify matters such as aesthetic and spiritual values, and to give views on the acceptability of the risks inherent in the various proposed standards and willingness to pay for necessary measures. Also, in situations where ambient quality is largely governed by the quality of effluent from one or very few sources, the setting of ambient quality standards becomes, in effect, also the setting of effluent quality standards, and the equity and bargaining considerations outlined more fully below may be aired at this stage.

Risk acceptability. The acceptability of a risk may depend not only on the character of the use that is at risk, but also on the attributes of the risk itself. Jacobson has constructed a table illustrating this point (Table II). These considerations, applied by Jacobson to the case of risks associated with acid rain, could be applied equally to other pollution situations. Consider, for example, the case of a body of water supporting a fishery that is threatened by a waterborne discharge. Consideration of the economic importance of the fishery to the community will indicate a pressure toward a higher standard if the fishery is vital to the sustenance of a native community or if income from tourists who visit the area for fishing is an economic factor in the community, than if it is used only for recreational purposes by local people. Given, however, that *one* of these situations is the case, for example, that the fishery is vital to, and used only by, a native community, Jacobson's analysis predicts that more protection against risk will be demanded if, for example, the type of damage predicted is rare, that is, alien to experience and therefore fear-inducing, rather than common, or if the pollution would come from an industrial plant owned by outsiders (innocent party at risk) rather than from the community's own waste collection system (polluter at risk).

Table II. Public Acceptance of Environmental Risks

Less Acceptable	*More Acceptable*
Catastrophic	Subtle
Imminent	Deferred
Permanent	Temporary
Irreversible	Recoverable
Probable	Unlikely
Rare	Common
Obvious	Intangible
Unpredictable	Predictable
Abstruse	Understood
Quantifiable	Nonquantifiable
Global	Localized
Involuntary	Voluntary
Consequence of human action	Consequence of natural processes
Innocent party	Polluter at risk

(Reproduced with permission from (1981) vol. 31 *Journal of the Air Pollution Control Association* 1071.)

Benefit–cost judgments. Here too is a point at which the public can comment on whether the protection of certain uses or the maintenance of a certain quality is "worth it." Several situations recently outlined in the Vancouver press may be combined to illustrate the choices that are available. In the first instance it was reported that air pollution caused by the coincidence of an inversion layer in the atmosphere with a weekend during which outdoor burning of leaves and other garden debris was permitted resulted in problems for area residents with asthma or air passages that are easily irritated. Another study told of two women whose allergies to environmental pollutants were so severe that they routinely use gas masks when near the fumes given off by cars. Consider, then, two proposed sets of air quality standards, the first intended to make the air safe and comfortable to breathe, even for those suffering from asthma, emphysema, etc., at nearly all times, to be implemented by alternatives to outdoor burning such as extra municipal pickups for garden debris, the second intended to make the air safe even for those with extreme environmental allergies, to be implemented by such measures as ending outdoor burning plus retrofitting of pollution-control devices on older autos and increased controls on stationary industrial sources. The first standard probably would be perceived as desirable, because the benefits would be fairly widespread, including many of the elderly, and the costs fairly modest. The second standard probably would be rejected as benefiting too few and imposing large costs on the vast majority. Somewhere in between lies the level that a broad cross section of the public might feel is a correct balance.

Effluent Standards

The object of the next stage of the standards-setting process is to move from a statement of the desired condition of the air or water to standards defining limits on discharges to the resource that will permit the desired state to be attained. Ambient standards and effluent standards sometimes have been regarded as alternative approaches to regulation, but this view is incorrect. The approaches are supplementary and each is necessary; an ambient standard alone is unenforceable because it gives no indication of cause and effect nor any guidance to either regulatory body or the regulated about the necessary courses of action, and an effluent standard lacking a basis in an ambient quality goal has no reasonable foundation in reality—it is the equivalent of the parental "Because I said so!"

Like the setting of ambient standards the setting of effluent standards requires both technical and nontechnical input.

Technical Considerations

Mathematical models. The science and art of constructing mathematical models to relate ambient quality to inputs of pollutants and to pollutant removal mechanisms inherent in the resource has made large advances over the last several decades. Before the widespread use of computers for such simulations, the possibilities for modelling were very limited and were restricted to cases involving only a few pollutants, sources of pollution inputs, and simple removal mechanisms. Present-day knowledge enables regulatory agencies to take account of more types of pollutants, a greater number of sources within an airshed or watershed, and more sophisticated behaviours of pollutants once they have entered the resource. The literature on the construction and use of mathematical models for investigations of air and water quality control is voluminous, and no attempt will be made here to review it. The regulatory agency will choose among the available approaches according to the complexity of the situation, the ease of gathering input data necessary for application of the model to the situation, and the ability of the model to produce results that approximate closely conditions in the "real world."

Many of the mathematical models used for pollution control have been intended to minimize an objective function, usually the cost of control measures, subject to a set of constraints, the most important of which is the desired quality of the pollution-receiving resource. Other constraints may include minimum treatment requirements, uniformity of treatment requirements, and prohibition of certain methods of treatment.

The greater utility of mathematical models lies not in that they give one "correct" answer, but that they permit, with very modest expenditures of extra time and money, sensitivity analyses that can yield much information about the response of the cost function to changes in the input data, the assumptions about pollutant behaviour and fate, or the constraints, and can therefore generate a number of options for further consideration.

The end product of the modelling process, therefore, will be, for an already-determined ambient quality standard, one or more sets of constraints with the attendant values generated by the model for the quality of each point source of pollutants and the costs entailed.

Form of the effluent standard. Popel has pointed out that fixed standards, i.e., standards expressed by one fixed value that is never to be exceeded, are not appropriate measures for water pollution control, because a fixed standard will always be exceeded, with the probability of exceedence decreasing with increased laxity of the standard. His analysis can be applied to air pollution as well. The input parameters for treatment facilities are highly variable because of variations in the processes generating the wastes, and these input variations may cause differences in response of the treatment process, amplifying the variations. Popel suggests that the appropriate measure is a combined standard consisting of a standard value and a permissible probability of excedence, and that stratified random sampling of effluent data be used for control. The combined standard also has the advantage of using all the data collected in judging conformity of effluent quality to standard, not merely the highest single value in a time period, and thus provides a more truly representative idea of compliance. This does not, of course, suggest that extreme values be disregarded altogether, because these values can be quite critical in their effects.

Coordination of control efforts in various media. Another technical consideration, and one that is often overlooked and sometimes very difficult to perform because of the lack of administrative mechanisms for doing so, is the coordination of pollution control efforts to protect air, water, and land. Pollutants removed from a waste source must still be disposed of somewhere, somehow. Some methods of pollutant removal and disposal may amount to little more than intermedia transfers of problems. Consider, for example, an aqueous effluent treatment system that produces an effluent meeting standards for discharge to a receiving water as well as a sludge containing high concentrations of toxic chemicals. The sludge may be incinerated, with release of toxics to the air, or disposed of on land in such a way that the toxics may be leached out and returned to an aqueous environment. An effective means of accounting for such side-effects may be to rule out certain types of disposal options, such as sludge incineration, in constructing the mathematical models, when it appears that they may lead to substantial side effects.

Feasibility of effluent standard compliance. Like ambient standards, effluent standards generally should be set at levels that make the monitoring of compliance possible. However, in the case where serious reservations exist about the safety of extremely low or even non-detectable amounts of a substance, a very low or even "no-discharge" standard may be set and the cooperation of industry in the form of process change and of other government entities in restricting sale or use of the substance may be sought. Garber, in a paper deeply critical of the effects of US PL 92-500 on waste discharge practices of the City of Los Angeles, cites the following case: The imposed limit on mercury in discharges to the ocean off California implies an average contribution of only 0.4 mg mercury per person per day in the population of three million served by the main municipal treatment plant. It is Garber's opinion that the personal use of medicinals such as merthiolate and mercurochrome would be significant in this context, and that achievement of this effluent standard would require a legislative ban on these and other commonly-used products containing mercury. A ban so widely affecting commerce would, of course, be well beyond the powers of local authorities in Canada as well as the US. When faced with a dilemma such as this, the regulatory authority may consider re-thinking its proposed standards, making sure that they have a firm basis in scientific data, and, if a very stringent standard still seems called for after re-examination, may wish to set a more lenient interim standard and reserve pressure for conformity with the more stringent standard until conformity is in fact possible. An alternative means for controlling substances that may be present in industrial discharges in less-than-detectable concentrations is that of requiring the industry to submit periodic materials balances for the questionable substances. Quantities of the substances accounted for in waste products, plus any unaccounted-for differences between amounts acquired and amounts in output, would be presumed to have been discharged to the environment.

Nontechnical Considerations

Equity. The fundamental fairness of pollution control regulation is an important issue at this stage of the standards-setting process. As Lyon stated in 1965, "In any democratic country regulatory activity is attuned to the concept of equity. This concept is found in many other regulatory endeavours and is one that is always the approach most likely to gain general public acceptance. It is also a concept which very often is difficult to explain or justify in scientific terms."

Bargaining. A final non-technical consideration in the process of setting effluent standards is the bargaining process between the regulators and the regulated. While this is only one consideration at the final stage of the rational model of idealized standards-setting discussed in this section, it is, according to Thompson, actually the essence of the regulatory process in Canada. He states that "no matter how normative measures are expressed in a statute—whether as policy guidelines or as command prohibitions—the end result in the case of environmental regulation is a bargaining process."

The bargaining process also can act as an interface between the technology and economics of pollution control, which until this stage have been considered in isolation, and the economies of the country and the world. Because of the perceived need for confidentiality about financial matters, this may be the first opportunity given to the regulatory authority to consider the effects of proposed effluent standards and prospective expenditures on a particular discharger's competitive position within the Canadian economy, and, if standards for an entire industry are being set, to consider collectively that industry's position in the world market.

Finally, the bargaining process can vividly draw attention to the weak points of the scientific and economic information supporting the standards-setting process. Often, bargaining will take place precisely because such weak points exist and leave room for maneuvering.

Beyond the Effluent Quality Standard— Technology-Based Effluent Standards

Technology-based effluent and emission standards are defined by Freeman as "quantitative" limits placed on all dischargers, where quantities are determined by reference to the available technology defined in terms of what is "practical," "possible," or "achievable." These limits are designated without reference to any ambient standards, balance of benefits and costs, or other guiding principles.

The reasons for the adoption of the technology based approach are many and complex. One group of reasons centres around the practical difficulties of using a water-quality-based model of the regulatory process. Here are a few brief excerpts from the comments of some of the men who guided this approach into legislation: "One of the major problems with water quality standards was ... the fact that they were unenforceable." "The reason why water quality standards were not enforceable is that, at that time, and I think it is still true today, it was impossible to infer from stream characteristics, water quality, goals, standards ... . By and large, water quality standards were measured in terms of four pollutants—biochemcial oxygen demand, suspended solids, fecal coliform, and pH. There was a growing recognition in 1972 that they weren't sufficient." Freeman observes that technology-based standards are usually perceived as simplifying matters. A less kind observation might paraphrase the attitude as, "It's too hard to do it right, so let's not even try."

The other pressures leading to the adoption of technology-based standards were more political and related to the specific conditions in the US in 1972. Again, these same Congressional staffers: "... there were a number of things that were going on in the area of water pollution control that set the stage for another congressional look at the subject. Among these was the concern that abatement was not proceeding at the pace that anybody would consider acceptable under the *Water Quality Act* of 1965 ... . Another perception was more a function of the general political climate of that time. Earth Day ... brought about a general concern that the government at all levels was not doing enough for environmental quality ... ."

While some of the motivation came from the philosophical position that disposal of wastes is not a legitimate "use" for water resources, by far the greatest part seems to have come from the perceived need to adopt an uncomplicated approach that would produce results—fast.

How has it worked? Apparently, not too well. According to Freeman, the benefits claimed for this approach have been largely illusory. From the standpoint of how quickly water quality has improved, he says, this approach was not necessarily more successful than the water quality based approach because it has had its own problems in information gathering, procedural delays, and legal challenges. Language such as "best practical" and "reasonable cost" leaves a great deal to administrative discretion and leaves the door open to bargaining. Numerous issues have arisen: Should "exemplary" plants or a cross section of existing plants be used to determine "practicable" standards? Should guidelines give specific numerical values? Should in plant process changes be considered? So much for simplicity and quick results.

Another difficulty is that technology-based standards discourage innovation in treatment processes and encourage reliance on the prescribed technologies even when they seem unlikely to produce the desired quality of effluent. The latter is a particularly important point from the standpoint of enforcement, because a discharger that can demonstrate that in good faith it relied on the required technology is in a fairly safe position even should its effluent cause identifiable problems.

The following extract illustrates (in the case of Ontario) how the standard-setting process fits into the legislative framework.

Canadian Environmental Law Association and Ontario College of Family Physicians "Environmental Standard Setting and Children's Health"
(Toronto: CELA and OCFP Environmental Health Committee—Children's Health Project, 2000), at 3-4, 107-8, and 174-77

Risk Assessment and the Precautionary Principle

[This section is a] critical review of the theoretical foundations of standard setting, namely the processes of risk assessment and risk management. The focus is on the use of risk assessment for deriving health-referenced standards. By the late 1970s, risk assessment became the regulatory tool of choice that increasingly replaced early decision-making that, in some cases, banned very hazardous substances (such as DDT and PCBs) due to their inherent toxicity. Instead, risk assessment enabled continued use of toxic chemicals at scientifically sanctioned "acceptable" levels. During the process of bringing risk assessment in greater synchrony with the increased knowledge of environmental health issues, attention has focused on continually refining rather than replacing risk assessment. Criticisms and some fundamental limitations of the system have been identified for well over 10 years and have yet to be adequately addressed. One of the first problems identified was the disproportionate focus in risk assessment towards managing cancer risks. It was not until the mid-1980s that the US Environmental Protection Agency (EPA) began to add some consideration of developmental risks into its risk assessment protocol. More fundamental limitations concern the numerous stages wherein inference and judgment are applied to compensate for large gaps in data and methodologies rendering risk assessment anything but a wholly objective scientific exercise.

Critical problems with risk assessment surround the characterization of exposure and dose-response. For the vast majority of chemicals, we do not know exactly how much of a particular substance, or combination of substances, to which people will be exposed in the course of its/their use, emission and path through the environment. It is also exceedingly difficult to determine what the relationship is between the amount that reaches the tissues and the response of the body to that dose.

More fundamentally, risk assessment enables risk calculations that allow for "acceptable" levels of chemical exposure that may cause one-in-a-million or one-in-ten-thousand risks (of cancer, birth defects, etc.) across a population. However, this game of odds becomes useless if further research confirms the suspicion that chemicals such as endocrine disruptors are capable of exerting population-wide effects at current levels of exposure. Nor is it appropriate to make such calculations for chemicals that are persistent and bioaccumulative. Risks will continue to increase for chemicals that do not break down and which accumulate in animal fat, breast milk, etc. Such risks will affect some people more seriously than others depending on the flow of persistent chemicals through the environment. The predicted avenues of exposure and the health endpoints that are used to assess risk clearly have implications for the ability of ensuing policy decisions to protect children's health.

Provincial Regulation

Ontario's *Environmental Protection Act* (*EPA*) is the principal statute governing air quality in the province. It establishes a general prohibition against discharging contaminants into the natural environment in excess of the amounts permitted by the regulations. "Contaminant" is defined to include a substance that causes an "adverse effect." "Adverse effect" is defined to include, among other things, "harm or material discomfort to any person"; "an adverse effect on the health of any person" and "impairment of the safety of any person." Because of the regulations, emissions may be permitted in accordance with a Certificate of Approval issued by the Ministry of the Environment (MOE). Specific provisions are provided for Certificates of Approval for all stationary sources that emit, or have the potential to emit outdoor air contamination. Certificates of Approval are legally-binding licences that set out the conditions under which a facility can operate, including maximum permissible contaminant emission levels. The Ministry of the Environment has established standards and guidelines that inform the setting of these emission limits, as described below.

Ambient Air Quality Criteria

Ambient Air Quality Criteria (AAQC) are established under the EPA and limit total atmospheric contaminant levels. The Criteria are established for different time periods and set the maximum average contaminant concentration that is permissible during a particular time period. Hence, a one hour AAQ Criterion for a contaminant would limit the average atmospheric quantity of the contaminant that is present during a one-hour period at a particular point or receptor. AAQC are based on either human health or environmental effects, whichever is the most sensitive, and are normally set at a level that is not expected to cause adverse effects to a sensitive receptor, based on continuous exposure. Consequently, socio-economic factors including costs and technological feasibility are not considered in the setting of an AAQC. If odour or irritant effects are experienced at levels below health effects, then the AAQC are established based on that more sensitive impact. The Criteria are not themselves standards, but they may become indirectly enforceable by way of being included in a particular Certificate of Approval issued to a particular applicant for a specific facility or mobile source. Where relevant, they are used to guide the setting of individual Certificate of Approval limits. Where National Ambient Air Quality Objectives (see below) exist, they inform the setting of AAQC. The Canada Wide Standards [CWS] process under CCME has largely usurped development of additional National Ambient Air Quality Objectives (NAAQO), in the sense that the federal government is devoting its resources to the CWS process although the authority to enact NAAQO is still in place. The Ontario Ministry of the Environment expects that in the future as new standards are developed, ... all of the criteria will be adopted as standards and there will no longer be air "guidelines" in use. This approach will be more consistent with current practice and more consistent with enforceability requirements.

Point of Impingement Standards

Regulation 346 under the EPA sets out Point of Impingement (POI) standards for non-vehicular contaminant sources. These legally-binding standards limit the contaminant content of the emissions that are produced by individual facilities. A point of impingement is the location at which a contaminant first makes contact with a sensitive receptor following emission. The receptor may be human, animal or plant. For any given emission source, there exist multiple points of impingement, as the contaminant reaches different receptors (people, plants, wildlife) that are situated at different distances and in different directions form the emission source. Schedule 1 to Regulation 346 establishes Point of Impingement limits for a number of contaminants. These standards are maximum average contaminant concentrations that are permitted over a half hour period at the Point of Impingement. They may not be exceeded unless an emission source is explicitly exempted by regulation.

Regulation 346 sets out, in its Appendix, formulae to calculate the concentration of a contaminant at the different possible points of impingement, depending on variables including source concentration and a range of relevant environmental conditions, such as weather. In order to determine if it is in compliance with POI standards, an industry calculates its POI concentrations using these formulae, for the range of points of impingement that are relevant to its situation. The industry then compares the *highest* POI contaminant concentration calculated with the Regulation 346 standard.

Once an Ambient Air Quality Criterion is developed for a particular contaminant, it is used by the MOE to set a Point of Impingement standard, via a series of established mathematical relationships. For example, a 24 hour AAQ Criterion is multiplied by 3 in order to derive a 24 hour POI limit. Similarly, an annual AAQ Criterion is multi-plied by a factor of 15 to determine the annual POI limit. According to the MOE, these relationships between AAQC and POI standards are well developed. The limi-tation of this method, however, is that it fails to consider background contaminant levels. In other words, it works well for an individual facility, but does not take into account the emissions produced by other facilities. It does not guarantee, therefore, that if the POI limits derived in this manner were met by all contaminant sources, that the AAQ Criterion for total atmospheric contaminant levels would also be satisfied. According to the MOE, this is only a concern for a few contaminants such as nitrous oxides and particulate matter, where background levels are significant. For other con-taminants, background levels are apparently minimal. However, it should be noted that among the contaminants of greatest concern for respiratory impacts on children are nitrous oxide and particulates.

Because POI standards apply to existing sources, some socio-economic issues are sometimes considered by the MOE in their development. The MOE considers whether the POI standards are "technically feasible" and whether the "costs" of implementa-tion are balanced by their "benefits." However, new sources may be required to be built to the more recent POI standards where applicable.

Point of Impingement Guidelines

The provincial Ministry also makes use of Impingement Guidelines. Like POI stand-ards, they are used to review Certificate of Approval applications and to approve new and modified emission sources. However, in contrast to POI standards, they do not automatically apply to emission sources and are only legally-binding when incorpo-rated into a Certificate of Approval. While POI standards are developed for substances that are identified as being of relatively greater risk to human health and the environ-ment, based on release quantities, the number of sources, and the potential for expo-sure at levels that may cause adverse effects, guidelines apply to substances that are released from relatively few sources and which the Ministry has determined are best managed on a case-by-case basis. POI guidelines are generally set to avoid adverse human health and environmental effects and accordingly, are not informed by socio-economic factors. As indicated above, the MOE expects to move toward use of stand-ards only as the newer standards are developed.

[There is also a standard-setting process at the federal and intergovernmental level. This is in context of the Canada-Wide Accord on Environmental Harmonization, which has been developed and managed by the CCME. The accord and its environ-mental standards subagreement are described as follows in the Children's Health Project report, at 107-8.]

Canada-Wide Accord on Environmental Harmonization

In 1993, the CCME identified harmonization of environmental management in Canada as a top priority and developed the Canada-Wide Accord on Environmental Harmonization ... . On January 29, 1998, all jurisdictions except for Quebec signed the

Accord. While not a statute, the Accord holds the potential to have a dramatic impact on the way that standards are developed at both the federal and provincial levels.

The Accord is a multilateral umbrella agreement, whose intent is to provide a framework for achieving harmonization. It provides a framework for the development of ancillary Sub-agreements on specific areas of environmental management.

[One of these subagreements is the Canada-Wide Environmental Standards Sub-Agreement.]

Canada-Wide Environmental Standards Sub-Agreement:
Canada-Wide Standards

The Canada-Wide Environmental Standards Sub-agreement "set out the principles underpinning the development of Canada-wide Standards (CWS) for environmental quality and human health, and commits the governments to participate in their development. Such standards could include guidelines and objectives, as well as legally enforceable standards." The focus of the Sub-agreement is on "ambient standards, so that all Canadians can expect a common high degree of environmental quality." Ambient standards are described as levels of environmental quality for specific media (for example, air, water, soils, or sediment).

One of the stated underpinnings of the development and attainment of Canada-wide Environmental Standards is the Precautionary Principle. The agreement states that, "where there are threats of serious or irreversible environmental damage, lack of full scientific certainty shall not be used as a reason for postponing the development and implementation of standards."

The Sub-agreement "calls for governments to establish priorities for the development of CWSs and to allow for public involvement." The priority setting phase consists of three stages; nomination, screening, and selection.

In November of 1999, the ministers agreed on draft Canada-Wide Standards for four priority pollutants: particulate matter; ground-level ozone; benzene; and mercury. Ministers agreed to take the standards back to their Cabinet colleagues, who have six months to consult on these before they are finalized and formally adopted at the CCME meeting in the spring of 2000.

Provincially, Ontario has posted three Notices of Proposal for Policy on its *Environmental Bill of Rights* Registry Web Site. Particulate Matter and Ozone are combined in one proposal, while Benzene and Mercury each have their own proposal. Consultations are occurring in early 2000 ... .

Currently, additional CWSs are under development for dioxins and furans; petroleum hydrocarbons; mercury from other sources; and benzene in air.

QUESTIONS

1. What are the advantages and disadvantages of specifying contaminant standards in regulations and making the breach of any standard an offence? If standards are directly enforceable in this way, should they be in the form of ambient standards or effluent standards? Would it be more efficient and effective not to specify standards in regulations,

and instead publish standards in guideline form, so that they may be adopted, if appropriate, as terms and conditions in operating licences or approvals?

2. What form should public participation in standard setting take? Should public
hearings be held? If so, at what stage or stages of the process? Would it suffice to invite
interested individuals or groups to submit written comments on proposed standards? If
standard setting does involve some form of government–industry bargaining, is there a
place for public involvement?

3. How can federal Canada-wide standards be implemented and enforced under provincial regulatory statutes?

V. INTERPRETATION OF ENVIRONMENTAL STATUTES

1. The ordinary principles of statutory interpretation, which involve reading the relevant words in their entire context and in their grammatical and ordinary sense harmoni-
ously with the scheme and object of the Act and the intention of Parliament, apply to the
interpretation of environmental legislation.

2. Since the scope of discretionary powers under environmental statutes is often at
issue, purpose clauses assume particular importance.

In *Quebec (AG) v. Canada (NEB)* (1994), 14 CELR (NS) 1, at 30 (SCC), Iabobucci J said:

> I am of the view that the Court of Appeal erred in limiting the scope of the National Energy
> Board's environmental inquiry to the effects on the environment of the transmission of
> power by a line of wire across the border. To limit the effects considered to those resulting
> from the physical act of transmission is an unduly narrow interpretation of the activity
> contemplated by the arrangements in question. The narrowness of this view of the Board's
> inquiry is emphasized by the detailed regulatory process that has been created. I would find
> it surprising that such an elaborate review process would be created for such a limited
> inquiry. As the Court of Appeal in this case recognized, electricity must be produced, either
> through existing facilities or the construction of new ones, in order for an export contract to
> be fulfilled. Ultimately, it is proper for the Board to consider in its decision-making process
> the overall environmental costs of granting the licence sought.

3. "Environmental quality" was interpreted as including social as well as biophysical
elements in *Friends of the Oldman River Society v. Canada (Minister of Transport)*
(1992), 7 CELR (NS) 1, at 25 (SCC), where La Forest J stated:

> I cannot accept that the concept of environmental quality is confined to the biophysical
> environment alone; such an interpretation is unduly myopic and contrary to the generally
> held view that the "environment" is a diffuse subject matter: See: *R v. Crown Zellerbach
> Canada Ltd.*, [1988] 1 SCR 401, 3 CELR (NS) 1, 25 BCLR (2d) 145, 40 CCC (3d) 289, 48
> DLR (4th) 151, 84 NR 1. The point was made by the Canadian Council of Resource and
> Environment Ministers, following the "Brundtland Report" of the World Commission on
> Environment and Development, in the *Report of the National Task Force on Environment
> and Economy*, September 24, 1987, at 2:

> > Our recommendations reflect the principles that we hold in common with the
> > World Commission on Environment and Development (WCED). These include the

fundamental belief that environmental and economic planning cannot proceed in separate spheres. Long-term economic growth depends on a healthy environment. It also affects the environment in many ways. Ensuring environmentally sound and sustainable economic development requires the technology and wealth that is generated by continued economic growth. Economic and environmental planning and management must therefore be integrated.

Surely the potential consequences for a community's livelihood, health and other social matters from environmental change are integral to decision-making on matters affecting environmental quality, subject, of course, to the constitutional imperatives, an issue I will address later.

4. The Supreme Court of Canada in the *Friends of the Oldman River* case held that the effect of the federal Environmental Assessment Review Process (EARP) Guidelines Order (subsequently replaced by the *Canadian Environmental Assessment Act*) was to add environmental factors to the decision criteria mentioned in s. 5 of the *Navigable Waters Protection Act*, notwithstanding that the Guidelines Order was merely delegated legislation and that it did not explicitly add environmental decision criteria to any powers under federal statutes. The issue was treated by the court as one of consistency between the Guidelines Order and the *Navigable Waters Protection Act* approval power. The test stated was whether the two statutes are contradictory, and the doctrinal similarity to the principle of paramountcy in constitutional division of powers cases was noted. According to La Forest J, broad interpretation of the Guidelines Order was consistent with its objectives and those of its parent *Department of the Environment Act* provisions—to make environmental assessment an essential component of federal decision making (see chapter 6, Environmental Assessment).

5. The contextual approach to statutory interpretation includes, as L'Heureux-Dubé J observed in *114957 Canada Ltée (Spraytech, Société d'arrosage) v. Hudson (Town)*, above, respecting the relevant values and principles enshrined in both customary and conventional international law. She concluded that there may be sufficient state practice to support arguments that the precautionary principle is a principle of customary international law. Thus, the principle must be respected in determining whether s. 410 of the Quebec *Cities and Towns Act*, RSQ, c. C-19, which empowered municipalities to pass bylaws for the "peace, order, good government, health and welfare ... of the municipality" authorized a pesticides bylaw that included a prohibition on pesticide use.

6. In *R v. Jopp Ventures Corp.* (2001), 40 CELR (NS) 262 (BCSC), the court rejected the trial judge's conclusion that charges of introducing "waste" into the environment against the Jopp composting operation, which collected organic materials including packaging, lumber, construction debris, manure, and yard cuttings, composted these materials and sold the compost, should be dismissed because these materials were recyclable and thus not "waste" under the Act or were "yard waste" and not "municipal solid waste."

Under the British Columbia *Waste Management Act*, RSBC 1996, c. 482, s. 1(1),

"waste" means
    (a) air contaminants,
    (b) litter,

(c) effluent,

(d) refuse,

(e) biomedical waste;

(f) special wastes, and

(g) any other substance designated by the Lieutenant Governor in Council,

whether or not the type of waste referred to in paragraphs (a) to (f) or designated under paragraph (g) has any commercial value or is capable of being used for a useful purpose;

"municipal solid waste" means

(a) refuse that originates from residential, commercial, institutional, demolition, land clearing or construction sources, ... [and]

"recycled material" means

(a) compostable waste, other than wood waste, from residential, commercial and institutional sources,

(b) used white goods,

(c) auto hulks,

(d) used tires,

(e) used lead acid batteries,

(f) used glass containers,

(g) used tin plated steel containers,

(h) used aluminum containers,

(i) used cardboard packaging,

(j) used newspapers and magazines,

(k) used high density polyethylene containers, and

(l) any substance prescribed as a recyclable material by the Lieutenant Governor in Council.

Under s. 1 of the *Compost Regulation*, BC reg. 334/93,

"composting facility" means a municipal solid waste management facility or a yard waste management facility where the waste is processed using composting technology ... ;

"yard waste" means vegetative matter resulting from gardening, horticulture, landscaping or land clearing operations, including materials such as tree and shrub trimmings, plant remains, grass clippings, trees and stumps, but does not include demolition waste, contaminated organic matter or significant amounts of animal feces.

Smith J followed the British Columbia Court of Appeal's decision in *British Columbia (Minister of Environment, Lands and Parks) v. Alpha Manufacturing Inc.* (1997), 150 DLR 193, in which Esson JA said, at para. 18:

[u]ndoubtedly there can be situations in which discarded material is put through some form of treatment or some process which alters its character and characteristics to the point where it could no longer be classified as waste. In this case, the discarded material was subjected to a process to make it suitable to be used as foundation material by giving it the requisite degree of solidity and by ... "preventing pollution of the local environment." That process, in my view, did not alter its character as discarded material so as to take it out of the category of waste ... .

He also noted the definition of "municipal solid waste" and concluded that

> [t]he trial judge was wrong in relation to "municipal solid waste," which is given a defini-
> tive, restrictive meaning by the words "means ... refuse that originates from residential,
> commercial, institutional, demolition, land clearing or construction sources": see: Driedger,
> EA, *Construction of Statutes*, 2d ed. (Toronto: Butterworths, 1983) ... . Accordingly, her
> conclusion—that refuse emanating from commercial sources is not municipal solid waste if
> it is compostable—is not supportable because compostable refuse is not excluded from the
> definition of municipal solid waste.

According to Smith J, the trial judge also erred in concluding that the materials in
question were "yard waste" and not "municipal solid waste" because

> s. 2(5) of the *Compost Regulation* provides:
>
>> (5) A person who produces or uses compost in accordance with this regulation is
>> exempt from section 3(2) ... of the Act.
>
> Obviously, the legislative intent is that "yard waste" is "waste" under the Act. Otherwise,
> there would be no need to exempt it from the operation of s. 3(2) of the Act.

Further, the trial judge's interpretation of "yard waste" was found to be "strained"
under the fundamental purposive approach to statutory interpretation in view of the
Waste Management Act's underlying policy of controlling, ameliorating, and, where
possible, eliminating the deleterious effects of pollution.

VI. THE QUASI-CRIMINAL OFFENCE MODEL

A. Overview of the Fisheries Act

The other major federal environmental regulatory regime is that under the *Fisheries Act*
(see K. Webb, *Pollution Control in Canada: The Regulatory Approach in the 1980s*
(Ottawa: Law Reform Commission of Canada, 1988)). Under this regulatory system,
which establishes industry-specific regulatory limits for contaminant discharges, greater
emphasis continues to be given to enforcement through prosecution of quasi-criminal
offences. Quasi-criminal offences or "strict enforcement" are a traditional and fundamental
element of the provincial regulatory model outlined above. They are therefore examined
in this chapter, while the broader range of enforcement and compliance policies and
instruments are considered in chapter 9. Though the vehicle used here is the main offence
provision under the federal *Fisheries Act*, analogous legal issues arise in the case of
offences under the provincial regulatory statutes, and some of these are considered below.

The *Fisheries Act* includes several classic regulatory offence provisions and there is a
long history of prosecution of these offences. In fact, there is even a dedicated report
series, the Fisheries Pollution Reports (FPR) (available on the Web at Environmental
Law Centre, http://www.elc.ab.ca/) that was initiated by the enforcement section of
Environment Canada in the 1970s.

In the following section, these *Fisheries Act* offence provisions are adopted as models
to look at a range of interpretive and evidentiary issues that have arisen in prosecutions
under these sections; emphasis will be on s. 36(3).

B. The Major Offences

Harmful alteration, etc., of fish habitat

35(1) No person shall carry on any work or undertaking that results in the harmful alteration, disruption or destruction of fish habitat.

Alteration, etc., authorized

(2) No person contravenes subsection (1) by causing the alteration, disruption or destruction of fish habitat by any means or under any conditions authorized by the Minister or under regulations made by the Governor in Council under this Act.

Deposit of deleterious substance prohibited

36(3) Subject to subsection (4), no person shall deposit or permit the deposit of a deleterious substance of any type in water frequented by fish or in any place under any conditions where the deleterious substance or any other deleterious substance that results from the deposit of the deleterious substance may enter any such water.

Deposits authorized by regulation

(4) No person contravenes subsection (3) by depositing or permitting the deposit in any water or place of

(a) waste or pollutant of a type, in a quantity and under conditions authorized by regulations applicable to that water or place made by the Governor in Council under any Act or other than this Act; or

(b) a deleterious substance of a class, in a quantity or concentration and under conditions authorized by or pursuant to regulations applicable to that water or place or to any work or undertaking or class thereof, made by the Governor in Council under subsection (5).

Note the elements of the s. 36(3) offence that must be proven by the Crown beyond a reasonable doubt. They are

1. a person (natural or artificial)
2. deposited (act) or permitted the deposit of (omission)
3. a deleterious substance
4. in water frequented by fish "or in a place or under conditions where such deleterious substance or another deleterious substance that results from the deposit may enter water frequented by fish."

"Deposit" is defined as any "discharging, spraying, spilling, leaking, seeping, pouring, emitting, emptying, throwing, dumping or placing" (s. 34(1)).

- Does this include only intentional deposits?
- Is dredging contaminated material from a waterbody and depositing it in another part of the waterbody a "deposit"? (See *Société pour Vaincre La Pollution v. Canada (Minister of Finance)* (1997), 22 CELR (NS) 64 (FCTD)).
- What about when silt stirred up from a stream bed by the operation of heavy equipment in the water settles on fish eggs located on another part of the stream bed? (See *R v. Stearns-Roger Engineering Co.*, [1974] 3 WWR 285; 1 FPA Pt. 1-1 (BCCA)).

"Deleterious substance" is defined in s. 34(1)(a) as any substance that,

if added to any water[, would] degrade or alter or form part of a process of degration or alteration of the quality of the water so that it is rendered or is likely to be rendered deleterious to fish or fish habitat or to the use of man of fish that frequent that water.

A critical issue that is largely settled but nevertheless continues to arise in the factual circumstances of cases is the "mixing zone" or "teaspoon of oil in the ocean" issue. The following decision of the BC Court of Appeal is the leading authority.

R v. MacMillan Bloedel (Alberni Ltd.)
(1979), 47 CCC (2d) 118; [1979] 4 WWR 6549; (1979), 2 FPR 182 (BCCA)

SEATON JA: The appellant was charged that it did unlawfully deposit a deleterious substance in water frequented by fish, contrary to s. 33(2) [now s. 36(3)] of the *Fisheries Act*. It was acquitted in the Provincial Court but an appeal was taken to the County Court where the acquittal was set aside and a conviction entered. This appeal from conviction is restricted to a question of law alone.

The appellant says that the County Court judge erred in his interpretation of the phrase "water frequented by fish," in his interpretation of the phrase "deleterious substance," and in denying the appellant's applicant to reopen the case.

The charge arose out of a spill of about 170 gallons of bunker C oil during unloading at the appellant's deep sea dock at Alberni Inlet. A suction valve was not closed when it ought to have been and the oil spilled beneath the dock. The appellant was prepared for this sort of accident and the response was prompt. Very little oil spread beyond the dock and the cleanup was carried out relatively quickly. If an offence was committed when the oil was spilled, the containment of the oil and the prompt cleanup would be relevant to the sentence but not the conviction.

[Seaton JA referred to and quoted the definitions of "deleterious substance" and "fish" ("includes shellfish, crustaceans and marine animals").]

The first argument arises out of the words "water frequented by fish." The learned trial judge concluded that this oil was not deposited in water frequented by fish for these reasons:

The evidence established that the deep sea dock was in that part of the Alberni Inlet which forms the estuary of the Somass River, that is, the intertidal waters where the fresh water of the River and the salt water of the Inlet intermingle. ... The lower reaches of the Somass River are spawning grounds for four species of salmon, namely, sockeye, chum, coho, and spring, and the habitat of Steelhead trout. Adult salmon migrate up the river in the summer and fall, even as late as the end of the year in the case of coho salmon. Salmon fry could be found in the waters of Alberni Inlet from the 1st of February until the latter part of the summer depending upon water temperature and other conditions. They would feed in the shallow waters along the shoreline. On the 9th February, 1977, a fisheries office had carried out an inspection of the waters of the Inlet and had found freshly hatched chum salmon fry in the shallow waters of the Inlet including the water of Lupsi Kupsi Point some 200-250 yards from the deep sea dock. Sculpins had been observed off the deep sea dock during tests carried out in 1975-76. On the day of the spill, 15th February, 1977, and during the following four or five days when the clean-up operation was carried out, there was no evidence of fish being under or around the deep sea dock. As the Crown's evidence showed that salmon fry was normally found in the shallow waters of shorelines, no reasonable inference could therefore be drawn that salmon fry were present in the water beneath the deep sea dock on the 15th February, 1977, or during the subsequent clean-up. Mr. Kier submitted that it was irrelevant that no dead fish were observed as a result of the spill. However, it seems to me that if salmon fry had been present under the dock during this incident their dead carcases would have been very much observed. The absence of carcases means either there were no fish under the dock or if there were the oil was not deleterious.

On this evidence and applying the interpretation of "water frequented by fish" above, I find (a) that the water of the estuary of the Somass River in the Alberni Inlet in which the deep sea dock is located is water frequented by fish; (b) that the particular water beneath the deep sea dock was *not* frequented by fish; (c) that the oil spill was contained in the water beneath the deep sea dock and did not endanger the fish frequenting other parts of Alberni Inlet. The Crown has therefore failed to prove that the oil was deposited in "water frequented by fish" as alleged in both courts.

I think that approach too narrow. It restricts the enquiry to commercial fish present at the moment of the spill in the very drop of water into which the oil was spilled. I am not prepared to accept any of those restrictions. The definition of "fish" is given in the Act and it is broad. The section does not speak of "water in which there are fish" but of "water frequented by fish." To restrict the word "water" to the few cubic feet into which the oil was poured would be to disregard the fact that both water and fish move.

I turn now to what is meant by "deleterious substance." It is the appellant's submission that to prove this charge the Crown must show that after the spill the water was made deleterious. That was what the learned Provincial Court judge said:

> The definition of "deleterious substance" is not very satisfactory because it begs the question when it states a "deleterious substance means (a) any substance that if added to water … it is rendered deleterious to fish … ." According to Dr. Birtwell one drop of bunker sea oil in the middle of the ocean can be potentially deleterious to fish. This may well be so but what the Crown has to establish in view of the words in the definition "so that *it is* rendered deleterious to fish" (emphasis added).

Deleterious means "physically or morally harmful or injurious" (Oxford International Dictionary at 474). In my view, then, the degradation of the water must be shown to be harmful or injurious to fish.

Dr. Birtwell's evidence showed that there were many factors to be taken into account in determining whether bunker sea oil rendered water deleterious to fish, but there was little, if any, evidence of these factors with respect to the water under the dock into which the oil was spilled. Two samples of this water (Exhibits 4 and 5) were collected by the fisheries officers but there was no evidence of any test upon them for toxicity. Dr. Britwell's opinion on the toxicity of bunker sea oil in water was stated in broad terms based on tests carried out by others. As most of the conditions affecting that toxicity were not proven with respect to the water under the dock, I cannot find that that water was in fact rendered deleterious.

The learned County Court judge rejected that approach and I think he was right in so doing. Section 33(2) prohibits the deposit of a deleterious substance, not the deposit of a substance that causes the water to become deleterious. The argument to the contrary is based on the definition of "deleterious substance."

. . .

What is being defined is the substance that is added to water, rather than the water after the addition of the substance. To re-phrase the definition section in terms of this case, oil is a deleterious substance if, when added to any water, it would degrade or alter or form part of a process of degradation or alteration of the quality of that water so that water is rendered deleterious to fish or to the use by man of fish that frequent that water. Applying that test to the findings of fact here, bunker C oil is a deleterious substance. Once it is determined that bunker C oil is a deleterious substance and that it has been deposited, the offence is complete without ascertaining whether the water itself was thereby rendered deleterious. I do not think that the words "that water" in the definition section mean the water into which it is alleged the accused deposited the substance. Those words refer back to "any water," at the beginning of the definition; the hypothetical water which would degrade if the oil was added to it.

The appellant says that the purpose of this legislation is to prevent waters being rendered deleterious to fish and that if given the plain meaning of the words, an absurdity will result. It is said that if a teaspoon of oil was put in the Pacific Ocean and oil was a deleterious substance, that would constitute an offence. In its submission that absurdity can be avoided by reading the Act to require that the water be made deleterious. There are some attractions to that reasoning, but I think that the result would be at least as unsatisfactory. Nothing could be done to prevent damage to the water that fell short of rendering the water deleterious. To prove that the damage had gone that far would be difficult indeed.

Had it been the intention of Parliament to prohibit the deposit of a substance in water so as to render that water deleterious to fish, that would have been easy to express. A different prohibition was decided upon. It is more strict. It seeks to exclude each part of the process of degradation. The thrust of the section is to prohibit certain things, called deleterious substances, being put in the water. That is the plain meaning of the words used and is the meaning that I feel bound to apply.

I would dismiss the appeal.

QUESTION

"Waters frequented by fish" is defined to mean "Canadian fisheries waters" (s. 34(1)). Also, s. 40(5)(b) states that

no water is "water frequented by fish," as defined in subsection 34(1), where proof is made that at all times material to the proceedings the water is not, has not been and is not likely to be frequented in fact by fish.

Is it necessary that the Crown prove that fish are actually present in the receiving water?

C. Regulatory Offences

The s. 36(3) offence is an example of a regulatory offence, a category that has been distinguished from "true crimes." Regulatory offences, according to Cory J in *R v. Wholesale Travel Inc.*, [1991] 3 SCR 154, at 219, are intended to protect the public or broad segments of the public by preventing future harm through the enforcement of minimum standards of care and conduct. The consequence is that the concept of fault is based on a reasonable standard of care that does not, as in a true criminal offence, imply moral blame.

1. Strict Liability

In *R v. Sault Ste Marie (City)*, [1978] 2 SCR 1299, the Supreme Court identified three classes of offences: *mens rea*, strict liability, and absolute liability. Section 36(3), like the overwhelming majority of environmental offences, has been held to fall into the strict liability class since it does not contain language such as "knowingly" or "wilfully," even though an express "all due diligence" defence was repealed in 1991. An absolute liability characterization would have required relatively clear statutory language to the effect that guilt should follow from proof of the prohibited act.

2. Due Diligence

Strict liability offences such as s. 36(3) are proven by the prosecution establishing the doing of the prohibited act. Then, however, it is a complete defence for the accused to establish on a balance of probabilities that he or she took all reasonable care. This is also expressed as "due diligence" or "no negligence." Proof of due diligence requires more than general instructions and cautions to employees or agents. The care expected must reflect the diligence of a reasonable professional possessing the expertise suitable to the activity in question. Relevant factors include the gravity of the harm, the available alternatives, the likelihood of harm, the skill required, and the extent to which the accused could control the causal elements of the offence. Due diligence may require proper construction, operation, and maintenance of facilities using the best and most advanced techniques to prevent environmental damage. However, compliance with written directions of a fisheries officer has been held to be due diligence. See *R v. Western Forest Industries Ltd.* (1978), 9 CELR 57; 2 FPR 269 (BC Prov. Ct.). The directions, in effect, mark out the base due diligence requirements so that substantial compliance will be sufficient and harm resulting from the directed activities will be considered to have been foreseen by the fisheries officials when issuing the orders. Though corporate environmental management systems that include elements outlined by Ormiston J in *R v. Bata Industries Ltd.* (1992), 7 CELR (NS) 245 (Ont. Prov. Ct.) (quoted below), may be significant in establishing due diligence, attention to measures to reduce risks relevant to the specific offence is critical: *R v. Imperial Oil Ltd.* (2000), 36 CELR (NS) 109 (BCCA).

The next case raises the question, due diligence in relation to what? The subsequent case illustrates in an "on the ground" way (note the original, unedited oral judgment), how some of these issues arise and are dealt with by provincial courts. (In part, this was a private prosecution prosecuted by the Sierra Legal Defence Fund; for a discussion about private prosecutions, see chapter 9.)

R v. MacMillan Bloedel Ltd.
(2001), 38 CELR (NS) 141 (BCSC)

[As part of its Queen Charlotte Islands logging operations, MacMillan Bloedel stored bulk diesel fuel and gasoline in above-ground tanks, each containing several thousand gallons. Underground hot-dipped galvanized steel pipes installed in the 1960s led from the tanks along Crabapple Creek (a fish habitat) to a fuelling station approximately 200 feet away belonging to the BC Ministry of the Environment. In 1993, in response to a complaint about the risk of diesel fuel from the pipes entering the creek, MacMillan Bloedel, under the supervision of the ministry, dug up and inspected the pipes. The pipes were tested by scraping them at intervals by hand and with a wire brush and by tapping them with a hammer. They were found to be in good condition, so they were cleaned and they continued to be used. Subsequently, the company developed protocols, including audits to identify, monitor, and improve environmental risks in its operations. As part of this environmental management system activity, underground pipes were identified in a report by an internal auditor as the company's most pressing environmental problem and it was recommended that the Crabapple Creek pipes be either reinstalled above ground or placed in a secondary sleeve to facilitate early leak detection. However, the division manager disagreed and no action was taken because the lines had been inspected in 1993 and all reasonable steps had been taken to avoid spills.

In 1997, one of the pipes failed, resulting in the discharge of diesel fuel into the creek, and the company was charged under s. 36(3) of the *Fisheries Act.*

The evidence at trial was to the effect that there was a reasonable risk that sooner or later the pipes would fail. However, the unchallenged evidence of a metallurgical expert was that the failure was caused by microbiologically influenced corrosion that began when the pipes were uncovered and scraped for inspection and was exacerbated when the lines were subsequently cleaned. The process of microbiologically induced corrosion was not well understood in 1993.

MacMillan Bloedel was convicted at trial on the basis that it did not prove on a balance of probabilities that it took reasonable care to prevent the spill. The company appealed.]

CATIFF J: The appellant submits that as the trial judge found that MB held an honest belief that the pipes were sound at the time of their rupture, MB should have been acquitted. The pipes were found to be in good condition in 1993, but in his 1995 report Mr. Pillsbury recommended they be replaced. This was because the pipes were aging and had a finite lifespan and to replace them with pipes above ground would mean easier access and inspection. While MB was in the course of replacing other pipelines in the Queen Charlottes there were no specific plans to replace the pipelines in question.

The Crown submits that it was not reasonable to continue to believe that the pipelines, although found to be sound in 1993, would continue to be sound and not require replacement, particularly in view of Mr. Pillsbury's report. The pipes were about 40 years old in 1997, which was at the near end of their lifespan. What concerned the trial judge, of course, was that there was no evidence of any plan to deal with them.

The cause of the rupture and consequent offence was however, microbiological corrosion, a phenomenon not well understood in 1993 and held by the trial judge to be a condition which MB could not have anticipated. The condition was apparently caused, or contributed to, by uncovering and scraping the pipes when they were inspected in 1993. The deterioration of the pipes from this cause was accordingly not reasonably foreseeable to MB. What was foreseeable was the deterioration of the pipes from age—in time they would eventually wear out—perhaps sooner than later. As I say, the lack of any specific plan to deal with this inevitable problem concerned the trial judge and it may be that MB can be justifiably criticised in this regard. But the offence itself was not caused by the pipes reaching the end of their lifespan, but rather because of a specific and unforeseeable condition. To blame MB for taking inadequate steps to replace aging pipes with new ones seems to me to be legally irrelevant in light of what actually happened, which was not a break down from old age, but was a rupture caused by a different and unanticipated cause. I add that the trial judge did not find that MB should have acted to replace the pipes by the time the spill occurred on 16 May 1997, but only that he had heard no evidence at the trial, some two or three years later, of any specific plan to do so. If the pipes had been so aged as to require replacement at or before the time of the spill the situation might have been different, but this was not the finding of the trial judge.

For the foregoing reasons I would allow the appeal, set aside the conviction and direct that a verdict of acquittal be entered.

Appeal allowed.

Fletcher v. Kingston (City)
[1998] OJ no. 6453 (Prov. Ct.)

[The city of Kingston operated a municipal landfill from the 1950s to the early 1970s. After closing the landfill, the city created a recreational area on the site. Subsequently, it was discovered that leachate from the site was entering the Cataraqui River. An Ontario Ministry of the Environment inventory and study ranked the site highest in terms of detrimental environmental effects through groundwater and surface water contamination. In the 1990s, citizens pressed the city and the ministry to take action and the ministry, in turn, put pressure on the city to develop an abatement plan. Finally, a citizen volunteer group, directed by Janet Fletcher, with the assistance of the Sierra Legal Defence Fund, carried out sampling at the site and had the samples analyzed.

As a result, a private information was laid in 1997 charging the city under s. 36(3) of the *Fisheries Act*. A parallel investigation by the ministry's investigative branch led to the laying of additional charges under the *Fisheries Act*. At the trial, the latter charges were prosecuted by the Crown while the private charges were prosecuted by counsel for the Sierra Legal Defence Fund.

The court first considered whether the *actus reus* was proven. This involved an assessment of the evidence and a consideration of the following arguments: (1) that the leachate substance must be shown to make the water into which it is introduced deleterious to fish, and (2) that the testing procedures used by the prosecutor were unreliable.]

BELL PROV. J (orally):

Actus Reus of the Charges

[I]t would seem that MacMillan Bloedel has been applied in Ontario and this Trier of Fact, having considered both arguments and examined the relative case law submitted by both Crown and the Defence, concludes that the [private] Prosecution and the Crown need only prove, in this element of the charge, that substance induced, toxic liquid by the Prosecution and toxic leachate by the Crown be deleterious or harmful to the fish.

. . .

The Defence attempts to discredit the methods used in the testing procedures by alleging that a pH shift results from the standard procedures utilized in warming the samples of effluent to fifteen degrees centigrade before the bioassays are performed. PH shift, I should explain to those who were not here for all of the trial, is the measurement of acidity or alkalinity of the samples and a pH of seven is a neutral, halfway in between. They claim that the resultant pH shift results in the increase in temperature of the effluent samples produces greater portions of unionized ammonia as opposed to the ionized portion which their experts claim is the toxic element of ammonia, that is, the unionized portion is the toxic element of ammonia. Through their expert's testimony, they further claim that the protocol which lays down precise methods for dealing with the testing, including doing the tests at fifteen degrees centigrade temperature and warming or cooling the samples to achieve this temperature and using rainbow trout as the fish in the bioassay tests is not what is required in this element of the charge.

. . .

However, having assessed the arguments and considered the reasoned counter arguments by the Prosecution and the Crown which negated these claims, again by charts, calculations and reference to other studies, this Trier of Fact must conclude that any change in the protocols, that is, laying down a method of testing which has been well established should take place in the scientific realm.

The so called protocols are the 1990 publications of Environment Canada: (1) the Biological Test Method. Acute Lethality Test Using Rainbow Trout and that is Exhibit 18 filed in this trial, and (2) The Biological Test Method—Determining Acute Lethality of Effluents to Daphnia Magna, Exhibit 19. They were developed with input and guidance from many scientific authorities throughout Canada and North America, were reviewed before publication and comments and suggestions were actively sought from the academic, scientific, industrial and laboratory community before final review. They were updated with amendments in 1996. This was a 1990 publication first of all. In the scientific realm, a serious challenge to an accepted protocol would involve experimentation, publication in an acknowledged periodical, attempted replication of the challenger's experimental results by other experts and an eventual forum of the experts in the field. Undoubtedly, a successful challenge by scientific experts would result in an immediate amendment to the protocol. The protocol, Exhibit 18 ... , specifically notes the conditions under which testing must be done, among them a temperature of fifteen degrees centigrade plus or minus one centigrade degree. So, what is acceptable is a range of temperature between fourteen degrees centigrade and sixteen degrees centigrade. ... [T]he same document also gives the rationale for using rainbow trout, which focuses on their availability, the knowledge of how toxicants affect them, and the extensive data bank for comparisons, etcetera. Since they have been used extensively throughout North America for more than two decades, a lot is known about them. Similar procedures are set out in section four of the Daphnia Magna protocol, Exhibit 19.

This Court, based on that evidence, declines to make a ruling which impinges on the well researched, referenced and reasoned methodology of such documents as "The Protocol," which has such widespread scientific support. By happenstance, in looking at all of the data, the Court does not agree with the Defence's arguments in support of the pH shift as causing the deaths in the bioassays. The argument of the Defence is entirely theoretical and scientific experts who wish to overturn accepted science, in this court's opinion, have to do more than testify in Court.

[The court found that seven of the eight counts were proven. One count was dismissed because there was uncertainty on the evidence as to the dates of analysis.]

Reasonable Doubt

A further issue in this argument arises when there is competing expert evidence. Counsellor Doody cites an Ontario Court of Appeal decision, *Regina v. Molnar* (1990) in which Mr. Justice Lacouriere states that it is a mistake for the Trier of Fact to choose which expert evidence he prefers. He goes on to say, citing *Regina v. Platt* (1981). "The only safe way of directing the jury was either to tell them that before they accepted the opinion of the Prosecution's pathologist"—this was a death situation and the two pathologists were testifying—so, "before they accepted the opinion of the Prosecution's pathologist, they must feel sure he was correct, or else to tell them they were to assume the Defence pathologist was right and therefore approach the case on the other evidence solely ... ."

• • •

Do I believe that the Ministry of the Environment and Beak Laboratories used the same methodology on these samples as they did on thousands of others according to their testimony? Yes, I believe they applied the same protocol. Secondly, do I believe that the Crown and Prosecution witnesses engaged in some conspiracy against the City and conducted these tests using some extraordinary method to "cook" the results in these particular samples? No. The Court does not believe that. The evidence confirms their adherence to the methodology to protocols. I can find no evidence of a lack of objectivity.

The Court, after analyzing the data presented, considering the arguments put forth by both sides and consulting the relevant case law rejects the reasonable possibilities at issue and has no reasonable doubts as to the commission of the *actus reus* in seven of the eight charges as outlined above.

Due Diligence Defence

[The court rejected the argument that the court, in assessing due diligence, is limited to the charge period.]

Mrs. Mirka Januszkiewicz was hired by the City as an Environmental Engineer in December of 1991. She holds accreditation in the Ontario Society of Professional Engineers and attests to a background in various aspects of the Environmental Sciences as well as having taken extra courses in Environmental Law and courses in management and operation of both landfill sites and sewage treatment plants and this comes from the examination in-chief of Mrs. Januszkiewicz.

As a result of Mr. Meunier's memo, Mirka Januszkiewicz gives evidence that she visited the site in May of 1992, saw puddles on the golf course and took samples which she had analysed for B-Tex compounds (Benzene Toluene etcetera). The Crown cites this as an example of foreseeability because these are typical products of the decomposition of landfill wastes.

Now, Jim English, an Environmental Technician with the City wrote to Mirka Januszkiewicz on the 27th of September 1993, apparently about the upcoming CH2M-Hill Report, Exhibit 30. He suggests certain additions to the informations with respect to the metals: arsenic, mercury and selenium, and ends with the warning, "I suspect this is an interesting can of worms." Now Mirka Januszkiewicz either misinterprets the remark or ignores it. However, the import of this memo is that Mirka Januszkiewicz knew about the study and the upcoming Hill Report before her 1st of November, 1994 contact with Alice Verbaas of the Ministry. This exhibit also contains a phone message to Mirka Januszkiewicz from Mr. Williams who worked for the CH2M-Hill Report and was so noted on the memo.

The Cataraqui River Conservation Authority agrees to permission for dumping of street sweepings on the Belle Park site for a one year period from the 16th of September 1993 to the 16th of September 1994 under certain conditions, which is Exhibit 170(b). These conditions include a trench and berm to trap sediments from the fill site so that only clear water enters the marsh area. Mirka Januszkiewicz, in her evidence, proffers the trench and berm as part of measures to control leachate run-off. However, evidence in cross-examination with reference to Exhibit 53, that was the big map, and photographs, specifically Exhibit 22, shows them to be up slope from the seeps, that is up slope from the water.

Alice Verbaas, an Abatement Officer with the Ministry of the Environment provides the Hill Report to Mirka Januszkiewicz on the 1st of November, 1994 advising her that the Ministry of the Environment wants some action on this. She gives the City 60 days to come up with a proposal to implement the Hill Report's recommendations which was to further monitor surface and ground water flows from the site. The report also indicated the estimated discharge as 161 litres per minute from the north and 55 litres per minutes from the south.

Now, Mirka Januszkiewicz, in her evidence, claims ignorance of the possible leachate problems in the landfill site. Mrs. Januszkiewicz and Mrs. Verbaas had numerous contacts during the period 1993 to January 1997 since they, along with other officials, were involved in several environmental projects: the Ravensview Sewage Treatment Facility, the Forcemain Problem and the street sweeping dumping to name the most prominent. Alice Verbaas states that the landfill site problem was also mentioned at these meetings. Mrs. Januszkiewicz's evidence is very vague on these points.

Alice Verbaas writes Parks Canada in an attempt to obtain federal funding for the City to do monitoring and remediation planning. In her letter dated the 10th of November 1994, which is Exhibit 59, ... she indicates that the Ministry of the Environment's concern about the leachate problem and also notes complaints that have been received about the staining and a copy of this memo was sent to Mrs. Januszkiewicz. Now, she claims ignorance about any great problems at the landfill and states that the Ministry of the Environment never indicated they received complaints. They never indicated to her that they received complaints. Now, the Court feels that the information was there for the reading, not only in this instance, but others as well.

Alice Verbaas also states that in her ongoing contacts with Mrs. Januszkiewicz on behalf of the City, they never disputed the facts of the Hill Report. She also states that anyone familiar with landfill site management should know that either the site had to be engineered to make a cap of impermeable material, clay, over the landfill to prevent the rainwater percolation through the material which produces leachate or to find some method of containing the leachate and dealing with it. She felt that the City would choose either of these in any plan they formulated.

When asked about suggestions that the City was given permission to shelve the landfill site so as to carry on with other more critical projects like the Ravensview Project, she answered that a more senior level of management dealt with this type of arrangement. Moreover, if there was such a deal worked out, it would be committed to paper in the form of a contract and signed by all parties. The existence of such a contract was unknown to her and has not been entered as evidence by the defence.

Another example of the City's knowledge of the problem was the revelation that Andrew Landy was retained to sample and prepare a report dated the 17th of May, 1996, Exhibit 166. Now, Mrs. Januszkiewicz admits in cross-examination that she did not read the report. She was too busy at the time, but approved Mr. Landy's invoices for payment. The analysis of the results were sent along to Mr. English for interpretation and this is Exhibit 170, ... which she never received nor repeated her request. Now, the Court acknowledges that Mirka Januszkiewicz may have been let down by her staff in this case. However, it asks itself, who is the professional here? Who supposedly has the knowledge? As more evidence comes forth about site visits in good weather where she sees no leachate staining and the paltry records of expenses, a few hundred dollars for environmental concerns at the site from 1992 to 1996 inclusive, the Court has to assume that Mirka Januszkiewicz was either incredibly naive about this discipline or that she was hopeful in suppressing any concerns until the City was prepared to deal with it. Subsequently, Mr. Rose of Malroz testified that there were exceedances for the phenols on Mr. Landy's samples and high levels of ammonia.

In August 1996, a letter from Mirka Januszkiewicz and Mr. Segsworth regarding the City's long term management plan for Belle Island, Exhibit 33, which was submitted to council and passed on the 10th of September 1996, it predominately deals with the after uses of the park, the golf course and it talks about kite flying and hiking trails and only, incidentally at the end, paragraph nine deals with the issue of leachate.

How does the Court interpret such a document taken in the context of this trial? Were the co-signers of this document so out of touch or so ignorant of the realities that they assumed the generalized platitudes of this so called long term management plan would be acceptable to the environmental concerns or was each senior city bureaucrat concerned only with his own turf and the Works Department concerned with the street sweepings and the Recreation Department concerned with the golf course and kite flying, which had the most clout? That Mrs. Januszkiewicz and the environmental portfolio were, at best, afterthoughts. Although it is difficult to maintain perspective and objectivity through a trial such as this one, this document, this long term management plan submitted eighteen months after it was asked for is a sort of a flag of arrogance in the Court's mind.

Secondly, it virtually ignores the concerns of the Abatement Officer of the Ministry of the Environment expressed in several contacts with the city through Mirka Januszkiewicz.

Thirdly, it seems to challenge the Ministry of the Environment that these are the established activities on the site. Do not interrupt them.

Now, the Court asks itself—maybe the Court should not ask itself this, but were the City politicians well served by their senior bureaucrats in this debacle. One interpretation of these events makes the so called management plan a power struggle in which the Environment Department lost out. Another interpretation, ignore the problem, continue stonewalling. It is an expense to avoid or thirdly, was there no correct analysis of the potential problem despite all signals to the contrary?

Before dealing with the charge period, the Court will comment on the issue in connection with the *actus reus* portion of the charges. Foreseeability: How could the City take any action to prevent the discharge if they did not know about any problems at the landfill site? I believe the foregoing treatise of the events and evidence prior to the 5th of December 1996 is sufficient in detail and self evident for the Court to conclude that Mirka Januszkiewicz and the City were aware of the leachate flow to the waters of the Great Cataraqui River and for reasons known only to the defendants chose to ignore it. The defence's issue of foreseeability and ignorance of the problem is negated on the evidence.

After the sharing of concerns by the Sierra Legal Defence Fund, Neil Rickey had contact with Mirka Januszkiewicz on several occasions in January. And again, Mirka Januszkiewicz's interpretation of the events and Neil Rickey's differ, but eventually a message got through and Malroz Engineering was retained to do site investigations in February of 1997. To the credit of both Mirka Januszkiewicz and the City, the whole process of site characterization and remediation was fast-tracked. An estimated

1.7 million dollars was spent in 1997 and 1998, about $200,000 up to the 6th of May 1997 on the project, which was the fourth charge of the Crown.

Although remediation in the form of damming the effluent discharge and pumping it to a sanitary sewer system was not completed until all but one of the charge dates, the 6th of May 1997, had occurred, the effluent was characterized by the analysis of many samples and eventually permanent below frost pipelines conveyed it to the sanitary sewer system, that is the Malroz Report, Exhibits 156(a) and 156(b) plus Exhibits 107 through to Exhibit 154.

In conclusion, the Court rejects the defendants' position that they were duly diligent in respect to preventing the discharges. The Court can find no evidence of a comprehensive plan, not even one of effective monitoring of the closed landfill site to detect discharges. Certainly, no effective resources were committed to even dealing with the problems on a haphazard basis.

Therefore, the Court registers a conviction on the four charges against the City from the Prosecution, that is the Sierra Legal Defence Fund and Janet Fletcher charges and three counts against the City on the Crown's charges dated the 10th and 19th of February 1997 and the 6th of May 1997, the three counts against Mirka Januszkiewicz also dated the 10th and 19th of February and the 6th of May 1997.

D. Other Offence Provisions

1. Proof of Harm

If a cyanide solution used in a leaching extraction plant for recovering gold and silver from mine tailings is, as a result of heavy rain, spilled into the surrounding environment and the company responsible is charged, does the Crown have to prove actual injury or harm to the surrounding environment? This issue was considered in *R v. Seraphim* (1997), 23 CELR (NS) 87 (BCCA). At the time, the relevant provisions of the British Columbia *Waste Management Act*, SBC 1982, c. 41, read as follows (emphasis added):

> 3(1) For the purposes of this section, the conduct of an industry, trade or business includes the operation by any person or facilities or vehicles for the collection, storage, treatment, handling, transportation, discharge, destruction or other disposal of waste.
>
> (1.1) Subject to subsection (3), no person shall, in the course of conducting an industry, trade or business, *introduce or cause or allow waste to be introduced into the environment.*
>
> 1(1) *"waste" includes*
>> (a) air contaminants,
>> (b) litter,
>> (c) *effluent,*
>> (d) refuse,
>> (e) special wastes, and
>> (f) any other substance designated by the Lieutenant Governor in Council,
>
> whether or not the type of waste referred to in paragraphs (a) to (e) or designated under paragraph (f) has any commercial value or is capable of being used for a useful purpose; ...
>
> "effluent" means a *deleterious* material flowing in or out of works; ...

"environment" means the air, land, water and all other external conditions or influences under which man, animals and plants live or are developed; ... .

1(2) For the purposes of this Act, introduction of waste into the environment means depositing the waste on or in or allowing or causing the waste to flow or seep on or into any land or water or allowing or causing the waste to be emitted into the air.

The Act contained no definition of "deleterious."
Subsequently, the definition of effluent was amended to provide as follows:

"effluent" means a substance that is discharged into water or onto land and that ...
(f) damages or is capable of damaging the environment."

The court allowed the appeal and set the original convictions aside on the ground that "deleterious" means that the substance released must be shown to be injurious to plant or animal life present at the time and place of the release; there was no evidence of such injury. Would the result in *Seraphim* be different under the amended definition of "effluent"?

Similarly, if an offence provision states that "no person shall discharge or cause the discharge into water of any material that may impair the quality of the water," does discharge into Lake Ontario of a small quantity of mineral oil contaminated with PCBs contravene this provision? See *R v. Toronto Electric Commissioners* (1991), 6 CELR (NS) 301.

In *R v. Inco* (2000), 41 CELR (NS) 9 (Ont. CA), the court stated that the appropriate test for "may impair" requires consideration of the nature of the material, the nature and circumstances of the discharge, including quantity and concentration, and the time period of the discharge and noted that

[i]nherently toxic substances will always fail that test, reflecting zero tolerance for discharging materials that, by their nature, may impair water quality. If the material in the discharge is not inherently toxic, then it will be necessary to consider the quantity and concentration of the discharge as well as the time frame over which the discharge took place.

2. Corporations

Corporations can be convicted of *mens rea* environmental offences on the "identification" theory under which liability is attributed to a corporation through its directing mind: *R v. Safety Kleen Canada Inc.* (1997), 22 CELR (NS) 202 (Ont. CA), applying *R v. Canadian Dredge and Dock Co. Ltd.*, [1985] 1 SCR 662. Key is the capacity of "directing minds" to exercise decision-making authority in implementing corporate policy, as opposed to merely carrying out that policy. A corporation can also be party to or aid and abet a *mens rea* offence. Corporations are liable for strict liability offences in the same way that individual persons are.

Does the following provision in the Alberta *Environmental Protection and Enhancement Act*, RSA 2000, c. E-12, establish a corporate directing mind for the purpose of a *mens rea* offence? Does it directly attribute lack of due diligence to a corporation as a result of acts of directors, officers, officials, employees, or agents? Or does it merely speak to the question of who can commit a corporate *actus reus*?

239. For the purposes of this Act, an act or thing done or omitted to be done by a director, officer, official, employee or agent of a corporation in the course of his employment or in the exercise of his powers or the performance of his duties shall be deemed also to be an act or thing done or omitted to be done by the corporation.

3. Corporate Officers and Directors

1. CEPA 1999 provides:

280(1) Where a corporation commits an offence under this Act, any officer, director or agent of the corporation who directed, authorized, assented to, acquiesced in or participated in the commission of the offence is a party to and guilty of the offence, and is liable to the punishment provided for the offence, whether or not the corporation has been prosecuted or convicted.

Where a director but not the corporation is charged under s. 280 (which is similar to s. 218 of the Alberta *Environmental Protection and Enhancement Act* and s. 78.2 of the *Fisheries Act*), is it necessary to prove the director's *mens rea* where the corporate offence is one of strict liability? See *R v. Swendson* (1987), 51 Alta. LR (2d) 277 (QB). What *actus* amounts to "acquiescence"? Should passive conduct or omissions be sufficient?

2. Ontario's *Environmental Protection Act* adopts a different approach (s. 280(2) of CEPA 1999 is similar), where directors may be held liable as principals, not parties:

194(1) Every director or officer of a corporation that engages in an activity that may result in the discharge of a contaminant into the natural environment contrary to this Act or the regulations has a duty to take all reasonable care to prevent the corporation from causing or permitting such unlawful discharge.

(2) Offence. Every person who has a duty under subsection (1) and who fails to carry out that duty is guilty of an offence.

(3) Liability to conviction. A director or officer of a corporation is liable to conviction under this section whether or not the corporation has been prosecuted or convicted.

Is this a strict liability offence, so that by proving the *actus reus* the Crown shifts the burden to officers or directors to establish due diligence on a balance of probabilities, or must the Crown prove failure to exercise reasonable care? In *R v. Commander Business Furniture Inc.* (1992), 9 CELR (NS) 185, at 250-51, the Ontario Provincial Court adopted the latter interpretation, disagreeing with the previous Provincial Court decision in *R v. Bata Industries Ltd.*, above.

3. In *Bata*, Ormiston J set out criteria for assessing the due diligence of officers and directors that became part of environmental law folklore and spawned a corporate environmental management industry. He said, at 287-88:

I ask myself the following questions in assessing the defence of due diligence:

(a) Did the board of directors establish a pollution prevention "system" as indicated in *Regina v. Sault Ste. Marie*, i.e. Was there supervision or inspection? Was there improvement in business methods? Did he exhort those he controlled or influenced?

(b) Did each director ensure that the corporate officers have been instructed to set up a system sufficient within the terms and practices of its industry of ensuring compliance with environmental laws, to ensure that the officers report back periodically to the board on the operation of the system, and to ensure that the officers are instructed to report any substantial non-compliance to the board in a timely manner?

I reminded myself that:

(c) The directors are responsible for reviewing the environmental compliance reports provided by the officers of the corporation but are justified in placing *reasonable* reliance on reports provided to them by corporate officers, consultants, counsel or other informed parties.

(d) The directors should substantiate that the officers are promptly addressing environmental concerns brought to their attention by government agencies or other concerned parties including shareholders.

(e) The directors should be aware of the standards of their industry and other industries which deal with similar environmental pollutants or risks.

(f) The directors should immediately and personally react when they have noticed the system has failed.

Within this general profile and dependent upon the nature and structure of the corporate activity, one would hope to find remedial and contingency plans for spills, a system of ongoing environmental audit, training programs, sufficient authority to act and other indices of a pro-active environmental policy.

E. Other Defences

Defences available to *mens rea*, strict, or absolute liability offences include

- *Act of God.* Proof that the act was caused by an extraordinary natural event over which the accused had no control and that could not be foreseen or avoided.
- *Act of a third party.* Normally the act of a stranger that could not have been foreseen or avoided with due diligence.
- *Officially induced error.* A mistake of law based on reasonable but erroneous advice of a government official.
- *Necessity.* Proof that the offence was committed because of emergency circumstances that made compliance impossible.
- *Raising doubt.* Raising doubt as to the Crown's case.

F. Sentencing

In *R v. United Keno Hill Mines* (1980), 10 CELR 43 (Yukon Terr. Ct.), Stuart TCJ wrote an essay outlining the principles for sentencing in environmental cases. These continue to be applied. The following case is an example.

R v. Neptune Bulk Terminals (Canada) Ltd.
(2001), 37 CELR (NS) 282 (BC Prov. Ct.)

[Neptune Bulk Terminals ("Neptune") pleaded guilty to discharging some 26.6 tonnes of canola oil into Burrard Inlet, waters frequented by migratory birds, contrary to s. 35(1) of the federal Migratory Birds Regulations, CRC 1978, c. 1035. The spill occurred during the transfer of canola oil, by means of pumping the oil through pipes from a storage tank to a ship. Neptune employees discovered the spill, informed superiors, and mobilized cleanup equipment. The employees contacted environmental protection agencies, reported the spill to senior company management, deployed a boom intended to contain the oil, and hired a firm specializing in spill cleanup. Neptune cooperated with federal enforcement officers. Eventually, nearly seven tonnes of canola oil and water mixture was recovered from the inlet, but not before 23 migratory birds were oiled, of which 16 died.

Neptune's engineering consultants analyzed the ruptured hose/pipe connector that was the source of the spill and concluded that it was severely degraded and weakened with many cracks and that the failure was due to the corrosion of steel reinforcing wires in the pipe. Though the consultant noted that annual pressure tests and routine visual inspection was essential for maintenance, there was no written maintenance procedure for the piping. Neptune did have a site contingency plan that contemplated possible canola oil spills, but there were no written operating procedures for loading canola oil into ships. Subsequently, after the cleanup was completed, consultants were hired to review loading procedures, to conduct employee training, and to relocate the hose/piping system from under the dock to an onshore location. In total, approximately $130,000 was spent.]

MOSS PROV. J: Counsel has referred to a number of cases. I will not review each case. From them I draw these important principles of sentencing for environmental cases.

Aggravating Factors

1. The nature of the environment affected—Although this spill occurred in an industrial section of the Vancouver waterfront, the foreshore of Vancouver's famous Stanley Park waterfront is only a short distance away, as is the waterfront area of West Vancouver extremely nearby. All the waters concerned are frequented by migratory birds.
2. The extent of the actual injury inflicted—Sixteen migrating seabirds were recovered either dead or beyond saving. It would be naïve to assume that every bird adversely affected was recovered. Accordingly, the damage to migratory birds is a serious consideration.
3. Was the event reasonably foreseeable? In my view, the answer is yes! Had there been a reasonable ongoing inspection system in place, it is quite probable that this type of spill could have been avoided.

Mitigating Factors

1. Remorse—The actions of the Defendant *post-spill* were prompt and efficient. Money does not seem to have been a limiting factor on their remedial efforts. I accept that the Defendants are remorseful.

2. Corporate executives from Neptune Terminals appeared personally in Court when the plea was entered. They have accepted responsibility for the problems created.
3. The spill was voluntarily reported to the environmental authorities. The Defendant did not seek to avoid liability for the spill.
4. Neptune Terminals is by all appearances a fairly large long-term corporate citizen located on the north Vancouver industrial waterfront.
5. Neptune Terminals has no prior record for any like transgression.

Conclusions

An effective *deterrent* to a company such as the Defendant, Neptune Terminals, considering the actual and potential damage inflicted to the environment, the rather large size of this spill, together with the factors mentioned, both mitigating and aggravating, in my view, a fine of $5,000 should be imposed. As well, there will be a Court Order under sec. 16(8) of the *Migratory Birds Convention*, 1994, requiring the Defendants to pay the further sum of $25,000.00 to Her Majesty, The Queen, as represented by Environment Canada for the purposes of the conservation and protection of migratory birds on the south coast of the Province of British Columbia. Unless either party objects, I grant Neptune Terminals thirty (30) days to pay the total of $30,000.00.

FURTHER READINGS

J. Benedickson, *Environmental Law* (Toronto: Irwin Law, 2002), chapters 8 and 9.

S. Berger, *The Prosecution and Defence of Environmental Offences* (Aurora, ON: Canada Law Book) (looseleaf).

J. Swaigen, *Regulatory Offences in Canada: Liability and Defences* (Toronto: Carswell, 1992).

W. Tilleman, "It's a Crime: Public Interest Laws (Fish and Game Statutes) Ignore Mens Rea Offices—Toward a New Classification Scheme" (1989) vol. 16, no. 3 *American Journal of Criminal Law* 279.

CHAPTER SIX

Environmental Assessment*

William A. Tilleman

I. INTRODUCTION

A. What Is Environmental Assessment?

"Human Welfare itself depends on the health of ecosystems—for the very good reason that our bodies, like our industries, are maintained by constantly taking in and digesting parts of the external world. When the quality of the environment deteriorates, so do we, along with our economies. This simple linkage has often been overlooked, but now its truth is coming home." State of Canada's Environment (Ottawa: Minister of Supply and Services Canada, 1991), at 1-3.

In Canada, environmental assessment is a public legal process to "look before you leap"—to weigh the merit of human activity against its potential harm to the environment. Although major environmental reviews have been conducted in most parts of Canada, there are still areas like northern Canada where such reviews, or at least coordinated assessments, have not yet been conducted.

This chapter focuses on federal assessments and policy issues within impact assessment; it does not discuss the intricacies of the provincial environmental assessment regimes in effect across Canada. Not only does each province have a distinct regime, but some provinces also have more than one regime, varying according to territories and sectors. Federally, the distinction between law and planning has assumed tremendous importance in recent years because of the federal tradition of referring the most significant proposals and projects to independent, expert panels for public review and hearings on environmental significance. What panels or governments consider to be good planning or environmental assessment practice may not coincide with what the courts conclude to be good law. Environmental assessment must have ambitious but fair objectives if it is to address successfully the many public interests in the environment and balance them against the goals of economic development.

*   I acknowledge the extensive input of my previous co-authors: Paul Emond (1st edition) and Rod Northey (2d edition). The best parts of this chapter that remain from previous versions are theirs. I also would like to thank my articling student, Wendy Gazard, for her assistance with updating this chapter.

B. Environmental Assessment Law in Context

Environmental assessment is unlike other environmental laws in the breadth of its procedural requirements. For example, it encompasses the control of pollutants, resource use, and approvals, as well as land-use planning laws. Environmental assessment also goes beyond discharge laws by making provision to examine more fully the effects of emissions, including social and cultural effects, and cumulative effects. In relation to land-use planning laws, environmental assessment includes consideration of zoning requirements, but also makes provision to examine alternative sites to determine a preferred location in light of potential advantages and disadvantages. In short, environmental assessment is intended to be a thorough process to address all fundamental environmental issues. Where a proposed action does not stand up to this scrutiny due to missing a key procedural step, environmental assessment should stop the action from proceeding.

There is no single model of environmental assessment. However, most of the critical environmental assessment issues may be understood by focusing on three questions:

1. will a proposal cause a significant adverse environmental effect;
2. if yes, is there any alternative that may offer a less significant adverse effect; and
3. having regard to all reasonable alternatives, overall, which alternative is overall the most appropriate for that project in a specific environmental setting?

II. BACKGROUND: HISTORY AND LEGISLATION

A. National Environmental Policy Act

The first legislation to insist on a comprehensive environmental approach was the US *National Environmental Policy Act* (NEPA), which required consideration of alternatives for any major federal action that may significantly affect the quality of the human environment. This legislation (42 USC, ss. 4321 et seq.), which has been copied in one form or another by almost 100 countries worldwide, set an entirely new course for environmental law—one of multi-disciplinary environmental planning. NEPA's environmental assessment requirements (s. 4332) were succinctly stated, making provision to

(A) utilize a systematic, interdisciplinary approach which will insure the integrated use of the natural and social sciences and the environmental design arts in planning and in decision making which may have an impact on man's environment;

(B) identify and develop methods and procedures which will insure that presently unquantified environmental amenities and values may be given appropriate consideration in decision making along with economic and technical considerations;

(C) include in every recommendation or report on proposals for legislation and other major Federal actions significantly affecting the quality of the human environment, a detailed statement by the responsible official on

(i) the environmental impact of the proposed action,

(ii) any adverse environmental effects which cannot be avoided should the proposal be implemented,

(iii) alternatives to the proposed action,

(iv) the relationship between local short-term uses of man's environment and the maintenance and enhancement of long-term productivity, and

(v) any irreversible and irretrievable commitments of resources which would be involved in the proposed action should it be implemented. ...

(E) study, develop, and describe appropriate alternatives to recommended courses of action in any proposal which involves unresolved conflicts concerning alternative uses of available resources.

B. Relationship of Legal Requirements to Planning Processes

From the outset, one of the most difficult issues raised by NEPA was the relationship between environmental assessment law and environmental assessment planning processes. To implement NEPA, the US government supplemented its requirements through regulations by the Council on Environmental Quality (43 FR 55990, November 28, 1978) and various regulations setting out agency-specific procedures. Under this approach, one must nevertheless distinguish between legal requirements and the step-by-step process used to meet these legal requirements. NEPA and its implementing regulations put courts in the delicate position of determining which aspects of the process were legal, requiring a "hard look" at correctness, and which aspects were factual or technical, requiring simply a reasonable approach.

This issue remains alive today under all of the Canadian environmental assessment regimes. Different laws involve different answers to the question of what is required to be done correctly and what is required to be done reasonably. This distinction should be considered for each situation raising an environmental assessment issue.

C. Environmental Assessment and Review Process Guidelines Order

In Canada, the starting point for federal environmental assessment was a task force on environmental assessment, which produced a report in 1972. The federal response to the task force report was to initiate the environmental assessment and review process (EARP) in 1973, through Cabinet policy. To implement the EARP, the government established the Federal Environmental Assessment Review Office (FEARO) in April 1974 (now the Canadian Environmental Assessment Agency). The focus of the EARP was public review of significant projects, programs, and activities. The first public review was conducted on the original Point Lepreau nuclear power generation station in New Brunswick in 1975. The most important environmental assessment in Canadian history was conducted in the 1970s through a federal public inquiry chaired by Justice Thomas Berger. The result was a landmark hearings process and an overall recommendation not to proceed with a proposed pipeline project until land claims and other issues were settled. Other related studies that followed the Berger Inquiry examined the proposed northern pipelines intended to deliver natural gas from the Arctic Ocean to southern markets.

In 1984, following internal and external review of the EARP, the government approved the Environmental Assessment and Review Process Guidelines Order, SOR/84-467, under the authority of the *Government Organization Act, 1979*. At this time, the guidelines order was conceived of as simply a planning tool for government actions and not a legally binding directive. However, in 1989, to the surprise of many, including the federal minister of the environment, the Federal Court of Canada ruled that the guidelines order was legally binding. Subsequent court decisions suggested that it applied to proposals that have an environmental effect on any area of federal jurisdiction. See *Rafferty-Alameda #1* (1989), FCJ 301; aff'd. (1989), FCJ 530 (CA); and *Friends of the Oldman River Society v. Canada (Minister of Transport)* (1992), 7 CELR (NS) 1 (SCC).

Over time, court challenges raised a number of problems with the guidelines order, affecting its application, administration, and enforcement: *Friends of the Oldman River Society v. Canada (Minister of Transport)*; *Friends of the Island Inc. v. Canada (Minister of Public Works)* (1993), 11 CELR (NS) 253, aff'd. 18 CELR (NS) 1 (FCA); *Naskapi-Montagnais Innu Assn. v. Canada (Minister of National Defence)* (1991), 5 CELR (NS) 287 (FCTD); and *Canadian Wildlife Federation Inc. v. Canada (Minister of the Environment)* (1990), 6 CELR (NS) 89 (FCA) (*Canadian Wildlife Federation II*).

D. Canadian Environmental Assessment Act

1. 1992-1995: Enacting the Canadian Environmental Assessment Act

An initial draft of the proposed *Canadian Environmental Assessment Act* (CEAA) was released in 1990 and, following a typically lengthy committee process that made many modifications to the draft bill and a further process of Senate hearings, the CEAA was given royal assent in June 1992. However, political issues resulted in the federal government's postponement of its proclamation. In 1994, the federal government changed and the new government determined that the CEAA should be proclaimed. Following more legislative hearings and amendments, the CEAA was finally proclaimed in force on January 19, 1995. At that time, four regulations required to implement the CEAA were also promulgated: the Inclusion List Regulations, SOR/94-637, the Law List Regulations, SOR/94-636, the Exclusion List Regulations, SOR/94-639, and the Comprehensive Study List Regulations, SOR/94-638.

2. Components of the CEAA's Environmental Assessment Process

The CEAA distinguishes the environmental assessment "document" from the environmental assessment "process." Roughly put, the environmental assessment document is the written result (a screening report or comprehensive study report) to be used in the environmental assessment process. The environmental assessment *process* required by the CEAA is set out in s. 14, which is quoted below. It includes, as applicable, screening or comprehensive study, mediation or panel review, preparation of necessary reports, and design and implementation of a follow-up program.

Thus, the CEAA environmental assessment process makes provision for a two-stage assessment of a project's environmental effects. These stages are self-directed assessment (screening or comprehensive study), and public review (mediation or panel review). An assessment consists of three parts: (1) conducting the assessment, (2) preparing an assessment report, and (3) taking a course of action on the project.

a. Form of Assessment

The first matter requiring attention is determining the appropriate form of self-directed assessment.

Screening. Screening is the basic level of environmental assessment within the CEAA, applying to almost all approval decisions made under acts listed in the law list regulations, such as the *Atomic Energy Control Act*, the *Canadian Agricultural Products Act*, the *Canadian Environmental Protection Act 1999*, the *Canada Wildlife Act*, the *Fisheries Act*, the Indian and Northern Affairs Legislation (for example, the *Canada Petroleum Resources Act*), the *National Energy Board Act*, the *National Parks Act*, the *National Transportation Act*, the *Navigable Waters Protection Act*, and the *Territorial Lands Act*. A screening may be avoided only where more substantial forms of assessment are employed from the outset, such as comprehensive study (s. 21) or direct referral to the minister for panel review or mediation (s. 29).

Comprehensive study. Certain types of projects require comprehensive study from the outset. All such projects are identified in the comprehensive study list regulations. Projects designated for comprehensive studies include major projects such as national parks; water management; oil, gas, or mineral resources; pulp and paper mills; smelters; defence works; navigable waterways; and waste management.

Panel review. The panel review is the most extensive type of environmental assessment under the CEAA. The panel has various legal duties, including (1) gathering information for the eventual hearing; (2) conducting hearings with a broad participation mandate; (3) preparing a report on its assessment of the impacts, including cumulative effects and monitoring; and (4) submitting the report with recommendations to the minister and the responsible authority.

Mediation. Mediation is an alternative to a panel review, but it has only been used once on a trial basis. See chapter 14.

b. Avoiding Duplication: One Project, One Assessment

The second matter that requires attention from the outset is whether the project falls within the jurisdiction of more than one decision maker. At least in theory, the CEAA makes provision to avoid duplication in all stages of assessment, using an approach described as "one project, one assessment." Section 4 states:

> 4. The purposes of this Act are ...
>
> (b.1) to ensure that responsible authorities carry out their responsibilities in a coordinated manner with a view to eliminating unnecessary duplication in the environmental assessment process ... .

To avoid duplication of environmental assessments, the CEAA provides that all "responsible authorities" for a project should "together determine" their respective duties and functions under the Act or seek the advice of the Canadian Environmental Assessment Agency (s. 12(2)). The Coordination by Federal Authorities Regulation, SOR/97-181, sets out guidance on coordinating environmental assessments that have more than one responsible authority or that involve several authorities possessing specialist or expert knowledge relevant to the environmental assessment.

There may be more than one responsible authority for a single project. The potential for multiple responsible authorities arises where, under s. 5 of the Act, the CEAA applies to a project for more than one reason (for example, both federal funding and a federal approval). Therefore, the CEAA makes provision for identifying a lead responsible authority so that only one environmental assessment is carried out (ss. 12(1) and (2)).

For projects subject to federal and *other* (that is, provincial) environmental assessment, the CEAA makes provision for federal authorities to carry out screenings or comprehensive studies in cooperation with provincial governments, other provincial statutory bodies, and any body constituted pursuant to land claims agreements or self-government legislation (ss. 12(4) and (5)). These provisions are complemented by provisions in provincial environmental assessment regimes and may be governed by CCME-sponsored harmonization subagreements. However, their ability to merge or stand alone with land claims legislation has not yet been tested. This includes major projects in most of northern Canada and involves portions of Yukon, the Northwest Territories, and Nunavut.

c. Conducting an Assessment

The CEAA does not prescribe a precise process for carrying out screening or comprehensive study. To carry out an assessment, the CEAA assigns the principal duty to "responsible authorities," which can delegate the administration of the assessment. Delegation may facilitate intergovernmental cooperation where a province, a provincial statutory body, a land claims body, or a self-government statutory body has the responsibility to assess a project (s. 12(4)). The only responsibility that may not be delegated is the ultimate responsibility to make a decision about the project's course of action (s. 20 (screening) and s. 23 (comprehensive study)). The authority to delegate means that the responsible authority may transfer certain actions associated with carrying out an assessment, such as preparing reports, to the proponent of a project.

However, the CEAA does not assign the responsibility for carrying out the environmental assessment to the "proponent." Instead, the Act assigns the responsibility for the process to the "responsible authority" that must make a federal decision on the project, which is generally the same entity as the "federal authority" that was identified, under s. 5, in determining whether the CEAA applied to the project. For example, a federal authority issuing a licence for a project may be deemed the authority responsible for its environmental assessment. In short, the only circumstance where CEAA decisions are "proponent driven" is where the federal government is proposing to carry out a project.

All further action by the federal government is halted until the assessment is concluded (s. 11). The CEAA also makes limited provision for proponents to be subject to the special application of the Act through ss. 46, 47, and 48. Where a project is subject to public review under ss. 46 (trans-provincial environmental effects), 47 (international environmental effects), or 48 (aboriginal lands and other federal lands), the minister may issue an order and seek an injunction against a proponent to prohibit the proponent from doing any act or thing until the assessment is completed (ss. 50 and 51).

d. Major Provisions of the Act

Canadian Environmental Assessment Act
SC 1992, c. 37

Responsible Authority

11(1) Where an environmental assessment of a project is required, the federal authority referred to in section 5 in relation to the project shall ensure that the environmental assessment is conducted as early as is practicable in the planning stages of the project, and before irrevocable decisions are made, and shall be referred to in this Act as the responsible authority in relation to the project.

(2) A responsible authority shall not exercise any power or perform any duty or function referred to in section 5 in relation to a project unless it takes a course of action pursuant to paragraph 20(1)(a) or 37(1)(a).

12(1) Where there are two or more responsible authorities in relation to a project, they shall together determine the manner in which to perform their duties and functions under this Act and the regulations.

(2) In the case of a disagreement, the Agency may advise responsible authorities and other federal authorities with respect to their powers, duties and functions under this Act and the manner in which those powers, duties and functions may be determined and allocated among them.

(3) Every federal authority that is in possession of specialist or expert information or knowledge with respect to a project shall, on request, make available that information or knowledge to the responsible authority or to a mediator or a review panel.

(4) Where a screening or comprehensive study of a project is to be conducted and a jurisdiction has a responsibility or an authority to conduct an assessment of the environmental effects of the project or any part thereof, the responsible authority may cooperate with that jurisdiction respecting the environmental assessment of the project.

. . .

Environmental Assessment Process

General

14. The environmental assessment process includes, where applicable,

(a) a screening or comprehensive study and the preparation of a screening report or a comprehensive study report;

(b) a mediation or assessment by a review panel as provided in section 29 and the preparation of a report; and

(c) the design and implementation of a follow-up program.

15(1) The scope of the project in relation to which an environmental assessment is to be conducted shall be determined by

(a) the responsible authority; or

(b) where the project is referred to a mediator or a review panel, the Minister, after consulting with the responsible authority.

(2) For the purposes of conducting an environmental assessment in respect of two or more projects,

(a) the responsible authority, or

(b) where at least one of the projects is referred to a mediator or a review panel, the Minister, after consulting with the responsible authority,

may determine that the projects are so closely related that they can be considered to form a single project.

(3) Where a project is in relation to a physical work, an environmental assessment shall be conducted in respect of every construction, operation, modification, decommissioning, abandonment or other undertaking in relation to that physical work that is proposed by the proponent or that is, in the opinion of

(a) the responsible authority, or

(b) where the project is referred to a mediator or a review panel, the Minister, after consulting with the responsible authority,

likely to be carried out in relation to that physical work.

16(1) Every screening or comprehensive study of a project and every mediation or assessment by a review panel shall include a consideration of the following factors:

(a) the environmental effects of the project, including the environmental effects of malfunctions or accidents that may occur in connection with the project and any cumulative environmental effects that are likely to result from the project in combination with other projects or activities that have been or will be carried out;

(b) the significance of the effects referred to in paragraph (a);

(c) comments from the public that are received in accordance with this Act and the regulations;

(d) measures that are technically and economically feasible and that would mitigate any significant adverse environmental effects of the project; and

(e) any other matter relevant to the screening, comprehensive study, mediation or assessment by a review panel, such as the need for the project and alternatives to the project, that the responsible authority or, except in the case of a screening, the Minister after consulting with the responsible authority, may require to be considered.

(2) In addition to the factors set out in subsection (1), every comprehensive study of a project and every mediation or assessment by a review panel shall include a consideration of the following factors:

(a) the purpose of the project;

(b) alternative means of carrying out the project that are technically and economically feasible and the environmental effects of any such alternative means;

(c) the need for, and the requirements of any follow-up program in respect of the project; and

(d) the capacity of renewable resources that are likely to be significantly affected by the project to meet the needs of the present and those of the future.

(3) The scope of the factors to be taken into consideration pursuant to paragraphs (1)(a), (b) and (d) and (2)(b), (c) and (d) shall be determined

(a) by the responsible authority; or

(b) where a project is referred to a mediator or a review panel, by the Minister, after consulting the responsible authority, when fixing the terms of reference of the mediation or review panel.

(4) An environmental assessment of a project is not required to include a consideration of the environmental effects that could result from carrying out the project in response to a national emergency for which special temporary measures are taken under *Emergencies Act.*

. . .

Screening

18(1) Where a project is not described in the comprehensive study list or the exclusion list, the responsible authority shall ensure that

(a) a screening of the project is conducted; and

(b) a screening report is prepared.

(2) Any available information may be used in conducting the screening of a project, but where a responsible authority is of the opinion that the information available is not adequate to enable it to take a course of action pursuant to subsection 20(1), it shall ensure that any studies and information that it considers necessary for that purpose are undertaken or collected.

. . .

20(1) The responsible authority shall take one of the following courses of action in respect of a project after taking into consideration the screening report and any comments filed pursuant to subsection 18(3):

(a) subject to subparagraph (c)(iii), where, taking into account the implementation of any mitigation measures that the responsible authority considers appropriate, the project is not likely to cause significant adverse environmental effects, the responsible authority may exercise any power or perform any duty or function that would permit the project to be carried out ...

(b) where, taking into account the implementation of any mitigation measures that the responsible authority considers appropriate, the project is likely to cause significant adverse environmental effects that cannot be justified in the circumstances, the responsible authority shall not exercise any power or perform any duty or function conferred on it by or under any Act of Parliament that would permit the project to be carried out in whole or in part; or

(c) where

(i) it is uncertain whether the project, taking into account the implementation of any mitigation measures that the responsible authority considers appropriate, is likely to cause significant adverse environmental effects,

(ii) the project, taking into account the implementation of any mitigation measures that the responsible authority considers appropriate, is likely to cause significant adverse environmental effects and paragraph (b) does not apply, or

(iii) public concerns warrant a reference to a mediator or a review panel,

the responsible authority shall refer the project to the Minister for a referral to a mediator or a review panel in accordance with section 29.

Comprehensive Study

21. Where a project is described in the comprehensive study list, the responsible authority shall

(a) ensure that a comprehensive study is conducted, and a comprehensive study report is prepared and provided to the Minister and the Agency; or

(b) refer the project to the Minister for a referral to a mediator or a review panel in accordance with section 29.

· · ·

28. Where at any time the Minister is of the opinion that

(a) a project for which an environmental assessment may be required under section 5, taking into account the implementation of any appropriate mitigation measures, may cause significant adverse environmental effects, or

(b) public concerns warrant a reference to a mediator or a review panel, the Minister may, after offering to consult with the jurisdiction, within the meaning of subsection 12(5), where the project is to be carried out and after consulting the with responsible authority or, where there is no responsible authority in relation to the project, the appropriate federal authority, refer the project to a mediator or a review panel in accordance with section 29.

· · ·

Decision of Responsible Authority

37(1) The responsible authority shall take one of the following courses of action in respect of a project after taking into consideration the report submitted by a mediator or a review panel or, in the case of a project referred back to the responsible authority pursuant to paragraph 23(a), the comprehensive study report:

(a) where, taking into account the implementation of any mitigation measures that the responsible authority considers appropriate,

(i) the project is not likely to cause significant adverse environmental effects, or

(ii) the project is likely to cause significant adverse environmental effects that can be justified in the circumstances,

the responsible authority may exercise any power or perform any duty or function that would permit the project to be carried out in whole or in part and shall ensure that those mitigation measures are implemented; or

(b) where, taking into account the implementation of any mitigation measures that the responsible authority considers appropriate, the project is likely to cause significant adverse environmental effects that cannot be justified in the circumstances, the responsible authority shall not exercise any power or perform any duty or function conferred on it by or under any Act of Parliament that would permit the project to be carried out in whole or in part.

(2) Where a responsible authority takes a course of action referred to in paragraph (1)(a), it shall, notwithstanding any other Act of Parliament, in the exercise of its powers or the performance of its duties or functions under that other Act or any

regulation made thereunder or in any other manner that the responsible authority considers necessary, ensure that any mitigation measures referred to in that paragraph in respect of the project are implemented.

(3) Where the responsible authority takes a course of action referred to in paragraph (1)(b) in relation to a project,

   (a) the responsible authority shall file a notice of that course of action in the public registry established in respect of the project pursuant to section 55; and

   (b) notwithstanding any other Act of Parliament, no power, duty or function conferred by or under that Act or any regulation made thereunder shall be exercised or performed that would permit that project to be carried out in whole or in part.

QUESTION

Examine the CEAA, SC 1992, c. 37. How do you know what type of environmental assessment a project requires? When will it be a screening, a comprehensive study, or a panel review? How does the public or the proponent move from one kind of environmental assessment to another? Is this decision only left to the minister or is it left to the responsible authority? How are these changes made? Can the responsible authority transfer a project from a screening to a panel review? Who can?

3. Amendments to the CEAA (2002)

Section 72 of the CEAA requires that five years after its coming into force the minister must undertake a comprehensive review of the operation of the Act and submit a report to Parliament along with any recommended changes. This review was initiated on December 14, 1999 with the release of a discussion paper and a series of in-depth studies on specific topics, followed by extensive consultations. On March 20, 2001, the resulting report entitled *Strengthening Environmental Assessment for Canadians* (Ottawa: CEAA, 2001) was tabled in Parliament, along with Bill C-19, *An Act to Amend the Canadian Environmental Assessment Act* (later Bill C-9, 37th Parl. 2d Sess., 2002). The proposed amendments aim to achieve the three main goals identified by the review process: (1) provide a greater measure of certainty, predictability, and timeliness to all participants in the process; (2) enhance the quality of assessments; and (3) ensure more meaningful public participation. Specific changes have been tabled in certain key areas, including

- focusing the Act on those projects with a greater likelihood of adverse environmental effects;
- improving coordination among federal departments and agencies when several are involved in the same assessment;
- reaffirming and enhancing cooperation with other governments in conducting environmental assessments where jurisdictions overlap;
- increasing certainty in the process in order to reduce the potential for project delays and cost increases;
- improving compliance with the Act;
- strengthening the role of followup to ensure that sound environmental protection measures are in place for the project;

- improving the consideration of cumulative effects (the combined effects of many projects in a region over a long period of time);
- providing convenient, more timely access to reports and other information about an assessment;
- strengthening the incorporation of aboriginal perspectives in the federal process; and
- expanding opportunities for public participation.

Although reaction to these amendments, especially those aimed at increasing transparency and improving public involvement in the planning process and at review, was largely favourable, some groups expressed concerns that they do not go far enough. For example, the Environmental Planning and Assessment Caucus (EPAC) of the Canadian Environmental Network criticized the proposed legislation for failing to entrench some fundamental principles of planning for sustainability, such as the inclusion of requirements to consider alternative development approaches for all projects and to conduct environmental assessment at the regional planning and policy levels. The EPAC maintained that without these strategic planning tools the Canadian public and project proponents will continue to be at odds over environmental sustainability as each project is proposed.

See M. Hébert, "Bill C-19, An Act To Amend the Canadian Environmental Assessment Act" (April 17, 2001, Library of Parliament, LS-402E), Parliamentary Research Branch, available online at http://www.parl.gc.ca/.

QUESTIONS

How effective has the CEAA been since its inception in 1995? Re-read the proposed amendments to the CEAA listed above and ask yourself if these amendments (for example, cumulative effects and monitoring) are so important, why are they being proposed now? What will other proposed changes (such as the public registry) do to the ability of citizens to gather information about projects?

4. The Role of the CEA Agency

The Canadian Environmental Assessment Agency oversees the implementation of the CEAA. The agency is independent of Environment Canada, although still under the direct supervision of the minister of the environment. The agency provides advice to governments and proponents on carrying out environmental assessments, but has no decision-making powers in respect of projects. The agency's Web site is http://www.ceaa.gc.ca/.

E. Conducting Environmental Assessments Across Canada

1. Division of Powers

The constitutional division of powers effects two of the fundamental environmental assessment questions: (1) Which requirements are needed when different regimes are triggered? and (2) What may be required of each regime once triggered? The most important case on environmental assessment and the constitutional division of powers is the guidelines order case of *Friends of the Oldman River Society*, above. This case illustrates the difficulty of determining the precise limits of federal and provincial environmental assessments for projects with no interprovincial or extraterritorial effects. The case also referenced the American precedent (NEPA). Perhaps the most important aspect of the *Friends of the Oldman River Society* decision is its conclusion that the scope of the environmental assessment may vary depending on the constitutional powers involved. This conclusion reflects the basic Canadian constitutional principle that the environment is not exclusively within the mandate of either level of government. Nevertheless, the case pointed out the obvious federal powers over impact assessment.

2. Federal Jurisdiction

Section 5 of the CEAA states that the federal process under the Act applies to "projects" where a federal authority

(a) is the proponent of the project ... ;

(b) makes or authorizes payments or guarantees a loan ... ;

(c) has the administration of federal lands and sells, leases or otherwise disposes of those lands ... ; [and]

(d) issues a permit or licence, grants an approval or takes any other action for the purpose of enabling the project to be carried out ... ,

unless the project is exempted (s. 7(1)(a) and s. 59(c)), or is in response to an emergency (ss. 7(1)(b) and (c)). Constitutionally, the federal government is a major landowner in the Canadian north and offshore. Hence, its decision making on such lands always triggers environmental assessment. Throughout Canada, the federal government manages other lands such as national parks and federal infrastructure, including railways, airports, and ports. Thus, projects involving the federal government as proponent also require environmental assessment.

There are other sources of power. A third source of federal constitutional authority is its spending power. Where the federal government spends money on projects, such spending triggers environmental assessment. A fourth source of federal authority is its regulatory authority through its constitutional jurisdiction over international and interprovincial works, undertakings, and trade and its jurisdiction over navigable waterways, fisheries, agriculture, and nuclear energy. Thus, where the federal government must make a regulatory decision affecting these aspects of the environment, environmental assessment is triggered. CEAA regulations, known as the law list regulations, designate dozens of federal permits, licenses, and approvals under various federal Acts. If carrying out a project involves a federal authority taking a law list action, the project is subject to the CEAA.

Decision makers that qualify as "federal authorities" whose actions can trigger s. 5 are defined in s. 2 as (1) a minister of the federal Crown, (2) an agency of the government of Canada or any other body established by or pursuant to an act of Parliament that is ultimately accountable through Cabinet to Parliament for the conduct of its affairs, (3) certain corporations under the *Financial Administration Act*, and (4) any other body prescribed by regulation. Thus, decisions of the federal Cabinet are not automatically subject to the CEAA, but may be subject to the CEAA through regulations.

3. Harmonization with Provincial Jurisdiction

The divergent principles at work in provincial environmental assessment regimes make it difficult to outline a common approach. It should simply be noted that provincial, territorial, and land claims regimes exist and their principles of application and administration differ, sometimes significantly, from those of the CEAA. The federal government has nevertheless attempted to coordinate with provincial and northern governments to avoid duplication in assessments.

The CCME has played a lead role in negotiating policies for the coordination of joint and overlapping assessments. Under its auspices the provinces (except Quebec) have reached agreement on an Environmental Assessment Sub-Agreement, which acts as a framework for bilateral federal–provincial environmental assessment harmonization accords. See the CCME Web site at http://www.ccmc.ca/.

4. Strategic Environmental Assessment: Policy and Program Assessment

Strategic environmental assessment is another term for environmental assessment of a program or policy. This term distinguishes policy or program assessments from environmental assessments of projects and other physical activities. More strategic environmental assessments are now being done from a policy perspective in Canada. Under the NEPA, the United States has required strategic environmental assessment from the outset. But in Canada, the CEAA applies to projects under specific circumstances only:

1. there must be a "project" that is not exempt, and
2. the project must fall within the general principles of application of the CEAA.

There is a 1999 Cabinet Directive on the Environmental Assessment of Policy, Plan and Program Proposals, which is a non-binding guideline used by federal departments and agencies for strategic environmental assessment. Available online at http://www.ceaa.gc.ca/.

NOTES AND QUESTIONS

1. Perhaps the most important question left unanswered by the preceding material is, just what was the environmental assessment process designed to accomplish? As you read the balance of the chapter, ask yourself *which* of the following five alternatives best describes the process.

a. The environmental assessment process is principally a device to help *governments* generate more and higher quality information about potential environmental effects. In other words, it is a process designed to assist the traditional decision makers.

b. The environmental assessment process is principally a device designed to empower *persons* and enable them to participate more effectively in the decision-making process. Under this model, whether a proposed activity proceeds and on what terms and conditions, is the result of a clash of interests: those for and those against a project. Environmental assessment facilitates decision making by providing opposing interests with a formal opportunity to participate in the "clash."

c. The environmental assessment process represents a restructuring of the way in which *proponents* make decisions about what to do, where to do it, and how to do it. Under this model, proponents are no longer able to do what they wish—they must comply with environmental and other regulatory standards. Now, decision-making responsibility is shared or perhaps even given up to a process that will determine whether a proposed undertaking is appropriate.

d. The environmental assessment process is a *planning* process that attempts to predict or anticipate potential environmental harm and, where possible, to mitigate or avoid the harm. The rationale behind this model is that it is cheaper for planners to avoid environmental problems than it is to proceed without regard for potential environmental harm.

e. Finally, and very much the opposite of 4, the environmental assessment process is a *post-hoc evaluative* process that recognizes that one can never predict the future. Thus, rather than trying to predict and avoid environmental harm, the environmental assessment process provides the ongoing supervision a project. This "monitoring" model also assumes an ability to adjust environmental regulation in the light of actual experience.

2. It will come as no surprise to learn that the advent of environmental assessment has raised a number of fundamental questions about its interaction with other planning and regulatory processes. How does environmental assessment fit with land-use planning processes, public enquiries, royal commissions, or expropriation procedures? What is the relationship between regulatory initiatives that flow from environmental assessment and those that come from within departments and other regulatory agencies such as the National Energy Board? Is there any relief for the inevitable overlap and duplication? What can be done to identify and resolve the inefficiencies, inconsistencies, and delays?

3. Should environmental assessments apply to legislative actions?

4. How do the normal s. 5 "action" triggers apply to policy reviews? Assuming that we can credibly undertake strategic environmental assessments, why should we be reviewing policy or ministerial decisions (which are political) such as the *decision* to create parks?

5. As the environmental assessment concept has evolved over time, a number of tensions have arisen among those charged with designing and administrating the process. For example, the continuing push to broaden the scope of the environmental assessment process and to recognize the systematic, interrelated nature of environmental issues clashes with the countervailing desire to make it more focused and efficient. Can the process assess everything well, and if not, what do we trade off?

6. Are there some environmental values that are too important to be left to a process that does not provide guaranteed environmental results? Compare the Canadian position with that expressed in the US case *Calvert Cliffs Coordinating Committee v. US Atomic Energy Commission*, 449 F. 2d 1109 (1971):

NEPA, first of all, makes environmental protection a part of the mandate of every federal agency and department. The Atomic Energy Commission, for example, had continually asserted, prior to NEPA, that it had no statutory authority to concern itself with the adverse environmental effects of its actions. Now, however, its hands are no longer tied. It is not only permitted, but compelled, to take environmental values into account. Perhaps the greatest importance of NEPA is to require the Atomic Energy Commission and other agencies to *consider* environmental issues just as they consider other matters within their mandates. This compulsion is most plainly stated in Section 102 ... .

The question here is whether the Commission is correct in thinking that its NEPA responsibilities may "be carried out in toto outside the hearing process"—whether it is enough that environmental data and evaluation merely "accompany" an application through the review process, but receive no consideration whatever from the hearing board.

We believe that the Commission's crabbed interpretation of NEPA makes a mockery of the Act. What possible purpose could there be in the Section 102(2)(C) requirement (that the "detailed statement" accompany proposals through agency review processes) if "accompany" means no more than physical proximity—maintaining no more than the physical act of passing certain folders and papers, unopened, to reviewing officials along with other folders and papers? What possible purpose could there be in requiring the "detailed statement" to be before hearing boards, if the boards are free to ignore entirely the contents of the statement? NEPA was meant to do more than regulate the flow of papers in the federal bureaucracy. The word "accompany" in Section 102(2)(C) must not be read so narrowly as to make the Act ludicrous. It must, rather, be read to indicate a congressional intent that environmental factors, as compiled in the "detailed statement," be *considered* through agency review processes. Beyond Section 102(2)(C), NEPA requires that agencies consider the environmental impact of their actions "to the fullest extent possible." The Act is addressed to agencies as a whole, not only to their professional staffs. Compliance to the "*fullest*" possible extent would seem to demand that environmental issues be considered at every important stage in the decision making process concerning a particular action—at every stage where an overall balancing of environmental and nonenvironmental factors is appropriate and where alterations might be made in the proposed action to minimize environmental costs.

5. Canada's Land Claims Agreements

One of the first examples of binding legislation on environmental assessment resulted from the 1975 *James Bay and Northern Quebec Agreement* (Quebec: Éditeur Officiel du Québec, 1976), an agreement between the Canadian and Quebec governments and the Cree and Inuit of northern Quebec. This agreement was ratified through federal and provincial legislation. Under this framework of agreement and legislation, the two governments were required to carry out environmental assessments of projects in areas subject to the agreement.

Since that time, a number of similar negotiations have occurred in northern Canada, resulting in additional commitments to supporting legislation. For example, the federal *Mackenzie Valley Resource Management Act*, SC 1998, c. 25, authorizes an environmental assessment process applicable to the area subject to a comprehensive 1992 land claim agreement between the federal government and the Gwich'in First Nation.

One of the newest territories in Canada is Nunavut. In the *Nunavut Land Claims Agreement* (Ottawa: Indian and Northern Affairs Canada, 1993), one of the key articles provided for the establishment of the Nunavut Impact Review Board. The broad environmental assessment mandate of this board is found in article 12.2.5:

In carrying out its functions, the primary objectives of NIRB shall be at all times to protect and promote the existing and future well-being of the residents and communities of the Nunavut Settlement Area, and to protect the ecosystemic integrity of the Nunavut Settlement Area. NIRB shall take into account the well-being of residents of Canada outside the Nunavut Settlement Area.

NOTES AND QUESTIONS

1. Is the Nunavut environmental assessment mandate the same as the *Calvert Cliffs* approach?

2. Do these land claims agreements, which are constitutionally entrenched, harmonize with the CEAA? Section 12.2.2 of the *Nunavut Land Claims Agreement*, as enacted in the *Nunavut Land Claims Agreement Act*, SC 1993, c. 29 (NLCA), states

> Where there is any inconsistency or conflict between any federal, territorial and local government laws, and the Agreement, the Agreement shall prevail to the extent of the inconsistency or conflict.

Under the CEAA, certain federal projects require a comprehensive study report (CSR). Assuming that the project is in Nunavut (which has no land claims CSR procedure or requirement), and it is sent to a full public review under the NLCA, is it inconsistent for a responsible authority to suggest under the CEAA that a CSR *also* be completed in Nunavut?

3. How does the Nunavut mandate differ from the purposes of the CEAA? Section 12.2.5 of the *Nunavut Land Claims Agreement* quoted above relies on the imperative of "ecosystemic integrity." Is this requisite significant?

4. An additional matter of developing interest is the role of traditional knowledge in environmental assessment. Because many of the largest resource projects proposed in Canada occur in the northern lands occupied by aboriginal peoples, it has been extremely important for governments to take special measures to encourage the participation of affected communities. Early federal environmental assessments were translated into appropriate aboriginal languages and hearings made express provisions to facilitate participation. More recently, federal panels have included aboriginal members; an example is the federal–provincial environmental assessment of a proposed transmission line in northern Manitoba where a majority of panel members were aboriginal. Land claims legislation also requires cultural matters to be taken into account. Section 12.2.24 of the *Nunavut Land Claims Agreement* states:

> *Public Hearings* [for impact assessment]
>
> 12.2.24 In designing its by-laws and rules of procedure for the conduct of public hearings, NIRB [Nunavut Impact Review Board] shall:
>
> (a) to the extent consistent with the broad application of the principles of natural justice and procedural fairness, emphasize flexibility and informality, and, specifically
>
> (i) allow, where appropriate, the admission of evidence that would not normally be admissible under the strict rules of evidence, and
>
> (ii) *give due regard and weight to the tradition of Inuit oral communication and decision-making; and*
>
> (b) *with respect to any classification of intervenors, allow full standing to a DIO* [designated Inuit organization]. [Emphasis added.]

5. Traditional and cultural knowledge is part of the impact assessment hearings in northern Canada. Yet, how does traditional knowledge take over from scientific assessments? Does it fill in "gaps" or does it replace the judgment of other experts? For biophysical or socioeconomic impacts? When and how?

6. Although the federal government has recognized the importance of aboriginal participation, is there any guarantee of intervener funding by relying exclusively on the land claims agreements?

III. WHAT "PROJECTS" ARE SUBJECT TO ENVIRONMENTAL ASSESSMENT?

A. Background

Perhaps the first issues to be addressed with regard to environmental assessment in Canada are matters of application and scope. To whom and to what does the process apply, and how broad is the process?

1. To Whom Does the Process Apply?

A law has to be clear and certain to be applied fairly and properly. Some argue that none of the environmental assessment processes make it particularly easy to answer the question "am I and/or my proposed activity subject to the Act?" One reason for this is that the status of the person (usually corporate or organizational) tends to be more important than the proposed activity. For example, the Ontario process applies to public persons (government departments and crown corporations) in one way, and to private persons in another. The federal process applies to persons who receive federal financial assistance, but not to those who do not. Certain Crown corporations are required to comply with the process, others are not.

2. Definition of "Project"

Project means a proposed physical work and any related construction, operation, modification, decommissioning, abandonment, or undertaking or, where prescribed by regulations known as the inclusion list regulations, "a physical activity not relating to a physical work" (s. 2). Thus, the definition of project is clearly limited to physical changes, not plans or transactions. For projects that involve physical works, the CEAA requires assessment of all related works and undertakings (s. 15).

Friends of the Oldman River Society v. Canada (Minister of Transport)
(1992), 7 CELR (NS) 1, at 21-52 (SCC)

[The province of Alberta applied to the federal minister of transport for an approval to construct a dam on the Oldman River, which was granted pursuant to s. 5 of the *Navigable Waters Protection Act*, RSC 1985, c. N-22. The federal minister considered the impact of the dam on marine navigation but did not subject the application to an environmental assessment as provided in the EARP guidelines order, SOR/84-467. The Friends of the Oldman River Society applied for *certiorari*, as well as *mandamus*, to quash the approval and require both the minister of transport and the minister of fisheries and oceans to comply with the guidelines order. The application was dismissed at the trial division but the Federal Court of Appeal reversed this decision, quashing the approval and ordering the ministers to comply with the guidelines order.]

LA FOREST J:

Statutory Validity of the Guidelines Order

Is the Guidelines Order Authorized by s. 6 of the Department of the Environment Act?

The word "guidelines" cannot be construed in isolation; s. 6 must be read as a whole. When so read it becomes clear that Parliament has elected to adopt a regulatory scheme that is "law," and thus amendable to enforcement through prerogative relief.

Alberta also argues that the *Guidelines Order* is *ultra vires* on the ground that the scope of the subject matter covered in the delegated legislation goes far beyond that authorized by the *Department of the Environment Act*. More specifically, it contends that the authority to establish guidelines for the purposes of carrying out the minister's duties related to "environmental quality" does not comprehend a process of environmental impact assessment, such as found in the *Guidelines Order*, in which the decision-maker is required to take into account socio-economic considerations. Rather, it is argued, the Act only permits the enactment of delegated legislation that is strictly concerned with matters relating to environmental quality as understood in a physical sense.

I cannot accept that the concept of environmental quality is confined to the biophysical environment alone; such an interpretation is unduly myopic and contrary to the generally held view that the "environment" is a diffuse subject matter see: *R v. Crown Zellerbach Canada Ltd.*, [1988] 1 SCR 401 [alternative citations omitted]. The point was made by the Canadian Council of Resource and Environment Ministers, following the "Bruntland Report" of the World Commission on Environment and Development, in the *Report of the National Task Force on Environment and Economy*, September 24, 1987, at p. 2:

> Our recommendations reflect the principles that we hold in common with the World Commission on Environment and Development (WCED). These include the fundamental belief that environmental and economic planning cannot proceed in separate spheres. Long-term economic growth depends on a healthy environment. It also affects the environment in many ways. Ensuring environmentally sound and sustainable economic development requires the technology and wealth that is generated by continued economic growth. Economic and environmental planning and management must therefore be integrated.

Surely the potential consequences for a community's livelihood, health and other social matters from environmental change are integral to decision-making on matters affecting environmental quality, subject, of course, to the constitutional imperatives, an issue I will address later.

I have therefore concluded that the *Guidelines Order* has been validly enacted pursuant to the *Department of the Environment Act*, and is mandatory in nature.

Inconsistency with the Navigable Waters Protection Act and Fisheries Act

The appellants Alberta and the federal ministers argue that the *Guidelines Order* is inconsistent with, and therefore must yield to, the requirements of the *Navigable Waters Protection Act* for obtaining an approval under s. 5 of that Act. Specifically, they say, the Minister of Transport is confined by the Act to a consideration of matters pertaining to marine navigation alone, and that the *Guidelines Order* cannot displace or add to the criteria mentioned in the Act. Alberta also submits that the *Guidelines Order* is similarly inconsistent with the *Fisheries Act*, but for the reasons set out later I do not find it necessary to address that issue.

· · ·

The inconsistency contended for is that the *Navigable Waters Protection Act* implicitly precludes the Minister of Transport from taking into consideration any matters other than marine navigation in exercising his power of approval under s. 5 of the Act, whereas the *Guidelines Order* requires, at a minimum, an initial environmental impact assessment. The appellant ministers concede that there is no explicit prohibition against his taking into account environmental factors, but argue that the focus and scheme of the Act limit him to considering nothing other than the potential effects on marine navigation. If the appellants are correct, it seems to me that the minister would approve of very few works because several of the "works" falling within the ambit of s. 5 do not assist navigation at all, but by their very nature interfere with, or impede navigation, for example, bridges, booms, dams and the like. If the significance of the impact on marine navigation were the sole criterion, it is difficult to conceive of a dam of this sort ever being approved. It is clear, then, that the minister must factor several elements into any cost-benefit analysis to determine if a substantial interference with navigation is warranted in the circumstances.

It is likely that the Minister of Transport, in exercising his functions under s. 5, always did take into account the environmental impact of a work, at least as regards other federal areas of jurisdiction, such as Indians or Indian land. However that may be, the *Guidelines Order* now formally mandates him to do so, and I see nothing in this that is inconsistent with his duties under s. 5. As Stone JA put it in the Court of Appeal, it created a duty which is "superadded" to any other statutory power residing in him which can stand with that power. In my view the minister's duty under the *Guidelines Order* is indeed supplemental to his responsibility under the *Navigable Waters Protection Act*, and he cannot resort to an excessively narrow interpretation of his existing statutory powers to avoid compliance with the *Guidelines Order*.

· · ·

A broad interpretation of the application of the *Guidelines Order* is consistent with the objectives stated in both the order itself and its parent legislation—to make environmental impact assessment an essential component of federal decision-making. A similar approach has been followed in the United States with respect to their *National Environmental Policy Act*. As Pratt J put it in *Environmental Defense Fund Inc. v. Mathews*, 410 F. Supp. 336 (DCC, 1976), at p. 337:

> NEPA does not supersede other statutory duties, but, to the extent that it is reconcilable with those duties, it supplements them. Full compliance with its requirements cannot be avoided unless such compliance directly conflicts with other existing statutory duties.

To hold otherwise would, in my view, set at naught the legislative scheme for the protection of the environment envisaged by Parliament in enacting the *Department of the Environment Act*, and in particular s. 6.

Nor do I think s. 3 of the *Guidelines Order*, which requires that the assessment process be initiated "as early in the planning process as possible and before irrevocable decisions are taken," is in any way inconsistent with s. 6 of the *Navigable Waters Protection Act*.

NOTE

In *Friends of the West Country Assn. v. Canada (Minister of Fisheries and Oceans)*, [2000] 2 FC 263 (FCA) (the *Sunpine* case), the Federal Court of Appeal held that it was up to the responsible authority to determine the scope of the project to be assessed (s. 15). Once the scope of the project to be assessed is defined, s. 15(3) of the Act—which says the assessment shall be conducted on any other undertaking "in relation to" the physical work—cannot be used to expand the scope and do a more wide-ranging assessment. Thus, in *Sunpine*, once it was decided that the scope of the environmental assessment was to look at two bridges, only undertakings in relation to the construction of the bridges (for example, staff housing) were included; the scope could not be expanded to look at the effects of the roads that connected the bridges or the logging that would result from the project's completion.

B. Major Federal Actions: CEAA ss. 5(1)(a)-(d)

As noted previously, the federal process under the CEAA applies to "projects" where a federal authority is the proponent of the project; makes or authorizes payments; sells, leases, or otherwise disposes of federal lands; or issues a permit or licence, grants an approval, or takes any other action for the purpose of enabling the project to be carried out unless the project is exempted or is in response to an emergency.

A project is defined in s. 2(1) of the Act to mean:

> (a) in relation to a physical work, any proposed construction, operation, modification, decommissioning, abandonment or other undertaking in relation to that physical work, or
>
> (b) any proposed physical activity not relating to a physical work that is prescribed.

Prescribed projects or classes of projects comprise the comprehensive study list (s. 2(1)). A comprehensive study means a study conducted pursuant to s. 21 of the CEAA—that is, a study that considers both the factors that are to be examined in a screening (s. 16(1)), as well as the additional factors set out in s. 16(2), namely a consideration of

(a) the purpose of the project;

(b) alternative means of carrying out the project that are technically and economically feasible and the environmental effects of any such alternative means;

(c) the need for, and the requirements of any follow-up program in respect of the project; and

(d) the capacity of renewable resources that are likely to be significantly affected by the project to meet the needs of the present and those of the future.

In addition, where the governor in council is satisfied that a project is likely to have significant adverse environmental effects, by regulation, it may require a comprehensive study to be conducted of the project. A "significant" environmental effect is not defined in the Act, although "environmental effect" is (see s. 7(1)).

C. Exemptions

Under s. 7, the CEAA provides limited exemptions from environmental assessment. There are two categories of statutory exemption: projects carried out in response to emergencies and projects receiving federal funding where the funding is provided in advance of specific details on the project. Section 7 also makes provision for exempting regulations, known as the exclusion list regulations. Under the terms of the CEAA, projects on the exclusion list must fit at least one of three grounds of exclusion:

- environmental assessment of the project is inappropriate for reasons of national security;
- the federal role in authorizing the project is minimal; or
- the potential environmental effects of the project are insignificant.

The present exclusion list regulations state that they are relying upon the third ground for exemption only. Under s. 60, the CEAA also provides for an exceptional form of exemption from the requirements of the Act or regulations where the federal Cabinet determines that compliance with a provision in the Act or regulations is inappropriate.

NOTES

1. Proposed amendments to s. 7 would provide that an environmental assessment is also not required if the project involves one of the entities that will be required by separate regulation to carry out an alternative environmental assessment process in relation to the project. The entities to which the exemptions would apply if all conditions were met are the Canadian International Development Agency, designated Crown corporations, designated harbour commissioners or commissions and port authorities, and other entities designated by regulation. See M. Hébert, above.

2. The text of NEPA does not provide a specific list of exemptions from environmental assessment. Instead, US courts, in deciding whether federal agencies are required to perform assessments, have found it necessary to interpret the Act in order to decide

whether proposals for legislation and other major federal actions significantly affect the quality of the human environment. Therefore, judicial interpretation is needed to determine whether an environmental assessment should be carried out or whether an exemption should apply. One of the most significant statements in this regard can be found in decision of the US Supreme Court in *Andrus, Secretary of the Interior, et al. v. Sierra Club et al.*, 442 US 347 (1979). The respondents, three organizations with interests in the preservation of the environment, brought an action alleging that proposed budget cuts to the National Wildlife Refuge System would adversely affect the operation and maintenance of a national program aimed at the restoration, preservation, development, and management of wildlife, including threatened and endangered species and their habitats. The respondents argued that by putting the wildlife refuges and the operation of the program at risk, the funding cutbacks would significantly affect the quality of the human environment, and therefore an environmental impact statement was required under s. 102(2)(C) of NEPA. To determine whether an impact statement was necessary, the court had to decide the issue of whether the language of s. 102(2)(C) was meant to encompass requests for "appropriations"—that is, authorizations by Congress permitting federal agencies to incur obligations and to make payments out of the Treasury for specified purposes. In other words, under NEPA, is a funding decision a "proposal for legislation" or does it fit into the category of "other major Federal actions?" The court found that federal agencies were not required to prepare environmental impact statements because appropriation requests do not fall into either category within the meaning of the statute. Referring to both the traditional separation drawn by Congress between "legislation" and "appropriation," and the interpretation of NEPA found in the regulations formulated by the Council on Environmental Quality, the court held that funding decisions do not constitute proposals for legislation. Neither do they constitute proposals for major federal actions, since appropriation requests do not propose federal actions, but merely fund actions already proposed.

IV. TIMING: WHEN DOES IT APPLY?

The timing of environmental assessment within federal decision making is set out in s. 11 of the CEAA:

> (1) Where an environmental assessment of a project is required, the federal authority referred to in section 5 in relation to the project shall ensure that the environmental assessment is conducted as early as is practicable in the planning stages of the project and before irrevocable decisions are made … .
>
> (2) A responsible authority shall not exercise any power or perform any duty or function referred to in section 5 in relation to a project unless it takes a course of action pursuant to paragraph 20(1)(a) or 37(1)(a).

The critical term in environmental assessment timing is "irrevocable decision." In *Quebec v. Canada (National Energy Board)* (1994), 14 CELR (NS) 1, Iacobucci J of the Supreme Court had this to say regarding irrevocable decisions and the proper timing of assessments:

The main goal of the Process created by the EARP Guidelines Order is that "the initiating department shall, as early in the planning process as possible and before irrevocable decisions are taken, ensure that the environmental implications of all proposals for which it is the decision-making authority are fully considered and where the implications are significant, refer the proposal to the Minister for public review by a Panel" (s. 3). The overarching purpose of the EARP Guidelines Order is to avoid, in situations in which multiple regulatory steps impinge on an undertaking or proposal, disregard for the fundamentally important matter of the protection of the environment. (Para. 67)

The Federal Court has dealt with the issue of timing in a number of cases since the enactment of the CEAA. For example, the case of *Bowen v. Canada (Attorney General)*, [1998] 2 FC 395 (TD), involved the premature decision of the minister of Canadian heritage to close and decommission airstrips located within the Banff and Jasper National Parks before CEAA assessments were done. The court found that in conducting an environmental screening Parks Canada had followed the wrong kind of environmental assessment process and, instead, a comprehensive study was necessary under the circumstances. Campbell J had this to say about the timing requirement contained in s. 11 of the CEAA: "I find that in observance of this provision, the comprehensive environmental study must be carried out before any decision is made to decommission."

Similarly, in *Tsawwassen Indian Band v. Canada (Minister of Environment)* (1998), 145 FTR 1; aff'd. [2001] FCJ no. 515; (2001), FCA 58, the Tsawwassen First Nation brought an application for judicial review of the granting of an ocean disposal permit to the Vancouver Port Corporation in relation to their Deltaport Container Terminal Project. The applicants argued that by conducting a limited screening, the minister erred in law by failing to comply properly with the provisions of the CEAA. In their view, an assessment of the project as a whole, rather than one limited to the effects of the disposal of dredged material, was required under the Act. The court disagreed and held that since the project was not in the proposal stage, but had been completed and fully operational by June 1997, the CEAA's environmental assessment requirements did not apply. On the issue of timing, the court held that the relevant provisions of the CEAA (ss. 8(1), 9, 10(1), 11(1), 54(1), and 54(2)) make it clear that environmental assessments are intended only to apply to proposed projects still in the planning stages—that is, projects for which irrevocable decisions have not yet been made. On appeal, Linden JA confirmed the finding of the Trial Division and concluded:

> [T]he word "project," as defined by the CEAA, applies only to projects where legal construction has not yet begun. In this case, the disposal work in question was completed in November 1995. The request by the appellant for the establishment of a board of review was made on December 13, 1995, two months after notice of the amendment was advertised in the Canada Gazette on October 14, 1995 and one month after completion of the authorized ocean disposal work. Consequently, the Minister has no duty to appoint a review panel or to conduct an assessment of a work which has been completed .... . [T]he provisions of CEAA are only applicable to proposed projects, not completed ones.

Sunshine Village Corporation v. Superintendent, Banff National Park
(1995), 15 CELR (NS) 278 (FCTD)

[This case involved a dispute about a proposed expansion of one of Canada's premier ski areas in one of Canada's most popular national parks. A national environmental group, the Canadian Parks and Wilderness Society (CPAWS), opposed the expansion, notwithstanding that the expansion was within an area zoned in the park as "recreational." CPAWS filed a judicial review action to stop tree clearing for ski runs on Goat's Eye mountain, after Sunshine Village had signed a construction agreement with Parks Canada that, as Sunshine Village argued, was fully studied, approved, and underway.]

JOYAL J: I need not elaborate further on that approach to that aspect of the case before me. Admittedly, an environmental assessment of the Goat's Eye proposal was made under the [EARP] Guidelines. What is done is done. Having found, however, that the proposal met the test, that a construction agreement was duly executed, that an initial implementation was carried out, I fail to see where any further impediment under the Guidelines may be raised at this time.

To argue a contrary position, in my view, would mean that whichever way the winds of politics blow, any proposal is subject at all stages of any development programme to a regulatory guillotine: should a proposal be approved under the EARP Guidelines, and the regulatory body, Parks Canada, acts in conformity with it and issues implementation authorizations necessary for it under its own regulatory process, the way would still be open for the exercise of ministerial discretion under section 13 [s. 28 CEAA]. Perhaps there are other provisions under Parks Canada regulations to order a public review or otherwise postpone the implementation, but with respect, s. 13 would not be one of them.

In my view, public concerns over environmental issues should not be made a matter of whim by anyone purporting to act under the authority of either the EARP Guidelines or the authority of the *National Parks Act* and its large volume of regulations. It would mean that no matter the many processes to which an applicant must submit, there is no finality to any proposal. This is especially relevant when dealing with a development which is planned not in relation to a wilderness area or to carve out some commercial use from pristine parks territory, but is earmarked for an area which has been specially "designated" under the *National Parks Act* Schedule as a recreational ski area.

The question of timing was also a central issue in the controversial case of *Hamilton-Wentworth (Regional Municipality) v. Canada (Minister of the Environment)*, 2001 FCT 381; aff'd. 2001 FCA 347, which dealt with the extension of the Red Hill Creek expressway outside of the city of Hamilton. The expressway extension completed a major transportation corridor that had been undertaken in stages by the regional municipality since the early 1960s. The necessity of conducting a new and separate environmental assessment under the newly enacted CEAA on the extension was dependent on the interpretation of the timing provisions of the CEAA. The region maintained that the project was continuous and ongoing, and that, as such, s. 74(4) of the CEAA, which exempts projects from the Act's requirements "[w]here the construction or operation of a physical work or the carrying out of a physical activity was initiated before June 22, 1984," applied. The applicants argued that the new extension should be assessed separately under the CEAA since the actual physical construction of the expressway, properly equated with a "shovel hitting the ground," was initiated after the s.74(4) cutoff date. The court disagreed and rejected the applicants characterization of what initiates the construction of a project. Dawson J held instead that the term "construction" encompasses a whole series of preliminary steps, including the acquisition and clearing of land, imposition of building restrictions, and securing of funding and approvals—that is, actions dedicated to and prerequisites to the actual physical step of construction. The court noted that since 1963 the regional municipality had taken numerous steps toward the completion of the project, including the enactment of the Official Plan Amendment designating the route right of way and incorporating plans for the freeway, the acquisition of property from landowners and approvals from governments and boards, the identification and protection of additional lands required for future interchanges, and the notification of affected landowners. Dawson J explained that what is "[c]rucial ... to the determination of whether a step is part of the initiation of construction ... is whether the action is both a necessary prerequisite to a 'shovel hitting the ground' and is dedicated to a particular project so that it evidences an irrevocable decision to proceed with the project."

The decision of the trial court was affirmed on appeal. In the words of Richard CJ,

> We agree with the Applications Judge's conclusion that the construction of the expressway was initiated prior to June 22, 1984, even though actual building had not at that time started. In a project of this complexity, it is simplistic to attach undue significance to when "the shovel hit the ground".... .
>
> [W]e agree with Dawson J's further conclusion that the application of the CEAA is excluded by subsection 11(1). In our opinion, the decision in Tsawwassen Indian Band ... cannot be distinguished from the facts of this case. Here, too, the advanced stage of the project, including its partial construction, meant that by January 1, 1995, there was no "project" in existence within the meaning of the Act for which an environmental assessment was required. We do not regard as a material distinction the fact that, in the case at bar, minor changes had been made to the design of the project.

During the trial, the respondents raised the argument that the phrase "irrevocable decision" in s. 11(1) refers only to decisions made by responsible authorities and not to decisions made by project proponents. The court refused to accept this narrow interpretation. To do so, Dawson J stated, would not only render s. 11(2) unnecessary, it would be inconsistent with previous judicial interpretations and with the Canadian Environmental Assessment Agency's own understanding of the CEAA process. In making this final determination, Dawson J relied on the wording of the agency's operational policy statement, which refers to both responsible authorities and the proponent as being better placed than the agency to "define potential solutions to a problem, and to establish the viability of alternatives."

The decision in *Hamilton-Wentworth* has raised a significant degree of concern among many, in particular, the Canadian Environmental Assessment Agency. In a presentation to the Standing Committee on Environment and Sustainable Development, the agency reviewed the case and expressed deep concerns that the Federal Court's reasoning "runs counter to the purpose of the CEAA, to ensure that the environmental effects of projects receive careful consideration before federal decisions are taken." The agency's primary concern is the determination that the CEAA does not apply to the Red Hill Creek project "because it would be a retroactive application of CEAA to a project for which irrevocable decisions were made prior to the coming into force of the Act in January 1995." In explaining their interpretation of the phrase "irrevocable decisions" and the reasoning behind it, the agency stated:

> We have always interpreted these words in section 11 as referring to the "irrevocable decisions" of federal authorities. Justice Dawson concluded that it has a broader meaning. She held that the term included decisions made by the municipal government, which is the proponent of the Expressway ... . She concluded that the Expressway was not a "project" for the purposes of CEAA because irrevocable decisions had been made to initiate construction prior to 1995 and therefore the construction of the Expressway was no longer "proposed"... .
>
> We had long thought that the issue of whether the Act applies to projects in advanced stages of planning was settled by litigation under ... the EARPGO ... . The results of the *Rafferty-Alameda* and *Oldman River Dam* cases were very clear:
>
> - The federal environmental assessment process had to be applied before departments could make the decision which was the EARPGO trigger.
> - It did not matter whether the federal decision was sought early or late in the planning stages of a project—or even in the implementation stages of a project. The federal assessment process had to be applied whenever the federal decision was sought.
> - The application of the federal assessment process was not affected by the decisions of others—whether they were provincial or municipal governments, proponents or anyone else ... .
>
> Whether CEAA applies to a project cannot simply depend on whether the *proponent*, the province or anyone else has already made a decision in relation to it. If so, proponents might plan their projects in such a way as to make "irrevocable decisions" before seeking federal decisions and in doing so, they could attempt to prevent application of CEAA ... .
>
> [O]ne of the reasons why the government decided not to seek leave to appeal the Federal Court of Appeal decision is because Bill C-19 provides a timely opportunity to propose amendments to ensure that the original intent of the Act is met. We believe that it is important to clarify two things in CEAA: First, a project continues to be "proposed" as long as a federal decision in relation to the project has not yet been made. Second, the decisions of others do not affect the application of the federal assessment process.

The agency proposed that any amendments to the CEAA should specifically address the questions surrounding the issue of "irrevocable decisions" and the definition of "project" by clearly stating that decisions by other bodies would not count as "irrevocable decisions," and that the environmental assessment process would apply at the time that a federal decision is sought even if a project were in the advanced planning stages.

Interestingly, the proposed amendments to the CEAA, which have been tabled in the House of Commons, do not contain provisions clarifying the terms "project" or "irrevocable decision." It appears that projects will continue to be exempt from review if any "irrevocable decisions" were made prior to June 1995. The issue whether the CEAA applies to projects where construction was initiated prior to this date will depend on the particular facts of each case, with the determination of what actually constitutes "construction" now based on developing common law and any statutory changes that do get through the House and Senate.

NOTE

Consider the implications of the methodology for unfinished highway projects, described by F.P. Grad, *Treatise on Environmental Law*, vol. 2 (New York: Matthew Bender, 1990), chapter 9, s. 02[2]c, at 9-122, 9-132 as follows:

> The segment issue is a recurring issue in highway planning and construction, and though rules have been formulated relating to the appropriate segment of highway for EIS [environmental impact statement] purposes, the determination in a specific case will depend on the particular facts. There is general agreement that NEPA requires an EIS at the earliest practicable time, so that the environmental analysis will contribute fairly to the planning process. The courts in dealing with the segmentation issue, have reflected the requirement of the Act that the preparation of an EIS must not become a mere ritual but ought to contribute to the accomplishment of the purposes of the Act. ... . The decision to plan for a major network of highways can be regarded as preliminary, because the real impact decisions will not be made until the precise route of a particular segment is settled upon. This may, however, circumvent the intent of the Act, because there would be no assessment of the environmental impact of the project taken as a whole. An agency that wanted to circumvent the clear intent of the Act would be able to point to the relatively minor environmental damage threatened by any one part of the project, ignoring the major impact of the project as a whole. The decision that a new highway system is needed should be subject to environmental impact considerations, just as the decision to build a particular stretch of road ... . In *Swain v. Brinegar*, the Seventh Circuit reviewed the adequacy of an environmental impact statement which covered only a segment of the highway project. Since the proposed federal action included the funding of the entire project, the court found that the environmental impact statement prepared was inadequate. In its view, NEPA requires federal decision-makers to consider environmental consequences of their actions before deciding to proceed. The environmental impact statement must enable them to take a pragmatic and realistic view of the scope of the contemplated action. The court looks for certain key attributes of the highway proposal; whether the highway has independent utility, whether it has logical termini and whether it forecloses any avenues for expansion. Since the answers to these three questions were in the affirmative, an environmental impact statement was required to cover the entire project. The court also relied on *SCRAP II* for the proposition that the scope of the environmental impact statement must be at least as broad as the scope of the federal action being taken. Since the proposed federal action consisted of the entire forty-two mile highway project, the statement had to consider the whole project ... . In summary, the application of NEPA to highway projects requires the preparation of an EIS that is coextensive in its coverage with the terms of the federal grant. When the grant covers a major project, so must the EIS. When the grant covers only a short stretch

of highway, the EIS need not cover the entire route, even though there may be some planning—though not yet a proposal—for the entire length. The assertion that a short stretch of road is not part of a larger highway project is subject to a number of tests. Does the proposed road have independent utility? Does it have logical termini? And, is it of sufficient length for the consideration of appropriate alternatives?

V. SCOPE OF ENVIRONMENTAL ASSESSMENT

A. Alternatives Requirement

Consideration of alternatives is the heart of good environmental planning and is essential whenever a project under the CEAA is likely to cause significant adverse effects. Several environmental assessment panel review decisions have grappled with a consideration of alternatives under the CEAA. See Report of the Alberta Energy and Utilities Board—Canadian Environmental Assessment Agency Joint Review Panel: Cheviot Coal Project, Mountain Park Area, Alberta (June 1997), at 20, and the Joint Public Review Panel Report: Sable Gas Projects, Canadian Environmental Assessment Agency, National Energy Board, et al. (October 1997), at 87.

A recent case from the Federal Court of Appeal shockingly appears to endorse a narrow approach to this issue. See *Alberta Wilderness Assn. v. Express Pipelines Limited* (1996), 137 DLR (4th), at 181 (FCA). Under s. 16 of the CEAA, every review panel "must include a consideration" of a number of listed factors, such as cumulative effects, the need for the project, mitigation measures, and alternatives to the project. However, in the *Sunpine* case, above, the courts had already decided that the minister and the responsible authority had the discretion to decide on the scope of each of these factors (s. 16(3)) as they fix the review panel's terms of reference (s. 33). Thus, in *Express Pipelines*, the court held that it was a discretionary decision for the minister and the responsible authority to decide which "alternative means" of conducting a project a panel can consider. This approach was upheld in the *Cheriot Mine* case (*Alberta Wilderness Assn. v. Cardinal River Coals Ltd.* (1999), 15 Admin. LR (3d) 25 (FCTD), where the only alternative to an open pit coal mine that the panel was allowed to consider was an underground mine, and other alternatives—such as a different location—were not open for review.

In contrast, NEPA requires impact statements to consider "alternatives to the proposed action." The requirement that agencies consider alternatives is critical to NEPA's implementation, and the Council on Environmental Quality regulations refer to the alternatives requirement as the "heart" of the environmental impact statement: see CFR, s. 1502.14. Consider s. 16 of the CEAA in light the following principles from US courts interpreting NEPA:

- US courts have developed a "rule of reason" standard, which "requires an agency to set forth only those alternatives necessary to permit a reasoned choice … . The touchstone of our inquiry is whether an EIS's selection and discussion of alternatives fosters informed decision-making and informed public participation." See *California v. Block*, 690 F. 2d 753 (1982), and *NRDC v. Morton*, 458 F. 2d 827 (CADC Cir. 1972), at 835-37.

- An EIS must consider not every possible alternative, but every reasonable alternative; the existence of a viable but unexamined alternative renders EIS inadequate. See *Citizens for Better Henderson v. Hodel*, 768 F. 2d 1051 (1985), and *Vermont Yankee Nuclear Power Corp. v. NRDC*, 435 US 519 (1978).
- "The evaluation of 'alternatives' mandated by NEPA is to be an evaluation of alternative means to accomplish the *general* goal of an action; it is not an evaluation of the alternative means by which a particular applicant can reach *his* goals." Nor does it limit an agency to the consideration of only one of those alternatives that it could adopt or put into effect. See *Van Abbema v. Fornell*, 807 F. 2d 633 (CA 7th Cir. 1986), *Trinity Episcopal School Corp. v. Romney*, 523 F. 2d 88 (1975) (CA 2d Cir.), and *NRDC v. Morton*, 458 F. 2d 827 (CADC Cir. 1972), at 835-37.
- The duty to consider alternatives exists independently of the duty to prepare an EIS, and so continues even if the EIS makes a finding that effects are insignificant. See *Sierra Club v. Alexander*, 484 F. Supp. 455 (DC NY 1980).

NOTES AND QUESTIONS

1. The alternatives assessment does not require crystal ball inquiries. It does, however, mean that decision makers must take a "hard look" at all reasonable means of avoiding or minimizing significant adverse environmental effects *before* making their decisions. How do these US decisions and notes above compare to the Federal Court of Appeal's decision in *Express*, above? Is there any reason why serious consideration of alternatives is required under NEPA in the United States, but not under the CEAA in Canada?

2. A second issue raised by the CEAA is *when* to address alternatives. Not requiring consideration of "need for" and "alternatives to" assessment early in the initial planning of projects was seen to severely prejudice objective consideration of those issues: see, for example, Robert B. Gibson, "Comments on Bill C-13 as currently proposed (with amendments introduced by the federal government on October 10, 1991)" for submission to the Legislative Committee on Bill C-13, November 7, 1991, at p. 1.

3. The American practice of alternatives is evolving. See "Forty Most Asked Questions Concerning CEQ's NEPA Regulations," 46 Fed. Reg 18026 (1981). See also *Friends of the Ompompanoosuc v. FERC*, 968 F. 2d 1549 (2nd Cir. 1992), *Norfolk v. EPA*, 761 F. 2d 867 (D. Mass. 1991); aff'd. 960 F. 2d 143 (1st Cir. 1992), *N.W. Resources Information Center Inc. v. National Marine Fisheries Service*, 56 F. 3d 1060 (9th Cir. 1995), and *Alaska Wilderness Recreation & Tourism Assn v. Morrison*, 67 F. 3d 723 (9th Cir. 1995).

B. Cumulative Effects

The importance of cumulative effects is underscored by a federal court decision that found a requirement to consider cumulative effects under the guidelines order, even though there was no explicit requirement to consider such effects at that time: see *Sunshine Village Corporation v. Canada (Minster of Heritage)* (1996), 20 CELR 171, at 202-3 (FCA). The CEAA requires consideration of cumulative effects for all assessments. Section 16 states:

16(1) Every screening or comprehensive study of a project and every mediation or assessment by a review panel shall include a consideration of the following factors:

(a) the environmental effects of the project, including the environmental effects of malfunctions or accidents that may occur in connection with the project and any cumulative environmental effects that are likely to result from the project in combination with other projects or activities that have been or will be carried out ... .

Although the phrase "cumulative effects" is not defined in the CEAA, the Canadian Environmental Assessment Agency has defined cumulative environmental effects as "the effects on the environment, over a certain period of time and distance, resulting from effects of a project when combined with those of other past, existing, and imminent projects and activities." Under s. 16(3), the responsible authority determines the scope of the factors listed in paragraphs 16(1)(a) to (e), including the scope of the cumulative environmental effects to be considered.

In *Friends of the West Country Assn. v. Canada (Minister of Fisheries and Oceans)*, [2000] 2 FC 263 (CA), an assessment of the cumulative effects resulting from the construction of two proposed bridges was at issue. The court had this to say about the operation of s. 16:

[P]aragraph 16(1)(a) does not specify which other projects or activities are to be considered ... . The scoping of other projects or activities to be taken into account is left to the discretion of the responsible authority under subsection 16(3) and paragraph 16(1)(a) places no mandatory duty in that regard on the responsible authority ... .

Implicit in a cumulative effects assessment under paragraph 16(1)(a) are effects from both the project as scoped and other projects or activities. Sunpine argued that if there were no adverse environmental effects from the project as scoped, there could be no cumulative effects as envisaged by that paragraph. While on its face this argument is compelling, I am not sure it is possible to rule out that a federal project, while creating no adverse effects itself, could exacerbate adverse effects of other projects. In any event, a finding of insignificant effects as was made here still implies some effects from the bridge projects themselves. It is not illogical to think that the accumulation of a series of insignificant effects might at some point result in significant effects. I do not say that is the case here. I only observe that a finding of insignificant effects of the scoped projects is sufficient to open the possibility of cumulative significant environmental effects when other projects are taken into account.

The issue of cumulative effects was further examined in the following case.

Bow Valley Naturalists Society v. Canada (Minister of Canadian Heritage)
[1999] FCJ no. 1422 (TD); aff'd. [2001] 2 FC 461 (CA)

[At trial, the Bow Valley Naturalists Society sought an application for judicial review of the decision of the acting superintendent of Parks Canada, made pursuant to s. 20(1)(a) of the CEAA, which held that the adverse environmental effects of the development of a proposed meeting facility by Canadian Pacific Hotels (CP Hotels) at the Chateau Lake Louise in Banff National Park would likely not be significant. The applicants argued primarily that the environmental assessment, which had been delegated by the responsible authority to the proponent, had not properly dealt with the assessment of cumulative effects. The assessment had considered the effects of the construction of a meeting facility for which a licence was being sought, but not those resulting from the construction of other facilities CP Hotels had included in their long-range plan. The applicants contended that because the assessment failed to take into account possible future projects that may impact Lake Louise and its environs, the CEAA had not been fully complied with and until this occurred the decision should be set aside and the minister prohibited from issuing any permits or approvals authorizing CP Hotels to proceed with the construction of the facility. However, the trial court dismissed the application on the grounds that the environmental assessment had met the requirements of the CEAA and that the superintendent had not committed any reviewable error either in fact or in law that would justify the court's intervention.

On appeal, the question of how cumulative effects fit into the environmental assessment process was dealt with thoroughly by the court.]

LINDEN JA: The *Canadian Environmental Assessment Act* was not intended to eliminate any and all development in the national parks. One of its stated purposes is to ensure sustainable development. Neither was the Act intended to provide a rigid structure for conducting environmental assessments, as each set of circumstances requires a different type of assessment, different scoping and different factors to be taken into consideration. While the dictates of the law must be followed, the process is a flexible and sometimes confusing one … .

The environmental assessment of CP's proposed meeting facility resulted in the production of numerous volumes of documents. Voluminous studies were undertaken by experts who considered a large number of different factors including cumulative effects. Public consultation was done. While the wording of the decision of the responsible authority is not as tidy, precise and lucid as one might wish it to be, I am not persuaded that, in the light of all the evidence, it was so unreasonable that it must be quashed. The Court must ensure that the steps in the Act are followed, but it must defer to the responsible authorities in their substantive determinations as to scope of the project, the extent of the screening and the assessment of the cumulative effects in the light of the mitigating factors proposed. It is not for the judges to decide what projects are to be authorized, but, as long as they follow the statutory process, it is for the responsible authorities … [to do so].

Consequently, even though the decision and its reasons leave much to be desired, and even though they are often untidy, confusing and lacking in specificity, I cannot conclude that the cumulative effects aspect of the decision of Parks Canada being judicially reviewed was unreasonable or that the Trial Judge erred in his decision in that regard. It is not necessary for the decision to be a model of legal analysis. Nor is it required, in order to comply with the Act, to consider fanciful projects by imagined parties producing purely hypothetical effects.

NOTES AND QUESTIONS

1. Are the cumulative effects decisions consistent?

2. What kinds of effects are cumulative? Direct effects? Indirect effects? How and when do cumulative effects "hit the radar screen"? Is it in the scoping exercise? How do you describe the affected environment? How do you determine environmental consequences when you are required to look beyond the current proposal?

3. This chapter began with a focus on *planning*. In terms of planning, when does the cumulative effects requirement arise? Does it arise when there are already projects in close proximity to the proposed project and the additional effects of a *new* project need to be studied against the existing projects? Or does it arise when several projects are planned together in the same area, and are therefore reasonably forseeable, but are not yet built? Would this not be a significant matter that requires all proposed projects to assess cumulative effects? If the issue is to be studied, do the responsible authorities release all information in their files relative to unpermitted but planned projects so that these studies can be professionally done?

4. When does the cumulative effects requirement cross the point of speculation?

5. In light of the decision in *Bow Valley Naturalists Society*, above, is the s. 16 requirement to carry out a cumulative effects assessment essentially nullified by the fact that s. 16(3) gives the minister and the responsible authority the complete discretion to decide whether other future projects should be included in the environmental assessment? Why or why not? See *Sunpine*, above, and *Cheriot Mines*, above.

6. How does the issue of cumulative effects deal with projects that are split or segmented—that is, whether they should be or not?

C. Significance

The CEAA requires a special form of evaluation compared to other environmental approval processes. Subsection 16(1) requires that screenings and comprehensive studies consider the significance of the effects associated with a project. The CEAA Responsible Authority Guide (available on the Web at http://www.ceaa-acee.gc.ca/0011/0001/0008/guide_e.htm) presents this evaluation as a three-part test: (1) Are the environmental effects *adverse*? (2) Are the adverse environmental effects *significant*? and (3) Are the significant adverse environmental effects *likely*?

According to the Responsible Authority Guide, significance must be determined objectively, having regard for scientific and technical information. In considering the third part of the test, it should be noted that the CEAA provides different requirements concerning likelihood in s. 16. For example, paragraph 16(1)(a) requires a description of environmental effects and accidents that *may* occur, but requires a description of cumulative effects that *are likely to* occur. It is not clear how s. 16 assessment requirements (possible effects) relate to choices about the course of action to be taken in s. 20 (screenings), 23 (comprehensive study), or 37 (panel review or mediation).

How does the CEAA deal with projects that may have the potential for significant effects? In answering the question, the CEAA regime for *significance* shares many similarities with that of the guidelines order and with NEPA. Under the guidelines order, the most important decision on significance was Muldoon J's decision in *Canadian*

Wildlife Federation v. Canada (Minister of Environment) (1990), 6 CELR (NS) 89 (FCA). In that case, the court was faced with an assessment document that used different environmental effects terminology from the guidelines order terminology of "significant" and "insignificant," including, for example, "moderate" effects. According to the court:

> It seems clear that as between significant and insignificant effects, "moderate impacts" must be taken clearly to mean "not insignificant." Effects which are not insignificant ["minimes"] must obviously be significant ["important"] effects, in second place of importance among the significant adverse effects. Conversely, to be insignificant, an adverse effect cannot be moderate, but rather must be without significance. To describe an adverse effect, or impact, as "moderate" is to mean that it is of significance, although not so seriously adverse as some others may be. By definition, that which is of moderate effect cannot be of insignificant effect. It cannot be "minime" if it be of moderate importance. So, the Court must take it to be the authors' meaning that moderate impacts are significant adverse environmental effects.

The CEAA defines both "environment" and "environmental effect" in s. 2:

> "environmental effect" means, in respect of a project,
>
> (a) any change that the project may cause in the environment, including any effect of any such change on health and socio-economic conditions, on physical and cultural heritage, on the current use of lands and resources for traditional purposes by aboriginal persons, or on any structure, site or thing that is of historical, archaeological, paleontological or architectural significance, and
>
> (b) any change to the project that may be caused by the environment, whether any such change occurs within or outside Canada.

> "environment" means the components of the Earth, and includes:
>
> (a) land, water and air, including all layers of the atmosphere,
>
> (b) all organic and inorganic matter and living organisms, and
>
> (c) the interacting natural systems that include components referred to in paragraphs (a) and (b).

It is important to understand the relationship of these terms in complying with the requirements of s. 16(1) to "consider" the environmental effects of the project. The definition of "environmental effect" references the environment and thereby incorporates its definition. A major issue of debate is the determination of what terms are included in the definition of "environmental effect" that are not included in the definition of the "environment." To date, no case has addressed this question. A second important aspect of the definition of "environmental effect" is the requirement to consider both the impact of the project on the environment and the impact of the environment on the project. Is this latter requirement equivalent to requiring a description of the environment? How may it differ? Recently, in *Bowen*, above, the court affirmed that the terms of s. 16(1) should receive a "liberal" interpretation.

This raises the question of whether the mitigation or compensation measures must in fact prevent potentially adverse environmental effects from becoming significant or whether it is sufficient that these measures merely could prevent environmental effects from becoming significant. The question was answered in *Curragh Resources Inc. v. The Queen in Right of Canada* (1992), 87 DLR (4th) 219 (FCTD), at 242, per Joyal J:

Section 14 [of EARP] puts an obligation on initiating departments to ensure that mitigation and compensation measures are applied to prevent potentially adverse environmental effects from becoming significant. As will be discussed below, there are two kinds of adverse environmental effects in the Panel provisions of the *Guidelines Order*: significant or insignificant. Consequently I interpret "effects from becoming significant" in section 14 as another way of saying that mitigation and compensation measures must be taken to make the adverse effects "insignificant." It follows that if a mitigation measure, needed to make the adverse effect "insignificant," is, for one reason or another, unable to be implemented, the adverse effect will be significant and there will be no other option but to submit the project to full review or even, as is the case under s. 12(f), to possible abandonment. When the adverse effect is significant the project cannot proceed without modification or public review by a panel. ...

Again, the US law provides a contrasting position. The question of what is and what is not a significant effect is addressed in the following regulations enacted under NEPA.

National Environmental Policy Act (NEPA) Regulations
40 CFR, Part 1508

1508 Terminology and Index

1508.27 "Significantly" ... requires consideration of: ...

(a) *Context*. This means that the significance of an action must be analyzed in several contexts such as society as a whole (human, national), the affected region, the affected interest, and the locality. Significance varies with the setting of the proposed action. For instance, in the case of a site-specific action, significance would usually depend upon the effects in the locale rather than in the world as a whole. Both short and long-term effects are relevant.

(b) *Intensity*. This refers to the severity of impact. Responsible officials must bear in mind that more than one agency may make decisions about partial aspects of a major action. The following should be considered in evaluating intensity:

(1) Impacts that may be both beneficial and adverse. A significant effect may exist even if the Federal agency believes that on balance the effect will be beneficial.

(2) The degree to which the proposed action affects public health or safety.

(3) Unique characteristics of the geographic area such as proximity to historic or cultural resources, park lands, prime farmlands, wetlands, wild and scenic rivers, or ecologically critical areas.

(4) The degree to which the effects on the quality of the human environment are likely to be highly controversial.

(5) The degree to which the possible effects on the human environment are highly uncertain or involve unique or unknown risks.

(6) The degree to which the action may establish a precedent for future actions with significant effects or represents a decision in principle about a future consideration.

(7) Whether the action is related to other actions with individually insignificant but cumulatively significant impacts. Significance exits if it is reasonable
to anticipate a cumulatively significant impact on the environment. Significance cannot not be avoided by terming an action temporary or by breaking it
down into small component parts.

(8) The degree to which the action may adversely affect districts, sites, highways, structures or objects listed in or eligible for listing in the National Register
of Historic Places or may cause loss or destruction of significant scientific,
cultural or historical resources.

(9) The degree to which the action may adversely affect an endangered or
threatened species or its habitat that has been determined to be critical under
the *Endangered Species Act of 1973*.

(10) Whether the action threatens a violation of Federal, State, or local law
or requirements imposed for the protection of the environment.

NOTES AND QUESTIONS

1. Do levels of significance depend on the particular resource (or area) that is under
scrutiny? What if public concern alone is high and controversial? Is that not significant
enough, at least from a political perspective? See s. 28 of the CEAA.

2. How do you determine significance for cumulative effects of connected projects?
Who makes the determination?

3. Does significance (or lack of it) have to be proven? Would it make sense to allow
the significance test to proceed as long as there is a reasonable scientific belief that a
project might cause a significant adverse environmental effect?

D. Transboundary Assessments: The ESPOO Convention on Transboundary Impact Assessment

International recognition of transboundary environmental impacts is longstanding. Canada
and the United States, for example, have been interested in addressing such impacts since
the early part of this century. With the integration of the European Community since
World War II, the support for effective transboundary laws has increased. These two
communities form the core of the Convention on Environmental Impact Assessment in a
Transboundary Context, signed in Espoo, Finland in 1991 (30 ILM 800 (1991)). Although the ratification process has been slow, the Convention has recently come into
force. (See F.P. Grad, *Treatise on Environmental Law*, above, s. 13.03(6)(c)). The CEAA
authorizes the use of joint review panels with foreign states: see ss. 40 and 41.

QUESTIONS

The definition of environmental effect includes *ex juris* impacts. How can we undertake
environmental impact studies relative to other jurisdictions and still respect sovereignty
principles? On the other hand, how can we study international projects that export
Canadian resources without also carefully reviewing all of the significant environmental
effects? If we fail to examine effects outside Canada for projects leaving Canada, is the

ultimate planning decision skewed in favour of allowing the proponent to benefit from all of the economic effects, while recognizing for planning purposes only part of the environmental effects?

VI. ROLE OF THE PUBLIC DURING A FEDERAL ENVIRONMENTAL ASSESSMENT
A. Public Registry

Section 55(1) of the CEAA provides:

> 55(1) For the purpose of facilitating public access to records relating to environmental assessments, a public registry shall be established and operated in a manner to ensure convenient public access to the registry and in accordance with this Act and the regulations in respect of every project for which an environmental assessment is conducted.

And the preamble to the CEAA provides in part:

> AND WHEREAS the Government of Canada is committed to facilitating public participation in the environmental assessment of projects to be carried out by or with the approval or assistance of the Government of Canada and providing access to the information on which those environmental assessments are based ... .

In the *Sunpine* case, above, the Federal Court of Appeal interpreted the CEAA's public participation requirements. In 1994, Sunpine Forest Products Limited identified a need for a permanent road to transport logs to its Strachan mill. The necessary route crossed two rivers, and as a result of the requirement to obtain federal approval to construct bridges over navigable waters, federal environmental assessments were triggered pursuant to s. 5(1)(d) of the CEAA. A public registry was established, pursuant to s. 55(1), but was located over two thousand miles away from the project in Sarnia, Ontario. At trial, the motions judge made the following findings of fact:

> A representative or representatives of the applicant requested that, in light of the remoteness of the registry from the site of the bridge projects, copies of all materials on the registry be provided to the applicant. Copies of some materials were provided but copies of other materials were not provided for the stated reasons of cost and the amount of work and duplication of the materials. The applicant's representative or representatives were invited to make an application for the materials under the *Access to Information Act*.

He concluded:

> Given that the materials were requested for the purpose of the public consultation provided for in subsection 18(3) of the CEAA and that the period provided for such consultation was quite short, the recommendation to make use of the *Access to Information Act* procedures was completely inappropriate and, more importantly, not in keeping with the obligation under section 55 of the CEAA and the related commitment recited in the preamble to the CEAA.

On appeal, Rothstein JA had this to say regarding the operation of s. 55(1):

> The establishment and manner of operation of the public registry under subsection 55(1) is subject to the exercise of discretion by the responsible authority. While cost is a factor to be

considered, and there is no proximity requirement for a public registry, subsection 55(1) does require that convenient public access to the registry must be ensured. If a public registry is not established and operated in close proximity to the relevant geographic area of the environmental assessment, other reasonable means, e.g. e-mail, faxes, placing a set of timely material filed in the registry with an agent in close proximity to the projects for access by the public, must be provided to comply with subsection 55(1). Even under the most deferential standard of review, the actions of the Coast Guard with respect to access to the public registry were patently unreasonable.

B. Mediation and Panel Review

For the CEAA, public review means either mediation (an untested process) or panel review. Panel reviews provide a public forum to assess a project's potential environmental effects and are managed by unbiased persons independent of the federal government. See the CEAA, ss. 30 and 33. Panel reviews also make provisions for affected members of the public to retain independent experts. Panel reviews should proceed in a fair and informed way to produce a recommendation to the government.

Under either mediation or panel review, affected or interested members of the public should be able to receive copies of all relevant materials. Further, all courses of action on a project taken by the responsible authority are public, as are mediation and panel review reports. The public has a right to know the course of action pursued in relation to the project, the mitigation measures to be implemented for the project, the extent to which the authority has adopted the recommendations of mediation or panel review reports, and the followup program that is designed for the project.

Screening. Participation in screening assessments is discretionary; there is no regulation providing for participation in a screening. Thus, a person has to request permission from the responsible authority to force early public involvement, hoping that the proponent will acquiesce. For screening reports and class screening reports, the responsible authority may not take any action before giving the public an opportunity to examine and comment upon the report (ss. 19 and 22).

Comprehensive study. Public participation in the assessment process for a comprehensive study is mandatory. Section 22 of the CEAA directs the authorizing agency to facilitate public access to the report by publishing notice of the date and place that the comprehensive study report will be available, and informing the public of their ability to file comments on the conclusions and recommendations of the report. The courses of action open to the minister after consideration of the report and any comments filed, are laid out in s. 23, which states that "where, it is uncertain whether the project, taking into account the implementation of any appropriate mitigation measures, is likely to cause significant adverse environmental effects, ... that cannot be justified in the circumstances, [or] public concerns warrant a reference to a mediator or a review panel, the Minister shall refer the project to a mediator or a review panel in accordance with section 29."

Panel review. The CEAA provides no clearly stated role for the public in the selection of panel members or in the establishment of terms of reference for the panel. However, the CEAA requires the panel to hold a hearing in a manner that gives members of the public an opportunity to participate (s. 34). Section 39 states:

34. A review panel shall, in accordance with any regulations made for that purpose and with its term of reference,

(a) ensure that the information required for an assessment by a review panel is obtained and made available to the public;

(b) hold hearings in a manner that offers the public an opportunity to participate in the assessment;

(c) prepare a report setting out

(i) the rationale, conclusions and recommendations of the panel relating to the environmental assessment of the project, including any mitigation measures and follow-up program, and

(ii) a summary of any comments received from the public; and

(d) submit the report to the Minister and the responsible authority.

Participant funding. The CEAA makes it a requirement that there be a participant funding program for panel reviews and mediation. Section 58(1.1) states:

58(1.1) For the purposes of this Act, the Minister shall establish a participant funding program to facilitate the participation of the public in mediations and assessments by review panels.

VII. EVALUATING ENVIRONMENTAL ASSESSMENTS IN CANADA

The International Study of the Effectiveness of Environmental Assessment (1996) was established to review the question whether environmental assessment can respond to the demands of a changing world and remain a relevant and effective tool for sustainable development in the 21st century. The study, which was launched in 1993 as a joint initiative of the CEA Agency and the International Association for Impact Assessment (IAIA) (http://www.iaia.org/), found that the environmental assessment process has produced positive as well as negative results.

On the positive side, the study identified three trends in environmental assessment process development and application. The first is the widespread application of environmental assessment systems by a significant number of developing countries and countries in transition. The second trend involves the emergence of a second generation of integrated environmental assessment processes in some industrialized countries that is more closely linked to national planning and decision-making practices. Third, there is a rapidly evolving trend to apply the environmental assessment process to policies, plans, and programs; a practice termed strategic environmental assessment. Strategic environmental assessment is regarded as an effective method for incorporating environmental considerations into the highest level of development decision making.

Although the study found many promising EA developments, there is still much fine tuning to be done in order to strengthen the process and achieve optimum effectiveness. The study found that four elements must be incorporated into the process to achieve effective environmental assessment applications:

1. appropriate timing in initiating assessments to ensure consideration of reasonable alternatives;

2. clear directions or guidelines for priority issues such as time lines and public participation;
3. quality information encouraged by compliance with procedural guidelines and "best practices"; and
4. increased receptivity of decision makers and proponents to EA (environmental assessment) results through effective communication and extended accountability.

The study concludes:

Broad, fundamental social changes—in globalization, deregulation, privatization, and public sector operations—carry profound implications for EA practice in the near term. They may signal, for example, the need for international EA standards and for new modes of EA guidance and monitoring for local authorities, businesses and consumers. They may bring increased pressures for process efficiency and "fast-track" approaches.

Looking further ahead, the long-term reference point is sustainability of development. Decisions taken over the next generation—decisions that can be informed by EA processes—may well determine whether society becomes a sustainable one, or whether it overshoots resource and environmental thresholds.

FURTHER READINGS

Council on Environmental Quality (CEQ), "The National Environmental Policy Act: A Study of Its Effectiveness After 25 Years" (Washington, DC: CEQ, Executive Office of the President, 1997).

J. Hanebury, "Environmental Impact Assessment and the Constitution" (2000) vol. 9 *Journal of Environmental Law and Practice* 169.

S. Hazell, *Canada v. The Environment* (Toronto: Canadian Environmental Defence Fund, 1998).

B. Hobby et al., *Canadian Environmental Assessment Act: An Annotated Guide* (Aurora, ON: Canada Law Book, 1995).

B. Karkkainen, "Toward a Smarter NEPA: Monitoring and Managing Government's Environmental Performance" (2002) vol. 102, no. 4 *Columbia Law Review* 903.

CHAPTER SEVEN

Public Participation and Judicial Review*

Chris Tollefson

I. INTRODUCTION

Over the last decade or so, the public has come to play a much larger role in environmental decision making. This expansion has occurred on various fronts including land-use planning processes, environmental assessment, pollution and resource permitting procedures, and public interest environmental litigation. Increasingly, it is said that environmental politics in Canada are undergoing a process of "legalization"; that informal, policy-based processes for making decisions affecting the environment are being replaced by more formal, law-based processes that explicitly contemplate a role for citizens and citizens groups. As we shall see, however, not all observers and affected interests support these developments.

II. PUBLIC PARTICIPATION AND THE PUBLIC INTEREST

R. Anand and I.G. Scott, QC
"Financing Public Participation in Environmental Decision Making"
(1982) vol. 60 *Canadian Bar Review* 81, at 87-94

Access to Justice

The objection that encouraging public participation would have the effect of stirring up unmeritorious litigation is only one aspect of a wider attack on "public interest" advocacy that is commonly mounted by critics who argue that conflict resolution is the sole legitimate purpose of civil actions. Another aspect of this approach is the

* The author gratefully acknowledges the research and editorial assistance of Carole Aippersbach, Molly Grindley, and John Unrau.

assumption that when claims are not enforced through litigation it is because they are unimportant to the affected individuals.

. . .

It is clear that the failure to advance a particular cause in a given piece of litigation often results from barriers to legal redress that have nothing to do with the merit of the cause or the relative importance of the harm that is perceived by the "victim." Economic barriers to participation in decision-making are well documented in all forms of litigation and apply most severely to those who suffer in addition from social, psychological and cultural impediments to the redressing of their grievances.

Additional barriers present themselves in the case of public interest groups. Professor Michael Trebilcock has identified three such barriers that have analogous effects on environmental groups. Firstly, the environmental concerns of the average citizen are spread across a great range of projects, issues and locations. On the other hand, a business interest that is concerned with the particular project, issue or location has "a sufficiently concentrated stake in any prospective regulation of it to make [its] views known very forcefully to government."

. . .

Secondly, unlike highly concentrated producer interests, environmental interests are not generally homogeneous. Most environmentalists are also both consumers and producers of goods and services, and in these roles will often see things differently.

. . .

The third barrier is commonly known as the "free rider" phenomenon. Olson, for example, argues that unless the membership in a public interest group is small, or unless some special incentive is provided to encourage individuals to act in the common interests of the group, rational and self-interested individuals will not act to achieve their common or group interests ... . In the result, public interest groups never achieve the strength that their number of potential beneficiaries would indicate since many of the possible contributors of money, time and expertise either require or are permitted to take a "free ride" at the expense of existing members.

It is by overcoming these "barriers to litigation" that the encouragement of public participation achieves the significant benefit of obtaining confidence in our system of civil justice. A significant "process" value is attached by the community to enhanced public involvement in collective decision-making.

. . .

Private Enforcement of Public Rights

A common response to the argument for increased citizen involvement in environmental decision-making is the assertion that intervenors have no useful purpose to serve, given that the public agencies such as administrative tribunals, and courts have been entrusted with the dual roles of regulators of industry and representatives of the public interest. Yet enforcement of public policies can be achieved by private individuals by supplementing the work of the various tribunals or by "energizing the agencies."

. . .

[T]hree principal factors ... combine to produce what has become known as agency "capture" by regulated interests. Firstly, the limited resources that are allocated to administrative agencies, considered in relation to the sheer mass of activity that is required to monitor and test proposals and applications, necessitates close co-operation between the regulator and the regulated industry. Administrative boards thus become dependent upon industry as providers of information. A second cause of industry orientation is the dependence of regulatory agencies on the regulated interests for political support. Independent tribunals cannot rely upon the government to protect them from legislative attack and must therefore develop their own constituencies that are capable of generating support in the legislatures. In this regard, a natural ally can often be found in the regulated interests.

Most importantly, two other characteristics of the administrative process have combined to form a third source of agency deference to industry positions. ... "Governmental agencies rarely respond to interests that are not represented in their proceedings." The mere setting up by governments of regulatory agencies is insufficient to protect the public interest.

. . .

At the very least, even if the interests of the regulated industry and the adjudicator do not fully coincide, it is clear that the "public interest" which is the theoretical mandate of the decision-maker is not unitary. It has diverse and indeed countervailing components, and so the environmental tribunal or court cannot be expected to become its guardian with unqualified success. Public intervention "softens the artificial two-sidedness which is often a by-product of the adversarial adjudicative process."

Improvement of Administrative and Judicial Processes

Four distinct benefits accrue to the investigative and adjudicative processes as a result of increased public participation.

Firstly, public participation provides decision-makers with a greater range of ideas and information on which to base their decisions ... . This substantive contribution to environmental decision-making has two aspects. Firstly, public participants bring important factual information and legal submissions to the attention of the adjudicator ... . The second element of substantive contribution is the presentation of a viewpoint or perspective that is not otherwise available to the decision-maker. Intervenors are often able to put forward a legal or factual argument which places a unique emphasis or interpretation upon existing issues or causes the tribunal to examine a new issue.

. . .

The second major benefit is that public participation can enhance public acceptance of judicial and administrative decisions ... . Public acceptability, in turn, can be expected to increase the implementation and enforcement of judicial and administrative decisions that rely upon public co-operation.

Third, problems of agency dependence on industry for political support may be alleviated by the broad participation of other parties. Such participation may promote the actual autonomy of the agency both by giving it a broader perspective from which to view its own role, and by providing alternative potential bases of political support.

Fourth, the presentation of alternative view points at the board or lower court level is said to induce these decision-makers to be more thorough in their analyses and to articulate more clearly and precisely the reasons for their decisions. These improvements may in turn contribute to the building of a record on which a reviewing or appellate court might reverse the initial decision.

While the goal of making bureaucracies more open and accountable to the public is generally uncontroversial, there is less support for the idea that we should aspire to a similar openness and accountability in our court system.

J. Moffet
**"Judicial Review and Environmental Policy: Lessons for Canada
from the United States"**
(1994) vol. 37 *Canadian Public Administration* 140, at 158-59

Who Will Use the Courts?

The principle of individual empowerment is one of the main reasons enhanced access to the courts is advocated in Canada. However, the experience with NEPA demonstrates that enhanced opportunities for environmental litigation do not necessarily increase citizen participation. The scientific and technological complexity of the issues involved generally mean that environmental litigation is too costly and time-consuming for the average citizen, or even for most small interest groups. Indeed, NEPA litigation is more often commenced by government and industry than by environmental interests.

The NEPA experience also suggests that environmental litigation will not necessarily produce the right type of cases to ensure systemic policy changes. Many environmental plaintiffs have been NIMBY groups, focusing on particular projects. Litigation concerning policies threatening more general and diffuse environmental considerations has been restricted to a few major environmental organizations.

. . .

Finally, it is not clear whether such organizations exist in Canada with sufficient resources to engage in enough litigation to present a widespread threat to entrenched government processes ... . A new emphasis on environmental litigation in Canada might serve only to divert limited resources from existing lobbying, educational, and scientific efforts into costly and time-consuming litigation.

Can the Courts Change Bureaucratic Behaviour?

The capacity of the courts to change values and behaviour is unclear. The preponderance of the sociology literature suggests that courts on their own can have little effect. On the other hand, anecdotal evidence from environmentalists suggests that early NEPA litigation did help mobilize the American environmental movement. At present, however, litigation at best raises the salience of specific issues. And it is unlikely to do more in Canada, where public environmental concerns are already pronounced. In any event, there is little evidence that litigation has had a positive effect on bureaucratic values. By reinforcing the credibility of the internal analysts, the threat of litigation may have helped indirectly. However, the surveys and case studies reviewed above indicate that the threat of litigation has made American bureaucrats defensive and frustrated, and has engendered negative feelings towards environmental legislation in general.

Embarking on reforms aimed at enhancing public participation requires grappling with the difficult question of defining the "public interest." There are some who would contend, for example, that so-called public interest pursuits are not "somehow less self-serving" than economic pursuits, nor "untainted by self-interest." Such critics point out that "there are many definitions of the public interest." See, for example, W.T. Stanbury, "A Sceptic's Guide to the Claims of So-Called Public Interest Groups" (1993) vol. 36 *Canadian Public Administration* 580.

Others defend the concept of the public interest, claiming that public interest groups can be clearly distinguished from other interest groups—such as economic and professional associations: their intention is to benefit persons outside their membership, their members are usually individuals, membership is open to all, and they are typically organized on a "democratic," not a "bureaucratic" basis. See, for example, S.D. Phillips, "Of Public Interest Groups and Sceptics: A Realist's Reply to Professor Stanbury" (1993) vol. 36 *Canadian Public Administration* 606.

These issues—whether the "public interest" can be defined and whether public interest groups are significantly different from other lobby groups, such as industry associations—have important implications for environmental law. Consider, in this connection, C. McCool's article on the public interest and costs law reform, below.

QUESTIONS

1. Is public participation, as some of its proponents would be prepared to argue, an unqualified human good?

2. Is it inconsistent, as a matter of principle, to support enhanced public participation in bureaucratic but not in judicial decision-making venues? Are there reasons one might support enhanced public participation in one venue and not in the other?

3. Until we are entirely clear about what is the "public interest" and who is positioned to benefit from public-interest-oriented law and policy reforms, should we be cautious about implementing such initiatives?

III. ADMINISTRATIVE LAW AND JUDICIAL REVIEW: AN OVERVIEW

A. What Is Administrative Law?

Administrative law is a body of law that governs government officials and administrative tribunals that are charged with the power to make decisions or pass regulations that affect people's rights or interests.

All governmental decision makers that are statutorily vested with such powers, whether directly or indirectly, must comply with the principles of administrative law. In the environmental context, this means that a broad range of *decisions* are subject to administrative law requirements. Examples would include approvals granted by Cabinet or individual ministers, the construction of public works and major mining or forestry projects, pollution-permitting decisions made by environmental tribunals or ministry staff, as well as land-use-related approvals issued by local government. Administrative law requirements also bind "subordinate law makers"—bodies and officials that have a statutorily delegated power *to make regulations*—in the exercise of their lawmaking function. Illustrations from the environmental context would include Cabinet or ministerial regulations governing waste, water, air, and wildlife management, as well as local government zoning bylaws.

Administrative law, like many other areas of law, is an amalgam of common law and legislation. It sets the rules that public authorities must follow in making decisions or enacting regulations, provides avenues for adversely affected parties to challenge these decisions or regulations, and, where an authority has acted unlawfully, prescribes available remedies.

B. The Role and Nature of Environmental Tribunals and Other Administrative Decision Makers

The complexity and scope of matters that are subject to modern environmental regulation has meant, of necessity, that responsibility for making important decisions affecting the environment is delegated by statute to ministerial officials or specially constituted administrative tribunals. Typically, the initial decision (for example, to issue a pollution permit or resource development licence) rests with a senior bureaucrat designated under the relevant statute and employed by the ministry responsible for regulating the activity in question. Most statutes provide for an internal appeal from decisions made at this level either to a more senior decision maker within the ministry or to an environmental or resource appeal *tribunal*.

These tribunals, as well as the bureaucrats making the initial decisions, must follow particular procedures in making their determinations. Usually these procedures are set out in some detail in statutes and rules governing their activities. These decision makers are also required to conduct themselves in accordance with the common law principles of *procedural fairness*. What is procedurally fair is said to depend on three main factors: the nature of the decision to be made, the relationship between the decision maker and the individual, and the effect of the decision on the individual's rights. Generally, fairness will require, at a minimum, notice before a final decision is made and an opportunity to be heard.

C. Supervision of Administrative Action

When reviewing tribunal decisions, courts will often defer to a tribunal's discretion, particularly where the tribunal has a demonstrated expertise for, and experience in, dealing with the relevant subject matter. In determining what level of deference should be applied, courts are also mindful of whether the legislature has sought to shield the tribunal's decisions from review by inserting a *privative clause* in the tribunal's constituting statute. In every case, before reviewing the tribunal's decision itself, courts resolve the deference question by determining, on a sliding scale, by what *standard of review* they will assess the decision.

It should be underscored, however, that courts will not defer to an administrative decision or regulation (often referred to collectively as "administrative action") that is beyond the powers of the responsible authority. Tribunals and other public decision makers are creatures of statute. Their powers are granted and defined by statute; they may act only within the confines their statutory *jurisdiction*. Lack of jurisdiction renders an administrative action *ultra vires*, and may entitle the challenging party to a remedy. All administrative action is subject to review for lack of jurisdiction by the superior courts under their inherent jurisdiction. This is the essence of the concept of *judicial review*. Each Canadian jurisdiction has its own procedural rules governing judicial review. Judicial review of federal boards and tribunals falls either to the Federal Court of Appeal (see s. 28(1) of the *Federal Court Act*, RSC 1985, c. F-7) or the Federal Court Trial Division (see s. 18 of the *Federal Court Act*). Provincial superior courts, as courts of inherent jurisdiction, have jurisdiction to review in all cases other than those under the Federal Court's jurisdiction.

In undertaking judicial review, courts frequently emphasize that their task is to review the legality of a decision or regulation, not its merits. The most common legal grounds upon which judicial review is sought include

1. substantive *ultra vires* (decisions or actions that are outside a body's statutory powers);
2. failing to consider relevant considerations or considering irrelevant considerations;
3. unlawful fettering of discretion;
4. real or apprehended bias;
5. breach of procedural fairness;
6. exercising discretion for an improper purpose or in bad faith;
7. unlawful subdelegation of a discretionary power; and
8. in restricted circumstances, errors of law and/or fact.

A closely related question is that of remedy. The principal remedies available on judicial review are fourfold: (1) an order quashing the administrative action (*certiorari*); (2) an order prohibiting the action (*prohibition*); (3) an order requiring the authority to act (*mandamus*); and (4) an order declaring existing rights, duties, or powers (*declaratory relief*).

To preserve their rights pending the hearing of their application for review, litigants may also seek interim injunctive relief (although public interest litigants often find it difficult to obtain such relief for reasons to be discussed later). It should be noted that, even where the petitioner successfully establishes that grounds for judicial review exist, courts have discretion to deny relief for various reasons, including that the jurisdictional breach is slight, that the application for review is premature, or that alternative remedies (that is, other avenues of appeal) have not been exhausted: see, for example, *Berg v. BC* (1991), 48 Admin. LR 82 (SCC).

This lattermost point raises the important distinction between appeals and judicial review. Sometimes a statute will expressly provide for an appeal to the courts for a party aggrieved by an administrative decision. Often, to pursue this avenue, the aggrieved party will be required first to obtain the court's *leave* (permission). For the purposes of statutory appeals and apart from common law standard of review principles discussed below, the principles governing judicial review do not apply; the existence, scope, and nature of the appeal mechanism is governed entirely by the relevant statute.

IV. THE ADMINISTRATIVE PROCESS

In the first instance, decisions affecting the environment are made within the bureaucracy by ministerial officials charged with responsibility for exercising statutory powers relating to environmental protection, public health, and resource development. Whether the decision relates to waste permitting, locating landfill sites, or resource development, usually a statutory appeal lies to an administrative appeal board.

Rationales for conferring appellate jurisdiction on these tribunals include:

1. *efficiency and flexibility* (tribunals are regarded as being more procedurally expeditious than courts, able to operate on a more informal basis, and offering greater potential for alternative dispute resolution);
2. *openness* (tribunals are perceived as offering enhanced opportunities for public-interest-oriented citizen participation);
3. *expertise* (tribunal membership can be tailored to equip the tribunal to deal with the complex legal and scientific issues raised by the decisions being appealed from); and
4. *experience* (tribunals are in a position to develop a sensitivity to the broader policy considerations relevant to their jurisdiction).

Since appointments to such tribunals are made at the discretion of Cabinet, a perennial concern is tribunal independence. Because these tribunals exercise quasi-judicial powers, and rely on public confidence effectively to discharge these powers, there has been considerable debate over how to minimize the inevitably political dimension of the appointments process, see: W. Tilleman, "Environmental Appeal Boards: A Comparative Look at the United States, Canada and England" (1996) vol. 21 *Columbia Journal of Environmental Law* 1, at 18-29.

Another recurring issue in this area concerns tribunal rules and procedures. Although they are appellate bodies, often tribunals will "retry" the matter before them afresh as a *trial de novo*. This means that the parties are entitled to call evidence instead of merely relying on the written record relating to the decision on appeal. Most tribunals also possess a broad discretion to confirm, alter, or overturn the decision under appeal. Tribunals are not expected to follow the legal formalities and rules of evidence that govern court proceedings. To expedite the hearing process (which will often involve unrepresented laypersons), many tribunals issue policy directives with respect to hearing procedures. In some provinces, notably Ontario and Alberta, such hearings are also subject to statutory codes of procedure. Perhaps most important, all tribunals are bound by a common law duty of procedural fairness to the parties appearing before them, the discharge of which is overseen by the superior courts.

Unlike courts, tribunals are not ordinarily empowered to impose costs awards against unsuccessful public interest participants. Indeed, in some instances, tribunals are vested with the power to promote public participation affirmatively by providing intervenor funding. Conventional wisdom suggests that "participation before administrative agencies … is intended to be far more liberal than standing before courts" (Tilleman, above, at 57). That this should be so seems to accord with the role and purpose of tribunals as an alternative means of airing public policy disputes. Bearing this in mind, consider the following materials dealing with tribunal standing.

J. Sherman, M. Gismondi, and M. Richardson
"Not Directly Affected: Using the Law To Close the Door on Environmentalists"
(1996) vol. 31, no. 1 *Journal of Canadian Studies* 102, at 103

A recent decision taken by the Public Health Advisory and Appeal Board of Alberta (PHAAB) denied one individual and two environmental groups standing to appeal the approval of the design and location of a large industrial waste facility in the County of Athabasca in northern Alberta. The PHAAB denied standing on the grounds that these Albertans were not "directly affected" by the development because they could not demonstrate an effect upon themselves "more direct than a general affect [sic] on the population at large." The challenge to the public's right to speak to the PHAAB was initiated by the developer of the waste facility, Alberta-Pacific Forest Industries (Alpac), whose lawyer characterized the "opposition" by environmentalists as "unwavering" and "unrelenting."' Local environmentalists, on the other hand, saw Alpac's challenge to their standing as a tactic to block critical analysis of the company's development.

The PHAAB is an administrative tribunal that hears appeals from the public on decisions made by local health units. Tribunals take "many forms, govern many types of public and private issues and vary radically in their procedures. They may be long-standing permanent bodies dealing with a broad range of questions [such as the PHAAB] or they may be one-time *ad hoc* agencies created to consider only one significant question (e.g., the environmental aspects of a new pipeline or the deaths of babies at a hospital)." They are designed to hear from the public, and from experts and specialists, before coming to a decision in the public interest.

According to liberal political theory, public hearings held by administrative tribunals "extend public participation beyond the electoral process and enhance citizen access to administrative processes of government." The tribunal is claimed to be "an independent and objective forum … impartial and economically disinterested in the issues at hand … operated according to quasi-judicial procedures, which not only encourage public access, but ensure fairness and a balance among competing forces." Effective public participation at the local tribunal level is not often discussed in the sustainable development literature, although it is recognized in political science and planning literature.

Is public access to tribunals being eroded? Writing in 1989, Andrew Roman argued in *Effective Advocacy before Administrative Tribunals* that "even in the courts of law, which tend to be far more formal than tribunals, the question of standing is becoming increasingly unimportant as a barrier to access." Yet in 1993, the decision by Alberta's Public Health Advisory and Appeal Board to deny standing to certain dissenting parties set a precedent in Alberta that is now limiting the ability of environmental and public interest groups, and individual citizens, to raise a range of important issues before various resource extraction, environmental and public health boards. The interpretation of "directly affected" emerging in Alberta may not be restricted to this province, but could be used as a precedent in other provinces.

NOTE

The decision of the PHAAB to deny standing in the above case was upheld by the Alberta Court of Appeal in reasons rendered on January 24, 1996. The "directly affected" test approved by the court in *Friends of the Athabasca Environmental Assn. v. Alberta (Public Health Advisory and Appeal Board)*, [1996] AJ no. 47 (CA) has since been applied in other Alberta cases, including *Martha Kostuch v. Environmental Appeal Board and Director of Air and Water Approvals Division* (1996), 21 CELR (NS) 257 (Alta. QB). In that case, judicial review was sought after the Environmental Appeal Board (EAB) dismissed an appeal of an amendment to a cement plant approval on the grounds that the applicant was not "directly affected" by the amendments and therefore lacked standing to appeal the amendments.

The court held that the EAB applied the correct test when it had stated:

> Two ideas emerge from this analysis about standing. First, the possibility that any given interest will suffice to confer standing diminishes as the causal connection between an approval and the effect on that interest becomes more remote. This first issue is a question of fact, i.e., the extent of the causal connection between the approval and how much it affects a person's interest. This is an important point; the Act requires that individual appellants demonstrate a personal interest that is directly impacted by the approval granted. This would require a discernible effect, i.e., some interest other than the abstract interest of all Albertans in generalized goals of environmental protection. "Directly" means the person claiming to be 'affected' must show causation of the harm to her particular in interest by the approval challenged on appeal. As a general rule, there must be an unbroken connection between one and the other.

Marceau J went on to note that a "history as an environmental advocate does not in my view entitle the Applicant to special status in the sense of being for that reason alone 'directly affected.'" He also disagreed that "the EAB should more readily grant status to public interest groups where as here very few if any persons can show a direct causal connection because there are no residences within about 20 miles," concluding that "if the Legislature had so intended they could have done so. Instead they chose to curtail the right of appeal and that is the Legislature's prerogative."

A contrasting approach to standing, albeit premised on different statutory language, is illustrated by the following case heard by the BC Forest Appeals Commission (FAC).

In the matter of an appeal under section 131 of the Forest Practices Code of British Columbia, SBC 1994, c. 41
(unreported decision 95101(a) available from the FAC
at http://www.fac.gov.bc.ca/)

A Panel of the Forest Appeals Commission

David Perry, Panel Chair

Between: Forest Practices Board (Applicant) and Ministry of Forests and Riverside Forest Products Ltd. (Respondent) and Cariboo-Chilcotin Conservation Council (Applicant)

[Riverside Forest Products was issued a stop work order and remediation order regarding damaging road construction and hauling. A review panel overturned the decision; on appeal, the Cariboo-Chilcotin Conservation Council (CCCC) applied for intervenor status, a matter within the discretion of the commission, pursuant to s. 131 of the Act.]

In deciding whether intervenor status should be granted under sub-section 131(9) of the Act the CCCC and Riverside submit, and the Commission agrees, that the test is whether the applicant has a valid interest in participating and can be of assistance in the proceedings ... .

In this case CCCC has provided some indication that they have a valid interest in participating. They represent a coalition of groups in the Cariboo-Chilcotin area that have a particular interest in the protection of the environment and sustainable development. The Commission is satisfied that the CCCC being a local group with a particular environmental interest does have a valid interest in participating in this procedure.

The second prong of the test is whether the CCCC can be of assistance in the proceedings. Riverside submits that the CCCC will not be of assistance to the proceeding because their interest is already represented by the Board. Riverside suggests that the legislature provided the Board with its broad authority to bring appeals before the Commission for the very reason that they represent the public interest and therefore represent the CCCC's interest. The Board itself has submitted that it does not agree with this characterization of the Board's role. Indeed the Board's own Values and Guiding Principles which are found at page 14 of the Board's 1995 Annual Report state that, "The Board will represent the public's interests, not those of any single group." The Commission cannot agree that the Board will represent the CCCC's interests. Had the legislature anticipated that the Board would have such a broad mandate it surely would not have provided for intervenors within the same legislative scheme.

· · ·

The question still remains can the CCCC be of assistance to these proceedings. The CCCC submits that they bring a unique environmental perspective to the proceedings. This is particularly so in that they are active users of the provincial forest that is the subject of this appeal. The Commission notes that the Preamble to the Act provides:

> WHEREAS British Columbians desire sustainable use of the forests they hold in trust
> for future generations;
> AND WHEREAS sustainable use includes ...
>   (c) balancing productive, spiritual, ecological and recreational values of forests to meet
> the economic and cultural needs of peoples and communities, including first nations ... .

Considering the above, it is the decision of the Commission that a local environmental coalition can be of assistance to the proceedings and in particular may be of assistance in determining the meaning and scope of "damage to the environment" as it is used in section 45 of the Act.

The final question to consider is to what extent should the CCCC be permitted to participate. Riverside submits that the participation should be in writing and that it should be limited to the interpretation of section 45 of the Act. The CCCC submits that full submissions including an environmental perspective be put before the Commission. The Board submits that they do not object to the CCCC application because the CCCC may choose to raise issues that the Board will not.

Riverside suggests that the Commission should come to the same conclusion that the Forest Appeal Board reached in *MacMillan Bloedel Ltd. v. Chief Forester*, June 19, 1992. In that case, the Appeal Board was considering an application for intervenor status by the Sierra Club of Western Canada into an appeal under the *Forest Act*. The appeal was over the annual allowable cut that had been arrived at between the licensees and the Ministry. The Appeal Board granted the Sierra Club limited standing to provide written argument only. Their reason for doing so was that the Board did not want to prejudice the parties by forcing them to respond to grounds of attack other than those which they chose to raise.

There are, however, differences between that case and this one. In this case the Act specifically provides for intervenors while the *Forest Act* does not. Similarly, in this case there is an issue under appeal that can benefit from the balancing of ecological interests against economic interests as is contemplated in the Preamble. The *Forest Act* has no such provision. Finally, the issue under appeal in the *MacMillan Bloedel* case was contractual in nature. In this case it is not.

Given the above it is the decision of the Commission that the Commission will benefit from the full participation of the CCCC as it applies to the appeal that has been commenced by the Board.

[Intervenor status granted.]

QUESTION

Do you agree, in general, that administrative tribunals should adopt a more liberal approach to standing than the courts?

V. JUDICIAL REVIEW

A. Standard of Review

A key threshold issue to be addressed in judicial review applications is the standard of review against which the tribunal's decision should be assessed. Over the last two decades, courts have generally tended to show greater deference to the decisions of administrative tribunals. Where courts conclude that a deferential approach is warranted, they will only interfere with a tribunal's decision if they deem it to be "patently unreasonable." Conversely, where they conclude that less deference is appropriate, they will scrutinize the tribunal's decision more rigorously.

Standard of review was a central issue in the following case involving a challenge to a decision by the Alberta EAB to embark on a hearing concerning PCB emissions from the Swan Hills incinerator. The facility's operator (Chem-Security) claimed that the issue of emissions had been previously addressed by another permitting tribunal and, as such, was not a "new matter" properly under the EAB's jurisdiction, as set out in its empowering legislation, the *Environmental Protection and Enhancement Act* (EPEA).

Graham v. Alberta (Director, Chemicals Assessment & Management, Environmental Protection)
(1996), 22 CELR (NS) 141, at 145-51 (Alta. QB)

MEDHURST J: What is the standard of review applicable to the Environmental Appeal Board's decision?

. . .

Effective September 1, 1996 the *EPEA* has been amended so that the Act now contains a broad privative clause limiting judicial review. However, regardless of whether a statute contains a built-in statutory limit such as a private clause, there is a strong tradition of courts showing curial deference to administrative bodies which possess a high degree of expertise.

In *Pezim v. British Columbia (Superintendent of Brokers)* (1994), 22 Admin. LR (2d) 1 (SCC), Iacobucci J at p. 9 stated:

> where there is no privative clause and where there is a statutory right of appeal, the concept of the specialization of duties requires that deference be shown to decisions of specialized tribunals on matters which fall squarely within the tribunal's expertise ... .

The question then is whether the EAB is entitled to curial deference? In making that decision it is necessary to determine whether the question in issue is a jurisdictional question or a question of law within the administrative tribunal's jurisdiction.

The method for distinguishing jurisdictional questions from questions of law within the administrative tribunal's jurisdiction was addressed by the Supreme Court of Canada in the *CBC* case [*ACTRA v. Canadian Broadcasting Corp.* (1995), 121 DLR (4th) 385], at p. 397:

> In distinguishing jurisdictional questions from questions of law within a tribunal's jurisdiction, this court eschewed a formalistic approach. Rather, it has endorsed a "pragmatic and functional analysis," to use the words of Beetz J in *UES Local 298 v. Bibeault*, [1988] 2 SCR 1048 ... . In that decision Beetz J noted, at p. 1086, that it was relevant for the reviewing court to examine:
>
> > "not only the wording of the enactment conferring jurisdiction on the administrative tribunal, but the purpose of the statute creating the tribunal, the reason for its existence, the area of expertise of its members and the nature of the problem before the tribunal."
>
> The goal is to determine whether the legislature intended that the question in issue be ultimately decided by the tribunal, or rather by the courts.

Counsel for the EAB in its brief applies the factors enumerated by Beetz J in *Bibeault*. I believe a number of these arguments support a finding that the EAB is a specialized board entitled to curial deference.

· · ·

[After noting (1) the broad wording of the enactment and (2) the omnibus environmental protection purposes of the EPEA, the court noted:]

(iii) Reason for the EAB's Existence

The EAB was created in order to hear the appeals which arise pursuant to the *EPEA* and *Government Organization Act*. Part 3 of the *EPEA* grants the EAB broad discretion to deal with the issues that may arise from a notice of objection filed pursuant to the *EPEA*, including the power to hear and determine appeals on a wide variety of regulatory decisions in relation to environmental matters.

(iv) Area of Expertise of EAB Members

The members of the EAB are appointed by the Lieutenant Governor in Council. Counsel for the EAB in their brief state that EAB members are appointed by virtue of their qualifications, abilities and experience and that in the course of fulfilling the EAB's environmental mandate, the members are exposed to technical and scientific matters, and consequently develop a body of expertise in the area.

(v) Nature of the Problem Before the EAB

Counsel for the EAB submits the nature of the question which was before the EAB was one of statutory interpretation. A matter within the realm of expertise of the EAB which required the EAB to analyze a question of mixed fact and law.

Given that the Supreme Court of Canada has endorsed a "pragmatic and functional approach" to determining the intention of the legislature, I believe the recent amendments to the *EPEA* which have added a broad privative clause to the Act can and must be taken into consideration when determining whether the EAB is entitled to curial deference.

. . .

I believe a pragmatic and functional analysis of the factors set out above will lead to the court concluding that the question in issue i.e. the interpretation of s. 87(5)(b)(i), is a question of law which was intended by the legislature to be ultimately decided by the EAB rather than the court. The Supreme Court of Canada in *Pezim v. British Columbia (Superintendent of Brokers)* ... , states at p. 27-28 that:

> There exist various standards of review with respect to the myriad of administrative agencies that exist in our country ... . The courts have developed a spectrum [of standards of review] that ranges from the standard of reasonableness to that of correctness. Courts have also enunciated a principle of deference that applies not just to the facts as found by the tribunal, but also to the legal questions before the tribunal in the light of its role and expertise. At the reasonableness end of the spectrum, where deference is at its highest, are those cases where a tribunal protected by a true privative clause is deciding a matter within its jurisdiction, and where there is no statutory right of appeal ... . At the correctness end of the spectrum, where deference in terms of legal questions is at its lowest, are those cases where the issues concern the interpretation of a provision limiting the tribunal's jurisdiction (jurisdictional error) or where there is a statutory right of appeal which allows the reviewing court to substitute its opinion for that of the tribunal and where the tribunal has no greater expertise than the court on the issue in question, as for example in the area of human rights.

Accordingly, in my view the proper test to be applied to the review of the decision of the EAB is the standard of patent unreasonableness.

B. Grounds for Review

As discussed above, there are a limited number of recognized grounds upon which courts are prepared to review administrative action. In the federal realm, these grounds for review have been codified in s. 18(1) of the *Federal Court Act*; in most other jurisdictions, however, these grounds are defined through precedent. The next case provides an illustration of a number of these grounds for review.

Halfway River First Nation v. British Columbia (Ministry of Forests)
(1997), 39 BCLR (3d) 227 (SC)

DORGAN J: Pursuant to the *Judicial Review Procedure Act*, RSBC 1996 c. 241, the Halfway River First Nation ("Halfway") seeks review of a decision of the District Manager ("Lawson"), Fort St. John Forest District, Ministry of Forests, made September 13, 1996. The decision approved the application of Canadian Forest Products Ltd. ("Canfor") for Cutting Permit 212 ("CP212").

The decision under review was the culmination of a lengthy informal process over 4 years. The Halfway Nation are descendants of the Hudson Hope Beaver people who were signatories to Treaty 8 in 1900. Canfor is the licensee under a forest licence in the Fort St. John timber supply area which lies within the boundaries of the area covered by Treaty 8.

Halfway asserts that in addition to its reserve land, it uses an area immediately adjacent to its reserve referred to as "Tusdzuh" for such traditional purposes as hunting, gathering plants for food and medicinal purposes, and spiritual ceremonies. The Halfway Nation asserts this area is integral to the maintenance of its traditional culture and indeed its sustenance. In 1995, Halfway filed a treaty land entitlement claim with the Federal Government in respect of the Tusdzuh area. Apparently, finality has not yet come to that process.

Pursuant to the applicable legislation and its licence, each year Canfor submits harvesting proposals in respect of five-year periods. In its application which resulted in the decision under review, Canfor applied to the Ministry of Forests for approval to harvest trees within the CP212 area. CP212 is located within the Tusdzuh area.

It is the responsibility of the District Manager (in this case Lawson) of the forestry district in which the proposed harvest is located (in this case Fort St. John) to deal with Canfor's application. On September 13, 1996 Lawson approved the application for harvest within CP212.

In December 1996, Canfor proceeded to commence its harvesting operations and the Halfway Nation erected a roadblock. Canfor responded with an application to this Court for an injunction. The parties agreed that the injunction application may be argued following delivery of these reasons.

Halfway argues that the approval of CP212 violates principles of administrative law and infringes their Aboriginal and Treaty Rights. [Discussion of aboriginal and treaty rights has been omitted.] The administrative law issues which arise are:

1. Did Lawson commit an error by failing to consider relevant considerations or by considering irrelevant considerations;
2. Did Lawson unlawfully fetter his discretion;
3. Was there real or apprehended bias on the part of Lawson such as to disqualify him;
4. Did Lawson commit an error of fact; [and]
5. Did Lawson violate principles of procedural fairness by failing to adequately consult with Halfway or by failing to provide Halfway with sufficient notice of his decision; ... .

Consideration of Relevant and Irrelevant Considerations

Relevant Considerations

While failure to consider relevant factors may provide a basis for impugning the exercise of discretion, an exercise of discretion will only be *ultra vires* if the decision-maker overlooked a relevant factor that its enabling statute expressly or, more usually, impliedly obliged it to consider ... .

The enabling statutes are the *Forest Act*, RSBC 1979, c. 140 (the "*Act*") and the *Forest Practices Code of British Columbia Act*, SBC 1994, c. 41 (the "*Code*").

The *Act* in s. 12(f) provides that cutting permits may be issued by the District Manager pursuant to a forest licence, and that their issuance must be in accordance with the *Act* and the *Code*. The preamble of the *Code* implies an obligation to consider a variety of factors in approving cutting permits ... [and] the three considerations the petitioner alleges that Lawson failed to take into account all fall within the preamble, namely, archaeological sites, impacts on wildlife, and use of the area by Halfway.

However, Lawson's Reasons for Decision suggest that he did consider these factors. With respect to wildlife values, all the blocks were reviewed on September 13 by Lambert, a biologist with the MOE. According to Lambert's affidavit, all of his concerns regarding potential impacts on wildlife were addressed. With respect to archaeological sites, Lawson notes that changes were made to the cutting permit to avoid an old pack trail and that the Cultural Heritage Overview Assessment ("CHOA") identified no other sites. Finally, with respect to interference with Halfway's use of the area Lawson considered the impact of harvesting on hunting, fishing and trapping, relying on information provided by the MOE. He also considered the impact of increased access, noting that Canfor would deactivate all roads.

Irrelevant Considerations

. . .

In certain circumstances, the court may review the exercise of discretion by an administrative decision-maker on the grounds that it was based on irrelevant considerations ... . While a tribunal may consider irrelevant circumstances, where a decision is based entirely or predominantly on irrelevant factors it may be subject to judicial review.

In the present case, Lawson appears to have taken into consideration the following factors in making his decision:

(a) The fact that the cutting permit application was consistent with Canfor's approved Five Year Development Plan.
(b) The fact that CP212 complied with the *Forest Practices Code*, as required by s. 12(f) *Forest Act*.
(c) The impact on fish and wildlife populations as determined from the Lambert Report and other information provided by BCE staff.
(d) The impact of the proposed harvesting on trapping, as determined from information provided by BCE staff.
(e) The Protection of Aboriginal Rights Policy.
(f) The Cultural Heritage (Ethnographic) Overview Assessment.
(g) The impact of improved access to the area on Native hunting.

These are all relevant considerations and therefore even if Lawson's decision was based in part on the factors suggested by the petitioners, it cannot be said to have been entirely or even predominantly based on irrelevant factors. Moreover, with respect to the factors specified by the petitioners, they are all either irrelevant or were not given any weight by Lawson:

(a) Timing of the decision: This was a factor in determining when the decision was made but not what the decision was.
(b) Political pressure from Canfor: There is no evidence that this had any impact on Lawson's decision and in any event there was pressure from the Halfway Band as well.
(c) Canfor's situation: I accept the argument of Canfor's counsel that as the cutting permit applicant, Canfor's circumstances must be relevant. Moreover, this factor would fall under paragraph (c) of the preamble to the *Forest Practices Code*.
(d) Government policy: This goes to the issue of fettering discretion and in any event can be a relevant factor.
(e) Threat of litigation: There is no evidence this had any impact and both sides were threatening litigation.

Fettering of Discretion

The petitioners submit that Lawson fettered his discretion by:

(a) Treating the government leave policy of not halting resource development pending TLE Claims as binding upon him.
(b) Refusing to consider the option of halting all logging in CP212 (adopting an inflexible policy).
(c) Arbitrarily setting September 13 as the date on which a decision with respect to CP212 would be made.

The petitioners also submit that Lawson's discretion was fettered by his superiors (the Minister of Forests and others).

Government Policy

A decision-maker's discretion may be fettered where he or she makes a decision with reference to the policy of another government body ... . Similarly, a decision-maker's discretion may be fettered where he or she simply complies with a direction from a superior, rather than making his or her own decision on the merits ... . Here, the district manager has the authority to halt logging in the area to protect First Nations' rights. The fact that Aboriginal and Treaty Rights are at stake is also significant.

Inflexible Policy

[A] decision-maker may not adopt an inflexible policy or guideline but rather must make each decision on its merits. ... [O]n the whole of the record I am satisfied that Lawson fettered his discretion by treating the government policy of not halting development as a given and by simply following the direction of the Minister of Forests not to halt development. This is particularly evident from p. 4 of his Reasons for Decision which reads:

In December 1995 the Minister of Forests advised both ourselves and the Halfway Band that it is not the policy of the provincial government to halt resource development pending resolution of the Treaty Land Entitlement (TLE) Claim and that we must honor legal obligations to both the Forest Industry as well as First Nations. This fact was again reiterated by Janna Kumi, Assistant Deputy Minister, Operations, upon her meeting with the Halfway Band in January 1996.

September 13 Date

Finally, setting September 13 as the date for deciding on CP212 in no way fettered Lawson's decision. He was still free to either approve or not approve the application on its merits.

Bias

. . .

Actual Bias

. . .

The courts have held that the accumulation of improprieties by a decision-maker may prove real bias. The improprieties alleged in this case are more limited. I have already rejected allegations that Lawson considered irrelevant considerations and failed to consider relevant considerations. Allegations of error of law have not been made out. The remaining alleged improprieties are insufficient to establish real bias.

Reasonable Apprehension of Bias

Attitudinal bias arises where a decision-maker has pre-judged an issue and has not brought an open mind to the decision-making process. The rule against bias disqualifies decision-makers with attitudinal biases ... .

While all administrative tribunals owe a general duty of fairness to the parties whose interests they must determine, the content of that duty varies given the nature of the decision, that is those of a judicial or quasi-judicial nature at one end of the spectrum and those of a legislative nature at the other. However, the right to be treated fairly is an "independent and unqualified right" ... .

In that case [*Newfoundland Telephone Co. v. Newfoundland (Board of Commissioners of Public Utilities)*, [1992] 1 SCR 623, at 645; 89 DLR (4th) 289, at 304] Mr. Justice Cory set out the test for reasonable apprehension of bias (at 636):

> The duty to act fairly includes the duty to provide procedural fairness to the parties. That simply cannot exist if an adjudicator is biased. It is, of course, impossible to determine the precise state of mind of an adjudicator who has made an administrative board decision. As a result, the courts have taken the position that an unbiased appearance is, in itself, an essential component of procedural fairness. ... The test is whether a reasonably informed bystander could reasonably perceive bias on the part of an adjudicator.

Given the nature of the decision in question, I have concluded that the District Manager must comply with a high standard of fairness which in the context of bias means that even a reasonable apprehension of bias would be sufficient to disqualify him.

[A] further statement by Lawson is of concern. In his letter to Chief Metecheah dated August 29, 1996 Lawson states "I must inform you that if the application is in order and abides by all Ministry regulations and the *Forest Practices Code* I have no compelling reasons not to approve their application." This statement strongly suggests that Lawson had already concluded that there was no infringement of Treaty or Aboriginal Rights. His only remaining concerns about the application were with respect to compliance with MOF and Code requirements. He requests information on Aboriginal and Treaty Rights with respect to future Canfor activities but makes no reference to such rights vis-à-vis CP212. The only conclusion to be drawn from this letter is that Lawson had already decided that there was no infringement of Halfway's rights.

This evidence indicates that once the Development Plan was approved, all applications for cutting permits within it will likely be approved as well and is evidence which supports a finding of a reasonable apprehension of bias.

Error of Fact

Generally, certiorari will not issue to correct an error of fact. There are, however, two exceptions to this rule ... .

The first permits review where there is a complete absence of evidence for a material finding of fact since a decision without any evidence is arbitrary and therefore reviewable. This constitutes jurisdictional error. The test for determining if there is no evidence was set out by McLachlin J in *Re McInnes and Simon Fraser University* (1984), 3 DLR (4th) 708 (BCCA):

> If the decision is to be upheld, there must be some evidence logically capable of supporting the conclusion to which the tribunal has come. Such evidence is sometimes referred to as evidence which "reasonably" supports the conclusion ... the conclusion must be one to which the tribunal could reasonably have come on the evidence. Such language does not, in my view, authorize the court to embark on the exercise of weighing and evaluating evidence which was properly received by the committee and which possesses some probative value. The court of review remains confined to the initial question of whether there is some evidence capable of supporting the committee's conclusion.

In the present case it cannot be said that there was no evidence supporting Lawson's finding that Aboriginal and Treaty Rights would not be infringed. Lawson had the CHOA report and information provided by BCE staff regarding the impact of harvesting on the traditional activities of hunting, trapping and fishing.

Secondly, the court may review a patently unreasonable error of fact since this affects the jurisdiction of the tribunal. A decision is patently unreasonable only where it is evidently not in accordance with reason or is clearly irrational. As stated by Cory J in *Canada v. PSAC*, [1993] 1 SCR 941, at 963-64:

Thus, based on the dictionary definition of the words "patently unreasonable," it is apparent that if the decision the Board reached, acting within its jurisdiction, is not clearly irrational, that is to say evidently not in accordance with reason, then it cannot be said that there was a loss of jurisdiction.

Given the limited evidence available to Lawson, the factual conclusions which he reached as to infringement of Treaty 8 or Aboriginal Rights is unreasonable. There was some evidence supporting his findings, however, Lawson had no information from Halfway. How can one reach any reasonable conclusion as to the impact on Halfway's rights without obtaining information from Halfway on their uses of the area in question?

Given the importance attached to Treaty and Aboriginal Rights, in the absence of significant information and in the face of assertions by Halfway as to their uses of CP212, it was patently unreasonable for Lawson to conclude that there was no infringement.

The Duty of Fairness and the Right To Be Heard

It is settled law that where a decision is administrative in nature, the parties are entitled to procedural fairness. However, the courts have moved away from classifying decisions as administrative, legislative or quasi-judicial and then applying principles of fairness based on this classification. In moving away from the classification noted above, the courts now tend to look at three factors in determining whether and to what extent a duty of fairness is owed: the nature of the decision to be made; the relationship between the administrative body and the individual; and the effect of the decision on the individual's rights: … .

Given that Lawson's decision was final in that no appeal is provided for in the Act or the Code, that the decision is specific in that it relates to a particular permit and an application for that permit made by a specific person or entity, that the relationship between the Provincial Government and its representative, in this case the District Manager, and Halfway is fiduciary in nature and that there is evidence to suggest that harvesting in CP212 could significantly affect Halfway's very way of life, I have concluded that the highest standards of fairness should apply.

Generally, fairness will require that notice be given and an effective opportunity to be heard be provided. Given the circumstances of this case, the duty of fairness ought to include an obligation on the District Manager to make all reasonable efforts and provide every opportunity for Halfway to be heard. Consultation must be meaningful and the district manager must take into serious consideration the information provided by Halfway and Halfway's rights in general. This is very similar to the consultation requirement associated with the MOF's fiduciary duty to Halfway.

In addition, procedural fairness requires that Halfway be given notice of the decision to be made. The evidence shows that Halfway had notice of the proposed harvesting in CP212 through the following mechanisms:

[A listing in paragraphs (a) to (h) of various forms of constructive and actual notice given to Halfway is omitted.]

(i) A meeting with Lawson on May 13, 1996 during which Lawson provided Halfway with a map of Canfor's proposed harvesting activities, including blocks in CP212.

(j) A letter dated August 27, 1996 from Lawson to Halfway indicating a decision would be made September 13, 1996 on the approval of CP212.

(k) A letter dated August 29, 1996 from Lawson to Halfway setting out Canfor's logging plans. ...

Paragraph (i) is the only true advance notice that Halfway had of Canfor's plans for the winter of 1997. It is not notice that Lawson would make his decision on September 13.

The letters dated August 27 and 29, 1996 (paragraphs (j) and (k)) cannot be considered adequate notice of Canfor's application given the late date at which they were sent. Moreover, in reply the petitioners noted that blocks are routinely added, deleted or altered by the applicant prior to application; therefore Halfway cannot comment until it sees the application. Canfor's application regarding the cut blocks in issue was not provided to Halfway until after Lawson had approved it.

Given these circumstances, notice was inadequate.

Decision to approve application quashed.

NOTES

1. An appeal of Dorgan J's decision was partially successful. See *Halfway River First Nation v. British Columbia (Ministry of Forests)* (1998), 178 DLR (4th) 666 (BCCA). The Court of Appeal held that the district manager had not fettered his discretion by reference to an "inflexible government policy" of not halting resource development pending the resolution of treaty claims. In the court's view, the government's policy did not preclude a full consideration of whether the permit application met with the requirements of the regulations, the Act, and the Code, and whether the hunting rights of the First Nation were taken into account. Nor, in the court's view, was there a reasonable apprehension of bias. The district manager performed both investigative and adjudicative functions and, as such, it was appropriate for him to offer tentative opinions about the case on the merits. It also concluded that notice was adequate because given the nature of the process, it was not possible to set out in advance the exact date on which the final decision would be made.

Nonetheless, Finch JA found that Halfway had been denied the right to be heard and that the district manager had erred in concluding that aboriginal and treaty rights would not be infringed.

2. As previously discussed, administrative agencies—including Cabinet itself—are also subject to judicial review in the exercise of their statutory power to make regulations. The following decision is a case in point.

Aluminum Co. of Canada v. Ontario (Minister of the Environment)
(1986), 19 Admin. LR 192, at 199-204 (Ont. SC)

MONTGOMERY J: The applicant, Aluminum Company of Canada, Limited ("Alcan"), seeks an order declaring s. 6 of Ontario Reg. 623/85 and ss. 1(1)(b) and 1(2) of Ontario reg. 633/85 *ultra vires* the Lieutenant Governor in Council.

Softdrink cans are the issue. Under earlier regulations only refillable bottles were allowed. Steel cans became permissible but aluminum cans were excluded. After 4 years of experimentation with recycling, Alcan convinced the Ministry of the Environment ("MOE") that aluminum cans were environmentally viable.

The government, by Order in Council, delayed the implementation of aluminum cans for 2 years to allow the steel industry in Hamilton to develop a thin rolled steel for softdrink cans. Alcan says this delay is costly to it and Alcan should not be kept out of the market.

. . .

[Ulterior Motive; Improper Purpose]

It is contended that the power delegated to the executive must be exercised for the purposes of the statute and not for an irrelevant purpose or in bad faith.

Reliance is placed upon the statement of Mr. Justice Rand in *Roncarelli v. Duplessis*, [1959] SCR 121, at p. 140:

> In public regulation of this sort there is no such thing as absolute and untrammelled "discretion," that is that action can be taken on any ground or for any reason that can be suggested to the mind of the administrator; no legislative Act can, without express language, be taken to contemplate an unlimited arbitrary power exercisable for any purpose, however capricious or irrelevant, regardless of the nature or purpose of the statute. Fraud and corruption in the Commission may not be mentioned in such statutes but they are always implied as exceptions. "Discretion" necessarily implies good faith in discharging public duty; there is always a perspective within which a statute is intended to operate; and any clear departure from its lines or objects is just as objectionable as fraud or corruption. Could an applicant be refused a permit because he had been born in another province, or because of the colour of his hair? The ordinary language of the legislature cannot be so distorted. ...

It is argued that once the MOE determined that aluminum cans were environmentally sound by virtue of a scheme of recycling, it was beyond the scope of the executive to impose a timetable for the aluminum cans to be implemented because that decision was based upon economic and political considerations outside the scope of the Act.

It is conceded that the paramount purpose of aluminum cans not being used until September 1987 is to protect the steel industry and protect jobs in the Hamilton area. Mr. Heintzman says this ulterior motive is fatal to the regulations.

That matter was addressed by the Supreme Court of Canada in *Thorne's Hardware Ltd. v. R* (1983), 143 DLR (3d) 577. There, an Order in Council enacted under the *National Harbours Board Act*, RSC 1970, c. N-8 extended the boundaries of St. John's

Harbour to include private property. Irving Oil Limited, the parent company, argued that the Order in Council was passed for improper motives, namely to permit the National Harbours Board to collect harbour dues and that it was expropriation without compensation. Mr. Justice Dickson (as he then was) wrote on behalf of the Court [at 581]:

> Decisions made by the Governor in Council in matters of public convenience and general policy are final and not reviewable in legal proceedings.
>
> Although, as I have indicated, the possibility of striking down an Order in Council on jurisdictional or other compelling grounds remains open, it would take an egregious case to warrant such action. This is not such a case. ...

In my view, the executive established a regulatory scheme to implement the use of aluminum cans for softdrinks for the first time. As part of that scheme it decided to delay the use of such cans until September 1987. There is no evidence of bad faith. The scheme was dependent upon recycling to avoid litter. The MOE has been satisfied on that count. It is not the function of this Court on judicial review to tell the executive when parts of its regulations shall be implemented. In my view, when the scheme came within the scope of the Act there was nothing unreasonable about the conduct of the executive in concerning itself with an ailing segment of the economy and the preservation of jobs. To adopt words of Chief Justice Dickson this is not such an "egregious case" as to warrant judicial intervention.

· · ·

In my view, as earlier stated, the scheme for use of disposable softdrink containers is contained in the statute and simply delaying the advent of aluminum cans in the marketplace albeit for purpose of assisting an ailing segment of the economy is not, in my view, so extraneous as to cause the Order in Council to be void. ... This case merely involves the temporary delay of the introduction of a, as of now, non-existent market for the sale of aluminum softdrink cans.

For these reasons I would dismiss the administrative attack on the regulations.

QUESTION

Canadian courts have traditionally given Cabinet and Cabinet ministers a broad berth in the exercise of their discretionary powers, while keeping bureaucratic discretion under much closer check. What rationale(s) support this approach? Do you agree with such an approach?

VI. PUBLIC PARTICIPATION AND JUDICIAL REVIEW
A. Public Interest Standing

Over the last two decades, courts have gradually liberalized the law of public interest standing. Important landmarks in this evolution, traced by Cory J in the excerpt that follows, include the standing trilogy of *Thorson*, *McNeil*, and *Borowski*, enactment of the Charter in 1982, and the extension of public interest standing principles to non-constitutional cases in *Finlay* in 1986. The Supreme Court of Canada's decision to deny standing to the Canadian Council of Churches, which had sought to challenge changes to federal immigration laws on behalf of current and future refugee claimants, is seen by some as evidence that we may be in the twilight of this liberalizing trend.

Canadian Council of Churches v. R
(1992), 88 DLR (4th) 193, at 201-4 (SCC)

The Question of Standing in Canada

Courts in Canada, like those in other common law jurisdictions, traditionally dealt with individuals. For example, courts determine whether an individual is guilty of a crime; they determine rights as between individuals; they determine the rights of individuals in their relationships with the state in all its various manifestations. One great advantage of operating in the traditional mode is that the courts can reach their decisions based on facts that have been clearly established. It was by acting in this manner that the courts established the rule of law and provided a peaceful means of resolving disputes. Operating primarily, if not almost exclusively, in the traditional manner, courts in most regions operate to capacity. Courts play an important role in our society. If they are to continue to do so care must be taken to ensure that judicial resources are not overextended. This is a factor that will always have to be placed in the balance when consideration is given to extending standing.

On the other hand there can be no doubt that the complexity of society has spawned ever more complex issues for resolution by the courts. Modern society requires regulation to survive. Transportation by motor vehicle and aircraft requires greater regulation for public safety than did travel by covered wagon. Light and power provided by nuclear energy require greater control than did the kerosene lamp.

The State has been required to intervene in an ever more extensive manner in the affairs of its citizens. The increase of State activism has led to the growth of the concept of public rights. The validity of government intervention must be reviewed by courts. Even before the passage of the *Charter* this court had considered and weighed the merits of broadening access to the courts against the need to conserve scarce judicial resources. It expanded the rules of standing in a trilogy of cases; *Thorson v. Canada (Attorney General)*, [1975] 1 SCR 138, *McNeil v. Nova Scotia (Board of Censors)* (1975), [1976] 2 SCR 265 and *Borowski v. Canada (Minister of Justice)*, [1981] 2 SCR 575. Writing for the majority in *Borowski*, Martland J set forth the conditions which a plaintiff must satisfy in order to be granted standing [at 598 SCR]:

> [T]o establish status as a plaintiff in a suit seeking a declaration that legislation is invalid, if there is a serious issue as to its invalidity, a person need only to show that he is affected by it directly or that he has a genuine interest as a citizen in the validity of the legislation and that there is no other reasonable and effective manner in which the issue may be brought before the Court.

Those then were the conditions which had to be met in 1981.

In 1982, with the passage of the *Charter*, there was for the first time a restraint placed on the sovereignty of Parliament to pass legislation that fell within its jurisdiction.

The *Charter* enshrines the rights and freedoms of Canadians. It is the courts which have the jurisdiction to preserve and to enforce those *Charter* rights. This is achieved, in part, by ensuring that legislation does not infringe the provisions of the *Charter*. By its terms the *Charter* indicates that a generous and liberal approach should be taken to the issue of standing. If that were not done, *Charter* rights might be unenforced and *Charter* freedoms shackled. The *Constitution Act, 1982* does not of course affect the discretion courts possess to grant standing to public litigants. What it does is entrench the fundamental right of the public to government in accordance with the law.

. . .

The question of standing was first reviewed in the post-*Charter* era in *Finlay v. Canada (Minister of Finance)*, [1986] 2 SCR 607. In that case Le Dain J, speaking for the court extended the scope of the trilogy and held that courts have a discretion to award public interest standing to challenge an exercise of administrative authority as well as legislation. He based this conclusion on the underlying principle of discretionary standing which he defined as a recognition of the public interest in maintaining respect for "the limits of statutory authority."

The standard set by this court for public interest plaintiffs to receive standing also addresses the concern for the proper allocation of judicial resources. This is achieved by limiting the granting of status to situations in which no directly affected individual might be expected to initiate litigation. In *Finlay*, it was specifically recognized that the traditional concerns about widening access to the courts are addressed by the conditions imposed for the exercise of judicial discretion to grant public interest standing set out in the trilogy. Le Dain J put it in this way, at 631 [SCR]:

> [T]he concern about the allocation of scarce judicial resources and the need to screen out the mere busybody; the concern that in the determination of issues the courts should have the benefit of the contending points of view of those most directly affected by them; and the concern about the proper role of the courts and their constitutional relationship to the other branches of government. These concerns are addressed by the criteria for the exercise of the judicial discretion to recognize public interest standing to bring an action for a declaration that were laid down in *Thorson, McNeil* and *Borowski*.

Should the Current Test for Public Interest Standing Be Extended?

The increasing recognition of the importance of public rights in our society confirms the need to extend the right to standing from the private law tradition which limited party status to those who possessed a private interest. In addition, some extension of standing beyond the traditional parties accords with the provisions of the *Constitution Act, 1982*. However, I would stress that the recognition of the need to grant public interest standing in some circumstances does not amount to a blanket approval to grant standing to all who wish to litigate an issue. It is essential that a balance be struck between ensuring access to the courts and preserving judicial resources. It would be disastrous if the courts were allowed to become hopelessly overburdened as a result of the unnecessary proliferation of marginal or redundant suits brought by well-meaning organizations pursuing their own particular cases certain in the knowledge that their cause is all-important. It would be detrimental, if not devastating, to our system of justice and unfair to private litigants.

The whole purpose of granting status is to prevent the immunization of legislation or public acts from any challenge. The granting of public interest standing is not required when, on a balance of probabilities, it can be shown that the measure will be subject to attack by a private litigant. The principles for granting public standing set forth by this court need not and should not be expanded. The decision whether to grant status is a discretionary one with all which that designation implies. Thus, undeserving applications may be refused. Nonetheless, when exercising the discretion the applicable principles should be interpreted in a liberal and generous manner.

NOTES

1. Whether the judgment in *Canadian Council of Churches* (*CCC*) will usher in a more conservative judicial approach to public interest standing is unclear. To date, most courts have not interpreted *CCC* as limiting or altering the *ratio* in *Finlay*. For example, in *Shiell v. Atomic Energy Control Board* (1995), 33 Admin. LR (2d) 122 (FCTD), the applicant sought judicial review of a licence issued to a uranium operation. Despite the applicant's 20-year involvement in environmental issues surrounding the uranium industry, the court refused her standing because of her lack of a "direct personal interest." Because she lived "several hundred miles" from the respondent's operation, the court— emphasizing the Supreme Court of Canada's concern over the "allocation of scarce judicial resources" from *Finlay* and *CCC*—held that "the decision will not affect her in any way different from that felt by any other member of the general public."

2. The basic *Finlay* test for discretionary public interest of standing was also applied in *Algonquin Wildlands League v. Ontario (Minister of Natural Resources)* (1996), 21 CELR (NS) 102. There, environmental groups brought a judicial review application arguing timber harvesting activities that had been authorized by the Ontario minister of natural resources violated a provincial forest sustainability law. They also brought a motion to stay the minister's decisions pending the disposition of the judicial review application. The court held:

It is uncontradicted that both applicants are nonprofit public interest environmental organizations with a history of responsible involvement in forest and land use planning issues in the Temagami area. The issues raised by the applicants are justiciable and in my opinion there is no other reasonable or effective manner in which the issues are likely to be brought before the court. It was suggested that the Minister of the Environment might attack the decisions but that seems to me to be highly unlikely. It was also suggested that members of the community could have brought the matter before the court and had not done so. It is also uncontradicted that the members of the applicants include many persons, who either live in Temagami or frequent the area for pleasure or business. It is clear from the material that there is considerable controversy in the area and that many members of the community support or at least do not oppose the government actions. As I have said it seems to me that unless someone, like the applicants, bring these issues to the court, the court will not be asked to address them. Accordingly if the applicant can overcome the hurdle that these are serious issues to be tried, I would be prepared to grant them standing to bring the application.

3. The question of public interest standing has been considered in the face of government inaction, as well as that of governmental action.

Society for the Preservation of the Englishman River Estuary v. Nanaimo (Regional District)
(1999), 28 CELR (NS) 253 (BCSC)

[The petitioner sought an order compelling the attorney general to require the Nanaimo regional district to undertake an environmental assessment of a dam that the latter was constructing. The petitioner argued that the nature of the proposed construction triggered a legal requirement for an assessment under the *Environmental Assessment Act*, RSBC 1996, c. 119. The district and the attorney general applied to dismiss the claim on the basis that the petitioner lacked standing.]

MACAULAY J: Is the petitioner entitled to public interest standing either for the purpose of seeking a declaration or mandamus?

. . .

In my view, the statutory scheme is comprehensive and the duty of enforcement has been relegated to the minister and the Attorney General. Public involvement, on the other hand, is triggered by the initiation of the assessment process. The Act contains nothing to suggest that the legislature intended that public interest groups would be actively involved in enforcing the legislation. As will be seen, this factor militates against the exercise of my discretion in favour of granting public interest standing to the petitioner ... .

The respondents advance two arguments. First, the petitioner is not entitled to public interest standing. Second, mandamus is not available as s. 5 [which prohibits a project proponent from proceeding without a required environmental assessment permit] does not create any special public duty owed to the petitioner. In other words, mandamus is not available to ensure that public authorities follow laws of general application ... . The Attorney General maintains that a private party is not entitled to seek a declaration, or enforce "penal" legislation, and relies primarily on *Gouriet v. Union of Post Office Workers and others*, [1977] 3 All ER 70 (HL) and *Carruthers and Whelton v. Langley*, [1986] 69 BCLR 24 (CA) ... . While I prefer to characterize the legislation as regulatory in nature, I consider it significant that the allegations against the respondents could attract penal consequences in the event of prosecution and conviction.

I have concluded that the Supreme Court of Canada has not extended the scope of public interest standing to the point that the principles set forth in *Gouriet* and *Carruthers* are no longer applicable ... . In my view, granting standing to a private litigant seeking to enforce a statute of general application against a public body extends the doctrine of public interest beyond its generally accepted parameters. This is particularly so where the public authority responsible for the enforcement of the statute decides in good faith not to place the issue before the court ... .

Here the petitioner seeks to enforce a public right ... . The petitioner has a concern about the alleged adverse environmental impact of the project, but no special interest in the decision whether or not to enforce the Act. The Minister, or the Attorney General, is uniquely suited, as representative of the public interest, to make this decision. There can be no doubt that either is more effectively able to bring the issue before the court than the petitioner. A decision made in good faith not to enforce or prosecute militates heavily against exercising my discretion in favour of the petitioner ... .

A similar result obtained in *Manitoba Naturalists Society Inc. v. Ducks Unlimited Canada*, [1992] 2 WWR 377 (Man. QB) where ... the court accepted that only the Attorney General could apply to the civil courts for injunctive relief against contraventions of a statute that creates an offence, as such wrongs are public in nature. Two factors were considered significant: first, the penalties that may flow from the violation of an injunction, if granted; and second, the granting of an injunction in the circumstances was "tantamount to a decision, based on a civil standard of proof, that the respondent has committed an offence under the Act" (at 384). Although the relief claimed here is a declaration and mandamus, failure to comply with an order for mandamus might also give rise to penalties. More fundamentally, a finding by this court that the respondents failed to comply with s. 5(1) of the *Environmental Assessment Act* is tantamount to a conviction for an offence pursuant to s. 76(2)(a) of the Act [which makes it an offence to fail to comply with s. 5(1) of the Act].

NOTE

In contrast, consider *Sierra Club of Canada v. Canada (Minister of Finance)*, [1999] 2 FC 211 (FCTD), where the petitioner sought judicial review of the government's refusal to subject the sale of nuclear reactors to China to a full environmental assessment. Evans J stated:

since environmental assessment legislation typically imposes obligations and liabilities on public authorities and proponents of projects subject to it, it would seem to follow that only they may challenge a failure by government to subject a project to an assessment in contravention of the Act. This surely cannot be right. If it were, it would mean that, for all practical purposes, governmental failure to require an environmental assessment when such an assessment is mandated by the legislation would be immune from judicial review for all intents and purposes. As understood today, the rule of law should be concerned to ensure that the legality of governmental inaction is as subject to challenge in the courts as are allegations of over-reaching by public officials.

B. Availability of Interim Injunctive Relief

While courts have displayed an increasing willingness to grant standing to public interest litigants, they have been much less sympathetic to arguments that existing legal doctrine should be adapted to accommodate public interest litigation in other ways. One area where this has been particularly true concerns the availability of interim injunctive relief.

Algonquin Wildlands League v. Ontario
(1996), 21 CELR (NS) 102

SAUNDERS J: The stay order sought is analogous to an injunction. There is no dispute as to the general nature of the test to be applied. It is the test set out in *RJR-MacDonald Inc. v. Canada (Attorney General)* (1994), 111 DLR (4th) 385 (SCC). It is a threefold test:

(i)   Is there a serious issue to be tried?;
(ii) Would the applicants suffer irreparable harm if the stay were refused?; [and]
(iii) What is the balance of convenience? That is which of the parties would suffer the greater harm from the granting or refusing the interim relief ... .

Initially this is the test with the lowest threshold. As stated in *RJR-MacDonald* at p. 411 unless the case on the merits is frivolous or vexatious or is a pure question of law, the judge as a general rule should go on to the next stage. The nature of the issues may be revisited at the end of the day when reaching a conclusion on the balance of convenience test. In dealing with this issue, the court should do no more at this stage than make a preliminary investigation of the merits. Indeed it is undesirable to go into the merits in any detail, having regard for the fact that they will be fully canvassed by the panel.

The applicant's attack on the municipal action is based on a noncompliance with the *Crown Forest Sustainability Act, 1994* [SO 1994, c. 25], and the conditions imposed by the Environmental Assessment Board. In my opinion the applicants have raised issues of statutory interpretation and ministerial conduct which are not frivolous and which require consideration before they can be determined. It is accordingly appropriate to pass to the second stage ... .

The applicants allege irreparable harm, in effect, on the simple straightforward position, that once you cut down a tree you cannot put it back. The extent or even the existence of the harm is disputed by the respondents. Furthermore the Minister submits that even if there were to be harm demonstrated, there has been no harm to these applicants, which the Minister submits is a necessary element of the test ... .

The cases suggest that the three tests should be considered in order and that if the applicant fails at any stage, that should be the end of the matter. It is important to note that neither the applicants in *Metropolitan Stores* nor the applicants in *RJR-MacDonald* were public interest applicants. The cases cited by the Minister in support of the submission that the irreparable harm must be suffered by the applicants either involved the issue of standing or were not binding on this court. It would be a rare case where a public interest applicant such as the organizations which are making this application would directly suffer irreparable harm. It would be illogical to grant these applicants standing and then turn around and deny them relief because they had not suffered harm. It would seem to me that a better approach would be to consider the public interest harm alleged by the applicants along with the harm to the respondents at the third stage of the inquiry. In my opinion there is nothing in the passage of Mr. Justice Beetz that would be inconsistent with that approach, bearing in mind that in *Metropolitan Stores* there was no public interest applicant. In short, in this situation, we should skip stage two and move to stage three. ...

The third stage is the balance of convenience or as it is sometimes called the balance of inconvenience. The factors to be considered vary from case to case. In this case the public interest is very much involved. The applicants say there would be irreparable harm to the public interest if this stay is not granted. Conversely the respondents say there would be irreparable harm to the public interest if the stay were to be granted.

As I have said the applicants take the simple and straightforward position that if you cut down the trees you cannot put them back. The respondents dispute there will be any significant harm or indeed any harm at all. There is considerable conflicting evidence on this point and it is not possible to make any meaningful determination. For the purpose of this motion, I am prepared to assume there will be some irreparable harm to the natural growth and wildlife in the area in spite of the efforts to keep it to a minimum.

The harm to the respondents is of a different nature. The Crown will be hampered in pursuing its policy for the use of Crown lands. Crown revenue will be at least deferred and perhaps lost. It is uncontradicted that needed wood supply will be unavailable and the Goulard mill will not be able to operate at full capacity. It is also uncontradicted that if this occurs there will be loss of employment which will have a ripple effect in the community. Again it is hard to quantify the extent of the harm, but it must be assumed that there will be some harm.

What is going on here is part of a world wide controversy or debate carried on in an effort to achieve a sustainable environment. In assessing the balance of convenience it is suggested in *RJR-MacDonald* that the court in determining whether to grant or withhold interlocutory relief should have regard not only to the harm which the parties contend they will suffer, but also to the nature of the relief sought, the nature of the legislation which is under attack, and where the public interest lies. To this I would add the nature of the authority of the Ministry which is under attack. This was not an issue in the *RJR-MacDonald* case, but in my opinion is an appropriate member of the group.

For a number of years the Ministry and interested segments of the public have been struggling with the issue of forest management. It is the obvious goal of all to achieve and maintain a sustainable environment while balancing the interests of the various segments. It is a complicated, ongoing and developing process. The details are set out in the material filed. In the course of argument it was not suggested that there had been anything other than good faith on the part of all parties to this application. The cutting of the forest at Owain Lake is clearly part of a comprehensive government policy with respect to the use of its land carried out in accordance with the principles I have tried to describe. While the applicants raised serious issues with respect to the compliance with the legislation and with the Environmental Assessment Board conditions, they have not, as submitted by the respondents for the industry, demonstrated anything that is substantially inconsistent with the draft manual or any connection between the alleged deficiencies and the alleged harm. The government action has been consistent with its declared policy.

In all of the circumstances I considered the balance favours the respondents. In my opinion it would be inappropriate to interfere with the action of the government, even for a short time. The motion therefore will be dismissed.

Environmentalists were met with a similar result in earlier litigation concerning logging in the lower Tsitika Valley on Vancouver Island. In May 1991 MacMillan Bloedel began cutting a roadway into the valley in preparation for future logging. In June 1991 the Western Canada Wilderness Committee launched an action claiming the road building was unlawful. It contended that the Ministry of Forests had no authority to issue a road building permit to the company until the ministry had approved the logging activities that the road would support. When their application for judicial review was dismissed in the BC Supreme Court, the Wilderness Committee filed an appeal and sought an injunction against further road building until the appeal was heard.

This injunction application was dismissed by Toy JA (in chambers). He held that the balance of convenience weighed against granting the injunction sought: (1991), 4 BCAC 296. Among the factors that he said supported this conclusion were that

1. the applicants had no direct or indirect interest that would be adversely affected if the road building continued;
2. the applicants had not proffered an undertaking to indemnify the company as to damages; and
3. completion of the road in this remote location would not amount to irreparable harm.

Toy JA's decision prompted critical commentary, an excerpt of which follows.

S.A.G. Elgie
"Injunctions, Ancient Forests and Irreparable Harm: A Comment on Western Canada Wilderness Committee v. A.G. British Columbia"
(1991) vol. 25 *UBC Law Review* 387, at 389-98

Direct, Distinct Interest

. . .

The reasoning of the Court in *WCWCII* has the effect of opening the courthouse doors to public interest plaintiffs but immediately routing them into the basement. While their lack of a distinct interest is no longer a barrier to standing, it will be weighed against them in awarding interlocutory injunctions. There is no rational foundation for such differing treatment. It runs contrary to the principles enunciated in *Finlay*. The Supreme Court made it clear that public interest plaintiffs were fully entitled to injunctive relief, if they satisfied the usual criteria. In doing so, the Court affirmed "the public interest in the maintenance of respect for the limits of administrative authority." Such respect is undermined if public interest plaintiffs are handicapped in their pursuit of injunctive relief against illegal government action.

Security for Damages

A second consideration of the Court of Appeal in denying injunctive relief was that, while the plaintiffs in *Bolton* were required to give an undertaking to pay any damages incurred if the appeal were unsuccessful, "no such undertaking was proffered on this application."

. . .

Most public interest plaintiffs are private citizens or non-profit citizens' groups like the Wilderness Committee. They generally have no economic stake in the outcome of the litigation. They are bringing an action to protect the environment, from which other members of the public will benefit as "free riders." Such plaintiffs simply cannot afford to reimburse a large company like MacMillan Bloedel for losses associated with an interlocutory injunction. If such a requirement is imposed, it will deter most citizens' groups from raising legitimate challenges to the legality of government action.

There is ample precedent establishing that plaintiffs who raise a "substantial issue" and are "acting in the public interest ... to preserve the status quo" ought to be relieved of the obligation to pay damages should their injunction later be dissolved. In fact, the BC Court of Appeal declined to require security from natives who were successful in obtaining a preliminary injunction against logging on Meares Island.

. . .

Irreparable Harm

The primary consideration which led Toy J to deny injunctive relief was his assessment that the logging of 400 more metres of road would not constitute "irreparable harm." Here lies the crux of the decision.

An irreparable injury is "a material one, and one that *could not be adequately remedied by money damages*." Unfortunately, the judgment says very little about why the effects of logging in the Tsitika would not be irreparable. There is some indication that "the remote area" in which the road was slated served to diminish the effect. If this is so, then it is difficult to understand. Wilderness areas, by definition, are remote. That is the very reason why they are prized by many people. Another possible explanation is that the amount of ancient forest in question, approximately one acre, was comparatively small. However, by the same token, the prejudice to MacMillan Bloedel was correspondingly small. Moreover, this factor simply does not explain how the loss of the forest would be reparable.

The effects of logging, and in fact most types of environmental harm, are not reparable, at least not for many generations. While many people think of BC's coastal ancient forests primarily in terms of recreation, their value runs far deeper. These forests provide a unique home to a rich and biologically diverse matrix of plant and animal species.

. . .

Leading scientists have concluded that it takes between 200 and 750 years for a coastal ancient forest to re-establish these essential characteristics. During the hundreds of years it takes to regain its old-growth features, the forest is unable to support the rich diversity of species which formerly inhabited it. Moreover, some logged-over forests will never be able to regain their old-growth characteristics ... . Simply put, when an old-growth forest is cut, hundreds of years must pass before the biological diversity of the area returns. In the interim, no amount of human effort or money can replace it.

. . .

Denying interlocutory injunctive relief to environmental plaintiffs in cases similar to *WCWCII* ensures that any ultimate court victory will be a hollow one. The purpose of interlocutory injunctions is to avoid this very problem.

Recently, there are indications that courts are reconsidering their approach to the issues of "undertakings" and "irreparable harm."

NOTES

1. In *Friends of Stanley Park v. Vancouver (City) Board of Parks and Recreation* (2000), 10 MPLR (3d) 25 (BCSC), the applicant sought an interim injunction to halt a road widening project in Vancouver's Stanley Park. Although he dismissed the application, Davies J offered these views with respect to the undertaking requirement:

> As I said during argument, it seems to me that if an applicant who applies for injunctive relief in a matter concerning serious public interests is able to establish a serious question to be tried, and that the balance of convenience, including the public interest, favours the granting of injunctive relief, such relief should not generally, at the interlocutory stage, be rendered ineffectual by reason of the fact that the applicant may not have the financial wherewithal to provide a viable undertaking as to damages. Had the applicants been successful in obtaining an interim injunction in this case, I would have exercised my discretion to allow that injunction without an undertaking as to damages.

2. Courts have also been increasingly willing to regard logging activity in parks as irreparable for the purposes of applications for injunctive relief. See C. Tolefson, "Advancing an Agenda? Recent Developments in Public Interest Environmental Law in Canada" (2002) *UNB Law Journal* 1. In *Caddy Lake Cottagers Assn. v. Florence-Nora Access Road Inc.* (1998), 126 Man. R (2d) 230 (CA), the court opined that if the injunction was not granted, irreparable harm would ensue in that "damages will not compensate for a destroyed forest" and that a failure to grant such relief would trigger a "non-reversible process, even in the event that the applicant [were ultimately] successful." Similarly, in *Friends of Point Pleasant Park v. Canada (Attorney General)* (2000), 188 FTR 280 (TD), the petitioners sought an interim injunction pending an application to block a plan to log trees suspected of being infested with spruce beetle. In granting the injunction, O'Keefe J stated:

> The applicants maintain that irreparable harm will be caused because if the interlocutory injunction is not granted and the judicial review application succeeds, then 10,000 trees would have been cut down under an invalid order. These trees could not be replaced in a person's lifetime, as many are older trees and the harm caused to the applicants' interests

could not be repaired. As well, the applicants argued that an award of damages would not replace the trees. The applicants also allege irreparable harm to themselves as individuals and as representing the public interest. Based on the above facts, I find that the applicants will suffer irreparable harm.

C. Costs and Public Interest Litigants

An analogous area is the liability of public interest litigants for adverse costs awards, as the following excerpt discusses.

C. Tollefson
"When the 'Public Interest' Loses: The Liability of Public Interest
Litigants for Adverse Costs Awards"
(1995) vol. 29 *UBC Law Review* 303, at 304-5, 314-19

Traditionally, Canadian courts have followed the English approach in awarding costs. In so doing, they have applied a "two-way" costs rule under which a litigant's liability for or entitlement to costs depends on whether the litigant is judicially deemed to have succeeded in the litigation. Increasingly, however, courts are being asked to recognize an exception to this rule where the unsuccessful party is "a responsible public interest litigant." Proponents of a "one-way" public interest costs rule, often referred to as the "public interest costs exception," invoke American jurisprudence where this approach to allocating costs has become well established and has displaced, for this and other designated types of litigation, the so-called "American rule" under which each side bears its own legal fees.

. . .

[The article goes on to discuss *Sierra Club v. Chief Forester and MacMillan Bloedel* (1993), 22 Admin. LR (2d) 129, a challenge to the ecological sustainability of the manner in which the chief forester had calculated the company's allowable timber cut. The BC Supreme Court dismissed the case and awarded costs against the Sierra Club (1994), 117 DLR (4th) 395.]

More than in any previous Canadian decision, the reasons bring into focus the challenges associated with developing costs principles that accommodate the growing phenomenon of public interest litigation. It is readily apparent that the Sierra Club made a very favourable impression upon Smith J both in terms of the novelty and public importance of its arguments and, more generally, in terms of the able manner in which it conducted the litigation. Yet, in the final result, he was not persuaded that he had grounds to depart from the ordinary rule that costs follow the event.

In reaching this conclusion, Smith J declined to recognize the existence of a public interest costs exception which he feared would give rise to the dangerous principle that public interest litigants "should be insulated from an award of costs in all cases." In his view, public policy concerns relating to the importance of fostering responsible public interest litigation were "a relevant factor" in allocating costs but they did not have the "status of a principle." According to him, the proper judicial approach was a discretionary one, involving the weighing of this and other "relevant and important factors."

Factors Favouring an Award of Costs

Like many public interest lawsuits, the *Sierra Club* proceeding was declaratory in nature; its goal was to seek clarification of a law that the petitioner believed was not being properly interpreted or applied. In adjudicating the suit, the court was therefore not being asked to attribute fault or award damages. As such, this was not a case in which the fault-based compensation rationale for awarding costs could tenably be advanced, nor was it advanced.

Nor was this a case in which the circumstances of the suit, or the manner in which it was conducted, justified imposing costs on the losing party as a form of punishment or to serve as a deterrent to others. As public interest litigation becomes more prevalent, it is likely that there will be cases where these circumstances exist, but, as Smith J's reasons make plain, they were not present here.

This leaves only a spoils-based compensation rationale: the notion that as a matter of established policy, the law should protect the right of a successful party to be, in Smith J's words, "partially compensated for the expense to which it has been put by the unsuccessful litigant."

The central reason why Smith J concluded that MacMillan Bloedel should be awarded its costs, on the apparent basis of this spoils rationale, lay in its status as "a private citizen, not a public agency." According to Smith J, even though MacMillan Bloedel was not being sued directly in the proceeding and was added as a party at its own request, it had no other "practical option" due to the "dramatic financial consequences" for the company had the petitioner prevailed. Moreover, in his view, the fact that MacMillan Bloedel had this private, pecuniary interest in the litigation, an interest which was qualitatively different from that of the petitioner and of the government, made its legal claim to costs all the more compelling.

While it is difficult to think of MacMillan Bloedel as a "public agency," it is equally difficult to think of it as merely a "private citizen." The reality is that it is neither. Given its substantial private financial resources (especially relative to the petitioner) and the substantial nature of its stake in the public resource at the centre of the case, to award costs to MacMillan Bloedel on the basis of its supposed status as a private citizen is to substitute a conclusion for an analysis.

· · ·

In cases like *Sierra Club*, the fact that a private interest has a financial stake in a challenged government decision militates strongly in favour of their being granted party status if they so desire. Determination of whether they ought to be entitled to costs if successful is a distinct, less straightforward matter. Insofar as the interest of the private party *is* entirely congruent with that of government, and there is no basis for questioning the capacity of government to defend the suit, there is good reason to question whether the private interest should be rewarded merely for exercising its right to participate in the litigation. This is particularly so when that reward has a broader cost in terms of access to justice for public interest litigants.

It is also critical to bear in mind the unique nature of the issues characteristically presented in cases of this kind. These cases usually involve challenges to the way government has allocated rights in public resources to private interests for the purposes of profit, whether that "resource" is a right to pollute the air, to harvest Crown timber or to dam a river. There is a strong public interest in ensuring that these arrangements are subjected to regular and careful public supervision, including judicial scrutiny. For a corporation like MacMillan Bloedel to participate as a respondent—voluntarily or otherwise—in litigation, as in *Sierra Club*, is a relatively small price to pay for holding rights to and profiting from a valuable public resource.

. . .

Factors Favouring a Costs Exemption

In concluding that costs should be awarded to MacMillan Bloedel, Smith J considered several factors that favoured the opposite result.

. . .

A strong argument against awarding costs was that, in pursuing the litigation in a responsible and able manner, the petitioner was performing a valuable public service. In British Columbia, the issue at the centre of the lawsuit—the rate and manner in which the provincial government authorizes private logging on public lands—was and remains a key political issue. The proposition that the *Forest Act* obliged the Chief Forester to set the AAC in an ecologically sustainable manner was, as Smith J acknowledged, both "novel" and of "public benefit." Moreover, he also recognized that while the petitioner's views with respect to "land use and forest management" were not "universally shared," they were held by a "large number of people in this province."

The public benefit question also has implications extending beyond the specific issue that the case put before the courts. To the extent that the litigation provided an opportunity for environmental interests to hold government legally accountable for forest policy in a public forum, a useful social function was served. The utility of this function is particularly evident in relation to environmental disputes which, in the words of another British Columbia Supreme Court Justice, tend "to provoke confrontations outside the law" of which the conflict in Clayoquot Sound is but one illustration. In short, there is a compelling argument that public interest is served by the application of costs rules in a manner that encourages the resolution of environmental disputes in a responsible manner through established legal channels.

Determination of the costs issue in *Sierra Club* also presented serious questions relating to the accessibility of justice for public interest litigants.

. . .

Adverse costs awards are one of the most significant barriers to realizing the promise of access to justice held out by liberalized rules of standing. Financing complex and protracted public interest litigation against government or private interests, of the type that is particularly prevalent in the environmental context, is an enormous challenge for any potential public interest litigant. When the prospect of being liable for the defendant's legal costs is factored into the equation, all but the best-financed (or, possibly, judgment-proof) litigants will be deterred from proceeding except in those rare instances where a successful outcome is a virtual certainty.

One of Smith J's concerns about recognizing a public interest costs exception was definitional: whether it was desirable or even possible to define and apply such a principle when, as he put it, "there are many 'public interests'" and many who hold "different perceptions of the public interest." In the article that follows, the author argues that despite this definitional uncertainty we should not shy from the challenge of costs law reform.

C. McCool
"Costs in Public Interest Litigation: A Comment on Professor Tollefson's Article, When the 'Public Interest' Loses: The Liability of Public Interest Litigants for Adverse Cost Awards"
(1996) vol. 30 *UBC Law Review* 309, at 313-16

Mr. Justice Smith was *precisely* right when he noted in the BC Supreme Court *Sierra Club* reasons (as quoted by the Court of Appeal) that "there are many 'public interests'" and "there are many who have a different perception of the public interest."

I would argue against a definition of the public interest that limits its application to those cases raising, and those people arguing, particular positions. This is, however, an identifiable view. There is a body of academic work about what is called "critical" or "creative lawyering," the "rebellious idea of lawyering" and "the new public interest law." It is implicit in the analysis of many that the public interest lawyer is on one identifiable side of a political line drawn through the world.

In many cases this is true. Those of us who are often identified as being public interest practitioners frequently argue from predictable positions on behalf of low-income and disadvantaged groups and individuals. This is because both society and the law frequently exclude our clients from the mechanisms and institutions that govern our collective lives. It would be wrong, however, to conclude from this that "the public interest" has a definable *content* in any particular situation. This would lead to the result, for instance, that in a natural gas rate case in which environmentalists argue for higher rates to fund conservation efforts, and ratepayer groups argue for lower rates to protect the financially disadvantaged, only one of them is arguing in the public interest. This is patently absurd.

Further absurdities would be created if "public interest" were defined so as to exclude those who argued against the federal government in the *Little Sisters* case, even though their position may well be in conflict with that of the "public interest" intervenors in support of the prosecution in *R v. Butler*. The conclusion must be that our definition of "public interest" does not depend on adopting or promulgating any one position within the confines of a particular case. The "public interest" lawyer is not the same as a "movement" lawyer, just as the public interest is not synonymous with any particular political movement. In addition, I would argue that the public interest is not something that can only be legitimately advanced by those who have no "special" or "direct" interest in it. This is, however, a commonly-accepted delineator of public interest litigants:

> a public interest group is an organization which has no personal, proprietary or pecuniary interest in the outcome of the proceeding, and which has as its object the taking of public or litigious initiatives seeking to affect public policy in respect of matters in which the group is interested ... and to enforce constitutional, statutory or common law rights in regard to such matters.

This quotation from *Reese v. Alberta* serves to illustrate an unnecessarily narrow view of public interest litigants. The fact that a litigant has a personal, proprietary or pecuniary interest in the outcome of a proceeding does not diminish any public interest value that may be present in the issues and circumstances of the case.

· · ·

If I am right, then we cannot determine the presence of the public interest either from the content of the positions advanced by the parties (or intervenors) to litigation, or from the presence or absence of a personal or direct interest in the outcome of the litigation. The possibilities might then appear to be open-ended, a dizzying prospect that may make the courts' reluctance to exercise a "public interest" exception to the award of costs more understandable.

The subject of the litigation must surely determine whether a public interest exists and whether that interest might lead a court to the positive exercise of its discretion to depart from the normal practice of awarding costs. A purely private dispute between neighbours as to, for example, the possible nuisance value of a structure on one's city lot may have no ramifications for those living on another block. If, however, some part of the case were to turn on a municipal bylaw that prohibits the adoption of a certain style of architecture, design and construction, the argument may become cloaked in issues of discrimination, racism and bigotry. This would take it out of the realm of the purely personal and put it into the public sphere. We would also expect a public interest approach to display "a perspective of group interest rather than individual interest."

· · ·

In attempting to delineate "public interest" the concern is with much more than just property interests. What is of interest is the notion that something can "become clothed with a public interest when used in a manner to make it of public consequence, and affect the community at large" and must therefore be "controlled by the public for the common good." This type of analysis would free us from the need to classify the dominant litigant as a private party, government or some variation thereof.

The question then would not be whether MacMillan Bloedel or Rogers Cable systems are more like individual human beings or more like governments, but whether or not they own or control something that is of public consequence and must therefore submit to being controlled for the public good. If they do and that thing or matter of public consequence then becomes the subject of litigation, the court should give serious consideration to excusing the public interest litigant from costs that it would otherwise have to pay.

Despite the views expressed by Smith J in *Sierra Club*, in similar cases courts have exercised their discretion to shield public interest litigants from adverse costs awards.

Valhalla Wilderness Society v. British Columbia (Ministry of Forests)
(1997), 4 Admin. LR (3d) 120 (BCSC)

[The applicant sought a declaration that various logging permits issued by the province to Slocan Forest Products were invalid. When this application was dismissed, Slocan sought an order for costs.]

PARIS J: It seems reasonable that the court should not in effect condone the bringing of actions without any legal merit, even by persons whose motivation is their perception of the public interest. As Smith J pointed out in the *Sierra* case "there are many 'public interests.'" In the attempt to accommodate or compromise between various interests within the community, the best policy for elected government to follow is often a difficult question on which reasonable persons can differ and which the court will be reluctant to second guess without compelling legal or constitutional grounds ... .

However, the watershed reserves argument raised serious legal issues and issues of unquestionable public interest ... . The resolution of the issues required a legal analysis of the interplay between the provisions of the *Land Act* and the *Forest Act* and a careful examination of government documents going back several years ... .

The financial consequences to the parties of an order for costs is not reason by itself to not award costs to a successful party. However, I believe it is a factor along with others that can be considered. As mentioned, the petitioner is a public advocacy group and there was evidence submitted that an order for costs against it would affect or eliminate some of its projected activities ... . I think it is reasonable to infer that the financial consequences of the proceedings will be far more significant for the petitioner than for the respondent ... .

Finally, I note that, as far as I know, the petitioner has at all times acted responsibly and within the law, in particular by attempting to vindicate its position through the courts ... .

In the result, for the foregoing reasons, namely, those related to the watershed reserves argument, the question of financial impact on the parties and the responsible actions of the petitioner, I exercise my discretion under Rule 57(9) and order that all parties will bear their own costs of the proceedings.

In addition to excusing public interest litigants from adverse costs awards, courts are increasingly being asked to award costs to test case litigants even when they are unsuccessful at trial. This is particularly so in constitutional challenges; see, for example, *Singh v. Canada (Attorney General)*, [1999] 4 FC 583 (TD).

Moreover, in recognition of the daunting expenses often associated with test case litigation against government, courts have shown a willingness to order "costs advances" where such an order is deemed necessary to ensure that the case is properly argued. To date, orders of this kind have been confined to the context of Charter litigation. See *Spracklin v. Kichton* (2001), 203 DLR (4th) 222 (Alta. QB) and aboriginal rights cases (below).

BC (Ministry of Forests) v. Okanagan Indian Band
[2002] 1 CNLR 57 (BCCA)

[The Crown commenced legal action against the band to enjoin it from harvesting timber on Crown lands; the band defended by asserting aboriginal rights to the timber in question. When the Crown succeeded in having the matter converted to a trial, the band applied to have its trial costs borne by the Crown.]

NEWBURY JA: [T]he court has the jurisdiction in appropriate circumstances to order costs in advance but that jurisdiction is "narrow and restricted to exceptional cases." In my view, the circumstances of this case are "special" or "exceptional." The "test case" nature of these proceedings has already been noted, and the public importance in this Province of the issues to be tried is obvious. It is clearly in the public interest that the applicability of the Forest Practices Code to lands and activities claimed as aboriginal be determined, and be determined on all the available evidence. The proceedings were initiated and are being pursued by the Minister against the Bands, and there is no doubt that counsel who have experience in aboriginal law are required to put forth the Bands' position. These facts remove this case from the realm of ordinary litigation where costs do generally follow the event, and financial hardship is not a proper ground for ordering otherwise ... . More importantly, the honour of the Crown is at stake in dealings between it and aboriginals ... . In my view, it is simply unrealistic for the Crown in this case to fold its hands and say that the Bands will have to manage without counsel.

I therefore propose to order that the Crown, in any event of the cause, pay such legal costs of the Bands as the Chambers judge orders from time to time ... .

NOTES

1. The Federal Court Rules, which govern all proceedings in the Federal Court, address the question of costs. Prior to 1998, rule 1408 gave discretion to award costs to a party only when there were "special reasons" to do so. When the rules were amended, rule 400 expanded that discretion and required the consideration of a number of factors in the decision, including the importance and complexity of the issues, the result of the proceeding, the conduct of the parties, and whether the public service of resolving the issue

supports a cost award. The effect of this change is as yet unclear, since the relatively limited jurisprudence under the rule is somewhat contradictory.

2. For example, in *Canadian Environmental Law Assn. v. Canada (Minister of the Environment)*, [2001] FCJ no. 1110, the court, in explaining its decision to impose costs despite the lack of any submissions on the issue, stated:

> I must admit that my preference was not to award costs against a public interest group in circumstances such as those existing in [the case at bar], but I felt that with the change in the Rules I had to apply the usual rule and award costs to follow the event.

3. In contrast, see *Harris v. Canada*, [2001] FCJ no. 1876, where the court awarded costs to an unsuccessful public interest litigant, stating:

> This individual's effort in bringing forward this litigation has permitted further light to be cast on events that had become a concern for Canadians across this country. Though ultimately unsuccessful in this instance, public institutions and the confidence which they carry can only be strengthened by close scrutiny of government actors by responsible citizens.
>
> The question of costs is of considerable significance when rationally deciding whether to bring an action. Where a plaintiff lacks a personal, proprietary or pecuniary interest in an action the plaintiff is effectively deterred from bringing the action, notwithstanding he or she may have, as a matter of law, public interest standing. ... This recognizes that absent an award of costs public interest status may be of theoretical but not practical effect.

4. See also *Inverhuron & District Ratepayers v. Canada* (2001), 273 NR 62 (FCA).

VII. STRATEGIC LAWSUITS AGAINST PUBLIC PARTICIPATION

C. Tollefson
"Strategic Lawsuits and Environmental Politics:
Daishowa Inc. v. Friends of the Lubicon"
(1996) vol. 31, no. 1 *Journal of Canadian Studies* 119

One of the most troubling developments in American public law over the last two decades has been the proliferation of lawsuits commenced and maintained for the purpose of "chilling" public participation in decision-making processes, particularly those affecting the environment. Cases of this kind have come to be known as SLAPP Suits ("Strategic Lawsuits Against Public Participation"). In the United States, "hundreds perhaps thousands" of SLAPPS are filed every year. Typically brought by corporate interests, these suits target citizens and citizen organizations for taking part in lawful demonstrations and boycotts, reporting health or environmental offences, circulating petitions, even for attending public meetings.

. . .

Traditionally, Canadians have enjoyed far fewer opportunities to participate in environmental decision making. This is changing. Both at the federal and provincial levels, recent legislative initiatives have conferred rights of participation analogous to those common in American regimes. In addition to lobbying for legally recognized participation rights, Canadian environmentalists have become increasingly effective in influencing public opinion and exercising political power through "extra-legal" means such as demonstrations, boycotts and information campaigns. As the capacity of Canadian environmentalists and other social activists to wield political and economic power grows, so too does the incentive for corporate interests to respond by bringing "strategic lawsuits." Recent experience bears this out.

Fraser v. Saanich (District)
(1999), 32 CELR (NS) 143 (BCSC)

[The plaintiff, who owned a small nursing home, sued the district of Saanich and eight local residents after her application for a municipal permit to expand the facility was turned down. The defendant residents had circulated a petition opposing the expansion and lobbied the district to this end. The defendants applied under rule 19(24) of the BC Rules of Court to have the claim dismissed summarily. The Chambers Judge granted their motion, and proceeded to consider the question of costs.]

SINGH J (orally): In order for this claim to be dismissed under Rule 19(24)(a) the court must be satisfied, absolutely, beyond a doubt, that the claim discloses no cause of action. The court must proceed on the premise that the allegations of fact contained in the Statement of Claim are true ... . While neighbourhood participation in municipal politics often places an almost adversarial atmosphere into land use questions, this participation is a key element to the democratic involvement of said citizens in community decision making ... . This type of activity often produces unfavourable results for some parties involved. However, an unfavourable action by local government does not, in the absence of some other wrongdoing, open the doors to seek redress on those who spoke out in favour of that action. To do so would place a chilling effect on the public's participation in local government.

If the process itself here was flawed, or disclosed bad faith on the part of the District of Saanich, the plaintiffs can take appropriate action against the District of Saanich. However, to place blame on the community group involved is doomed to failure where there has been no, and I repeat, no pleading of any material facts that could support any such claim of wrongdoing. If the plaintiffs wish to support such a claim surrounding the democratic activities of others, it would be necessary to provide at least some factual underpinning. The plaintiffs have not done so, as yet, at all.

What I am faced with is the bald assertion that the neighbourhood residents were negligent, that they colluded, conspired, breached fiduciary duty, acted in bad faith, and as well, interfered with breached contractual relations. There is no allegation that during this process the neighbourhood residents breached any proper procedure set out by the District or made any false statements ... . I have no difficulty, therefore, in finding that it is "plain and obvious" that the plaintiffs' Statement of Claim discloses no reasonable claim and contains radical defects ranking with those listed in Rule 19(24). It has no merit against those defendants. The action against the neighbourhood residents is dismissed ... .

Counsel for the neighbourhood residents has argued that the claim against his clients is in the nature of a SLAPP suit, an acronym for Strategic Lawsuit Against Public Participation. It is a meritless action filed by a plaintiff whose primary goal is not to win the case but rather to silence or intimidate citizens who have participated in proceedings regarding public policy or public decision making ... . I find, therefore, finally, that this action not only contains an unreasonable claim, is meritless and devoid of any factual foundation, but also has been used as an attempt to stifle the democratic activities of the defendants, the neighbourhood residents. I find the plaintiffs' conduct reprehensible and deserving of censure by an award of special costs.

Although in this case, the court was prepared to dismiss the alleged SLAPP suit summarily, the high standard for securing dismissal at this stage established in *Carey Canada Inc. et al. v. Hunt*, [1990] 2 SCR 959 (that is, "plain and obvious"), means that many putative SLAPP suits end up proceeding to trial. This has prompted commentators to promote the enactment of anti-SLAPP legislation.

C. Tollefson
"Strategic Lawsuits and Environmental Politics:
Daishowa Inc. v. Friends of the Lubicon"
(1996) vol. 31, no. 1 *Journal of Canadian Studies* 119

Even if the courts ultimately decide to extend the protection of the *Charter* to SLAPP targets, there is still a compelling need for direct legislative response to the SLAPP problem. SLAPP suits characteristically represent an attempt to convert economic power into legal advantage at the expense of democratic participation. In recognition of this, the goal of anti-SLAPP legislation must be to protect democratic participation by countering the corrosive effects of money in the legal process. In recent years, legislation of this kind has been enacted in nine American states.

An initial priority is to facilitate early identification and dismissal of SLAPP suits. The first step would be to recognize a statutory right of public participation that has legal force in dealings both with government and with other "private" parties. To provide optimal protection, the right should be framed as broadly as possible so as to encompass the diverse ways in which citizens participate directly or indirectly in the processes of government. The right should therefore include, but not be limited to, the right to communicate with all levels and arms of government (including the judiciary) on matters of public policy. Communication should be defined to include traditional lobbying activities as well as other forms of participation including demonstrations, boycotts and the pursuit of judicial and administrative remedies. Communications directed at other members of the public should also be specifically protected. Exclusions should be limited to acts which are manifestly criminal, or are contrary to quasi-criminal legislation, and to acts intended to cause physical harm to persons or property.

Such legislation would also prescribe the remedies available to a person who believes that their statutory right to participate is being threatened by a SLAPP suit. The best approach is to allow the party who is being sued to make a special pretrial motion to have the suit dismissed. The motion would be heard expeditiously, primarily on the basis of material then in the court file, without witnesses being called. It would be up to the party claiming to be the SLAPP target to show that the activities for which they were being sued fell within the terms of the right to participate under the legislation. At this point, the onus would shift to the filer to establish on the balance of probabilities that the suit is not a SLAPP.

The burden of defending SLAPPs will be considerably less onerous if reforms of the type just described are implemented. However, the legal work necessary even to prepare a summary dismissal application can be considerable. Moreover, not all SLAPPs can be disposed of summarily. In all but the clearest cases courts may hesitate to dismiss a claim. In these circumstances, the prospect of recovering an award of costs at the end of the proceeding does little to relieve the more immediate day to day financial hardship felt by SLAPP targets. For these reasons, and because of the important public values imperiled by SLAPP suits, a strong argument can also be made that state-funded legal representation should be available to applicants who are able to satisfy legal aid administrators that they may be a SLAPP target ... .

Finally, anti-SLAPP legislation must clearly prescribe that the purpose of costs awards, where a SLAPP suit has been summarily dismissed or dismissed following a trial on its merits, is to compensate the target fully for litigation-related expenses. Although these reforms would cause most potential SLAPP filers to reflect carefully before proceeding, they are an inadequate response in a situation where a filer has acted in bad faith or otherwise abused the legal process. In this scenario, an award of costs which merely compensates the target for his or her legal expenses does not go far enough. To relieve a target in this situation from the necessity of pursuing a separate claim for abuse of process, therefore, anti-SLAPP legislation should incorporate a SLAPP-back provision. A provision of this kind would allow a target not only to seek and be awarded costs from a filer, but also to recover ordinary and punitive damages where the evidence establishes that the SLAPP was filed in bad faith or otherwise represents an abuse of the legal process.

NOTE

In 2001, the BC government enacted the *Protection of Public Participation Act*, SBC 2001, c. 19 (PPPA), which incorporated several of the reforms advocated above. The PPPA created a broad statutory right of public participation encompassing all communications to government and the general public on issues of public interest while excluding, *inter alia*, actions that harmed persons or property, violated a court order, or were otherwise judicially considered to be an "unwarranted interference with the rights or property of a person." The common law of defamation was also changed to broaden the protection for communications falling within the statutory definition of "public participation." Under the PPPA, a court could summarily dismiss a suit where it was satisfied, on a balance of probabilities, that the suit targeted conduct that fell within this definition *and* that the suit was being pursued for an "improper purpose" (that is, not to prevail at trial but rather to chill public participation). The PPPA also conferred discretion on a court to order the filer of the suit to post security (representing the full amount of costs and damages to which a defendant might ultimately be entitled), if it concluded that there was a "realistic possibility" that the defendant could meet these two conditions if the suit went to trial. The PPPA had been on the books for only a few months when it was repealed by the newly elected Liberal government. To date the PPPA is the only anti-SLAPP law enacted in Canada, although 21 such laws are now in force in the United States.

FURTHER READINGS

J. McKenzie, *Environmental Politics in Canada* (Oxford: Oxford University Press, 2002).

C. Tollefson, "SLAPPs: Developing a Canadian Response" (1994) vol. 73 *Canadian Bar Review* 200.

M. Valiante and P. Muldoon, "A Foot in the Door: A Survey of Recent Trends in Access to Environmental Justice," in S. Kennett, ed., *Law and Process in Environmental Management* (Calgary: Canadian Institute of Resources Law [CIRL], 1993), 142.

CHAPTER EIGHT

Pollution Prevention and Environmental Liability: The Evolution of the Law of Toxic Real Estate, Contaminated Lands, and Insurance

Joseph F. Castrilli

I. INTRODUCTION

For over a decade a variety of advisory and regulatory bodies have raised concerns about the environmental contamination of land in Canada. The National Round Table on the Environment (NRTEE) and the Economy has stated:

> Across Canada, thousands of contaminated sites lie abandoned or underutilized, the results of a century of industrialization. Their current condition poses health and economic threats. Many of these sites have not been identified because of insufficient information on the environmental condition of land. Although many of these sites are capable of being cleaned up economically and brought into productive use, the rate of clean-up is slow.

See *State of the Debate on the Environment and the Economy: Greening Canada's Brownfield Sites* (Ottawa: NRTEE, 1998), at 3.

In a similar vein, the Canadian Council of Ministers of the Environment (CCME) noted:

> Decades of human activity have left a legacy of contaminated land throughout Canada. Virtually every sector of the Canadian economy has contributed to the problem, ranging from resource industries (mining and forestry), heavy industries (steel-making) and petro-chemical production to small manufacturing plants and retail gasoline stations. Historical practices, most of them environmentally unacceptable today, have created current conditions that could potentially harm human health and the environment.

See *Guidance Document on the Management of Contaminated Sites in Canada* (Winnipeg: CCME, 1997), at 1.

An early attempt to recommend a consistent nation-wide approach to governments on how to address the problem was the CCME's principles on contaminated site liability. See *Contaminated Site Liability Report: Recommended Principles for a Consistent Approach Across Canada* (Winnipeg: CCME, 1993). The CCME principles addressed such matters as (1) adopting the "polluter pays" principle in framing contaminated site remediation policy and legislation; (2) defining and exempting persons potentially responsible for cleanup; (3) developing factors to address the allocation of responsibility; (4) issuing certificates of compliance when cleanup is satisfactorily completed; and (5) applying fairness principles to any regime adopted.

The 1990s saw governments across the country begin to address questions of land contamination, particularly issues relating to remediation and liability. A number of provinces enacted legislation regulating the problem and incorporated many of the CCME principles into their regimes. Laws adopted in several provinces in the 1990s addressed such matters as (1) investigation and identification of contaminated sites; (2) persons responsible for remediation; (3) development of remediation plans; (4) joint, several, absolute, and retroactive liability; (5) apportionment or allocation of remediation responsibility; and (6) cost recovery from responsible persons by those who incur remediation costs.

As a result of these legislative initiatives, the sale, ownership, and management of lands contaminated with toxic substances, wastes, and other hazardous materials increasingly occupied the interest of the real estate, business, industrial, and financial communities due to the potential for liability for cleanup and compensation costs. Potentially responsible persons within these sectors began seeking means of limiting their liability through a variety of measures designed to mitigate and, if possible, prevent pollution from activities within their ownership, management, or control.

Among the measures developed on a voluntary basis by the private sector have been environmental audits and environmental management systems. Both these measures are internal evaluations of company activity designed to verify compliance with legal requirements, company policies, and standards, as well as to identify compliance problems, weaknesses in management systems, or areas of environmental risk. The reasons for the development of these voluntary private sector efforts include the need to (1) avoid future corporate and personal civil and administrative liability for environmental cleanup and compensation by determining whether current operations are in compliance with environmental laws; (2) establish a defence of due diligence to possible quasi-criminal liability by putting in place a proper system of environmental management; and (3) obtain financing from lending institutions that may require as a condition of such funding an environmental audit or development of an environmental management system. See R. Cotton et al., "Environmental Considerations in Business Transactions" in *Canadian Environmental Law*, 2d ed. (Markham, ON: Butterworths, 1991), and J.D. Wolfe, "Environmental Management Systems: Due Diligence and State of the Art—ISO 14000," in Law Society of Upper Canada, *Advanced Environmental Law* (Toronto: Continuing Legal Education, LSUC, 1996).

More recently, a second generation of land remediation legislation has begun to evolve in Canada to address "brownfields," or abandoned or underutilized properties where past actions have caused real or suspected environmental contamination. Regarded as a subset of contaminated sites, brownfields are viewed as sites that exhibit good potential for other uses and economically viable business opportunities. See NRTEE, *Greening Canada's Brownfield Sites*, above, at 4. The impetus for brownfield laws is twofold. First, it arises from increased concern in government and the private sector over the impact of stringent contaminated site legislation on the ability and willingness of the real estate, business, industrial, and financial communities to engage in the environmental cleanup of abandoned or orphaned lands. Second, it arises from a desire to avoid residential, commercial, and industrial development in new "greenfield" areas, when rehabilitated lands could be used.

This chapter provides an overview of three interrelated areas of the law that have developed to address these matters: (1) private rights of action between purchasers, vendors, and other persons involved in the sale of toxic real estate; (2) regulatory control of, and civil and administrative liability for, contamination of land involving potentially responsible parties such as owners, operators, parent corporations, lenders, receivers, receiver-managers, trustees in bankruptcy, and liquidators; and (3) insurance coverage for damage arising from environmentally contaminated property.

II. TOXIC REAL ESTATE

A. The Liability of Vendors—Contract Principles

The liability of vendors to purchasers for the sale of contaminated real estate may arise under contract principles. The following case illustrates the application of the doctrine of *caveat emptor* and the circumstances under which a vendor has a duty to disclose information regarding the contaminated state of a property.

Tony's Broadloom & Floor Covering Ltd. v. NCM Canada Inc.
(1995), 17 CELR (NS) 22, at 24 (Ont. Ct. Gen. Div.)

The plaintiff purchaser, Tony's Broadloom and Floor Covering Ltd. ("Tony's Broadloom"), in Trust, moved for summary judgment to rescind an agreement of purchase and sale, primarily on the ground that the vendor failed to advise the plaintiff that the land had been contaminated by varsol, which, in the plaintiffs' submission, was a latent defect.

The defendant vendor, SKD Company ("SKD"), brought a cross-motion for summary judgment to dismiss the plaintiff's action, primarily on the ground that the defect was patent, and, in any event, the contamination did not prevent the purchaser from continuing to use the land for its current use as a factory. ...

Issues

1. Is hazardous waste contamination of industrially zoned land a patent or a latent defect?

2. Is the vendor of land contaminated by hazardous waste obliged to disclose such defect to the purchaser when no inquiry is made by the purchaser, and the vendor is unaware of the purchaser's intention to use the land for anything other than its current use?

Law

Patent or Latent Defect

The distinction between a patent and latent defect is described by Ron Milner Stonham in his text, *The Law of Vendor and Purchaser* (Sydney: The Law Book Co. of Australia Pty. Ltd., 1964), at p. 29:

> A patent defect is a defect which a purchaser is likely to discover if he inspects the property with ordinary care. A latent defect is one which a purchaser, inspecting the property with ordinary care, would not be likely to discover. Whether a defect is patent or latent is a question of degree ... . It is not enough that there exists on the land an object of sense, that might put a careful purchaser on inquiry; but, in order to be a patent defect, the defect must either be visible to the eye, or arise by necessary implication from something visible to the eye. [Citations omitted.]

Similarly, in 42 *Halsbury's Laws of England*, 4th ed. (London: Butterworths, 1983), s. 51, under the subheading *Disclosure by the Vendor—Defects of Quality* it is stated at p. 47:

> Defects of quality may be either patent or latent. Patent defects are such as are discoverable by inspection and ordinary vigilance on the part of a purchaser, *and latent defects are such as would not be revealed by any inquiry which a purchaser is in a position to make before entering into the contract for purchase.*
>
> The vendor is not bound to call attention to patent defects; the rule is "caveat emptor." Therefore a purchaser should make inspection and inquiry as to what he is proposing to buy. *If he omits to ascertain whether the land is such as he desires to acquire, he cannot complain afterwards on discovering defects of which he would have been aware if he had taken ordinary steps to ascertain its physical condition. ...* [Emphasis added.]

I am of the view that a reasonable purchaser, purchasing industrially zoned land which it knew, or ought to have known, was used as a factory, and upon which it intended to construct a residential development, would have exercised its right to inspect the Property to discover whether there was any contamination before submitting an offer to purchase. Further, a prudent purchaser would have seen the pipes on the Property, and would have inspected the contents of the shed on the Property, and would have been drawn to inquire of the vendor for what purpose these structures existed.

Thus, I find that since the varsol contamination was readily discoverable by the purchaser in these circumstances, it constitutes a patent defect. The rule of caveat emptor applies to contracts of sale of land. The purchaser takes that which he sees, or which, as a prudent and diligent purchaser, he ought to have seen, and is not entitled to have anything better ... . In the case of a patent defect, as distinguished from a latent defect as to quality or condition, and where the means of knowledge are equally open to both parties, and no concealment is made or attempted, a prudent purchaser will inspect, and exercise ordinary care—caveat emptor: V. Di Castri, *The Law of Vendor and Purchaser*, at p. 173.

Caveat emptor applies where an inspection by a reasonably competent person would have revealed the defect. The purchaser made no inquiry of the vendor as to whether the Property was fit for development as a residential complex. ... The vendor had no indication from the purchaser that the purchaser did not intend to continue the extant use of the Property as a factory.

I am asked to determine whether the vendor's silence regarding the varsol contamination, and, in particular, in not proferring to the purchaser the contents of the May Letter and the August Report, amounted to fraudulent or negligent misrepresentation. In other words, was there a positive duty on the vendor to come forward with the information that the land was contaminated by varsol, notwithstanding that the contamination would not affect the purchaser's ability to carry on employing the land for its current use?

The plaintiff charges that the vendor has perpetrated fraud. I disagree. There may indeed be a moral obligation to have disclosed the contamination; there is no legal obligation to have done so, where the contamination does not render the land unusable for any purpose, and where the vendor took no steps to conceal the contamination. ...

There is no fiduciary relationship between the vendor and purchaser in the negotiation of a contract for the sale and purchase of land. Prima facie the vendor is not obliged to disclose matters, not being defects in title, merely affecting the value or price or the use to which the property may be put, whether such defects be patent or latent: Stonham, *The Law of Vendor and Purchaser, supra*, at p. 221.

I note the result in *John Levy Holdings Inc. v. Cameron & Johnstone Ltd.* (1992), 26 RPR (2d) 130, appeal dismissed March 24, 1993 (Ont. CA), where Philp J found that while contaminants on the property in that case exceeded [Ministry of the Environment] guidelines for agricultural/residential/parkland use, the contaminants did not affect the current use of the property, which was commercial/industrial. As the vendor had no way of knowing the purchaser's intention to some day rezone the property to develop a residential condominium complex, the vendor was not bound to disclose the fact that the property was contaminated for the purpose of this higher use ... . If the purchaser intended to use the property for residential purposes after seeking planning approval, the onus was on the purchaser to ensure that the Property could be so used. The plaintiff should have: (i) conducted a proper inspection of the Property before entering the agreement of purchase and sale; (ii) asked the vendor pertinent questions particularly related to the pipes and equipment in the shed, and, (iii) insisted that a provision be inserted in the agreement, making it conditional on the Property being appropriate for residential use. See *McGeek Enterprises Ltd. v. Shell Canada Ltd.* (1991), 6 OR (3d) 216. ...

In the circumstances, I am unable to find that there was a legal duty on the vendor to advise the purchaser about the May Letter and the August Report, both of which disclose that varsol contamination of the Property is an ongoing problem.

[The plaintiff's motion was dismissed. The defendant's cross-motion was granted because the court found the defect to be patent, as it was readily discoverable by reasonable inspection.]

NOTES AND QUESTIONS

1. The Ontario Court of Appeal affirmed the decision of White J in *Tony's Broadloom*, at (1996), 31 OR (3d) 481, at 487-88. That court would have treated the presence of the contaminant as neither a latent nor a patent defect in the property because the vendors had no reason to believe that the purchasers would use the property for any purpose other than an industrial one. The purchasers "got exactly what they bargained for—industrial land. Their undisclosed intention to use the property for residential purposes does not alter the bargain" they made, or "create a latent defect in the industrial property" that the purchasers agreed to acquire. The Court of Appeal went on to suggest that if the panel was wrong and the presence of the contaminant was a defect, then they agreed with the conclusion at trial that the defect was a patent one because it would have been readily discoverable by the purchasers had they exercised reasonable vigilance in the circumstances. In the context of this case, reasonable vigilance would have included inspection of the property and inquiries of the vendors, and local and provincial authorities, as well as the taking of soil samples early enough in time to learn of the existence of the contaminant before closing. Instead, according to the appeal court, the purchasers "chose not to disclose their intended use of the property and to take no steps to satisfy themselves that the property could be used for that purpose."

2. A more recent toxic real estate case exemplifying the application of the doctrine of *caveat emptor* is *801438 Ont. Inc. v. Badurina* (2000), 34 RPR (3d) 306 (Ont. SCJ). In *Badurina*, the court dismissed the purchaser's action against the defendant vendor because the court found that the latter made no representations as to the environmental condition of vacant land or its development potential. The court held that the purchaser could in any event have readily ascertained for itself the condition and development potential of the property and that of adjacent derelict and contaminated property. The *Badurina* court also affirmed the proposition that what constitutes a defect in the quality of land must be determined in the context of the intended use of the land.

3. Some provinces have responded to the problems posed by the doctrine of *caveat emptor* by imposing disclosure requirements on vendors of real property. In British Columbia, amendments to the *Waste Management Act*, RSBC 1996, c. 482, s. 26.1(7) require a vendor who knows or reasonably should know that real property has been used for an industrial or commercial purpose to provide a site profile to a prospective purchaser of the property and, subject to the regulations, to a manager of the Ministry of Environment, Lands, and Parks. Pursuant to the Contaminated Sites Regulations, BC reg. 375/96, s. 3(7), a vendor of real property must provide a site profile to a prospective purchaser at least 30 days before the actual transfer of real property. The regulations also exempt vendors from the requirement to provide a site profile if (1) the purchaser waives the requirement in writing; (2) at the time of contract for purchase and sale, the subject property of the sale is used primarily for residential purposes; or (3) the property has never been zoned for any use other than residential. The regulations further set out the information that must be included in a site profile, including identification of areas of the site that are of potential environmental concern.

B. The Liability of Vendors—Tort Principles

Vendors may also be liable under tort principles. The doctrine of *caveat emptor* does not apply to fraudulent representations or conduct. Where a defect is latent and may pose a risk of danger to life, health, or the environment, the failure of a vendor to disclose this information to a purchaser may constitute fraud allowing the purchaser to sue for deceit.

Sevidal v. Chopra
(1987-88), 2 CELR (NS) 173, at 190 (Ont. HC)

[Prior to entering into an agreement of purchase and sale, the vendors failed to disclose to the purchasers the existence of radioactive material in the neighbourhood. Before closing, the vendors learned that the subject property itself also was contaminated with radioactive material but did not disclose this information to the purchasers.]

OYEN J:

Liability of the Chopras

The issues with respect to the Chopras relate to disclosure. Did the Chopras owe a duty to the Sevidals to disclose the presence of radioactive material in the McClure Crescent area before the agreement to purchase was signed, or to disclose the discovery of radioactive material in the backyard of 63 McClure Crescent before the closing?

Here we are dealing with a latent defect. Latent defects with respect to the sale of land, have been described succinctly in 42 *Hals.* (4th ed.), p. 47, para. 51:

> latent defects are such as would not be revealed by any inquiry which a purchaser is in a position to make before entering into the contract for purchase.

Redican v. Nesbitt, [1924] SCR 135, ... stands for the proposition that the doctrine of caveat emptor does not apply to fraud, error in substantialibus or where there is a warranty, contractual condition or collateral contract.

In reviewing whether a cause of action existed in the case of *McGrath v. Maclean* (1979), 22 OR (2d) 784 ... (Ont. CA), Dubin JA, at p. 791-92 [OR], quoted favourably from a lecture by Professor Bora Laskin, as he then was, ... :

> Does the vendor have any duty of disclosure in matters of quality and fitness which do not constitute defects of title? Here we deal with the classical notion of caveat emptor as applied to the physical amenities and condition of the property unrelated to any outstanding claims of third parties or public authorities such as would impinge on the title. *Absent fraud, mistake or misrepresentation, a purchaser takes existing property as he finds it*, whether it be dilapidated, bug-infested or otherwise uninhabitable or deficient in expected amenities, unless he protects himself by contract terms. ...
>
> *I do not propose to dwell on fraud, mistake or misrepresentation save to make a few observations about the way in which, if established, they relieve a purchaser from the binding effect of caveat emptor. Fraud can be a rather elastic conception, and there are*

cases which show a tendency to find fraud when there has been concealment by the vendor of latent defects. Rowley v. Isley, [1951] 3 DLR 766, a British Columbia decision entitling a purchaser to rescind (even after paying the price and taking possession) where there was a failure to disclose infestation by roaches, illustrates the proposition, and goes quite far in allowing rescission after the transaction had been closed. *On the other hand, a latent defect of quality going to fitness for habitation and which is either unknown to the vendor or such as not to make him chargeable with concealment or reckless disregard of its truth or falsity will not support any claim of redress by the purchaser. He must find his protection in warranty.* [Dubin JA's emphasis.]

. . .

An exception to the general rule of caveat emptor will be found where there is fraud or fraudulent misrepresentation and, where there is such a finding, failure on the part of the vendor to disclose will give rise to a cause of action.

Fraud arises when a statement is made "knowingly, or without belief in its truth, or recklessly, careless whether it be true or false": Per Lord Herschell in *Derry v. Peek* (1889), 14 App. Cas. 337 (HL) at p. 374. Fraud can also arise where there is active concealment, *Abel v. McDonald, infra.* Finally, fraud arises where there is failure to disclose a potential danger, *Rivtow Marine, infra; McGrath v. Maclean, supra; CRF Holdings, infra; Ford v. Schmitt, infra.*

Counsel for the Sevidals argued that failure to disclose the presence of radioactive contamination both in the area and later on the property itself amounted to a fraudulent misrepresentation, and that the Chopras intended to deceive the Sevidals. ...

[M]any of the cases turn on their ... facts. ...

In *CRF Holdings Ltd. v. Fundy Chemical International Ltd.* ... , [1982] 2 WWR 385 ... (BCCA) [leave to appeal to the Supreme Court of Canada refused (1982), 42 NR 358], the vendor told the purchaser that certain slag on the property would make excellent fill, when in fact the vendor knew that the slag was radioactive. In reviewing the law with respect to representation only of favourable aspects of a property, Anderson JA referred to several cases at p. 420 [WWR]:

> where it has been held that to knowingly represent only favourable aspects without disclosing the fact that those favourable aspects are substantially qualified by restrictions and unfavourable aspects, known to the person making the representation, amounts to fraud. ...

Anderson JA went on to hold at p. 421 that, even in the absence of a positive fraudulent misrepresentation, the failure to disclose the inherently dangerous nature of the thorium waste was fraudulent. He cited the judgment of Ritchie J in *Rivtow Marine Ltd. v. Washington Iron Works Ltd.,* [1974] SCR 1189: ... :

> Even from the earliest times articles dangerous in themselves as well as articles which were made dangerous by reason of some defect known to the manufacturer were excepted from this general rule ... based on the fact that the vendor of the article who knew it to be defective was guilty of fraud or deceit and for this reason liable to any one who suffered as a result of an injury. ...

I agree with the approach taken by Judge Kurisko in *Ford v. Schmitt,* Ont. Co. Ct., Waterloo, Doc. No. 11124/82, November 30, 1984. In that case the purchaser refused to close when she learned that the house was insulated with urea formaldehyde foam insulation ("UFFI"). Both the vendor and the agent independently knew about the UFFI and that it had been banned by the government. The agent told the vendor that he would disclose the type of insulation only if asked. The Judge held that the failure to disclose the detrimental facts concerning the insulation was a fraudulent and material misrepresentation upon which the purchaser relied to her detriment. The Judge was satisfied that the vendor realized that disclosure of UFFI would adversely affect the price and the chance of a sale. The requisite intention to defraud was therefore imputed to the vendor.

[The court reviewed additional cases.]

. . .

I am influenced by the obiter of Dubin JA [in *McGrath, supra*]. In that case, he uses an example of a situation where a vendor would have a duty to disclose. That example is closer to our fact situation than any of the other cases I have cited. At p. 792, after he has quoted from Professor Laskin's lecture, *supra*, he says:

> I am prepared to assume that, in an appropriate case, a vendor may be *liable to a purchaser* with respect to premises which are *not new* if he *knows* of a *latent defect which renders the premises unfit for habitation*. But, as is pointed out in the lecture above referred to, in such a case it is *incumbent upon the purchaser to establish that the latent defect was known to the vendor, or that the circumstances were such that it could be said that the vendor was guilty of concealment or a reckless disregard of the truth or falsity of any representations* made by him. It is to be observed that that is quite a different case than the one founded on the principle of *M'Alister (or Donoghue) v. Stevenson, supra*.
>
> Similarly, I am prepared to assume that there is *a duty on the vendor to disclose a latent defect which renders the premises dangerous in themselves, or that the circumstances are such as to disclose the likelihood of such danger, e.g., the premises being sold being subject to radioactivity*. Again, however, under such circumstances the cause of action is not dependent on the principles enacted in *M'Alister (or Donoghue) v. Stevenson*. [Emphasis added.]

To return to the case before me, and dealing first with the issue of whether the Chopras should have disclosed the existence of radioactive material in the area prior to entering into the agreement of purchase and sale, I find, based on the principles enunciated in the cases to which I have referred, that they should have. They knew about the potentially dangerous latent defect prior to the signing of the agreement. The fact that at the time the agreement was signed the latent defect was only known to be on property in the immediate area and not on the property itself, provides no excuse for non-disclosure. The Chopras were guilty of concealment of facts so detrimental to the Sevidals that it amounted to a fraud upon them, and, therefore, the Chopras are liable in deceit.

In considering the second issue of whether the Chopras should have disclosed the discovery of radioactive material on their property prior to closing, the principles enunciated in the cases would apply equally but even more forcefully to them when the discovery was made on their property a week prior to closing but there is one further aspect which must be addressed before I make my finding: whether there is a duty to disclose a change of circumstance after the agreement is signed but before closing.

In the cases already set out, the vendor knew of the latent defect prior to the signing of the agreement. In this case, I have found as well that the Chopras knew of the latent defect in the immediate area prior to the signing of the agreement but I want to deal separately with whether they should have disclosed the latent defect on their property which they knew nothing about when they signed the agreement but which they discovered was there at least a week prior to closing.

. . .

In *Abel v. McDonald*, [1964] 2 OR 256, (CA), ... when the purchasers moved in they discovered that the basement floor had dropped several inches from the time they had inspected the property before signing the offer. Aylesworth JA found fraud through active non-disclosure on the part of the vendors. He indicated that active non-disclosure meant that, with the knowledge that the damage to the premises had occurred after the agreement was signed, the vendors actively prevented that knowledge from coming to the notice of the purchasers.

In the case before me, while there may not have been quite the same non-disclosure as in the *Abel* case, the comments of McFarlane JA in *Sorenson v. Kaye Holdings*, *supra*, at p. 208 [BCLR] apply:

> where, as here, the claim is for damages for fraud, it is my opinion that the court must consider the whole of the dealings between the parties from [the first meeting] until their contract was carried through to completion.

In all the circumstances of this case, I find that the Chopras had a duty to disclose the change of circumstances to the Sevidals prior to closing. Accordingly, with regard to the second issue, I find that the Chopras should have disclosed the discovery of radioactive material on their property, and I find the Chopras were guilty of concealment of facts so detrimental to the Sevidals that it amounted to a fraud upon them. Therefore, the Chopras are liable in deceit.

NOTES

1. In *Godin v. Jenovac* (1993), 35 RPR (2d) 288 (Ont. Ct. Gen. Div.), a vendor failed to disclose the existence of a closed municipal landfill in the vicinity of the subject property. The court held that there was no duty to disclose this information to the purchaser in the absence of any evidence that the site posed a health hazard or danger. Similarly, in *Ceolaro v. York Humber Ltd.* (1994), 37 RPR (2d) 1 (Ont. Ct. Gen. Div.), a vendor developer failed to advise condominium purchasers that the property was formerly a site for sewage treatment that had been subject to extensive remedial engineering to remove a methane gas hazard. The *Ceolaro* court followed *Godin* and distinguished *Sevidal* on the basis that there was no duty on the vendor to disclose the information unless there was a health or safety risk.

2. Vendors also may be liable under other tort principles such as negligent misrepresentation and negligence. In *Sassy Investments Ltd. v. Minovitch* (1996), 21 CELR (NS)

126 (BCSC), vendors of a gasoline station were liable for negligently misrepresenting to the purchasers that they had monitored and recorded the gasoline inventory at the station, and liable in negligence for failing to complete inventory records and not exercising the requisite degree of care in controlling the gasoline inventory, when uninventoried gasoline leaked from the station's underground pipes and contaminated the wells of nearby residents.

C. The Liability of Real Estate Agents and Solicitors

It is possible for real estate agents or lawyers to attract environmental liability in any type of land transaction. Real estate agents may be liable in contract or tort if they fail to exercise a reasonable degree of care and skill that persons of ordinary prudence and ability might be expected to show in the capacity of agent. Solicitors in real estate transactions also may be liable in contract or tort if they fail to exercise the due care and attention expected of the reasonably competent solicitor. The *Sevidal* case illustrates the application of these principles in an environmental context to both real estate agents and solicitors.

Sevidal v. Chopra
(1987-88), 2 CELR (NS) 173, at 203 (Ont. HC)

OYEN J:

Liability of Antonio and Northgate

The issue with respect to Antonio is: did she meet the appropriate level of competence expected from a real estate agent for the work which she undertook for the Sevidals?

[The court found that the real estate agent exercised the appropriate level of competence with respect to finding a suitable house and property for the Sevidals, except for the radioactivity problem, which the court found that the agent did not know about until after the agreement was signed. The court further held that it could not find that the agent ought to have known of the problem. The court also found that neither the agent's employer, Northgate, the Sevidals' lawyer, Clapp, nor the loan mortgage officer knew of a radioactivity problem at McClure Cresent although all of them were experienced in dealing with real estate in the Scarborough area. Moreover, the court found that nothing would have alerted Antonio to the fact that the McClure Crescent development was any different from numerous others in the Scarborough area.]

Having the waiver of the condition [regarding financing] signed before the mortgage was applied for is a different situation. In *Charter-York Ltd. v. Hurst; Hurst v. Charter-York Ltd.* (1978), 2 RPR 272 (Ont. HC) [leave to appeal to Supreme Court of Canada dismissed (1979), 28 NR 616n (SCC)], Labrosse J considered the claim of a vendor against his real estate agent based on a breach of the obligations under the listing agreement. At p. 279 with respect to the standard of care required by a real estate agent under the contract, he cited with approval an extract from 22 *Hals*. (3d ed.), at pp. 47-48:

> All agents, whether paid or unpaid, skilled or unskilled, are under a legal obligation to exercise due care and skill in performance of the duties which they have undertaken, a greater degree of care being required from a paid than from an unpaid, and from a skilled than from an unskilled, agent. The question in all such cases is whether the act or omission complained of is inconsistent with that reasonable degree of care and skill which persons of ordinary prudence and ability might be expected to show in the situation and profession of the agent.

Labrosse J also found at p. 280 that the standard of care by the agent and the quantum of damages in the *Charter-York* case would be the same whether the breach was based in contract or in tort. His reasoning would be applicable to this case and I adopt it.

The Sevidals were immigrants to Canada. They were purchasing their first home and they were unfamiliar with the laws affecting the purchase. Antonio had immigrated from their homeland and spoke the same dialect. The Sevidals relied on her to a large extent as their real estate agent. Antonio was the Sevidals' agent. The Chopras were represented by another agent. In view of my earlier findings that Antonio failed to explain the waiver and that the Sevidals did not understand it, I find that, in having the Sevidals sign the waiver before the mortgage was applied for, Antonio did not meet the level of competence expected of her.

[The court found that the Sevidals' loss was foreseeable because the agent took the chance of removing the condition expecting that, in her experience, the mortgage would not be refused and even if it were she could arrange other financing.]

Nevertheless she knew she was exposing the Sevidals to some risk which, I have found, she failed to explain to them. The uncontraverted testimony of Clapp was that, if the condition had remained, he would have had no difficulty in getting the Sevidals out of the transaction once the radioactivity problem in the area was discovered. By her action, Antonio prevented the Sevidals from using the condition in a manner in which their lawyer testified it could have been used to prevent loss to them. Antonio, therefore, is responsible for the resulting loss.

[As Antonio was an employee of Northgate, acting within the scope of her duties, the court also found Northgate responsible for the acts of its employee.]

Liability of Clapp

The issues with respect to Clapp are: first, what was his retainer and, second, did Clapp meet an appropriate level of competence expected from a solicitor for the work which he undertook?

The work which Clapp first undertook for the Sevidals was to attempt to get them out of the transaction. Although the closing would not take place for more than 2 months after the Sevidals saw Clapp, within 2 days the Sevidals sought the advice of a government agency on the radioactivity. Based on that advice the Sevidals instructed Clapp to proceed with the transaction which he did.

Counsel for the Sevidals urged me to find that Clapp did not meet the appropriate level of competence expected in the circumstances in that: (1) He did not explore all the potential avenues for getting the Sevidals out of the transaction and he failed to get them out of it; (2) He did not consult counsel expert in contested real estate transactions; (3) He did not check independently the advice given to them, he did not advise them to get that advice in writing and he made no further inquiry even of the Sevidals about the radioactivity problem after he had been instructed to complete the transaction.

Although their counsel complained that Clapp did not consult experts, the Sevidals' counsel chose not to call any solicitor expert in the real estate field to give evidence as to what a reasonably competent solicitor would have done in the circumstances.

LeDain J describes the standard of care required of a solicitor in *Central & Eastern Trust Co. v. Rafuse*, [1986] 2 SCR 147 ... as "that of the reasonably competent solicitor, the ordinary competent solicitor and the ordinary prudent solicitor."

I have reviewed the advice given by Clapp to the Sevidals in their first interview. I have reviewed the steps he took on their behalf in the 2 days after that interview before their instructions changed. I have considered the care he took to make sure that he did not put them in anticipatory breach of contract. I have reviewed his acceptance of their reliance on the advice given to them by the AECB [Atomic Energy Control Board], and I have reviewed as well the work done on behalf of the Sevidals in connection with the completion of the transaction. In particular, I have considered Clapp's evidence as to how he conducts a real estate transaction to see if his general approach to real estate transactions meets a reasonably acceptable standard. In my view it does. I have also considered the extent of Clapp's knowledge of the real estate field based on his testimony that most of his practice is in the residential real estate field.

I find that Clapp did consider, to the extent necessary in the 2 days after he was retained, the avenues open to the Sevidals for backing out of the transaction. I have no doubt that, had the Sevidals not changed their instructions to him, he would have continued to pursue his original retainer in an appropriate fashion and would have continued to advise them when the next appropriate step was contemplated.

Since Clapp himself had substantial experience in the residential real estate field, I do not find it was necessary for Clapp, before his retainer changed, to consult a person more experienced than himself.

I find as well that it was reasonable for Clapp not to make independent inquiries of AECB since Mrs. Sevidal had told him she had been advised by a responsible government agency that there was no contamination on the property at 63 McClure Crescent.

[The court found that Clapp carried out his duties in acting for the Sevidals as a reasonably competent solicitor. He was not careless in his advice to, or representation of, them.]

D. The Liability of Government Agencies

Government may attract environmental liability in the context of real estate matters as a vendor or purchaser of land or as a regulator.

The case of *Heighington v. Ontario* (1990), 4 CELR (NS) 65, at 67 (Ont. CA) considers the situation of regulatory negligence. The provincial department of health became aware in the 1940s that soils on the subject property had high levels of radioactive contamination. The province expropriated the lands in the 1950s and a provincial crown housing agency, unaware of the contamination, leased the land to builders in the 1970s who subdivided the land into lots to construct houses. In 1980 radiation levels exceeding acceptable limits were found in some of the yards of the subdivision. The owners and former owners of residences in the subdivision brought action against the province in negligence and were successful at trial (1987), 2 CELR (NS) 93 (Ont. HC). The province appealed the trial judgment, but the Court of Appeal held that the *Public Health Act*, RSO 1937, c. 299, "imposed a duty on the Department of Health to take such measures as necessary to abate conditions injurious or dangerous to health," and that "in all the circumstances, the provincial officials were negligent in that, in breach of the *Public Health Act*, they failed to take reasonable steps to cause to be removed such radioactive material including contaminated soil, as might endanger the health of future occupants of the land."

NOTES AND QUESTIONS

1. In the *Sevidal* case, the Atomic Energy Control Board (AECB) was found liable in negligent misrepresentation. The agency, pursuant to statutory powers under the former *Atomic Energy Control Act* (now *Nuclear Safety and Control Act*, SC 1997, c. 9), assumed responsibility for disseminating information about radioactivity in the area. However, the agency gave the Sevidals inaccurate information about whether there was radioactive soil on the property. In addition, the agency failed to give the family other pertinent information about the status of ongoing investigations, in part because of an agency policy of non-disclosure about soil contamination except to landowners, a policy not communicated to the Sevidals. Because the Sevidals had sought advice in order to help them make a judgment whether to back out of the transaction, the agency's representations failed to meet the standard of care required in the circumstances and contributed to the damages suffered by the Sevidals (at 197-200). The agency also was found liable in negligence because there was a sufficient relationship of proximity between the agency and the public due to the agency's assumption of responsibility to provide information to the public regarding radioactivity in the area. A duty of care arose because it was also within the contemplation of agency employees that carelessness on their part would be likely to cause damage to the Sevidals. The agency was not protected in this instance by characterization of its conduct as the formulation of policy. The court noted that the agency had a right, as a matter of policy, to decide to whom information would be disseminated. In this case, however, the agency provided some incomplete and inaccurate information to the Sevidals without advising them of the agency's policy of non-disclosure, which would have alerted the family to the need to make other inquiries. "The actions of the AECB almost set a trap for the unwary purchasers. Parliament certainly never intended a public authority to exercise its policy-making powers in such a way that non-disclosure of the policy would mislead a member of the public who made an appropriate inquiry" (at 200-3).

2. Because of concerns that the federal government not attract liability upon the purchase or sale of land, the Treasury Board of Canada has adopted a management policy on federal contaminated sites. The policy requires that (1) before federal departments or agencies acquire or dispose of real property, they must ascertain its environmental condition; and (2) when disposing of federal real property departments and agencies must, upon request, disclose available environmental information on the property to potential purchasers. See *Treasury Board Federal Contaminated Sites Management Policy* (Ottawa: Treasury Board Canada, 2002).

3. What difference, if any, would the Treasury Board policy have had on the outcome of the *Sevidal* case had the policy been in effect at the time and been applied by the AECB?

III. CONTAMINATED LAND

In addition to private rights of action by purchasers against vendors and others in connection with the sale of toxic real estate, a variety of other parties with interests in contaminated lands increasingly are subject to a myriad of controls and liabilities imposed by legislatures, regulators, and courts. Liability may attach to the interests of owners, operators, parent corporations, lenders, receivers, receiver-managers, trustees in bankruptcy, liquidators, or governments. A preliminary issue that all such potentially responsible parties must face is the level of cleanup that must be achieved.

A. The Cleanup Standard

Determining "how clean is clean" has been an ongoing debate in the context of the cleanup of contaminated lands. Federal–provincial bodies, such as the CCME, have developed a variety of guidelines and standards to address contaminants in soil and groundwater. In some provincial jurisdictions, these standards have been adopted as regulations. In others, they have been retained as guidelines. The following case illustrates the extent to which remediation may be required to satisfy civil liability claims.

Tridan Developments Ltd. v. Shell Canada Products Ltd.
(2002), 57 OR (3d) 503 (CA)

[Appellant S operated a service station in Ottawa adjacent to a car dealership owned by respondent T. In 1990, 9000 litres of gasoline leaked from an underground fuel line on S's property. S undertook remediation of its property in accordance with government standards applicable at the time, but did not remove all of the contaminated soil. In 1991, T discovered that some of the gasoline had migrated to its property. S accepted responsibility for the cleanup of T's property, but a dispute arose as to the appropriate level of cleanup. The trial judge held that T was entitled to have its property remediated to a pristine condition and assessed that cost at $550,000. The trial judge further awarded T $350,000 for loss of property value due to the stigma associated with the contamination. S appealed the assessment of damages.]

The Facts

. . .

Several sets of Ministry of Environment (MOE) guidelines were in place during the period between the spill and trial. ... [T]he "Guideline for Use at Contaminated Sites in Ontario," revised February 1997 ("1997 MOE guideline") ... currently applies. Its stated purpose is to provide

> advice and information to property owners and consultants to use when assessing the environmental condition of a property, when determining whether or not restoration is required, and in determining the kind of restoration needed to allow continued use or reuse of the site. The ministry has provided the guideline, along with the supporting documentation, to assist landowners in making decisions on soil and/or groundwater quality for proposed or existing property uses.

Under the 1997 MOE guideline, the level of permissible pollutants varies depending on whether the property is used for agricultural, residential or commercial purposes. The relevant criteria for land used for commercial purposes is set out in Table B. Within Table B, permissible concentration levels vary depending on whether the groundwater is used for drinking purposes and on whether the soil at the contaminated site is fine, medium or [coarse]. Lower concentration levels of pollutants are permitted for [coarse] grain soil, since pollutants can travel more easily through [coarse] soil than fine soil.

No one suggests that the guidelines supplant the common law standard of compensation for injury to land. However, Shell asserts that the MOE guideline represents a reasonable standard to apply to commercial lands that are contaminated but unaffected for the purpose being served. The difference in cost between meeting the 1997 MOE guideline and achieving a site which is clean of all contaminants, referred to in the evidence as a pristine site, is approximately $250,000, mostly referable to the amount of soil that must be removed and replaced.

Damages for Reparation of the Tridan Property

The trial judge found that the plaintiffs were entitled to have their property remediated to pristine condition and assessed the cost of doing so at $550,000. ...

The trial judge might have relied upon those expert witnesses supporting the MOE guidelines as a reasonable measure of reparation and thus the damages suffered. This is a commercial property on a busy thoroughfare and unlikely to ever be a site for residential use. It might be concluded that, in a practical sense, Tridan is not likely to need or want to clean its soil at depth of every particle of pollutant. However, in the circumstances of this case, I cannot say the trial judge erred in deciding that Tridan was entitled to reparation to a pristine state. Where a product that may cause mischief escapes to a neighbour's property, there is responsibility "for all the damage which is the natural consequence of its escape." See *Rylands v. Fletcher* (1866), [1861-73] All ER Rep. 1 at 7 ... . Of course, they must be reasonable. On all the evidence, it is fair to conclude that the damages would not be eliminated by reparations to the point of the MOE guidelines. There would be residual loss of value, referred to as stigma, which would be reduced, as the trial judge found, or eliminated, as I am about to find, by remediation to the pristine level.

Stigma

An analysis of all the evidence brings me to the conclusion that there is no support for the trial judge's conclusion that there is a residual reduction of value in a pristine site caused by the knowledge that it was once polluted. It would appear that the trial judge simply misapprehended the evidence of the two principal witnesses for Tridan [who testified that there would be no impact on market value if the site were cleaned to a pristine condition]. ...

In sum, the evidence compels me to conclude that there is no stigma loss at the pristine cleanup level. This conclusion also makes sense of the trial judge's holding that cleanup to the pristine standard was justified in this case. If the trial judge's assessment of stigma damage at $350,000 is taken as the diminution in value at cleanup to the guideline standard, then the more economical route is to proceed to the pristine level at an additional cleanup cost of $250,000 with no stigma damage.

In my view, the only reasonable conclusion from the totality of the evidence is that a pristine site has no residual loss of value and ... the judgment should be amended to reduce the amount awarded by $350,000.

[The court allowed the appeal in part.]

NOTES AND QUESTIONS

1. *Tridan* establishes two important propositions. First, in appropriate circumstances, a defendant who permits a contaminant to migrate offsite may be required to remediate the neighbour's property back to its original pristine condition, even if that remediation level is more stringent or protective than standards established by government cleanup guidelines. Second, while a court can order the cleanup of neighbouring land to a pristine condition, landowners that benefit from such a 100 percent remediation cannot claim that there is a contamination stigma attached to their land thereafter that warrants additional damages.

2. Ontario recently has enacted Bill 56, the *Brownfields Statute Law Amendment Act, 2001*, SO 2001, c. 17, which will amend several environmental, planning, and municipal laws in the province. As part of the amendments, Bill 56 will establish rules for contaminated site assessment and cleanup. In particular, Bill 56 would amend the *Environmental Protection Act*, RSO 1990, c. E.19, to do three things. First, it would make environmental site assessment and cleanup to prescribed standards mandatory where there is a change in land use from industrial/commercial to residential/parkland. Second, it would authorize regulations to provide clear rules for site assessment, cleanup, and standards for contaminants based on a proposed land use. This change would largely codify MOE's 1997 guidelines into standards having the force of law. Third, it would require the acceptance of a site-specific risk assessment by MOE as prepared by a certified professional and allow for conditions to be placed on the use of a property.

3. If a *Tridan* fact situation were to occur following the coming into force of Bill 56, would contaminated site cleanup to prescribed standards, as opposed to pristine conditions, take precedence in a civil action for damages? See D. Mahoney, "Contaminated Property and Brownfields in Ontario: Statutory Obligations and Opportunities," in *Contaminated Properties and the Redevelopment of Brownfield Sites* (Ottawa: Canadian Bar Association, 2002), 11.

B. Liability Principles

In theory, the 1993 CCME principles for contaminated site liability, above, endorsed two competing approaches to the application of liability under legislation in Canada. One approach is exemplified by the adoption of the "polluter pays" principle. A second approach is exemplified by the adoption of notions of "fairness" and the need to "allocate" liability on the basis of such factors as level of contribution to the problem.

In practice, provincial legislation and its interpretation by the courts has attempted to straddle both approaches. For example, in British Columbia, liability for remediation of a contaminated site is absolute, retroactive, joint, and several under the *Waste Management Act*, RSBC 1996, c. 482, s. 27(1). However, the Act also allows potentially responsible persons to seek an opinion from an allocation panel, established under the statute, regarding the responsible person's share of liability (s. 27.2). Moreover, regulations under the statute clarify the statute's liability principles by making it clear that nothing in the Act shall be construed as prohibiting the apportionment of a share of liability to one or more responsible persons, by the government or a court, where justified by available evidence. See Contaminated Site Regulations, BC reg. 375/96, s. 34(1)(2). Accordingly, competing provisions in the Act and regulations temper the broad liability that otherwise may be imposed on those responsible for the remediation of contaminated sites in British Columbia.

In contrast, the laws of other provinces that purport to adopt principles of fairness and allocation of contaminated site liability on the basis of fault may be interpreted differently by the courts. In *Legal Oil & Gas Ltd. v. Alberta (Minister of Environment)* (2000), 34 CELR (NS) 303 (Alta. QB), an environmental protection order, under s. 113 of Alberta's *Environmental Protection and Enhancement Act*, RSA 2000, c. E-12, was issued to an oil well owner to clean up a spill. The spill had migrated offsite and contaminated neighbouring land decades before the law was enacted. Section 113 authorizes a director of the provincial environment ministry to issue an order to the person responsible for the substance where the director is of the opinion that a release of a substance into the environment has occurred and the release has caused an adverse effect. The owner contended that any contamination of these lands occurred before it took possession and acquired ownership of the well. Following a hearing by the provincial Environmental Appeal Board, the minister of environment adopted the recommendation of the board to affirm the order. The owner applied for judicial review of the minister's approval of the order. The court had this to say about the issue of retrospectivity:

> The Applicants submit that ministerial approval of the Director's order has the effect of determining that s. 102 [now 113] of the Act is retrospective in its application. They argue that as the Act does not expressly state that it operates with respect to transactions which

occurred prior to its enactment, the Board should have applied the presumption against retrospective application. ...

However, the Board ... concluded that to the extent the [order] has a retrospective element, s. 102 of the Act is intended to operate in that fashion.

I do not consider the conclusion of the Board in relation to this issue to be patently unreasonable, particularly given that the Supreme Court of Canada has recognized an exception to the presumption against retrospective application when the purpose of the provision is to protect the public rather than to punish (*Barry v. Alberta (Securities Commission)*, [1989] 1 SCR 301 ... . Section 102 of the Act certainly falls in the "protection of the public" category.

NOTES AND QUESTIONS

1. The liability principles recognized under British Columbia's *Waste Management Act* have been vigorously defended. See W. Braul, "Liability Features of Bill 26" (1994) vol. 4 *Journal of Environmental Law and Policy* 139, at 158-73, noting that the liability principles under the Act of absolute, retroactive, and joint and several liability are found generally in Canadian environmental legislation. They have also been vigorously criticized. See R. Crowley and F. Thompson, "Retroactive Liability, Superfund and the Regulation of Contaminated Sites in British Columbia" (1995) vol. 29 *UBC Law Review* 87, at 106-16, approving the Act's allocation panel process and related provisions that seek to limit liability, but arguing for more reasonable, fair, and efficient apportionment of responsibility between the province, local beneficiaries, and past responsible persons.

2. Recently, the British Columbia government has initiated a review of the Act. In the terms of reference for the review, the issue of joint and several, absolute, and retroactive liability is identified for examination because it "may lack fairness and has resulted in investors being fearful of investing in, or redeveloping contaminated land in" the province. See BC Ministry of Water, Land and Air Protection (BCMWLAP), *Terms of Reference for Minister's Advisory Panel on Contaminated Sites* (Victoria: BCMWLAP, 2002). Other stakeholders, however, have taken a different view. They suggest that the principles of joint and several, retroactive, and absolute liability are "essential components" of the contaminated sites regime that give effect to the "polluter pays" principle and ensure that such sites are not abandoned to become a taxpayer and community burden. See West Coast Environmental Law (WCEL), *Polluter Pays and the Public Interest: A Submission to the Minister's Advisory Panel on Contaminated Sites* (Vancouver: WCEL, 2002), at 2-3. In September 2002, the Interim Report of the Advisory Panel recommended that a "fair, principled and efficient process" be established for allocating and apportioning liabilityon the basis of a set of equitable principles defined in the legislation, similar to the approach currently used in Manitoba. The new process would replace the current principles of liability. See Advisory Panel on Contaminated Sites (APCS), *Interim Report* (Victoria: APCS, 2002), at 17.

3. The process in Manitoba referred to by the BC Advisory Panel is established under the *Contaminated Sites Remediation Act*, CCSM 1996, c. C205. Following the identification of remediation measures as necessary at a contaminated property, the Act authorizes the province to issue remediation orders to potentially responsible persons (PRPs). The

Act sets out a process for apportionment of liability among PRPs based on a set of factors derived from the 1993 CCME principles for contaminated site liability. The factors include: (1) the polluter pays principle, (2) subjective or objective knowledge of the person regarding the contaminated state of the property, (3) effect on fair market value or permitted uses of the site, (4) reasonable steps, if any, taken to prevent contamination, (5) whether the site was disposed of knowing it was contaminated, (6) compliance with industry standards in handling contaminants, and (7) steps that the PRP took to limit contamination and notify regulatory authorities after becoming aware of the contamination (ss. 1(1)(c) and 21). PRPs only are responsible for their proportionate share of remediation costs as determined by agreement, or following a provincial apportionment hearing. They are not jointly and severally liable for cleanup unless they are in default (s. 30). Is it sound environmental policy for Manitoba law to contemplate that less than 100 percent of remediation liability could be allocated among PRPs, leaving the provincial taxpayer responsible for the costs of remaining "orphaned" shares? See J. Stefaniuk, "The Green Greenfields of Home: Contaminated Site Legislation in the Prairie Provinces—An Overview," in *Contaminated Properties and the Redevelopment of Brownfield Sites*, at 3.

4. In practice, the fairness approach to allocating contaminated site remediation liability has been used infrequently in Manitoba and Alberta. Instead, the other rules that have been used in these provinces are based on joint and several liability, do not provide for apportionment of liability, lack criteria for achieving fairness among PRPs, and are more reliant on government discretion. Which approach to liability principles makes for better environmental policy: a regime where the ground rules are stringent, detailed, transparent, and applied consistently? Or a regime that in theory adopts fairness principles, but in practice relies on the discretion of government as to when they will be applied? See C. Chiasson, "British Columbia Case Highlights Differing Contaminated Site Philosophies" (2001) vol. 11 *Journal of Environmental Law and Policy* 287, at 291-92 (comparing British Columbia and Alberta) and Stefaniuk, above (referring to Manitoba).

C. Parties Liable

As noted above, liability may attach to the interests of owners, operators, parent corporations, lenders, receivers, receiver-managers, trustees in bankruptcy, liquidators, or governments.

1. Owners and Operators—Past and Present

Many provinces have vested ministries of the environment with broad authority to order the cleanup of contaminated property, including soil and groundwater. These orders are often directed at owners and operators of sources of contamination. Some of these jurisdictions also have attempted to apply their legislative powers to past owners and operators. The following case exemplifies judicial treatment of current and past owners and operators under early versions of these statutory authorities.

Canadian National Railway Co. v. Ontario
(1992), 6 CELR (NS) 211, at 214, 218 (Ont. Ct. Gen. Div.)

[On land owned by CNR, AP Inc. operated a wood treatment business in Thunder Bay harbour from 1974 to 1982. At that point, AP Inc. assigned the lease and sold the business to NWP Inc., and took back a mortgage by way of sublease to secure the sale. Over the years soil, groundwater, and sediments in and around the site became contaminated by creosote and other chemicals arising from current and past operations at the site. In 1987, a director of the Ministry of the Environment issued a control order under the *Environmental Protection Act*, RSO 1980, c. 141, as amended, to study and clean up the problem to CNR (the landowner), AP Inc. (the past plant owner and operator), and NWP Inc. (the current plant owner and operator), all of whom appealed the order to the province's Environmental Appeal Board. The board confirmed the order against CNR and NWP Inc., both of whom appealed to the Divisional Court, while the director appealed the dismissal of the order against AP Inc.]

PER CURIAM: The issues before the Court are as follows:

(1) Is an owner who has never occupied the site at any relevant time, an owner or occupant or person in charge, management or control of the source of contaminant?

(2) Is a former owner or occupant responsible? ...

(4) Was there any evidence that NWP participated in the contamination? ...

The relevant provisions of the Act are as follows:

1(1) In this Act, ...

(m) "person responsible" means the owner, or the person in occupation or having the charge, management or control of a source of contaminant; ...

6. When the report of a provincial officer, a copy of which has been served upon the person responsible for a source of contaminant, contains a finding that a contaminant added to, emitted or discharged into any part of the natural environment by any person or from any source of contaminant exceeds the maximum permissible amount, concentration or level prescribed by the regulations, contravenes section 13 or is a contaminant the use of which is prohibited by the regulations, the Director may issue a control order directed to the person responsible therefor. ...

[Section 17 of the Act authorized the director to order "a person who owns or who has management or control of an undertaking or property" to implement specified procedures.]

113(1) The Director may, where he is authorized by this Act to issue an order known as a "control order," order the person to whom it is directed to do any one or more of the following, namely,

(a) to limit or control the rate of addition, emission or discharge of the contaminant into the natural environment in accordance with the directions set out in the order;

(b) to stop the addition, emission or discharge of the contaminant into the natural environment, ...

(c) to comply with any directions set out in the order relating to the manner in which the contaminant may be added, emitted or discharged into the natural environment;

(d) to comply with any directions set out in the order relating to the procedures to be followed in the control or elimination of the addition, emission or discharge of the contaminant into the natural environment; ...

(g) to study and to report to the Director upon, ... measures to control the discharge into the natural environment of the contaminant specified in the order.

I—Ownership, Occupation and Control of a Source of Contaminant

The purpose of the Act is to provide for the protection and conservation of the natural environment and should be liberally construed. The Board found that the environmental problem was caused by the continuous, past and present drippings from the retort area, as well as the presence of contaminated soil on site, which allows contaminants to seep into the lake, as well as different spills which presumably occurred over the past years.

Section 1(1)(c) defines "contaminant" as something resulting directly or indirectly from the activities of man that impairs the environment. Section 1(1)(p) defines "source of contaminant" as anything that discharges a contaminant into the natural environment. Section 1(1)(k) defines "natural environment." ...

We are of the opinion that, on a proper reading of the Act, the source of contaminant must be some source outside the natural environment and not from a source that is part of the natural environment itself. Otherwise, contaminated lake water, changed by the natural water cycle to cloud and then to rain upon land, then by seepage into the land or drainage to a river, and then to another lake, would make that latter lake water and all the intervening moisture, whether it be cloud, rain, soil or river, all sources of contaminant for which persons would be responsible. It would make persons responsible even if they had no knowledge of there being a contaminant or, if they did, where it came from, because they were the owner, occupant or in charge of the land or river or the other lake. The same analogy could apply to a situation where a person owns land located between a farm and a lake. If the farmer uses excessive fertilizer, it could become a contaminant that seeps through the farm soil or runs into the abutting land or seeps into the soil of the abutting land, and through it into the lake. The intervening property owner would have no knowledge, either of the contaminant or its location. The contaminant entered the natural environment on the farm, and the owner of the in-between lands could not be said to be the owner of the source of contaminant. It would be an undue and improper strain upon the interpretation of the definition of a natural environment in s. 1(1)(k) to read it as being disjunctive, and to cover natural movements of contaminant from one part of the natural environment to another.

In the present case, the Board made findings of fact as to where and how the contaminant exists. These must be recognized by the Court. However, as stated in

Rockcliffe Park Realty Ltd. v. Ontario (Director, Ministry of the Environment) (1975), 10 OR (2d) 1, … (CA), at p. 15 [OR], before s. 6 or s. 7 (or, for that matter, s. 17) can be invoked, it must be shown that a person has been responsible for the discharge into the natural environment in that the contaminant entered the natural environment from the equipment or spillings from the operation on the site. Once in the soil, or in the water, it is in the natural environment. Seepage thereafter, from the soil or subsoil into the lake, is not from a source of contaminant within the meaning of the Act. For these reasons, even if CN, being owner of the soil as opposed to the plant, was found to be an owner within the definition of "person responsible," it is not so responsible because the soil is not the source of contaminant.

The Board found that the CN employee on the site was there for no other purpose than to ensure that the work done by NWP and prior lessees was to CN's specifications, and that the Director had never approached CN directly with its concerns until the December 1987 order. There was evidence that CN owned the creosote supplied to NWP for use on the site. The Board made no findings on this latter point. On these facts and evidence and the lease documents previously referred to, it is clear that CN had no direct occupation or the charge, management or control of the undertaking carried on by NWP, which was found to be the source of the contaminant. CN was therefore not a person responsible, unless it could be said that a person responsible includes a person who had the potential power to gain occupation or control of a source of contaminant. …

The Board made no finding that the covenant of maintenance and repair in the lease was breached. More will be said of breach of covenant when we deal with Abitibi. Failing an actual breach of covenant, CN had no right, let alone an obligation, to re-enter the lands or to take possession thereof or of the plant thereon. CN was therefore not in occupation, nor did it have the charge, management or control of the source of contaminant. The future possibility of obtaining occupation or control cannot be read [into] the Act. …

II—Is a Former Owner or Occupant Responsible?

The Board found that Abitibi [AP Inc.] was a former owner and operator of the plant. We agree with the Board's conclusion that s. 1(1)(m) and s. 6 are restricted to present owners or operators. The order is directed to the person responsible for the source of contaminant. That is the person who can best obey the order and co-operate with the Ministry in arranging for studies on the site, or to take remedial measures. A former owner normally would have no right to re-enter the premises to obey any order. Section 17 provides that a person who owns or has management or control of an undertaking may be ordered to do certain listed things, all of which refer to things in the future. Section 113, while broad in its opening words as to whom the order may be directed, lists the specific acts that can be ordered. They all relate to matters in the future. We are of the opinion that none of them are applicable to a former owner or operator. Therefore, Abitibi is not subject to liability on the basis of having been a prior owner, even if it did contaminate the natural environment during such prior ownership. …

We also agree with the Board that, even if it could be said that some of the existing contaminant was owned by Abitibi, it does not make Abitibi liable. The liability lies upon the person responsible for the source of the contaminant, not upon the owner of the contaminant. The source of the contaminant differs from the contaminant itself. We have already stated that the movement of contaminant, that is already in the natural environment, to another part of the natural environment, does not make the first area the source of contaminant for the second. ...

IV—Was There Any Evidence that NWP Participated in the Contamination?

From the evidence, it would appear that NWP has taken many active steps to reduce or contain the contamination, and that the plant is operating in a more environmentally satisfactory manner now than prior to its purchase thereof. NWP is the owner of the plant and is in control and management thereof. If the plant is a source of contaminant during NWP's ownership, it is responsible therefor.

The Board made a finding of fact that the contamination was caused by the continuous operation of the NWP plant, which includes the present drippings from the retort area and the different spills, and that there was contaminated soil on the site. This Court can only interfere with that finding if there was no cogent evidence on which it could come to that conclusion.

There was ample evidence of contamination in the soil on the site but, as we have held, this soil is not the source of contaminant. ...

In addition, NWP, as occupant of the soil, is responsible for its condition even if it results from a prior occupant's conduct. (See *Sedleigh-Denfield v. O'Callaghan*, [1940] AC 880 at p. 897.) NWP is also the "owner" of the soil within the definition of "person responsible," because it had the possession or dominion over it. (See *Wynne v. Dalby*, ...)

[The court held that for these reasons and no matter how unfair it may appear to NWP, it was properly included within the order.]

NOTES AND QUESTIONS

1. The Ontario Court of Appeal affirmed the decision of the Divisional Court in *CNR* at (1992), 8 CELR (NS) 1, at 5-6. With respect to CNR, the Court of Appeal agreed with the Divisional Court that in the factual circumstances of the case, the soil that constitutes the natural medium through which the contaminant percolates is not a "source of contaminant" within the meaning of s. 6 of the Act, and that CNR was not, as a result of its interest as a reversionary owner of the contaminated soil, a "person responsible for a source of contaminant" under that section. With regard to AP Inc., the Court of Appeal agreed with the Divisional Court that ss. 6 and 17, as drafted at the time, were restricted to present, not former, owners and operators, and that the director's order could not be addressed to AP Inc. as a result of activities conducted by it during the period of its ownership or operation prior to 1982. The Court of Appeal further noted that although

not determinative of the issue, amendments to the *Environmental Protection Act* passed in 1990 applicable to ss. 6 and 17 (now ss. 7 and 18, RSO 1990, c. E.19) extend the scope of these provisions to previous owners and occupiers, and to persons who "had" the charge, management, or control of a source of contaminant, undertaking, or property. The Court of Appeal agreed that the order was properly directed to NWP Inc., as the owner and person in control and management of the plant that the board had found was a continuing source of the contamination.

2. If the 1990 amendments had been in force at the time of the 1987 order in *CNR*, what would be the result for AP Inc.? What about CNR? Do the 1990 amendments change CNR's legal position?

3. Bill 56, Ontario's new Brownfields law, above, which amends several pieces of environmental, planning, and municipal legislation, will provide liability protection from future environmental orders for current and past owners and operators (those in charge, management, or control) of contaminated property who follow the prescribed site assessment and cleanup process. This would include filing a record of site condition with the province under the new site registry, using a certified consultant, and following other requirements to be prescribed by regulation (SO 2001, c. 17, adding part XV.1, s. 168.7 to the *Environmental Protection Act*, RSO 1990, c. E.19).

4. Other provinces have developed extensive contaminated site liability provisions for owners and operators. British Columbia's *Waste Management Act* (Part 4—Contaminated Site Remediation) treats current and past owners and operators as persons responsible for remediating contaminated sites, subject to certain exemptions. Excerpts from the statute follow.

Waste Management Act
RSBC 1996 (Supp.), c. 482

26(1) In this Part: ...

"*operator*" means ... a person who is or was in control of or responsible for any operation located at a contaminated site, but does not include a secured creditor unless the secured creditor is described in section 26.5 (3); ...

"*owner*" means a person who is in possession of, has the right of control of, occupies or controls the use of real property, including, without limitation, a person who has any estate or interest, legal or equitable, in the real property, but does not include a secured creditor unless the secured creditor is described in section 26.5(3); ...

Division 3—Liability

Persons responsible for remediation at contaminated sites

26.5(1) Subject to section 26.6, the following persons are responsible for remediation at a contaminated site:
  (a) a current owner or operator of the site;
  (b) a previous owner or operator of the site; ... .

Persons not responsible for remediation

26.6(1) The following persons are not responsible for remediation at a contaminated site: ...

    (d) an owner or operator who establishes that

        (i) at the time the person became an owner or operator of the site,

            (A) the site was a contaminated site,

            (B) the person had no knowledge or reason to know or suspect that the site was a contaminated site, and

            (C) the person undertook all appropriate inquiries into the previous ownership and uses of the site and undertook other investigations, consistent with good commercial or customary practice at that time, in an effort to minimize potential liability,

        (ii) while the person was an owner of the site, the person did not transfer any interest in the site without first disclosing any known contamination to the transferee, and

        (iii) the owner or operator did not, by any act or omission, cause or contribute to the contamination of the site;

    (e) an owner or operator who owned or occupied a site that at the time of acquisition was not a contaminated site and during the ownership or operation the owner or operator did not dispose of, handle or treat a substance in a manner that, in whole or in part, caused the site to become a contaminated site.

NOTES AND QUESTIONS

1. British Columbia's contaminated site liability provisions for current and past owners and operators are modeled on the 1980 US *Comprehensive Environmental Response, Compensation, and Liability Act* (CERCLA), 42 USCA, s. 9607(a). CERCLA makes the following persons potentially responsible parties: "(1) the owner and operator of a vessel or facility; or (2) any person who at the time of disposal of any hazardous substance owned or operated any facility at which such hazardous substances were disposed of." CERCLA contains similar exemptions from liability to those in BC's legislation. Recent amendments to CERCLA in January 2002 add exemptions for *bona fide* prospective purchasers and contiguous property owners; they also clarify the innocent purchaser defence added to the law by amendments in 1986. See E.E. Smary, "The New Federal Superfund Amendments—New Transactional and Brownfield Standards in the United States," *Contaminated Properties and the Redevelopment of Brownfield Sites*, at 3-8.

2. Recently, the British Columbia APCS has recommended that the *Waste Management Act* should narrow the range of persons currently caught within s. 26.5 of the Act and the definitions of "owner" and "operator" in s. 26. According to the advisory panel, "responsibility should be connected primarily to a person's control over and causal link to the activity or substance causing the contamination, rather than to considerations of who has the 'deepest pockets.'" See APCS, *Interim Report*, at 15-16. What are the advantages and disadvantages of this approach to identifying potentially responsible persons? Is the deepest pocket not that of the taxpayer who will be forced to pay for cleanups if those with some connection to, or who benefited from activity on, a contaminated

site are exempt from liability? Moreover, if the net of potentially responsible persons is narrowed will this encourage or undermine the trend to act preventively in business practices by performing due diligence inspections and environmental audits on property?

2. Parent Corporations

There are a number of liability theories that may be applicable to parent corporations under contaminated site legislation. One theory is based on simply owning shares in a subsidiary. A second theory is based on the control exercised by the parent over the subsidiary. The following case explores these theories.

Beazer East, Inc. v. British Columbia (Environmental Appeal Board)
(2000), 36 CELR (NS) 195 (BCSC)

[Wood treatment operations had taken place on property in Burnaby, British Columbia from 1931 to 1982, resulting in contamination of the property. For a number of years during this period, Beazer East, Inc. (BEI) was the parent corporation (through share ownership) of the operator of the wood treatment facility. In 1997, after the coming into force of the contaminated site remediation provisions of the *Waste Management Act*, a manager for the provincial environment ministry issued a site remediation order to BEI as a previous owner, operator, and producer. BEI appealed the order to the board. The board upheld the order against BEI as a previous owner and operator, but not as a producer. BEI petitioned the court for (1) an order quashing or setting aside the remediation order and those portions of the Board's decision finding BEI to be a previous owner and operator, and (2) a declaration relieving the company of responsibility for remediation of the site.]

Was Beazer a Previous Owner?

[T]he relevant portion of the definition of "owner" [under the *Waste Management Act* follows]:

> "owner" means a person who is in possession of, has the right of control of, occupies or controls the use of real property [s. 26(1)]. ...

The first issue to be determined is whether a parent corporation can be an "owner" by virtue of its share ownership in its subsidiary. Although this was not the conclusion of the Board, it is the Manager's position that the correct interpretation of the definition leads to such a conclusion. ...

In support of its position that a parent corporation can be an "owner" by virtue of its share ownership in the subsidiary, the Manager relies primarily on the decision of the Supreme Court of Canada in *Atco Ltd. v. Calgary Power Ltd.*, [1982] 2 SCR 557. At issue in that case was whether Atco Ltd. required the consent of the Public Utilities Board of Alberta before it could acquire shares in Calgary Power Ltd. In order to decide whether the consent was required, it was necessary to determine whether Atco

Ltd. was an owner of a public utility. The Court concluded that Atco Ltd. was the owner of a public utility because it owned the majority of the shares in a company which, in turn, owned almost all of the shares of three companies which were public utilities.

In the Alberta legislation, the phrase "owner of a public utility" was defined to mean "a person owning, operating, managing or controlling a public utility." The focus was whether Atco Ltd. controlled a public utility. The genesis of the Court's reasoning is as follows:

> In the discharge of its varied functions it is difficult to appreciate how the Board can maintain a sound and comprehensive regulatory position so as to discharge its duty to the public at large in the regulation of public utilities and their owners, unless a broad interpretation is accorded to the words adopted by the legislature in s. 98. In my view, the words "owner of a public utility" must, by reason of s. 2, *supra*, include a person without legal ownership in the system but having the power to control (p. 575).

. . .

In the present case, there are no ... provisions of the [*Waste Management*] *Act* which suggest a legislative intent to give the words in the definition of "owner" a meaning broader than their ordinary meaning. Indeed, there are provisions which indicate that the Legislature intended to give them their ordinary meaning. Further, the legislative purpose of remedying contaminated sites will not be defeated by giving the words their ordinary meaning.

The Board concluded that Beazer had "the right of control of ... the use of real property." It did not expressly consider dictionary definitions of the word "right." ...

To be a right within the meaning of the Act, it is my view that it must be a right recognized by law. Put another way, it must be a legally enforceable right. A parent corporation does not have the legal right to control a subsidiary's use of its assets. ...

Of course, a parent corporation may have de facto control over the use of a subsidiary's assets. With the knowledge that a parent corporation can change the directors of a subsidiary and that the directors can change the officers, the management of the subsidiary may follow the directions of the parent corporation with respect to the use of its assets because the officers realize that they may be removed if they ignore those directions. However, there is a difference between a right to control and an ability to control. ...

It was open to the Legislature to define "owner" to include persons who had the capacity or ability to control the use of real property but it chose to confine the definition to persons who had the right of control of the use of the property (and persons who occupied the property or who actually controlled the use of the property). ...

Was Beazer a Previous Operator?

[T]he relevant portion of the definition of "operator" [under the *Waste Management Act* follows]:

> "operator" means ... a person who is or was in control of or responsible for any operation located at a contaminated site [s. 26(1)]. ...

The Board disagreed with the Manager's position that a parent corporation can be said to have "control of" or be "responsible for" an operation on a site by virtue of its ownership of 100% of the shares, and it examined the meaning of those terms. For the reasons I gave in connection with the interpretation of the term "owner," I agree with the Board's conclusion in this regard. ...

I agree with the Board's conclusion that the words "in control of" in the definition relate to factual control of "any operation" on the contaminated site and that there is no reason to give the words a restricted meaning so to require that there be actual control of day to day operations. I referred to the Legislature's treatment of secured creditors when considering the definition of "owner" and it also provides guidance with respect to the interpretation of the definition of "operator." Like the definition of "owner," the definition of "operator" states that it does not include a secured creditor unless it is described in s. 26.5(3). In the exclusions in s. 26.5(3), clause (c) provides that a secured creditor is not responsible for remediation if it "participates only in purely financial matters related to the site." This suggests that the Legislature intended the phrase "in control of ... any operation" in the definition of "operator" to have a broad meaning. As the Legislature found it necessary to exclude participation in financial matters by secured creditors, the Legislature must have intended the phrase "in control of ... any operation" to be sufficiently broad to cover control of financial operations at a contaminated site. ...

In general terms, it is my view that the intention of the Legislature was to include persons who made decisions or had the authority to make decisions with respect to any operation on the site. These are the persons who are potentially culpable because they were the ones who made or could have made decisions in relation to operations on the site, which may have included operations that caused or contributed to the contamination. A person who makes the decisions with respect to an operation is "in control" of the operation and a person who has the authority to make the decisions with respect to an operation is "responsible" for the operation. In my opinion, a person who is responsible for an operation is one who is accountable for the operation but the accountability is not necessarily legally enforceable. ...

In the end result, it has not been demonstrated that the Board gave an incorrect interpretation to the definition of "operator," although its reference to legal authority suggests that it may have interpreted the definition too narrowly. ...

In its decision, the Board reviewed the evidence at length and concluded that while none of the indicia were determinative in and of themselves, the totality of the evidence showed that Beazer had the requisite "control of" and "responsibility for" "any operation" at the Site.

[In conclusion, the court held that Beazer was a previous operator by virtue of its control of an operation at the site.]

NOTE

The court in *Beazer* also was asked to "lift the corporate veil" in order to impose liability on the parent company. In rejecting this approach, Tysoe J stated: "In my view, this case is not about lifting the corporate veil in the sense of making the shareholders of a corporation liable for the actions of the corporation. Rather, this case is about interpretation of the Act" (at 222). However, courts in other jurisdictions have imposed liability on parent corporations by piercing the corporate veil or assigning tort liability directly to the parent company. In the international investment context, what are the implications for parent corporations with foreign subsidiaries under various statutory, corporate, or tort theories of responsibility? See W. Braul, "Parent Corporation Liability for Foreign Subsidiaries" (2001) vol. 4, no. 4 *Environment Law* 258.

3. Lenders

Lenders potentially can be held liable for the costs of remediating the contaminated property of those who borrow from them if they assume the ownership of the property or exercise control or management of the property. Realizing on security taken on assets that happen to be environmentally contaminated lands may constitute "control" sufficient for lenders to incur liability for cleanup costs. *CNR* was one of the first environmental cases in Canada to consider the situation of mortgagees in this context.

Canadian National Railway v. Ontario
(1992), 6 CELR (NS) 211, at 218 (Ont. Ct. Gen. Div.)

III—Is a Mortgagee Who Is Not an Owner or
Person in Control, Responsible?

The Board made a finding of fact that NWP [present occupier and mortgagor] had breached the covenant in the mortgage to keep the plant in a good state of repair. The Director therefore submits that Abitibi [past occupier and mortgagee] did not take the necessary, reasonable steps to remedy the situation because it did not exercise its rights to declare the mortgage in default and enter and take control of the plant and stop further contamination. For the purpose of this case, we see no difference between a mortgage of the lease and a mortgage of land in the more normal situation.

As there was evidence of further contamination after the granting of the mortgage, the Board could express its opinion as to a default. However, such finding or opinion is not legally binding. Whether or not there was a default of the covenant sufficient to warrant a re-entry is a question of fact and law to be determined by a court. We do not find it necessary or proper to determine any such default in this case. The Board had no power to move from its own finding of default to its stated position that the mortgagee had the power to re-enter.

In the present case, the Board stated as follows [p. 184, ante] [[1990] OEAB no. 37, file nos. SINO.001.88, SINO.031.88, SINO.033.88, and SINO.034.88]:

> In economic terms, it has great control over the mortgagor since if the mortgagee decided to require the mortgagor to observe the *Environmental Protection Act* in the same way that it obliges him or her to purchase insurance or to pay the property taxes, this would greatly improve the level of compliance with the *Environmental Protection Act*.

There are good reasons why a mortgagee might want to impose such conditions in the mortgage agreement. The non-compliance with the *Environmental Protection Act* obviously diminishes the value of the security given and potentially could render the property unsalable. However, the wisdom of such practices cannot determine whether the Ministry can recover directly from the mortgagee the costs of compliance with the *Environmental Protection Act*. However, if it can be said that a right of re-entry upon default gives the mortgagee a sufficient right of "control," it is a sufficient right of control upon the mortgagor and not upon the source of contaminant. Paragraph 1(m) refers to control on the source of contaminant. It is the Board's view that a mortgagee's control is not direct enough upon the source of contamination to justify a finding that the mortgagee is a person responsible pursuant to Section 1.

For the Act to automatically cover mortgagees who are not in possession, the definition at paragraph 1(m) should be amended to provide for "owner, persons having a security interest or being in charge, management or control."

The Board did not find that the mortgagee had a sufficient, direct control of the source of the contamination to find Abitibi responsible, and deleted it from the order. We disagree with the Board's statement that the right of re-entry would give control only of the mortgagor. Mortgages usually contain both personal and property remedies. The right of re-entry under this mortgage is a property remedy and, if properly exercised, gives the mortgagee the possession and therefore the control of the property. Once in control of the property, it could be a person responsible under the Act if, at that time, it was found that the plant was the source of contaminant.

Counsel for the Director conceded that there would be no responsibility upon an innocent third-party lender under the Act, but submitted that Abitibi's connection with, and knowledge of, the site warranted a finding of responsibility. The fact that the technical, legal ownership of the plant is in the mortgagee does not make it an owner within the definition of a person responsible. To be an owner within the meaning of the Act, and subject to the serious responsibility imposed by it, there must be possession or dominion over the facility or property. (See *Wynne v. Dalby* (1913), 30 OLR 67, 16 DLR 710 (CA) at 74 [OLR].) There was no such possession or dominion by Abitibi in this case. We do not believe it makes any difference whether a mortgagee such as Abitibi had knowledge of the contamination or not. If a mortgagee has taken no active steps with respect to gaining or obtaining control of the property, it is not responsible.

In our opinion, Abitibi is not responsible as mortgagee. At best, it had the right to obtain control in the future through its remedies under the mortgage. It was not actually in control of the plant at the time of the order. [The Act is] stated in the present and not the future tense.

NOTES AND QUESTIONS

1. The Divisional Court appeared to leave open the possibility that if a mortgagee takes "active steps with respect to gaining or obtaining control of property" short of actual possession, this may bring it within the ministry's jurisdiction for purposes of being served with an order. However, the Ontario Court of Appeal, while affirming the

Divisional Court's decision, did not adopt this part of its reasoning. The Court of Appeal held that Abitibi's position as a holder of security not in possession did not bring it within s. 6 of the Act as a person having "charge, management or control of a source of contaminant" within the definition of "person responsible" in s. 1(1)(m), or within s. 17 as a person having "management or control of an undertaking or property" (*Canadian National Railway v. Ontario* (1992), 7 OR (3d) 97 (CA)). Does the Court of Appeal judgment suggest that nothing less than actual possession would have made the mortgagee subject to an order?

2. In *Ontario (Attorney General) v. Tyre King Tyre Recycling Ltd.* (1992), 9 OR (3d) 318 (Gen. Div.), it was held that a mortgagee not in possession could not be found negligent in respect of a fire that took place at a tire dump owned by its mortgagor because such a mortgagee does not have the requisite control over the property. Having the power to acquire control is insufficient to support a finding of negligence against a mortgagee. Do *CNR* and *Tyre King* implicitly reward lenders who do nothing about environmental problems, and penalize those lenders who do get involved? See M.D. Faieta, "Case Comment: Canadian National Railway v. Ontario" (1992), 6 CELR (NS) 237.

3. In *King (Township) v. Rolex Equipment Co.* (1992), 8 OR (3d) 457 (Gen. Div.), the court held that a mortgagee of land not in possession but with an illegal garbage dump on the property must decide whether it will remove the waste from the property. Where the mortgagee declines to do so, the court may appoint a receiver over the mortgagee's objections to remove waste and allow the receiver to recover the cost of removal in priority to the mortgagee's interest. The court indicated that without the removal of the waste from the property, the property was worthless because it could not be sold. Moreover, it was against the public interest that a community continue to contend with a garbage dump because a secured creditor with the greatest interest in the property refuses to take any action. Though the Ontario courts have held that an environment ministry order cannot be issued to a mortgagee not in possession, does the *Rolex* case indirectly cause the same impact on mortgagees as a remedial order issued directly to them? See D. Estrin, *Business Guide to Environmental Law* (Scarborough, ON: Carswell, 1992), at 9-20 to 9-24. On the other hand, is it in the public interest to have the ministry remedy the situation with tax dollars and then allow the mortgagee to reap the benefit by selling the property at a vastly improved price? See F. Carnerie, "Case Comment on King v. Rolex— Private Law Duties and Private Interests: The Role of Mortgagees in Waste Removal" (1992), 9 CELR (NS) 1.

4. The following case illustrates actions that a mortgagee may take without having possession of property that will constitute "charge" and "control" sufficient to attract some liability for cleanup under environmental requirements.

Re Karge
(1997), 21 CELR (NS) 5, at 9 (Ont. Env. App. Bd.)

[K sold his farm property in 1990 and took back a second mortgage on the property. The new owner, S, brought tens of thousands of used tires to the site without requisite environmental approval, buried many of them at the site as a temporary measure with the knowledge of the environment ministry, and then abandoned the property when the site began to threaten groundwater in the area. K began trying to sell the property, and was renting it to another person when the ministry issued an order to K in 1995 to remove the tires. K appealed the order to the province's Environmental Appeal Board].

Does Mr. Karge Have Charge and Control of the Land Containing the Waste?

Section 43 of the *Environmental Protection Act* provides that where waste has been deposited upon, in, into or through any land or land covered by water or in any building that has not been approved as a waste disposal site, the Director may order an owner or previous owner, an occupant or previous occupant or a person who has or had charge and control of such land or building to remove the waste and to restore the site to a condition satisfactory to the Director.

The words "charge" and "control" in this provision are not defined in the Act, nor are there any court decisions interpreting these words in the context of this section. The Director does not take the position that Mr. Karge has charge and control by virtue of holding a mortgage on the property. However, the Director argues that Mr. Karge exercised charge and control of the land by collecting rent from one or more tenants of the property and by offering the property for sale.

. . .

Ontario Courts have held in various contexts that a mortgagee does not have control of land by virtue of its rights under the mortgage unless and until it exercises those rights [*Canadian National Railway, supra*].

. . .

Unless the Court of Appeal's decision in the CN case can be taken to apply to section 43 of the *EPA* and to stand for the proposition that nothing short of actual possession will put a mortgagee in charge and control, the case law gives insufficient assistance in determining what will constitute charge and control by a lender under s. 43. In our view, however, "charge and control" in section 43 cannot be synonymous with possession, since section 43 also refers to "occupant," which connotes possession. If the Legislature intended to limit charge and control to occupation or possession of land, the word occupant would cover this. Therefore, there are actions that a mortgagee can take without having possession that will constitute charge and control under s. 43.

. . .

In our view, Mr. Karge need not actually take possession of the property to exercise charge and control. The acts of authorizing persons to occupy the property, accepting rent from them, and attempting to evict them, and restoring the property to its previous condition, for the purpose of protecting his investment in the property represent a degree of charge and control which is minimal, but still falls within the meaning of this phrase.

NOTES AND QUESTIONS

1. Despite the finding of liability in *Re Karge*, much of the liability imposed on K was relieved by the board because (1) K had not been involved in burying the tires; and (2) the ministry had been involved in overseeing their deposit and then had failed to act in a

timely manner to remedy subsequent problems. The board applied fairness principles first enunciated by it in *Re 724597 Ontario Ltd.* (1994), 13 CELR (NS) 257 and upheld in *Re 724597 Ontario Ltd.* (1995), 18 CELR (NS) 137 (Ont. Ct. Gen. Div.). Does the board's application of fairness principles and the court's endorsement of the board's jurisdiction to do so, notwithstanding a finding of liability, have the potential to create more orphaned sites; foster poorer environmental practices by owners, lenders, and others; and have a chilling effect on the ministry's issuance of orders? See J.D. Coop, "Beyond 'Appletex': The Status of 'Fairness' Litigation and the Challenges Posed by the Doctrine of 'Fairness'" (1996) vol. 7 *Journal of Environmental Law and Policy* 115, at 145-48.

2. Due to the magnitude of concern in the business and financial community about the potential liability of lenders, for a number of years, Ontario's Ministry of the Environment had been entering into individual agreements with lenders to (1) facilitate cleanup of contaminated lands and (2) minimize environmental liability. However, the business and financial communities had continuing concerns. As a result, in 1993 the ministry created a multi-stakeholder working group to provide advice on ways to achieve greater certainty for lenders. Reporting in 1995, the working group produced a discussion paper that recommended development of a standard or global agreement between the ministry and lenders. The purpose of the global agreement would be to provide lenders with assurance about the scope of their potential environmental liability for all properties on which they hold security and want to realize. Generally, the global agreement was designed to facilitate the ability of lenders to conduct environmental investigations of and otherwise protect the value of, and prepare for sale, real property on which they held security without attracting environmental liability or reaping windfall profits. In practice, however, concerns developed with the global agreement process. Although the global agreement appeared to exempt lenders from liability for cleanup, subject to certain exceptions, the global agreement also contained a provision that the ministry interpreted as requiring lenders to enter into site-specific supplementary agreements that were more onerous for lenders than the global agreement. For example, the ministry used the global agreement to prohibit the management or sale of property unless a lender would agree to provide a reserve fund through a supplementary agreement. Consequently, there was concern in the financial community that the consistency sought by the ministry in developing a global agreement applicable to all lenders that would prevent creation of new abandoned sites, would be lost if the ministry sought more onerous supplementary agreements in each case. This was of particular concern because there was no authority for the agreement process under any statute administered by the ministry.

3. To resolve this unsettled state of affairs, Ontario recently enacted Bill 56, the *Brownfields Statute Law Amendment Act, 2001*, which codifies the global agreement concept as a matter of Ontario law. In this regard, Bill 56 includes two categories of amendments to the *Environmental Protection Act* designed to protect secured creditors. The first category will provide secured creditors with protection from environmental liability while they protect their security interests. In particular, secured creditors not in possession are permitted to undertake a variety of prescribed actions without attracting liability for specific ministry orders. These actions include investigating and providing services to property, paying taxes, collecting rent, and responding to the presence or discharge of a contaminant on the property (s. 168.17). The second category will protect

secured creditors when they foreclose on a property. Secured creditors that foreclose on a property are protected from the issuance of a ministry order for five years from the date of foreclosure unless they engage in gross negligence, wilful misconduct, or other circumstances that may be prescribed by the regulations (s. 168.18).

4. Despite the amendments, Bill 56 has not eliminated the potential of imposing environmental liability on secured creditors in Ontario. The amendments allow the ministry to issue orders to a secured creditor who has foreclosed on a property where the province believes that a contaminant on the property poses a danger to human health or safety, serious risk of impairment to the natural environment, or serious risk of injury to property (s. 168.20). Although these instances are characterized as "exceptional circumstances" under Bill 56, will this characterization eliminate liability concerns in the financial community? See R. Curpen, S. Elliot, and D. Kirby, "Ontario Brownfields Bill Passed with Mixed Opinions" (2002) vol. 5, no. 2 *Environment Law* 290, at 293-94.

5. Other jurisdictions have also dealt with the issue of lender liability directly through legislation. British Columbia's *Waste Management Act*, RSBC 1996, c. 482 (Part 4—Contaminated Site Remediation) treats lenders as persons responsible for remediating contaminated sites, subject to certain exemptions. Statutory excerpts follow.

Waste Management Act
RSBC 1996, c. 482

26(1) In this Part:

"*secured creditor*" means a person who holds a mortgage, charge, debenture, hypothecation or other security interest in property at a contaminated site. ...

Division 3—Liability

Persons Responsible for Remediation at Contaminated Sites

. . .

26.5(3) A secured creditor is responsible for remediation at a contaminated site if

(a) the secured creditor at any time exercised control over or imposed requirements on any person regarding the manner of treatment, disposal or handling of a substance and the control or requirements, in whole or in part, caused the site to become a contaminated site, or

(b) the secured creditor becomes the registered owner in fee simple of the real property at the contaminated site, but a secured creditor is not responsible for remediation if it acts primarily to protect its security interest, including, without limitation, if the secured creditor

(c) participates only in purely financial matters related to the site,

(d) has the capacity or ability to influence any operation at the contaminated site in a way that would have the effect of causing or increasing contamination, but does not exercise that capacity or ability in such a way as to cause or increase contamination,

(e) imposes requirements on any person if the requirements do not have a reasonable probability of causing or increasing contamination at the site, or

(f) appoints a person to inspect or investigate a contaminated site to determine
future steps or actions that the secured creditor might take.

NOTES AND QUESTIONS

1. The attempt to limit the liability of lenders under BC law is based on CERCLA
(s. 9607(a)(2), above), as amended in 1996. See W. Braul, *Liability Features of Bill 26*,
above, at 151-55. As long as the lender has not participated in management, it is not
liable under CERCLA, even if it later forecloses. However, the lender must seek to sell at
the "earliest practicable, commercially reasonable time, on commercially reasonable
terms, taking into account market conditions and legal and regulatory requirements." See
CERCLA, 42 USCA, s. 9601(20)(E).

2. Pursuant to the Contaminated Site Regulations, BC reg. 375/96, s. 25, secured
creditors in British Columbia also will not become responsible for contaminated site
remediation if they impose requirements on persons to comply with environmental laws;
participate in loan workout actions; take steps to preserve, protect, and enhance the value
of secured assets or reduce environmental contamination; or undertake realization proceedings, as long as they do not become the fee simple owner of the contaminated site.

3. Compare the Ontario, BC, and US approaches to issues of lender liability. Which
approach is preferable? To what extent can cautious lenders prevent potentially "dirty"
developments by refusing financing?

4. Receivers and Receiver-Managers

Receivers are appointed by creditors or pursuant to court order to take possession and
control of the property of bankrupt or insolvent persons. Receiver-managers have the
further responsibility of carrying on the business of the debtor. Receivers and receiver-
managers can attract environmental liability where such properties are contaminated and
made the subject of cleanup orders under environmental legislation. The following case
was the first in Canada to find that the costs of environmental cleanup take priority over a
secured party's claim in the distribution of the assets of an insolvent party.

Panamericana de Bienes y Servicios SA v. Northern Badger Oil & Gas Ltd.
(1992), 7 CELR (NS) 66, at 69 (Alta. CA)

LAYCRAFT CJA: The issue on this appeal is whether the *Bankruptcy Act*, RSC 1985,
c. B-3, prevents the court-appointed receiver-manager of an insolvent and bankrupt
oil company from complying with an order of the Energy Resources Conservation
Board of the province of Alberta. The order required the receiver-manager, in the
interests of environmental safety, to carry out proper abandonment procedures on
seven suspended oil wells. In Court of Queen's Bench, Mr. Justice MacPherson held
[at 191 Alta. LR] that the order requiring "the abandonment and the securing of potentially dangerous well sites is at the expense of the secured creditors' entitlement"

under the *Bankruptcy Act* and is "beyond the province's constitutional powers." He directed the receiver-manager not to comply with the order. For the reasons which follow, I respectfully disagree with that conclusion and would allow the appeal by the board.

. . .

[T]he direct issue in this litigation, in my opinion, is whether the *Bankruptcy Act* requires that the assets in the estate of an insolvent well licensee should be distributed to creditors leaving behind the duties respecting environmental safety, which are liabilities, as a charge to the public.

. . .

IV Did the Board Have a Provable Claim in the Bankruptcy?

There are two aspects to the question whether the board had a "provable claim" in the bankruptcy. The first is whether Northern Badger had a liability; the second is whether that liability is to the board so that it is the board which is the creditor. I respectfully agree that Northern Badger had a liability, inchoate from the day the wells were drilled, for their ultimate abandonment. It was one of the expenses, inherent in the nature of the properties themselves, taken over for management by the receiver. With respect, I do not agree, however, that the public officer or public authority given the duty of enforcing a public law thereby becomes a "creditor" of the person bound to obey it.

The statutory provisions requiring the abandonment of oil and gas wells are part of the general law of Alberta, binding every citizen of the province. All who become licensees of oil and gas wells are bound by them. Similar statutory obligations bind citizens in many other areas of modern life. Rules relating to health, or the prevention of fires, or the clearing of ice and snow, or the demolition of unsafe structures are examples which come to mind. But the obligation of the citizen is not to the peace officer, or public authority which enforces the law. The duty is owed as a public duty by all the citizens of the community to their fellow citizens. When the citizen subject to the order complies, the result is not the recovery of money by the peace officer or public authority, or of a judgment for money, nor is that the object of the whole process. Rather, it is simply the enforcement of the general law. The enforcing authority does not become a "creditor" of the citizen on whom the duty is imposed.

[The court noted that although the board had the power under the *Oil and Gas Conservation Act* to do the abandonment work itself and become a creditor for the sums expended, it had not done so. Rather it was simply enforcing observance of a part of the general law of Alberta.]

In my view, the board is not, at this point, a "creditor" of Northern Badger with a claim provable in its bankruptcy. The problem presented by this case is not to be solved, therefore, by determining whether the board ranks as a creditor of Northern Badger before or after the secured creditors. Rather it must be determined whether the receiver, which was the operator of the oil wells in question, had a duty to abandon them in accordance with the law.

V The Duties of the Receiver

A receiver appointed by the court must act fairly and honestly as a fiduciary on behalf of all parties with an interest in the debtor's property and undertaking. The receiver is not the agent of the debtor or the creditor or of any other party, but has the duty of care, supervision and control which a reasonable person would exercise in the circumstances. The receiver may be liable for failure to exercise an appropriate standard of care. ...

It is also clear that the receiver takes full responsibility for the management, operation and care of the debtor's assets, but does not take legal title to them. ...

A further factor affecting the obligation of a court-appointed receiver is the receiver's status as an officer of the court; the standard required because of that status is one of meticulous correctness. ...

In the present case it is clear that almost from the commencement of the receivership, the receiver was aware of the obligation, in law, of Northern Badger to see the oil and gas wells properly abandoned. The correspondence from the board detailed the obligation for the proper operation of the wells and the ultimate abandonment of them. ...

VI Conclusion

In my opinion the board had the power, when authorized by the Lieutenant Governor in Council, to order the abandonment of the wells by some person. The order was clearly within the general regulatory scheme, and within the expressed purposes, of both of the statutes regulating the oil and gas industry. ...

The receiver has had complete control of the wells and has operated them since May 1987, when it was appointed receiver and manager of them. It has carried out for more than three years activities with respect to the wells which only a licensee is authorized to do under the provisions of the *Oil and Gas Conservation Act*. In that position, it cannot pick and choose as to whether an operation is profitable or not in deciding whether to carry it out. If one of the wells of which a receiver has chosen to take control should blow out of control or catch fire, for example, it would be a remarkable rule of law which would permit him to walk away from the disaster saying simply that remedial action would diminish distribution to secured creditors.

While the receiver was in control of the wells, there was no other entity with whom the board could deal. An order addressed to Northern Badger would have been fruitless. That is so because, by order of the court, upon the application of the debenture holder, neither Northern Badger nor its trustee in bankruptcy had any right even to enter the well sites or to undertake any operation with respect to them. Moreover, under the regulatory scheme for Alberta oil wells, only a licensee is entitled to produce oil and gas. The receiver cannot be heard to say that, while functioning as a licensee to produce the wells and to profit from them, it assumed none of a licensee's obligations. ...

The Alberta legislation regulating oil and gas wells ... is a statute of general application within a valid provincial power. It is general law regulating the operation of oil and gas wells, and safe practices relating to them, for the protection of the public. It is not aimed at subversion of the scheme of distribution under the *Bankruptcy Act* though it may incidentally affect that distribution in some cases. It does so, not by a direct conflict in operation, but because compliance by the receiver with the general law means that less money will be available for distribution.

NOTES AND QUESTIONS

1. The Alberta Court of Appeal's affirmation of the Board's order in *Panamericana* resulted in the receiver-manager having to allocate approximately $200,000 from the funds realized on the sale of the bankrupt company's assets for proper environmental cleanup and sealing of the abandoned wells. This left virtually nothing to be distributed to the secured creditor. What if the cleanup had cost more than the funds available to the receiver-manager from sale of the bankrupt's assets? Would the receiver-manager have been liable for the difference?

2. In 1997, Parliament answered this question by enacting a series of amendments to the *Bankruptcy and Insolvency Act*, RSC 1985, c. B-3, ss. 14.06(2)-(8) (SC 1997, c. 12, s. 15). These amendments expanded and extended to receivers (and interim receivers), the protection from personal liability already available under the statute to trustees in bankruptcy. In particular, the amendments remove from receivers personal liability under federal or provincial law for any environmental condition or damage that arose before the receiver's appointment. For environmental conditions or damage arising after the appointment, liability only attaches to the receiver if there has been gross negligence or wilful misconduct. In addition, if an order is made under federal or provincial law requiring the receiver to remedy an environmental condition, the receiver may comply with the order, abandon the property, contest the order, or apply for a stay of the order. The purpose of the application for a stay of the order is to allow the receiver the opportunity to assess the economic viability of complying with the order (s. 14.06(5)). If the receiver abandons any interest in the real property (for example, if the costs of remedying environmental damage exceed the value of the property), the costs to remedy the damage do not rank as a cost of administration but are only an unsecured claim (s. 14.06(6)). However, any federal or provincial government claim for the costs of remedying environmental damage affecting real property of the debtor is a secured claim and ranks in priority to all other claims (s. 14.06(7)).

3. Have the 1997 amendments struck the right balance between protecting the public from environmental harm and protecting receivers (and trustees in bankruptcy) and the social function that they perform in a bankruptcy? See D. Saxe, "Trustees' and Receivers' Environmental Liability Update" (1998), 49 CBR (3d) 138.

4. The environmental liability of receivers also has been expressly limited in provincial legislation. Under Alberta's *Environmental Protection and Enhancement Act*, SA 2000, c. E-12, s. 107, receivers or receiver-managers are defined as "persons responsible" who can be issued environmental protection orders in connection with contaminated sites. However, s. 240(3) limits the liability of receivers or receiver-managers to the value of the assets that they are administering unless the situation identified in the order resulted from or was aggravated by their gross negligence or willful misconduct.

5. British Columbia does not obligate receivers to personally remediate sites that were contaminated on the date that the receiver became the owner or operator of the site unless the receiver exercised control or imposed requirements over persons regarding the management of substances, was grossly negligent or guilty of wilful misconduct in the exercise of such control, and the control requirements caused the site to become contaminated. The Contaminated Sites Regulation, BC reg. 375/96, s. 26(3) requires a receiver to carry out remediation at a contaminated site only to the extent of available funds and only during the term of the appointment. Under the regulation, available funds refers to those funds left after the receiver and secured and trade creditors have been paid, and borrowed funds by the receiver have been taken into account (s. 26(1)).

6. Bill 56, Ontario's new "brownfields law" that amends the *Environmental Protection Act*, limits the province's authority to issue a cleanup order to a receiver unless the order arises from the gross negligence or willful misconduct of the receiver, or other circumstances to be prescribed by the regulations. This is the case even in situations of environmental emergency if the receiver also notifies the province within a prescribed time period after being served with the order of its abandonment or disposal of interest in the property to which the order relates, or if the order has been stayed under the federal bankruptcy legislation. See SO 2001, c. 17, ss. 168.19(1) and 168.20(1), (2), and (7).

7. Compare the above laws from Alberta, British Columbia, and Ontario with federal requirements under the *Bankruptcy and Insolvency Act*. Has consistency in approach across the country been achieved on the issue of the liability of receivers for environmental damage? To what extent, if any, are any of the above provincial laws pre-empted by the 1997 federal amendments? Note that the provincial rules also apply to trustees in bankruptcy.

8. Injured third parties also have applied to the courts for leave to commence actions against receivers and receiver-managers for environmental damage arising from the management of the bankrupt's business. See *Mortgage Insurance Co. of Canada v. Innisfil Landfill Corp.* (1996), 20 CELR (NS) 19 and 37; (1997), 23 CELR (NS) 288 (Ont. Ct. Gen. Div.—Comm. List). The Bill 56 amendments, above, do not protect receivers from civil liability. Should they?

5. Trustees in Bankruptcy

Federal bankruptcy and insolvency law permits trustees in bankruptcy to be appointed by courts to administer the estates of bankrupt persons. Property owned by the bankrupt becomes the responsibility of the trustee for the purposes of selling assets and distributing the sale proceeds to creditors. If the bankrupt's property is contaminated, a trustee confronts the same potential liability problems faced by other potentially responsible persons. However, even before amendments by Parliament to federal bankruptcy law, the courts had been prepared to treat trustees somewhat better than other potentially responsible parties, as illustrated by *Re Lamford Forest Products Ltd.* (1992), 8 CELR (NS) 186, at 188 (BCSC). In that case, a bankrupt sawmill made a voluntary assignment in bankruptcy in 1990. The site was contaminated with heavy metals and other toxic substances as a result of lumber treatment activities connected with the sawmill business. A provincial pollution abatement order was issued to the company that if complied with would absorb, if not exceed, all the proceeds without payment to secured or other creditors. If the order was not complied with, substantial penalties would follow. The official receiver brought a motion for directions, and the court held:

> The balancing of values in this case falls in favour of protecting the health and safety of society over the rights of creditors, as it did in the *Bulora* and the *Panamericana* case, but there is also a need in modern society for trustees to take on the duty of winding up insolvent estates. ... [N]o trustee can be found who will take on the bankruptcy of Lamford without a guarantee that he or she will be entitled to trustee's fees to be deducted from the amount paid out under the order, and will have no personal liability for the costs of cleanup of the contaminated site ... . I direct that in the event that there are insufficient funds to meet the requirements of the order, the payment of funds pursuant to the order must be subject to a reduction equal to the amount of the trustee's fees.

Amendments in 1992 to the *Bankruptcy and Insolvency Act*, RSC 1985, c. B-3, s. 14.06(2) (SC 1992, c. 27, s. 9(1)) exempted a trustee in bankruptcy from personal liability under environmental legislation if the harm occurred before the trustee's appointment, or after the appointment, unless the damage occurred as a result of the trustee's failure to exercise due diligence.

QUESTIONS

Did the 1992 amendments to the Act codify the result in *Lamford* respecting exempting the trustee from liability for pre-appointment environmental contamination? In 1997, further amendments to the Act extended this exemption from liability to receivers and receiver-managers. In addition, the 1997 amendments also changed the standard of care during administration of the bankrupt's estate for trustees (and receivers or receiver managers) from due diligence to gross negligence or wilful misconduct. Do you agree with the standard of care chosen? See V. Dumoulin and A.M. Sheahan, "Environmental Liability: Proposed Amendments to the Bankruptcy and Insolvency Act" (1996) vol. 5 *Digest of Environmental Law and Environmental Assessment* 85, at 86, 105-6.

6. Liquidators

Although amendments to federal bankruptcy and insolvency laws have limited the liability of receivers and trustees in bankruptcy for environmental damage to property, other federal statutes that regulate the windup and restructuring of businesses have not limited the liability of those responsible under these laws for liquidation of such estates.

For example, in *Canadian Deposit Insurance Corp. v. Canadian Commercial Bank* (2000), 34 CELR (NS) 127 (Alta. QB) a liquidator was appointed to wind up the bank's estate. The liquidator applied to the court for direction regarding its potential liability arising from environmental claims against properties owned by the bank in the United States, that were realized by the liquidator during the course of the liquidation. The court examined the scope of the protection offered by s. 76(2) of the *Winding-up and Restructuring Act*, RSC 1985, c. W-11 (WURA), which states:

> (2) The liquidator is not liable to any person whose claim has not been sent in at the time of distributing the assets or part thereof under.

The court also reviewed ss. 14.06(2)-(8) of the *Bankruptcy and Insolvency Act*, above, relating to the limitation of environmental liability afforded to trustees and receivers under that Act, and similar provisions under the *Companies' Creditors Arrangement Act*, RSC, 1985, c. C-36, noting that sections in these Acts "expressly protect the representative of creditors from environmental claims" but there is no such section in WURA. The court held that it "should not assume that Parliament intended ... WURA to be interpreted as including sections that were not expressly included" and that "[a]ccordingly, the only interpretation which Parliament could have intended for s. 76(2) is one which excludes protection of the liquidator against environmental claims arising during the liquidation."

Given the similarity in purposes among the various federal statutes examined in this case and the decision of Parliament to limit the environmental liability of trustees in bankruptcy and receivers under federal bankruptcy and insolvency laws, one may question what policy rationale, if any, justifies the continued environmental liability of liquidators under WURA. See F. Coburn and G. Manning, *Toxic Real Estate Manual* (Aurora, ON: Canada Law Book, 2001), at II-46.4.

7. Government

In theory, any level of government may be liable for environmental cleanup of contaminated land. In practice, municipal governments may be more exposed than any other government level for several reasons. First, municipalities may have abandoned or derelict land within their territory. Second, municipalities are responsible for both controlling and fostering real property development and redevelopment under provincial planning and related legislation. Third, municipalities may acquire property as a result of unpaid municipal taxes.

Accordingly, to facilitate the redevelopment of brownfields, some provinces have enacted legislation that limits municipal environmental liability in a manner that parallels the protections provided to secured creditors and their representatives. Bill 56, Ontario's brownfields law, which amended the province's *Environmental Protection Act*, exempts municipalities from a variety of environmental orders for the following activities:

Environmental Protection Act
SO 2001, c. 17

168.12(2) ...

1. Any action taken for the purpose of conducting, completing or confirming an investigation relating to non-municipal property. ...

2. preserving or protecting non-municipal property [for example, provision of various necessities, services, and securities]. ...

3. responding to [health or safety dangers to persons, risks to the environment, or damage to any property from the presence of] contaminants on, in or under property. ...

4. [exercising] a right under any Act to collect rent or levy by distress in relation to an unpaid amount. ...

5. [acting] for the purpose of the *Municipal Tax Sales Act*. ...

6. [acting] for the purpose of [ensuring building code and fire protection compliance].

NOTES AND QUESTIONS

1. The law reforms also allow municipalities, who become owners of contaminated properties because of failed tax sales, from becoming subject to environmental orders with respect to the properties for five years. However, municipalities can lose this protection if there is gross negligence or wilful misconduct by the municipality or if there are exceptional circumstances such as harm or risk to persons, the natural environment, or other property (ss. 168.13 and 168.14). Also, there are other exceptions to the liability protections offered and there is no protection from civil (or quasi-criminal) liability. Some commentators have described the protections offered to municipalities and other potentially responsible persons as "qualified immunities" that may or may not result in the redevelopment of brownfields. Do you agree? See Mahoney, above, at 7-12. See also Curpen et al., "Ontario Passes Brownfields Bill with Mixed Opinions," above, at 294.

2. What are the environmental risks and benefits associated with rapid facilitation of brownfield redevelopment? See J.F. Castrilli, "Hazardous Wastes and Brownfields," in *Sixth Annual Report on Ontario's Environment* (Toronto: Canadian Institute for Environmental Law and Policy, 2002), 55, at 69-70.

IV. INSURANCE

As private actions and government regulatory initiatives increase the scope and magnitude of environmental liability for contaminated lands, potentially responsible persons are seeking insurance protection to cover the costs of environmental claims and government orders. The extent to which comprehensive general liability insurance, special purpose environmental impairment liability insurance, or other types of insurance provide coverage for such persons is governed by exclusion clauses contained in these insurance policies. As this chapter already has noted, governments themselves may face environmental liability. The following case illustrates the effect of a pollution exclusion clause in a policy of insurance in the context of a claim of negligence against the government.

R v. Kansa General Insurance Co.
(1994), 13 CELR (NS) 59 (Ont. CA)

[In 1988 a landowner commenced an action against an adjacent landowner R.K. and her tenants alleging that environmental pollutants had escaped from their lands onto the plaintiff's. R.K. issued a third-party claim against the Crown alleging the negligence of its officers in responding to the pollution problem. The Crown advised its insurer, KGI, of the third-party claim. KGI undertook to defend the claim without prejudice to its right to dispute coverage or indemnity in light of the pollution exclusion clause in the insurance policy. KGI subsequently asked the Crown to assume defence of the proceedings. The Crown applied for an order requiring KGI to defend the action. A motions judge held that the pollution exclusion clause applied only to exclude coverage to an insured who actively engaged in polluting activities. He ordered

KGI to defend the action without prejudice to its right to deny coverage at a later time if the Crown was shown to be a polluter within the meaning of the exclusion clause. KGI appealed the order to defend.

KGI had issued a comprehensive general liability insurance policy ("Policy") to the Crown, which provided that the insurer would pay all sums that the insured became obliged to pay for damages arising from property damage caused by accident or occurrence as covered by the Policy.

The Policy contained the following exclusion:

This Policy shall not apply to claims arising out of:

(i) the discharge, dispersal, release or escape of smoke, vapours, soot, fumes, acids, alkalis, toxic chemicals, liquids or gases, waste materials or other irritants, contaminants or pollutants into or upon land, the atmosphere or any water of any description no matter where located or how contained, or into any water-course, drainage or sewage system.

The Court of Appeal held that American cases are not persuasive in the Canadian context and would not form a sound basis for the interpretation of the pollution exclusion clause in the Policy, because the pollution exclusion clauses in those cases were all less absolute than the clause in question, which excluded coverage even for sudden and accidental pollution.]

LABROSSE JA: Even if I assume, for the sake of argument, that the pollution exclusion clause in the Policy operates only against an "active" or "actual" polluter, the Crown is faced with a serious difficulty in light of s. 14(1) of the *Environmental Protection Act*, RSO 1990, c. E.19. ...

Section 14(1) creates three kinds of polluters: those who discharge a contaminant, those who cause the discharge of a contaminant and those who permit the discharge of a contaminant. The Crown concedes that, if the allegations of the Krieser claim [R.K.] are made out, it would be included in the third class of polluter. Under Ontario law, the passive polluter who permits pollution to take place is just as much a polluter as the active polluter who discharges or causes the discharge of pollution. The Crown's argument that it could not be considered an active polluter, within the meaning of the American cases, therefore does not assist it under Ontario law.

There is no dispute between the parties regarding the principles which are relevant to the insurer's duty to defend. They were stated by McLachlin J in *Nichols v. American Home Assurance Co.*, [1990] 1 SCR 801. The duty to defend arises when the allegations in the pleadings raise claims which might be payable under the agreement to indemnify in the insurance contract: the mere possibility that a claim may succeed is sufficient. If there is any ambiguity in the contract, it must be resolved in favour of the insured. The duty to defend is broader than the duty to indemnify since it is not necessary for the insured to establish that the obligation to indemnify will, in fact, arise in order to trigger the duty to defend.

The Policy issued to the Crown provided very broad coverage. The insurer agreed to pay all sums which the insured became obligated to pay, by law or by agreement, for damages arising from property damage caused by an accident or occurrence. The claim to which the Policy refers, in relation to the insurer's duty to defend, is any action brought against the Crown for an occurrence under the Policy. ... [I]t has been conceded that the Crown's alleged negligence in fulfilling its regulatory duty falls within the definition of "occurrence" under the Policy and, therefore, obliges Kansa [KGI] to defend the Krieser claim. The exclusion clause, however, denies coverage where the claim arises out of the discharge of pollutants upon land. The issue then becomes whether the Crown's alleged regulatory negligence falls within the pollution exclusion clause. The negligence relates to a failure to recognize, advise and respond to environmental contamination. The third party seeks contribution and indemnity for damages caused by the unstemmed pollution as a result of the Crown's failure to act.

The Crown argues that the Krieser claim is one of regulatory negligence rather than a claim for pollution. The exclusion is for claims in which it is possible to trace a continuous chain of causation, unbroken by the interposition of a new act of negligence, between the discharge of pollutants and the losses sustained by the claimant. The losses alleged in the Krieser claim were caused by the Crown's intervening acts of negligence in failing to disclose and advise, in failing to respond to the pollution problem and in failing to fulfil its statutory duty: the exclusion clause, therefore, is inapplicable to Krieser's claim against the Crown.

The appellant's position is that the words "claims arising out" in the exclusion clause refer to the event or occurrence from which the claim arose (i.e. the pollution) and not the cause of action alleged against the insured (i.e. the negligence). The appropriate test for determining whether damages arise out of a claim is to apply the chain of causation test. The regulatory negligence of the Crown is not an intervening act which takes the occurrence or the damages outside the scope of the pollution exclusion clause. Damages resulting from a failure to regulate or a failure to warn of the release of pollutants constitute damages arising from the discharge of pollutants. The Crown's alleged negligence was merely incidental to the primary event of pollution and constituted a continuing cause rather than a new and independent cause giving rise to the loss.

. . .

To succeed the appellant must, therefore, show that the Krieser claim is based on circumstances in which it is possible to trace a continuous chain of causation, unbroken by the interposition of a new act of negligence, between the pollution at #39 Fenmar Drive and the damages sustained by Rose Krieser. In my opinion, the Crown's alleged negligence cannot be divorced from the discharge of pollutants which caused the damages and, therefore, the claim falls within the exclusion. The damages claimed by Rose Krieser arise from the contamination of the lands at #39 Fenmar Drive and the alleged regulatory negligence does not constitute an intervening act, ... which breaks the chain of causation. The fact that it is the negligence of the Crown's officers in carrying out their regulatory duty to enforce the environmental legislation rather than the negligence of the Crown's officers in, for example, transporting toxic material which gave rise to the discharge of pollutants, does not change the nature of the occurrence and, hence, of the claim. The regulatory negligence can do no more than exacerbate the damages: there would be no loss without the pollution.

[The court allowed the appeal, set aside the order, and dismissed the Crown's application for a declaration that Kansa must defend the third party claim brought against the Crown.]

NOTES AND QUESTIONS

1. *Kansa* is one of the first cases in Canada to consider absolute pollution exclusion clauses in a comprehensive general liability insurance policy. What are the implications of this decision for insurance coverage of environmental damage? See A.R. Hudson and J.K. Friesen, "Environmental Coverage Under Comprehensive General Liability Insurance Policies in Canada" (1995) vol. 5 *Journal of Environmental Law and Practice* 141, 156-60.

2. Special purpose environmental liability insurance policies that attempt to cover, not exclude, pollution increasingly are considered by persons engaging in activities with a high risk of environmental harm. However, these policies present their own problems for insured persons and insurers. See D.R. Cameron, *Environmental Concerns in Business Transactions: Avoiding the Risks* (Toronto: Butterworths, 1993), at 79; and L.A. Reynolds, "New Directions for Environmental Liability Insurance in Canada" (1996) vol. 6 *Journal of Environmental Law and Practice* 89.

3. The use of environmental insurance policies is also seen as a method to facilitate redevelopment of brownfields because it can facilitate transactions by reducing risk and uncertainty for developers and lenders. See D. Kirby, S. Elliot, and K. Dobson, "Insurance Is a Risk Management Tool for Brownfields" (2001) vol. 4, no. 4 *Environment Law* 263, at 265.

4. What role do insurers play in ensuring that the "polluter pays"? To the extent that an insurer provides environmental liability impairment insurance coverage to high-risk industrial and commercial interests under strict standards, does the insurer effectively become a *de facto* environmental regulator? Is that good or bad? See L. Reynolds, above, at 207-10.

FURTHER READINGS

Commissioner of the Environment and Sustainable Development (CESD), *The Legacy of Federal Contaminated Sites* (Ottawa: CESD, 2002).

"Remediation and Restoration of Contaminated Land," chapter 11, in J. Benedickson, *Environmental Law*, 2d ed. (Toronto: Irwin Law, 2002).

CHAPTER NINE

Enforcement and Compliance*

Linda F. Duncan

I. INTRODUCTION

While considerable attention has been dedicated toward achieving sustainable development through improved environmental protection standards, environmental indicators, pollution prevention, and the avoidance of development-related disputes, one component of this complex equation continues to be underappreciated. That component is enforcement and compliance. A dichotomy of views persist on the respective merits of strictly enforced regulatory models versus voluntary or market-driven models for achieving sustainable development. Most Canadian environmental regimes, however, have adopted some form of middle ground: experience proving that the most practicable and efficacious route is some combination of strategic enforcement action and measures to foster "voluntary compliance."

This chapter first clarifies the terms "enforcement" and "compliance" and then surveys a selection of triggers for effective enforcement and recent Canadian innovations toward an improved environmental enforcement and compliance regime, including

1. the international drivers for effective domestic environmental enforcement action;
2. a sampling of the diverse enforcement and compliance strategies and approaches toward a framework for effective enforcement;
3. a trend toward greater delegation of enforcement roles;
4. innovative approaches to sanctioning environmental violators; and
5. examples of private enforcement initiatives.

II. DEFINING ENFORCEMENT AND COMPLIANCE

At the outset, it is helpful to have a clear understanding of the terms "enforcement" and "compliance" and the evolution in their usage in Canada. Enforcement is commonly and, in many instances, inaccurately equated with one limited response to non-compliance,

---

* The author gratefully acknowledges the research assistance of Leesa Sylyski and Andrea Hilland, as well as the kind assistance provided by Erica Gerlock, Alberta Justice.

namely the prosecution and incarceration of offenders. In practice, this is an oversimplistic and dated view of the breadth and variety of mechanisms now used by Canadian environmental authorities to ensure that standards and targets are observed. This narrow characterization of enforcement (and its purported limitations) is used as the premise for replacing traditional enforcement—"command and control"—with other, more flexible means.

Similarly, the term "compliance" has often been misconstrued and misapplied. During the early period of environmental regulation, agencies commonly measured and reported environmental compliance using vague guidelines that were outside the constructs of the law. See B. Smart, *Beyond Compliance: A New Industry View of the Environment* (Washington, DC: World Resources Institute, 1992). This approach followed naturally from a largely technical perspective within many agencies that most environmental non-compliance represents a mere technical blip on monitoring records. Accordingly, the response deemed appropriate has often been technical advice, not intervention. The result, according to some legal scholars and practitioners, was constructive deregulation by virtue of a persistent pattern of non-enforcement. See J. Swaigen, *Regulatory Offences in Canada: Liability & Defences* (Scarborough, ON: Carswell, 1992).

Not surprisingly, supporters of a non-interventionist philosophy embrace private, non-regulatory systems for establishing and verifying "standards" of practice. Industry-led initiatives such as voluntary codes of practice, and the ISO 14000 environmental management system seek to replace government-dictated standards with industry-dictated, self-imposed, non-binding, and self-audited guidelines shrouded in regulatory terminology (for example, standards, certification, and compliance).

As a counterpoise to this shift to self-regulation, enforcers and the public have sought more strategic means for responding to violators.

L.F. Duncan
"Effective Environmental Enforcement: The Missing Link to
Sustainable Development"
(LLM thesis, Dalhousie University, Dalhousie Law School, 1999),
at 13-18 (edited)

Enforcement

Enforcement is any government or private action or intervention taken to determine or respond to non-compliance. While enforcement is commonly equated with criminal prosecution, this is neither an accurate nor complete portrayal of environmental law enforcement. For many jurisdictions, environmental enforcement now characteristically involves a wide array of administrative, criminal and mediative tools to effect compliance, and to mitigate or prevent environmental damage.

For example, enforcement includes procedures to screen new or existing laws or permits to ensure compliance in the most cost efficient manner. Enforcement includes policies and programs to encourage or recognize voluntary efforts towards compliance (audit privilege, self-reporting), government surveillance and private enforcement action. Some have suggested enforcement also includes the means to establish liability or responsibility for harm. (C. Wasserman, *Proceedings of the Third International Conference on Environmental Enforcement*, vol. I, April 25-28, 1994, Oaxaca, Mexico (Washington, DC: US EPA et al., 1994), at 16).

Enforcement is more than punishment after the fact. It includes the process of creating binding standards or imposing liability. It includes accountability for ensuring compliance, inclusive of the obligation to comply, and the duty to enforce. It includes the rights and responsibilities associated with exercising enforcement powers.

It is similarly important to understand that the measurement of effective enforcement reflects more than the tally of enforcement actions or compliance statistics. It also includes less tangible and more complex concepts such as environmental results and deterrence. As noted by one experienced US Environmental Protection Agency enforcement official:

> The primary goal of environmental enforcement is to ensure compliance in order to protect the environment and public health. However, despite the central importance of compliance rates and the aggregate level of enforcement activity, they are not, by themselves, the only indicators of a healthy enforcement program. Other measures may indicate whether or not the overall environmental benefits of laws and regulations are being achieved. While a lot has been analyzed and written about the US environmental protection effort, we are still learning about the efficacy of our programs and our concept of environmental "success" continues to be both dynamic and evolving. As EPA's environmental enforcement program has matured, the concept of "success" itself has become more complex and multi-faceted. It encompasses not only the concept of high rates of compliance and aggregate numbers of enforcement actions, but also the important, albeit more difficult to measure, concept of environmental results and deterrence. (R. van Heuvelen, "Successful Compliance and Enforcement Approaches," Proceedings of the Third International Conference on Environmental Enforcement, Vol. I, April 25-28, 1994, Oaxaca, Mexico, [unpublished] at 163)

Compliance

Compliance is the achievement of a prescribed process or standard. For those governments operating within a system premised on the "Rule of Law," compliance is understood to mean observation of the law. Some enforcement and compliance policies have specifically endorsed this direct connection to adherence to law. For example, the *Canadian Environmental Protection Act Enforcement and Compliance Policy* states that "[c]ompliance means a state of conforming with the law" (Minister of the Environment, Government of Canada, May 1998).

While such statements may appear axiomatic, many governments have deemed it necessary to issue enforcement and compliance policies to replace compliance ratings based on imprecise guidelines or shifting technical objectives. It is now widely accepted that a more accurate and consistent measurement of compliance is adherence to a legally imposed and consistent standard. Compliance objectives can be prescribed by statute, regulation, license or permit, compliance agreement (where provided for by law) or through administrative directives or court order.

Determinations of compliance are also not limited to measurement of adherence to specified pollution standards. It is equally significant to regulations which implement alternative implementation strategies such as economic or market instruments. For example, when implementing a system of pollution control through trading effluent rights or opportunities, government must first establish minimum effluent standards and then establish a system for trading permits or marketing surplus, and maintain a monitoring system for both the pollution levels and an audit of the trading. There is growing appreciation for the complexity of compliance assessments for market approaches.

Compliance also relates to procedural rules. By way of example, compliance is achieved if a government agency responsible for conduct of an environmental assessment of a proposed project ensures that the procedures dictated by law are observed, such as appointment of an unbiased and qualified panel, opportunities [are] accorded to the affected public to participate and recommended conditions are implemented. (See: *Friends of the Oldman River v. Canada (Minister of Transport)*, [1992] 1 SCR 3).

Accountability for compliance with prescribed codes of conduct is also recognized as a critical determinant for liability and compensation. Clear evidence of this can be found in judicial decisions on director liability for environmental damages including determinations on factors such as due diligence. (See for example: *R v. Bata Industries* (1992), 70 CCC (3d) 394 (Ont. Prov. Ct.). Similarly, the courts have held that with the decision to impose standards comes the duty to ensure compliance, that is, to inspect and enforce. (See for example: *Swanson Estate v. Canada* (1990), 19 ACWS (3d) 810 (FCTD).

Compliance, then, is the end objective or result. Enforcement is a means to achieve that end. Failure to understand the significance of enforcement in the environment and development equation will, it is argued, relegate sustainable development to a mere theoretical construct.

Compliance and Enforcement Policy for the Canadian Environmental Protection Act, 1999

(Ottawa: Environment Canada, 2001) (Available on the Web at http://
www.ec.gc.ca/CEPARegistry/documents/policies/candepolicy/toc.cfm.)

What Are Compliance and Enforcement?

The terms "compliance" and "enforcement" are used many times throughout the Enforcement and Compliance Policy for the Act. It is therefore useful to make their meanings clear.

Compliance means the state of conformity with the law. Environment Canada will secure compliance with the *Canadian Environmental Protection Act, 1999* through two types of activity: promotion and enforcement.

Measures to promote compliance include communication and publication of information, consultation with parties affected by the Act.

Enforcement activities include:

(1) Inspection and monitoring to verify compliance;
(2) Investigations of violations;
(3) Measures to compel compliance without resorting to formal court action, such as directions by the Minister or enforcement officers, ticketing, and environmental protection compliance orders by enforcement officers; and
(4) Measures to compel compliance through court action, such as injunctions, prosecution, court orders upon conviction, and civil suit for recovery of costs.

NOTE

Thorough discussions of alternative definitions of and approaches to the terms "enforcement" and "compliance" are offered in the proceedings of the international forums sponsored by the International Network on Environmental Compliance and Enforcement (INECE) (accessible in hard copy and on the Web at http://www.inece.org/).

III. INTERNATIONAL OBLIGATIONS AND COMMITMENTS FOR EFFECTIVE ENVIRONMENTAL ENFORCEMENT

As signatory to numerous multilateral agreements (Rio Declaration (1992) vol. 31 *International Legal Materials* 874 and Agenda 21, UN Doc. A/Conf.151/26/Rev.1 (1993)) and international conventions (Biodiversity Convention (1992) vol. 32 *International Legal Materials* 818; CITES (1975), CTS 32, Heavy Metals Protocol to the LRTAP Treaty, http://www.unece.org/env/lrtap/), Canada has committed to effectively enforcing and maximizing compliance with Canadian environmental laws and regulations. These various international laws and instruments contain commitments not only to enact effective, enforceable environmental laws but also to allocate the requisite powers, resources, and measures both to promote compliance and to ensure timely, appropriate responses to violators.

**United Nations Conference on Environment and Development
"Developing Effective National Programmes for Reviewing and
Enforcing Compliance with National, State, Provincial and
Local Laws on Environment and Development"**
(1993), chapter 8.21, Agenda 21, UN. Doc. A/conf.151/26/rev.1

Each country should develop integrated strategies to maximize compliance with its laws and regulations relating to sustainable development, with assistance from international organizations and other countries as appropriate. The strategies could include:

(a) Enforceable, effective laws, regulations and standards that are based on sound economic, social and environmental principles and appropriate risk assessment, incorporating sanctions designed to punish violations, obtain redress and deter future violations;

(b) Mechanisms for promoting compliance;

(c) institutional capacity for collecting compliance data, regularly reviewing compliance, detecting violations, establishing enforcement priorities, undertaking effective enforcement, and conducting periodic evaluations of the effectiveness of compliance and enforcement programmes;

(d) Mechanisms for appropriate involvement of individuals and groups in the development and enforcement of laws and regulations on environment and development.

North American Agreement on Environmental Cooperation
(entered into force on January 1, 1994)
(United States–Canada–Mexico) (1993) vol. 32 *International Legal Materials* 1480

Article 5: Government Enforcement Action

(1) With the aim of achieving high levels of environmental protection and compliance with its laws and regulations, each Party shall effectively enforce its environmental laws and regulations through appropriate governmental action, subject to Article 37, such as:

(a) appointing and training inspectors;

(b) monitoring compliance and investigating suspected violations, including through on-site inspections;

(c) seeking assurances of voluntary compliance and compliance agreements;

(d) publicly releasing non-compliance information;

(e) issuing bulletins or other periodic statements on enforcement procedures;

(f) promoting environmental audits;

(g) requiring record keeping and reporting;

(h) providing or encouraging mediation and arbitration services;

(i) using licenses, permits or authorizations;

(j) initiating, in a timely manner, judicial, quasi-judicial or administrative proceedings to seek appropriate sanctions or remedies for violations of its environmental laws and regulations;

(k) providing for search, seizure or detention; or

(l) issuing administrative orders, including orders of a preventative, curative or emergency nature.

(2) Each Party shall ensure that judicial, quasi-judicial or administrative enforcement proceedings are available under its law to sanction or remedy violations of its environmental laws and regulations.

(3) Sanctions and remedies provided for a violation of a Party's environmental laws and regulations shall, as appropriate:

(a) take into consideration the nature and gravity of the violation, any economic benefit derived from the violation by the violator, the economic condition of the violator, and other relevant factors; and

(b) include compliance agreements, fines, imprisonment, injunctions, the closure of facilities, and the cost of containing or cleaning up pollution.

NOTES AND QUESTIONS

1. The North American Agreement on Environmental Cooperation (NAAEC), above, further obligates its council (of North American cabinet-level government representatives) to encourage effective enforcement by Canada, as a party, of its environmental laws and regulations, compliance with those laws and regulations, and technical cooperation. To facilitate implementation of this obligation, the council established the North American Working Group on Environmental Enforcement and Compliance Cooperation (EWG). The EWG provides a forum for exchange of information and expertise and joint enforcement action among senior environmental enforcement officials of the three countries. The EWG also prepares the mandatory annual report on the parties' enforcement obligations. (See the Commission on Environmental Cooperation, http://www.cec.org/.)

It is generally understood that one of the reasons for creating the NAAEC as a side agreement to the North American free trade agreement (NAFTA) (1993) vol. 32 *International Legal Materials* 289 and 605, was the need to defray any unfair economic or trade advantages that may be gained by any of the three countries through deregulation or non-enforcement of its environmental laws. This objective is reflected in part V of the NAAEC, which establishes a multi-tiered process of consultations and arbitration of allegations of a persistent pattern of failure by a party to effectively enforce its environmental laws. Potential penalties include monetary penalties or trade sanctions. The NAAEC makes specific provision for application of the obligations under the agreement to provinces (annex 41).

2. What potential limitations are inherent in the NAAEC for the exercise of Canada's rights to assert claims related to non-enforcement?

3. Who is obligated to respond to and is potentially liable for any allegation of a persistent pattern of non-enforcement by a province of one or more of its environmental laws under the NAAEC?

4. What are the potential implications under the NAAEC of a policy of delegation of monitoring and enforcement of federal laws to provincial authorities?

IV. THE ROLE OF ENFORCEMENT IN IMPLEMENTING ENVIRONMENTAL LAW

A. Introduction

K. Harrison
"Is Cooperation the Answer? Canadian Environmental Enforcement in Comparative Context"
(Spring 1995) vol. 14, no. 2 *Journal of Policy Analysis and Management* 221, at 222

Competing Models of Regulatory Enforcement

As Hawkins has observed, "law may be enforced by compulsion and coercion, or by conciliation and compromise." In the last decade, a substantial literature has emerged on these two competing regulatory enforcement styles, alternatively labeled conciliatory or cooperative on the one hand, and adversarial, legalistic, or deterrence-oriented on the other. The distinctiveness of the two approaches is easily overstated, since even the cooperative approach relies on the implied threat of coercion. Nonetheless, there appear to be at least two characteristic differences.

The first concerns regulators' response to noncompliance. Adversarial regulators tend to rely more heavily on formal sanctions, such as administrative penalties and civil or criminal prosecution, while their cooperative colleagues are more inclined to negotiate informal compliance schedules with polluters. As a result, the cooperative style of enforcement is characterized by personal, even amicable, relations between regulator and regulated. Compromise and consensus normally prevail over the winner-take-all stakes of litigation.

A second difference lies in how strictly regulators define compliance in the first place. The legalistic approach to enforcement relies heavily on the definition of compliance found in the "black letter law." In contrast to this "rule-bound rigidity," cooperative regulators are more inclined to interpret rules flexibly, particularly when they believe that polluters are making good faith efforts to comply.

Although diverse approaches to enforcement have been documented within countries, and even within agencies, comparative studies have noted a unique predisposition for coercive enforcement among US regulatory agencies. The existence of distinct models of enforcement provokes two questions: What factors lead regulators to adopt one model or the other, and which approach is more effective? With respect to the first question, previous authors have pointed with varying degrees of emphasis to the characteristics of the regulator's environment including political culture, institutions, and legal framework—that can either constrain or invite regulators' discretion with respect to enforcement.

The focus of this article is the second question, however. Is there reason to believe that one approach is more effective than the other given the inevitable scarcity of administrative resources? As Hoberg has noted, past studies that have hailed the merits of cooperative enforcement have offered surprisingly little by way of empirical support.

In their classic critique of US regulatory enforcement, Bardach and Kagan harshly criticize the US propensity to "go by the book," arguing that the inflexible, prosecution-oriented approach is not only inefficient in treating minor and significant violations equally, but counterproductive in provoking antagonistic relationships between regulators and the regulated. In other words, there is no need to actually employ the proverbial stick if the donkey can be motivated by ear stroking and the mere threat of the stick. Although the authors convincingly document the flaws of the US approach, their conclusion that cooperative enforcement would be more effective rests on an unbalanced comparison between the real-world US experience and an idealized model of cooperative enforcement.

Canadian students of enforcement have also praised the cooperative enforcement model. Although acknowledging disappointing results in practice, they argue that the solution is to strengthen, rather than reject, the bargaining process. However, their support for cooperative enforcement rests on an untested assumption that firms will be willing to comply with standards and deadlines that they helped to negotiate in the first place.

. . .

The Canadian Experience

Environmental enforcement in Canada to date has been characterized by cooperation both between industry and government and between the two levels of government. According to Thompson:

> [B]argaining is the essence of the environmental regulatory process as it is practiced in Canada ... the norms of conduct are the subject of negotiation and renegotiation between the regulator and the regulated right down to the moment of compliance or noncompliance. In this sense, rules stated in statutes or regulations are merely points of departure for negotiating modifications of behaviour; and "compliance" or "noncompliance" means "agreement" or "disagreement."

The typical response to noncompliance with environmental standards has been for government/officials and the regulated firm to negotiate a schedule for firms to gradually come into compliance, taking into account both the severity of environmental impacts and the polluter's ability to afford the necessary controls. Prosecution has been used only sparingly as a last resort. Indeed, up to 1988, there were only ten prosecutions under four of the five major federal environmental statutes combined. Legal action under the fifth, the *Fisheries Act*, has been more common in the case of accidental spills, but prosecution of noncompliant continuous discharges has been rare.

The enforcement process has been characterized by intergovernmental cooperation as well. The federal government generally conceded the leading role in enforcement to the provinces during the 1970s and 1980s, although federal involvement was somewhat greater in the coastal provinces. In Atlantic Canada, for instance, joint meetings between industry, federal officials, and provincial officials were commonplace. The result historically was a closed and informal three-way relationship between federal and provincial governments and regulated firms. A spokesperson for one Atlantic pulp and paper company explained that, "most of the meetings between industry, the feds and the province take place at this [restaurant] table. ... A lot of business takes place over a coffee" [personal interview].

Conclusion

In the case of the pulp and paper industry, the cooperative Canadian approach to enforcement has delivered disappointing results compared to the more adversarial US approach. This study therefore casts doubts on the relatively untested assumption that cooperative enforcement is equally if not more effective than the adversarial approach. While definitive conclusions await pooled data analysis of the pulp and paper and other industries, the case study does suggest the need for more critical examination of the effectiveness of cooperative regulatory regimes.

It might be argued that the problem in Canada lies not in cooperative enforcement per se but in the particular Canadian version of it. Scholz has demonstrated formally that the ideal enforcement officer is generally forgiving, yet vengeful in response to persistent noncompliance. Canadian regulators have been abundantly forgiving, but seldom vengeful. However, while the Canadian model of cooperative enforcement may fall short of the ideal, it nonetheless represents an empirical point of reference to the real-world performance of adversarial US regulators.

A related challenge might arise from those who argue that there are two distinct characteristics of enforcement—cooperativeness, and stringency. In other words, the problem may not be that the Canadian regulators are more cooperative than their US counterparts, but that they simply are less stringent. However, there is reason to question whether stringency and cooperativeness are in fact independent. Vengeful behavior is an anathema to a culture of cooperation for several reasons. Enforcement officers may interpret voluntary compliance as unwillingness to entertain proposals for prosecution, and thus continue to pursue negotiated compliance beyond the limits of genuine good faith efforts. In addition, students of cooperative enforcement have often observed that officials persist with fruitless negotiations because they perceive resorting to prosecution as a personal failure. The personal relationship between regulator and polluter that characterizes cooperative enforcement also can generate sympathy for the polluters' plight among regulators, a subtle form of "capture."

Finally, the relatively junior officials in regional offices who engage in day-to-day compliance negotiations may be especially receptive to threats of job loss from polluters, given their own organizational vulnerability. Such threats clearly were influential in Canadian regulators' willingness to grant mills ever more time to comply. An Environment Canada report argued in 1988 that critics of the federal government's enforcement of pulp mill effluent regulations "ignore that government officials probably have decided against prosecution out of compassion for the hundreds, and sometimes thousands, of Canadians who could lose their livelihood as a result of overly zealous enforcement." It is noteworthy, however, that in the United States, where the adversarial enforcement regime precluded similar concessions, not a single mill closure has been attributed to environmental regulations, even though similar threats of job losses were registered by US mills.

While this study represents only a first step in a research agenda to more systematically compare the effectiveness of different enforcement approaches, one can speculate about whether it would be possible to combine the strengths of both models. A compromise solution may be to administratively separate the functions of technical support and enforcement. Compliance officers could be encouraged to explain regulatory requirements and offer technical support to polluters in a cooperative manner, while enforcement officials could be expected to enforce standards in a more adversarial manner. While this compromise captures some of the purported advantages of cooperative enforcement, it forgoes others. For instance, there would be no opportunity to circumvent any "unreasonableness" inherent in formal standards by flexibly interpreting requirements and deadlines for individual sources, arguably the feature of the cooperative enforcement model given greatest emphasis by Bardach and Kagan. In response, however, it can be argued that a first step, one more consistent with democratic accountability, is simply to write more reasonable standards in the first place. It is true that no formal regulation can account for every eventuality, however. In that regard, market-oriented instruments such as tradeable permits may offer promise, since they can allow firms with particularly high control costs to meet reduction requirements at a more reasonable price by purchasing credits from someone else.

A credible threat of prosecution is essential if cooperative enforcement is to be effective. Yet for the reasons noted above, the culture of cooperative enforcement may undermine that credibility. The Canadian experience with environmental enforcement suggests that with no stick in sight, carrots and ear stroking make for a fat and quite immobile donkey.

B. Strict Enforcement (Pollution as Crime)

Those who support the need for strict enforcement, particularly the prosecution of environmental offences, generally base their argument on one or more of the following theories: strict enforcement is necessary to punish violators, to deter other potential violators, to reverse a persistent pattern of non-compliance, and/or to punish those who would otherwise be "free riders." The legal principles relevant to the prosecution of environmental offences are considered in chapter 5.

"Undermining the Law: Addressing the Crisis in Compliance with Environmental Mining Laws in BC"
(Vancouver: West Coast Environmental Law and Environmental Mining Council of BC, 2001), at 11, 50-51, and 53

Benefits of Prosecution

The impacts of prosecution are numerous. Allowing private prosecutions to proceed would send a signal to polluters that the government is serious about environmental protection. Lawbreaking should not be tolerated. If government does not have the resources to enforce the law, then permitting citizens to do so is entirely consistent with the spirit and intent of these laws. Someone needs to hold polluters accountable. We have already established that the threat of punishment is a meaningful deterrent for polluters. It provides reassurance to law abiders that their efforts to comply with the law will not be in vain, as it operates as a disincentive to "free riders" who would otherwise disregard the law while some companies work to ensure compliance. Finally, it encourages companies to shift toward pollution abatement technology.

The mere exercise of commencing a prosecution can also be efficient under certain conditions. According to one government prosecutor, a prosecution can be concluded in less than a year, whereas the process of investigating and negotiating to achieve compliance can take a number of years. The deterrent effect alone of laying a charge may result in pollution abatement, regardless of the result. Finally, the use of private prosecutions as a tool recognizes that in some circumstances, "no amount of persuasion or administrative action will bring to light the deliberate and surreptitious activities going on in certain industries the way a prosecution can." Based upon the Environment Canada study, if only one half of a percent to two percent of all polluters end up in court, this hardly constitutes a drain on the justice or the court system.

As one official bluntly stated in reference to a particular problem mine, "the company knows we don't have the resources to follow-up on the prosecution so they're laughing at us." While we are not advocating that all violators be brought directly before a judge, it is clear that the court system (both in terms of number of polluters who appear before a judge and level of fines levied) is underutilized. According to one commentator:

> Regulatory targets will respond according to the size of the potential penalty, discounted by the probability that they will escape liability. Hence regulators may generate the appropriate level of compliance by adjusting either the likelihood of detection and conviction, or the size of the penalty.

Given that only one per cent of identified polluters will face a judge, and the court's record of imposing low fines, the deterrent capacity of the court is negligible. Unless the threat of prosecution becomes real for a company, and as long as a court ordered fine is negligible relative to business profits, it is not likely that polluters will change their behaviour.

. . .

The Role of the Court

We routinely assume that those who break the law face the consequences of their actions in court. As we have seen, however, there are many instances where infractions go unnoticed or unidentified. Court is a last resort for dealing with non-compliance, and very few violators ever appear before a judge. In part, this is because the prosecution process is perceived as time consuming and costly. However, if used promptly and effectively, prosecutions can be an efficient remedy. Perhaps the strongest deterrent to a chronic polluter is the stigma and cost associated with a strong conviction. Court is a key means to ensure that compliance is taken seriously.

According to Environment Canada, enforcement of standards is part of an extended process of research, communication, negotiations and, if necessary, punitive action. It identifies eight stages to its enforcement cycle, which can take anywhere from 5 to 10 years. In practical terms only one half to two percent of all polluters will be prosecuted for violating environmental legislation, and only ½ to 2 percent of the polluters in an industry group will actually be convicted and fined.

. . .

It is arguable that the low number of charges and fines means that compliance with the law is generally good. While this would be a comforting conclusion to draw it is an unlikely one. Both the federal and provincial governments admit that they do not have adequate resources to enforce their laws. The number of repeat offenders on the NC [non-compliance] Reports, the fact that internal investigations files reveal more permit breaches than are reported, and the steady decline in inspections and monitoring indicate that the low number of charges and fines means that there are significant but often hidden problems with compliance.

NOTES AND QUESTIONS

1. Some scholars have suggested that failed commitment to effective enforcement can have the intentional or inadvertent effect of altering standards or deregulation. See J. Swaigen, *Regulatory Offences in Canada*, above. B.M. Mitnick, in *The Political Economy of Regulation: Creating, Designing and Removing Regulatory Forms* (New York: Columbia University Press, 1980), at 421-22, argues that deregulation may be effected through quite insidious means, including cuts to resources, expertise, and facilities necessary to monitor and enforce.

> A form of deregulation through non-enforcement can occur if a regulatory unit's budgetary or other support is cut, so that the unit is simply unable to enforce the regulation ... such a tactic could successfully elude the difficulties of getting deregulation through the legislative process. Selective cuts in support, with consequently consecutive non-enforcement, or shift in enforcement priority, can therefore be a way to control regulatory performance and, possibly, to avoid major attacks for the regulation's supportive clientele.

What, if any, implications are there for the application of the principle of "rule of law," where policies dictate against the enforcement of prescribed environmental standards?

2. For references to the significance of the role of deterrence in sentencing environmental violators, see *R v. United Keno Hill Mines* (1980), 10 CELR 43 (Yuk. Terr. Ct.); *R v. Cottonfelts Ltd.* (1982), 2 CCC (3d) 287 (Ont. CA), at 295; and *R v. Van Waters & Rogers Ltd. & Rogers Ltd.* (1998), 220 AR 315 (Prov. Ct.), where Fradsham J cites J. Swaigen and G. Bunt, *Sentencing in Environmental Cases* (Ottawa: Law Reform Commission of Canada, 1985): "There appears to be a substantial role for punishment and denunciation of conduct in the sentencing of environmental offenders." See also *R v. Alberta Public Works (Dewar Western Inc.)* (2001), 51 WCB (2d) 189 (Alta. Prov. Ct.), where the court observed that "taking such unacceptable risks must be unconditionally discouraged through appropriately harsh penalties."

3. An extensive review of sentencing principles and their application by Canadian courts is offered in S.D. Berger, *The Prosecution and Defence of Environmental Offences*, vol. II (Aurora, ON: Canada Law Book) (looseleaf).

4. It may be noted that a growing number of citizen submissions have been filed under article 14 of the NAAEC, above, alleging failure of the Government of Canada to enforce federal environmental laws, among them CEPA 1999, the CEAA, and the federal *Fisheries Act*, RSC 1985, c. F-14. See, for example, NAAEC Submissions: Friends of the Oldman River (SEM-97-006), BC Mining (SEM-98-004), and BC Logging (SEM-00-004). In a number of instances, submitters have alleged that Canada failed to observe its official enforcement and compliance policies. Submissions, official responses and completed factual records are available online at the Commission for Environmental Cooperation Web site, http://www.cec.org/. See also Quebec Environmental Law Center, "Discussion Paper for Fisheries and Oceans, ENGO Concerns and Policy Options Regarding the Administration and Delegation of Subsection 35(2) of the *Fisheries Act*,

proposed Subsection 35(3) and Consequences for Federal Environmental Assessment," prepared for the *Fisheries Act* Working Group, Canadian Environmental Network, January 1996.

5. It is noteworthy that Canadian empirical studies indicate that over 90 percent of businesses state that their primary motivation for establishing environmental management systems was compliance with regulations. Approximately 70 percent cite potential directors' liability—a factor also related to environmental laws. Only 25 percent claim to have been motivated by voluntary programs. See KPMG Management Consultants, *Canadian Environmental Management Survey 1996* (Toronto: KPMG, 1996). Similar findings are reported in D. Saxe, *Environmental Offences: Corporate Responsibility and Executive Liability* (Aurora, ON: Canada Law Book, 1990) and D. Saxe, "Voluntary Compliance v. Enforcement? Why the Threat of Legal Action Is Important" (1996) *Hazardous Materials Management* 62.

C. Enforcement and Compliance Policies

The majority of federal and provincial agencies responsible for the administration of laws for the protection of the environment have issued enforcement and compliance directives that clarify their polices and programs; these directives include such things as criteria for official responses to violations. The first significant publicly disclosed enforcement policy was the enforcement and compliance policy tabled before Parliament in 1986 in tandem with the enactment of CEPA, 1985 in 1988. In tabling the policy, Tom McMillan, then federal minister of the environment, said "A good law, however, is not enough. It must be enforced—ruthlessly if need be."

Since the tabling of this policy, a plethora of similar policies have been issued by federal and provincial departments. Among the most recently issued is the enforcement and compliance policy for the fish habitat provisions of the federal *Fisheries Act*, below. The titles to these polices, compared with those of previously issued polices, reflect the general shift by these and other departments toward increased reliance on voluntary, as opposed to interventionist, responses to non-compliance.

**Fisheries Act, Habitat Protection and Pollution Prevention Provisions,
Compliance and Enforcement Policy**
(Ottawa: Government of Canada, July 2001), at 3

Introduction

[L]aws and regulations are not sufficient in themselves; they must be administered and enforced in a fair, predictable, and consistent manner. Those who administer the laws and those who must comply with them need to understand how the government intends to achieve compliance with the legal requirements. For these reasons, this *Compliance and Enforcement Policy* has been developed for the habitat protection and pollution prevention provisions of the *Fisheries Act*.

...

The *Policy* explains what measures will be used to achieve compliance with the *Fisheries Act* habitat protection and pollution prevention provisions. It sets out principles of fair, predictable, and consistent enforcement that govern application of the law, and responses by enforcement personnel to alleged violations. This policy also tells everyone who shares a responsibility for protection of fish and fish habitat—including governments, industry, organized labour and individuals—what is expected of them.

Guiding Principles

The following general principles govern application of the habitat protection and pollution prevention provisions of the *Fisheries Act*:

(a) Compliance with the habitat protection and pollution prevention provisions and their accompanying regulations is mandatory.

(b) Compliance will be encouraged through communication with parties affected by the habitat protection and pollution prevention provisions.

(c) Enforcement personnel will administer the provisions and regulations in a manner that is fair, predictable, and consistent. Rules, sanctions and processes securely founded in law will be used.

(d) Enforcement personnel will administer the provisions and accompanying regulations with an emphasis on preventing harm to fish, fish habitat or human use of fish caused by physical alteration of fish habitat or pollution of waters frequented by fish. Priority for action to deal with suspected violations will be guided by
  • the degree of harm to fish, fish habitat or human use of fish caused by physical alteration of habitat or pollution of waters frequented by fish, or the risk of that harm; and/or
  • whether or not the alleged offence is a repeat occurrence.

(e) Enforcement personnel will take action consistent with this *Compliance and Enforcement Policy.*

(f) The public will be encouraged to report suspected violations of the habitat protection and pollution prevention provisions of the *Fisheries Act*.

...

Responses to Alleged Violations

Enforcement measures are directed towards ensuring that violators comply with the *Fisheries Act* within the shortest possible time and that violations are not repeated.

Enforcement personnel will respond to suspected violations. They will take into account the harm or risk of harm to fish, fish habitat and/or human use of fish. If they determine that there is sufficient evidence a violation has occurred, they may take enforcement action.

Criteria for Response to Alleged Violations

If enforcement personnel are able to substantiate that an alleged violation of the habitat protection or pollution prevention provisions of the Act has occurred and there is sufficient evidence to proceed, they will decide on an appropriate action, applying the criteria below.

Nature of the Alleged Violation

Factors considered in assessing the nature of an alleged violation will include:

(a) The seriousness of the damage or potential damage to fish habitat, the fishery resource, or the risks associated with the human use of fish;
(b) The intent of the alleged violator;
(c) Whether it is a repeated occurrence; and
(d) Whether there were attempts by the alleged violator to conceal information or otherwise circumvent the objectives and requirements of the habitat protection and pollution prevention provisions.

Effectiveness in Achieving the Desired Result with the Alleged Violator

The desired result is compliance with the Act in the shortest possible time and with no further occurrence of violations, in order to protect fish and fish habitat and human use of fish. Factors to be considered include:

(a) The alleged violator's history of compliance with the habitat protection and/or pollution prevention provisions;
(b) The alleged violator's willingness to co-operate with enforcement personnel;
(c) Evidence and extent of corrective action already taken; and
(d) The existence of enforcement actions by other federal or provincial/territorial authorities.

. . .

Prosecution

Prosecution is the preferred course of action where evidence establishes that:

(a) The alleged violation resulted in risk of harm to fish or fish habitat;
(b) The alleged violation resulted in harmful alteration, disruption or destruction of fish habitat (not authorized by the Minister of Fisheries and Oceans);
(c) The alleged violator has previously received a warning for the activity and did not take all reasonable measures to stop or avoid the violation;
(d) The alleged violator had previously been convicted of a similar offence.

Enforcement personnel will examine each case to determine whether a warning, a direction by a Fishery Inspector, Ministerial Order or injunction is the appropriate alternative to prosecution. Prosecution may still be the enforcement action chosen, in accordance with the criteria set out in "Response to Alleged Violations," above. Prosecution will always be pursued where evidence establishes that:

(a) There is evidence that the alleged violation was deliberate;
(b) The alleged violator knowingly provided false or misleading information to enforcement personnel;
(c) The alleged violator obstructed enforcement personnel in the carrying out of their duties or interfered with anything seized under the Act;
(d) The alleged violator concealed or attempted to conceal or destroy information or evidence after the alleged offence occurred;
(e) The alleged violator failed to take all reasonable measures to comply with a direction or an order issued pursuant to the Act.

NOTES AND QUESTIONS

1. A number of official reviews have been conducted on the adherence by government officials to their respective enforcement and compliance policies. In 1998 the federal parliamentary Standing Committee on Environment and Sustainable Development completed a review of Environment Canada's enforcement responsibilities, policies, and practices of various federal environmental laws. The final report, *Enforcing Canada's Pollution Laws: The Public Interest Must Come First!* (Ottawa: Standing Committee on Environment and Sustainable Development, 1998), identifies a number of problems and inadequacies and makes a series of recommendations to improve the enforcement and compliance record. One of the objectives of the review was a consideration of the effect of the harmonization initiative of the CCME (http://www.ccme.ca/). Among the issues examined are the delegation of federal enforcement authority, the trend toward voluntary compliance, and roles afforded private citizens in enforcing federal laws. These issues are discussed below.

2. Where a government issues an official enforcement and compliance policy, or where enforcement responses or other measures (for example, mitigation) are prescribed in law, what liability issues may arise for a department or agency that fails to observe those prescribed responses for a particular suspected or actual violation? See *Environmental Resource Center et al. v. Canada (Minister of the Environment)*, 2001 FCT 1423, and the citizen enforcement submissions to the Commission for Environmental Cooperation (http://www.cec.org/).

V. DELEGATION OF ENFORCEMENT RESPONSIBILITIES

A trend in the enactment or revision of both federal and provincial environmental laws has been to incorporate provisions enabling the delegation of enforcement powers and responsibilities to other departments, other orders of government (now commonly called "jurisdictions"), private parties, or to First Nations.

Yukon Environment Act
SY 1991, c. 5

Partnership with the Government of Canada

54. The Commissioner in Executive Council may make agreements with the Government of Canada ...

(b) on cooperation concerning monitoring, decision-making, investigations, emergency response or any other aspect of environmental management; ... .

Partnership with Yukon Municipalities

55. The Minister may make agreements with municipalities ...

(d) on integration or consolidation of approval processes, inspections, enforcement, or any aspect of the administration of this Act or a schedule A enactment; ... .

Delegation

60(1) The Minister may, in writing, delegate to any employee of a department of the Government of the Yukon or a municipality the exercise of any power conferred or duty imposed on the Minister under this Act or the regulations. ...

Transfer of Administration

61(1) Subject to the *Public Service Commission Act*, the Minister may, with the approval of the Commissioner in Executive Council transfer the administration of a provision of this Act or the regulations to ...

(b) a municipality;

(c) the Government of Canada; or

(d) any other organization ... .

In other instances, accountability for enforcement has been altered by the delegation of enforcement powers and responsibilities through multilateral or bilateral federal–provincial agreements under which designated "lead parties" are to assume responsibilities otherwise available or imposed. One such agreement is the CCME *Inspections and Enforcement Sub-Agreement* (accepted in principle June 6, 2000), below. It introduces a unique concept whereby responsibility for government intervention, in this instance, to inspect or enforce federal and provincial environmental laws, is to be assumed by the government that is considered "best situated." Criteria for determining which level of government is best situated to respond include the scale, scope, and nature of the environmental issue; physical proximity; available resources; and interprovincial, interterritorial, and international considerations.

**Canadian Council of Ministers of the Environment
Inspections and Enforcement Sub-Agreement**
(Winnipeg: CCME, May 2001) (Available online at
http://www.ccme.ca/assets/pdf/insp_enfsubagr_e.pdf.)

This Sub-Agreement covers inspection and enforcement activities undertaken to verify and ensure compliance with environmental protection laws. This agreement includes the provisions of the Canada-wide Environmental Inspections Sub-agreement which it now replaces.

1. Objectives

1.1 Consistent with the Canada-wide Accord on Environmental Harmonization and Annexes, and to enhance environmental protection, the objectives of this Sub-Agreement are:

1.1.1 To achieve a consistent, high level of compliance with environmental protection laws across Canada, and

1.1.2 To serve as an enabling framework for future bilateral and multilateral implementation agreements that:

    i. deliver a range of inspection and enforcement activities across Canada that are fair, consistent and predictable;

    ii. provide a cooperative work sharing approach for inspection and enforcement activities related to environmental protection laws, where appropriate;

    iii. identify a process to set priorities for inspection and enforcement programs; and

    iv. provide an efficient and cost effective approach to inspection and enforcement activities in Canada.

2. Scope

2.1 This Sub-agreement applies to inspection and enforcement activities undertaken for the purpose of achieving compliance with environmental protection laws.

2.1.1 "environmental protection laws" in this Sub-Agreement mean any act, statute or regulation, or provision thereof, the primary purpose of which is the protection of the environment, or the prevention of a danger to human life or health in the context of environmental quality.

2.1.2 "inspection activities" in this Sub-Agreement means any actions taken by governments, such as site visits, examining substances, processes, products or wastes, taking samples for analysis, examining records or other information, responding to complaints and review of self-reported information to verify that the operations and activities of the regulated community (regulatee) are in conformity with the law.

2.1.3 "enforcement activities" in this Sub-Agreement means any actions taken by governments to gather evidence associated with potential violations, to undertake preparatory work for court actions and all sanctions and follow-up associated with responses to violations of the law.

2.2 The focus of this Sub-Agreement is on areas where federal, provincial and territorial governments have the environmental protection laws and the ability to take action in similar situations. Based on assessment of which government is best-situated, implementation agreements may encompass inspection and enforcement activities related to environmental provisions in any other legislation administered by signatory Ministers as agreed to by the respective governments.

3. Principles

3.1 In addition to principles identified in the Canada-wide Accord on Environmental Harmonization and Annexes, implementation agreements under this Sub-Agreement will reflect the following:

3.1.1 Legal Applicability: Governments acknowledge that all federal, provincial and territorial environmental legislation continues to apply regardless of which jurisdiction carries out the inspection and enforcement activities.

3.1.2 Transparency: Inspection and enforcement information will be exchanged between and among governments. Reports on inspections, and enforcement responses will be publicly available following the principles enumerated in section 6.4 below. [Not reproduced.]

3.1.3 Risk Based Approach: Governments will set priorities for inspection and enforcement activities in consideration of environmental and health risks, compliance levels and other factors relating to enhancing environmental protection.

4. Approach

4.1 Implementation agreements will provide flexibility in determining the respective roles and responsibilities of governments.

4.1.1 In the context of this Sub-Agreement, the inspection and enforcement functions of the federal government include international borders and obligations, transboundary domestic issues, federal lands and facilities, products/substances in Canada-wide trade and commerce, and other matters specific to the federal government.

4.1.2 In the context of this Sub-Agreement, the inspection and enforcement functions of provincial and territorial governments include industrial and municipal facilities and discharges, application of laws on provincial and territorial land, waste disposal and destruction, and other matters specific to provincial and territorial governments.

4.1.3 For the purpose of this Sub-Agreement, the activities set out in 4.1.1 and 4.1.2 may be varied based on a best-situated assessment as per criteria outlined in 4.1.4 and as agreed to by governments through development of specific implementation agreements.

4.1.4 In assessing which government is best situated, governments agree to give consideration to applicable criteria such as:

    i. scale, scope and nature of the environmental issue;

    ii. equipment, infrastructure and laboratory capacity to support activities;

    iii. physical proximity;

iv. efficiency and effectiveness;

v. human and financial resources to deliver obligations;

vi. scientific, technical and analytical expertise;

vii. ability to address local needs;

viii. interprovincial, inter-territorial/international considerations and obligations;

ix. government already performing inspection and enforcement activities; and

x. existing agreements

4.2 Notwithstanding each government's jurisdiction and the best situated to act concept, governments agree to provide mutual support utilizing the strengths and capabilities of each jurisdiction throughout implementation of this Sub-Agreement.

4.3 Irrespective of agreements to divide the delivery of such activities between or among the governments, each government will maintain an inspection and enforcement capacity.

5. Accountability

5.1 Governments entering into implementation agreements under this Sub-Agreement remain ultimately accountable and legally responsible for the enforcement of their own environmental protection laws.

Standing Committee on Environment and Sustainable Development
Enforcing Canada's Pollution Control Laws:
The Public Interest Must Come First!
(Ottawa: House of Commons Standing Committee on Environment and
Sustainable Development, 1998), at 1-2 and 40-41

5. The Committee was also interested in studying enforcement because of the harmonization initiative currently being carried out by the Canadian Council of Ministers of the Environment (the CCME). This initiative has been of particular concern to the Committee because it seeks to reassign, by administrative agreement, the functional responsibility for Canada's environmental laws to one or the other level of government.

6. The first phase of the CCME's harmonization initiative, consisting of a main Accord and three of ten proposed Sub-agreements, was completed and signed by the Ministers of the Environment on 29 January 1998. The Sub-agreement on enforcement is among the seven Sub-agreements that had not been developed. It is, however, scheduled to be completed during the current, second round of negotiations. The Committee therefore thought it would be useful to undertake this study on enforcement to see if recommendations ought to be made before the Sub-agreement on enforcement is finalized and ratified.

· · ·

123. During its hearings last fall on the CCMEs harmonization initiative, the Committee heard many concerns about the proposed initiative and made a number of findings based on the evidence before it. Among other things, the Committee [in 1997] concluded that:

(a) There is insufficient evidence of overlap and duplication of environmental regulations and activities between the federal and provincial/territorial governments, thus making it doubtful that greater administrative efficiency and cost savings would be achieved under the agreement.

(b) The provinces might eventually assume a considerable number of functions under the Accord and Sub-Agreements, thus leaving the federal government with only a limited set of responsibilities of considerably less importance than its current environmental protection role.

(c) A significant devolution of federal environmental protection powers to the provinces and the territories might engender weaker environmental protection in Canada.

(d) Rather than assuring that environmental practices and regulations of the two levels of government are complementary, the ultimate effect of the Accord and Sub-agreements will be to eliminate one level of regulations and practices.

124. The Committee continues to have serious misgivings about the harmonization initiative. Nothing said in this current round of hearings has made us look more favourably upon the initiative. If anything, Environment Canada's poor enforcement record under the bilateral agreements, as well as the problem of loss of operational capacity have strengthened our belief that the Accord and Sub-agreements may be ill-advised.

125. [T]he Sub-agreement on Enforcement is in the process of being developed. Although the Committee had recommended that the full package be finalized before ratification of the Accord and the three completed Sub-agreements (standards, inspections and environmental assessments), this advice was not heeded and the first phase of the initiative was signed on 29 January 1998. In its report, the Committee questioned the wisdom of moving ahead on the Sub-agreement on inspections in the absence of the one on enforcement. Pointing out that the two went hand in hand, it was our position that the two should be dealt with together. This was not done. Nonetheless, the Committee believes that the forthcoming Sub-agreement on enforcement deals with too important an area for it to go ahead at this time. The Auditor General has agreed to prepare a report on the effectiveness of the existing environmental agreements with the provinces and territories. The Committee views the tabling of his report in Parliament as a desirable pre-condition to the signing of the Sub-agreement on enforcement, for it will provide Canadians with a thorough and independent assessment of the existing strengths and weaknesses of the existing agreements and thus allow informed decisions to be made on the provisions that should be included in the Sub-agreement on enforcement.

Environmental Resource Centre et al. v.
Canada (Minister of Environment)
2001 FCT 1423

[The Environmental Resource Centre and two other non-governmental organizations (NGOs) brought judicial review applications to challenge environmental decisions by the federal ministers of environment and fisheries and oceans in relation to a project by Suncor Energy Inc. to expand its northern Alberta oil sands mining and bitumen upgrading facility. The plaintiffs challenged the main decision of the minister of the environment (MOE) under s. 23 of the CEAA, above, that, based on the information in the required comprehensive study report (CSR) by Suncor, the cumulative environmental effects of the project will be insignificant. This decision would require that the project be referred back to the ministry of fisheries and oceans (the responsible decision-making authority (RA) under the CEAA) for *Fisheries Act* approval and that it need not be referred for mediation or public review by an assessment panel. A major basis for the MOE's conclusion was Suncor's participation in a provincial initiative, the regional sustainable development strategy (RSDS), a voluntary, consensus-based process involving companies operating in the region, federal and provincial government agencies, affected municipalities, First Nations, and NGOs.]

HENEGAHN J: [The minister of the environment] has no legislative control over the process in the event of its abandonment. In my view, reliance by the MOE upon provincial regulatory powers and initiatives, including the RSDS and industry based initiatives including the CEEMI [provincial Cumulative Environmental Effects Management Initiative], which are beyond enforcement or control by the federal authorities, amounts to a misinterpretation of her duty to consider mitigation factors when she reviewed the CSR. She erred in her interpretation of the Act.

However, if I am in error in this conclusion, I will consider her decision as an exercise of ministerial discretion. Viewed from that perspective, the question is whether the decision is reasonable.

I am not satisfied that reliance upon processes over which she has no control constitutes a reasonable exercise of authority or discretion.

Reliance by the MOE on the RSDS as a mitigation measure cannot be characterized as a discretionary decision over the choice of science to be relied on in the preparation of the CSR. While the record contains references to RSDS as being an example of the science of adaptive management, the fact remains that this is a process over which the MOE has no control and in which she participates only as a voluntary stakeholder, together with representatives from other federal departments. Although section 12 of the *CEAA* specifically recognizes reliance by federal authorities upon actions taken in the provincial sphere for some purposes, there is nothing in that section or elsewhere which allows the MOE or any federal RA to discharge their respective obligations by voluntary participation in provincial regulatory processes and initiatives.

NOTES AND QUESTIONS

1. At least one court challenge has been filed alleging that the *Canada-wide Accord on Environmental Harmonization* and various federal–provincial accords are unconstitutional. See *Canadian Environmental Law Assoc. v. Canada (Minister of the Environment)*, [1999] 3 FC 56 (FCTD).

2. In other instances, as in *Environmental Resource Centre*, above, challenges have been brought before the courts related to alleged improper reliance by federal departments

on processes delivered under the mandate of provincial laws. In addition, a number of submissions have been filed under the NAAEC, alleging that specified arrangements made between federal and provincial governments related to the delegation of enforcement responsibilities violate the NAAEC's Article 5 obligation for effective enforcement. See, for example, submission SEM-96-003 (*Friends of the Oldman River*) and factual record for submission SEM-97-001 (*BC Aboriginal Fisheries Commission et al.*).

3. What, if any, constitutional challenges could be raised by virtue of reliance on the principle enunciated in the harmonization accord of a "best situated" government?

4. What potential impacts, if any, could the harmonization accord have on Crown liability for damages arising from failure to intervene to inspect or enforce environmental laws? See, for example, *Swanson Estate v. Canada* (1990), 19 ACWS (3d) 810 (FCTD); *Kamloops (Municipality) v. Neilson*, [1984] 2 SCR 2; and *Tock v. St. John's Metropolitan Area Board*, [1989] 2 SCR 1181.

VI. ALTERNATIVE APPROACHES TO ENFORCEMENT AND COMPLIANCE

Over the past decade, Canadian environmental law has evolved to incorporate a number of alternative mechanisms to ensure compliance or to respond to violations. On the continuum of enforcement and compliance measures, Canadian environmental agencies have increasingly tended to opt for the less interventionist, more negotiable responses, including negotiated compliance agreements and industry self-monitoring, reporting, and audits. Additional challenges are placed on enforcers by a reliance on alternative standard-setting mechanisms, for example, ISO 14000, sectoral agreements, or emission-trading regimes. A counterpoise to this official "backing off" has been an increased incidence of citizen-initiated suits, including private prosecutions and judicial review proceedings to force government enforcement action.

Some Canadian jurisdictions have enhanced their capabilities to respond in a constructive manner to environmental violations by revising their environmental laws to expand the toolbox of available enforcement responses. Counted among the more innovative new tools are administrative penalties, expanded sentencing powers, and a mechanism for negotiated compliance agreements. This has permitted innovation in sentencing, such as a condition that a convicted company obtain ISO 14000 Environmental Management System certification (*R v. Prospec Chemicals Ltd.* (1996), 19 CELR (NS) 178 (Alta. Prov. Ct.)) and judicial prohibitory, remedial, or planning orders following conviction under provisions such as s. 291 of CEPA, 1999.

While it may be premature to assess the relative efficacy of these diverse approaches to compliance, recent surveys and studies suggest a trend to increased rates of non-compliance in those jurisdictions giving preference to "voluntary" measures, or where significant cuts have been made to environmental enforcement budgets. See, for example, Sierra Legal Defence Fund, *Polluter's Haven, Air and Wastewater Violations in the Lake Ontario Basin* (July 2002); Sierra Legal Defence Fund, *Pulping the Law, How Pulp Mills are Ruining Canadian Waters with Impunity* (November 2000); Sierra Legal Defence Fund, *Ontario, Yours To Pollute, A Report on Ontario's Wastewater Violations 1995-2000* (October 2001) (all are available online at http://www.sierralegal.org/); and

West Coast Environmental Law Association (WCEL) and Environmental Mining Council of BC, *Undermining the Law: Addressing the Crisis in Compliance with Environmental Mining Laws in BC* (Vancouver: WCEL et al., 2001) (available online at http://www.wcel.org/). The shift away from strict enforcement has also attracted intensified scrutiny by government-established review bodies with a mandate to review the enforcement policies and programs of federal and provincial agencies. See, for example, the Standing Committee on Environment and Sustainable Development, *Enforcing Canada's Pollution Laws: The Public Interest Must Come First!*, above, and the Environmental Commissioner of Ontario (ECO), *Having Regard: Annual Report 2000-2001* (Toronto: ECO, 2001), available online at http://www.eco.on.ca/.

A. Negotiated (Legally Binding) Compliance

Negotiated (legally binding) compliance agreements have taken a variety of forms in Canada. Until recently, negotiations occurred on two levels, both through informal discussions. The first involved consultations between a regulatory body and the violating industry; the second involved consultations held by government with an industry sector and affected community to review potential scenarios in order to improve the overall record of compliance or environmental performance. While the first scenario rarely engages the public, it has become common in the latter scenario to also invite representatives of affected communities or NGOs to the table.

More recently, amendments have been made to environmental laws to provide a legal framework for negotiated compliance agreements or schedules. One example is the recently added provision for compliance agreements under CEPA, 1999, a mechanism that attracted considerable discussion and debate.

Voluntary Measures To Ensure Environmental Compliance:
A Review and Analysis of North American Initiatives
(Montreal: Commission for Environmental Cooperation (CEC), 1998), at 25
(reprinted in (Fall 1998) *North American Environmental Law and Policy*)

Federal Government Proposals

The *Canadian Environmental Protection Act* (CEPA) does not specifically refer to "voluntary compliance" in its Enforcement and Compliance Policy. It allows enforcement officials limited discretion to respond to non-compliance with measures other than prosecution. Instead of inviting an offender to submit a proposal for returning to compliance, federal inspectors are limited to giving written warnings. Warnings may be used when the degree of harm or potential harm to the environment, human life or health appears to be "minimal." The regulator must consider the nature of the violation and the effectiveness of a warning in enjoining the violator to achieve compliance. Factors to be considered include the violator's history of compliance and willingness to cooperate, any corrective or enforcement action already taken, and the importance of consistency.

In December 1995, the federal government announced its intention to amend CEPA to include negotiated settlements as part of its new, integrated approach to compliance and enforcement:

> The term "negotiated settlement" refers to an agreement reached between a regulatee and a regulator. The goal of negotiated settlements is to increase compliance and decrease the need to prosecute or seek an injunction. The settlement is made after the regulatee has been found to have broken the law, in this case, CEPA and/or its accompanying regulations. Instead of prosecuting or taking another enforcement action, the regulator negotiates with the regulatee to identify the steps that the regulatee will take to ensure that another violation will not occur. The agreement takes as a starting point that the regulatee will correct the violation. It is important to note that compliance with the law is not negotiable—the regulatee must comply. The only thing being negotiated is the steps that the regulatee will take to return to a state of compliance with the law and to ensure that the violation does not recur.

Negotiated settlements offer the regulatee and the regulator an opportunity to agree on such things, as, for example, the regulatee's commitment to set up better monitoring mechanisms, improve pollution prevention or pollution control measures, or changes to the production process to reduce the possibility of future offenses. Negotiated settlements can also specify the type of corrective measures that the regulatee will take to clean up environmental damage resulting from the offense or the restitution that the regulatee will offer. Settlements can include a time frame for the regulatee's actions, a requirement to file status reports with the regulator, and a list of specific consequences if the regulatee fails to live up to the terms of the settlement. Negotiated settlements do not stand alone. Under a renewed CEPA, they would be one enforcement mechanism among a spectrum of options and would be used in conjunction with an administrative penalty scheme either to supplement the monetary penalty or to replace it.

As is the case with administrative monetary penalties, negotiated settlements in various forms, including assurances of voluntary compliance, compliance plans, consent orders and consent agreements, are not new to North American law. For example, such assurances are used in Canada in provinces such as British Columbia, Newfoundland and Quebec in relation to business and trade practices. Compliance plans exist under the Ontario *Occupational Health and Safety Act*. Consent agreements are found in the federal *Canadian Human Rights Act* and *Competition Act*, and both the Ontario *Business Practices Act* and *Discriminatory Business Practices Act*. The Alberta *Agricultural Service Board Act* provides for "negotiations." The US Environmental Protection Agency uses consent orders and consent agreements.

Canadian Environmental Protection Act, 1999
SC 1999, c. 33

Environmental Protection Alternative Measures

296(1) Environmental protection alternative measures may be used to deal with a person who is alleged to have committed an offence under this Act only if it is not inconsistent with the purposes of this Act and the following conditions are met:

(a) the measures are part of a program of environmental protection alternative measures authorized by the Attorney General, after consultation with the Minister,

(b) the offence alleged to have been committed is an offence under this Act except an offence under

(i) paragraph 272(1) or (b), in respect of subsection 16(4), 81(1), (2), (3) or (4), 82(1) or (2), 84(2) or 96(4), section 99, subsection 106(1), (2), (3) or (4), 107(1) or (2), 109(1) or (2), 119(1), 148(1), 202(4) or 213(4) or section 227 or 228,

(ii) paragraph 272(1)(c), (d) or (e),

(iii) subsection 273(1), if the offence is committed knowingly, or

(iv) subsection 274(1) or (2);

(c) an information has been laid in respect of the offence;

(d) the Attorney General, after consulting with the Minister, is satisfied that they would be appropriate, having regard to the nature of the offence, the circumstances surrounding its commission and the following factors, namely,

(i) the protection of the environment and of human life and health and other interests of society,

(ii) the person's history of compliance with this Act,

(iii) whether the offence is a repeated occurrence,

(iv) any allegation that information is being or was concealed or other attempts to subvert the purposes and requirements of this Act are being or have been made, and

(v) whether any remedial or preventive action has been taken by or on behalf of the person in relation to the offence;

(e) the person has been advised of the right to be represented by counsel,

(f) the person accepts responsibility for the act or omission that forms the basis of the offence that the person is alleged to have committed;

(g) the person applies, in accordance with regulations made under section 309, to participate in the measures;

(h) the person and the Attorney General have entered into an agreement within the period of 180 days after the Attorney General has provided initial disclosure of the Crown's evidence to the person

(i) there is, in the opinion of the Attorney General, sufficient evidence to proceed with the prosecution of the offence; and

(j) the prosecution of the offence is not barred at law.

. . .

298(1) An agreement may contain any terms and conditions, including, but not limited to,

(a) terms and conditions having any or all of the effects set out in section 291 or any other terms and conditions having any of the effects prescribed by the regulations that the Attorney General, after consulting with the Minister, considers appropriate; and

(b) terms and conditions relating to the costs of laboratory tests and of field tests, travel and living expenses, costs of scientific analyses and other reasonable costs associated with supervising and verifying compliance with the agreement.

(2) Any governmental or non-governmental body may supervise compliance with an agreement.

299. An agreement comes into force on the day on which it is signed or on any later day that is specified in the agreement and continues in force for the period, not exceeding three years, specified in the agreement.

300(1) Subject to subsection (5), the Attorney General shall consult with the Minister before entering into an agreement and shall cause the agreement to be filed, as part of the court record of the proceedings to which the public has access, with the court in which the information was laid, within 30 days after the agreement was entered into.

(2) A report relating to the administration of or compliance with an agreement shall, immediately after all the terms and conditions of the agreement have been complied with or the charges in respect of which the agreement was entered into have been dismissed, be filed with the court in which the agreement was filed in accordance with subsection (1).

301. A copy of every agreement and report referred to in subsection 300(2) and every agreement that has been varied under subsection 303(1), or a notice that the agreement or report has been filed in court and is available to the public, shall be included in the Environmental Registry.

B. Negotiated (Voluntary) Compliance

A second category of negotiated agreements involve those that provide non-binding commitments to environmental improvements beyond or outside regulatory requirements. Some authors have recommended adoption of legislated frameworks and principles to ensure consistency and fairness in their application and increase the level of public acceptability of these alternative "compliance" instruments.

A number of voluntary environmental approaches (VEAs) or voluntary non-regulatory initiatives (VNRIs) have been introduced by government or industry either to establish environmental performance "standards" or objectives, to reward investment in environmental measures beyond regulatory requirements, or to provide mechanisms for alternative routes to compliance.

Among those tools that directly or indirectly address compliance are

1. compliance policies that provide for negotiated compliance plans and agreements;
2. lender liability agreements;
3. audit privilege policies and allowances;
4. polices adopting private standard-setting and audit schemes (for example, ISO 14000 certification, Canadian Chemical Producers' Association Responsible Care program, Accelerated Reduction/Elimination of Toxics (ARET) multistakeholder process);

5. memoranda of understanding;
6. provisions enabling greater flexibility or innovation in sentencing; and
7. challenge programs (for example, the Climate Change Voluntary Challenge and Registry Program (VCR Inc.).

While many of the mechanisms adopt mandatory language such as "standards" and "verification of compliance," only a subset of these initiatives actually target compliance with legally binding standards. The remainder target improved environmental management or performance. Widely diverse views have been expressed on the appropriateness of the moniker "voluntary compliance" for these instruments. While some laud the concept, others deem the term an oxymoron.

A.R. Lucas
"Voluntary Initiatives for Greenhouse Gas Reduction"
(2000) vol. 10 *Journal of Environmental Law and Practice* 89, at 93-96

Fundamental Problems

Apart from unreasonable expectations, there are several fundamental problems. One is the persistent idea that voluntary initiatives are complete alternatives to formal legally enforceable regulatory measures in achieving or "complying" with emission standards. A second problem is lack of clarity in using such terms as "voluntary programs" and "voluntary compliance." "Voluntary" can include commitments made voluntarily rather than imposed under regulatory authority but nonetheless intended to achieve regulatory compliance. An example is a negotiated compliance agreement between a government regulator and a permittee within the legal authority of the regulator but alternative to imposed permit conditions or coercive enforcement action such as administrative penalty or prosecution. This latter category of voluntary actions caused a Canadian multistakeholder organization that studies voluntary approaches to characterize voluntary actions as "Voluntary or Non-Regulatory Initiatives" (VNRIs).

. . .

Voluntary or Non-Regulatory Initiatives (VNRIs)

There may be alternative methods or manners of meeting environmental requirements that are expressed in essentially qualitative terms in licenses or permits. The non-compliance threshold may be reached only when, for example, release of contaminant in excess of permit limits has occurred and there has been a failure to exercise all due diligence in taking action to prevent the non-compliance. This is a consequence of the legislative use of strict liability offences to compel compliance with environmental requirements. Thus, in principle, compliance may become voluntary at some difficult-to-identify point when it is likely that a court would recognize that all due diligence has been exercised.

With these shades of "voluntary" in mind, it must be remembered that consensual actions in the context of regulatory processes are not strictly voluntary. Rather, a negotiated compliance agreement, for example, may simply be one technique, in addition to coercive regulatory actions, to achieve regulatory compliance. The threat of coercive action is a prime motivator for voluntary "non-regulatory" arrangements.

J. Moffet, B. Davis, and B. Mausberg
"Supporting Negotiated Environmental Agreements with Statutory and Regulatory Provisions: An Overview for Ontario"
(Toronto: Environmental Defence Canada, 2002), at 1-3 and 9

1.2 Negotiated Environmental Agreements

Negotiated environmental agreements are a subset of voluntary environmental approaches (VEAs). VEAs are schemes where parties (primarily companies) make commitments to improve their environmental performance beyond existing legal requirements. The distinctive feature of negotiated environmental agreements is that they involve commitments for environmental performance developed through bargaining between a public authority and industry. As such, they can be distinguished from both "public voluntary programs" and "unilateral commitments." Public voluntary programs involve commitments designed by a government agency and in which individual firms are invited to participate (e.g., ARET, VCR). Unilateral commitments are set by industry independently of any negotiation (e.g., Responsible Care). Neither involves bargaining.

This paper also distinguishes "self-regulation" from negotiated environmental agreements. For the purpose of this paper, self-regulation is considered the control by an association of the conduct of its members. These arrangements can take various forms, but typically involve clear statutory delegation to a specified body of the powers to control certain aspects of the conduct of a profession (e.g., doctors, lawyers, accountants) or group of actors within a sector (e.g., the recent delegation to Marina operators in Ontario of the power to self-regulate certain environmental issues). The distinction between these arrangements and agreements can be fuzzy. Indeed, this paper identifies some aspects of self-regulation models as options to consider for negotiated agreements. The basic distinction, again, however, is that self-regulation does not entail bargaining; instead it is a form of delegated authority within clearly prescribed parameters.

There are numerous important and controversial issues about when to use and how to design negotiated environmental agreements. This paper takes no position as to the overall merit of a VEA in any given situation. Rather, it focuses only on the (heretofore overlooked) issue of what role statutory and regulatory provisions could play in enhancing the effectiveness, efficiency and credibility of such agreements.

. . .

2.1 Ensuring that Statutory and Regulatory Linkages Address the Needs of Stakeholders

. . .

Each interested party will want a statutory or regulatory framework to augment the particular characteristics of agreements in which they are most interested. Conversely, each stakeholder will want to ensure that any statutory or regulatory framework does not have an adverse effect on one of those characteristics. Thus, for example, industry participants will want a statutory or regulatory framework to help reduce transaction costs, enhance the certainty with respect to the impact their agreement might have on existing or future regulatory obligations, strengthen the likelihood of equitable treatment or reduce the chances of free riders. While an explicit legal framework can be expected to provide enhanced clarity and certainty, industry will also be concerned about excessive legal requirements that render agreements virtually identical to regulations thereby eliminating the benefits of flexibility associated with an agreement.

Similarly, governments can be expected to be interested in a statutory or regulatory framework for negotiated environmental agreements if such a framework helps them to reduce their administrative costs, either by achieving performance equivalent to that required in existing regulations with less enforcement required or through environmental gains beyond their immediate regulatory control. Governments may also want a legal linkage to enhance their ability to respond to public demands for accountability. As is discussed below, governments also will want to ensure that any formalization of agreements respects basic legal considerations and avoids increasing the likelihood of such problems as officially induced error or inappropriate fettering of discretion.

Finally, the interested public likely will support a statutory or regulatory framework that ensures that agreements contain clear targets with which the public agrees (ideally, which they have helped negotiate), requires participants to provide the public with credible assurances of improved performance or reduces the likelihood of free riders.

. . .

In theory, an explicit linkage to statutory or regulatory provisions could help address each of the interests of the various stakeholders described above. For example, by providing clear legal approbation of an agreement, an explicit linkage to statutory or regulatory provisions could enhance the profile of an agreement, thereby enhancing its credibility with stakeholders and the likelihood that targeted actors will join the regime. A statutory or regulatory framework for agreements related to a given issue could help ensure consistency among similar agreements and avoid concerns about "regulatory capture" … . Statutory or regulatory provisions concerning penalties for non-compliance could increase the likelihood of compliance with the terms of the agreement and decrease the chance of free riders. And finally, credibility, participation rates and compliance levels could all be augmented by the provision of a clear set of incentives or a legal requirement to impose alternative regulations if the agreement does not address the given issue effectively.

The case for explicit regulatory integration is not unequivocal, however. Linking negotiated environmental agreements (or any form of voluntary environmental activity) to a statute or regulation can raise various important problems. For example, providing an explicit statutory or regulatory linkage may actually strengthen each of the following concerns identified by critics about negotiated environmental agreements:

(a) To the extent that statutory recognition of an agreement provides a signal to the public that the government is satisfied that a given issue (risk) will be addressed adequately, it may increase the potential for government liability should the agreement prove to be ineffective.

(b) If the agreement addresses behaviour that would otherwise be subject to regulatory control, such a linkage may increase the potential for officially induced error.

(c) Agreements that purport to circumscribe future government intervention in a given area may give rise to concerns about fettering the government's discretion to act.

(d) Individualized agreements providing differentiated approaches to the same issue may generate concerns about fairness and the rule of law.

(e) Legislative approval of agreements negotiated bilaterally between industry and government where that approval does not also require procedural safeguards equivalent to those provided for the development of regulations may enhance concerns about regulatory capture or lack of transparency.

(f) From industry's point of view, a heavy regulatory hand (or perception thereof) that blurs the distinction between an agreement and a regulation may be a disincentive to participate in an agreement.

· · ·

One of the key issues with respect to negotiated environmental agreements is how to ensure compliance. In most cases, governments promote compliance through incentives and by providing a credible threat of more direct intervention if the agreement is not effective. In addition, in some cases it may be possible to ensure that the agreement itself: a) is legally binding, and b) contains explicit penalty provisions for non-compliance.

· · ·

3.2.5 Authorize Regulatory Exemptions or Relaxations

There are numerous examples of ways in which jurisdictions have revised legislation to provide for regulatory-related incentives for participating in a voluntary program.

• *Relaxed or streamlined regulatory requirements.* Voluntary environmental agreement statutes can authorize the government to alter the basic regulatory requirements in return for strong environmental performance commitments in an agreement. Various US state programs authorize the permitting agency to negotiate the removal of mutually identified administrative burdens for program participants. For example, a 1997 Oregon law authorizes the Oregon Department of Environmental Quality to issue "Green Permits" that may waive regulatory requirements, authorize consolidated reporting and provide other benefits for participating facilities that can demonstrate certain requirements, including a superior track record, public reporting and community engagement and a commitment to beyond compliance performance levels. In addition, "Custom Waiver Permits" allow limited waivers of regulatory requirements if the waiver is needed to help the facility perform significantly better than otherwise required. Non-compliance with any of these permits is subject to the same penalties as non-compliance with a regular permit.

• *Reduced reporting.* Various US State programs as well as both the US *Clean Air Act* and the *Clean Water Act* authorize reduced reporting requirements for parties engaged in specified activities that lead to beyond compliance performance. By analogy, a statute could authorize a similar reduction in reporting for facilities that have negotiated an environmental agreement of a specified form and content.

• *Reduced inspections.* The proposed legislation in support of Wisconsin's Green Tier program provides that the government will inspect participating facilities "at the lowest frequency permitted by [the relevant law]" (section 7(f)).

• *Deferred enforcement (audit privilege).* Various jurisdictions have developed "audit privilege" policies or statutory rules over the past decade. Essentially, these policies provide that the government will not enforce violations discovered during a voluntary audit if the offending party reports the violation and corrects it within a specified period of time. Again, the proposed Wisconsin Green Tier legislation provides an interesting example of an audit privilege rule that is provided to participants in a voluntary program based on the negotiation of environmental agreements. Section 10(r) of the proposed Act provides that the government will not enforce any violation identified by an audit conducted by a Green Tier participant if the violation is corrected within 90 days of the audit.

Audit privilege policies are highly contentious, particularly with respect to whether they should apply to one-off incidents that have serious repercussions (such as major water contamination). In theory, it should be possible to include detailed provisions in an agreement to address these difficult issues.

NOTES AND QUESTIONS

1. An excellent overview of the varied approaches adopted by environmental agencies in Canada, the United States, and Mexico for triggering voluntary compliance is provided in the 1998 report of the Commission for Environmental Cooperation, *Voluntary Measures To Ensure Environmental Compliance: A Review and Analysis of North American Initiatives*, excerpted above. In a second publication, *Voluntary Codes: Private Governance, the Public Interest and Innovation*, due for a 2003 release, editor and contributor K. Webb offers a more positive spin on the potential for "voluntary compliance" instruments, arguing that they have had and can have a demonstrable environmental benefit when used constructively. See also Industry Canada, "An Evaluation Framework for Voluntary Codes," available online at http://strategis.ic.gc.ca/pics/ca/evalu.pdf.

2. A considerable amount of analysis has been directed at alternative policies and approaches to improving the compliance record of the Canadian pulp and paper industry. An analysis conducted by Environment Canada of alternative responses to continual violations in the antisapstain and heavy duty wood preservative industry raises questions about the efficacy of voluntary initiatives and gives credence to interventionist measures.

In a program report, P.K. Krahn, acting head of the inspections division, Environment Canada, Pacific and Yukon region, stated:

> Environment Canada's Pacific and Yukon regional office has implemented a compliance and enforcement program which has developed over the last 15 years into four primary stages: Problem definition and Scientific Assessment: Compliance Promotion and Inspection: Strategic Enforcement Initiatives and Prosecution: Compliance Maintenance. These can be divided into 8 distinct phases. The compliance process takes place over a 5 to 7 year period depending on the industry and has resulted in dramatic reductions in the discharges of harmful substances and increases in compliance with the Federal *Fisheries Act* and the *Canadian Environmental Protection Act*. Three case studies of the Antisapstain Industry, Pulp and Paper Industry, and Heavy Duty Wood Preservation Industry which included 154 of the largest industrial facilities in British Columbia demonstrate that compliance promotion combined with progressive use of stronger enforcement tools leads to compliance with federal environmental legislation.
>
> The design of this process results in less than 0.5% to 1.5% of the facilities in any of the industry groups being subjected to prosecution and maximizes the use of other enforcement tools such as inspections, warning letters and direction letters. The sole reliance on voluntary compliance was demonstrated to be ineffective for these sectors in achieving even a marginally acceptable level of compliance or benefit to the environment.
>
> • • •
>
> Properly designed and applied compliance and enforcement programs resulted in a significant expenditure/cost ratio. Expenditures by industry to comply with the regulatory initiatives were demonstrated to exceed the federal government costs for the program by ratios that were greater than 70:1. In one case study the heavy duty wood preservation expended over $39,000,000 to comply with environmental requirements as a result of a $600,000 expenditure on a strategic enforcement program under the Fraser River Action Plan.
>
> • • •
>
> A review of 19 different regulatory groups found that those industrial sectors which relied solely on self monitoring or voluntary compliance had a compliance rating of 60% vs. the 94% average compliance rating for those industries which were subject to federal regulations combined with a consistent inspection program. Voluntary compliance programs and peer inspection programs could not achieve satisfactory levels of compliance.

(From "Enforcement vs. Voluntary Compliance: An Examination of the Strategic Enforcement Initiatives Implemented by the Pacific and Yukon Regional Office of Environment Canada 1983 to 1998," DOE FRAP 1998-3, Regional program report 98-02 (Vancouver: Government of Canada, 1998) (available online at http://www.rem.sfu.ca/ FRAP/9803.pdf). See also Sierra Legal Defence Fund, *Pulping the Law: How Pulp Mills Are Ruining Canadian Waters with Impunity* and K. Harrison, "Is Cooperation the Answer?" above.

3. A thorough analysis of the efficacy of alternative approaches to compliance with environmental mining laws in British Columbia is provided in WCEL et al.'s, *Undermining the Law: Addressing the Crisis in Compliance with Environmental Mining Laws in BC.*

4. Where there is reliance on a voluntary mechanism to achieve compliance with an environmental standard, what are the implications for responding to free riders? What are the implications, if any, of reliance by governments on voluntary or non-interventionist routes to compliance for the observance of the principle of "rule of law"? Can you identify potential conflicts for environmental agencies employing traditional enforcement responses while simultaneously promoting the use of voluntary measures such as ISO 14000?

5. Identified problems or constraints with voluntary mechanisms have included lack of transparency and limited rights of third parties (P. Muldoon and R. Nadarajah, "A Sober Second Look," in R. Gibson, ed., *Voluntary Initiatives: The New Politics of Corporate Greening* (Peterborough, ON: Broadview Press, 1999)); potential impact on standard of care and an inability to respond to free riders (CEC, *Voluntary Measures to Ensure Environmental Compliance: A Review and Analysis of North American Initiatives*, above); lack of political accountability (CEC, *Environmental Management Systems and Compliance: Report to the Council of the Commission for Environmental Cooperation on Results and Recommendations Pursuant to Council Resolution 97-05 by the North American Working Group on Environmental Enforcement and Compliance Cooperation* (Montreal: CEC, June 1998)); efficacy (R. Hornung and M. Bramley, *Federal and Provincial Government Inaction on Climate Change During a Period of Rising Industrial Emissions* (Ottawa: Pembina Institute, March 2000), A.R. Lucas, "Voluntary Initiatives for Greenhouse Gas Reduction: The Legal Implications" (2000) vol. 10 *Journal of Environmental Law and Practice* 89, and K. Webb, "Voluntary Initiatives and the Law," in Gibson, above); and implications for enforcement and compliance programs, policies, and responses (CEC, *Council Resolution 97-05: Future Cooperation Regarding Environmental Management Systems and Compliance*).

6. Is it possible to apply consistent indicators to evaluate and report on the relative effectiveness of "command and control" versus "voluntary compliance" measures for achieving effective environmental enforcement? For a discussion of the problems posed in evaluating the effectiveness of voluntary compliance programs, see CEC, *Indicators of Effective Environmental Enforcement: Proceedings of a North American Dialogue* (Montreal: CEC, March 1999).

VII. PRIVATE ENFORCEMENT

A. Citizen Suits

Canadian citizens are accorded some rights and opportunities for legally challenging the exercise by federal and provincial governments of their powers and responsibilities for the enforcement of, or adherence to, environmental laws. These rights are provided within domestic statutes and international agreements, examples of which are provided below. There is a growing body of precedent involving citizen suits seeking judicial intervention directed at forcing governments to take action to enforce environmental laws.

North American Agreement on Environmental Cooperation
(entered into force on January 1, 1994)
(United States–Canada–Mexico) (1993) vol. 32 *International Legal Materials* 1480

Article 6: Private Access to Remedies

(1) Each Party shall ensure that interested persons may request the Party's competent authorities to investigate alleged violations of its environmental laws and regulations and shall give such requests due consideration in accordance with law.

(2) Each Party shall ensure that persons with a legally recognized interest under its law in a particular matter have appropriate access to administrative, quasi-judicial or judicial proceedings for the enforcement of the Party's environmental laws and regulations.

(3) Private access to remedies shall include rights, in accordance with the Party's law, such as:

(a) to seek sanctions or remedies such as monetary penalties, emergency closures or orders to mitigate the consequences of violations of its environmental laws and regulations;

(b) to request that competent authorities to take appropriate action to enforce that Party's environmental laws and regulations in order to protect the environment or to avoid environmental harm.

Canadian Environmental Protection Act, 1999
SC 1999, c. 33

Environmental Protection Action

22(1) An individual who has applied for an investigation may bring an environmental protection action if

(a) the Minister failed to conduct an investigation and report within a reasonable time; or

(b) the Minister's response to the investigation was unreasonable.

(2) The action may be brought in any court of competent jurisdiction against a person who committed an offence under this Act that

(a) was alleged in the application for the investigation; and

(b) caused significant harm to the environment.

(3) In the action, the individual may claim any or all of the following:

(a) a declaratory order;

(b) and order, including an interlocutory order, requiring the defendant to refrain from doing anything that, in the opinion of the court, may constitute an offence under this Act;

(c) an order, including an interlocutory order, requiring the defendant to do anything that, in the opinion of the court, may prevent the continuation of an offence under this Act;

(d) an order to the parties to negotiate a plan to correct or mitigate the harm to the environment or to human, animal or plant life or health, and to report to the court on the negotiations with a time frame set out by the court; and

(e) any other appropriate relief, including the costs of the action, but not including damages.

B. Private Prosecution

Yukon Environment Act
SY 1991, c. 5

19(1) An adult person resident in the Yukon may institute a private prosecution in respect of an offence under this Act or a regulation under this Act or under a Schedule A enactment or a regulation under a Schedule A enactment.

L.F. Duncan
Enforcing Environmental Law: A Guide to Private Prosecution
(Edmonton: Environmental Law Centre, 1990), at 7

Who Can Launch a Private Prosecution?

General Right

It is a general rule of law that anyone can commence a private prosecution. The *Criminal Code*, the federal law which regulates the conduct of actions before the criminal courts, specifically provides that anyone, who on reasonable grounds believes that a person has committed an offence, may commence a prosecution by swearing an information (more commonly known as the charge).

. . .

Barriers

Despite the preservation of the common law right of a private citizen to initiate a prosecution, some barriers do exist. The Attorney General and the courts exercise broad powers which can impact upon the right to proceed. Certain laws may also curtail or restrict the right to lay an information. For example, the Alberta *Petty Trespass Act* prohibits prosecution under the Act unless the information is laid by the owner or occupier of land or his servant. Other laws provide for the intervention by the Crown or the courts later in proceedings.

Prior Consent of the Attorney General

Many laws require the prior consent of the federal or provincial Attorney General before a prosecution can be initiated. In such cases the consent must be obtained before the information is laid. The decision by the Attorney General to grant or deny his [or her] consent is completely within his [or her] discretion. It has been argued that the exercise of discretion by the Attorney General may be subject to review. No reasons are required however and the courts have demonstrated a reluctance to review the exercise of these discretionary powers.

Where consent is granted it is provided in the form of an Attorney General's *fiat*. It need not necessarily be in writing. However, any procedural requirements imposed by statute must be complied with and specific reference must be made to the alleged offence, the accused and time and place of the offence.

The *Criminal Code* includes many provisions requiring prior consent of the Attorney General. [O]ther federal and provincial statutes include provisions which require prior consent of the Attorney General before the commencement of prosecution ... .

The right of provincial legislators to impose conditions on the right to initiate a private prosecution has been questioned by the courts. To date, however, the courts have confined their interventions to situations where the provinces have attempted to restrict prosecutions under the *Criminal Code*.

Kostuch v. Kowalski
[1991] 6 WWR 160 (Alta. QB); aff'd. [1993] 6 WWR 696 (Alta. CA)

MILLER ACJQB: Suffice it to say that the matter arises from a rather complex and protracted web of legal proceedings initiated by Dr. Martha Kostuch in an attempt to stop construction of the Oldman River Dam. Litigation first arose in August 1988 when Dr. Kostuch initiated her first information under the *Fisheries Act*, RSC 1985, c. F-14 against the then Minister of the Environment, Kenneth Kowalski, and two construction companies working on the project, W.A. Stephenson Construction (Western) Ltd. and SCI Engineering and Constructors Inc. A second information was sworn in January 1990; a third in February 1990; a fourth in April 1990; a fifth and sixth on May 4, 1990, and a seventh, the one before this Court, on July 24, 1990.

· · ·

In considering the first ground of appeal in this application, it becomes critical to identify what test is the applicable one to use in weighing whether or not the actions of Kostuch in initiating the last information on July 4, 1990, constituted an abuse of process of the court.

Because of the history of this matter, it is important, at the outset, to clarify what is actually happening in this application for there are two different types of proceedings which have been before the courts and it may be that the test and the burden of proof are different depending on which type of application we are now addressing.

The first category of proceeding was an application by Kostuch to lift a stay of proceedings which had been entered by the Attorney General. The second category is this type of application to the court to enter a stay of proceedings against a prosecution initiated either by the Crown or, as in this case, by a private citizen.

· · ·

The Flagrant Impropriety Test

In an application to lift a stay of proceedings the courts have generally been loath to interfere with the discretion of the officer of the Crown, the Attorney General unless there has been some clear evidence of flagrant impropriety.

. . .

Generally, the degree of impropriety to be met before the court will intervene to reverse an action by the Attorney General is very extensive. It must border on corruption by the Crown, violation of the law, bias against the particular offence, or prejudice against the accused or the victim.

. . .

The Abuse of Process Doctrine

On the other hand, the law governing the court's intervention to enter a stay in the face of a seemingly legitimate prosecution has followed an entirely different course. It has evolved around the doctrine of abuse of process where the application to the court to enter a stay is measured against whether there has been an abuse of process on the part of the party swearing the information in preparation for proceeding with the prosecution.

. . .

Moving then to the application of the doctrine of abuse to the matter before this court, the task becomes one of balancing the competing societal interests in ensuring effective prosecution of criminal matters, on the one hand, and in avoiding an affront to notions of fair play and decency on the other. In making this determination, the court must decide on which side of the balance the administration of justice would best be served and whether this is one of those "clearest of cases."

. . .

Fradsham Prov. J reviewed all of the matters before him to determine that proceeding with the prosecution would not be an affront to fair play or decency and that it was not the result of oppressive or vexatious proceedings on the part of the private prosecutor. He considered what would be in the best interests of the administration of justice.

His conclusion is reached after review of the factors to be considered in arriving at a decision on abuse of process. Keeping in mind the onus on the applicants to prove that the affront to fair play and decency outweighs the societal interests in the effective prosecution of the case before the court, he summarizes at 152 that:

> Dr. Kostuch has not attempted to abuse the process of this court. On the evidence before me she has, through her counsel, attempted to utilize, in the most proper and professional manner, those rights given to her under our legacy of the common law and the provisions of the *Criminal Code*. On two occasions she has convinced judicial officers that a prosecution is warranted—on two occasions that prosecution has been thwarted by the Attorney General. In both cases, the reasons behind the actions of the Attorney General, though not on the evidence before me motivated by malafides, were faulty. She again seeks the assistance of this court—that is not an abuse of the process but a very proper use of the process.

Fradsham Prov. J was correct in this part of his decision applying the doctrine of abuse of process and in deciding that this was not one of those "clearest of cases." ...

The end result of my decision is that the information sworn by Kostuch dated July 24, 1990, should be allowed to proceed through the system in the usual course of events.

NOTE

Recent successful private prosecutions have resulted in substantial penalties against environmental offenders. In *Fletcher v. Kingston (City)*, [1998] OJ no. 6453; [1999] OJ no. 5705; and [2002] OJ no. 2324 (QL) (Prov. Ct.), charges originating from a private information were prosecuted by counsel for the Sierra Legal Defence Fund. Other charges were prosecuted by a provincial Crown prosecutor. It resulted in convictions and fine of $125,000 (under appeal); see the discussion in chapter 5. In *R v. City of Hamilton*, September 18, 2000 (unreported), a case involving a private informant alleging deposit of toxic leachate into a creek, a record penalty of $450,000 was assessed for an environmental offence committed by a municipality. See also *Landry (Private Prosecutor) v. United Aggregates Ltd.*, [1999] OJ no. 5121 (QL) and [2001] OJ no. 345.

C. Citizen Oversight of Government Enforcement Policy and Practice

A number of mechanisms are enshrined in Canadian domestic law and international and multilateral agreements to which Canada is party that empower citizens to trigger processes wherein environmental enforcement policies and practices are publicly scrutinized. Some of these include the processes under the *Auditor General Act*, RSC 1995, c. A-17, whereby "federal departments may be asked to explain federal policy, investigate an environmental infraction, or examine their enforcement of federal environmental legislation" (see *2000 Report of the Commissioner of the Environment and Sustainable Development*, http://www.oag-bvg.gc.ca/environment/); CEPA, 1999, above; and the NAAEC, above. These procedures require governments to publicly disclose information and to account for their actions in response to alleged violations of specified environmental laws. Consequently, as an alternative or precursor to launching private legal actions, individuals can choose to "force" official enforcement action by exercise of these petition-type processes.

Canadian Environmental Protection Act, 1999
SC 1999, c. 33

17(1) An individual who is resident in Canada and at least 18 years of age may apply to the Minister for an investigation of any offence under this Act that the individual alleges has occurred.

. . .

18. The Minister shall acknowledge receipt of the application within 20 days of the receipt and shall investigate all matters that the Minster considers necessary to determine the facts related to the alleged offence.

19. After acknowledging receipt of the application, the Minister shall report to the applicant every 90 days on the progress of the investigation and the action, if any, the Minister has taken or proposes to take, and the Minister shall include in the report an estimate of the time required to complete the investigation or to implement the action, but a report is not required if the investigation is discontinued before the end of the 90 days.

North American Agreement on Environmental Cooperation
(entered into force on January 1, 1994)
(United States–Canada–Mexico) (1993) vol. 32 *International Legal Materials* 1480

Article 14: Submissions on Enforcement Matters

(1) The Secretariat may consider a submission from any non-governmental organization or person asserting that a [state] Party is failing to effectively enforce its environmental law, if the Secretariat finds that the submission:

(a) is in writing in a language designated by that Party in a notification to Secretariat;

(b) clearly identifies the person or organization making the submission;

(c) provides sufficient information to allow the Secretariat to review the submission, including any documentary evidence on which the submission may be based;

(d) appears to be aimed at promoting enforcement rather than at harassing industry;

(e) indicates that the matter has been communicated in writing to the relevant authorities of the Party and indicates the Party's response, if any; and

(f) is filed by a person or organization residing or established in the territory of a Party.

(2) Where the Secretariat determines that a submission meets the criteria set out in paragraph 1, the Secretariat shall determine whether the submission merits requesting a response from the Party. In deciding whether to request a response, the Secretariat shall be guided by whether:

(a) the submission alleges harm to the person or organization making the submission;

(b) the submission, alone or in combination with other submissions, raises matters whose further study in this process would advance the goals of this Agreement;

(c) private remedies available under the Party's law have been pursued; and

(d) the submission is drawn exclusively from mass media reports.

Where the Secretariat makes such a request, it shall forward to the Party a copy of the submission and any supporting information provided with the submission.

NOTES AND QUESTIONS

1. In the NAAEC's enforcement submission process, above, if the CEC secretariat considers that a submission, in light of a party government's response under art. 14 (21), warrants developing a factual record, it makes a recommendation with reasons to the CCME. The council may then, by a two-thirds vote, request that the secretariat do so. There are a few guidelines for the preparation of factual records, but under art. 15, information provided by a party government must be considered and relevant information may be considered that is publicly available; that is submitted by interested persons, NGOs, or the joint public advisory committee established under the agreement; or that is developed by the secretariat or by independent experts. What is reasonably clear is that factual information, not the making of findings or recommendations, is contemplated.

The secretariat prepares a draft factual record, and after receiving comments from the party governments, the secretariat submits a final factual record to the council. By a two-thirds vote, the council may make the factual record available to the public. This is the final stage in the process. There is no decision or recommendation. The factual record serves as a spotlight on the enforcement issues that are raised. For a review of the process and suggestions for research concerning process effectiveness, see D.L. Markell, "The Commission for Environmental Cooperation's Citizen Submission Process" (2000) vol. 12 *Georgetown International Environmental Law Review* 545. Opinions are widely divided on the utility of the citizen submission process under the NAAEC. For additional perspectives, see, for example, C. Tollefson, "Games Without Frontiers: Investor Claims and Citizen Submissions Under the NAFTA Regime" (2002) vol. 27 *Yale Journal of International Law* 141; M.R. Goldschmidt, "The Role of Transparency and Public Participation in International Environmental Agreements: The North American Agreement on Environmental Cooperation" (2002) vol. 29 *Boston College Environmental Affairs Law Review* 343; J.H. Knox, "A New Approach to Compliance with International Law: The Submissions Procedure of the NAFTA Environmental Commission" (2001) vol. 28 *Ecology Law Quarterly* 1.

2. In his article "Advancing an Agenda? A Reflection on Recent Developments in Canadian Pubic Interest Environmental Litigation" (2002) vol. 51 *UNB Law Journal* 1, at 2, C. Tollefson offers this comment on the role played by private environmental litigators:

> Sometimes these groups litigate with a view to restraining government action; other times, they intervene to defend the exercise of government power. Almost invariably, however, I would contend that their participation in the litigation process is motivated or defined by a particular vision of social and political ordering. In other words, not only are they seeking vindication of their rights on the merits as is typical in private litigation, they are also mindful of and aspire to advance broader principles, interests and values.

FURTHER READINGS

J. Benedickson, *Environmental Law*, 2d ed. (Toronto: Irwin Law, 2002), chapter 7.

F. Gertler, "Lost in (Intergovernmental) Space: Cooperative Federalism in Environmental Protection," in S. Kennett, ed., *Law and Process in Environmental Management* (Calgary: Canadian Institute of Resources Law [CILR], 1993).

D. Saxe, *Environmental Offences: Corporate Responsibility and Executive Liability* (Aurora, ON: Canada Law Book, 1990).

K. Webb, ed., *Voluntary Codes: Private Governance, the Public Interest and Innovation* (Ottawa: Carleton University Research Unit for Innovation, Science and the Environment, 2003).

CHAPTER TEN

The Economic Approach*

J. Owen Saunders

I. INTRODUCTION

If there is one social science that can claim dominance in terms of its influence on social policy over the last century, it is certainly economics. Much of this dominance is explained by the success of the economic model, a model that, more than any other social science, attempts to replicate the approach found in the physical sciences or, more precisely, that found in physics. The model provided by physics is particularly attractive to policy makers because it is deductive—that is, one begins with a description of the universe in terms of laws. From these laws, one can then predict how the universe will react to given shocks. Not surprisingly, the explanatory powers claimed by economics have attracted the interest of lawyers, as witnessed by the explosion of literature on economic analysis of law over the past two decades, especially in the United States, but increasingly also in Canada.

Economic approaches to social policy have played a particularly important role with respect to environmental policy, although not without some controversy. This controversy relates especially to the argument that some of the environmental problems for which an economic approach is advocated should not be treated in this way. Specifically, for example, it is sometimes argued by environmental advocates that the use of effluent charges as a means of dealing with pollution is in some sense improper, insofar as they can be seen as condoning pollution rather than condemning it. Similarly, it is sometimes argued that an "economic" approach to issues such as wilderness preservation is inappropriate, insofar as national parks should not have a price put on them; and, indeed, as we will see in this chapter, there is some emerging evidence that the market approach to issues such as the latter does have considerable drawbacks.

Many environmental issues are of special theoretical interest for economists for another reason; they are often raised as examples of market failure, or, put differently, of exceptions to the "normal" model that economists use to describe the world. Not all

* I would like to acknowledge with thanks the research assistance of Carla Tait, who served as a student research assistant in the Canadian Institute of Resources Law during the summer of 2002. I would also like to acknowledge the secretarial assistance of Patricia Albrecht and Sue Parsons of the Institute.

instances of market failure are of particular relevance to environmental issues. For example, this chapter does not address the important examples of market failure dealing with monopolies. However, at least two prominent examples of market failure are of special interest here; these are public goods and, even more significantly, spillover effects. The excerpt below refers to the latter as externalities, although some economists would classify both these types of failure as examples of externalities; the point we are concerned with below, however, is less one of semantic exactitude than a comprehension of the concepts involved. As will be seen, the failure of the market is rooted in an inability to assert ownership over a particular resource. As a result, the market fails to provide the "correct" signals, and the good is not produced in the optimal quantities.

II. MARKET FAILURE

B.C. Field and N.D. Olewiler
Environmental Economics, **1st Canadian ed.**
(Toronto: McGraw-Hill Ryerson, 1995), at 69-78

External Costs

When entrepreneurs in a market economy make decisions about what and how much to produce, they will normally take into account the price of what they will produce and also the cost of items for which they will have to pay: labour, raw materials, machinery, energy, and so on. We call these the *private* costs of the firm, they are the costs that show up in the profit-and-loss statement at the end of the year. Any firm, assuming it has the objective of maximizing its profits, will try to keep its production costs as low as possible. This is a worthwhile outcome for both the firm and society because inputs always have opportunity costs; they could have been used to produce something else. Furthermore, firms will be alert to ways of reducing costs when the relative prices of inputs change.

But in many production operations there is another type of cost that, while representing a true cost to society, does not show up in the firm's profit-and-loss statement. These are called *external costs*. They are called "external" because, although they are real costs to some members of society, they will not normally be taken into account by firms when they go about making their decisions about output rates. Another way of saying this is that there are costs that are external to firms but internal to society as a whole.

One of the major types of external cost is the cost inflicted on people through environmental degradation. An example is the easiest way to see this. Suppose a paper mill is located somewhere on the upstream reaches of a river and that, in the course of its operation, it discharges a large amount of wastewater into the river. The wastewater is full of organic matter that arises from the process of converting wood to paper. This waste material gradually is converted to more benign materials by the natural assimilative capacity of the river water but, before that happens, a number of people downstream are affected by the lower quality of water in the river. Perhaps the waterborne residuals reduce the number of fish in the river, affecting downstream fishers. The river may be also less attractive to look at, affecting people who would like to swim or sail on it. Worse, the river water perhaps is used downstream as a source of water for a public water supply system, and the degraded water quality means that the town has to engage in more costly treatment processes before the water can be sent through the water mains. All of these downstream costs are real costs associated with producing paper, just as much as the raw materials, labour, energy, etc., used internally by the plant. But from the mill's standpoint these down-stream costs are *external costs*. They are costs that are borne by someone other than the people who make decisions about operating the paper mill. At the end of the year the profit-and-loss statement of the paper mill will contain no reference whatever to these real downstream external costs.

If we are to have rates of output that are socially efficient, decisions about re-source use must take into account both types of costs—the private costs of producing paper plus whatever external costs arise from adverse environmental impacts. In terms of full social cost accounting:

Social Costs = Private Costs + External (Environmental) Costs.

. . .

Most of the cases of environmental destruction involve external costs of one type or another. Electricity generating plants emit airborne residuals that affect the health of people living downwind. Users of chemicals emit toxic fumes that affect people living in the vicinity. Developers build on land without taking into account the degra-dation of the visual environment of local inhabitants, and so on. Nor is it only busi-nesses who are responsible for external environmental costs. When individuals drive their automobiles, exhaust gases add to air pollution, and when they dispose of solid waste materials (like old batteries), they may affect the quality of the local environment.

There are many different types of environmental externalities. Most, but not all, are expressed through physical linkages among parties involved, polluter and people damaged. The simplest is where there are just two parties involved—one polluter and one person suffering damages. An upstream pulp mill and a downstream firm that uses the river water in its production operations is an example. There are cases of single polluters and multiple damaged parties, such as a power plant that emits SO_2 affecting a group of community residents living downwind. Other cases involve mul-tiple polluters but only one damaged party, for example, the runoff from many farms that affects the well water of a household. And finally there are many cases where both polluters and parties damaged are many in number, for example, urban air pol-lution stemming from automobile emissions: each driver is both a producer and a recipient of the externality. The same is true of global phenomena, such as the green-house effect.

There are some externalities that do not involve physical linkages. Degradation of the scenic environment through thoughtless land development is an example. And there are some externalities that involve neither physical linkages nor close proxim-ity. People in one part of a country, for example, may feel loss when those in another region cause damage to an important environmental resource, for example, a unique species of animal or plant. This brings up a problem that we will state but not solve. What is the limit, if any, to be placed on external damage that people may legitimately claim? A person may suffer damages when someone in her vicinity plays their stereo too loudly, but can she legitimately claim that she suffers damages if, for example, they adopt a lifestyle with which she doesn't agree? If people in Victoria pollute the waters of their harbours, may residents in Edmonton claim that they have been damaged? If fishers in Newfoundland exhaust the cod stock to support their families, can people in Winnipeg justifiably claim that they have been damaged? The legal doctrine of "standing" is relevant to these situations. A private citizen may bring suit on environmental cases if that person is able to show that he or she is in fact being damaged by the activity in question. Few such suits for environmental damages have been initiated in Canada. For all the hypothetical situations noted above, it would be unlikely that standing would be granted by the courts because it would be difficult to show that individuals in a distant city were damaged. However, a resident of Victoria who operates a tourist business that has been adversely affected by the presence of sewage in Victoria waters would be more likely to be granted standing. These examples bring up a very important point. A person may feel worse off if fish stocks have been depleted or oceans polluted. They might even be willing to pay some amount of money to clean up the oceans or restock the fish. But, they still have no standing in the courts. The legal doctrine of standing is thus incompatible with the economist's use of willingness to pay as a measure of value. Values established through legal cases may not fully represent the value people are willing to pay for environmental quality.

· · ·

External Benefits

An external benefit is a benefit that accrues to somebody who is outside, or external, to the decision about consuming or using the good or resource that causes the externality. When the use of an item leads to an external benefit, the market willingness to pay for that item will understate the social willingness to pay.

· · ·

As another example of an external benefit, consider a farmer whose land is on the outskirts of an urban area. The farmer cultivates the land and sells his produce to people in the city. Of course, the farmer's main concern is the income he can derive from the operation, and he makes decisions about inputs and outputs according to their effect on that income. But the land kept in agriculture produces several other benefits, including habitat for birds and other small animals, and scenic values for passers-by. These benefits, while internal from the standpoint of society, are external from the standpoint of the farmer. They don't appear anywhere in his profit-and-loss position: they are external benefits of his farming decisions. In this case the agricultural value of the land to the farmer understates the social willingness to pay to have the land in agriculture.

When economists discuss the rudiments of supply and demand, we usually use as examples very simple goods that do not have external benefits. Farmers produce and supply so many million apples per year. Individual and market demand curves for apples are easy to comprehend. If we want to know the total number of apples bought, we can simply add up the number bought by each person in the market. Each person's consumption affects no one else. In this case the market demand curve will represent accurately the aggregate marginal willingness to pay of consumers for apples. But in cases involving external benefits, this no longer holds. We can see this by considering a type of good that inherently involves large-scale external benefits, what economists have come to call "public goods."

Public Goods

Consider the provision of national defence services. Once the defence system with all its hardware and people are in place, everyone in the country receives the service. Once the services are made available to one person, others cannot be excluded from making use of the same services. This is the distinguishing characteristic of a *public good*. It is a good which, if made available to one person, automatically becomes available to others.

Another example of a public good is clean air. If the air around a city is free of serious contaminants, anyone in the city can breathe the air without diminishing its availability to all other people within the city. Note carefully that it is not the ownership of the supplying organization that makes a public good public. Although our two examples require government involvement, a public good is distinguished by the technical nature of the good, not by the type of organization making it available. For example, radio signals are free to anyone with a receiver. But most radio stations are privately owned.

We are interested in public goods because environmental quality is essentially a public good. If the quantity of stratospheric ozone is increased, everyone worldwide benefits. Private markets are likely to undersupply public goods, relative to efficient levels. To see why, let's take another very simple example: a small freshwater lake on the shores of which there are three occupied homes. The people living in the houses use the lake for recreational purposes but, unfortunately, the water quality of the lake has been contaminated by an old industrial plant that has since closed. The contaminant is measured in parts per million (ppm). At present the lake contains 5 ppm of this contaminant. It is possible to clean the water by using a fairly expensive treatment process. Each of the surrounding homeowners is willing to pay a certain amount to have the water quality improved. Table 4-2 shows these individual marginal willingnesses to pay for integer values of water quality. It also shows the total marginal willingness to pay, which is the sum of the individual values.

The table also shows the marginal cost of cleaning up the lake, again just for integer values of water quality. Note that we have increasing marginal cost, as the lake becomes cleaner the marginal cost of continued improvement increases. Marginal cost and aggregate marginal willingness to pay are equal at a water quality of 2 ppm.

At levels less than this (higher ppm), aggregate marginal willingness to pay for a cleaner lake exceeds the marginal cost of achieving it, hence from the standpoint of these three homeowners together, improved water quality is desirable. But at quality levels better than 2 ppm, total willingness to pay falls below marginal costs. Thus 2 ppm is the socially efficient level of water quality in the lake.

Table 4-2 Individual and Aggregate Demand for Lowering Lake Pollution

| | Marginal willingness to pay ($ per year) | | | | |
Level of contaminant (ppm)	Homeowner A	Homeowner B	Homeowner C	Total	Marginal cost of cleanup
4	110	60	30	200	50
3	85	30	20	140	65
2	70	10	15	95	95
1	55	0	10	65	150
0	45	0	5	50	240

. . .

Having identified the efficient level of water quality, could we rely on a competitive market system, where entrepreneurs are on the alert for new profit opportunities, to get the contaminant in the lake reduced to that level? Suppose a private firm attempts to sell its services to the three homeowners. The firm goes to person A and tries to collect an amount equal to that person's true willingness to pay. But that person will presumably realize that once the lake is cleaned up, it's cleaned up for everybody no matter how much they actually contributed. And so A may have the incentive to underpay, relative to their true willingness to pay, in the hopes that the other homeowners will contribute enough to cover the costs of the cleanup. But, of course, the others may react in the same way. When a public good is involved, each person may have an incentive to "free ride" on the efforts of others. A free rider is a person who pays less for a good than her/his true marginal willingness to pay, a person who underpays, that is, relative to the benefits they receive.

Free riding is a ubiquitous phenomenon in the world of public goods, or in fact any good the consumption of which produces external benefits. Because of the free-riding impulse, private, profit-motivated firms will have difficulty covering their costs if they go into the business of supplying public goods. Private firms will be unable to determine a person's true willingness to pay for the public good. Thus, private firms will normally *under supply* goods and services of this type, if they can supply the good or service at all. Environmental quality improvements are essentially public goods. Since we cannot rely on the market system to provide efficient quantities of "goods" of this type, we must fall back on some type of nonmarket institution involving collective action of one type or another. In the lake example, the homeowners may be able to act collectively, perhaps through a homeowner association, to secure contributions for cleaning up the lake. Of course, the free-rider problem will still exist even for the homeowner's association, but if there are not too many of them, personal acquaintance and the operation of moral pressure may be strong enough to overcome the problem. When there are many thousands or millions of people, however, as there usually are in most environmental issues, the free-rider problem may be handled effectively only with more direct collective action through a governmental body that has taxing power. It is not that we wish completely to replace market processes in these cases. What we want to do is add sufficient public oversight to the market system that we do finally end up with efficient levels of environmental quality that are equitably distributed.

R.L. Heilbroner
Understanding Microeconomics, **2d ed.**
(Englewood Cliffs, NJ: Prentice-Hall, 1972), at 145-48

Controlling Externalities

So far we have pointed out how a market system generates externalities and how difficult it is to decide what to spend on reducing pollution or improving the environment. Now let us turn to another, equally important matter: the problem of choosing among various ways of lessening harmful production or consumption activity.

Basically, there are three main ways in which we can control external costs.

1. We can *regulate* the activity which creates it.
2. We can *tax* the activity that creates it.
3. We can *subsidize* the polluter to stop (or lessen) his activity.

Regulation

Faced with the ugly view of smoke belching from a factory chimney, sludge pouring from a mill into a lake, automobiles choking a city, or persons being injured by contaminants, most ecologically concerned persons cry for regulation. Pass a law to forbid smoky chimneys or sulferous coal; pass a law to make mills dispose of their wastes elsewhere or purify them; pass a law against automobiles in the central city; pass a law against DDT.

Sometimes regulation *is* the cheapest and easiest and most effective means of bringing pollution to a halt. If the pollution is extremely dangerous (as in the case of radiation damage or mercury poisoning or DDT), then outright prohibition may be the proper solution. Strict laws against just such abuses have recently been passed by most states and by the federal government; still stricter ones may follow.

But regulation is not always the indicated solution. In some cases (smoke from trash fires or from private chimneys, private garbage disposal, littering, etc.) the regulations may be too expensive or too difficult to enforce. A law that is semi-enforced is often worse than no law at all, since it encourages an attitude of deliberate law-evasion. In other cases, severe regulation may bring results that are not in the best social interests of the community. The only way to stop *all* smoke from a particular factory may be to discontinue production in that factory. With that drastic step, society would gain well-being from the absence of smoke, but *it would lose the well-being derived from goods and services the factory produced*. Hence, as in our earlier diagram, when the aim of social policy is not to eliminate all pollution, but to hold it to socially acceptable levels (levels at which marginal costs and benefits are equal), regulation may not be the instrumentality best adapted to the purpose.

Taxation

Then what about taxation? An alternative to regulating a polluter, whether an industry or individual, is to allow him to pollute all he pleases but to make him pay for each "unit" of pollution he creates. For instance, we can powerfully discourage factories from burning high sulfur content fuel if we tax them for each unit they buy; or we can discourage the abandonment of old cars by charging a considerable sum (say $100) as a special "environment tax" payable on the purchase of a new car, which is returnable to the purchaser if he trades in his car or disposes of it to certified automobile disposal yards, but which he forfeits if he simply abandons his car. Very high deposits on beer cans and bottles would also serve as a "tax" to deter throwing these objects away.

As we have mentioned, taxes cannot be used as a means of pollution control when the pollutant is very dangerous, since the antipollution tax, by its very intent, is a license to permit pollution activity but to make it more expensive. Hence it is important to understand the reasoning behind the use of taxes as an antipollution measure.

Pollution taxes are an effort to impose a cost where previously none was levied. Thus *taxes, by making a free good no longer free, attempt to "internalize" externalities*; that is to force the firm (or person) who creates a negative externality to pay for it himself (or have his customers pay for it) instead of foisting the charges upon the community. If the tax is appropriately figured, it should raise the marginal private costs of carrying on the activity to equal the social costs that the activity imposes on the community.

The use of a tax graduated by degrees of pollution has much to recommend it where it is technically and administratively possible. Such a tax permits the polluting companies to increase their profits by focusing their technology on the elimination of pollution—a most effective incentive. Ideally, in other words, we can use the tax mechanism to allow the market itself to include *all* costs and thus to allocate resources in the public interest, with the efficiency inherent in the pricing mechanism.

Subsidies

But taxes, like regulation, are *not* always effective. For example, taxes on fumes or unpleasant smells coming from a factory or an effluent from a mill require that we have accurate devices for monitoring the amount of pollutant. Moreover, since the pollution damage may vary from still days to windy ones, ideally the tax should be steeper on some days (or hours) than on others—a difficult arrangement for technical reasons. When municipalities are sources of pollution (from city incinerators or sewage systems), who is going to tax the city? Here the solution lies either in state or federal regulation or in state or federal subsidies to help municipalities bear the cost of environmental improvement. Where effective taxation is technically difficult (and where outright regulation may not be effective either), a solution to the problem may be to *pay* the polluter to install antipollution equipment. That is, we might offer him an outright payment or subsidy to stop polluting.

The problem with subsidies is that the public may resent paying taxes to induce someone to stop doing something it feels he shouldn't be doing in the first place. But there are times when subsidy may nonetheless be the easiest way of bringing about a desired result. For example, it may be very difficult to suppress the emission of dangerous but invisible fumes from car exhausts either by regulation (which will take care of new cars, but not old ones) or by taxation (who can tell which car is polluting?). But it might be possible to reduce this dangerous form of pollution by installing the necessary equipment *free*, along with a windshield sticker. This would of course be a subsidy, but it might also be the best means of dealing with a difficult problem.

The Ubiquity of Externalities

Our discussion of the control over externalities has barely scratched the surface of a broad and complex problem. But it is not our purpose here to explore that problem fully, so much as to relate the subject of environmental damage and repair to the market system itself. For we will remember that we began to look into the problem of externalities as part of our first overview of the market. Now it is time to come to a few preliminary judgments.

1. *The market is a very poor allocator of resources for which there is no price tag attached.* That is, the market allows "free goods" to slip through its meshes entirely unnoticed. Hence there is a tendency for marketers—firms and individuals—to overuse free goods, even when in fact these goods have become scarce.

2. *The market is not equipped to take into account the social as well as the private costs and benefits of economic activity.* Hence a market allocation of activity typically leads to too much production of "bads" and not enough of "goods"; that is, to the production of goods or services to the point at which *social cost* is greater than the social benefit (even though the *private* cost may be just equal to the private benefit). For example, a factory may be making money in a fully competitive market, but only because the wastes it pours into the rivers are not charged to it as a cost.

3. *Externalities*—that is, costs and benefits for which no allowance is made in the prices of goods or services—*are virtually omnipresent.* The employee in a pleasant office treats his family well and adds well-being to the community; the employee in an unpleasant establishment gets drunk, beats his wife and children, and imposes additional police costs on the town. One man builds a beautiful house and embellishes the neighborhood; another builds an eyesore, runs the neighborhood down, and sends his sensitive neighbors fleeing.

4. *Through taxation and subsidy, it is possible to "internalize" a considerable amount of the externalities of a market system*; that is, to impose costs on (or to allot benefits to) those who would not otherwise be fully charged or recompensed for the social results of their activity through the marketplace alone. When taxes or subsidies cannot be used, regulation (provided it can be enforced) can reduce pollution or control other externalities.

5. *Control over pollution and improvement of the environment are matters to which an economic calculus applies.* Indeed, the more conscious we become of the ubiquity of the ecological problem and the vast amounts that must eventually be spent to improve our environment, the more important it becomes to think in terms of balancing marginal costs and benefits, as best we can figure them, and to make intelligent use of such ideas as the social discount rate.

NOTE

A special aspect of externalities of particular interest to environmental and natural resources management is the problem of common property resources, which is perhaps best illustrated by the "tragedy of the commons." As will be seen in the excerpt below from Hardin's classic article, the word tragedy is used here in its original sense from Greek drama—that is, a disaster that is seen to be unfolding but that nevertheless cannot be prevented. In the case of the tragedy of the commons, the tragedy must be played out, although the instinct for pursuing one's own self-interest must inevitably lead to the ruin of all.

G. Hardin
"The Tragedy of the Commons"
(1968) vol. 162 *Science* 1243, at 1244

The tragedy of the commons develops in this way. Picture a pasture open to all. It is to be expected that each herdsman will try to keep as many cattle as possible on the commons. Such an arrangement may work reasonably satisfactorily for centuries because tribal wars, poaching and disease keep the numbers of both man and beast well below the carrying capacity of the land. Finally, however, comes the day of reckoning, that is, the day when the long-desired goal of social stability becomes a reality. At this point, the inherent logic of the commons remorselessly generates tragedy.

As a rational being, each herdsman seeks to maximize his gain. Explicitly or implicitly, more or less consciously, he asks, "What is the utility *to me* of adding one more animal to my herd?" This utility has one negative and one positive component.

1) The positive component is a function of the increment of one animal. Since the herdsman receives all the proceeds from the sale of the additional animal, the positive utility is nearly +1.

2) The negative component is a function of the additional overgrazing created by one more animal. Since, however, the effects of overgrazing are shared by all the herdsmen, the negative utility for any particular decision-making herdsman is only a fraction of −1.

Adding together the component partial utilities, the rational herdsman concludes that the only sensible course for him to pursue is to add another animal to his herd. And another; and another … . But this is the conclusion reached by each and every rational herdsman sharing a commons. Therein is the tragedy. Each man is locked into a system that compels him to increase his herd without limit—in a world that is limited. Ruin is the destination toward which all men rush, each pursuing his own best interest in a society that believes in the freedom of the commons. Freedom in a commons brings ruin to all.

NOTE

Much of the discussion to this point has focused on the problems associated with the failure of the market to deal with situations where the prices of certain factors are not adequately accounted for in the production decision, whether for physical or technical reasons (for example, the difficulty in asserting ownership rights over the undoubtedly valued right to enjoy a mountain sunset) or as the result of the legal system's allocation of property rights. In both cases, the failure is attributable to the inability to deprive others of access to and enjoyment of some attribute of property. Not surprisingly, then, where the problem is rooted in the particular allocation of property rights, economists—and lawyers—have looked to the legal system that allocates such rights for a solution. In the case of the commons, for example, an obvious solution is to vest the property rights in one owner—possibly the state—who would then manage the pasture in a way that maximizes the long-run benefits of the land. This might be done by operating the pasture directly or by charging for grazing rights under any number of systems.

As will be seen later in this chapter, a solution to externalities predicated on a clear and enforceable allocation of property rights has applications for many situations other than those illustrated by Hardin's article. At this point, however, we must address a preliminary question regarding the allocation of such rights—namely, what does economics tell us about who should be the recipient of such rights if we are to pursue an economically efficient (though not necessarily "fair") result? Let us take the example of a large steel mill polluting surrounding agricultural land, with significant damage accruing to the crops. Assuming that we wish to internalize the negative externalities created by pollution from the mill by allocating enforceable rights to air quality, does it matter to whom such property rights are given? For example, does it make a difference whether the legal system on the one hand imposes no penalty on the factory owner for polluting the air (effectively allowing for appropriation of the air quality "resource" by the steel mill), or, on the other hand, penalizes such pollution by allowing the farmer to sue for the damages to the crop yield? It might appear to be intuitive that the "correct" (optimal) result for society is achieved where the factory owner is forced to bear the costs of the pollution. In fact, the Coase Theorem, discussed below, suggests that, subject to certain important assumptions relating to transactions costs, the initial allocation of rights is unimportant to the economically efficient outcome for society; whether the rights are allocated to the farmer or the factory owner, the same (efficient) result will be achieved. This does not mean, of course, that the farmer and factory owner are unaffected by the result, only that society's welfare *as a whole* will not be affected. The important point for society's welfare, then, is that rights be allocated; to whom they are allocated may raise questions of fairness, but not of economic efficiency.

A.M. Polinsky
An Introduction to Law and Economics, **2d ed.**
(Toronto: Little, Brown & Co., 1989), at 11-14

The Coase Theorem

One of the central ideas in the economic analysis of law was developed in an article by Ronald Coase in 1960 ["The Problem of Social Cost" (1960) vol. 3 *Journal of Law and Economics* 1]. This idea, which has since been named the *Coase Theorem*, is most easily described by an example. Consider a factory whose smoke causes damage to the laundry hung outdoors by five nearby residents. In the absence of any corrective action each resident would suffer $75 in damages, a total of $375. The smoke damage can be eliminated in either of two ways: A smokescreen can be installed on the factory's chimney, at a cost of $150, or each resident can be provided an electric dryer, at a cost of $50 per resident. The efficient solution is clearly to install the smokescreen since it eliminates total damage of $375 for an outlay of only $150, and it is cheaper than purchasing five dryers for $250.

Zero Transaction Costs

The question asked by Coase was whether the efficient outcome would result if the right to clean air is assigned to the residents or if the right to pollute is given to the factory. If there is a right to clean air, then the factory has three choices: pollute and pay $375 in damages, install a smokescreen for $150, or purchase five dryers for the residents at a total cost of $250. Clearly, the factory would install the smokescreen, the efficient solution. If there is a right to pollute, then the residents face three choices: suffer their collective damages of $375, purchase five dryers for $250, or buy a smokescreen for the factory for $150. The residents would also purchase the smokescreen. In other words, the efficient outcome would be achieved regardless of the assignment of the legal rights.

It was implicitly assumed in this example that the residents could costlessly get together and negotiate with the factory. In Coase's language, this is referred to as the assumption of *zero transaction costs*. In general, transaction costs include the costs of identifying the parties with whom one has to bargain, the costs of getting together with them, the costs of the bargaining process itself, and the costs of enforcing any bargain reached. With this general definition in mind, we can now state the simple version of the Coase Theorem: If there are zero transaction costs, the efficient outcome will occur regardless of the choice of legal rule.

Note that, although the choice of the legal rule does not affect the attainment of the efficient solution when there are zero transaction costs, it does affect the distribution of income. If the residents have the right to clean air, the factory pays $150 for the smokescreen, whereas if the factory has the right to pollute, the residents pay for the smokescreen. Thus, the choice of the legal rule redistributes income by the amount of the least-cost solution to the conflict. Since it is assumed for now that income can be costlessly redistributed, this distributional effect is of no consequence—if it is not desired, it can be easily corrected.

Positive Transaction Costs

The assumption of zero transaction costs obviously is unrealistic in many conflict situations. At the very least, the disputing parties usually would have to spend time and/or money to get together to discuss the dispute. To see the consequences of positive transaction costs, suppose in the example that it costs each resident $60 to get together with the others (due, say, to transportation costs and the value attached to time). If the residents have a right to clean air, the factory again faces the choice of paying damages, buying a smokescreen, or buying five dryers. The factory would again purchase the smokescreen, the efficient solution. If the factory has a right to pollute, each resident now has to decide whether to bear the losses of $75, buy a dryer for $50, or get together with the other residents for $60 to collectively buy a smokescreen for $150. Clearly, each resident will choose to purchase a dryer, an inefficient outcome. Thus, given the transaction costs described, a right to clean air is efficient, but a right to pollute is not.

Note that in the example the preferred legal rule minimized the effects of transaction costs in the following sense. Under the right to clean air, the factory had to decide whether to pay damages, install a smokescreen, or buy five dryers. Since it was not necessary for the factory to get together with the residents to decide what to do, the transaction costs considered—the costs of the residents to get together—did not have any effect. Under the right to pollute, the residents had to decide what to do. Since the residents were induced to choose an inefficient solution in order to avoid the cost of getting together, the transaction costs did have an effect. Thus, even though no transaction costs were actually incurred under the right to pollute since the residents did not get together, the effects of transaction costs were greater under that rule.

We can now state the more complicated version of the Coase Theorem: If there are positive transaction costs, the efficient outcome may not occur under every legal rule. In these circumstances, the preferred legal rule is the rule that minimizes the effects of transaction costs. These effects include the actual incurring of transaction costs and the inefficient choices induced by a desire to avoid transaction costs.

The distributional consequences of legal rules are somewhat more complicated when there are transaction costs. It is no longer true, as it was when there were zero transaction costs, that the choice of rule redistributes income by the amount of the least-cost solution. In the example, if the residents have the right to clean air, the factory pays $150 for the smokescreen, whereas if the factory has the right to pollute, the residents pay $250 for five dryers.

Although the simple version of the Coase Theorem makes an unrealistic assumption about transaction costs, it provides a useful way to begin thinking about legal problems because it suggests the kinds of transactions that would have to occur under each legal rule in order for that rule to be efficient. Once these required transactions are identified, it may be apparent that, given more realistic assumptions about transaction costs, one rule is clearly preferable to another on efficiency grounds. The more complicated version of the Coase Theorem provides a guide to choosing legal rules in this situation.

NOTES AND QUESTIONS

1. One of the limitations of the Coase Theorem (and indeed, many would argue, of modern "welfare economics") is that it does not engage in any effective way the issue of interpersonal utility comparisons. Put differently, modern economists (unlike many of their 19th-century predecessors) have generally declined to address the question whether some distributions of costs and benefits are more "fair" than others. Economics provides no answer, for example, as to whether a pauper would get greater utility from an additional $100 of income than would a billionaire. To avoid this obstacle, economists sometimes assume that so long as the outcome of a particular action means that losers *could* be compensated and there remain net social benefits, then the welfare of society is increased. How reasonable is this assumption? How helpful is this approach to political decision makers in framing environmental policy?

2. How significant in practice are transaction costs likely to be with respect to environmental disputes? Is there an analogy here to the objections that have sometimes been levelled at the liberal concept of a "free market of ideas"—a concept that is central to much of our thinking on civil liberties?

FURTHER READINGS

R.H. Coase, "The Problem of Social Cost" (1960) vol. 3 *Journal of Law and Economics* 1.

H. Elliott, "A General Statement of the Tragedy of the Commons" (1997) vol. 18, no. 6 *Population and Environment: A Journal of Interdisciplinary Studies* 515.

R.W. Hahn, "The Impact of Economics on Environmental Policy" (2000) vol. 39, no. 3 *Journal of Environmental Economics and Management* 375.

N. Mercuro, ed., *Ecology, Law and Economics: The Simple Analytics of Natural Resource and Environmental Economics* (New York: University Press of America, 1997).

W.J. Samuels, "The Coase Theorem and the Study of Law and Economics" (1974) vol. 14 *Natural Resources Journal* 1.

J.J. Seneca and M.K. Taussig, *Environmental Economics*, 3d ed. (Englewood Cliffs, NJ: Prentice-Hall, 1984).

J.E. Wilen, "Renewable Resource Economics and Policy: What Differences Have We Made?" (2000) vol. 39, no. 6 Journal of *Environmental Economics and Management* 306.

III. COST–BENEFIT ANALYSIS

Much of the discussion in the previous section concentrated on the inefficiencies that were introduced by the failure of the marketplace to adequately reflect all the relevant costs and benefits inherent in the use of some resource or resources. The identification of all such costs and benefits, especially in the context of environmental decision making, is the subject of a large and often controversial literature on cost–benefit analysis. That this area of economics has generated such controversy should not be surprising. It is one thing, for example, to say that the loss of a wilderness area imposes a cost on society; it is quite another to attempt to quantify such a loss in monetary terms—not least because there is no identifiable market for wilderness that provides us with a price in the way that the costs of commonly traded goods are easily identified.

The first excerpt in this section describes the application of economic analysis, including cost–benefit analysis, to the management of public lands and resources. This is followed by a serious questioning of the ability of cost–benefit analysis to accurately value certain types of loss, including especially losses related to environmental degradation.

T.S. Veeman
"The Application of Economic Analysis to Public Land and Resource Management: An Overview"
in T.J. Cottrell, ed., *Role of Economics in Integrated Resource Management*, *Proceedings held October 16-18, 1985* (Hinton, AB: Alberta Forestry, Land and Wildlife, 1985), 17, at 17-24

Economics and Value

The Concept of Value

. . .

Since money is the current medium of exchange (and not gold, salt, or cigarettes as in previous times and places), the exchange value of a commodity is measured in terms of its price, that is, the quantity of money for which the commodity can be exchanged. The price or exchange value of goods, in turn, is determined simultaneously by considerations of supply (cost) and demand (utility or preference). Underlying the pattern of demand is the doctrine of consumers' sovereignty—the notion that each individual is the best judge of what he or she wants. Moreover, the marginal utility associated with goods is tied to a person's marginal willingness to pay. Implicit, too, is the assumption that the consumer's wants are insatiable—more is preferred to less. Such assumptions clearly can be criticized, but are unlikely to be abandoned completely.

The fact that goods have value can be ascribed ultimately to the scarcity of resources and the aspect that the resources have competing uses. If goods were available in unlimited supply, they would be free. Typically that is not the case, and price must serve as a rationing device for goods or resources, particularly those with exclusive property rights. In so far as the valuation of natural resources is concerned, it is also important to remember that natural resources are multi-attribute and thus have quantity, quality, time and space dimensions.

Economic values are regarded to be relative values and not "intrinsic" values. Economic values are typically couched in terms of opportunity cost. The value of an extra gun is the amount of butter you would be willing to give up to obtain the gun. Economists do not try to determine what something, like education or clean air, is worth in and of itself. Economic values are typically marginal or incremental values, rather than total values.

Types of Values

It is important, at the outset, to note that public decision-making with respect to public land and natural resources in Alberta must be as concerned with extra-market values as with market-determined values. Timber and wheat can be readily valued in terms of market prices, but the extra-market values associated with the recreational or watershed functions of public land must be imputed. It is analytically useful, following Charles Howe (1971), to distinguish four categories of values (or types of benefits and costs):

1. economic values for which market prices exist and for which these prices correctly reflect societal opportunity costs or true scarcity values; for example, farm or timber outputs which are not price supported
2. economic values for which market prices exist but for which the prices fail to reflect appropriate scarcity values or shadow prices; for example, price-supported commodities or labour inputs that would otherwise be unemployed
3. economic values for which no market prices exist but for which appropriate social values can be approximated in money terms, by inferring what consumers would be willing to pay for the product or service, either through direct surveys or indirect techniques such as the Hotelling-Clawson-Knetsch method of extra-market benefit estimation; for example, forest-based recreation or hunting and fishing
4. values for which it would be difficult to imagine any kind of market-like process capable of registering a meaningful monetary valuation; for example, the preservation of a beautiful view, historic site or way of life, or the destruction of a unique riverscape.

The ease with which values (benefits and costs) are estimated clearly diminishes as one moves down the preceding list. This is no argument, however, for the policy analyst to ignore values in categories 3 and 4.

General Approaches and Criteria for Resource Management

There are two basic types of resource management decisions: those relating to resource development, such as increasing the volume of water stored or expanding the agricultural or forest land base, and those relating to resource allocation such as allocating a fixed amount of a given natural resource among different uses or users at a point in time.

Such development and allocation decisions must often be made in the context of broad national and/or provincial goals relating to promotion of economic growth, creation of employment, enhancement of trade, greater price stability, a fairer distribution of income and environmental protection. A narrower range of economic criteria, particularly those relating to *efficiency* and *equity* (income distribution), is generally found to be useful especially in appraising the projects or policies of a provincial government department such as Alberta Energy and Natural Resources, Alberta Environment, or Alberta Agriculture.

Efficiency and Equity

The criterion or goal of efficiency deals essentially with the relationship of social benefits and social costs exclusive of their distribution. Any project having net social benefits greater than zero or, alternatively, having a benefit-cost ratio exceeding unity, passes the limited test of economic feasibility. A more stringent efficiency test requires that the project be compared with alternative projects or uses of scarce investment funds.

The goal of equity, on the other hand, refers to the incidence of social benefits and costs—in a nutshell, who reaps the benefits and who bears the costs? Any project or policy typically has impacts on the personal or size distribution of income (among income recipients such as individuals or households), the functional distribution of income (in terms of labor income, projects, and rent), and the spatial or regional distribution of income (say as between northern and southern Alberta).

The Market System and Pareto-Optimality

Economists extol the virtues of price systems as useful, de-centralized, administrative devices. It is also a tenet of economics that a perfectly competitive market system will tend to be efficient. Given the initial endowment of resources, which may be unequal, and given the state of technology, a Pareto-optimal state is achieved wherein total social product—"the size of the economic pie"—is maximized from our scarce resources. Pareto-optimality occurs when there is no way to make one economic agent better off without making someone else worse off, and is associated with a host of marginality conditions in production and consumption.

The concept of Pareto-optimality is of rather limited use as a criterion for public policy. Most projects or policies generate gains to some individuals and losses to others. This led, in the 1940s, to a further refinement of modern applied welfare economics—the "compensation principles" of Hicks and Kaldor. Any project or policy change improved social welfare, it was argued, if the gainers could (hypothetically) compensate the losers and there was some positive net gain remaining. Indeed, benefit-cost analysis rests on these very theoretical underpinnings—the "Pareto criterion with compensation." These refinements are not without criticism. Indeed, Arrow, the Nobel laureate, has argued that it is impossible to aggregate individual preferences into a social preference over various states of the world. Even "majority rule" can be shown not to be an ideal social welfare function. Despite these theoretical difficulties, economists continue to use benefit-cost analysis as a practical tool, and legislatures continue to use the principle of "majority rule."

. . .

Special Rules for Efficient Resource Allocation

I now wish to turn to more specific rules which should underlie resource allocation and which should help to ensure greater efficiency in the use of Alberta's public land and natural resources. Some of these rules were first outlined in a similar meeting in British Columbia by Peter Pearse (1975).

Rule 1. Take a social perspective. In the first place, the policy analyst must take a social, rather than a private, perspective with respect to any project or policy change. Private firms will undertake private feasibility studies which are based on private returns, costs and discount rates. Governments, at times, may only wish to study impacts on their revenues and expenditures. But generally in a study taken from society's point of view, other aspects must be considered. A social benefit-cost analysis, for example, must include external or unappropriated benefits which the private sector can not capture, and external or uncompensated costs imposed by the project or policy on third parties. Secondly, social analysis should consider and estimate the economic activity generated in industries which are linked forward, as with processing and distributing industries, and linked backward, as with input supply industries, to the primary activity such as logging or farming. Such stemming and induced secondary benefits are clearly important to regional income distribution and perhaps also, under special circumstances, to efficiency concerns. Thirdly, there is the distinct likelihood that social rates of discount will be lower than private rates.

Rule 2. Choose an appropriate accounting stance. Is the analysis to be undertaken from the national, provincial, regional or local point of view? Generally, a provincial accounting stance is appropriate because government departments such as Alberta Energy and Natural Resources are charged with managing resources from a provincial perspective and because provincial monies are being used to fund the project. A major implication here is that there may be beneficial impacts of projects on certain regions or communities within the province which would be included as efficiency benefits in a regional stance, but not in a provincial stance. In other words, the inclusion or exclusion of secondary benefits—economic activity which either stems from or is induced by the primary activity—is intimately related to the choice of a suitable accounting stance. Once an accounting stance is chosen, the analyst compares the state of the economy *with* the project with the state of the economy *without* the project, ensuring that any benefit sphere does in fact represent a net gain in economic activity and not merely a transfer of economic activity within the (provincial) jurisdiction.

Rule 3. Value goods and resources properly. For outputs and inputs in category 1 of Howe's classification, market prices do reflect true scarcity values. For such items, the central questions relate to whether the project itself may influence price levels and whether real prices of the item are expected to change over time.

· · ·

For outputs or inputs having distorted market prices (Howe's category 2), such prices should be corrected to reflect true societal scarcity values or opportunity costs. If a benefit-cost study is undertaken, it should be remembered that estimates of total benefits or total willingness-to-pay for project output should include consumer's surplus.

Rule 4. Be sure to consider extra-market values. The social analysis of any project or policy change must consider not only the more readily measured market values. The extra-market values (in Howe's category 3) must be included in the analysis. Benefits and costs in category 4 are not commensurable and must be included as qualitative factors in the overall analysis. A complete and proper evaluation of hydro-electric power from a Slave River Dam, for example, versus power from conventional, coal-fired, thermal production would require inclusion of the respective extra-market costs associated with the two alternatives.

Rule 5. For a natural resource with mutually exclusive uses, allocate the resource to the use which provides the highest net social benefits. If the public land manager, for instance, is faced with the question of whether a particular parcel of land should be allocated to agricultural use or forestry use, the use which provides the highest net social benefits should be chosen.

Rule 6. Where possible, use natural resources on a multiple-use basis. A considerable advance in the societal management of natural resources has occurred whenever single-use oriented government agencies have moved to multiple use of versatile resources.

· · ·

Economists then go further and employ the principle of "equimarginal value in use." This principle states that a natural resource, such as a parcel of land, should be allocated between two competing uses, such as grazing for cows or habitat for elk, such that the marginal value products of the two respective uses are equated.

Rule 7. Sometimes, no use of a natural resource may be the best use. It is unwise for society to allocate scarce capital and labor to the development of some natural resource if the discounted benefits of so doing are less than the discounted costs— unless there are other over-riding social objectives. Many physical scientists tend to equate the non-use of a natural resource with physical waste of the resource. However, it makes no social sense, at least in efficiency terms, to dam a river or cut a tree, if the benefits of this action are less than the costs.

Rule 8. Be wary of using secondary benefits to justify projects. The problem of secondary benefits has been the most troublesome and controversial aspect of benefit-cost studies, especially those relating to water projects, in Alberta. Economists argue that secondary benefits can only be counted as efficiency benefits within the efficiency analysis if resources are unemployed within the provincial economy and if the spinoff activity truly represents a net gain in economic activity within the province. Prior to 1982, it was clearly improper to include secondary benefits as legitimate efficiency benefits. Today, for their inclusion, the analyst must be convinced that the unemployment of resources would be chronic over the life of the project. Moreover, all projects generate secondary impacts, so a more useful question may be how many more secondary benefits Project A yields than Project B. In general, economists remain reluctant to justify projects in terms of their secondary benefits and would prefer to adjust primary costs of the project, such as labour costs during construction, in periods of cyclical unemployment. This is not to say that secondary benefits are unimportant in project evaluation. Their proper role relates to the objective of regional income distribution as well as to questions of repayment and pricing.

Rule 9. The evaluation and allocation of public goods requires special analytical treatment. It is difficult to impute individual demand curves for the services of public goods. In simulating the demand curves of individuals from direct questionnaires, there are typically biases in respondent's answers to questions concerning willingness-to-pay, either "free rider" bias or problems stemming from non-representative samples of the population. Once individual demand curves are obtained, the aggregate demand curve for the services of the public good is obtained through vertical and not horizontal summation of the demand curves of all individual users. With respect to pricing of a public good, welfare economics dictates that the efficiency price of a public good should be set equal to zero because the marginal cost of provision to another user is zero.

Rule 10. Avoid irreversibility in renewable resource use. It can certainly be argued that welfare economics and applied tools like benefit-cost analysis do not readily account for the welfare of future generations. In benefit-cost logic, any benefit or cost at some date 30 or 40 years in the future is rather minuscule in present value terms. However, this is not to say that the literature on resource economics is devoid of thinking on matters relating to future generations. In particular, Ciriacy-Wantrup (1968) and Krutilla and Fisher (1975), among others, have argued strongly for strategies in decision-making with respect to renewable resources that would avoid irreversibility (critical zones) in resource use and would "keep options open" for future generations.

NOTE

Cost–benefit analysis has been described as an "imprecise art." Some critics would go further and suggest that the use of this approach in dealing with many environmental benefits is so crude in practice as to be useless at best, and even positively misleading. Some recent literature on the estimation of non-pecuniary values suggests that many of our "intuitive" apprehensions about the pricing of what many of us consider "priceless" natural assets are not misplaced. As the following excerpt illustrates, some of the assumptions often employed by economists in the estimation of benefits and costs are subject to serious questioning. Moreover, they are assumptions that can dramatically alter the amount of compensation flowing from the cost–benefit evaluation.

J.L. Knetsch
"Economics, Losses, Fairness and Resource-Use Conflicts"
in M. Ross and J.O. Saunders, eds., *Growing Demands on a Shrinking Heritage: Managing Resource-Use Conflicts* (Calgary: Canadian Institute of Resources Law, 1992), 20, at 23-29

Economic Values and Their Assessment

The economic—pecuniary and non-pecuniary—importance of conflicting uses remains central to how resource use is allocated among competing claimants. However, given the uncertainties and lack of ready means of measurement, and the often-misunderstood nature of what is to be measured, many assessments have not necessarily raised the level of informed debate or improved proposed resolutions of resource conflicts. Quite apart from the obvious, and expected, self-serving exaggerations and biased assertions of interested parties, there are other more systematic worries about valuations and their use in judgments, allocation decisions, and regulatory reform.

The first is the fairly obvious discounting of less easily assessed non-pecuniary values in planning decisions, in litigation, and in reform proposals, relative to more easily appreciated—and more easily measured—financial data. Although there are numerous exceptions, courts, for example, still often treat some amenity values as "mere delights" and not the equal of commercial returns.

A second source of potential malassessment is the practice of taking various expenditures, or cost outlays, associated with the use or development of a resource to represent the value of the resource itself—a feature of what Tom Power has aptly called "folk economics." The usual accountings include such analysts' employment-generating activities as estimating tourist expenditures, studying local economic impacts, and using multipliers to determine so-called spin-offs. Although these are frequently done with great technical competence, this is not uniformly the case, and in nearly all cases they reflect narrow interests of local boosterism rather than resource values.

The common attribution of associated spending and secondary or spin-off impacts to the value of the resource prompting the expenditures leads to a nonsensical conclusion that a recreation facility located in some remote area is more valuable than an equally attractive one located close to users because it requires greater effort and cost to get to the more distant site. It is to say that a mineral deposit deeper in the earth is more valuable than one closer to the surface because more wage income will be generated in bringing the ore up to the processing facility. Such accountings give rise to poor decisions and to the spectacle of officials solemnly attempting to construct an economic justification for preserving an important historical, cultural, or environmental site by calling attention to the largely irrelevant spending by a few visitors, while totally ignoring large real losses in economic welfare that would accompany demise of the asset.

A further, related problem with the counting of expenditure impacts is that if these associated benefits are to be credited as part of the gains attributable to a particular project, then the expenditures, jobs, and income that are not realized because of the spending that is displaced by this use must surely be debited as part of the costs. It is clearly misleading to count the secondary gains without counting the secondary costs. While there may be an interest in increasing or maintaining economic activity in a particular area, the justification for projects contributing to this turns on the added value of having employment and income accruing in one area rather than in another region; the justification of economic feasibility or efficiency is not demonstrated by such one-sided accounting. The practice of crediting spin-off gains and ignoring commensurate losses resulting from the displaced spending leads not only to a further over-supply of wasteful projects, but blunts the search for ones that will more nearly satisfy both objectives of more productive use of economic resources and maintenance of activity in areas of deserving concern.

The pervasiveness of using local impacts as measures of resource values is in part attributable to another difficulty in sorting out more reasonable responses to a wide array of policy issues: the asymmetry of interests and incentives between parties having a large but diffuse interest in the results and those having a smaller but concentrated interest. Small groups representing specific interests are often able to impose costs of uneconomic alternatives on another group because these costs are spread among a larger number of individuals. As the loss to any single member of the larger group may be relatively small, there is little incentive for any single person to be too offended, to become very interested in the issue, to protest, or to attempt to persuade others of the wastefulness of the proposal. The larger returns to each in the small group provide quite the opposite incentive. This asymmetry often results in unbalanced information, a lack of critical review, and biased treatments of gains and losses.

There is also a too-easy assumption that market prices, which may adequately measure the value of a substitute, also measure the value to people who consider alternatives as being inferior to a particular holding to which they have a particular attachment. A compensation payment of the market price of another house, for example, is unlikely to leave a long-term resident as well off as before the taking of the person's home.

Gains and Losses

A further asymmetry that may often seriously compromise efficient and equitable choices of entitlements is the commonly unappreciated disparity between measures of positive and negative changes in economic well-being.

Something has economic worth only to the extent that people are willing to give up something else in order to acquire or keep it. The usual textbook suggestion is, for example, "The economic value of something is how much someone is willing to pay for it or, if he [or she] has it already, how much money he [or she] demands to part with it." There is little disagreement on this—welfare gains are correctly measured by the maximum sums that gainers would pay to obtain them and losses "are measured by the total number of dollars which prospective losers would insist on as the price of agreeing to adoption."

However, rather than the compensation measure, a second measure of loss is commonly used to weigh adverse impacts and assign entitlements: the maximum willingness of an individual to pay to avoid giving something up. The reasons for the common use of this second, and usually inappropriate, measure, are:

1. that its calculation is often more convenient than the correct compensation measure, and
2. that it is widely assumed that for all practical purposes the two measures will result in fully equivalent assessments.

Any disparity between the willingness-to-pay (WTP) and the compensation-demanded (willingness to accept, or WTA) measures is confidently expected to be negligibly small and of no practical importance: "the differences between compensating and equivalent measures are trivial," and "[a]s a practical matter it usually does not make much difference which of these two approaches ... is adopted."

As a result, it has become common practice to base assessments for all manner of policy and planning purposes on this presumption of evaluation equivalence. No reckoning of any difference is made, or thought to be necessary. The possibility of differing values is generally ignored in proposals to resolve resource-use conflicts and deliberations leading to the assignment of property entitlements, as well as in benefit-cost analyses, assessments of damages, and the setting of health, safety, and environmental standards.

There is, however, little evidence to support this traditional view of equivalence. Instead, the available evidence—which has been accumulating for a dozen or so years—supports an alternative view of large and systematic disparities. People value losses much more than they do commensurate gains.

The recent research studies are consistent in finding that people require payments to give up entitlements that are from about two or three to well over five times larger than the maximum sums they would agree to pay to retain the same rights. The differences are not trivial, and attempts to understand and deal with resource conflicts will be severely hindered by continuing to ignore them.

A useful summary of the findings from the research on gains and losses is provided by the choices made by two comparable groups of individuals participating in a simple experiment. Each individual in the first group was given a coffee mug and all were told that the mug was theirs to keep. They were then offered a four-hundred-gram Swiss chocolate bar of roughly comparable price in exchange for their mug.

The participants in the second group were offered the opposite choice. They were each initially given one of the large chocolate bars and then offered a mug in exchange for their chocolate bar. All other conditions were identical to those of the first group.

The participants in both groups had the identical opportunity of ending up with a coffee mug or a chocolate bar; there was no effort required to make any necessary trade and no uncertainty concerning the validity of the exchange offers.

Conventional economic assumptions about how people value gains and losses, which are the presumptions used in most economic analyses, including valuations of competing resource uses, offer a strong prediction of what should occur. The relative numbers of individuals preferring mugs to chocolate bars should be roughly equal in the two groups, as the relative preferences are not expected to be affected by which initial entitlement is awarded or by any difference in the value of gains and losses.

The results of the experiment showed a very different pattern of preferences from the one predicted by traditional economic principles. Rather than roughly equal proportions in each group preferring the chocolate bar and the mug, the numbers varied widely and systematically in accord with the direction of the necessary exchange.

Group	Prefer Mug	Prefer Chocolate
1. Give up mug for chocolate	89 percent	11 percent
2. Give up chocolate for mug	10 percent	90 percent

Nearly nine out of every ten (89 percent) of those individuals required to lose their mug in order to gain a chocolate bar (Group 1) indicated that they valued a mug more than the chocolate. Only one in ten favoured a loss of their chocolate bar to gain a mug (Group 2).

Participants' preferences were clearly not independent of the initial entitlement or the direction of trade offers, as is commonly assumed. The individuals taking part in this exercise valued a mug more than a chocolate bar when facing the prospect of losing the mug, but valued a mug less than the chocolate when given the choice of gaining a mug at the cost of giving up the chocolate.

The reference position of people in the experiment mattered very much in terms of whether the good was valued as a potential loss or as giving up a possible gain. In common with most experience, but in contrast with much of conventional economics, losses were worth more than fully commensurate gains.

The results of the simple coffee mug and chocolate bar exchange exercise are representative of a general finding from essentially all controlled tests of the equivalence proposition. An early example is the response of a sample of duck hunters in the United States who indicated that, on average, they would pay $247 each to maintain a wetland necessary to support present duck populations, but would demand a minimum compensation of $1044 to agree to its demise—a bit over a four-fold difference. In another early study, Thaler found that people placed very different values on a .001 change in risk to their life depending on the direction of the change. The compensation they demanded was one or two orders of magnitude greater to accept the risk (a loss) than the largest amount they were prepared to pay to eliminate an identical risk (a gain).

Similar disparities have now been reported by many investigators using a variety of methods to evaluate widely varied assets, and differences have been shown to be independent of transaction costs, repetition of trade offers, income effects, or wealth constraints. The results of the many tests and studies are consistent in showing that losses matter much more to people than commensurate gains, and that reductions in losses are more valuable than foregone gains.

While these findings have until recently not proven popular with many economic practitioners—an unfortunate social cost of their reluctance to give up conventional assertions—they seem in accord with the strong intuitions of most people. Oliver Wendell Holmes summarized this intuition many years before the recent studies were undertaken in these terms:

> It is in the nature of man's mind. A thing which you have enjoyed and used as your own for a long time, whether property or an opinion, takes root in your being and cannot be

torn away without your resenting the act and trying to defend yourself, however you came by it. The law can ask no better justification than the deepest instincts of man.

The empirical evidence seems to be consistent with Holmes' statement; it differs only in the finding that the reluctance to give something up does not necessarily occur only after "a long time." Once a reference position is perceived, people value gains and losses as departures from this neutral point, and motivations respond accordingly.

NOTES AND QUESTIONS

1. Professor Knetsch discusses some serious deficiencies in the way in which cost–benefit evaluation is typically undertaken. Other writers have reached similar conclusions, conclusions that have not been embraced wholeheartedly by the economics profession. The unease with which many view a cost–benefit approach to environmental values is reflected in the literature on contingent valuation in respects other than that illustrated in the Knetsch article. For example, one of the problems that has confronted researchers who have attempted to determine, on the basis of interviews, the price at which citizens could be "bought off" in return for decreased environmental quality is that a large proportion of those individuals selected for participation in the experiment refuse to participate—that is, they deny the very legitimacy of the approach being proposed. This is all the more remarkable given the fact that, as M. Sagoff as noted, "[s]ocial scientists have long known that the human subjects of their experiments go to great lengths to follow instructions and remain obedient to authority" to the point (in the well-known Milgram experiments) of torturing one another if instructed to do so. See M. Sagoff, *The Economy of the Earth* (Cambridge: Cambridge University Press, 1988), at 84. Is it admissible to consider, for example, what are the costs and benefits of strip mining if the result will be the despoilation of a national park—or the costs and benefits of fishing methods that lead to the incidental extinction of dolphins? If indeed some costs are in a sense "unthinkable," where and why do we draw the line?

2. What implications does the asymmetrical view of gains and losses have for environmental policy? Is it possible that how one structures the response to an environmental problem—as a loss or a gain—may affect its reception by the public? Suppose, for example, that a government must decide how to spend an extra million dollars in tax revenues as the result of a project that has a minor negative effect on the environment. Which is likely to result in greater satisfaction—rewarding the public with a tax cut or using the money in a rehabilitation effort? Conventional economics would suggest the former, because citizens are allowed to maximize their utility by spending the benefit as they see fit. But how is this answer altered if one characterizes the new tax break as a gain and the revenues spent on rehabilitation as the mitigation of a loss? In light of the differential evaluation of gains and losses, is it possible that by directing its expenditures to mitigating losses, a government could achieve equivalent or greater societal satisfaction than would be the case with even larger expenditures that are designed to compensate the public with a gain?

3. As with the Coase theorem discussed earlier, the cost–benefit approach also raises issues with respect to the fairness of the outcome that are typically not addressed by economists. For example, it has been shown that people generally regard as "unfair"

outcomes that result in one group gaining as the direct result of the imposition of a loss on another group—even in situations where economists would characterize the behaviour as "rational." Suppose a forest fire breaks out near an isolated town, and citizens rush to hose down their roofs to decrease the chance of house fires caused by sparks. Assume that there is only one hardware store in town, which has a limited number of hoses for sale. Faced with a sudden and dramatic increase in demand, conventional economics would suggest raising the price for hoses dramatically. Do you think that this economically efficient way of allocating resources in the face of increased demand would be regarded as an "acceptable" or "fair" solution? Would your answer be any different if the store announced that all additional profits from the increased price would be donated to the local fire department?

FURTHER READINGS

M.L. Cropper, "Has Economic Research Answered the Needs of Environmental Policy?" (2000) vol. 39, no. 3 *Journal of Environmental Economics and Management* 328.

H.E. Daly and J.B. Cobb Jr., *For the Common Good* (Boston: Beacon Press, 1989).

J.M. Hartwick and N.D. Olewiler, *The Economics of Natural Resource Use*, 2d ed. (Reading, MA: Addison-Wesley, 1998).

D. Kahneman, J.L. Knetsch, and R. Thaler, "Fairness as a Constraint on Profit Seeking: Entitlements in the Market" (1986) vol. 76 *American Economic Review* 728.

D.W. Pearce, *Cost–Benefit Analysis*, 2d ed. (London: MacMillan Press, 1983), chapters 1 and 2.

S.E. Rhoads, *The Economist's View of the World* (Cambridge: Cambridge University Press, 1985).

M. Sagoff, *The Economy of the Earth* (Cambridge: Cambridge University Press, 1988).

M. Sagoff, "Some Problems with Environmental Economics" (1988) vol. 10 *Environmental Ethics* 55.

IV. MARKET INSTRUMENTS

The section above dealt with the often-difficult evaluation of economic costs and benefits in environmental decision making. Even assuming, however, that one can accurately gauge the environmental costs associated with particular actions, there remains the important question of how best to intervene so as to assure that these costs are properly reflected in the marketplace. Much of environmental legislation has historically relied on command and control approaches to this end. To take the most simple example, once it is decided that a certain level of pollution is unacceptable to society, amounts above this level may be prohibited. Does economics have anything to tell us, however, about whether some approaches to limiting the levels of pollution (or of other types of environmental harm) are more effective than others? The excerpts below discuss different possible approaches to controlling environmental harm from the perspective of economic efficiency. Reference is made to recent experience in the United States with "economic" approaches to air pollution—where federal legislation has made possible the creation of a "market" in rights to pollute, a market that is philosophically objectionable to a number of environmentalists who feel that this in some sense "legitimises" actions that should be seen to be condemned rather than condoned by society. Despite such objections, the United States has recently extended the use of such methods under its *Clean Air Act*, and even among many environmentalists there is increasing interest in an approach that claims to avoid many of the disadvantages of the traditional command and control systems.

A. Scott
"Economic Incentives: The Problem of Getting Started"
in Canadian Society of Environmental Biologists, Alberta Chapter,
Economy & Ecology, The Economics of Environmental Protection (symposium
held February 19-20, 1985, University of Alberta, Edmonton), 75, at 75-79

Six "Economic" Approaches to Pollution Control

Much of this paper will be devoted to examining how an economic system of pollution control gets started, and what problems are likely to be encountered. The discussion centers on the system of transferable emissions rights, which is occasionally contrasted with the competing pollution-tax system.

In this section, however, I begin by examining a list of six methods of pollution control, all of which have important "economic" aspects. The purpose is to show why the tax and rights systems have especially strong claims to be called economic.

1. The Fines Approach

The first system relies on waste-disposal regulations backed up by fines for infractions. If the fines were proportional to the damage done, and/or to the amount of waste illegally emitted, then this system of control would be very similar to the tax system described below. Usually, however, the fine is set on some other basis, so that, although this system undoubtedly has an economic or financial dimension, it has not that economic design that is intended to give an incentive to firms to clean up to a sensible extent. Instead, this approach usually induces firms to behave in an all-or-nothing fashion.

2. The Regulatory Approach

I refer here to pollution regulation of the pollution-permit variety in effect in most Canadian provinces and under the federal *Fisheries Act*. Like the fines approach, it relies on the enforcement of rules or standards for polluter behavior. The economic aspect of this very common approach is to be found in the cost to the firm of complying with requirements that it install abatement technology.

Both these approaches, well-known to economic analysis, embody the principle that "the polluter should pay." This principle is often attributed to economic reasoning, because (especially in international competition among nations), it is supposed to prevent countries attracting industry by offering a haven to the dirtiest and most objectionable polluters. It is, accordingly, embodied not only in the environmentalists' United Nations' Stockholm Declaration of 1972 but also in the related economic adoption of the polluter-pays principle by a convention of the industrialized OECD countries. Canada signed both of these documents.

3. Government Grants, Subsidies, and Tax Reductions

Taxpayers will be aware that in most parts of Canada, as in most industrialized countries, the chief principle at work has not become the "polluter-pays" principle, but the "government pays" approach. Nor is subsidizing polluters a new policy. From the middle of the nineteenth century, pollution cleanups or abatement have been accomplished by publicly financed sewage works. These have been of great assistance in waste disposal by commercial establishments and small industries, most of which are encouraged simply to dump their wastes into large collection systems which then process the effluents and return them to rivers and lakes. Another waste disposal subsidy is likely to be embodied in our new policies on acid rain. One way for Ontario to cut its sulphur emissions is for its coal-burning plants to burn low-sulphur coal, such as that from western Canada. It seems likely that the transportation of such coal, now prohibitively costly, will be subsidized in part by government.

Of course such direct subsidies do not help with all kinds of waste disposal. In other cases, governments have indirectly lent a hand by profit-tax allowances and credits to encourage private abatement and to relieve industry of part of the burden. Such a tax remission is just a subsidy under another name. A subsidy policy is certainly "economic," but even it is not the type of economic incentive instrument to which this [Economics of Environmental Protection] conference is devoted.

Then what "economic" policy instruments *are* we talking about? The key to this mystery is that for the most part the subject called "the economics of pollution abatement" is not concerned with *who* pays. Its analysis is, therefore, concerned with a rather narrow range of policy instruments: that is, three instruments which all work the same way but place the burden of reducing the amount of pollution on three different classes of payer. There is, first, a tax proposal (number 4 below). It tends to place the payment burden on the polluting firm and its customers. Then there is a subsidy proposal (number 5). It tends to place the burden on the government and taxpayers. And finally there is a proposal for transferable-pollution rights, about which I will be speaking later (number 6). It tends to place the burden on the firm, but less so on the firms to whom the rights were first issued.

Economic analysts have shown that all three measures tend in the long run to work to the same conclusion. That is, they have shown that there exists a pollution tax rate, a pollution subsidy rate, and a quantity of pollution rights, all of which will bring about the same amount of private spending on abatement, and the same amount of remaining pollution not controlled. Thus, the three instruments are interchangeable.

Because economists have been concerned with showing this interchangeability, they have not been so interested in what they call the "distributional" question of who ought to pay. This disregard for the distribution of the impact is a frequent characteristic of scientific economies, tending to concentrate on what can be done at a certain minimum total cost rather than on who should bear the cost. Economists are proud of this restraint on their part. In avoiding questions about who ought to pay they leave for our political process the function of distributing and redistributing our total well-being by setting tax rates, grants, and transfers. I think we are lucky that these final questions, about who should be gainers and losers from any policy, are not left to them!

It is assumed that the following question is to be solved: how can we reduce the present level of pollution by inducing firms and plants to abate their emissions so that a desired target level of pollution is reached, in such a way as to choose those abatement processes and methods and to concentrate the abatement effort of the whole community in such plants as will minimize the cost of reaching the target?

The three instruments can be used interchangeably, and they will have the following needs. First, they cannot be put into operation until the authorities know quite a lot about a region's pollution problem. They must know in particular, which firms and plants are emitting wastes into the environment, and how much is being emitted per day or month. Second, they must have set for them a target level, or standard, of total emissions to which they wish to reduce the initial total flow. Third, they must have a capacity to continue to measure the amount each firm or plant is emitting while the policy is in effect, that is, indefinitely. Fourth, they must have a capacity to measure or monitor the *total* amount of pollution produced when the policy is operating.

This is how each "economic instrument" of policy would be operated:

4. The Emission Tax Approach

The authorities would impose a tax (a fee or charge) on each ton each firm was emitting. Thus, the more a firm dumped into the water, the sewers or the air, the more it would have to pay. The principle is that the firms would find it profitable to change the materials or fuels they use, the processes they follow or the products they make in such a way as to reduce their tax bill.

If the firms showed that they would rather pay the tax than abate their waste disposal sufficiently, the tax rate would have to be increased. The government or authority would get some revenue from this tax, but their chief purpose would be to press equally on all the firms until the amount of pollution was cut down to the target that the community had set for itself.

5. The Abatement Subsidy Approach

There are few examples of this kind of subsidy being tried. It would work the same way as a tax and can be described in almost the same language. The authorities would pay a fee to each firm for every ton the firm stopped emitting. Thus, the more a firm reduced its dumping into the water, the sewers or the air, the more subsidy it would receive. The principle is that the firms would find it profitable to change the materials or fuels they use, the processes they follow or the products they make in such a way as to increase their subsidy revenue.

If the firms showed that they would rather continue dumping their wastes into the environment than accept the subsidy, the subsidy rate would have to be increased. The government or the authority would incur some expense from this subsidy but its chief purpose would be to offer an equal inducement to all the firms until the amount of pollution was cut down to the target that the community had set for itself.

6. The Transferable Emissions Rights Approach

Few of these schemes exist, but more are being tried out. They are already at work in the fisheries. The authorities can proceed in several ways to induce the firms to cut down their dumping of wastes.

(i) The authorities can give to each firm a transferable entitlement equal to its initial amount of dumping. In that case, the authorities would announce a timetable of planned reductions in the amount of dumping that each certificate permits. Every firm would then have to abate pollution by changing materials or fuel they use, the processes they follow, or the products they make in such a way as to meet the maximum amount their certificate allows. However, the firms would also be free to buy a certificate from another firm. The principle is that the firms would find it profitable to cut down their emissions or buy certificates, whichever is cheaper. Some firms would cut down a lot, some would find it more profitable to keep on emitting some pollutants.

(ii) There is a second way this scheme can be brought into effect. As with the first, the authorities could give to each firm a certificate of entitlement equal to the initial amount of dumping. These certificates would be transferable. When they had been issued, the government would start a "buy-back" scheme. It would enter the market and make cash offers for certificates bearing entitlements at a certain number of dollars per ton of entitlement. At this price, some firms would be glad to sell part or all of their certificate to the government or other firms. The principle is that some firms would cut down their emissions in order to get the revenue from selling their pollution entitlements. The cash value of all remaining permits would tend to rise so that all other firms would begin to consider selling their certificates to the government or other firms until the target abatement of total pollution was reached.

(iii) The first two ways of using the transferable emission rights approach would allow the overall abatement to be phased in either quickly or slowly. Either by its policy of reducing the entitlement permitted by each certificate, or by reducing the total number of certificates outstanding, the authorities would deliberately move the polluters towards the overall target.

The third route is much more abrupt, and is the route usually presumed to be used in the economic and environmental literature. Using this route, the authorities can give away or sell just the right amount of pollution emission rights to industry by putting that amount up for auction. The principle is almost the same: the firms would find it profitable to cut down their emissions or bid for certificates from the government whichever was cheaper for them.

D.G. McFetridge
"The Economic Approach to Environmental Issues"
in G.B. Doern, ed., *The Environmental Imperative: Market Approaches to the Greening of Canada* (Toronto: C.D. Howe Institute, 1990), 84, at 95-102

Marketable Permits

Definition

Under a marketable-permit scheme, the appropriate level of environmental quality is defined in terms of allowable emissions. Permits are allocated to firms, generally on the basis of historic emissions or output. These permits enable the owner to emit a specified amount of pollution. Permits can be traded and sometimes banked. As a result, abatement is undertaken by the firms with the lowest abatement costs. Firms with higher costs buy the permits. This system minimizes the cost of achieving the desired level of abatement, provided that the market is competitive.

Examples

Marketable Effluent Permits: A system of marketable effluent permits was introduced in 1981 at Fox River, Wisconsin. The permits last for five years and allow the holder to discharge effluent with a specified biological oxygen demand (BOD). Permits were granted to two types of users: pulp and paper mills and municipal waste treatment plants. With only one trade in six years, however, the system has not been effective, for several reasons:

- trading is allowed only for those with a demonstrated inability to introduce abatement technology or for new entrants who in any case must install state-of-the-art abatement;
- the value of permits is uncertain since the acquiring party does not necessarily get the permit after it is reissued; and
- permits are a very small part of the regulatory structure.

Emissions Trading: The EPA [US Environmental Protection Agency] allows limited trading in the right to emit carbon monoxide, sulphur dioxide, and nitrous oxides. Trading may take any of four forms: netting, offsets, bubbles and banking.

- *Netting* allows new emissions from a plant provided they are offset by emission reductions elsewhere in the same plant. This is also called "internal trading."
- *Offsets* is the practice of allowing new emissions in areas in which air-quality standards have not been met provided they are offset by greater reductions in the same plant or other plants in the same area. Offsets can thus be obtained either by "internal or external trading."
- *Bubbles* are an aggregation of all sources of a given pollutant in a particular plant. Required emissions reductions can take place where it is least costly.
- *Banking* is the process by which emissions below a required level can be "saved" and used or sold in the future.

The cost savings from netting and bubbles, both of which involve only internal trading, are thought to be very large but are also uncertain. Most offset and banking trades have also been internal. These measures have also resulted in considerable cost savings.

External trading has been minimal and its cost-saving potential remains unrealized, for two apparent reasons. First, the program is an adjunct to an extensive system of environmental regulations that require, among other things, state-of-the-art abatement in all new plants. Second, the EPA has left the rights inherent in a permit deliberately ambiguous precisely to discourage external trading. The reason for this is, in turn, that external trading is visible, and it antagonizes environmentalists who (correctly) see grandfathered emissions permits as a right to pollute (at some level).

Lead Trading: During the 1982-87 period, the United States reduced the lead content of motor gasoline. Each refinery received lead rights equal to its current production times the current lead-control standard. If the lead content of a refiner's gasoline production was below the total allowed amount, remaining lead rights could be sold or banked.

This program is regarded as having been effective, since a considerable amount of trading in lead rights did occur and there was a significant refiner cost saving as a consequence. The program's success apparently was due to well-defined lead rights, in the sense that the lead content of gasoline could readily be monitored and because the lead content reduction goal was widely agreed upon and understood—that is, environmentalists accepted a limited "right to pollute" in this case. Moreover, lead rights were readily tradable.

Emissions Charges

Definition

In principle, an emissions charge is levied on a per-unit-of-pollutant basis. The unit charge can vary with the nature of the pollutant and with the concentration and time period of emission. Again, in principle, the fee should be equal to the damages imposed on competing users. In other words, the fees should be equal at the margin to the decline in the value of the resource to other users.

If emissions charges are set in this fashion, several results will follow:

- the value derived from emissions must be at least as great as the sum of the costs imposed on competing users;
- emissions abatement will be introduced to the point at which the cost of abatement equals the emissions fee; and
- investments in abatement will be distributed efficiently among polluters.

Examples

Emissions or effluent charges tend to differ significantly from the ideal. They are often not related directly to emissions and, as far as can be discerned, are not based on the damages inflicted on competing users. In France, for example, effluent charges do not vary with the volume or content of effluent, although the sewage tax is volume-related and discharge permits are priced according to discharge content. In West Germany, effluent charges cover a wide range of pollutants and are related to volume and concentration.

The Netherlands has the highest effluent charges of any industrial country. These are set on the basis of volume, concentration, and the nature of the discharge, with the actual emissions of large users being monitored. These charges are said to have been very effective in reducing water pollution.

User charges levied by waste-water processing utilities in the United States are based on volume and concentration. Hahn [R. Hahn, "Economic Prescriptions for Environmental Problems: How the Patient Followed the Doctor's Orders" (1989) vol. 3 *Journal of Economic Perspectives* 95] concludes that these charges are not enough to cover the cost of these facilities or to affect the behavior of polluters. In their earlier study, Baumol and Oates [W. Baumol and W. Oates, *Economics, Environmental Policy, and the Quality of Life* (Englewood Cliffs, NJ: Prentice-Hall, 1979)] cite evidence that conflicts with Hahn's conclusion on responsiveness. They find US studies to show elasticity of BOD discharge with respect to effluent fees of 0.5 and 0.8.

A number of Canadian cities levy effluent charges based on BOD, suspended solids, and grease. Some have found their system of charges to be effective and easy to administer [J. Chant, D.G. McFetridge, and D. Smith, "The Economics of the Conserver Society," in W. Block, ed., *Economics and the Environment: A Reconciliation* (Vancouver: Fraser Institute, 1990)]. Response elasticities of BOD and suspended solids discharge to changes in effluent fees on the order of 0.5 have also been found in Canada.

B. Stevens and A. Rose
"A Dynamic Analysis of the Marketable Permits Approach to Global Warming Policy: A Comparison of Spatial and Temporal Flexibility"
(2002) vol. 94, no. 1 *Journal of Environmental Economics and Management* 45, at 45-46

The trading of pollution rights is one of the more important innovations economists have contributed to environmental policy-making. Most of the analysis of marketable permits considers trading across entities, implicitly within a given time period, but there may also be gains from trade across time if permit banking and borrowing are allowed. Emissions trading emphasizes economic incentives and freedom of choice in the context of the workings of the market and thus capitalizes on the standard welfare economics result of achieving economic efficiency, or, under more modest goals, cost-effectiveness. Equity, in its various forms, can also be promoted by tailoring the initial distribution of permits.

The Kyoto Protocol has taken these themes into account. Although 38 industrialized countries (Annex B signatories) committed to targets and timetables for the reduction of greenhouse gases (GHGs), implementation is not limited to fixed quotas. Instead, several features of the Protocol, often referred to as "flexibility mechanisms,"

allow for various aspects of permit trading. Joint Implementation (JI) allows one Annex B country to sponsor a GHG mitigation project in another Annex B country and
receive credit against its own commitments. Likewise, the Clean Development
Mechanism (CDM) allows Annex B countries to sponsor similar projects in developing countries. The extension of the project-by-project arrangement to a multilateral
context would move the institution in the direction of a full-fledged permit market.

The Protocol also allows for banking of permits, or mitigation in excess of commitments in some periods, with the prospect of mitigation at levels lower than
commitments at some future date. Borrowing, however, is not explicitly mentioned.

. . .

While economic motivations emphasize unrestricted permit trading, non-economic
considerations have entered the policy debate to restrict flexibility. The main example, known as "supplementarity," would limit the amount of permit purchases and
sales. Some policymakers resent the prospect of a country "buying its way out" of its
Kyoto commitment. Others resent the prospects that, because of economic down-
turns, Russia and other former Soviet republics could sell permit allotments in excess
of their emissions at zero cost to themselves (so-called "hot air" permits) and would
be doing so without actually reducing global emission levels. The first argument
misses the point that countries buying permits do so at a positive price and that trading promotes efficient resource allocation. The second argument might be addressed
directly without restricting permit transactions.

QUESTIONS

1. One typically thinks of pollution permits being held by polluters. What about the
possibility of environmental organizations or trusts buying such permits as a means of
reducing the level of pollutants discharged? Would such an approach have some broader
appeal? For example, suppose that a government were to assign tradeable quantitative
rights to water use in a river basin, could one argue that an allocation of such rights
should also be made to environmental "consumers" as represented by some designated
organizations?

2. What potential does the pollution permit approach have for addressing
transjurisdictional environmental problems other than greenhouse gas emissions, especially for problems affecting the global commons? See D.W. Pearce and J.J. Warford,
World Without End: Economics, Environment and Sustainable Development (Oxford:
Oxford University Press, 1993).

FURTHER READINGS

H.M. Biggs, R.F. Kosobud, and D.L. Schreder, eds., *Emissions Trading: Environmental
Policy's New Approach* (New York: Wiley, 2000).

Canada, Task Force on Economic Instruments and Disincentives to Sound Environmental
Practices, *Economic Instruments and Disincentives to Sound Environmental Practices:
Final Report of the Task Force* (Ottawa: Environment Canada, 1994).

J.H. Dales, *Pollution, Property and Prices* (Toronto: University of Toronto Press, 1968).

R.W. Hahn and R.N. Stavins, "Incentive-Based Environmental Regulation: A New Era from an Old Idea" (1991) vol. 18 *Ecology Law Quarterly* 1.

J.E. Krier, "Marketable Pollution Allowances" (1994) vol. 25 *University of Toledo Law Review* 449.

Organisation for Economic Co-operation and Development, *Managing the Environment: The Role of Economic Instruments* (Paris: OECD, 1994).

C. Rolfe, *Turning Down the Heat: Emissions Trading and Canadian Implementation of the Kyoto Protocol* (Vancouver: West Coast Environmental Law Research Foundation, 1998).

T. Sandler, *Global Challenges: An Approach to Environmental, Political and Economic Problems* (Cambridge: Cambridge University Press, 1997).

T. Tietenberg, ed., *The Economics of Global Warming* (Aldershot, UK: Edward Elgar, 1997).

V. CONSUMER APPROACHES

The sections above have concentrated primarily on what can be considered interventions by government in the production process—whether that intervention is characterized by direct command and control, by the rearrangement of property rights, or by other economic incentives and disincentives. By concentrating on the supply side of the equation, however, we have largely ignored in this discussion possible measures directed at the demand side—that is, measures aimed at influencing the consumer directly. This final section addresses some of the emerging approaches that focus on the consumer, with special attention paid to the question of so-called eco-labelling. As with the case of tradeable emissions permits, this is an area that has received more attention in the United States than in Canada, especially in terms of litigation.

J.P. Kimmel Jr.
"Disclosing the Environmental Impact of Human Activities: How a Federal Pollution Control Program Based on Individual Decision Making and Consumer Demand Might Accomplish the Environmental Goals of the 1970s in the 1990s"
(1989) vol. 138 *University of Pennsylvania Law Review* 505, at 526, 527-29

Until now, most proposed economic charge approaches have sought to achieve environmental quality by targeting only the business sector of the economy. Proponents of such charge approaches assume that most externalities occur during production. The charge approach alters the cost variable of the producer's output equation in an effort to influence production decisions and create a more efficient market. The regulatory approach, while addressing economic factors, also targets only producers by implementing production constraints.

. . .

The consumer is an appropriate target of environmental enhancement legislation because consumer behavior greatly influences production decisions. Additionally, consumers themselves cause pollution while consuming and disposing of products.

Reducing the demand for highly polluting products could produce a number of environmental benefits. First, it would decrease aggregate pollutant emissions as either inefficient production decreased or more environmentally efficient methods of production, use and disposal were adopted. The direct regulatory approach cannot achieve these results because it fails to address pollution occurring through the use and disposal of products and packages. Additionally, targeting the demand component in producer decisions removes producers from the difficult position in which they are placed by both the regulatory and charge systems. Under those systems, producers face the same consumer demands, needs, and desires regardless of the additional costs of productions that are imposed. The result is that only one component of consumer demand—price—may be affected. The other factors of demand are left weighing in favor of continued consumption of the same products, regardless of their environmental impact.

Second, making the demand for products sensitive to the pollution generated throughout the product's life cycle would provide an incentive to producers and disposal firms to satisfy that demand by developing products and disposal methods that meet consumers' overall desires. Pollutants would be reduced because of the consumer demand for more environmentally efficient products and processes.

Third, a system operating within the free market by influencing consumer demand would be more efficient because a central planning agency would no longer be making pollution control decisions based on information that is nearly impossible to gather or assimilate. Each producer and consumer would make her own decisions based on market information that would guide those decisions toward environmental goals. Moreover, this approach recognizes that some pollution is an unavoidable by-product of economic and social progress; individual economic decision making will sometimes demand that certain products be produced regardless of their environmental impact. In those situations, however, costs could be imposed on the consumer to compensate society for the use and cleanup of the environment.

Finally, developing demand-driven economic incentives to encourage compliance with environmental goals greatly reduces the difficulties of attempting to force thousands of ambivalent producers to comply with regulatory standards. If the market in which producers sell their goods and services demands that those items be pollution-lean, the need to monitor producers disappears; voluntary compliance would be more certain.

NOTE

The now-common requirement in many jurisdictions for systems that provide for mandatory deposits for drink containers is the most obvious example of a policy that is designed to make transparent to consumers the social costs of their choices. It is possible, however, that one could go much further in this direction by imposing a range of product taxes on disposable products so as to reflect the costs to society of solid waste generation—in effect to take account of the negative externalities discussed earlier in this chapter. For a discussion of some proposals in this respect, see B.A. Bernheim, "Can We Cure Our Throwaway Habits by Imposing the True Social Cost on Disposable Products?" (1992) vol. 63 *University of Colorado Law Review* 953.

M.F. Teisl, B. Roe, and R.L. Hicks
"Can Eco-Labels Tune a Market? Evidence from Dolphin-Safe Labeling"
(2002) vol. 43, no. 3 *Journal of Environmental Economics and*
Management 339, at 339-41

The environmental characteristics of products have become increasingly important to consumers. Firms have responded by placing eco-labels on products that highlight the item's environmental attributes and by introducing new, or redesigned, "green" products. Governments and nongovernmental organizations have also responded by organizing, implementing, and verifying eco-labeling programs that cover thousands of products in more than 20 countries, while international efforts to standardize environmental labeling schemes have also emerged. From a policy perspective, one aim of eco-labels is to educate consumers about the environmental impacts of the product's manufacture, use, and disposal, thereby leading to a change in purchasing behavior and ultimately, to a reduction in negative impacts. Further, eco-labeling policies may promote environmental objectives without production site command and control methods and are seen as a way of meeting global environmental objectives while complying with international trade agreements.

In order for eco-labels to achieve policy objectives, consumers must hold preferences for certain environmental amenities and respond to the information presented on eco-labels by altering purchases toward eco-labeled goods. Their widespread use suggests that eco-labeling is perceived as an effective method of altering consumer behavior. However, few studies have attempted to identify the behavioral effectiveness of eco-labeling programs. Evaluating the policy effectiveness of eco-labeling programs requires understanding how information affects market behavior. Evaluating the economic efficiency of labeling programs requires measuring the benefits and costs of such information.

. . .

Labeling and Consumer Choice

Although implementation of eco-labels is widespread, research concerning its impact and effectiveness is limited and aggregate quantitative results are rare. Much of the research has measured effectiveness either by identifying changes in consumer awareness after exposure to label information or by asking consumers whether eco-labeling programs would affect their purchase behavior. However, a change in awareness does not necessarily translate into a change in behavior and consumers do not necessarily follow their own purchasing assertions.

Market-based research investigating other types of labels (e.g., nutrition labels, quality seals) has demonstrated that a change in labeling can change market behavior. However, the apparent effectiveness of these (non-eco) labeling programs may not be applicable to eco-labeling because these non-eco-labels provide information about the characteristics of the product. Eco-labels, like the dolphin-safe labels studied here, differentiate products with respect to characteristics of the product's production.

NOTES AND QUESTIONS

1. As suggested in the last excerpt, the growing sensitivity of consumers to environmental factors has not been lost on environmental and other groups. The possible sympathy of interests between commercial interests and environmental groups raises a number of controversial questions.

One issue is whether environmental groups should consider "alliances" with appropriate industries whereby they endorse environmentally acceptable products in return for financial rewards. This is an approach that has been adopted by environmental groups in the United Kingdom and the United States since the 1980s. While there may be some financial advantages to such an arrangement, however, there is also the obvious danger that the group itself may become "tainted" through its willingness to lend its name to commercial endeavours. Perhaps the best known example of this in Canada is the 1989 decision by Pollution Probe to endorse green products at Loblaws supermarkets in return for a fee tied to the volume of sales. The decision led to controversy both within Pollution Probe and within the environmental community generally. Ultimately the executive director of Pollution Probe resigned and the group ended its relationship with Loblaws. See G. Gallon, "The Green Product Endorsement Controversy: Lessons from the Pollution Probe/Loblaw Experience" (1991) vol. 18, no. 3 *Alternatives* 16. Should environmental groups have a role in endorsing some products as more "environmentally friendly" than others and, if so, how should this role be carried out?

2. The other side of the coin of product endorsement by environmental groups is consumer boycotts, which have proven remarkably effective for a number of high-profile issues. Consumer boycotts may take one of two primary forms. The first is a boycott of the product itself (for example, fur coats). The second is a general boycott against goods from a particular firm or country with which the product is associated. International consumer boycotts have been effective in influencing state behaviour in areas other than the environment. One could cite in this respect the widespread consumer boycott of South African products during the apartheid era, even before the imposition of international sanctions. In a similar vein was the consumer protest directed at Nestlés because of the controversy over its promotion of infant formulas in the Third World.

Consumer boycotts offer a special advantage in the context of international trade, where the major international agreement regulating trade practices—the General Agreement on Tariffs and Trade (GATT)—has little to say on environmental issues. Although there is some room for an "environmental exception" in the GATT—that is, an exception permitting trade-distorting measures that would otherwise be prohibited—the current phrasing is clearly deficient in light of our understanding of the environment. The GATT, however, is directed at government-induced distortions of trade; it imposes no restrictions on the rights of individuals to organize boycotts of foreign products, on whatever grounds. It thus allows for the imposition of consumer pressure on other states that might not be possible under normal trade legislation.

A good illustration of this is provided by the case of "dolphin-safe" tuna. In the Eastern Tropical Pacific Ocean, there is a phenomenon whereby dolphin tend to swim above schools of tuna; when purse seine nets are set to capture the tuna, the result is that they also catch the associated dolphins. One reaction to this in the United States was the introduction of legislation that, *inter alia*, prohibited the import of tuna where the fishing methods resulted in an unacceptable level of dolphin kills. In a resulting GATT dispute settlement panel hearing (which today would be held under the World Trade Organization) initiated by Mexico (the state that was effectively the target of the impugned provision), the panel report found that the US actions could not be justified under any GATT exceptions. However, the same report also found that US labelling provisions adopted to regulate the use of the term "dolphin safe" on canned tuna were permissible, in that they left the ultimate choice up to the market. In fact, of course, such regulation of information can provide an essential element in making consumer action effective. In the case of canned tuna, such consumer action in the United States did indeed prove highly effective. See *United States—Restrictions on Imports of Tuna*, GATT Dispute Settlement Panel Report, Submitted to the Parties 16 August 1991 (1991) vol. 30 *International Legal Materials* 1594.

3. Despite its approval of the US labelling provisions, the GATT panel's refusal in the *Tuna* case to approve US measures in their entirety has been criticized by a number of writers. See, for example, R.E. Housman and D.J. Zaelke, "The Collision of the Environment and Trade: The GATT Tuna/Dolphin Decision" (1992) vol. 22 *Environmental Law Reporter* 10268. However, such critiques, which often amount to the proposition that unilateralism is acceptable in international relations so long as it is in the interests of the environment, raise some difficult issues in their own right—for example, the question as to who should decide whether a particular policy is environmentally "correct." Moreover, there is at least some ground for fear that such unilateralism will be welcomed not necessarily on environmental grounds, but because of protectionist sentiment. It is significant, for example, that the US actions with respect to the Eastern Tropical Pacific tuna took place only after the US tuna fleet itself no longer operated in that area. In such cases, are consumers paying higher prices to protect the environment or to protect domestic industry? See J.O. Saunders, "Trade and Environment: The Fine Line between Environmental Protection and Environmental Protectionism" (1992) vol. 47 *International Journal* 723.

4. Given that such actions are typically imposed (or at least proposed) by developed states, while the target is typically developing states, it is not surprising that accusations of "green imperialism" have also been raised. How does one determine what is a "legitimate" effort to protect the environment and what is an improper attempt to interfere in the economic development policies of another state?

FURTHER READINGS

L. Barrera-Hernandez, "Consumer Behaviour and the Environment: An Environmental and Policy Approach" (1995) vol. 5 *Journal of Environmental Law and Practice* 161.

J.M. Church, "A Market Solution to Green Marketing: Some Lessons from the Economics of Information" (1994) vol. 79 *Minnesota Law Review* 245.

D.S. Cohen, "The Regulation of Green Advertising: The State, the Market and the Environmental Good" (1991) vol. 25, no. 2 *UBC Law Review* 225.

G. Gallon, "The Green Product Endorsement Controversy: Lessons from the Pollution Probe/Loblaw Experience" (1991) vol. 18, no. 3 *Alternatives* 16.

S. Gardner, "How Green Were My Values: Regulation of Environmental Marketing Claims" (1991) vol. 23 *University of Toledo Law Review* 31.

C. Kye, "Environmental Law and the Consumer in the European Union" (1995) vol. 7, no. 1 *Journal of Environmental Law* 31.

A.S. Rousso and S.P. Shah, "Packaging Taxes and Recycling Incentives: the German Green Dot Program" (1994) vol. 47 *National Tax Journal* 689.

CHAPTER ELEVEN

Environmental and Animal Rights*

Elaine L. Hughes

I. INTRODUCTION

Civil rights are widely accepted throughout North America as one means of achieving legal protection of the interests of minority or disadvantaged groups. It is not surprising, therefore, that environmental advocates have explored the possibility of adapting the civil rights model for use in the environmental area. This chapter provides an overview of a group of law reform ideas that are based on the concept of creating a legally enforceable civil right to environmental quality.

J. Swaigen and R.E. Woods
"A Substantive Right to Environmental Quality"
in J. Swaigen, ed., *Environmental Rights in Canada* (Toronto: Butterworths and CELRF, 1981), 195, at 197-98

Rightly or wrongly, members of the public and learned commentators alike have equated powerlessness with a lack of rights. Joseph Sax was one of the first reformers to clarify in the environmental context the difference between a regime in which the public has substantive rights and one characterized by government powers, unchecked discretion and mere procedural rights. In *Defending the Environment*, Sax describes the difference between a rights-based legal regime and one based on other considerations:

> The elaborate structure of administration middlemen we have interposed between the citizen and his interest in environmental quality has had another pernicious effect. It has dulled our sensitivity to the claim that citizens, as members of the public, have rights. The citizen who comes to an administrative agency comes essentially as a supplicant, requesting that somehow the public interest be interpreted to protect the

* The author gratefully acknowledges the research assistance of Omolara Oladipo, LLM.

environment values from which he benefits. The citizen who comes to court has quite a different status—he stands as a claimant of rights to which he is entitled.

Thus far neither our courts nor our legislatures have significantly faced up to the implications of public rights. They continue to be fixated on the administrative process as *the* mechanism for identifying and enforcing the public interest. The public remains an outsider, to be tolerated as a recipient of notices and participant at formal hearings, but not as a central player. Elaborate schemes are devised for studies by agencies and for coordination among them, but the administrative agency continues to be viewed as the key instrument of decision-making. Even the most sympathetic courts today recoil at the prospect of questioning an agency's discretion or its supposed expertise about the public interest. The public itself is thought to possess *no* expertise about the public interest.

The consequence of all this, as we shall see, is an incredible tangle of agencies with noble-sounding mandates and small budgets; court decisions which, in their reluctance to question administrative discretion, send cases back for interminable "further studies" or with directions for correcting little procedural blunders they have made; and proceedings that go on for years—and even decades. And when it is all over, we have, as at the beginning, a decision reflecting the agency's response to *its* political necessities—its insider perspective about the public interest.

Sax contrasted the position of the "supplicant" with the holder of rights. He pointed out how strange it would be if the owner of private property could not initiate action to enforce his individual property rights, but had to rely on some bureaucrat to vindicate them "when, and if, he determines them to be consistent with the public interest."

In a recent book advocating recognition of "fundamental" rights of individuals to be free from government interference, Ronald Dworkin describes this "rightless" kind of situation as one which does not provide each party to the process with treatment equal in respect and dignity.

Current Canadian environmental law and policy frequently mirror the kinds of situations and outcomes described by both Sax and Dworkin as characterizing rightless regimes. Substantive issues are often not approached directly. Because the system focuses on procedures rather than rights, it bogs down in orders requiring further studies and corrections of small procedural blunders, but fails to examine the merits of the environmental protection case. As in Sax's description of the American environmental decision-making context, the administrative agencies in Canada which attempt to interpret the public interest in a situation where one party has property rights and the other has none treat the right-holder with more concern and respect than they do the non-right-holder.

E. Hughes and D. Iyalomhe
"Substantive Environmental Rights in Canada"
(1998-99) vol. 30, no. 2 *Ottawa Law Review* 229, at 232-34

Even amongst rights advocates, there has been a longstanding debate about environmental rights. That debate can be divided into three major issues or groups of issues. The first is the realm of the theorist, centred on the question of whether environmental rights and duties exist and, if so, what is their nature? Regardless of whether any legal recognition exists, is there a moral right to a healthy environment? Is such a right individual or collective? Is it a positive or a negative right? Can we conceptualize such rights as anthropocentric (i.e., human rights to environmental quality) or ecocentric (animal rights, species' rights or rights for nature)? Do these rights extend to future generations? Are there duties that accompany the rights? What is an appropriate scope for such a right or group of rights, and is there a social consensus on this?

There is, of course, an extensive body of literature by philosophers, ethicists and political and legal theorists that discusses and debates these very questions. Often, the conclusions of the authors are shaped by their theory about the basis of rights—whether they arise from a social contract, from socio-economic utility, from the intrinsic worth of the individual, from some law of human nature, or from some other theoretical basis. As a generalization, analysts conclude that there are moral rights to environmental quality, although there is little agreement about the nature, scope or ambit of such rights. However, on occasions where the issue is raised, there is usually agreement that such rights should, like other civil rights, be legally enforceable, and that this would, potentially, prove useful in solving environmental problems.

This brings us to the second area of debate, then, which focuses on the question: if one chooses to make environmental rights legally enforceable, how can this best be done? Should the rights be procedural or "substantive"? Should they be statutory or constitutional? Should they be enforceable against government or private persons or both? In what forum should such rights be asserted? What remedies should be available? How should one resolve conflicts between environmental and other rights, such as property rights? In "hard" cases, should environmental rights provide a presumptive solution?

Again, there is a fairly substantial body of literature that puts forward a variety of answers to these questions. Generally speaking, one can say that the form of legal protection envisioned by writers in the area is shaped by the authors' views on the nature and scope of the moral right. Thus, for example, a different remedy might be suggested by someone who views environmental rights as collective rights than would be put forward by someone who views those rights as individual rights. Also influential is the writers' views about the nature of participatory democracy. For example, one might choose to have the courts as final adjudicator if one views their role as being that of an overseer of government, there to prevent abuse of authority by government officials and to ensure fairness and impartiality. On the other hand, one might view the courts as inappropriate policy-makers, and any expanded role of the judiciary as fundamentally undemocratic.

Clearly, then, the arena of environmental rights is filled with a wide variety of contentious issues, all of which must be settled in order to come up with a concrete proposal. Assuming, however, that a society can decide on the nature of environmental rights, their scope, and the form that they should take in law, one is then left with the third and most fundamental set of questions. Will better environmental protection actually result? Can it be achieved in a way that achieves distributive justice i.e., will it be equitable, just and fair? Is there a way to bring everyday reality into conformity with our catalogue of environmental rights? Finally, what are the social implications of recognizing environmental rights?

NOTES

As J. Castrilli has pointed out in "Environmental Rights Statutes in the United States and Canada" (1998) vol. 9 *Villanova Environmental Law Journal* 349, at 352, there remains a "fundamental and continuing dissatisfaction with the administrative and regulatory process as the exclusive source for implementing the public interest in environmentally-sound decision-making." As deregulation and privatization became common in the 1990s, the need for citizens to be able to hold government accountable, access the judicial process, and participate effectively in environmental decisions arguably became more urgent and important than ever before.

Proposals for improved rights generally fall into one of three categories:

1. *Procedural rights.* Since the 1970s, a number of procedural improvements in environmental law have been enacted in some jurisdictions, including improved standing rules before both courts and administrative tribunals, environmental impact assessment laws, access to information laws, intervener funding programs, improved class action rules, and regulatory legislation that creates statutory torts if breach of a rule causes personal injury or property damage. (See generally chapters 3 and 6.) However, there are continued calls for an expansion of participation or accountability rights, either (1) to ameliorate continuing procedural obstacles to pursuing environmental litigation (whether civil or criminal), or (2) to ensure better citizen participation in governmental and administrative decision-making processes, such as licensing. Such procedural rights are usually envisioned as statutory bills of rights.

2. *Substantive rights.* On the basis of American proposals, particularly the 1970 *Michigan Environmental Protection Act* (MEPA), Mich. Comp. Laws Ann. 324.1701-324.1706 (West 1997), many commentators have argued for creation of a "right to a healthy environment" as a legal right enforceable by individual citizens through lawsuits, and that would develop into a "common law of environmental quality" via judicial interpretation "in a manner similar to the development of the law of property or contracts." (Castrilli, above, at 371-72) Such a right might be enforceable against either private persons or government, whenever a reasonable level of environmental quality was violated. The rights are conceived of as individual rights; occasionally a collective right to environmental quality is proposed along with a corresponding government duty to protect the public interest or "public trust." Such proposals might be statutory or constitutional (for example, via incorporation into the *Charter of Rights and Freedoms*). Arguably, constitutionally protected aboriginal and treaty rights of the First Nations already include the protection of some environmental values.

3. *Non-human rights.* Several proposals have suggested environmental rights aimed at the protection of non-human life or protection of the environment per se. Proposals for extending legal rights to non-human entities often concentrate on justifying *why* such rights should be granted, although several also explore *how* one might accomplish such a goal. There is a substantial body of work that explores the links between animal welfare activism, animal rights and the environmental movement.

Each of these categories will be illustrated in the following materials. As you proceed, try to evaluate the strengths and weaknesses of both the individual proposals and the civil rights approach in general.

II. PROCEDURAL RIGHTS

Numerous attempts to obtain an "environmental bill of rights" have been made in Canada since the early 1970s. These have arisen primarily at the provincial level, in the form of proposed legislation that has been procedural or administrative in nature. Typically, the basic idea has been to try to address a number of the existing deficiencies in the present law. For example, one of the earliest proposals was made in Alberta in 1979: Bill 222, *The Environmental Bill of Rights*, 1st sess., 19th leg. Alta., included standing to bring private prosecutions, a statutory cause of action for pollution if it significantly decreased environmental quality, some provisions altering the burden of proof in civil actions, better access to information, and some provisions dealing with remedies. Other proposals were made periodically, including those in Ontario in 1979, 1980, 1987, and 1989, and Saskatchewan in 1982; each proposal continued to emphasize the improvement of procedural rights, including costs, intervenor funding, and judicial review of administrative decisions, although some also included a few "substantive" provisions.

However, each time such bills were introduced they either died on the order paper or were blocked by the majority government of the day. In fact, the only rights legislation successfully enacted in the 1970s and 1980s was section 19.1 of Quebec's *Environment Quality Act*, RSQ 1997, c. Q-2, which, in 1978, gave every natural person "a right to a healthy environment and to its protection ... to the extent provided for by this act and the regulations." However, this section created little more than a statutory tort, protecting residents only from violations of the legislative requirements. See generally chapter 4 and *Calvé v. Gestion Serge Lafrenière Inc.*, [1999] JQ no. 1334.

Finally, in 1990, the first "true" Canadian environmental rights legislation was enacted with the passage of the Northwest Territories' *Environmental Rights Act*, SNWT 1990, c. 28. The next year the Yukon Territory enacted more comprehensive environmental legislation that also included a set of environmental rights.

Environment Act
SY 1991, c. 5

4. This Act binds the Government of the Yukon.

5(1) The objectives of this Act are

(a) to ensure the maintenance of essential ecological processes and the preservation of biological diversity;

(b) to ensure the wise management of the environment of the Yukon;

(c) to promote sustainable development in the Yukon;

(d) to ensure comprehensive and integrated consideration of environmental and socioeconomic effects in public policy making in the Yukon;

(e) to recognize the interests of Yukon residents in regional, national and global environmental well-being;

(f) to utilize fully the knowledge and experience of Yukon residents in formulating public policy on the environment; and

(g) to facilitate effective participation by Yukon residents in the making of decisions that will affect the environment.

(2) The following principles apply to the realization of the objectives of this Act

(a) economic development and the health of the natural environment are interdependent;

(b) environmental considerations must be integrated effectively into all public decision-making;

(c) the Government of the Yukon must ensure that public policy reflects its responsibility for the protection of the global ecosystem;

(d) the Government of the Yukon is responsible for the wise management of the environment on behalf of present and future generations; and

(e) all persons should be responsible for the consequences to the environment of their actions.

(3) This Act shall be interpreted and applied to give effect to the objectives and principles of this section.

6. The people of the Yukon have the right to a healthful natural environment.

7. It is hereby declared that it is in the public interest to provide every person resident in the Yukon with a remedy adequate to protect the natural environment and the public trust.

8(1) Every adult or corporate person resident in the Yukon who has reasonable grounds to believe that

(a) a person has impaired or is likely to impair the natural environment; or

(b) the Government of the Yukon has failed to meet its responsibilities as trustee of the public trust to protect the natural environment from actual or likely impairment,

may commence an action in the Supreme Court.

. . .

9(1) It is a defence to an action under paragraph 8(1)(a) that

(a) the activity of the defendant that caused or is likely to cause the impairment of the natural environment was in compliance with a permit, licence or other authorization issued or a standard established (i) under an enactment; or (ii) under an Act of Parliament listed in Schedule B;

(b) the activity ... has not caused ... material impairment ... ;

(c) the defendant has established that there is no feasible and prudent alternative to the activity; or

(d) the activity of the defendant (i) has not impaired and is not likely to impair the natural environment outside residential property; and (ii) is caused or authorized by the person using the property as a residence.

(2) No action under subsection 8(1) shall be commenced after 15 years from the date the cause of action arises.

10(1) No person is prohibited from commencing an action under subsection 8(1) by reason only that he or she is unable to show

(a) any greater or different right, harm or interest than any other person; or

(b) any pecuniary or proprietary right or interest in the subject matter of the proceeding.

(2) No action under subsection 8(1) shall be dismissed on the ground that

(a) the public trust is not irrevocable or certain;

(b) a beneficiary cannot be identified; or

(c) an authority has the power to authorize an act which may impair the natural environment.

. . .

11. Where it is proved ... that the defendant released, at the material time, a contaminant of the type that caused the impairment, the onus shall be on the defendant to prove that he, she or it did not cause impairment.

12(1) [T]he Supreme Court may

(a) grant an interim, interlocutory of permanent injunction;

(b) grant a declaration;

(c) award damages;

(d) award costs; and

(e) grant such other remedy that the Supreme Court considers just.

[Subsection 2 sets out additional remedies, including mandatory monitoring, environmental restoration, preventive measures, suspension or cancellation of permits, and ordering environmental impact assessments.]

. . .

14(1) Any two persons resident in the Yukon, who believe on reasonable grounds that an activity is impairing or is likely to impair the natural environment may apply to the Minister for an investigation.

. . .

19(1) An adult person resident in the Yukon may institute a private prosecution in respect of an offence under this Act or a regulation under this Act ... .

(2) Where a private prosecution under subsection (1) results in a conviction, the court may order ... that all or a portion of the fine imposed, when collected, shall be paid to the person instituting the private prosecution ... .

. . .

20. ...

(2) No employer shall dismiss or threaten to dismiss, discipline, impose any penalty on, intimidate or coerce an employee because the employee ... [takes action under ss. 8, 14, 19, or other remedial sections as specified].

. . .

22(1) Any person or group of persons may complain to the Minister with respect to a decision, recommendation, act or omission of an authority having or exercising power of responsibility under this Act or a Schedule A enactment, including the exercise of a discretionary power. [Such complaints may be investigated and referred to mediation pursuant to s. 23.]

. . .

29. The Minister shall consult with affected interests in the development of a proposal to make, amend or revoke a regulation under this Act or a Schedule A enactment.

30(1) Subject to section 34, where the Commissioner in Executive Council proposes to make, amend or revoke a regulation under this Act or a Schedule A enactment, the proposal shall be referred to the Minister for public review, and the Minister shall then initiate a public review.

. . .

36. The Minister may establish participant funding programs ... .

37. Nothing in this Part affects any other remedies or defences available at law.

38(1) The Government of the Yukon is the trustee of the public trust.

(2) The Government of the Yukon shall, subject to this Act or a Schedule A enactment, conserve the natural environment in accordance with the public trust. ["Public trust" is defined in s. 2 as "the collective interest of the people of the Yukon in the quality of the natural environment and the protection of the natural environment for the benefit of present and future generations."]

NOTES AND QUESTIONS

1. What changes does the Yukon Act make to the rules of both tort and criminal law in relation to procedure, particularly in relation to standing, the onus of proof, remedies, and costs? For a summary of the significant features of the Act, see Hughes and Iyalomhe, above.

2. What legal effect, if any, do ss. 6 and 7 of the Yukon Act have? What is the purpose of including such provisions in the legislation? Note that s. 6 is the main "substantive" right to environmental quality in the statute, and there is no remedy for its breach. However, note that no personal injury or property damage is needed in order to commence an action under s. 8.

3. Hughes and Iyalomhe, above, argue that s. 8 of the Yukon Act is a "solid effort at an effective EBR" due to its emphasis on protecting biological processes, its availability to all adult citizens, its partial reverse onus, the ability to seek judicial review in advance of impairment, and its broad remedies directed toward environmental restoration. However, as they note (at 248),

[u]nfortunately, the entire scheme is undermined by section 9 of the Act, which prescribes the defences available to a rights-violator. In short, where actions are brought against impairing persons, it is a defence that the activity was licenced under any territorial and several major federal statutes, was confined to the polluter's residential property, or that it lacked a feasible and prudent alternative to the activity. The availability of possession of a permit or licence for the activity as a defence converts the section 8 cause of action into an ordinary statutory tort with little difference from those available in most environmental laws. It means that actionable impairment of environmental rights is confined to those cases where government standard-setting has accurately assessed the level at which such rights

might be infringed and has licenced only non-infringing activities. Thus, citizens whose rights are being impaired by a licenced activity have no enforceable rights at all, unless there is effective recourse to challenge government standard-setting. A licence to pollute is also a licence to violate environmental rights.

Do you agree?

4. Examine s. 9(1)(d) of the Yukon Act. Does this appear to be a suitable way to resolve a conflict between public environmental rights and private property rights? Are there any provisions to address distributive justice concerns? Is it possible to adequately protect environmental quality if environmental concerns do not have at least *prima facie* priority over private property interests? Swaigen and Woods, above, suggest (at 203-4) that a plaintiff should succeed on showing interference with his or her environmental rights, unless the defendant meets a reverse onus of proof that a compelling public or private interest exists, which justifies interference with the plaintiff's rights. How does s. 11 compare with this proposal?

5. An early draft of the Act contained a provision that would have provided for judicial review of the merits of government decisions under the Act. Section 22 was substituted for it. What would be the strengths and weaknesses of permitting judicial review of the correctness of administrative decisions? Are you confident that the courts are the right forum for resolving complex environmental problems, and dealing with their associated socioeconomic implications? Are judges trained accordingly?

6. Much of the land in the Canadian north is owned by the federal government or subject to aboriginal land claims agreements. What implications does this have for the applicability and constitutionality of the Northwest Territories and Yukon Acts or legislation implementing such land claims agreements?

7. Note how the environmental rights and remedies are intertwined with the notion of the public trust (see the discussion in chapter 12). The public trust doctrine seeks to ensure that government fulfills a duty to protect collective societal interests in environmental quality. As Swaigen and Woods, above, note (at 209-11), the public trust doctrine "appears to be useful as a remedy for citizens against government decisions, and useful for government against private activities, but it is not clear that it supports actions by private citizens against other private citizens" and, therefore, "falls short of the goals we have set for a substantive right: giving the citizen a *prima facie* right to environmental protection against government and private land owners, and giving these environmental rights as much weight as the landowner's proprietary right."

Alternatively, Hughes and Iyalomhe, above, have noted (at 249) that the Yukon Act s. 9 defences do not apply to s. 8(1)(b) public trust actions, and,

[a]s yet, this portion of the Yukon EBR remains untested, … it clearly has the potential to safeguard and protect environmental rights. While the action can be directed only at government and not private persons, it can be taken at the behest of rights holders and clearly includes collective and future interests in the protection of environmental quality, which is to be interpreted so as to achieve the objective of maintaining essential ecological processes. The section also liberalizes the concept of standing, since rights-holders are not obliged to show that they are directly affected by an act or omission, above any effect on the general public, before they can institute an action.

For an overview of the public trust doctrine in Canada, see J.C. Maguire, "Fashioning an Equitable Vision for Public Resource Protection and Development in Canada: The Public Trust Doctrine Revisited and Reconceptualized" (1996) vol. 7, no. 2 *Journal of Environmental Law and Practice* 1.

8. How helpful will it be for the public to have input into standard-setting activities, such as changes to environmental regulations (ss. 29 and 30)? The Yukon Act contemplates that a public review will take place before such changes are made, which may include public hearings. The result of the review is taken into account by the responsible minister in making a recommendation to Cabinet regarding the proposed regulations. It does not result in a binding decision.

As Swaigen and Woods, above, point out (at 196), "a right of the public to participate in a decision-making process or to have certain matters taken into consideration falls far short of a right to have a particular decision in a specific case." To be effective, should environmental rights dictate the results of the environmental decision-making process? Would such an approach be compatible with prevailing conceptions of how social policy should be determined in a representative democracy such as Canada?

9. Subsequent to the enactment of the Yukon legislation, other Canadian provinces initiated efforts to enact environmental bills of rights.

The Saskatchewan legislature had under consideration Bill 48 of 1992, *An Act To Provide a Charter of Environmental Rights and Responsibilities*. In 1993, the bill was reviewed by the provincial Standing Committee on the Environment; it recommended numerous changes and that Bill 48 itself not be reintroduced to the legislature. No new initiatives have resulted. See Standing Committee on the Environment, *Report on Environmental Rights and Responsibilities* (Leg. Assembly of Sask., 1993).

Also in 1992, British Columbia began the process of drafting a new *Environmental Protection Act*, which initially contained an environmental bill of rights. However, the environmental rights sections were deleted from the draft bill by late 1995, and the bill itself was withdrawn from the legislative agenda. See *Environmental Law Update* (Vancouver: Continuing Legal Education of BC, 1995), at 1.1.19.

10. Ontario also engaged in a lengthy process to develop an environmental bill of rights. (See, generally, Castrilli, above.) The resulting legislation received royal assent in December 1993 and was proclaimed in force in February 1994. Unlike other provincial efforts, the Ontario bill is not primarily directed toward improving the efficacy of environmental litigation. Instead, the Ontario *Environmental Bill of Rights* (EBR) focuses on increasing government accountability by way of political pressures, increased public participation in environmental decision making, and the creation of an environmental commissioner's office to oversee the Act's implementation. Judicial intervention is treated as a back-up measure when other processes, such as rights to request government review of policies or investigations of environmental harm, have failed. Access to information and "whistleblower" protection provisions are also included.

Environmental Bill of Rights, 1993
SO 1993, c. 28

Preamble

· · ·

The people of Ontario have as a common goal the protection, conservation and restoration of the natural environment for the benefit of present and future generations.

While the government has the primary responsibility for achieving this goal, the people should have means to ensure that it is achieved in an effective, timely, open and fair manner.

1. In this Act,

"environment" means the air, land, water, plant life, animal life and ecological systems of Ontario;

"instrument" ... means any document of legal effect issued under an Act and includes a permit, licence, approval, authorization, direction or order issued under an Act, but does not include a regulation;

"policy" means a program, plan or objective and includes guidelines or criteria to be used in making decisions about the issuance, amendment or revocation of instruments, but does not include an Act, a regulation or an instrument;

2(1) The purposes of this Act are,

(a) to protect, conserve and, where reasonable, restore the integrity of the environment by the means provided in this Act;

(b) to provide sustainability of the environment by the means provided in this Act; and

(c) to protect the right of a healthful environment by the means provided in this Act.

· · ·

5(1) An environmental registry shall be established as prescribed.

· · ·

6(1) The purpose of the registry is to provide a means of giving information about the environment to the public.

[Subsection 2 makes it clear that such information is to include things done under the Act.]

7. Within three months after the date on which this section begins to apply to a Ministry, the Minister shall prepare a draft Ministry statement of environmental values that,

(a) explains how the purposes of this Act are to be applied when decisions that might significantly affect the environment are made in the Ministry; and

(b) explains how consideration of the purposes of this Act should be integrated with other considerations, including social, economic and scientific considerations, that are part of decision-making in the Ministry.

8(1) [T]he Minister shall give notice to the public that he or she is developing the Ministry statement of environmental values.

(2) Notice under this section shall be given in the registry and by any other means the Minister considers appropriate.

[Subsection 3 specifies matters that must be included in the notice, including the contents of the draft statement and an invitation to the public to comment.]

* * *

9(1) [T]he Minister shall finalize the Ministry statement of environmental values and give notice of it to the public.

11. The Minister shall take every reasonable step to ensure that the Ministry statement of environmental values is considered whenever decisions that might significantly affect the environment are made in the Ministry.

15(1) If a Minister considers that a proposal ... for a policy or Act could, if implemented, have a significant effect on the environment and the Minister considers that the public should have an opportunity to comment, the Minister shall ... give notice of the proposal ... .

[Section 16 contains similar provisions relating to proposals for regulations. Sections 19-21 established a system to classify proposals for instruments as class I, II, or III, depending on the significance of their risk levels and potential harm to the environment. Class I instruments involve the least environmental impact and have a correspondingly less onerous schedule of notice and participation opportunities. Class II instruments are intermediate and may trigger public meetings, mediation, or other participating measures. Class III instruments involve high public interest, high environmental impact, and full public hearings.]

22(1) The Minister shall ... give notice to the public of a Class I, II or III proposal for an instrument ... .

* * *

35(1) A Minister who gives notice of a proposal under section 15, 16 or 22 shall take every reasonable step to ensure that all comments relevant to the proposal that are received as a result of the public participation process described in the notice of the proposal are considered when decisions on the proposal are made in the Ministry.

* * *

38(1) Any person resident in Ontario may seek leave to appeal from a decision whether or not to implement a proposal for a Class I or II instrument ... (if) the person seeking leave to appeal has an interest in the decision (and) another person has a right under another Act to appeal ... .

* * *

41. Leave to appeal a decision shall not be granted unless it appears to the appellate body that

(a) there is good reason to believe that no reasonable person ... could have made the decision; and

(b) the decision ... could result in significant harm to the environment.

* * *

[Section 49 establishes the office of an environmental commissioner. Pursuant to s. 59, the commissioner oversees implementation of the Act, monitors compliance and discretionary conduct of ministers, and assists ministries to comply with the legislation.]

. . .

61(1) Any two persons resident in Ontario who believe that an existing policy, Act, regulation or instrument of Ontario should be amended, repealed or revoked in order to protect the environment may apply to the Environmental Commissioner for a review of the policy, Act, regulation or instrument by the appropriate Minister.

(2) Any two persons resident in Ontario who believe that a new policy, Act, or regulation should be made or passed in order to protect the environment may apply to the Environmental Commissioner for a review of the need for the new policy, Act, or regulation by the appropriate Minister.

. . .

62. Within ten days of receiving an application for review, the Environmental Commissioner shall [refer it to the minister or ministers responsible for the matters raised in the application].

. . .

65. A Minister who receives an application for review from the Environmental Commissioner shall acknowledge receipt to the applicants within twenty days of receiving the application from the Commissioner.

[Sections 67-73 provide that within fixed time limits, the Mminister must determine whether the public interest warrants a review, provide written notice of the decision, and, if a review is conducted, state what action will be taken.]

74(1) Any two persons resident in Ontario who believe that a prescribed Act, regulation or instrument has been contravened may apply to the Environmental Commissioner for an investigation of the alleged contravention by the appropriate Minister.

[A process similar to that described above is followed in the case of requests for investigations.]

. . .

82. In this Part,
"public resource" means,
    (a) air,
    (b) water, not including water in a body of water the bed of which is privately owned and on which there is no public right of navigation,
    (c) unimproved public land,
    (d) any parcel of public land that is larger than five hectares and is used for,
        (i) recreation,
        (ii) conservation,
        (iii) resource extraction,
        (iv) resource management, or

(v) a purpose similar to one mentioned in subclauses (i) to (iv), and

(e) any plant life, animal life or ecological system associated with any air, water or land described in clauses (a) to (d).

. . .

84(1) Where a person has contravened or will imminently contravene an Act, regulation or instrument ... and the actual or imminent contravention has caused or will imminently cause significant harm to a public resource of Ontario, any person resident in Ontario may bring an action against the person in the court in respect of the harm and is entitled to judgment if successful.

(2) Despite subsection (1), an action may not be brought under this section in respect of an actual contravention unless the plaintiff has applied for an investigation into the contravention under Part V and,

(a) has not received one of the responses required under sections 78 to 80 within a reasonable time; or

(b) has received a response under sections 78 to 80 that is not reasonable.

. . .

85(1) For the purposes of section 84, an Act, regulation or instrument is not contravened if the defendant satisfies the court that the defendant exercised due diligence in complying with the Act, regulation or instrument.

(2) For the purposes of section 84, an Act, regulation or instrument is not contravened if the defendant satisfies the court that the act or omission alleged to be a contravention of the Act, regulation or instrument is authorized by an Act of Ontario or Canada or by a regulation or instrument under an Act of Ontario or Canada.

. . .

89(1) In order to provide fair and adequate representation of the private and public interests, including governmental interests, involved in the action, the court may permit any person to participate in the action, as a party or otherwise.

. . .

93(1) If the court finds that the plaintiff is entitled to judgment in an action under section 84, the court may,

(a) grant an injunction against the contravention;

(b) order the parties to negotiate a restoration plan in respect of harm to the public resource resulting from the contravention and to report to the court on the negotiations within a fixed time;

(c) grant declaratory relief; and

(d) make any other order, including an order as to costs, that the court considers appropriate.

(2) No award of damages shall be made under subsection (1).

. . .

103(1) No person who has suffered or may suffer a direct economic loss or direct personal injury as a result of a public nuisance that caused harm to the environment shall be barred from bringing an action without the consent of the Attorney General in respect of the loss or injury only because the person has suffered or may suffer direct economic loss or direct personal injury of the same kind or to the same degree as other persons.

...

118(1) Except as provided in section 84 and subsection (2) of this section, no action, decision, failure to take action or failure to make a decision by a Minister or his or her delegate under this Act shall be reviewed in any court.

(2) Any person resident in Ontario may make an application for judicial review under the *Judicial Review Procedure Act* on the grounds that a Minister or his or her delegate failed in a fundamental way to comply with the requirements of Part II respecting a proposal for an instrument.

...

120. This Act binds the Crown.

NOTES AND QUESTIONS

1. After reading the Ontario EBR, do you have a clear idea of citizens' environmental rights in the province? Can you articulate what environmental protection measures can be achieved under the EBR that could not have been achieved without it? Perhaps unsurprisingly, the EBR has been described as "byzantine," "peculiar," "complex," "contradictory," and "paradoxical." For an overview of the strengths and weaknesses of the EBR, see M. Winfield, G. Ford, and G. Crann, *Achieving the Holy Grail?: A Legal and Political Analysis of Ontario's Environmental Bill of Rights* (Toronto: CIELAP, 1995); M. Winfield, "A Political and Legal Analysis of Ontario's Environmental Bill of Rights" (1998) vol. 47 *UNB Law Journal* 325; and Castrilli, above.

2. In light of the EBR's complexity, a number of user's guides have been developed. See, for example, Pollution Probe, *Ontario's Environmental Bill of Rights Users Guide* (Ontario: Queen's Printer, 1995); P. Muldoon and R. Lindgren, *The Environmental Bill of Rights: A Practical Guide* (Toronto: Emond Montgomery, 1995); and D. McRobert and C. McAteer, *The Nuts, the Bolts and the Rest of the Machinery: A Guide to and Update on Ontario's Environmental Bill of Rights* (Toronto: ECO, 2001), also available online at http://www.lacieg2s.ca/law/canapp01.htm.

3. The Ontario EBR was phased in over a five-year period. During that time, successive government ministries became subject to the Act's provisions and, therefore, were to begin notifying the public of proposed Acts and policies, were required to classify instruments, and became subject to the application for review provisions. Also during the phase-in, additional statutes became prescribed, triggering the notification requirements, the request for investigation provisions, and the "whistleblower" protections. Recent legislative changes and alterations to Ontario's ministry structure have somewhat modified the original implementation schedule.

4. Notwithstanding that, as of April 1996, the Ontario Ministry of Natural Resources (MNR) became subject to the EBR, it failed to pass a regulation to classify its instruments into the class I, II, and III categories, which would trigger associated public participation rights. In June 2001, the Environmental Commissioner's office filed a special report with Legislative Assembly of Ontario detailing the MNR's "long string of broken promises." In July 2001, the MNR finally promulgated Ont. reg. 261/01 and classified its instruments. See ECO, *Broken Promises: MNR's Failure To Safeguard Environmental Rights*, available online at http://www.eco.on.ca/english/publicat/sp04.pdf.

5. A major issue in the development of the EBR was the choice to focus on political accountability, through mechanisms such as the statements of environmental values (ss. 7-11) and the Office of the Environmental Commissioner (ss. 49-59), rather than using judicial review of administrative decisions. For example, it has been pointed out that the commissioner has no power to engage in substantive policy and program reviews, and that there are no sanctions if ministries fail to comply with the legislation, apart from negative comments by the commissioner in reports to the legislature. Acts, policies, regulations, and instruments that are promulgated in defiance of the EBR process remain valid. Citizens are given no substantive rights, and have no direct method to effect environmental policy, apart from the complex s. 84 statutory tort. Class proceedings are prohibited except in public nuisance actions and no intervenor funding is provided. See Winfield et al. (1995) and Winfield (1998), above. In light of these concerns, do you think that the Ontario political accountability model is preferable to a judicial accountability model? In what forum would the "best" environmental decisions be made?

6. Ontario has undergone a change in government since the enactment of the EBR, and the new administration has engaged in substantial budget cuts (in the range of 40-50 percent), privatization schemes, and a markedly different policy agenda than its predecessor. In 1995, the Ministry of Finance was permanently exempted from the EBR's jurisdiction. The Environmental Commissioner of Ontario, in a special report to the legislature in October 1996 (http://www.eco.on.ca/english/publicat/sp02.pdf) noted:

> Ontario is undergoing a massive policy shift in environmental protection .... The Ministries are making remarkable changes to environmental safeguards either behind closed doors or with minimal public participation. This is a clear and unacceptable departure for the goals and purposes of the Environmental Bill of Rights.

Similar concerns were expressed again in the commissioner's 1996 annual report, *Keep the Doors Open to Better Environmental Decision Making* (Toronto: ECO, 1996), where it was noted (at 3) that

> [t]hroughout 1996, the ministries demonstrated an alarming lack of environmental vision. They failed to put their stated environmental values into action. Instead, their activities were characterized by omnibus-style legislation, cuts to environmental programs and the shift of environmental responsibilities to municipalities and the private sector.

Note that these same ministries, pursuant to s. 15, have the discretion to decide whether policies or Acts are environmentally significant and whether the public should have an opportunity to comment; if not, the citizen rights to notice and comment under the EBR do not apply. As noted by Diana Babor in "Environmental Rights in Ontario: Are Participatory Mechanisms Working?" (1998) *Colorado Journal of Environmental Law and Policy* 121, at 133,

> [w]hen a government perceives cost to be measurable only by a balance sheet, the importance of environmental rights is neither recognized nor advanced, and procedural safeguards, as upheld by the EBR, may consequently be treated as (costly) bureaucratic steps to be circumvented.

7. Over 60 percent of the statutes and regulations prescribed under the EBR were amended to some degree by August 2001. The *Environmental Approvals Improvement*

Act (SO 1997, c. 7), passed in 1997, expanded the ability of the Ontario Cabinet to exempt facilities from environmental protection legislation and allows Cabinet to create "deemed" or "standardized" approvals regimes to replace individual facility licenses, likely removing them from the EBR process. See McRobert and McAteer, above, at 20-22. In addition, since 1998 the increased use of a type of compliance order called a provincial officer's order, which is not a reviewable prescribed EBR instrument like other control orders, has decreased citizen appeal rights. (See McRobert and McAteer, above, at 28-29.)

8. The EBR has also failed to meet expectations in relation to the usefulness of statements of environmental values (SEVs). These were intended to be plans for implementation of the EBR's environmental protection purposes, but the SEVs were so vague and "underwhelming" that the commissioner became involved in a one-year review designed to aid improvements. Little progress was made and "in practice, the statements appear to be having little or no impact on Ministry behaviour or policies" (Winfield (1998), above, at 341).

9. To date, the s. 84 "harm to a public resource" action has been used only twice: *Braeker et al. v. The Queen et al.*, action filed in Ontario Superior Court, Owen Sound, July 27, 1998, File no. 33332/98 and *Brennan v. Board of Health for the Simcoe County District Health Unit*, action filed in Ontario Superior Court, Barrie, July 16, 1999, File no. 99-B222. Critics have noted that the barriers to bringing such an action are seen as "so high that they constituted a 'vortex of pain' ... and made use of the right virtually impossible." See: ECO, *EBR Litigation Rights Workshop Meeting Report* (Toronto: ECO, 2000), at 15. One of the major flaws in the process is the scope of available defences (Hughes and Iyalomhe, above, at 251-52):

> It is a defence to a section 84 claim that the defendant was duly diligent in attempting to comply with the infringed legislation, that the defendant had a licence or statutory authorization, or that the defendant "complied with an interpretation" of the permit that the court considers reasonable ... .
>
> Clearly, the Ontario EBR section 84 statutory tort suffers from the same limitations as the section 8(1)(a) statutory tort under the *Yukon Act*: action against impairment of environmental rights is limited to cases where government standards are exceeded, so protection of any rights that might nevertheless be violated is dependant upon effective recourse to challenge government standard-setting. In fact, the Ontario tort is even narrower, as even unlicensed activities that harm rights can be justified if the defendant is not negligent or acted on a "reasonable" interpretation of what they thought they were licenced to do.

10. Attempts to use public nuisance actions now that s. 103 of the EBR has removed some standing barriers may well be more successful. In a recent case, *Hollick v. Toronto (City)*, 2001 SCC 68, file no. 27699, the Supreme Court of Canada left open the use of class actions for such suits under Ontario's *Class Proceedings Act, 1992*, SO 1992, c. 6.

11. Despite its problems, the EBR has resulted in a number of successful applications for review and investigation. Also, despite concerns that the criteria to obtain leave to appeal instrument classifications (s. 41) were potentially insurmountable, the Ontario Environmental Review Tribunal has concluded that applicants need not prove their case on a balance of probabilities; rather "a lower standard of proof sufficient to show that their concerns have a real foundation" is sufficient. See *Re Barker* (1996), 20 CELR (NS)

72, at 81; and *Residents Against Company Pollution v. Ontario (Ministry of Environment & Energy)*, [1996] OEAB no. 29. Nevertheless, the many limitations of the Act and the government's tendency to simply ignore adverse reports by the commissioner have led many to the conclusion that Ontario has "opted for an environmental rights regime in name only" (Castrilli, above, at 425).

12. The Environmental Registry is available online at http://www.ene.gov.on.ca/envision/env_reg/ebr/english/index.htm, and the Environmental Commissioner of Ontario's Web site is http://www.eco.on.ca/. The registry has been a comparatively successful part of the regime, providing a broad level of public access to information.

13. The federal government has enacted similar procedural rights in CEPA 1999. As Hughes and Iyalomhe, above, note (at 253-54):

> The CEPA [1999] provisions closely parallel the Ontario EBR. Pursuant to section 17, any adult resident of Canada may apply to the Minister for investigation of any offence under the Act. The Minister investigates the complaint and has the discretion to discontinue the investigation if in his or her opinion the alleged offence is not substantiated or "does not require further investigation." If the investigation proceeds, the Minister refers the matter to the Attorney General for "any action that the Attorney General may wish to take."
>
> Section 22 of the Act provides citizens who have applied for an investigation with a right to bring an "environmental protection action" if the response to the investigation was unreasonable or unreasonably delayed. The action may be brought against anyone who committed an offence under the Act who "caused significant harm to the environment," unless that person has already been convicted, or is subject to "environmental protection alternative measures." The claimant, if successful, may obtain a declaration, a court order requiring preventive measures or requiring the defendant to refrain from misconduct, negotiated restoration plans or "any other appropriate relief" including costs (but not damages). The burden of proof remains on the plaintiff, undertakings to pay damages may be waived, intervenor standing and costs are discretionary, and the court has the discretion to stay or dismiss the proceedings in the "public interest" taking into account, *inter alia*, the adequacy of any government plan to address the issues raised.
>
> Available defences include: due diligence in complying with the Act, authorization under a federal statute or equivalent provincial legislation, officially induced mistake of law and "any other defences."
>
> As with the Ontario EBR and Yukon statutory torts, these provisions of the CEPA [1999] clearly allow citizens some room to seek redress when legislated standards are violated and the conduct constitutes an offence, and protecting environmental rights to some degree particularly when government is failing to enforce its laws. What is lacking is an ability to challenge rights-violating conduct that is licenced or to obtain judicial remedies when the standards themselves are inadequate.

See generally D. McRobert and R. Cooper, *The Environmental Registry, the Right To Request an Investigation and Environment Protection Acts Under CEPA* (Toronto: ECO, 2000).

14. The CEPA 1999 registry is available online at http://www.ec.gc.ca/CEPARegistry/. Although there is no exact equivalent to the Environmental Commissioner of Ontario, there is now a federal Commissioner of the Environment and Sustainable Development (CESD) within the auditor general's office. The federal commissioner conducts audits

and reports to Parliament, and there is a process for petitioning the CESD for assistance in obtaining information from federal ministries. See http://www.oag-bvg.gc.ca/domino/cesd_cedd.nsf/html/menu7_e.html.

15. Additional political accountability can result from the ability of Canadians to file a submission with the secretariat of the Commission on Environmental Cooperation (CEC), the oversight body established under the NAAEC. Governments must respond to such complaints and the CEC council can then require the creation of a factual record, which generates both public information and potential government embarrassment. See http://www.cec.org/citizen/index.cfm?varlan-english.

III. SUBSTANTIVE RIGHTS

J. Swaigen and R. Woods
"A Substantive Right to Environmental Quality"
in J. Swaigen, ed., *Environmental Rights in Canada* (Toronto: Butterworths and CELRF, 1981), 195, at 196, 199-200

The right to enter the forum is only the beginning. If participants in the forum find that one party—the party seeking to develop land or discharge pollutants—consistently comes to the forum armed with rights which compel a decision in his favour and against the environment, those without counter-balancing rights will become disillusioned and abandon the forum, seek other forums, retreat into apathy, strike out against the system, or demand similar rights.

There is evidence that the failure of institutional arrangements to result in decisions in favour of environmental protection has led to such disillusionment. The adjustments to the legal process that have taken place over the past decade have not led to a balancing of environmental concerns against private property rights, or against the discretion of government agencies to make decisions favouring immediate economic benefits over environmental protection. Perhaps this is the time to renew the search for a substantive right to environmental quality—one which ensures advocates of environmental quality more than a mere right to participate and entrenches environmental quality in the legal system as a value equivalent to private property rights and a fetter on government discretion to permit environmentally-harmful activities; a right that draws lines and sets limits on how much environmental degradation is permissible.

. . .

Rights may create a balance between competing interests or shift an existing balance. Sometimes a right may preclude any balancing of interests; for example, when a fundamental constitutional right prevents the majority from overriding the interest of an individual or a minority group, even to serve a public interest or provide some great benefit to the community. Even so, although the existence of a right may preclude a flagrant overriding of minority interests, it is doubtful that a right can ever be absolute. It seems rights will always be tempered by competing rights, whether private or public.

Describing the desired right as "substantive" is a shorthand way of indicating the effect environmentalists hope an environmental right will have. Substantive rights usually confer upon their holder status to participate in the making of decisions that affect the interest to which the rights relate. In an early attempt to describe the effects environmental rights might have, Christopher Stone identified three incidents of rights: (1) The right-holder can institute legal action. (2) Injury to the right-holder must be taken into account by the legal system. (3) Relief must run to the benefit of the right-holder. Dworkin suggests in addition that substantive rights lead to a result in favour of the right-holder in hard cases, even when no settled rule disposes of the matter. According to Dworkin, rights are important moral principles which lead to decisions which enhance the dignity and independence of the right-holder, even when these decisions may be contrary to political or economic expediency.

Those who search for a right to environmental quality hope it will confer more than a right to participate or some requirement of due process or natural justice before environmentally harmful decisions are taken. They want a right which will dictate a decision in favour of environmental protection in difficult cases. They hope this right will be equivalent to a civil liberty, on the one hand, constraining government actions harmful to the environment, and, on the other, equivalent to a property right, restraining the use of private property in ways that are incompatible with sound ecological management.

NOTE

A difficult issue is the need to define the *content* of the substantive environmental right(s) so that one can tell when the right is being infringed. Consider the following argument.

E. Hughes and D. Iyalomhe
"Substantive Environmental Rights in Canada"
(1998-99) vol. 30, no. 2 *Ottawa Law Review* 299, at 235-37

Our starting point is the proposition that environmental rights must include, at a minimum, the right to a level of environmental quality that will ensure humanity's survival. Whatever else we are, humans are biological organisms, and thus have certain basic biological needs that must be met either from the environment, or the energy, resources and inspiration it provides to fuel our technology and culture. At a basic biological level, as a species we need air, water, food, shelter materials and other humans to survive.

There are important *dimensions* to each of these environmental components that must be considered. First, there is a *quantitative* dimension: humans must have adequate supplies of air, water, food, shelter materials and other humans. Second, there is a *qualitative* dimension: these essentials must be uncontaminated, safe or reasonably clean. Finally, there is a *temporal* dimension. Our adequate supplies of reasonably

clean air, water, food, shelter and other humans must be sustained through generations to ensure our species' survival. Arguably, then, this is the level of environmental
quality which would meet the human species' most basic biological survival needs
and which is referred to in the literature as a "right to a reasonable level of environmental quality." This would also seem to comprise the minimum content of a collective right to environmental quality.

In Canada, human rights have generally been conceptualized as individual, rather
than collective. If we turn to the question of individual biological survival (rather than
species' survival), are there any other factors which require our consideration? Arguably, for individual survival some level of medical or health care is fundamental. Thus,
one sees reference to the "right to a healthy environment" expressed by many authors.

Additionally, each individual needs *access* to their fair share of the basic resources
outlined above; there is a notion of distributive justice which must be incorporated if
one accepts that individual welfare is "morally relevant and a legitimate purpose of a
just society." As moral rights, environmental rights would be universal rights of all
persons and, therefore, there should be a level of individual entitlement to environmental quality, without discrimination.

. . .

What positive measures need to be taken to secure such basic biological survival
rights? First, to supply the essentials of life, it is necessary to maintain essential biological processes. Thus, for example, humans need to have photosynthesis continue,
to supply atmospheric oxygen, and to maintain hydrological cycles, to supply fresh
water. Second, the only known way to maintain essential biological processes is to
maintain functioning ecosystems; there is no artificial or technological substitute. To
maintain functioning ecosystems (i.e. natural processes) scientific consensus tells us
to do things such as: preserve biological diversity, maintain soil fertility and the productive capacity of the land, protect the oceans, receive sunlight only at wavelengths
to which the planet's biology is accustomed, maintain climatic stability, and protect
ourselves and our environment from toxic contamination. Of course, scientific uncertainty makes the specifics of such a list debatable; one can only work with the best
scientific advice presently available. However, within the limits of scientific knowledge, such are the kinds of things that humans have rights to, if the right to environmental quality is to have any meaning, even at the level of mere survival.

Would people be satisfied with a level of environmental quality that merely ensured base survival? "Beyond basic life support, natural resources provide second-
level societal support to humans, without which societies … as we know them could
not develop." … It would seem impossible to make a comprehensive description of
the level of environmental quality necessary to sustain human culture, yet *some* level
of environmental amenities seem needed to ensure human well-being, beyond mere
health or physical survival. The best that most analysts seem to be able to do is to
describe this as a right to a level of environmental quality that is "beneficial" to human
culture, or which is sufficient to maintain *a* socioeconomic system (not necessarily
the [existing] socioeconomic system).

NOTES AND QUESTIONS

1. J. Sax contends, in "The Search for Environmental Rights" (1990) vol. 6 *Journal of Land Use and Environmental Law* 93, at 96, that there is a public duty to pass on our natural capital or collective inheritance to future persons to ensure them the freedom of thought, action, and choice that we hold dear as democratic values. See also H. Ralston, "Rights and Responsibilities on the Home Planet" (1993) vol. 18 *Journal of International Law* 251.

2. In the search to move from mere procedural rights to a substantive right to environmental quality, many obstacles need to be overcome. One of the greatest problems is how to make an environmental right "paramount" over, or at least *prima facie* as important as, other legal rights. As Swaigen and Woods, above, put it (at 204):

> To be substantive, it need not be absolute. However, it must have the same *prima facie* weight as a property right. This would give it substantial clout both against actions of the State and against private property rights. If this essential quality is not recognized, environmental rights will not be substantive in the same sense as property rights.

Attempts to fashion such a right, however, bring one face-to-face with the spectres of judicial and legislative conservatism. Experience suggests that when environmental concerns come into conflict with other values, such as economic interests, the environment is the traditional loser.

The American experience is illustrative. There, MEPA, above, was the first statutory bill of rights. Castrilli, above, describes MEPA's main provisions (at 373):

> In terms of procedural reform, MEPA allows "any person" to maintain an action "for declaratory and equitable relief against any person for the protection of the air, water, and other natural resources and the public trust in these resources from pollution, impairment or destruction." This liberal grant of standing effectively permits anyone to sue anyone. The substantive right created by MEPA entitles the plaintiff to succeed in an action upon making a prima facie showing that the defendant has caused, or is likely to cause, pollution, impairment or destruction to the environment. The plaintiff will prevail unless the defendant can rebut this showing by submitting evidence to the contrary or by way of "affirmative defense that there is no feasible and prudent alternative ... that is consistent with the promotion of the public health, safety, and welfare in light of the state's paramount concern for the protection of its natural resources." Where a defendant's challenged conduct is subject to an existing environmental standard that the courts find deficient in light of MEPA's requirements, the court can direct the agency to adopt a standard "approved and specified by the court," or remit the parties to appropriate administrative or other proceeding.

However, the threshold of harm that the courts have said is needed to be proved by a plaintiff to establish a *prima facie* case has, over time, risen. See *Kimberley Hills v. Dion*, 320 NW 2d 673 (Mich. CA 1982). This has led some commentators to question MEPA's effectiveness and strength: D. Lynch, "The Michigan Environmental Protection Act (MEPA)" (1991) *University of Detroit Mercy Law Review* 55. Similar problems have been experienced in other states with similar legislation, see A. Piela, "A Tale of Two Statutes: Twenty Year Judicial Interpretation of the Citizen Suit Provision in the Connecticut EPA and the Minnesota ERA" (1993) vol. 21, no. 2 *Boston College Environmental Law Review* 401.

3. Such problems have led many to argue that statutory bills of rights are too easily amended or repealed; other inconsistent legislation is not necessarily invalid; exemptions to ordinary statutes are too easily granted; and their provisions too easily are construed narrowly by courts intent on deference to the legislature. The solution suggested by many is to entrench environmental rights in the constitution.

The only real attempt to include such rights in Canada's constitution occurred in 1978, with Bill C-60, *Constitutional Amendment Act, 1978*, 3rd sess., 30th Parl., Canada. It included, *inter alia*, a reference in s. 4 to "the commitment of all Canadians to the balanced development of the land of their common inheritance and to the preservation of its richness and beauty in trust for themselves and generations to come." In a brief to a joint Senate/House of Commons committee studying the bill, the Canadian Environmental Law Association made several recommendations to try to strengthen the environmental provisions. Instead, the bill was never adopted and the later proposal, which eventually became the *Constitution Act, 1982*, contained no reference to environmental rights.

Assuming that one did wish to entrench environmental rights in the constitution, however, what form should such rights take?

D. Gibson
"Constitutional Entrenchment of Environmental Rights"
in N. Duple, ed., *Le droit à la qualité de l'environnement*
(Montreal: Quebec Amerique, 1988), 275, at 287

[In the text of the article, the author describes why he feels constitutional entrenchment of environmental rights is desirable, discusses what he thinks the nature of such rights should be, and explains the rationale behind the particular proposal he has formulated. The following excerpt contains the author's summary of his key points, followed by the text of his proposal.]

Summary

1. A constitutional guarantee of environmental protection in the Canadian Constitution is possible and desirable.

2. To be effective, such a guarantee must involve more than an empty declaration. There must be a means by which it can be implemented, and its implementation must be judicially reviewed.

3. Because effective environmental protection measures will vary from time to time, from place to place, and from one component of the environment to another, it would be impossible to include these detailed measures in a constitutional guarantee. The Constitution must, therefore, delegate the responsibility for creating and enforcing the guarantee to the ordinary legislative and administrative processes.

4. In the interests of both effectiveness and fairness, the protective measure that legislatures and governments are called upon to take must be equally applicable to governmental and non-governmental enterprises.

5. Although it would be impossible to specify all of the ingredients of an effective environmental protection program in the Constitution, it is desirable that the essential

elements be listed. These would include: the creation of an environmental protection agency for each jurisdiction, the establishment of minimum standards of environmental quality by such agencies, the effective enforcement of such standards, the right of residents of the jurisdiction to be informed of pending determinations by the agencies and to make representations to the agency on the subject.

6. To ensure that governments will live up to their obligation to create and enforce such programs, there should be a right of everyone, after a certain compliance period, to seek declarations from the courts as to the sufficiency of the compliance by a particular legislature or government.

7. Although such a constitutional guarantee could be created independently of all other constitutional rights, it would be convenient to enact it as part of the Canadian Charter of Rights and Freedoms, thereby gaining the benefit of the Charter's limitation and enforcement provisions.

Environmental Rights

15.1(1) *Right to Beneficial Environment.* Everyone has the right to a beneficial environment, and to enjoy its use for recreational, aesthetic, historical, scientific and economic purposes, to the extent reasonably consistent with:

(a) the equivalent rights of others;

(b) the health and safety of others; and

(c) the preservation of a beneficial environment in accordance with subsection (2).

(2) Everyone has a right to the preservation of a beneficial environment, so as to ensure its future enjoyment for the uses set out in subsection (1).

(3) For the purposes of this section, "environment" includes land, water, air and space, and the living things that inhabit them, as well as artificial structures and spaces that are beneficial to humans or to other components of the environment.

15.2(1) *Duty to Make and Enforce Environmental Laws.* The Parliament and Government of Canada, and the Legislatures and Governments of the Provinces have the duty, within their respective areas of jurisdiction, to make and enforce laws and programs for the implementation of the rights set out in section 15.1.

(2) *Content of Laws.* The laws and programs referred to in subsection (1) shall include, without restricting the generality thereof:

(i) the creation and maintenance of an environmental protection agency for each jurisdiction, responsible for determining minimum standards of environmental quality and preservation appropriate for each aspect of the environment, in each area of the jurisdiction, and to vary such standards, partially or wholly, temporarily or permanently, where the agency deems such variation to be advisable;

(ii) the creation of effective measures to enforce such minimum standards within the jurisdiction;

(iii) the right of everyone resident within the jurisdiction to be informed by the environmental protection agency, by means of appropriate public notice, of all pending determinations or variations of such minimum standards and allowing a reasonable time before each determination or variation is decided upon by the agency; and

(iv) the right of everyone resident within the jurisdiction to make representations of fact, law or policy to the environmental protection agency about any determination or variation of such minimum standards.

(3) *Scope.* The laws and programs referred to in subsection (1) shall apply to activities of the Crown, as well as to activities of private persons and organizations.

15.3 *Judicial Review.* After this section and sections 15.1 and 15.2 have been in force for more than one year, everyone has the right to apply under subsection 24(1) to a court of competent jurisdiction for a declaration that the Parliament or the Government of Canada, or the Legislature or Government of a province, has failed to fulfil some or all of the duties imposed by section 15.2.

NOTES AND QUESTIONS

1. Swaigen and Woods, above, suggest (at 233-34) that an effective substantive environmental right would have the following characteristics:

It must clearly state that citizens have standing not only against government but also against other citizens. If compliance with environmental regulations and procedures is not to be seen as an absolute defence, the legislation must provide for this. The defence should be abolished in many cases and qualified by balancing tests or by reference to other important considerations in others. If economic considerations alone are not to constitute a defence, the legislation must include a provision to this effect. To determine what levels of environmental quality are to be protected, the legislatures must specify a range of considerations, either setting standards or specifying the "rules of thumb" the courts must apply. The law must give the courts clear guidance. Discretion left to the courts must be a discretion to impose more stringent standards than existing ones, but not less stringent ones. Finally, in order to create a truly substantive right to environmental quality, the legislation must state that there is a substantive right which is equivalent to a property right.

Measured against this standard, what are the strengths and weaknesses of Gibson's proposed constitutional amendment? Using the same standard evaluate the strengths and weaknesses of the Ontario EBR, above?

2. What is the impact of suggesting that environmental rights be included in the Charter rather than some other part of the constitution? See Gibson, above, at 285-87. Given the explicit balancing test set out in s. 1 of the Charter, what limits on environmental rights could you foresee being argued successfully?

3. One of the major criticisms of constitutional entrenchment of environmental rights has been that the Charter is only applicable against government, while most pollution stems from private activity. The Gibson proposal tries to circumvent this problem but, in light of subsequent jurisprudence holding that the Charter is not applicable to the private sector, is such a proposal still feasible? Are there any alternative ways of amending the Charter that would permit a desirable balance to be struck between environmental rights and private polluters' existing rights? Gibson himself now suggests that "there is a strong case" for a separate constitutional document that would expressly apply to private activities, and is no longer convinced that amendments to the Charter are the best choice.

4. C. Stevenson, "A New Perspective on Environmental Rights After the Charter" (1983) *Osgoode Hall Law Journal* 390, offers the opinion (at 420) that

> [i]t is unlikely that such a constitutional right will be adopted by amendment of the Constitution for, even though it is widely recognized as a fundamental right, the political and economic climate is not conducive to its enactment.

Do you agree? In the 1991 constitutional proposals (*Shaping Canada's Future Together* (Ottawa: Supply and Services Canada, 1991)), the federal government proposed entrenchment of private property rights but not environmental rights. What impact on environmental quality would the constitutional guarantee of property rights have? Is such a proposal no more than a "backlash" reaction to lobbying for an environmental Charter amendment?

5. In the absence of a Charter amendment, are there any existing Charter rights that might protect aspects of environmental rights? Past suggestions include s. 7 (environmental degradation as a threat to the rights to life or security of the person, including health risks), s. 2 (wilderness preservation as a matter of conscience or religion) and s. 15 (unequal standards and enforcement as discrimination; differential impacts of toxic substances on the elderly or physically challenged). See Gibson, above, and W. Andrews, "The Environment and the Canadian Charter of Rights and Freedoms," in Duple, above (at 263). What are the limits to such arguments? See, for example, *Manicom v. County of Oxford* (1985), 14 CELR 99 (Ont. Div. Ct.).

6. Why might it be beneficial to constrain governmental discretion on environmental matters by constitutionally entrenching environmental rights? Andrews, above, points out one major rationale (at 270):

> Regarding environmental issues, however, [judicial] review is often hampered by the fact that the only party who can speak for the environment is the very government whose action, or lack of action, is the subject of the review. Although governments are politically accountable, this does not obviate the need for judicial review of government action. In my opinion, political accountability does not justify the government monopoly of the right to defend the environment.

7. Is it important, if only as a matter of expressing our national attitudes and aspirations, to include environmental values in the constitution? Why do Canadians seemingly place little value on a symbolic constitutional statement, insisting instead on a legally enforceable right?

8. Could better environmental protection be accomplished by non-Charter constitutional amendments that adjust the division of powers over environmental matters? How could this be accomplished? See D. Gibson, "Environmental Protection and Enhancement under a New Canadian Constitution," in S.M. Beck and I. Bernier, eds., *Canada and the New Constitution*, vol. 2 (Montreal: Institute for Research on Public Policy, 1983).

9. Could environmental rights be included in the constitutions of provinces? How would such an amendment to a provincial constitution be accomplished? What legal effect would it have? See F. Gertler and T. Vigod, "Environmental Protection in a New Constitution," submission by the Canadian Environmental Law Association to the Select Committee on Ontario in Confederation (Toronto: CELRF, 1991).

10. First Nations Canadians already have constitutionally entrenched rights. The extent to which these aboriginal and treaty rights can be used for environmental protection is discussed in the next section.

IV. ABORIGINAL RIGHTS AND THE ENVIRONMENT

R. Kapashesit and M. Klippenstein, in "Aboriginal Group Rights and Environmental Protection" (1991) vol. 36 *McGill Law Journal* 925, note (at 929):

> Care must be taken when attempting to generalize about the belief systems of hundreds of distinct Aboriginal groups in North America. However, Aboriginal environmental belief systems share a number of features which can be identified and considered. These include a lack of division between humans and the rest of the environment, a spiritual relationship with nature, concern about sustainability, attention to reciprocity and balance, and the idiom of respect and duty (rather than rights).

Protection of First Nations' cultures, therefore, will often serve to protect lifestyles that include what the authors call "aboriginal environmental ethics," which in turn could advance the goal of environmental protection. In the words of G. Erasmus, "A Native Viewpoint," in M. Hummel, ed., *Endangered Spaces: The Future for Canada's Wilderness* (Toronto: Key Porter Books, 1989), at 92

> Conservation has always been integral to the survival of indigenous peoples. Without renewable resources to harvest, we lose both our livelihood and our way of life. Aboriginal communities have everything to gain from conservation—and much to offer: a profound and detailed knowledge of species and ecosystems, ways of sharing and managing resources that have stood the test of time, and ethics that reconcile subsistence and co-existence.

In Canada, the central legal recognition of aboriginal rights is contained in s. 35 of the *Constitution Act, 1982* (being schedule B to the *Canada Act 1982* (UK), 1982, c. 11). It recognizes and affirms "the existing aboriginal and treaty rights of the aboriginal peoples of Canada," including those acquired through land claims settlements. Although such rights do not expressly include environmental rights, there is, nevertheless, some potential for a degree of environmental protection, particularly where wilderness preservation may be necessary to secure hunting, fishing, or trapping rights. In the following excerpts, the scope of s. 35 rights is outlined, after which the extent to which such group rights provide a measure of environmental protection is explored further.

M. Valiente
"Legal Foundations of Canadian Environmental Policy"
in D. VanNijnatten and R. Boardman, *Canadian Environmental Policy: Context and Cases*, 2d ed. (Don Mills, ON: Oxford University Press, 2002), 3, at 9-12

Certainly, recognition in s. 35(1) of the Charter of "existing Aboriginal and treaty rights" has had a major influence. Since 1982, most of the "rights" cases and some of the treaty cases (including the well-known *Marshall* decision in 1999 [[1999] 3 SCR

456]) have focused on claims by First Nations to resources, particularly fish and game, but also to timber.

In the first case to address Aboriginal rights under the Charter, *R v. Sparrow*, [1990] 1 SCR 1075 and later in *R v. Gladstone*, [1996] 2 SCR 723 the Supreme Court of Canada faced the controversial issue of who should get priority over a fishery resource, in *Sparrow* a rapidly shrinking one, once it was determined that an Aboriginal right existed. The Court determined that first priority should go to "conservation," to ensure that the resource would continue to be available for harvest. Once conservation of the resource was assured, priority should go first to the Aboriginal food fishery. After that, allocation becomes more difficult. The Court refused to recognize that the Aboriginal commercial fishery should be able to exclude non-Aboriginal commercial fishers but that other objectives such as "economic and regional fairness" and historical reliance on the resource should be weighed in the balance, in order to reconcile the place of Aboriginal societies within a larger Canadian society.

Also addressed in these cases is the ability of the government to interfere with s. 35 Charter rights, for example, through its fisheries regulations. The test for justifying such interference requires the government to establish a valid legislative objective and an approach that respects the Crown's special obligations. At a minimum, meaningful consultation is always necessary; in some circumstances, consent is required. As Chief Justice Lamer stated in *R v. Delgamuukw* [1997] 3 SCR 1010:

> The nature and scope of the duty of consultation will vary with the circumstances. In occasional cases, when the breach is less serious or relatively minor, it will be no more than a duty to discuss important decisions. ... Of course, even in these rare cases where the minimum acceptable standard is consultation, this consultation must be in good faith, and with the intention of substantially addressing the concerns of the Aboriginal peoples whose lands are at issue. In most cases, it will be significantly deeper than mere consultation. Some cases may even require the full consent of an Aboriginal nation, particularly when provinces enact hunting and fishing regulations in relation to Aboriginal lands.

Thus, because of their special status, the involvement of First Nations in decisions that affect their entrenched rights is profoundly different from, and judged by a much higher standard than, any other type of public or stakeholder consultation. This requires a fundamental shift in government administrative procedures.

Another route bringing First Nations into environmental decision-making is under terms of comprehensive land claims and self-government agreements. Fourteen such agreements have been finalized, with numerous others, primarily in northern Canada and British Columbia, at different stages of negotiation. These agreements are seen as "modern treaties" and therefore have constitutional status. Starting in 1975 with the James Bay and Northern Quebec Agreement (JBNQA), all of the comprehensive land claims agreements contain provisions regarding the sharing of resource and development decisions.

The Nunavut agreement is perhaps the most structured example, but it serves to illustrate the trend. Under the 1993 agreement, which formed the basis for the legislation establishing the new territory, several boards and tribunals were established, including the Nunavut Planning Commission, Water Board, Wildlife Management

Board, and Impact Review Board. For each, membership is determined by a set formula, which allocates places to persons nominated by each of the territorial government, the federal government, and Inuit organizations. This formula ensures Inuit voices are heard on all resource and development decisions.

NOTES AND QUESTIONS

1. The *Gladstone* decision, above, is one of a number of cases on the scope of s. 35 decided by the Supreme Court of Canada in 1996. Other significant contemporary cases include *R v. N.T.C. Smokehouse Ltd.*, [1996] 2 SCR 672; *R v. Van der Peet*, [1996] 2 SCR 507; *R v. Adams* [1996] 3 SCR 101; and *R v. Côté*, [1996] 3 SCR 139. For a general discussion see K. McNeil, "How Can Infringements of the Constitutional Rights of Aboriginal Peoples Be Justified?" (1997) vol. 8, no. 2 *Constitutional Forum* 33.

2. The analysis for justifying infringement of Aboriginal rights was first extended to treaty rights in *R v. Badger*, [1996] 1 SCR 771. See also *R v. Sundown*, [1999] 1 SCR 393 and *R v. Marshall*, above.

3. As Valiente notes, above, recent land claims settlements generally include regimes for the management of land, water, and wildlife. Aboriginal participation in management is guaranteed, and often environmental impact assessment review processes in which aboriginal peoples have representation are specified. While aboriginal peoples generally have equal representation on management boards and agencies, often these entities make "recommendations" to government, which continues to hold final decision-making discretion. For an overview of some of these schemes, see M. Muir, "Impact of Aboriginal Claims Agreements on Environmental Review in the Northwest Territories" (1991) vol. 1, no. 3 *Journal of Environmental Law and Practice* 283.

4. Impact and benefits agreements (IBAs), or agreements between project proponents and local aboriginal peoples, are common when resource developments may adversely effect the environmental or cultural resources of aboriginal lands and communities, and are designed to ensure that some benefits accrue to the local populace. They may be binding contracts, treated as conditions precedent for project approvals, enforceable terms of a land claims settlement, or non-binding prescriptions for creating a positive working relationship. See S. Kennett, *A Guide to Impact and Benefits Agreements* (Calgary: CIRL, 1999).

5. As Valiente notes, above, it is clear that the constitutional status of aboriginal rights entitles First Nations' peoples to a distinct and arguably more extensive decision-making process than the general public. Although it remains unclear exactly when either the federal and provincial Crown's duty to consult arises, the constitutional duty "is distinct from the obligation to consult based on statutory requirements and administrative law requirements of procedural fairness." See M. Ross, "The Dene Tha' Consultation Pilot Project: An Appropriate Consultation Process' with First Nations?" (2001) vol. 76, *Resources* 1, at 2. Likely, "any decision affecting the balance between Aboriginal and treaty rights and non-Aboriginal interests in natural resources ... requires prior consultation," and that consultation must be context-specific, have good faith, be meaningful, and minimize infringement of the rights. Additionally, the process must of course be designed to accord priority to the constitutional rights (Ross, above, at 5). See also *R v. Adams*,

above. Does this qualify as the kind of "substantive right" outlined by Swaigen and Woods, above? What if the duty to consult extends to corporations? See *Haida Nation v. British Columbia* (2002), 44 CELR (NS) 1 (BCCA).

6. See also *Paul v. BC Forest Appeals Commission*, [2001] 38 CELR (NS) 149 (BCCA); *Mikisew Cree First Nation v. Canada (Heritage)*, [2002] 1 CNLR 169 (FCTD); and *Taku River Tlingit First Nation v. BC*, [2002] 43 CELR (NS) 169 (BCCA).

J. Woodward and T. Syed
"The Importance of Aboriginal Rights and Perspectives for Species Protection and Habitat Conservation"
Paper presented at the National Conference on Aboriginal Law and Governance, Pacific Business and Law Institute, Vancouver, BC, June 21, 2000, at 4-14 to 4-23

The Nature of Aboriginal and Treaty Rights as Inherently Ecological

In this section, we will discuss four arguments for including habitat protection or general ecosystem management as part of the nature or content of an Aboriginal or treaty right. The greater the success of these arguments, the more constitutionally entrenched ecosystem conservation will be and the more opportunities that will exist for habitat protection. These different arguments should not be seen as watertight categories, since there is considerable overlap between them, but rather as different angles from which to approach the issues.

A Right to a Species Must Include an Implied Right to Habitat Conservation To Be Meaningful

The argument that a right to trap, hunt, etc. a species must include, in order to be meaningful, protection of that species' habitat draws upon numerous Supreme Court of Canada declarations emphasizing the importance of characterizing rights in a way that ensures that their exercise is meaningful. For example, *Sparrow* states that the first step in the inquiry of whether a right has been infringed is refer to the "character-istics or incidents of the right at stake," since without such a consideration, there is the danger that the right will be so narrowly construed as to make its content mean-ingless and its exercise impossible. Similarly, in *Sioui*, [1990] 3 CNLR 127 the Court found that to properly interpret the Hurons' freedom of exercise of religion and cus-toms guaranteed in their treaty, it had to supply a territorial component, since "for a freedom to have real value and meaning, it must be possible to exercise it some-where." These propositions were most clearly laid out in *Marshall*, where the Court summarized some of the jurisprudence on meaningful interpretation as follows:

> [I]n *Sundown*, ... , the Court found that the express right to hunt included the implied right to build shelters required to carry out the hunt. See also *Simon*, ... , where the Court recognized an implied right to carry a gun and ammunition on the way to exer-cise the right to hunt. These cases employed the concept of implied rights to support the

meaningful exercise of express rights granted to the first nations in circumstances where no such implication might necessarily have been made absent the *sui generis* nature of the Crown's relationship to Aboriginal people.

The pronouncements of implied rights are in keeping with the constitutional principles of giving a purposive interpretation of Aboriginal rights and of not determining such rights in a vacuum.

The case of *Westbank First Nation*, [1997] 2 CNLR 221 illustrates the potency of this doctrine of giving meaningful characterizations to Aboriginal rights. *Westbank* was an injunction application by Harold Derickson and the Westbank First Nation, who were seeking to prevent proposed logging by the Riverside and Weyerhauser companies within their traditional territory. They based their application upon their Aboriginal right to trap pine marten, one of the fur-bearing species they have traditionally harvested. The Nation argued that further logging in the area would, by destroying the pine marten's preferred habitat of old growth forests, endanger their Aboriginal right. Thus, they alleged that the Crown's issuance of the cutting permits to log the areas was an infringement of their right and consequently that all planned logging in the area should be restrained until the issues were fully determined at trial. Although Curtis J declined to grant the injunction, his reasons for doing so contain a number of very significant findings and suggest that further applications may meet with more success.

First, Curtis J characterized the Aboriginal right as the right "to trap a harvestable surplus of marten," which he then framed as the right "to trap marten in the territory *without risk of removing the species from the territory.*" Second, the fact that the recent trapping was of minimal economic value was not significant, given that it held "important cultural value." Third, it did not matter that the proposed logging would conceivably have the effect of improving the habitat for *other* fur-bearers included in the Westbank's claim; the fact that the habitat for the preferred species of pine marten was threatened was enough of a legal interest for the Westbank to see to protect.

The significance of these findings should not be underestimated. What we have here is an application of the above principles. Curtis J took the Westbank's ecological perspective seriously when characterizing the nature and content of their constitutional rights, and he characterized the right in a purposive and contextual manner, with the result being a broadening of an Aboriginal right to trap a species to include the protection of that species' habit. Through this approach, Curtis J made the right to trap pine marten truly meaningful. It is precisely what we, above, have urged as needed: the extension of legal principles deriving from cases of "direct" infringement of a right through regulation to those situations of "indirect" infringement.

. . .

Re-Thinking the Separation Between the Right to a Resource and Its Management

A slightly different tack than the implied right/meaningful interpretation approach above is the argument that rights or powers that may be separated under Western common law need to be integrated for Aboriginal rights. *Sparrow* emphasizes that when determining the scope of an Aboriginal right, courts must be careful to "avoid the application of traditional common law concepts of property as they develop their understanding of [...] the '*sui generis*' nature of Aboriginal rights." Thus, for example, "it would be artificial to try to create a hard distinction between the right to fish and the particular manner in which that right is exercised."

These remarks go directly to the view that the distinction between the right to use a resource and the right to manage and conserve it may be a false one from the perspective of many Aboriginal groups. As Emily Walter, Michael M'Gonigle and Celeste McKay have recently argued, the narrow construction of, for example, Aboriginal fishing rights to mean simply the right to harvest is only "consistent with the Western approach to economic exploitation of natural resources [where] exploitation and management are generally conceived as separate activities." This bears great implications for how rights to fish, hunt, etc. are properly conceived. As stated above, traditional common law categories are to be avoided when determining the scope of an Aboriginal right. In fact, the scope is best understood in light of the particular history and culture of the Aboriginal peoples whose right is at issue. Walter *et al.* suggest that in "traditional Aboriginal approaches to resources," the "use and management of salmon fisheries are integrated and inextricable." Surely, such an ecological perspective needs to inform how the "right to fish" is understood. The effect of incorporating such a perspective is arguably to broaden the characterization of the right to include the right to maintain an ecosystem conducive to the exercise of the right, perhaps through some form of management scheme. This suggests, to put it bluntly, that the current scope of the Aboriginal rights of many First Nations is being mischaracterized.

. . .

Establishing an Independent Aboriginal Right to a Healthy Ecosystem

A third possibility is that the "enhancement of Aboriginal rights" through the conservation of resources is to occur through the establishment of an independent Aboriginal right to a healthy ecosystem, such a right being "consistent with Aboriginal beliefs and practices." It is certainly very arguable that "simply" maintaining a balanced ecosystem is itself an element of a practice that is integral to the distinctive culture of many Aboriginal groups. In fact, this conclusion follows quite directly from the repeated recognition by the courts of the centrality of Aboriginal ecological values both to their culture and to an interpretation of their rights.

As stated above, part of the *Van der Peet* test for an Aboriginal right is that the element of a practice, custom or tradition be integral to the distinctive culture of the group claiming the right. However, it is important to note that the requirement that the element be "distinctive" does not mean it must be unique to the group in question. An Aboriginal group can have a custom in common with other groups and still claim that it is integral to its "distinctive" culture, as long as it is a defining characteristic of that culture. Put another way, the relation of a practice to a group's identity does not hinge on how different the practice is from that of other Aboriginal groups, but rather on how essential it is each group's own identity. Thus, many groups may have in common an element that is integral, in its own way, to each group's distinctive culture. This is likely the case with the place that the practice of maintaining a balanced ecosystem has in the identity of many First Nations.

· · ·

Broadening the Crown's Constitutional Fiduciary Duty To
Include an Obligation To Maintain a Healthy Ecosystem

Finally, there is the argument that, whether or not an Aboriginal group has an implied, broadened or independent right to a healthy ecosystem or habitat protection, there *is* a heightened responsibility on the part of the Crown to ensure that such conservation occurs in order to fully "enhance" the exercise of what Aboriginal rights do exist. This heightened responsibility has three sources.

First, there is the fact that section 35 [rights] are constitutional rights and thus require an extra measure of deference and protection from the government as compared to statutory or common law rights. Second, there is the special trust relationship which exists between the Crown and Aboriginal peoples generally and which specifically provides the "guiding principle" for section 35 rights. Thus, the government must act in a fiduciary capacity in ensuring that Aboriginal rights are properly conceived and protected. Finally, there is the *Aboriginal* nature of section 35 rights which means that in order to properly give full protection to these constitutional rights, the Crown as fiduciary needs to look to the Aboriginal perspective on the rights so that it can act to ensure that such rights are exercisable in their full meaning and scope.

NOTE

While many see traditional aboriginal ecological management as a model for conservation of wildlife and wildlife habitat, some commentators have noted the possibility of a divergence between environmental and aboriginal goals. Particularly controversial has been aboriginal hunting of endangered species, such as whales and bald eagles. Aboriginal leaders who favour resource development, such as logging and mining, for its often badly needed economic benefits, also find themselves at odds with those seeking to preserve traditional resources uses. How would you reconcile the rights of endangered species with the rights of endangered cultures? One option is the renegotiation of treaties to ensure the opportunity for both input and compensation if aboriginal peoples are to be asked for further cooperation for the benefit of endangered species. See O. Schwartz, "Indian Rights and Environmental Ethics" (1987) vol. 9 *Environmental Ethics* 291.

V. NON-HUMAN RIGHTS

All of the proposals examined to this point suggest that environmental rights should be *human* rights. These may be based on the need to protect human health or safety, or human interest in maintaining a certain level of environmental quality because of our use and enjoyment of nature. One might even go so far as to say humans might be given rights to preserve the environment for aesthetic, philosophical, or other non-utilitarian reasons. Yet what if we went one step further and granted legal rights to the environment itself? Should this concept be incorporated into our legal system? *Could* this concept fit within our legal framework? Would such a concept provide better environmental protection than other legal reforms? What about the rights of non-human animals that share our environment?

C.D. Stone
"Should Trees Have Standing?—Toward Legal Rights for Natural Objects"
(1972) vol. 45 *University of Southern California Law Review* 450, at 450-82

The legal rights of children have long since been recognized in principle, and are still expanding in practice. Witness, just within recent time, *In Re Gault*, guaranteeing basic constitutional protection to juvenile defendants, and the *Voting Rights Act* of 1970. We have been making persons of children although they were not, in law, always so. And we have done the same, albeit imperfectly some would say, with prisoners, aliens, women (especially of the married variety), the insane, Blacks, foetuses, and Indians.

Nor is it only matter in human form that has come to be recognized as the possessor of rights. The world of the lawyer is peopled with inanimate right-holders: trusts, corporations, joint ventures, municipalities, Subchapter R partnerships, and nation-states, to mention just a few. Ships, still referred to by courts in the feminine gender, have long had an independent jural life, often with striking consequences. We have become so accustomed to the idea of a corporation having "its" own rights, and being a "person" and "citizen" for so many statutory and constitutional purposes, that we forget how jarring the notion was to early jurists. ...

It is this note of the *unthinkable* that I want to dwell upon for a moment. Throughout legal history, each successive extension of rights to some new entity has been, theretofore, a bit unthinkable. We are inclined to suppose the rightlessness of rightless "things" to be a decree of Nature, not a legal convention acting in support of some status quo. It is thus that we defer considering the choices involved in all their moral, social and economic dimensions. ...

The fact is, that each time there is a movement to confer rights onto some new "entity" the proposal is bound to sound odd or frightening or laughable. This is partly because until the rightless thing receives its rights, we cannot see it as anything but a *thing* for the use of "us"—those who are holding rights at the time. ...

The reason for this little discourse on the unthinkable, the reader must know by now, if only from the title of the paper. I am quite seriously proposing that we give legal rights to forests, oceans, rivers and other so-called "natural objects" in the environment—indeed, to the natural environment as a whole.

· · ·

Now to say that the natural environment should have rights is not to say anything as silly as that no one should be allowed to cut down a tree. We say human beings have rights, but—at least as of the time of this writing—they can be executed. Corporations have rights, but they cannot plead the fifth amendment; *In Re Gault* gave 15-

year-olds certain rights in juvenile proceedings, but it did not give them the right to vote. Thus, to say that the environment should have rights is not to say that it should have every right we can imagine, or even the same body of rights as human beings have. Nor is it to say that everything in the environment should have the same rights as every other thing in the environment.

What the granting of rights does involve has two sides to it. The first involves what might be called the legal-operational aspects; the second, the psychic and socio-psychic aspects. I shall deal with these aspects in turn.

. . .

What It Means To Be a Holder of Legal Rights

[A]n entity cannot be said to hold a legal right unless and until *some public authoritative body* is prepared to give *some amount of review* to actions that are colourably inconsistent with that "right" ... . But for a thing to be *a holder of legal rights*, something more is needed than that some authoritative body will review the actions and processes of those who threaten it. As I shall use the term, "holder of legal rights," each of three additional criteria must be satisfied. All three, one will observe, go towards making a thing *count* jurally—to have a legally recognized worth and dignity in its own right, and not merely to serve as a means to benefit "us" (whoever the contemporary group of rights-holders may be). They are, first, that the thing can institute legal actions *at its behest*; second, that in determining the granting of legal relief, the court must take *injury to it* into account; and third, that relief must run to the *benefit of it*.

. . .

Toward Having Standing in Its Own Right

It is not inevitable, nor is it wise, that natural objects should have no rights to seek redress in their own behalf. It is no answer to say that streams and forests cannot have standing because streams and forests cannot speak. Corporations cannot speak either; nor can states, estates, infants, incompetents, municipalities or universities. Lawyers speak for them, as they customarily do for the ordinary citizen with legal problems. One ought, I think, to handle the legal problems of natural objects as one does the problems of legal incompetents—human beings who have become vegetable. If a human being shows signs of becoming senile and has affairs that he is de jure incompetent to manage, those concerned with his well being make such a showing to the court, and someone is designated by the court with the authority to manage the incompetent's affairs. The guardian (or "conservator" or "committee"—the terminology varies) then represents the incompetent in his legal affairs. Courts make similar appointments when a corporation has become "incompetent"—they appoint a trustee in bankruptcy or reorganization to oversee its affairs and speak for it in court when that becomes necessary.

On a parity of reasoning, we should have a system in which, when a friend of a natural object perceives it to be endangered, he can apply to a court for the creation of a guardianship.

· · ·

We make decisions on behalf of, and in the purported interests of, others every day; these "others" are often creatures whose wants are far less verifiable, and even far more metaphysical in conception, than the wants of rivers, trees, and land.

· · ·

Toward Recognition of Its Own Injuries

As far as adjudicating the merits of a controversy is concerned, there is also a good case to be made for taking into account harm to the environment—in its own right. As indicated above, the traditional way of deciding whether to issue injunctions in law suits affecting the environment, at least where communal property is involved, has been to strike some sort of balance regarding the economic hardships *on human beings*. ... Why not throw into the balance the cost *to the environment*? ...

[T]he traditional legal institutions have a more difficult time "catching" and confronting us with the full social costs of our activities ... (interests) too fragmented and perhaps "too remote" causally to warrant securing representation and pressing for recovery. ... There is no reason not to allow the lake to prove damages to them as the prima facie measure of damages to it. *By doing so, we in effect make the natural object, through its guardian, a jural entity competent to gather up these fragmented and otherwise unrepresented damage claims, and press them before the court even where, for legal or practical reasons, they are not going to be pressed by traditional class action plaintiffs.* Indeed, one way—the homocentric way—to view what I am proposing so far, is to view the guardian of the natural object as the guardian of unborn generations, as well as of the otherwise unrepresented, but distantly injured, contemporary humans. ...

[In addition] the guardian would urge before the court injuries not presently cognizable—the death of eagles and inedible crabs, the suffering of sea lions, the loss from the face of the earth of species of commercially valueless birds, the disappearance of a wilderness area.

· · ·

Toward Being a Beneficiary in Its Own Right

As suggested above, one reason for making the environment itself the beneficiary of a judgment is to prevent it from being "sold out" in a negotiation among private litigants who agree not to enforce rights that have been established among themselves. Protection from this will be advanced by making the natural object a party to an injunctive settlement. Even more importantly, we should make it a beneficiary of money awards. ... The natural object's portion could be put into a trust fund to be administered by the object's guardian ... the fund would be available to preserve the natural object as close as possible to its condition at the time the environment was made a rights-holder.

· · ·

Toward Rights in Substance

So far we have been looking at the characteristics of being a *holder of rights*, and exploring some of the implications that making the environment a holder of rights would entail. ... To flesh out the "rights" of the environment demands that we provide it with a significant body of (procedural and constitutional) rights for it to invoke when it gets to court.

NOTES AND QUESTIONS

1. Think about some of the practical details of Stone's proposal. Who would be a suitable guardian for a natural object? How would you judge what the environment "needed"? Is the government not already a "guardian" of the public interest? See Stone, above, at 464-73. What are the possible uses to which a damage award could be put? What sort of procedural rights would be needed for the environment to successfully bring an action? See Stone, above, at 480-87. In a rare attempt to apply Stone's thesis, a minority of the US Supreme Court in *Sierra Club v. Morton*, 405 US 727 (1972) considered the question of the environment's "right" to bring legal actions. Douglas J, in a dissenting judgment, held, *inter alia*, that

> Contemporary public concern for protecting nature's ecological equilibrium should lead to the conferral of standing upon environmental objects to sue for their own preservation. ...
>
> The river as plaintiff speaks for the ecological unit of life that is part of it. Those people who have a meaningful relation to that body of water ... must be able to speak for the values which the river represents and which are threatened with destruction. ...
>
> The voice of the inanimate object, therefore, should not be stilled. That does not mean that the judiciary takes over the managerial functions from the federal agency. It merely means that before these priceless bits of Americana ... are forever lost ... the voices of the existing beneficiaries of these environmental wonders should be heard.

2. What would be the appropriate "holder" of legal rights? Should it be an individual object (a lake or tree)? Should it be a species? Should it be an ecosystem or geographic area? For further reading, see G. Varner, "Do Species Have Standing?" (1987) vol. 9, *Environmental Ethics* 57; S. Lehmann, "Do Wildernesses Have Rights?" (1981) vol. 3, *Environmental Ethics* 129; S. Emmenegger and A. Tschentscher, "Taking Nature's Rights Seriously" (1994) vol. 6 *Georgetown International Environmental Law Review* 545.

3. What type of philosophical shift is needed in our social and legal systems to accept the notion of natural objects having rights? In another leading article from the same decade as Stone's, L. Tribe puzzled over the decision of Los Angeles County officials to plant over 900 plastic trees along a major boulevard. The plastic trees, of course, provided "shade, decoration and the aesthetic semblance of a natural environment." They also needed less space and care. As Tribe asked, "What's wrong with plastic trees?" Does your answer depend on your environmental ethic—the way you view the relationship between, and inherent value of, people and nature? See L. Tribe, "Ways Not To Think About Plastic Trees: New Foundations for Environmental Law" (1974) vol. 83, no. 7 *Yale Law Journal* 1315.

4. Stone's article provoked a storm of commentary. Much of it has focused not on the legal issue of "could we do this?", but on the related moral issue of "ought we to do this?" Many object to the idea that we should grant legal rights to "things" that lack, for example, preferences, capacity for suffering, sentience, or some other criterion of moral "consideration." Stone himself considers these issues to be distinct. In "Legal Rights and Moral Pluralism" (1987) vol. 9 *Environmental Ethics* 281, he notes (at 282-83):

> But legal considerateness is not the same as moral considerateness. Nor is the relationship one of congruence. They raise two separate issues. The legal issue involves the prerequisites of legal considerateness, including legal rights. As I explain, whether we can grant something legal rights is largely a matter of coherence, and there is nothing incoherent about granting rights to entities that lack interests (although doing so raises some special problems, none of which is beyond repair).
>
> The moral issue is this. Supposing (as Varner and I both do) that it is coherent to assign (some appropriate) legal rights to a tree or species: why *ought* we to do so? ... [I]t seems to me that the "rightness" of our preserving a species by such measures as giving it a legal right does not have to depend upon the species having a moral right to be preserved.

For an elaboration of Stone's arguments, see C. Stone, *Earth and Other Ethics* (New York: Harper & Row, 1987).

5. One alternative is the utilitarian view that environmental protection is desirable, but only to satisfy (morally relevant) human wants and welfare. D. MacDonald, *The Politics of Pollution* (Toronto: McClelland & Stewart, 1991), notes, at 264, that one of the dangers of the latter view is that when "we are not particularly concerned for the well-being of any species other than our own, except insofar as it meets human needs, surely it makes more sense to adapt to the damage we have wrought than to pay the price for environmental protection." Does it make any real difference to people alive today that passenger pigeons no longer exist? If the cost of environmental protection is so high that it seems prohibitive, what "rule" could we use to make policy decisions? In deciding how much protection will cost, how could one accurately place an economic value on the losses or damage to the environment? See Stone, above, at 473-80.

6. Could the same results be achieved by other kinds of reform to our legal system? Are "rights" the appropriate model? Are you confident that formal recognition of environmental rights would help transform our social and legal institutions, rather than becoming simply one more instrument for perpetuation of the existing power structures? For some explorations of these issues see J. Livingston, "Rightness or Rights?" (1984) vol. 22, no. 2 *Osgoode Hall Law Journal* 309; P. Elder, "Legal Rights for Nature—The Wrong Answer to the Right(s) Question" (1984) vol. 22, no. 2 *Osgoode Hall Law Journal* 285; and D.P. Emond, "Cooperation in Nature: A New Foundation for Environmental Law" (1984) vol. 22, no. 2 *Osgoode Hall Law Journal* 323.

7. How does this discussion relate to the question of animal rights? What do you think of an environmental ethic that respects nature without regard for the lives of the individual beings within the ecosystem?

D.W. St. Pierre
"The Tradition from Property to People: The Road to the Recognition of Rights for Non-human Animals"

(1998) vol. 9, no. 2 *Hastings Women's Law Journal* 255, at 257-60

A great deal of literature is devoted to the philosophical debate on whether or not animals deserve rights. This Note begins with the assumption that the life of an animal has inherent value which should be protected through the recognition of legal rights. The basis for this assumption lies at the intersection of science and philosophy. According to evolutionary theory, the difference between species is not one of distinct categories, but merely one of degree. There is nothing in this degree of difference that is so great as to justify the domination visited by our species upon other species of this planet. Humans do not possess any characteristics which are not shared by at least one other species. Non-human animals use tools, communicate with language, display emotions, have social relations, establish cultures, display rational thought and even exhibit altruism. The converse is also true. There are no shortcomings displayed by non-human animals that are not also reflected in human behavior. Our society values and protects the rights of every human—even the most severely mentally handicapped humans—some of whom lack both the capacity to use language and to think rationally, are given protection under the law. Currently, our society limits its circle of moral concern by imposing inherent value only on the lives of humans, without any rational basis for that limitation. In the spirit of social evolution, it is time to expand our circle of moral concern and respect the value of non-human life. Leaving the specific extent of rights for non-human animals to the philosophers, the general precepts to strive toward include freedom from imprisonment, as well as from the infliction of pain, suffering or death.

A meaningful discussion of rights requires a discussion of how rights are enforced or asserted. Yet, speaking of rights in terms of self-assertion creates a problem regarding the rights of animals. Since animals cannot speak for themselves, who is to assert their interests? Our legal system already confronts and resolves this problem when dealing with children, mentally incompetent individuals and others who are deemed unable to represent themselves. Guardians ad litem and next friends are appointed to advocate for the best interest of that individual and could serve the same purpose for non-human animals.

The current prevailing attitude towards non-human animals in this country can be described as legal welfarism. This is the notion "represented by and in various legal doctrines, that animals, which are the property of people, may be treated solely as means to ends by humans as long as this exploitation does not result in the infliction of 'unnecessary' pain, suffering, or death." As property, non-human animals are meant to be used in a reasonable and efficient manner. Consequently, the value of non-human animals is measured only in terms of their usefulness to humans, not in terms of any interests they may have in their own right.

Legal welfarism embraces the reasonable and efficient, but "humane" use of non-human animals. Animal welfarists work to improve the conditions under which animals are kept and used. However, their theory of humane use can be seen as a rhetorical concept because it would be difficult to find an individual specifically espousing a pro-cruelty ethic. Even the largest exploiters of animals might claim that they treat their animals well and have every incentive to do so.

The state regulates the use of animals through anti-cruelty statutes. Yet, cruelty statutes are designed to prevent "unnecessary" suffering, and do not create anything equivalent to "rights" for non-human animals. According to David Favre, the use of cruelty statutes to establish criminal sanctions seeks to fulfill three social goals: "first, to proscribe certain human actions as unacceptable in our society; second, to decide that a minimum level of care is due to any animal; and finally, to protect the economic interest that animals represent to their owners." Our legal system is structured, however, such that virtually any treatment of a non-human animal can be justified as some sort of "necessity." Arguably, the value of the life of a non-human animal is caught up in a cost benefit analysis so heavily weighted in favor of even the most frivolous human "benefit," that the protections provided by cruelty statutes are practically nonexistent.

NOTES AND QUESTIONS

1. In the 1970s two major streams of ethical argument arose that questioned both the efficacy and the morality of legal welfarism. First, "enlightened utilitarianism" was popularized by P. Singer in *Animal Liberation: A New Ethics for Our Treatment of Animals* (New York: NY Review, 1975 and Avon Books, 1977). His core argument is that because of a shared capacity to feel pain and suffer in any calculations of the utility of using animals their interests must be given equal consideration with human interests; failure to do so can rest upon nothing more than "speciesism" (prejudice akin to sexism or racism). Second, "animal rights" theories were advanced; the classic work in this area is by T. Regan, in *The Case for Animal Rights* (Berkeley, CA: University of California Press, 1983). The foundation for his theory is that it is the possession of consciousness and inherent value that gives moral rights to humans and other animals alike; the fact that we are "subjects of a life"—that is, that we all have a life that is better or worse for us (regardless of our value or utility to others), is what gives us the right not to be treated in ways that fail to accord respect to our interests. (See also T. Regan and P. Singer, eds., *Animal Rights and Human Obligations* (Englewood Cliffs, NJ: Prentice Hall, 1976).

2. How are animal welfare issues treated in environmental philosophy? A. Leopold's land ethic, expounded in *A Sand County Almanac* (Oxford: Oxford University Press, 1966), is a classic "holistic" environmental ethic that grounds itself in ecological principles, expounding that "a thing is right when it tends to preserve the beauty, integrity, and stability of the biotic community. It is wrong when it tends otherwise" (at 262). A "major tenet of holist philosophy is the notion that the primary locus of value resides not in the individual parts of nature, but, rather, in the whole to which the individuals belong": M. Kheel, "Licence to Kill: An Ecofeminist Critique of Hunter's Discourse," in C. Adams and J. Donovan, eds., *Animals and Women: Feminist Theoretical Explorations* (Durham, NC: Duke University Press, 1995), chapter 4, at 97. Accordingly, "holism maintain[s] that the well-being of the whole must always take precedence over the individual parts"

(Kheel, above, at 97). One result, as C. Miller notes in *Environmental Rights: Critical Perspectives* (London: Routledge, 1998), at 186, is that such

> [h]olistic approaches have invited the description "environmental facism" when they blithely subordinate individual organisms (humans not excluded) to the aggregate utility of the entire ecosystem. If reconciling the autonomy of individuals with social order is the perennial concern of political science, then the recognition that an individual organism and the ecosystem which sustains them may both be bearers of moral consideration has becomes comparably central issue in environmental philosophy.

P. Singer
"Not for Humans Only: The Place of Nonhumans in Environmental Issues"
in K.E. Goodpaster and K.M. Syre, eds., *Ethics and Problems of the 21st Century* (Notre Dame, IN: University of Notre Dame Press, 1979), at 191

We can now draw at least one conclusion as to how the existence of nonhuman living things should enter into our deliberations about actions affecting the environment: Where our actions are likely to make animals suffer, that suffering must count in our deliberations, and it should count equally with a like amount of suffering by human beings, insofar as rough comparisons can be made.

The difficulty of making the required comparison will mean that the application of this conclusion is controversial in many cases, but there will be situations in which it is clear enough. Take, for instance, the wholesale poisoning of animals that is euphemistically known as "pest control." The authorities who conduct these campaigns give no consideration to the suffering they inflict on the "pests," and invariably use the method of slaughter they believe to be cheapest and most effective. The result is that hundreds of millions of rabbits have died agonizing deaths from the artificially introduced disease, myxomatosis, or from poisons like "ten-eighty"; coyotes and other wild dogs have died painfully from cyanide poisoning; and all manner of wild animals have endured days of thirst, hunger, and fear with a mangled limb caught in a leg-hold trap. Granting, for the sake of argument, the necessity for pest control—though this has rightly been questioned—the fact remains that no serious attempts have been made to introduce alternative means of control and thereby reduce the incalculable amount of suffering caused by present methods. It would not, presumably, be beyond modern science to produce a substance which, when eaten by rabbits or coyotes, produced sterility instead of a drawn-out death. Such methods might be more expensive, but can anyone doubt that if a similar amount of human suffering were at stake, the expense would be borne?

Another clear instance in which the principle of equal consideration of interests would indicate methods different from those presently used is in the timber industry. There are two basic methods of obtaining timber from forests. One is to cut only selected mature or dead trees, leaving the forest substantially intact. The other, known as clear-cutting, involves chopping down everything that grows in a given area, and then reseeding. Obviously when a large area is clear-cut, wild animals find their whole living area destroyed in a few days, whereas selected felling makes a relatively minor disturbance. But clear-cutting is cheaper, and timber companies therefore use this method and will continue to do so unless forced to do otherwise.

. . .

For when an environmental decision threatens the lives of animals and birds, it almost always does so in a way that causes suffering to them or to their mates, parents, offspring, or pack-members. Often, the type of death inflicted will itself be a slow and painful one, caused, for instance, by the steady build-up of a noxious chemical. Even when death itself is quick and painless, in many species of birds and mammals it leaves behind survivors whose lives may be disrupted. Birds often mate for life in some species separating after the young have been reared but meeting again, apparently recognizing each other as individuals, when the breeding season comes round again. There are many species in which a bird who has lost its mate will not mate again. The behavior of mammals who have lost their young also suggests sorrow and distress, and infant mammals left without a mother will usually starve miserably. In other social species the death of one member of a group can cause considerable disturbance, especially if the dead animal is a group leader. Now since, as we have already seen, the suffering of nonhuman animals must count equally with the like suffering of human beings, the upshot of these facts is that quite independently of the intrinsic value we place on the lives of nonhuman animals any morally defensible decision affecting the environment should take care to minimize the loss of animal life, particularly among birds and mammals.

M. Kheel
"License To Kill: An Ecofeminist Critique of Hunters' Discourse"
in C. Adams and J. Donovan, eds., *Animals and Women: Feminist Theoretical Explorations* (Durham, NC: Duke University Press, 1995), at 110-11

Ecofeminism is still in the process of forging connections between feminism and the environmental movement. If ecofeminism is to rise to the challenge of its potential, it must begin to move beyond abstract statements concerning ethical conduct and thought. We have seen that it is not sufficient to rely on abstract language such as "holism," "biocentrism," or even "reverence" and "respect." We must begin to say what we mean by these words. When we speak of reverence and respect, we must ask "what precisely do we mean?" An emphasis on a spiritual sense of connection is, indeed, a praise-worthy goal. But a spiritual sense of connection must translate into genuine caring behavior for other living beings. Caring for other living beings cannot be conducted in the privacy of one's interior psychic state. It must take into account a genuine recognition of the response of the one we are caring for. Saying a prayer before you kill an animal is no more acceptable than saying a prayer before a rape. It is our actions, more than our state of mind, that are crucial in the realm of ethical conduct. If these actions flow only from a mentally constructed desire, they cannot take into account the needs of all parties in question. Moral actions must flow not only from the capacity to perceive our interconnection with others, but also from our ability to acknowledge—to morally attend to—the plight of other living beings as separate and distinct from our own needs and desires.

Environmental philosophy and the environmental movement as a whole have failed to incorporate a genuine concern for individual beings. Currently, no major environmental organization is willing to express opposition to hunting, and none takes a position on eating meat. But until the environmental movement and environmental philosophy develop a concern for individual beings, they will be living in the shadow of their violent past. Hunters currently kill more than 200 million animals every year. They cripple, harass, and orphan millions more. An ecofeminist ethic must deplore this, along with all other expressions of violence. It must seek to sever the connections that historically have bound the environmental movement to a practice of violence. An ecofeminist ethic must help us to realize that, since we do not need to hunt or eat meat for survival, we should do neither. Rather, we should all engage in a genuine celebration which recognizes that the best gift that we can offer to and receive from animals is their continued lives.

NOTES AND QUESTIONS

1. For recent arguments supporting animal rights, see T. Regan, *Defending Animal Rights* (Chicago: University of Illinois Press, 2001); G. Francione, *Animals, Property and the Law* (Philadelphia: Temple University Press, 1995); and S. Wise, *Rattling the Cage* (Cambridge, MA: Perseus Books, 2000).

2. For more on the animal welfare/environment overlap, see B. Norton, "Environmental Ethics and Nonhuman Rights" (1982) vol. 4 *Environmental Ethics* 17; M. Sagoff, "Animal Liberation and Environmental Ethics" (1984) vol. 22, no. 2 *Osgoode Hall Law Journal* 297; and T. Regan, *All that Dwell Therein: Animal Rights and Environmental Ethics* (Berkeley, CA: University of California Press, 1982).

3. For an overview of Canadian animal welfare law, see E. Hughes and C. Meyer, "Animal Welfare Law in Canada & Europe" (2000) vol. 6 *Animal Law* 23.

VI. CONCLUSION

This chapter has examined a number of suggestions for advancing environmental protection through law reforms based on a civil rights model. This might involve recognizing human rights to environmental quality, constitutionalizing environmental rights, granting rights to natural objects or animals themselves, or expanding existing rights (such as aboriginal rights) to indirectly achieve environmental protection.

As we have seen, all of these suggestions sit rather uneasily with our traditional "rights paradigm." As D. Saxe, *Environmental Offences: Corporate Responsibility and Executive Liability* (Aurora, ON: Canada Law Book, 1990), points out (at 18), "Human rights have usually been conceptualized ... as individual negative rights, rights of individuals to be free from interference by government. They are protected by limiting state action." She goes on to note (at 18-20) that environmental rights, on the other hand, "cannot be easily accommodated within this paradigm" because

1. private, rather than state, action is the principal cause of environmental harm;
2. environmental protection usually requires positive state action, not limits to it;
3. environmental rights are "quintessentially" public rights enjoyed by all, not rights to be claimed by some individuals to the exclusion of others;
4. the insidious and broad-ranging nature of environmental damage may be such that a breach of environmental rights may not produce serious injury to one particular individual, so a collective remedy may be necessary;
5. much environmental degradation is primarily a threat to future generations and non-human life;
6. environmental rights are positive rights that carry with them a corresponding duty on others to take steps to protect the environment, not merely to refrain from action;
7. we lack a societal consensus on the proper ambit of such rights; and
8. assertion of these rights does not give us guidance in making hard decisions about environmental protection.

Such concerns are not limited to the domestic debate. Internationally, there have also been calls for a "substantive human right to an ecologically-balanced environment [that] would place a duty on governments to preserve ecosystem balance for current and future generations" (Babour, above, at 132). There are several international declarations and regional treaties that make reference to environmental rights and there are several judicial and academic explorations of the extent to which environmental rights can be derived from existing human rights, such as the right to life.

The main arguments for creating an "autonomous" right to a healthy environment are, according to P. Birnie and A. Boyle, *International Environmental Law*, 2d ed. (Oxford: Oxford University Press, 2002), at 255, "the enhanced status it would give environmental quality when balanced against competing objectives and other human rights, including the right to property, and that it would recognize the vital character of the environment as a basic condition of life, indispensable to the promotion of human dignity and welfare, and to the fulfillment of other human rights." (See also N. Gibson, "The Right to a Clean Environment" (1990) *Saskatchewan Law Review* 5, at 16.) At the same time, however, they note that the difficulty of defining such rights and the anthropocentric nature of such rights, which focus on humans to the exclusion of other species and the environment per se, coupled with the potential that such rights will do little to add to the extensive regulation (via treaties) of international environmental matters, may make legal recognition of substantive environmental rights undesirable or redundant. On the other hand, when one examines cases where environmental and health concerns *have* been successfully linked to the enforcement of existing individual human rights, Birnie and Boyle, above, conclude (at 261): "where the failure of governmental action is a major source of environmental harm, human rights law, both national and international, has significant potential for remedying deficiencies in national regulation and enforcement."

Thus, the international debate has reflected many of the same concerns as the domestic debate. In many respects, it has also followed a similar path. The strongest environmental "rights" agreed to by states tend to be procedural rights, such as those in the 1998

Aarhus Convention on Access to Information, Public Participation in Decision-making and Access to Justice in Environmental Matters (reprinted in vol. 38 *International Legal Materials* 517), which is expected to be extremely influential on national laws and policies in Europe. "This approach rests on the view that environmental protection and sustainable development cannot be left to governments alone but require and benefit from notions of civic participation in public affairs already reflected in existing civil and political rights" (Birnie and Boyle, above, at 261). However, it is often only once such international instruments are implemented via domestic legislation that the new rights can really be used by public interest litigants to "make public bodies accountable for their actions under international law" (Birnie and Boyle, above, at 264).

Another, more fundamental problem must also be considered. Underlying all versions of the civil rights approach is an assumption that having "rights" is a good thing; that getting legally enforceable environmental rights will make things better than they are in our current state of "rightlessness." This assumption has, however, been criticized.

One problem with rights theory is that legal rights do not necessarily solve problems, they simply redefine them in ways that suggest legal solutions—even if those are not the best solutions. If we have a right to sue for violations of our environmental rights, we will tend to do so, obtaining, perhaps, damages. But maybe what is really needed to solve the problem of pollution is a change in political will or public education; our "rights" may not give us what we really *need*, nor disrupt the *status quo* in any significant way.

Another problem with rights is that the almost inevitable response is to claim competing rights, and usually the holder of the more powerful "right" wins. The classic example is the "environment versus jobs" rights contest. Who has more money and resources to put into rights-based litigation—corporations or environmental groups? What good is a right without the power to defend it? How can you be sure that environmental rights would prevail over other rights?

Another difficulty with rights discourse is that rights can be appropriated for uses other than those intended. We assume that a right to environmental quality will be used for the benefit of the environment—for wilderness preservation, endangered species protection, pollution control, and the like. What if a scientist claims a violation of environmental rights because a regulation prohibits the release of genetically engineered species, which the scientist claims will enhance environmental quality by increasing biodiversity and replacing extinct species?

Other criticisms of rights theory abound, but by now the point should be clear. If, as environmentalists, we advocate civil rights as a means of environmental protection, we should think in advance about the strengths and weaknesses of our approach. In a broad context, think about the social and legal implications of asserting environmental or animal rights. As D. MacDonald, *The Politics of Pollution*, above, points out (at 270), there are some problematic issues that environmentalism faces:

> How *do we*, within the constraints of political reality, both stop pollution of a river and treat a one-industry town with the fairness and social justice it deserves? How *do we* both protect the global environment and at the same time alleviate the all too real suffering and anguish that are the lot of the majority of our fellow citizens on the globe? In summary, what can

environmentalism suggest as a means of alleviating the pain of the dislocations and costs that would follow from implementation of its central thesis—that economic expansion must be slowed or stopped?

Finally, try to evaluate how much we can achieve with this approach compared with other proposals for law reform. As Birnie and Boyle, above, note (at 251):

> It is not clear that [the rights argument] leads necessarily to any greater protection for than the environment than is already available in ... law, or that could be made available simply through better regulation.

On the other hand, new rights are not the same as new rules (Birnie and Boyle, above, at 251), and if we are ever to achieve the "right" balance between environmental, social, and economic concerns, further exploration of the civil rights model is perhaps warranted.

FURTHER READINGS

P. Birnie and A. Boyle, *International Law & the Environment*, 2d ed. (Oxford: Oxford University Press, 2002), chapter 5.

J. Castrilli, "Environmental Rights Statutes in the United States and Canada" (1998) vol. 9 *Villanova Environmental Law Journal* 349.

G. Poelzer, "Aboriginal Peoples and Environment Policy in Canada: No Longer at the Margins," in D. VanNijnatten and R. Boardman, eds. *Canadian Environmental Policy: Context and Cases*, 2d ed. (Don Mills, ON: Oxford University Press, 2002).

T. Regan, *Defending Animal Rights* (Chicago: University of Illinois Press, 2001).

M. Winfield, "A Political and Legal Analysis of Ontario's Environmental Bill of Rights" (1998) vol. 47 *UNB Law Journal* 325.

CHAPTER TWELVE

Protected Spaces and Endangered Species*

Stewart Elgie

In wildness is the preservation of the world … . Life consists of wildness. The most alive is the wildest. Not yet subdued to man, its presence refreshes him … . When I would re-create myself, I seek the darkest wood, the thickest and most interminable and to the citizen, most dismal, swamp. I enter it as a sacred place, a Sanctum Sanctorum. There is the strength, the marrow, of Nature. In short, all good things are wild and free.

Henry David Thoreau (1851)

I. PARKS AND PROTECTED AREAS

A. The History of Parks

Most Canadians take for granted the fact that we have wilderness parks. However, parks, in the modern sense, are a relatively recent North American creation.

Today we look upon parks as special places that provide a sanctuary for both man and nature, places where some relief from everyday stress can be found. Special places serving contemplative or spiritual needs have existed in eastern cultures since 500 BC. The eastern religions of Shintoism, Taoism, and Buddhism held a reverence for nature not reflected in Christianity. Thus shrines such as the Bo Tree in Sri Lanka have protected nature and provided places for contemplation for more than 2000 years. In contrast, Christian theology often casts wilderness as the antithesis of paradise. [As exemplified in the writings of Joel: "The land is like the garden of Eden before them, but after them a desolate wilderness."]

Skipping a few centuries, we find new benchmarks in the royal forests and game preserves of England and France. The *Doomsday Book* of 1086 was perhaps the first inventory of lands, forests, and hunting preserves. Formal gardens such as Hyde Park (1536) and Richmond Park (established by Charles in 1637) were some of the earliest lands

---

* The author would like to thank Dayna Scott for her invaluable research assistance in updating this chapter.

to be called "parks." In the new world, Boston Common (1603) is often acknowledged as the first formal public open space in North America. The next major landmark was the establishment of Yosemite as a twenty-square-kilometre state park in California in 1864. This was followed by "the world's first instance of large-scale wilderness preservation in the public interest." On March 1, 1872, President Ulysses S. Grant signed an act designating over 8,000,000 hectares of northwestern Wyoming as Yellowstone National Park.

The establishment of Yellowstone National Park in the United States sparked a global interest in parks. In 1879 Royal National Park was established in New South Wales, Australia, and in 1894 Tongariro National Park was dedicated in New Zealand. Thus, by the turn of the century, the national-parks concept, as we know it today, was underway.

In Canada, Frederick Law Olmstead, the noted American landscape architect who was involved in the design of Central Park in New York in 1857, designed Mount Royal Park in Montreal in 1872. In Toronto, High Park was established in 1873, followed by Vancouver's Stanley Park in 1888. With the protection of Banff National Park in 1885, Niagara Falls in 1887, and Ontario's Algonquin Provincial Park in 1893, Canada, perhaps unwittingly, created "a system of parks."

Between 1885 and 1929, Canada established fifteen national parks. [In 1930, the *National Parks Act* was passed.] But with the transfer of natural resources in western Canada to the provinces in 1930, the national parks program ground to a halt. Only four parks were established in the next twenty years: Cape Breton Highlands in 1936, Prince Edward Island in 1937, Fundy in 1948, and Terra Nova in 1957. The next thirty years, though, saw the system double. The postwar boom, new cars, and new highways brought a new generation of visitors to North America's parks.

> H. Eidzvik, "Canada in a Global Context," in M. Hummel, ed., *Endangered Spaces: The Future for Canada's Wilderness* (Toronto: Key Porter Books, 1989)

Today, there are 39 national parks in Canada, 2 national marine parks, over 1,000 provincial parks, and a host of other types of conservation areas. Canada's parks protect many of the nation's most spectacular natural features, including the highest mountain (Kluane), the tallest tree (Carmanah Pacific), the largest inland delta (Wood Buffalo), the most northerly point (Ellesmere Island), the most southerly point (Point Pelee), the strongest tides (Fundy), and many endangered species, for which parks are the last refuge. Parks and protected areas are important for recreational, educational, cultural heritage, and ecological reasons.

B. The Idea of Wilderness in North America

The European settlers brought their attitudes toward nature with them to the new world. Wilderness, at first, was something to be conquered and subdued. North America's native people who had lived on, and from, the land for several thousand years had no concept of wilderness, at least in the European sense. The idea of protecting wild places or of exploiting them are concepts born in societies that see themselves as separate from, and above, nature. North American natives had evolved a lifestyle based on respect for the land and animals. They took what they needed to live, but never so much as to upset the natural balance.

The creation of the first national parks in the United States sprang largely from the birth of a philosophical belief in the value of wilderness. As the wild frontier was tamed, a kind of romantic reverence for wilderness emerged. Its early origins are found in the mid-1800s in the nature writings of people like Ralph Waldo Emerson ("nature is the symbol of the spirit") and Henry David Thoreau. Their writings later influenced President Theodore Roosevelt, who laid the foundations of the US national parks network around the turn of the 20th century.

Roosevelt was also greatly influenced by John Muir, a man who is associated more closely with wilderness thinking than anyone in North America, and perhaps the world. Beginning in the 1890s, after almost losing his sight in an accident, Muir journeyed up and down the west coast of North America from California to Alaska—mostly on foot. His articulate writings about the places he visited and about the value of wilderness had an almost religious zeal to them and influenced many people. Muir is most famous for his epic struggle to prevent Hetch Hetchy Valley in his beloved Yosemite Park from being dammed. "Dam Hetch Hetchy," he wrote, "as well dam for water tanks the people's cathedrals and churches, for no holier temple has ever been consecrated by the hand of man." Although Muir eventually lost, the battle marked the birth of his organization, the Sierra Club, as a potent wilderness advocate.

Although the frontier mentality began to wane in the United States around the turn of the 20th century, it remained very much a part of the Canadian psyche. The creation of Canada's first national park sprang less from philosophy and more from a desire for profit. In 1883, with the help of local natives, railway workers discovered Banff hot springs. The Canadian Pacific Railway (CPR) was quick to realize that the springs and the mountains could provide a popular and profitable destination for wealthy tourists. Anxious to enlist riders for the new railway, CPR president William Van Horne wrote to the prime minister, saying "the springs are worth a million dollars." That was enough to stir the fires of preservation in Sir John A. Macdonald, who set aside Banff Park because it would provide "large pecuniary advantage to the Dominion." The first *Rocky Mountain Parks Act*, SC 1887, c. 32, allowed industrial buildings, mining, and logging in the park, so long as they did not interfere with the tourist trade. Thus, the origins of Canada's national parks lie not in the preservationist zeal of a John Muir, but in the utilitarian desires of the CPR.

For most of the 20th century, Canadians have continued to view nature as something to be exploited for profit, even within parks. However, there have been some strands of wilderness thinking. The paintings of the Group of Seven, following World War I, helped to portray Canada's landscape as something more than just raw materials. During the 1930s, Grey Owl, an Englishman who retreated to the Canadian wilds and adopted a native persona, spoke and wrote eloquently about the need to preserve Canada's wildlife and wilderness. More recently, writers like W.O. Mitchell, Farley Mowat, Northrop Frye, and Margaret Atwood have helped to identify the soul of the nation with its wilderness, particularly the north. In the past three decades, Canada's frontier mentality has begun to give way, and an appreciation for wilderness has started to emerge.

C. Why Parks?

There are many reasons for creating parks. Seven of the main reasons are set out below. Note that each different reason entails a somewhat different vision of what a park is.

- *Recreation.* Parks offer prized opportunities for outdoor recreation. Different people prefer different types of recreation, ranging from wilderness hiking and canoeing, to mountain biking, skiing, and car camping.
- *Profit.* Tourism is big business. In 1987-1988, expenditures in national parks directly contributed over $1.5 billion to the Canadian economy.
- *Education.* Parks provide a living laboratory for the study and appreciation of ecosystems and their component species.
- *Spiritual value.* Certain places are viewed as sacred by some cultures, particularly native ones. For others, experiencing spectacular natural locations is of spiritual importance.
- *Cultural heritage.* Canadian cultural identity has been deeply influenced by wilderness. In the words of Canadian author Northrop Frye, "The real question is not who am I, but where is here?" If we lose wilderness, we lose the ability to understand this aspect of our past and ourselves.
- *Protecting ecosystems for human needs.* Protecting watersheds ensures the quality and flow of rivers. Intact forests help produce clean air and absorb atmospheric carbon (mitigating climate change). Preserving a wide diversity of species ensures a broad genetic pool for use in future agricultural, medicinal, and scientific research.
- *Intrinsic preservation.* All life has a right to exist for its own sake. Only by minimizing human intrusion in an area can it be allowed to function naturally.

Each of the first six reasons is based on an *anthropocentric* (human-centred) viewpoint. The first two reasons favour substantial use of parks, and extensive development of tourist facilities in some areas. The next four reasons favour limited human alteration of parks. The seventh reason also favours minimal human intrusion into parks, but stems from an *ecocentric* viewpoint.

Most parks are created for a mixture of the above reasons. Federal parks legislation has traditionally enshrined an anthropocentric view of parks, but has called for a balance between use and preservation. Recent amendments, discussed below, have added an ecocentric mandate as well.

The principal argument against the creation of parks is that they "lock up" valuable natural resources. Many national parks are rich in natural resources. As recently as the 1950s, lead, zinc, and silver were mined in the Rocky Mountain parks. There is a deposit of 500 million tonnes of gypsum in Wood Buffalo National Park. The parks also contain large quantities of high-grade timber. Of course, the extraction of natural resources conflicts with all of the above reasons for creating parks. Thus far, because of its vast size and abundant resources, Canada has been able to set aside parks while still satisfying the demands for resource extraction. In future years, as our natural resource stocks are depleted, there may be increasing pressure to develop resources inside parks.

D. Is Our Park System Adequate To Meet These Needs?

In designating land for parks, there are a number of important questions to be answered: How much? What size? Where? At what cost?

How much? The question of how much land to protect as parks is a political, scientific, and ethical question. The 1987 report of the UN World Commission on Environment and Development (the Brundtland commission) called for at least 12 percent of each country to be protected. In 1989, the World Wildlife Fund launched the Endangered Spaces campaign, calling for at least 12 percent of Canada's lands to be fully protected by the year 2000, with representative parks in each natural region. The federal government and all provincial and territorial governments committed to this target, although none has yet achieved it.

Very few of the world's countries have met this target. A few nations, including Tanzania, Costa Rica, Botswana, and Zimbabwe, have protected substantially more than 12 percent of their lands. Canada ranks well down the list with less than 8 percent of its lands protected. The United States, by comparison, has protected almost 10 percent of its land. With over 50 percent of its lands in a roadless condition, Canada has a unique opportunity among the world's countries to protect pristine areas (only 12 percent of US lands are in roadless condition). But opportunities for parks in Canada are dwindling quickly, particularly in the south.

What size? An ecosystem consists of a variety of organisms, existing in an interrelated web. It is difficult to put boundaries on an ecosystem, because many of its constituents—air, rivers, and migratory wildlife—will move in and out of any boundary. Still, in establishing parks, it is desirable to include an area sufficient to encompass viable populations of resident (as opposed to migratory) animal species. Doing so can be difficult. Some animals, such as bears and wolves, require 25 to 50 square kilometres per animal. A park not only must be of sufficient size, but should follow natural boundaries such as mountains or rivers that define the animals' range. A few of Canada's larger parks such as Wood Buffalo and Kluane support fairly intact ecosystems. Most, however, are too small, or fail to follow natural boundaries, and thus cannot support a full range of native species.

Where? Canada's landscape is a mosaic of numerous types of topography, vegetative cover, and geological makeup. It is important that protected areas cover a representative mix of all natural regions in the country. Parks Canada lists 39 different natural regions in the country (the World Wildlife Fund estimates that there are about 350). As of 2003, only 25 of those regions contain national parks (although some contain provincial parks), meaning that 14 new parks are needed to complete the parks system, which Ottawa had promised to do by 2000. A particular problem will be creating parks in areas accessible to Canada's major population centres.

Another challenge will be protecting aquatic areas. Traditionally parks have been used to protect terrestrial areas. However, one of the new developments in the conservation movement is the establishment of marine parks. The new *Canada National Marine Conservation Areas Act*, SC 2002, c. 18, aims to create the marine equivalent of the land-based national parks system. It affirms the need to establish a system of marine conservation areas representative of the oceans and Great Lakes. The *Oceans Act*, SC 1996, c. 31, also allows for the establishment of protected marine areas (by the minister of fisheries). So far, only two marine parks have been established. One particular challenge for managing marine parks is the fact that water and most aquatic species (other than plants) move freely across park borders.

At what cost? Creating new parks can be very expensive. For instance, South Moresby National Park, created in 1988, cost the federal government $106 million. Of that amount, $50 million went to the BC government, which owned the land, $26 million was paid to logging companies who held rights to log the land, and the remaining $30 million went to actual park costs.

One expense in creating a park is purchasing the land from the owner. Any government can expropriate lands without compensation if it wishes but, for political reasons, few governments do so. Most protected areas legislation in Canada provides for compensation to affected owners. If an Act says nothing, there is a presumption at common law that any government expropriation of property entails compensation. Since most provinces still have significant amounts of unoccupied Crown land, compensating landowners often is not a major expense in creating provincial parks, except near heavily populated areas. However, to create a national park, except in the territories, the federal government must purchase the land from the provincial Crown or private owners. That is why most of the large national parks in the western provinces, such as the Rocky Mountain parks and Wood Buffalo, were created before the federal government gave up ownership of public lands in 1930.

An even greater expense in creating a park can be compensating all rights holders who have an interest in the Crown land. One very important question is whether a person who holds a licence to mine or log on Crown land must be compensated when that land is set aside as a park.

The Queen in Right of British Columbia v. Tener et al.
(1985), 17 DLR (4th) 1 (SCC)

[The respondents received a Crown grant in 1937, giving them title to certain subsurface minerals and entitling them to use surface lands to extract the minerals. In 1973, the land in question was included in a class A provincial park (Wells Gray), which meant mining was not allowed. The respondents were informed that no further work on their mining claim would be permitted. They sought compensation for the alleged "expropriation."]

ESTEY J: That an interest in minerals is an interest in land is not contested. Expropriation or compulsory taking occurs if the Crown or a public authority acquires from the owner an interest in property.

. . .

This kind of legislative and executive action finds its counterpart in many community developments. ... Zoning illustrates the process. Ordinarily, in this country, the United States and the United Kingdom, compensation does not follow zoning either up or down. However, it has been said, at least in some courts of the United

States, that a taker may not, through the device of zoning, depress the value of property as a prelude to compulsory taking of the property for a public purpose. ... The same principle was applied in this country as long ago as 1913 by the Court of Appeal of Ontario in *Re Gibson and City of Toronto*, 11 DLR 529, at p. 536.

. . .

These authorities, however, do not deal squarely with the determination of the question as to whether an expropriation has occurred in the circumstances arising in this appeal, and if so, at what time did it do so. In the cases cited, the public authorities, as part of the acquisition process, formally invoked the expropriation legislation. Here, the notice, *supra*, while inviting some response by the respondents on the question of compensation, neither formally invoked the machinery of compulsory taking nor in precise terms invited a formal claim from the respondents. However, *the longstanding presumption of a right to compensation must be remembered* [emphasis added]. As Lord Atkinson stated in *Attorney-General v. De Keyser's Royal Hotel Ltd.*, [1920] AC 508, at p. 542, "unless the words of the statute clearly so demand, a statute is not to be construed so as to take away the property of a subject without compensation."

. . .

The respondents and their predecessors in title for many years conducted some kind of development work or operations on these lands. ... Eventually, as we have seen, the authorities advised the respondents in 1982 that no permit would be issued. The property rights which were granted to the respondents or their predecessors in title in 1937 were in law thereby reduced. The denial of access to these lands occurred under the *Park Act* and amounts to a recovery by the Crown of a part of the right granted to the respondents in 1937. This acquisition by the Crown constitutes a taking from which compensation must flow.

. . .

This process I have already distinguished from zoning, the broad legislative assignment of land use to land in the community. It is also to be distinguished from regulation of specific activity on certain land, as for example, the prohibition of specified manufacturing processes. This type of regulation is akin to zoning except that it may extend to the entire community. The imposition of zoning regulation and the regulation of activities on lands, fire regulation limits and so on, add nothing to the value of public property. Here the government wished, for obvious reasons, to preserve the qualities perceived as being desirable for public parks, and saw the mineral operations of the respondents under their 1937 grant as a threat to the park. The notice of 1978 took value from the respondents and added value to the park. The respondents are left with only the hope of some future reversal of park policy and the burden of paying taxes on their minerals. The notice of 1978 was an expropriation and, in my view, the rest is part of the compensation assessment process.

NOTES AND QUESTIONS

1. Following this decision, British Columbia rezoned Mr. Tener's mineral claim area as a "recreation area" within the park. Thus, mineral activity was permitted and his

compensation claim became moot. Do you agree that companies with licences to extract resources from *public* lands should be compensated for the full market value of the licence, including the future revenue it would have generated, if the land is made a park? (This is the normal rule.)

2. In 1992, the BC courts applied the *Tener* decision in a case stemming from a 1988 decision of the BC Cabinet to stop granting permits to mine in Strathcona Provincial Park on Vancouver Island. In that case, the Court of Appeal held that the *Tener* principle does not apply to a "mining claim," which under BC legislation is personal property (as opposed to a "Crown grant," which is an "interest in land"). In so deciding, the appeal court rejected as "outdated" the presumption of a right to compensation for the taking of any property interest in a park (*Cream Silver Mines Ltd. v. BC* (1992), 75 BCLR (2d) 324). See also *MacMillan Bloedel Ltd. v. British Columbia*, 2000 BCCA 422 (a logging company may bring an action for compensation against the government when its contract-based logging rights in an area are cancelled for the establishment of a park).

3. How far could the decision in *Tener* be stretched? Would stringent environmental legislation that severely restricted the use of property amount to a taking? In *Mariner Real Estate v. Nova Scotia (Attorney General)* (1999), 178 NSR (2d) 294 (CA), several landowners claimed compensation for "*de facto* expropriation" when the government of Nova Scotia designated their shorefront land as a specially protected beach under the *Beaches Act*, RSNS 1989, c. 32, as amended, and denied them permits to build single-family homes there. The Court of Appeal reasoned:

> Reliance was placed on *Tener* for the proposition that loss of economic value of land is loss of land. In my view, however, there is nothing in the judgments of either Estey or Wilson JJ in that case supporting this proposition. The case does stand for the proposition that whether an interest in land has been lost is to be judged by the effect of the regulation as opposed to its form. ... [B]oth judges linked their holding to the loss, in effect, of a traditionally recognized interest in land. ...
>
> It was clear in *Tener* that it was not the loss of the economic value of the minerals that constituted the interest in land taken, but the complete inability to exercise the right of access to, or withdrawal of, the minerals.

The court held that the landowners did not demonstrate a loss of all viable use of the property. For example, while their applications to build traditional homes were rejected, the ministry had indicated that other environmentally appropriate developments for sand dunes may be acceptable. Therefore, there was no de facto expropriation.

E. An Overview of Protected Areas in Canada

Approximately 11 percent of Canada's land base falls within some form of conservation area. Of this total, federal areas—national parks, national wildlife areas, and migratory bird sanctuaries—account for nearly 4 percent, and the remainder (over 7 percent) comes from provincial parks, wildlife areas, ecological reserves and other types of provincial conservation areas. Some of these areas are more protected than others—less than 8 percent exclude logging, mining, and hydro-electric development (which is the general definition of a protected area). The different types of conservation areas can be distinguished by examining two main factors.

1. *The purpose of the area.* The primary purpose of national and provincial parks is recreation (national parks have also had an ecosystem protection mandate since 1988). The type of recreation emphasized ranges from wilderness parks to roadside rest areas. The purpose of wildlife areas and migratory bird sanctuaries is to protect wildlife and habitat, although recreation is also allowed. The primary purpose of ecological reserves is to protect ecosystems for educational and scientific purposes.

2. *What non-recreational uses are permitted?* National parks do not allow logging, mining, or sport hunting (although a few parks allow aboriginal subsistence hunting). The same is not true of many provincial parks. Provincial wilderness areas and ecological reserves generally do not allow logging, mining, or sport hunting but many wildlife areas and migratory bird sanctuaries allow hunting and "commercial resource utilization."

All told, the national parks are the most protected areas in Canada. They account for about one-third of Canada's protected lands, if areas that allow logging, mining, and dams are excluded. The remainder of this section will examine three key issues in the management of protected areas, with particular emphasis on national parks: How are competing demands of different recreational users resolved? How are internal threats to parks managed (particularly logging and mining)? And how are external threats to parks managed?

F. Playgrounds or Sanctuaries? Resolving Demands of Competing Recreational Users in Parks

As noted above, there are a number of different reasons for establishing parks. Some reasons focus on maximizing opportunities for human recreation and enjoyment. Others focus on preserving intact ecosystems where humans are at best visitors. This tension is reflected in the newly revised *Canada National Parks Act*, SC 2000, c. 32 (CNPA). Section 4(1) of the CNPA sets out the overall mandate for park management:

> The national parks of Canada are hereby dedicated to the people of Canada for their benefit, education and enjoyment, subject to this Act and the regulations, and the parks shall be maintained and *made use of* so as to leave them *unimpaired* for the enjoyment of future generations. [Emphasis added.]

Similar wording is found in many provincial parks acts. The mandate embodies a fundamental paradox: parks shall be "maintained unimpaired" but are for "use." The Act seeks to have its cake and eat it too. Extensive use of parks invariably causes impairment. National parks policy attempts to meet both goals, resulting in inevitable conflicts.

1. Parks as Playgrounds

The growing interest in recreation and the environment in recent decades has brought more and more people from around the world into Canada's parks. In 1947, there were roughly 500,000 visitors to the national parks. In 1998, there were nearly 20 million—4 million in Banff alone. These visitors have brought with them an influx of tourist dollars that has helped to finance Parks Canada's budget. They also have brought steadily increasing demands on the parks' limited resources. Overuse is now a significant problem in some parks.

More visitors in parks mean more infrastructure used by more people. One major problem is roads. Roads fragment wildlife habitat. They also bring more cars into parks, which means more air pollution and more roadkill of animals (in the 1970s, Kootenay Park was losing almost 10 percent of its elk population annually to cars on the Trans-Canada Highway).

More visitors has meant greater development of townsites, complete with boutiques, restaurants, motels, sewage, and garbage. It also has meant increased demand for recreational facilities, such as ski hills and golf courses, which eat into pristine habitat. For instance, most of the montane (valley bottom) environment in Banff and Jasper, which comprises only 5 percent of these parks and is very fragile, is now covered with towns, tourist accommodations, airports, roads, and recreational facilities.

In the Rocky Mountain parks, the proliferation of recreational facilities has gotten so bad that, in 1988, Parliament amended the former *National Parks Act*, RSC 1985, c. N-14, to prohibit the approval of any new commercial ski areas. However, existing ski areas were allowed to develop within their lease boundaries. In 1992, a major expansion proposal by Sunshine Village ski area in Banff National Park lead to a lengthy legal battle between developers and environmentalists. Sunshine Village Corp. (SVC) wanted to increase the capacity of its commercial ski area by over 50 percent and sought approval to build new runs, lifts, and hotel and parking facilities. The proposed parking area was particularly problematic; it would be built in a narrow valley that was believed to be an important movement corridor for bears and wolves. The company obtained approval to begin clearing ski runs while the rest of the expansion proposal was still undergoing environmental assessment. This angered environmentalists, who promptly took Parks Canada to court, arguing that the agency was required to assess the "cumulative effects" of the entire proposal before deciding whether to approve any particular part. SVC countersued, claiming that Parks Canada was required to approve the entire proposal, without environmental assessment, because the environment minister had previously given it "preliminary approval." In the end, after four years of court hearings, the Federal Court of Appeal ruled that Parks Canada was required to assess the "cumulative impacts" of the overall proposal, and a public review panel was appointed to do so. SVC subsequently abandoned its long-range development proposal, although an expansion in one area did proceed. See *Canadian Parks and Wilderness Society v. Banff National Park (Superintendent)* (1994), 84 FTR 273 (FCTD); aff'd. (1996), 202 NR 132 (FCA) (the *Sunshine* case).

The *Sunshine* case was the first legal challenge to excessive recreational development in a national park and may mark a turning point in the struggle between recreational "use" and ecological protection in Canada's national parks. Since *Sunshine*, there have been several more cases about recreational development in national parks. See, for example, *Young v. Canada (Attorney General)*, [1999] FCJ no. 1290 (FCTD) (where the court upheld Parks Canada's decision to end river rafting on the Maligne River in Jasper because of impacts on harlequin duck nesting areas) and *Bow Valley Naturalists Soc. v. Canada (Minister of Heritage)*, [2001] 2 FC 461 (FCA) (where an environmental assessment of a proposed Lake Louise convention centre was not required to consider cumulative impacts from secondary development).

2. Parks as Wilderness

For many people, national parks represent one of the few remaining opportunities to experience solitude in a pristine wilderness setting. For such persons, hiking or canoeing is more than just a recreational outing, it is an opportunity to experience Canada in a way that the settlers and their native predecessors experienced it. Such an experience can contribute not only to mental and physical well-being, but can promote an appreciation of one's cultural heritage. In 1944, following a wilderness canoe voyage, Pierre Trudeau wrote: "I know a man whose school could never teach him patriotism, but who acquired that virtue when he felt in his bones the vastness of his land, and the greatness of those who founded it."

The United States passed the world's first *Wilderness Act* (now 16 USC) in 1964. The Act sets out a powerful and eloquent definition of wilderness:

> A wilderness, in contrast with those areas where man and his own works dominate the landscape, is hereby recognized as an area where the earth and its community of life are untravelled by man, where man himself is a visitor who does not remain. An area of wilderness is further defined to mean ... land retaining its primeval character and influence, without permanent improvements or human habitation, which is protected and managed so as to preserve its natural conditions ... 16 USC § 1131(c).

Since the Act's passage, more than 5 percent of the US lands have been protected as wilderness.

Canada does not have a *Wilderness Act* per se. Some provinces have created ecological reserves and wilderness areas, but these account for less than 0.2 percent of Canada's lands. The 1988 amendments to the former NPA (now CNPA) introduced the first vestige of federal wilderness legislation in Canada, stating

> 14(1) The Governor in Council may, by regulation, declare any region of a park that exists in a natural state or is capable of returning to a natural state to be a wilderness area.
>
> (2) The Minister may not authorize any activity to be carried on in a wilderness area that is likely to impair the wilderness character of the area.

This provision has the potential to give substantial protection to wilderness. However, as of 2003, only 4 of 39 national parks have had regions of the park designated wilderness areas.

3. Zoning: The Solution?

The principal response to the overuse of parks has been zoning. Section 11(1) of the CNPA requires the preparation, after public consultation, of a management plan for each park. Management plans must address park zoning. There are five different zones:

1. *Special preservation* (no motorized access or man-made facilities permitted);
2. *Wilderness* (only primitive visitor facilities and no motorized access permitted);
3. *Natural environment* (limited facilities and motorized access permitted);
4. *Outdoor recreation* (recreational facilities and motorized access permitted); and
5. *Park services* (includes towns and visitor facilities).

The majority of national park area is either in zone 1 or 2. For instance, the Banff management plan designates 4 percent of the park as special preservation and 93 percent as wilderness (almost all of this area has been legally designated as wilderness under the CNPA).

Over 90 percent of park visitors never get more than one kilometre off the road system—venturing no further than well-maintained roadside trails or campgrounds. The object of zoning is to concentrate this majority of park users, particularly high-impact users, within fixed areas of parks (zones 3 to 5). These areas are, in effect, written off as wilderness areas. The remaining areas (zones 1 and 2) accommodate those interested in a wilderness experience. If properly implemented, zoning can be an effective method of accommodating the growing number of park visitors while maintaining the parks in a primarily natural state. However, the national parks zoning requirements suffer from one major flaw—they have no legal force. Although zoning is required by the CNPA, the five zoning designations are not defined in the Act or the regulations: they stem from policy. As a result, park administrators and wayward individuals cannot be compelled to adhere to the limitations set out for a zone.

For a stirring comment on commercialization and overuse of parks, see E. Abbey, "Polemic: Industrial Tourism and National Parks," in *Desert Solitaire: A Season in the Wilderness* (New York: McGraw-Hill, 1968).

4. Maintaining "Ecological Integrity" as the First Priority

In the early 1990s, there was growing concern about the declining health of Canada's national parks. The situation was most serious in Banff. A host of major development proposals and massive visitor increases were taking a toll on the fragile ecology of Canada's oldest park. Already one species had gone extinct, and the long-term survival of others (including grizzly bears) was at risk. In 1994, the federal government appointed the Banff-Bow Valley task force to come up with management recommendations to maintain and restore the park's ecological integrity. Following the report of the task force in 1996, it was realized that the types of pressures facing Banff were also increasing in many other parks. As a result, in 1998, Minister of Canadian Heritage Sheila Copps appointed a blue-ribbon panel on conserving ecological integrity in Canada's national parks.

The panel concluded that the parks are under significant threat from sources both inside and outside of parks. Its key findings included the following two points.

- Canada's national parks are under stress, in some cases extreme stress. These stresses are real and serious although they are not necessarily apparent or immediate. Nature's capacity to absorb injury is not infinite. ... Our parks are at a crossroad. If we continue on our current path, we risk losing for all time access to the experience of protected nature, the wilderness we so cherish.
- Parks Canada must ... ensure that protecting ecological integrity is the first priority of all aspects of national parks management.

As a result of the panel's report, the CNPA (then in bill form) was amended by adding a strong requirement to make ecological integrity the first priority in all aspects of park management.

These provisions of the new CNPA came into force in February 2001, and were the subject of a legal challenge shortly thereafter.

Canadian Parks and Wilderness Society v.
Minister of Canadian Heritage et al.
(2001), 212 FTR 1 (FCTD)

[The Canadian Parks and Wilderness Society (CPAWS) sought judicial review of a decision of the minister of Canadian heritage to approve the construction and operation of a winter road, some 118 kilometres in length, through Wood Buffalo National Park. The road, which would follow an abandoned road allowance from the 1960s, was being built to provide a faster north–south transportation route for Fort Smith and other communities outside the park. The park management plan stated, and Parks Canada acknowledged, that the road "was not required for park management purposes." Parks Canada also acknowledged that the proposed road would result in "the loss of vegetation along the right of way, some degree of potential or actual erosion of fragile sandy soils, the exposure of some wildlife in the Park to poaching and to mortality caused by vehicle collisions and increased risk of harm to sensitive karst landscape." An environmental assessment by Parks Canada concluded that the proposed road "would not be likely to cause significant adverse environmental impacts."]

GIBSON J: Wood Buffalo National Park is 44,807 sq. km in size, the largest national park in the country and one of the largest in the world. ... In 1983, the Park was designated a World Heritage Site by the United Nations ... .

[The court first addressed CPAWS's argument that approval of the road contravened ss. 8(2) and 4(1) of the CNPA, which read

> 4(1) The national parks of Canada are hereby dedicated to the people of Canada for their benefit, education and enjoyment, subject to this Act and the regulations, and the parks shall be maintained and made use of so as to leave them unimpaired for the enjoyment of future generations.

and

> 8(2) Maintenance or restoration of ecological integrity, through the protection of natural resources and natural processes, shall be the first priority of the Minister when considering all aspects of the management of parks.]

· · ·

I agree with counsel for the respondents that the record, when read in its totality, is consistent with the Minister and her delegates according first priority to ecological integrity in arriving at the decision under review. That the decision is clearly not consistent with treating ecological integrity as the Minister's sole priority is clear. However, that is not the test. I reiterate: subsection 4(1) of the new Act requires a delicate balancing of conflicting interests which include the benefit and enjoyment of those living in, and in close proximity to, Wood Buffalo National Park. This is particularly so when that Park is as remote from services and facilities as is in fact the case and as is likely to remain the case for some time. In the circumstances, while Wood Buffalo National Park, like other National Parks, is dedicated to the people of Canada as a whole, it is not unreasonable to give special consideration to the limited number of people of Canada who are by far most directly affected by management or development decisions affecting the Park. I am satisfied that it was reasonably open to the Minister and her delegates to conclude that the interest of those people overrode the first priority given to ecological integrity where impairment of such integrity can be minimized to a degree that the Minister concludes is consistent with the maintenance of the Park for the enjoyment of future generations.

· · ·

Subsection 8(2) of the Act does not require that ecological integrity be the "determinative factor" in a decision such as that under review. Rather, it simply requires that ecological integrity be the Minister's "first" priority and, as indicated immediately above, I am satisfied on the totality of the evidence before the Court that it was her first priority in reaching the decision here under review. I acknowledge that the record before me does not disclose that the Minister and her delegates used the phrase "ecological integrity" in their decision making process, or, in fact, in the decision that is under review itself. That reality does not lead inexorably to a conclusion that ecological integrity was not considered or was not given a first priority. I am satisfied on the record that it is clear that ecological integrity was taken into account by the Minister and her delegates.

[The court then addressed CPAWS' argument that it was unlawful for Parks Canada to issue a permit to allow clearing of the road allowance for "non-park management purposes."]

[T]he Minister and her delegates have acknowledged in a number of places throughout the evidence before me that the winter road at issue is not required for park management purposes. ...

[S]ubsection 12(1) of the *National Parks General Regulations* [provides]:

> 12(1) The superintendent may issue a permit to any person authorizing the person to remove, deface, damage or destroy any flora or natural objects in a Park *for purposes of Park management.* [emphasis added]

While the winter road at issue may not, itself, be required for park management purposes, once a decision, the decision here under review, to authorize its construction within the park is taken, I am satisfied that "park management purposes" are expanded by the decision itself to comprehend what is necessary to implement the decision to allow the winter road, with the implied ongoing right to use and duty to maintain.

[The court rejected CPAWS' application and upheld the minister's decision.]

NOTES AND QUESTIONS

1. Do you agree with Gibson J's reasoning that making ecological integrity the "first priority" (as the CNPA requires) does not mean making it the "determinative priority"? If so, what *does* making it "the first priority" mean?

2. Gibson J's decision is under appeal, and the road through Wood Buffalo Park has not yet been constructed (as of spring 2003). This is because a local native band, the Mikisew Cree First Nation, was successful in its challenge to Parks Canada's approval of the road.

Mikisew Cree First Nation v. Canada (Minister of Canadian Heritage)
(2001), 214 FTR 48 (FCTD)

[The Mikisew Cree First Nation ("Mikisew") has reserve lands both within and near Wood Buffalo National Park ("WBNP"). The Mikisew claims its members' treaty rights to hunt, trap, and carry out traditional activities within WBNP will be effected by the construction of the road. Those impacts include a ban on hunting and trapping in a 200-metre-wide corridor along the 118 kilometre road; loss of wildlife due to increased access, poaching, vehicle collisions, and destruction of habitat; loss of vegetation; and other ecological impacts. First Nations people have inhabited WBNP for thousands of years. Since 1949, specific regulations have authorized traditional hunting, trapping, and fishing within the park.]

HANSEN J: In approving the road, did the Minister fail to conduct herself in accordance with her fiduciary and constitutional duties to Mikisew in breach of subsection 35(1) of the *Constitution Act, 1982*?
Subsection 35(1) of the *Constitution Act, 1982* ... reads as follows:

> 35(1) The existing aboriginal and treaty rights of the aboriginal peoples of Canada are hereby recognized and affirmed.

. . .

The text of Treaty No. 8 ... explicitly grants the First Nations the right to continue hunting and trapping as they had always done, throughout the tract surrendered, subject to conservation and limited geographic restrictions.

. . .

The plain language of Treaty No. 8 reveals only two limitations on the right to hunt and trap. ... First, there was a geographic limitation. The right to hunt could be exercised "throughout the tract surrendered ... saving and excepting such tracts as may be required or taken up from time to time for settlement, mining, lumbering, trading or other purposes." Second, the right could be limited by government regulations passed for conservation purposes.
The Supreme Court of Canada decision in *Badger*, [1996] 2 CNLR 77, held that whether the land has been "taken up" is a question of fact to be determined on a case-by-case basis. It turns on a determination of whether the lands in question have been put to a *visible use* that is *incompatible* with the exercise of the specific treaty rights claimed.

. . .

Does Use as a National Park Constitute a "Visible and Incompatible" Use?

The Minister submits that national parks were established to protect the ecological integrity of a particular representative example of the Canadian landscape as well as to protect and preserve flora and fauna within that area. ...
The Minister concludes that treaty rights to hunt and trap within the borders of WBNP are incompatible with the purpose of the Park. The Minister feels that preservation of the Park's ecology and wildlife would be compromised if all Treaty No. 8 Indians were able to hunt and trap in the Park.

The applicant relies on the holdings of the Supreme Court of Canada in *Badger*, *supra*, and *R v. Sundown*, [1999] 1 SCR 393 for the proposition that the exercise of First Nations treaty rights is not incompatible with the creation of the Park. ...

The Court in *Sundown*, *supra*, at 414, established that "the creation of a park is not necessarily incompatible with the exercise of hunting rights unless, perhaps, the park operates as a wildlife sanctuary that prohibits all hunting." ...

The applicant submits that the purpose of WBNP cannot be incompatible with hunting. The applicant points to the *Wood Buffalo National Park Game Regulations*, SOR/78-830 which allow both natives and non-natives to hunt in the Park during open season as long as they have a permit.

. . .

In my view, the lands of WBNP have not been "taken up" in a manner that is incompatible with a regulated right to hunt and trap by Mikisew. ...

The Minister's appeals to "ecological integrity" in this context are without merit. That is not to say hunting and trapping could never be found to be incompatible with the use of land as a national park. WBNP is a unique park; it is a vast and isolated wilderness. The exercise of hunting and trapping rights by Mikisew has coexisted with the use of the land as a national park since its inception.

[The court concluded that the construction of the road would infringe the Mikisew Cree's treaty rights to hunt and trap in WBNP and that the infringement was not justified.]

NOTE

Some have claimed that this decision opens the door to unregulated aboriginal hunting and trapping in parks. Do you agree? Under what conditions could such a right be established? How should the balance be struck between aboriginal rights to hunt and trap and the conservation goals of parks? Would the result in the case be different if the federal government had discharged its aboriginal consultation obligations properly? See the discussion in chapters 2 and 11.

G. Threats to Parks

Overuse is not the only threat to the integrity of parks—far from it. The 11 percent of Canada's lands within conservation areas is subject to severe encroachments, both from within and without.

1. Internal Threats

a. National Parks

Section 4 of the CNPA dictates that national parks be maintained "unimpaired for the enjoyment of future generations." Despite these lofty words, some parks are anything but unimpaired.

One problem is pollution. Sewage from townsites and ski areas in Banff and Jasper parks has significantly degraded water quality in the once-pristine Bow and Athabasca rivers. Dump sites for waste from towns and visitor facilities within parks attract bears and scar the park landscape. A number of parks are bisected by highways, and roadkills (and railroad kills) are a significant threat to park wildlife. Park highways are also used by trucks carrying dangerous cargo. An accident could cause a spill of toxic substances within a park. There is one section in the CNPA directed at pollution problems:

> 32(1) Where any substance that is capable of degrading the natural environment ... is discharged or deposited within a park, any person who has charge or control of the substance shall take reasonable measures to prevent any degradation of the natural environment... .

Do you think this section sets a standard adequate to ensure that parks remain unimpaired? What are "reasonable measures"? Would it be more effective to regulate hazardous activities before the fact, rather than after a discharge has occurred? Would this section cover pollution emanating from outside park borders? Who has "charge or control" of the substance?

Another problem is resource extraction, including logging, mining, and oil drilling. Many parks are rich in natural resources. In the parks' early years, resource extraction was sanctioned as long as it did not interfere with tourism. In the 1920s, the federal government avoided many resource conflicts by simply removing resource-rich areas from parks.

Resource extraction is now illegal in national parks, and has been since 1930 (one exception is "traditional renewable resource harvesting" by aboriginal people, which the CNPA specifically authorizes in some parks (s. 17)). However, the prohibition against resource extraction has frequently been honoured in its breach.

Between the 1930s and 1950s, mining of silver, lead, and zinc continued in Glacier, Yoho, and Kootenay parks. During the same era, commercial logging was taking place in Prince Albert, Riding Mountain, Wood Buffalo, and the four Rocky Mountain parks. Wood Buffalo and Riding Mountain even had sawmills in the parks. In 1964, Parks Canada stopped issuing new logging and mining permits and, by 1969, had bought up most of the existing rights. Still, logging rights remain in Banff and Terra Nova and Wood Buffalo parks. For more information, see L. Bella, *Parks for Profit* (Montreal: Harvest House, 1987).

Over the years, these violations of parks legislation had provoked public outcry, but never litigation (which has been used frequently to protect national parks in the United States). One reason was that, until the *Finlay* decision in 1986, only persons whose private property or economic interests were affected had standing to bring a judicial review action (*Minister of Finance v. Finlay*, [1986] 2 SCR 607). This ruled out action over parks, which, by definition, were public property. The *Finlay* decision extended standing to public interest groups. In 1992, for the first time ever, a lawsuit was launched challenging development activity within a national park. The Sierra Legal Defence Fund went to court on behalf of the Canadian Parks and Wilderness Society to strike down a federal licence permitting logging in Wood Buffalo Park. Before trial, the federal government conceded that the licence was illegal, and the federal court issued a consent judgment declaring the licence and the implementing order in council "invalid and unauthorized by the provisions of the *National Parks Act*" (in particular, s. 4) (*Canadian Parks and Wilderness Society v. Superintendent of Wood Buffalo National Park* (1992), 34 ACWS (3d) 618 (FCTD)). Future cases will be needed to determine exactly what other development activities violate s. 4. Would construction of new paved highway through a park violate s. 4? A new golf course? Is cattle grazing in Grasslands Park unlawful?

b. Provincial Parks

Resource extraction poses a far greater threat in provincial protected areas. All told, provincial parks and wildlife areas account for over 50 percent of Canada's conservation lands. In most provinces, wildlife areas are legally open to resource extraction. Of even greater concern are provincial parks—areas that one might expect to be protected from resource extraction. Most provinces' parks legislation contains an overall purpose clause that is similar to the one found in the CNPA. Ontario's *Provincial Parks Act*, RSO 1990, c. P.34, reads:

> 2. All provincial parks are dedicated to the people of Ontario ... for their healthful enjoyment and education, and the provincial parks shall be maintained for the benefit of future generations in accordance with this Act and the regulations.

What is the main difference between this provision and the parallel one in s. 4 of the CNPA, above? Similar dedications can be found in parks legislation in New Brunswick (*Parks Act*, SNB 1982, c. P-2.1, s. 2) and Saskatchewan (*Parks Act*, SS 1986, c. P-1.1, s. 3(1)). Nova Scotia's legislation contains a weaker version (*Provincial Park Act*, RSNS 1989, c. 367, s. 2(2)), as does British Columbia's, in regard to certain class A parks (*Parks Act*, RSBC 1996, c. 344, s. 5(3)).

Despite this strong wording in the dedication section, most provinces' parks legislation does not prohibit logging, mining, or other forms of resource extraction. That is not to say that resource extraction is actively occurring in most provincial parks. In most provinces resource extraction is presently not allowed in parks as a matter of policy, but policies are not enforceable and can be changed or ignored without public notice. Moreover, resource extraction is actively occurring in a number of provincial parks. For instance, Ontario's Algonquin Park, one of the most popular parks in Canada, is being logged extensively, and logging is occurring in several of Manitoba's provincial parks. Several mines have operated in Strathcona Park—British Columbia's oldest park—for decades. And oil drilling is occurring in Alberta's Dinosaur Park, a UN World Heritage Site.

Quebec appears to be one of the few provinces that excludes resource extraction in all provincial parks (RSQ, c. P-9, s. 7). However, Quebec has placed very little land in provincial park status. Most of its protected lands are in wildlife areas, where resource extraction is allowed. Check the provincial parks legislation in your area. Does it allow resource extraction? In what parks is such extraction occurring?

2. External Threats

The greatest threat to parks comes from activities outside their borders. No park is a self-contained ecosystem. All have air and water that flow in and out, and species that range beyond park borders. What goes on outside a park cannot help but have effect inside a park. This is known as the "island effect," because the park becomes an island of protection amidst a sea of development.

Examples are not hard to find. Vast expanses of clearcut forest surround Pacific Rim National Park—right up to its border. In fact, all of BC's national parks, as well as the four Rocky Mountain parks are bordered by logging operations. Such logging is not only a visual eyesore, it can damage a park's ecology. Logging near parks can affect water quality and soils within neighbouring parks, and many park animals rely on forest habitat outside the park.

Logging next to parks also opens up road access to hunters. Virtually tame park animals become subject to hunting when they wander beyond park borders; they are easy marks for poachers who illegally wander within park borders. The areas in British Columbia and Alberta around the Rocky Mountain parks support numerous hunting outfitters.

Water and air pollution originating outside park borders frequently enter parks. Many of the lakes in Ontario's Killarney Provincial Park are dead due to acid rain caused by the nearby INCO plant in Sudbury. Municipalities, pulp mills, and other industries upstream of parks discharge toxic pollutants into waters that flow into park rivers and lakes (as is happening in Wood Buffalo Park). Dams and water diversions have significantly affected the aquatic ecosystems of Wood Buffalo and Grasslands parks.

If our parks are to remain unimpaired islands amidst an increasingly developed landscape, solutions to the external threats problem must be found. One future solution is to create parks large enough to contain relatively complete ecosystems. In the meantime, the most effective solution is for park managers to coordinate with private owners, environmental authorities, and government land managers in areas around parks. Thus far, efforts to do so have met with little success. Department managers and private land owners perceive little benefit to their interests from restricting development in their areas in order to protect nearby parks. This problem is further exacerbated in the case of national parks, because it is generally provincial authorities who are in charge of land management and pollution control around park borders. Thus, the problem becomes one not only of coordinating between departments, but between different governments, often from opposing political parties.

In the United States, this problem has been addressed, to some extent, by law. The federal *Clean Air Act* and *Clean Water Act* call for particularly stringent regulation of emissions in the vicinity of national parks and wilderness areas. (See 42 USCA, ss. 7470(2), 7472, 7473(b)(1), 7475(d)(2)(C), and 7491.) Also, the *Wilderness Act* has been interpreted to require preservation of adequate water flows in wilderness areas (*Sierra Club v. Block*, 622 F. Supp. 842 (Col. DC, 1985), vacated on different grounds 911 F. 2d 1405).

Unfortunately, such laws are virtually non-existent in Canada. The federal *Fisheries Act*, RSC 1985, c. F-14 and *Navigable Waters Protection Act*, RSC 1985, c. N-22, which regulate water quality and quantity, and the air quality regulations under CEPA, make no special provision for parks. However, there is a little-known provision protecting water quantity in western national parks. The *Natural Resources Transfer Act* of 1930 (20 & 21 Geo. 5, c. 26) specifies that the provinces of British Columbia, Alberta, and Saskatchewan will not, by works outside of the boundaries of the [national] parks, reduce the flow of water within any of the rivers or streams within the same to less than that which the Minister of the Interior deems necessary adequately to preserve the scenic beauties of the said parks.

This provision appears to have been ignored, at least in recent decades.

3. The Public Trust Doctrine

Another legal approach, which has been used in the United States to address external threats to parks, is the public trust doctrine. The origins of the public trust doctrine lie in Roman and, later, English common law. The public had a right of access to all navigable waters for purposes such as fishing and navigation, and the sovereign had a duty to manage all navigable waters so as to uphold this right (*Gann v. Free Fishers of Whitstable* (1865), 11 HL Cas. 192). The Canadian courts have adopted this common law duty, but have neither expanded its scope nor explicitly labelled it as a trust obligation *(Rhodes v. Perusse* (1909), 41 SCR 264). US courts have done both.

In 1892, the US Supreme Court clearly stated that the government's duty to preserve public access to waters was a trust duty. In so doing, the court struck down the Illinois legislature's attempt to convey a large area of submerged land along the shore of Lake Michigan to a private railway (*Illinois Central Railway Co. v. Illinois*, 146 US 387 (1892)). Subsequent US courts have gone even further and have extended the public trust obligation to apply to public lands, particularly parks. For instance, in 1966, the Massachusetts Supreme Court declared unlawful a statute purporting to authorize construction of a private ski resort in a state park (*Gould v. Greylock*, 215 NE 2d 114 (1966)).

The US public trust doctrine is not an outright prohibition against government alienation of interests in public lands and waters. To do so, in effect, would be to give to the courts the policy-making role of elected legislatures. Rather, the doctrine has evolved to mean:

> When a state holds a resource which is available for the free use of the general public, a court will look with considerable skepticism upon any government conduct which is calculated either to reallocate that resource to more restricted uses or to subject public uses to the self interest of private parties.

See J. Sax, "The Public Trust Doctrine in Natural Resources Law" (1970) vol. 68 *Michigan Law Review* 471, at 484.

The public trust concept has been explicitly incorporated by statute in a number of US states. For a list, see J. Dimento, "Citizen Environmental Legislation in the States: An Overview" (1976) *Journal of Urban Law* 413. Several Canadian jurisdictions have passed or proposed legislation adopting the public trust concept (see chapter 11). For a more detailed treatment of the public trust doctrine in Canada and the United States, see J. Sax, "The Public Trust Doctrine in Natural Resources Law," above, C. Hunt, "The Public Trust Doctrine in Canada," in J. Swaigen, ed., *Environmental Rights in Canada* (Toronto: Butterworths and CELRF, 1981), and J. Maguire, "Fashioning an Equitable Vision for Public Resource Protection in Canada" (1997) vol. 7 *Journal of Environmental Law and Practice* 1.

The common law public trust doctrine has provided the intellectual roots for US courts to find a statutory public trust obligation flowing from parks legislation. The leading precedent for applying a public trust obligation to lands in and around national parks comes from the *Redwood Park* litigation.

Sierra Club v. Department of Interior
376 F. Supp. 90 (US Dist. Ct. 1974)

[Redwood National Park was created in 1968. The park sheltered some of the last remaining stands of California's magnificent 100-metre-high redwood trees—some of which had been growing for nearly 2000 years. Logging on the steep-sloped lands (both private and federal) surrounding the Park was seriously affecting soil stability and water quality within the park. The Sierra Club filed an action alleging that the secretary of the interior was violating his statutory trust obligation by failing to take action to protect the park's ecological resources.]

SWEIGERT District Judge: The *National Park System Act*, 16 USCA Sec. 1, provides for the creation of the National Park Service in the Department of the Interior which Service shall:

> promote and regulate the use of Federal areas known as national parks, ... by such means and measures as conform to the fundamental purpose of said parks, ... which purpose is to conserve the scenery and the natural and historic objects and the wildlife therein and to provide for the enjoyment of the same in such manner and by such means as will leave them *unimpaired for the enjoyment of future generations*. [Emphasis added.]

In addition to these general *fiduciary obligations* [emphasis added] of the Secretary of the Interior, the Secretary has been invested with certain specific powers and obligations in connection with the unique situation of the Redwood National Park.

The Redwood National Park was created on October 2, 1968 by the *Redwood National Park Act*, 16 USCA Secs. 79a-79j, "to preserve significant examples of the primeval coastal redwood (Sequoia sempervirens) forests and the streams and seashores with which they are associated for purposes of public inspiration, enjoyment, and scientific study."

Congress limited the park to an area of 58,000 acres ... and conferred upon the Secretary specific powers expressly designed to prevent damage to the park by logging on peripheral areas.

Title 16 USCA Sec. 79c(e) provides:

> In order to afford as full protection as is reasonably possible to the timber, soil, and streams within the boundaries of the park, the Secretary is authorized ... to acquire interests in land from, and to enter into contracts and cooperative agreements with, the owners of land on the periphery of the park and on watersheds tributary to streams within the park designed to assure that the consequences of forestry management, timbering, land use, and soil conservation practices conducted there-on, or of the lack of such practices, will not adversely affect the timber, soil, and streams within the park as aforesaid.

. . .

In *Rockbridge v. Lincoln*, 449 F. 2d 567 (9th Cir. 1971) our Circuit ... held that, in view of the trust relationship of the Secretary toward the Indians ... such discretion as was vested in the Secretary was not an unbridled discretion ... and, therefore, a cause for judicial relief under the *Administrative Procedure Act* was stated.

In view of the analogous trust responsibility of the Secretary of the Interior with respect to public lands as stated in *Knight v. United Land*, ... and the analogous legislative history indicating a specific set of objectives which the provisions of the *Redwood National Park Act* were designed to accomplish, we consider *Rockbridge, supra*, to be strongly persuasive to the point that a case for judicial relief has been made out by plaintiff.

We are of the opinion that the terms of the statute, especially § 79c(e), ... impose a legal duty on the Secretary to utilize the specific powers given to him whenever reasonably necessary for the protection of the park and that any discretion vested in the Secretary concerning time, place and specifics of the exercise of such powers is subordinate to his paramount legal duty imposed, not only under his *trust obligation* [emphasis added] but by the statute itself, to protect the park.

[The defendants' motion to dismiss was denied.]

NOTES AND QUESTIONS

1. In a second decision, the court determined that the secretary had violated his statutory and public trust obligations (*Sierra Club v. Department of Interior*, 398 F. Supp. 284 (US Dist. Ct. 1975)). The secretary had entered into cooperative agreements with several logging companies, as contemplated by the *Redwood National Park Act*, but the court found that the agreements were "so general and so full of qualifications as to render them practically meaningless and unenforceable" and were "inadequate to prevent or reasonably minimize damage to the resources of the Park resulting from timber harvesting operations." The court ordered the secretary to come up with a plan of action by a certain date, at which time the court would judge its adequacy. Does this remedy strike an adequate balance between the court's duty to review the legality of agency action and its duty not to take over the role of government?

2. In the third Redwoods case, after reviewing the department's proposal, the court held that it had met its statutory duties (*Sierra Club v. Dep't of Interior*, 424 F. Supp. 172 (1976)). Shortly after the case, Congress expanded Redwoods Park by purchasing the lands in dispute.

In Canada, the issue whether a public trust obligation exists over lands in and around a park has been explicitly addressed in only one case.

Green v. The Queen in Right of the Province of Ontario et al.
(1973), 2 OR 396 (HC)

LERNER J: From the statement of claim it appears that the plaintiff, Larry Green, is ... a researcher in the employ of "Pollution Probe" at the University of Toronto ... . Lake

Ontario Cement Limited ... entered into a written lease on January 12, 1968, with the Province of Ontario for a parcel of land containing 16.02 acres and forming part of the sand banks and some lands under the waters of West Lake in the Township of Hallowell, Prince Edward County. Pursuant to the lease, Lake Ontario Cement ... have the right to excavate sand ... for 75 years. ...

Some two years and three months later, pursuant to the authority of the *Provincial Parks Act*, the Province of Ontario established the "Sandbanks Provincial Park" as a provincial park within the meaning of said Act consisting of 1,802 acres, more or less, of land which coincidentally is adjacent to and adjoining the 16.02 acres *previously* leased to Lake Ontario Cement ... . The 16.02 acres have never been nor are they now, part of the said park lands so dedicated.

The statement of claim at para. 5 sets out s. 2 of the *Provincial Parks Act* which states:

> 2. All provincial parks are dedicated to the people of the Province of Ontario and others who may use them for their healthful enjoyment and education, and the provincial parks shall be maintained for the benefit of future generations in accordance with this Act and the regulations.

and on the basis of s. 2 alleges that it imposes a trust upon the Province of Ontario with regard to Sandbanks Provincial Park, to maintain that park in keeping with the "spirit" of s. 2 and that by permitting the use of the adjoining lands which the Province of Ontario had legally conveyed by leasehold to the other defendant were in breach of the trust implicit in s. 2 set out above.

· · ·

The plaintiff, in fact, is seeking a declaration of breach of a statutory trust which is not open to him unless he has a special interest above that of the general public ... .

It was also admitted by counsel for the plaintiff that but for the existence of s. 2 of the *Provincial Parks Act* there would be no basis for bringing the action. Notwithstanding the philosophical and noble intentions (my expression) of the Legislature to express in the pertinent section an ideological concept, no statutory trust has been created. It becomes necessary to break down the wording thereof: "All provincial parks are dedicated to the people of the Province of Ontario and others who may use them ... ." This simply makes it clear that all persons (and I presume that includes those lawfully in Canada) are entitled to make use of the parks without the inhibitions or restrictions of race, religion, creed or other prejudicial implications inimical to the welfare of society and particularly the people of Ontario. "... [A]nd the provincial parks shall be maintained for the benefit of future generations in accordance with this Act and the regulations" implies that the Province of Ontario is required to physically maintain the parks so dedicated. This view is confirmed and amplified by the provisions of s. 3(1) and all the subsections of s. 19 covering such things as the issuing of permits, the fees for the right to enter and use the parks, which are so complete as to make the power of the Province in the whole concept of park lands, absolute.

A reading of s. 2 together with s. 3(2) makes it clear that the subject-matter of the trust is not certain. Section 3(2) empowers the Province to increase, decrease or even put an end to or "close down" any park. There cannot be a trust as is alleged by the plaintiff herein unless the subject-matter of the trust is of certainty.

[T]he learned authority, Keeton in *Law of Trusts*, 9th ed. (1968), p. 5, [states]:

> All that can be said of a trust, therefore, is that it is the relationship which arises wherever a person called the trustee is *compelled* in Equity to hold property ... for the benefit of some persons ... in such a way that the real benefit of the property accrues, not to the trustee, but to the beneficiaries or other objects of the trust.

This statement when considered in the light of s. 3(2) and when coupled with s. 2 should make it clear that the Province of Ontario cannot be held to be a trustee. Section 3(2) cannot be construed as *compelling* the Province to hold these lands or for that matter any park lands, for any certain period of time or forever for the purposes that are alleged by the respondent to be read in to s. 2 of the *Provincial Parks Act*.

...

The action therefore as framed for breach of trust discloses no reasonable cause of action.

No one can be critical of resort to the Courts to remedy social wrongs or injustices by way of interpretation of law, either statutory or by precedent. This is desirable in our rapidly changing society and preferable to the lawless or anarchical way of seeking rectification of real as well as unreal injustices, inequities and abuses as practised in other jurisdictions. Nevertheless, if resort to the Courts is to be had, care must be taken that such steps are from a sound base in law otherwise ill-founded actions for the sake of using the Courts as a vehicle for expounding philosophy are to be discouraged.

Having first concluded that the plaintiff has no status to maintain this action and that the statement of claim discloses no reasonable cause of action, on reflection, I do not think it improper for me to find also that the action is vexatious and frivolous. I say this because the plaintiff had to know of the existence and terms of the lease and that it pre-dated by a substantial period of time, the establishment of Sandbanks Provincial Park.

[The action against all defendants was dismissed with costs]

NOTES AND QUESTIONS

1. The part of the judgment dealing with the public trust was *obiter* since the action was dismissed due to lack of standing. Would the case be dismissed due to lack of standing today?

2. The judge applies strict trust law to reach his finding (which the US court in *Sierra Club* did not do). He then accuses the plaintiffs of bringing an "ill-founded action for the sake of using the Courts as a vehicle for expounding philosophy." Compare the two judgments. Do differences in the facts or legislation explain the widely different decisions? If not, what does?

3. The judge's main reason for rejecting a trust duty was that, under the Ontario Act, Cabinet had the power to decrease the size of a park by order. In contrast, the CNPA requires an Act of Parliament to reduce the size of a park. Does this mean a trust duty exists under the CNPA?

4. Shortly after the *Green* decision, the province announced that it would expropriate Lake Ontario Cement's lease, although it claimed that the litigation played no role in its decision.

5. Note that in the *Redwoods* case the public trust obligation was supported, by analogy, by the trust obligation toward natives. In Canada, the courts have also found a "fiduciary duty" toward aboriginal people (*Guerin v. R* (1984), 13 DLR (4th) 321 (SCC)). Compare s. 8(1) of the *Indian Act* with s. 4(1) of the CNPA.

6. A recent case in British Columbia considered the issue of the Crown's jurisdiction to regulate activity *outside* the boundaries of a park. A tourist operator set up a float camp just outside Gwaii Haanas National Park in British Columbia. Parks Canada determined that the camp interfered with the wilderness experience within the park, and was inconsistent with plans to make the adjacent aquatic area a marine park. Parks Canada refused to issue the operator a "quota" to use the park for its kayaking and diving tours. The operator went to court, challenging Parks Canada's authority to make decisions based on activities occurring outside a park. The federal court, in *Moresby Explorers Ltd. v. The Attorney General of Canada* [2001] FCT 780, agreed with the operator, reasoning (at paras. 107-8):

> There is no principle of administrative law which allows a decision maker to claim authority over areas where it has none ... . If such considerations entered into the denial of quota for activities associated with the float camp, they would be extraneous considerations and would result in the decision being set aside. ...
>
> None of this detracts from the fact that there are legitimate conservation and ecological issues arising from unregulated float camp operation in remote areas which abut onto park lands. The mandate conferred on the Minister and the Superintendent to preserve the ecological integrity of the park lands gives them a legitimate interest in the conduct of operations in areas which impact on the park lands. But a legitimate interest is not the same as a right to prohibit that which is otherwise lawful in an area outside the park's jurisdiction by means of conditions attached to a park business licence. ... In my view, the mandate conferred by the *National Parks Act* does not extend to regulating behaviour outside park boundaries through the device of business licences on the ground of conservation.

The judge does not explain *why* the CNPA does not authorize Parks Canada to address activity outside a park that are detrimental to the park. Do you agree with the decision? Why/why not?

7. For an excellent overview of the issues surrounding Canada's parks, see M. Hummel, ed., *Endangered Spaces: The Future for Canada's Wilderness* (Toronto: Key Porter Books, 1989) and M. Hummel, ed., *Protecting Canada's Endangered Spaces* (Toronto: Key Porter Books, 1995).

II. ENDANGERED SPECIES

To keep every cog and wheel is the first precaution of intelligent tinkering.

Aldo Leopold, *A Sand County Almanac* (1949)

A. Defining the Problem

1. The Extent of the Problem

Species extinction has been a natural fact of life on earth for billions of years. Over 90 percent of the species that have inhabited the earth at one time are now extinct. Thus, extinction per se is not a problem. What is a problem is the alarming rate of extinction that has arisen in recent decades.

Although no one knows for certain, scientists estimate that, before the last few millennia, an average of 2 to 3 species of plants and animals went extinct every year worldwide. Natural processes were able to replace these species, and then some. Currently, conservative estimates are that we are losing 2 to 3 species *per day* worldwide, but the rate may be more like 2 to 3 species *per hour*. It is simply impossible to know for sure, since only 1.4 million out of an estimated 30 million species have been discovered.

Canada, because of its northern latitude, has fewer species than tropical countries. Having fewer species means that the loss of a small number of species will have more drastic effects on Canada's ecosystems than it would on more diverse, tropical ecosystems. In Canada, there are currently 240 plant and animal species officially listed as endangered or threatened (by comparison, the United States lists over 1,250). These include well-known species such as the beluga whale and wood bison, and lesser-known ones such as Furbish's lousewort. Even these alarming numbers vastly understate the problem. Lack of firm data means that many species suspected of being endangered have not yet been listed. Moreover, we may be driving countless species that we have not yet discovered to extinction. For instance, since 1991, University of Victoria scientists have discovered dozens of "new" species from a research platform in a single tree in Vancouver Island's Carmanah Valley.

One thing that all scientists can agree on is that the rate of extinction is rising rapidly. Today's endangered species are a prophecy of wide-scale extinctions in the future if current practices are not reversed soon.

2. Why Save Species?

There are many reasons for saving species, some anthropocentric, some ecocentric.

Ecosystem benefits. Wild plants and animals play an important role in maintaining the planet's ecological functions. Plants clean the air and preserve the carbon balance. Micro-organisms break down pollutants in water and on land, and renourish the soil. In short, all life is a complex, interrelated web. Humans are dependent upon other species for our survival. Just how many strands of the web we can cut before the web starts to collapse we do not know.

Food. Species of plants and animals make up virtually all the food we eat. We use less than 4 percent of known plant species for food. If we are to produce enough food to meet the needs of our rapidly growing population, we will need to explore the potential of many more species. Moreover, in parts of many countries around the world, including Canada, wild plants and animals still provide a major food source for native people.

Medicinal uses. Nearly half of the medicine prescribed in North America comes from natural species. Yet only a small percentage of the earth's species have been screened to determine their medicinal value. For instance, BC's Pacific Yew tree, long regarded as a weed and cut indiscriminately, has recently been found to contain taxol, which has become one of the most important drugs in fighting cancer.

Recreational and aesthetic benefits. Wildlife viewing is very popular—over 60 percent of Canadians enjoy it. In fact, bird watching is now the world's most popular hobby. Wildlife plays an important role in our national identity as Canadians. Wild animals adorn our currency, our artwork, even our flags. Wild species provide a sense of fascination, and awe, reminding us of our "wild" roots.

Economic benefits. Protecting species makes good sense ecologically, and economically. In 1991, Canadians spent an estimated $8.3 billion on wildlife-related activities, generating over $4 billion in tax revenue and over 200,000 jobs.

Ethical reasons. Many people believe that all species have an inherent right to exist. They find it arrogant for human beings, who have occupied the planet for only a tiny fraction of its history, to wipe out many other species simply to meet our own insatiable needs. This ethic has been best expressed by Aldo Leopold, *A Sand County Almanac* (1949), at 238-39 and 261:

> The first ethics dealt with the relation between individuals; the Mosaic decalogue is an example. Later accretions dealt with the relations between the individual and society. The Golden Rule tries to integrate the individual into society; democracy to integrate social organization to the individual.
>
> There is no ethic yet dealing with man's relation to land and the plants and animals which grow upon it. Land, like Odysseus's slave-girls, is still property. The land relation is still strictly economic, entailing privileges but not obligations. The extension of ethics to this third element in human environment is, if I read the evidence correctly, an evolutionary possibility and an ecological necessity. It is the third step in a sequence. ...
>
> All ethics so far evolved rest upon a single premise: that the individual is a member of a community of interdependent parts. ... The land ethic simply enlarges the boundaries of the community to include soils, waters, plants and animals, or collectively, the land. ...

For a more detailed discussion, see H. Doremus, "Patching the Ark: Improving Legal Protection of Biological Diversity" (1991) vol. 18 *Ecology Law Quarterly* 265. See also chapters 1 and 16.

3. Threats to Species

Human interference is the cause of most extinctions. The current rate of extinction is at least 1,000 times higher than the natural rate. The explosion of human population in recent decades has pushed human settlements into most corners of the planet, displacing many other resident species. Our increasing demand for resources has further accelerated the problem. Human consumption now captures over 40 percent of the Earth's "net primary productivity" (living matter produced by the sun's photosynthetic energy)—the basis of life on earth.

Habitat loss. The single most important cause of species extinction is destruction of habitat. Most species cannot exist outside their natural habitat. Over 80 percent of species decline in Canada can be traced to habitat loss. Seventy-five percent of Canada's original prairie has been paved over or plowed, including 99 percent of tall grass prairie. Southern Ontario, the most densely populated region in Canada, has lost more than 90 percent of its original Carolinian forests and wetlands, giving it the nation's highest concentration of endangered species. Coastal British Columbia is the most biologically diverse region in Canada, yet wide-spread clearcutting of its old growth forests is endangering the survival of species such as the spotted owl, northern goshawk, marbled murrelet, and grizzly bear.

Direct human exploitation. Hunting and harvesting of species is another major cause of extinction. Many species, such as the passenger pigeon, which once numbered in the billions and could blacken the sky for days, have been hunted to extinction. Many of the world's endangered species, including elephants and rhinoceros, are being hunted (legally and illegally). In Canada, some threatened species, such as the grizzly bear, are still open to hunting, and others are subject to poaching.

Pollution. Pollution of the air and water threatens numerous species. The poisoning of the Great Lakes and acidification of countless lakes in eastern Canada has reduced stocks of fish and other organisms. Pollution of rivers and coastal areas is placing increased stress on aquatic species. For example, beluga whales inhabiting the mouth of the St. Lawrence River absorb so much toxic pollution that when they die and wash up on shore, they often must be disposed of as hazardous waste. Another threat is climate change, which is predicted to significantly alter the planet's natural regions, resulting in substantial displacement of species. It already has caused a thickening of the ice sheet covering Canada's Arctic islands, resulting in the near extinction of the peary caribou.

This is not to say that all human-induced change must stop. To live, like all species, humans must affect other organisms. Species can tolerate some change, and most can adapt, given enough time. What must stop is the rate and extent of human intervention.

For further discussion, see C. Rankin and M. M'Gonigle, "Legislation for Biological Diversity: A Review and Proposal for British Columbia" (1991) vol. 25 *UBC Law Review* 277.

4. Endangered Species Legislation

Near the turn of the century, Canadian governments took measures to help save the beaver from excessive trapping and to protect the habitat of the rapidly disappearing bison. The signing of the Migratory Birds Convention, [1916] CTS 465 with the United States in 1916 was designed to protect migratory birds from overhunting and other threats. These isolated efforts have typified the approach to species protection for most of the past century. It was not until the 1970s that North American governments began to pass legislation to directly address the problem of overall species extinction.

B. US Legislation

The United States was the first country to pass legislation protecting endangered species. The *Endangered Species Act* (ESA) was passed in 1966 and was significantly strengthened in 1973 [16 USC § 1531 et seq.]. The current Act has three main steps:

1. listing of all endangered and threatened species;
2. designation and protection of critical habitat for all listed species; and
3. prohibition against "takings" of any listed species.

These three key requirements form the backbone of the Act; however, there are at least two other important provisions: the US Fish and Wildlife Service must develop a recovery plan for each listed species, and all federal agencies must "insure that actions authorized, funded or carried out by them do not jeopardize the continued existence of an endangered species."

One major strength of the US legislation is that its mandatory wording allows citizens to go to court, if necessary, to compel agencies to carry out their species protection duties. The importance of these citizen enforcement powers was demonstrated in the *Spotted Owl* litigation, which dealt with the Act's first two steps, listing and critical habitat designation.

Northern Spotted Owl (Strix Occidentals Caurina) et al. v. Hodel
716 F. Supp. 479 (US Dist. Ct. 1988)

ZILLY District Judge: A number of environmental organizations bring this action against the United States Fish & Wildlife Service ("Service") and others, alleging that the Service's decision not to list the northern spotted owl as endangered or threatened under the *Endangered Species Act* of 1973, 16 USC § 1531 et seq. ("ESA" or "the Act"), was arbitrary and capricious or contrary to law.

Since the 1970s the northern spotted owl has received much scientific attention, beginning with comprehensive studies of its natural history by Dr. Eric Forsman, whose most significant discovery was the close association between spotted owls and old-growth forests. This discovery raised concerns because the majority of remaining old-growth owl habitat is on public land available for harvest ... .

In 1987, 29 conservation organizations filed a ... petition to list the owl as endangered both in the Olympic Peninsula in Washington and in the Oregon Coast Range, and as threatened throughout the rest of its range.

In July 1987, the Service announced that it would initiate a status review of the spotted owl and requested public comment. The Service assembled a group of Service biologists, including Dr. Mark Shaffer, its staff expert on population viability, to conduct the review. The Service charged Dr. Shaffer with analyzing current scientific information on the owl. Dr. Shaffer concluded that:

the most reasonable interpretation of current data and knowledge indicate continued old growth harvesting is likely to lead to the extinction of the subspecies in the foreseeable future which argues strongly for listing the subspecies as threatened or endangered at this time.

The Service invited a peer review of Dr. Shaffer's analysis by a number of US experts on population viability, all of whom agreed with Dr. Shaffer's prognosis for the owl, although each had some criticisms of his work.

The Status Review was completed on December 14, 1987, and on December 17 the Service announced that listing the owl as endangered under the Act was not warranted at that time. This suit followed.

. . .

The Service's documents ... lack any expert analysis supporting its conclusion. Rather, the expert opinion is entirely to the contrary.

The Court will reject conclusory assertions of agency "expertise" where the agency spurns unrebutted expert opinions without offering a credible alternative explanation. Here, the Service disregarded all the expert opinion on population viability, including that of its own expert, that the owl is facing extinction, and instead merely asserted its expertise in support of its conclusions.

Accordingly, the United States Fish and Wildlife Service's decision not to list at this time the northern spotted owl endangered or threatened under the *Endangered Species Act* was arbitrary and capricious and contrary to law.

In June 1990—19 months after the court's decision—the Fish and Wildlife Service listed the spotted owl as a "threatened" species. However, the owl was not out of the woods yet. A second case focused on the failure of the service to designate the owl's critical habitat.

Northern Spotted Owl v. Lujan
758 F. Supp. 621 (US Dist. Ct. 1991)

ZILLY District Judge: Plaintiffs move this Court to order the federal defendants to designate "critical habitat" for the northern spotted owl. As defined under the ESA, "critical habitat" refers to geographic areas which are essential to the conservation of the spotted owl and which may require special management considerations or protection. 16 USC § 1532(5)(A)(i). ... The Secretary must consult with other federal agencies to ensure that governmental actions do not "result in the destruction or adverse modification" of land designated as critical habitat. 16 USC § 1536(a)(2).

. . .

The Secretary, through the Service, claims that critical habitat for the spotted owl was not "determinable" when, in June 1989, the Service proposed to list the owl as threatened or when it issued its final rule one year later. The federal defendants contend that, under these circumstances, they are entitled to a twelve-month extension of time pursuant to 16 USC § 1533(b)(6)(C).

The language employed in Section 4(a)(3) and its place in the overall statutory scheme evidence a clear design by Congress that designation of critical habitat coincide with the species listing determination. The linkage of these issues was not the product of chance; rather, it reflects the studied and deliberate judgment of Congress that destruction of habitat was the most significant cause of species endangerment.

. . .

This Court rejects as incongruous the federal defendants' argument that Section 4(b)(6)(C) authorizes an automatic extension of time merely upon a finding that critical habitat is not presently "determinable," even where no effort has been made to secure the information necessary to make the designation. To relieve the Secretary of any affirmative information gathering responsibilities would effectively nullify Congress' charge that the species listing and habitat designation occur concurrently, "to the maximum extent ... determinable." 16 USC § 1533(a)(3).

Indeed, the Service candidly acknowledged in its June 1989 proposed rule that it had not conducted the analyses required by Section 4(b)(2).

More is required under the ESA and the Service's own regulations than the mere conclusion that more work needs to be done.

. . .

The Service's actions in June 1990 merit special mention. In its final rule the Service stated that the northern spotted owl is "overwhelmingly associated" with mature and old-growth forests. The Service further stated that, at present rates of timber harvesting, much of the remaining spotted owl habitat will be gone within 20 to 30 years. Despite such dire assessments, the Service declined to designate critical habitat in its final rule, citing the same reasons it gave one year earlier. Whatever the precise contours of the Service's obligations under the ESA, clearly the law does not approve such conduct.

[The court ordered the service to publish its proposed critical habitat plan within 90 days and to designate critical habitat as soon as possible thereafter.]

NOTES AND QUESTIONS

1. The lead plaintiff in each case is the spotted owl itself. This is not because owls, or trees, have standing under US law. US courts have developed a principle of "standing for one means standing for all" to avoid frivolous challenges to the standing of some plaintiffs where at least one plaintiff clearly has standing. This principle allowed the spotted owl to be listed as the lead plaintiff, followed by other plaintiffs with standing.

2. The first decision involved a citizen petition to list the owl as endangered. Under the US *Endangered Species Act*, an agency must respond within a fixed time. Why do you think that this provision is in the Act? Is there a similar requirement in Canada's *Species At Risk Act*, SC 2002, c. 29 (SARA), discussed below?

3. The second decision focused on the requirement to designate critical habitat within one year of listing. Is there a similar requirement in Canada's SARA? Would this case have been successful under SARA? The *Spotted Owl* cases clearly illustrate the valuable role courts can play when an agency, for political reasons, is reluctant to carry out its legislative mandate.

4. The *Spotted Owl* cases involved the first two steps under the US *Endangered Species Act*. The third step is the prohibition against "taking" an endangered species. In 1979, the US federal court ruled that significant habitat destruction constitutes "taking" (*Palila et al. v. Hawaii Department of Land and Natural Resources*, 471 F. Supp. 985 (US Dist. Ct. 1979); aff'd. 639 F. 2d 495 (9th Cir. 1981)). In that case, the state of Hawaii challenged the constitutional jurisdiction of a federal statute (the ESA) to dictate the management of state lands. The court determined that protection of endangered

species was a matter of sufficient "national concern" to invoke the federal commerce power, and that the federal treaty-making power also supported the Act, including its application to state and private lands. Would the result have been the same under Canada's constitution?

5. The prohibition on "taking" became quite controversial in the late 1980s when it resulted in regulation of logging of old growth forests on private and state lands in Washington and Oregon, which were home to the spotted owl. A lawsuit by a coalition of timber-dependent communities challenged the validity of the regulation defining "take," arguing that the term should only cover direct physical injury to animals, not habitat destruction. The Federal Court of Appeal, by a 2-1 vote, accepted the plaintiffs' argument. This decision was appealed to the US Supreme Court.

Babbitt v. Sweet Home Chapter of Communities for a Great Oregon
115 S. Ct. 2407 (1995)

STEVENS J: Section 9 of the *Endangered Species Act* makes it unlawful for any person to "take" any endangered or threatened species. ... Section 3(19) defines the statutory term "take" [as meaning] "to harass, *harm*, pursue, hunt, shoot, wound, kill, trap, capture, or collect."

The ... regulations that implement the statute define the statutory term "harm":

> *Harm* in the definition of "take" in the Act means an act which actually kills or injures wildlife. Such act may include *significant habitat modification or degradation* where it actually kills or injures wildlife by significantly impairing essential behavioural patterns, including breeding, feeding, or sheltering. 50 CFR ss 17.3 (1994).

Respondents [assert] that Congress did not intend the word "take" in s. 9 to include habitat modification, as the Secretary's "harm" regulation provides.

The text of the Act provides three reasons for concluding that the Secretary's interpretation [of "harm" to include "significant habitat modification"] is reasonable. First, an ordinary understanding of the word "harm" supports it. The dictionary definition of the verb form of "harm" is "to cause hurt or damage to: injure." Webster's Third New International Dictionary 1034. In the context of the ESA, that definition naturally encompasses habitat modification that results in actual injury or death to members of an endangered or threatened species.

Second, the broad purposes of the ESA support the Secretary's decision to extend protection against activities that cause the precise harms Congress enacted the statute to avoid. ... As stated in s. 2 of the Act, among its central purposes is "to provide a means whereby the ecosystems upon which endangered species and threatened species depend may be conserved ... ."

[T]he Secretary reasonably construed the intent of Congress when he defined "harm" to include "significant habitat modification or degradation that actually kills or injures wildlife."

[The dissenting judges found, among other things, that destruction of a species' habitat merely impaired its ability to reproduce, but did not cause actual "harm" (beyond causing "psychic harm"). O'Connor J, in a separate opinion, challenged this finding, writing: "One need not subscribe to theories of 'psychic harm' to recognize that to make it impossible for an animal to reproduce is to impair its most essential physical functions and to render that animal, and its genetic material, biologically obsolete. This, in my view, is actual harm."]

NOTES AND QUESTIONS

1. Critics of the US ESA argued that the law was too ironclad in its blanket prohibition of any project that harmed an endangered species, regardless of the project's benefits. The problem was highlighted in 1978, when the US Supreme Court blocked construction of the Tellico Dam in Tennessee because of the discovery that it would destroy the habitat of a tiny, endangered fish, the snail darter (*TVA v. Hill*, 437 US 153 (6th Cir. 1978)). Over $100 million had been spent on the dam at that point. As a result of the controversy, a limited exemption procedure was inserted into the Act. A seven-member committee of cabinet ministers and senior officials (known as the "God Committee"), after holding hearings, may grant an exemption for a project if five of its seven members find that (1) there are no feasible and prudent alternatives to the project, (2) the benefits of the project clearly outweigh the benefits of alternative courses of action that would conserve the species or its critical habitat, and (3) the action is in the public interest (16 USC § 1536(h)(1)).

The committee has been convened only on three occasions. In its first decision, the committee denied an exemption for the Tellico Dam (although the project was later exempted by legislation). More recently, the committee decided to allow logging in 40 percent of spotted owl critical habitat.

2. For further information, see K.A. Kohm, ed., *Balancing on the Brink of Extinction: The Endangered Species Act and Lessons for the Future* (Washington, DC: Island Press, 1991); Oliver A. Houck, "The Endangered Species Act and its Implementation by the US Departments of Interior and Commerce" (1993) vol. 64 *University of Colorado Law Review* 277; K.A. Yagerman, "Protecting Critical Habitat under the Federal Endangered Species Act" (1991) vol. 20 *Environmental Law* 811; and J. des Rosiers, "Note: The Exemption Process Under the Endangered Species Act: How the 'God Squad' Works and Why" (1991) vol. 66 *Notre Dame Law Review* 825.

C. Canadian Legislation and Programs

1. The Federal Endangered Species Program

In the early 1970s, following passage of the US *Endangered Species Act*, two Canadian provinces (Ontario and New Brunswick) passed their own (weaker) legislation. The federal government did not. In the late 1970s, however, Canada established an unofficial committee to identify species at risk. The Committee on the Status of Endangered Wildlife in Canada (COSEWIC) consists of representatives of wildlife conservation agencies of the federal, territorial, and provincial governments, as well as three independent scientists. COSEWIC commissions status reports on species suspected of being at risk, then meets twice a year to assign the appropriate designation to each species. Possible designations include

- *Extinct:* a species formerly indigenous to Canada that no longer exists anywhere;
- *Extirpated:* a species no longer known to exist in the wild in Canada but existing elsewhere;
- *Endangered:* a species threatened with imminent extirpation throughout all or significant portions of its Canadian range;
- *Threatened:* a species likely to become endangered if the factors affecting its vulnerability are not reversed; and
- *Special concern:* a species that is particularly at risk because of low or declining numbers, because it occurs at fringe of its range, or for some other reason.

There are presently 415 species on COSEWIC's list (and 240 are listed as threatened or endangered). The list is growing at a rate of about 20-30 new species per year, and even these figures understate the extent of the problem. Due to limited resources and staff, COSEWIC has been unable to review many Canadian species suspected of being at risk.

COSEWIC's role in protecting species has been severely limited by the fact that it has no legal authority. Being listed by COSEWIC gives no legal protection to a species. Another problem is that COSEWIC only *lists* species; it does not develop recovery plans for them. In 1988, this problem was partially addressed by the creation of Recovery of Nationally Endangered Wildlife (RENEW), which is made up of representatives from federal and provincial wildlife agencies. RENEW's goal is to set up recovery teams for each vertebrate species listed as endangered or threatened by COSEWIC, and then come up with a recovery plan for the species. Unfortunately, only 21 recovery plans have been approved in the 15 years since RENEW was created. As with COSEWIC, RENEW's recovery plans have no legal force.

NOTES AND QUESTIONS

1. The COSEWIC's complete list of species at risk can be found online at http://www.speciesatrisk.gc.ca/ and at http://www.cosewic.gc.ca/.

2. Find four species at risk in your province. What are the reasons for their decline? Do any of them have approved recovery plans?

2. Federal Legislation

Bismarck once said, "there are two things you do not want to see made: legislation and sausages." These words aptly describe the evolution of federal endangered species legislation in Canada.

In 1992, at the Rio Earth Summit, Canada was the first western nation to sign, and later ratify, the Convention of Biological Diversity (1992) vol. 31 *International Legal Materials* 818. Article 8 of that convention provides that

Each nation shall, as far as possible and as appropriate: ...

(k) develop ... necessary *legislation* and/or other regulatory provisions for the protection of threatened species and populations.

The federal government initially took the position that this provision did not require Canada to pass endangered species legislation. Then, following a high-profile public campaign by conservationists, in 1994, the government announced its intention to de-velop an endangered species law. After two years of consultation, in October 1996, the *Canada Endangered Species Protection Act* was introduced in Parliament. This bill was never passed into law; it died on the order paper when an election was called in April 1997. A second bill was introduced in early 2000, but again it died on the order paper when an election was called later that year. Finally, the *Species At Risk Act* (SARA), excerpts of which are reproduced below, was passed by Parliament in December 2002.

The development of this law attracted a great deal of attention from the public, media, and industry, due in part to controversy about the US Act and its perceived effects on development. When you read the statute, you will note that in some places its drafting is quite complex. This is because the initial bill, already fairly complex, was significantly strengthened by Parliament's environment committee following extensive hearings. Then, when the bill was debated in Parliament, the government sought to reverse most of the committee's key changes. This lead to intense negotiations that produced compromise (and even more complex) wording. As you read the parts of the Act dealing with listing and habitat protection, think about how the same result could have been achieved with much simpler language.

Species At Risk Act
SC 2002, c. 29

Interpretation

2(1) The definitions in this subsection apply in this Act.
"competent minister" means

(a) the Minister of Canadian Heritage with respect to individuals in or on fed-eral lands that are ... national parks, national historic sites or other protected heritage areas ... ;

(b) the Minister of Fisheries and Oceans with respect to aquatic species, other than individuals mentioned in paragraph (a); and

(c) the Minister of the Environment with respect to all other individuals.
"critical habitat" means the habitat that is necessary for the survival or recovery of a listed wildlife species and that is identified as the species' critical habitat in the recovery
"habitat" means

(b) the area or type of site where an individual or wildlife species naturally occurs or depends on directly or indirectly in order to carry out its life processes or formerly occurred and has the potential to be reintroduced.
"List" means the List of Wildlife Species at Risk set out in Schedule 1.

"wildlife species" means a species, subspecies, variety or geographically or ge-netically distinct population of animal, plant or other organism, other than a bacterium or virus, that is wild by nature and ... is native to Canada.

...

Wildlife Species Listing Process

15(1) The functions of Committee on the Status of Endangered Wildlife in Canada are to

(a) assess the status of each wildlife species considered by COSEWIC to be at risk and, as part of the assessment, identify existing and potential threats to the species and

(i) classify the species as extinct, extirpated, endangered, threatened or of special concern [See the COSEWIC definitions of these terms, above.], ... or

(iii) indicate that the species is not currently at risk; ... .

(2) COSEWIC must carry out its functions on the basis of the best available information on the biological status of a species, including scientific knowledge, community knowledge and aboriginal traditional knowledge.

16. ...

(2) Each [COSEWIC] member must have expertise drawn from a discipline such as conservation biology, population dynamics, taxonomy, systematics or genetics or from ... aboriginal traditional knowledge of the conservation of wildlife species.

• • •

22(1) Any person may apply to COSEWIC for an assessment of the status of a wildlife species.

• • •

List of Wildlife Species at Risk

27(1) The Governor in Council may, on the recommendation of the Minister, by order amend the List in accordance with subsections (1.1) and (1.2) by adding a wildlife species, by reclassifying a listed wildlife species or by removing a listed wildlife species, and the Minister may, by order, amend the List in a similar fashion in accordance with subsection (3).

(1.1) Subject to subsection (3), the Governor in Council, within nine months after receiving an assessment of the status of a species by COSEWIC, may review that assessment and may, on the recommendation of the Minister,

(a) accept the assessment and add the species to the List;

(b) decide not to add the species to the List; or

(c) refer the matter back to COSEWIC for further information or consideration.

(1.2) Where the Governor in Council takes a course of action under paragraph (1.1)(b) or (c), the Minister shall, after the approval of the Governor in Council, include a statement in the public registry setting out the reasons. ...

(3) Where the Governor in Council has not taken a course of action under subsection (1.1) within nine months after receiving an assessment of the status of a species by COSEWIC, the Minister shall, by order, amend the List in accordance with COSEWIC's assessment.

• • •

29(1) If the Minister is of the opinion that there is an imminent threat to the survival of a wildlife species, the Minister must, on an emergency basis, after consultation with every other competent minister, make a recommendation to the Governor in Council that the List be amended to list the species as an endangered species.

...

Measures To Protect Listed Wildlife Species

32(1) No person shall kill, harm, harass, capture or take an individual of a wildlife species that is listed as an extirpated species, an endangered species or a threatened species.

33. No person shall damage or destroy the residence of one or more individuals of a wildlife species that is listed as an endangered species or a threatened species, or that is listed as an extirpated species if a recovery strategy has recommended the reintroduction of the species into the wild in Canada.

34(1) With respect to individuals of a listed wildlife species that is not an aquatic species or a species of birds that are migratory birds protected by the *Migratory Birds Convention Act, 1994*, sections 32 and 33 do not apply in lands in a province that are not federal lands unless an order is made under subsection (2) to provide that they apply.

(2) The Governor in Council may, on the recommendation of the Minister, by order, provide that sections 32 and 33, or either of them, apply in lands in a province that are not federal lands with respect to individuals of a listed wildlife species that is not an aquatic species or a species of birds that are migratory birds protected by the *Migratory Birds Convention Act, 1994*.

(3) The Minister must recommend that the order be made if the Minister is of the opinion that the laws of the province do not effectively protect the species or the residences of its individuals.

...

Recovery Strategy

37(1) If a wildlife species is listed as an extirpated species, an endangered species or a threatened species, the competent minister must prepare a strategy for its recovery.

38. In preparing a recovery strategy, action plan or management plan, the competent minister must consider the commitment of the Government of Canada to ... the principle that, if there are threats of serious or irreversible damage to the listed wildlife species, cost-effective measures to prevent the reduction or loss of the species should not be postponed for a lack of full scientific certainty.

39(1) To the extent possible, the recovery strategy must be prepared in cooperation with

(a) the appropriate provincial and territorial minister for each province and territory in which the listed wildlife species is found;

(b) every minister of the Government of Canada who has authority over federal land or other areas on which the species is found; ...

(d) every aboriginal organization that the competent minister considers will be directly affected by the recovery strategy.

...

41(1) If the competent minister determines that the recovery of the listed wildlife species is feasible, the recovery strategy must address the threats to the survival of the species identified by COSEWIC, including any loss of habitat, and must include

(a) a description of the species and its needs that is consistent with information provided by COSEWIC;

(b) an identification of the threats to the survival of the species and threats to its habitat that is consistent with information provided by COSEWIC and a description of the broad strategy to be taken to address those threats;

(c) an identification of the species' critical habitat, to the extent possible, based on the best available information, including the information provided by COSEWIC, and examples of activities that are likely to result in its destruction;

(c.1) a schedule of studies to identify critical habitat, where available information is inadequate;

(d) a statement of the population and distribution objectives that will assist the recovery and survival of the species, and a general description of the research and management activities needed to meet those objectives; ... .

42(1) [T]the competent minister must include a proposed recovery strategy in the public registry within one year after the wildlife species is listed, in the case of a wildlife species listed as an endangered species, and within two years after the species is listed, in the case of a wildlife species listed as a threatened species or an extirpated species.

...

Protection of Critical Habitat

58(1) Subject to this section, no person shall destroy any part of the critical habitat of any listed endangered species or of any listed threatened species—or of any listed extirpated species if a recovery strategy has recommended the reintroduction of the species into the wild in Canada—if

(a) the critical habitat is on federal land ... ;

(b) the listed species is an aquatic species; or

(c) the listed species is a species of migratory birds protected by the *Migratory Birds Convention Act, 1994.*

(2) If the critical habitat or a portion of the critical habitat is in a national park ... , a marine protected area under the *Oceans Act*, a migratory bird sanctuary ... , or a national wildlife area ... , the competent Minister must, within 90 days after the recovery strategy or action plan that identified the critical habitat is included in the public registry, publish in the Canada Gazette a description of the critical habitat or portion that is in that park, area or sanctuary.

(3) If subsection (2) applies, subsection (1) applies to the critical habitat ... described in the Canada Gazette under subsection (2) 90 days after the description is published in the Canada Gazette.

(4) If all of the critical habitat or any portion of the critical habitat is not in a place referred to in subsection (2), subsection (1) applies in respect of the critical habitat ... specified in an order made by the competent minister.

(5) Within 180 days after the recovery strategy or action plan that identified the critical habitat is included in the public registry, the competent minister must, after consultation with every other competent minister, with respect to all of the critical habitat or any portion of the critical habitat that is not in a place referred to in subsection (2),

(a) make the order referred to in subsection (4) if the critical habitat or any portion of the critical habitat is not legally protected by provisions in, or measures under, this or any other Act of Parliament ... ; or

(b) if the competent minister does not make the order, he or she must include in the public registry a statement setting out how the critical habitat or portions of it, as the case may be, are legally protected.

(5.1) Despite subsection (4), with respect to the critical habitat of a species of bird that is a migratory bird protected by the *Migratory Birds Convention Act, 1994* that is not on federal land ... or in a migratory bird sanctuary referred to in subsection (2), subsection (1) applies only to those portions of the critical habitat that are habitat to which that Act applies and that the Governor in Council may, by order, specify on the recommendation of the competent minister.

. . .

61(1) No person shall destroy any part of the critical habitat of a listed endangered species or a listed threatened species that is in a province or territory and that is not part of federal lands.

(1.1) Subsection (1) does not apply in respect of

(a) an aquatic species; or

(b) the critical habitat of a species of bird that is a migratory bird protected by the *Migratory Birds Convention Act, 1994* that is habitat referred to in subsection 58(5.1).

(2) Subsection (1) applies only to the portions of the critical habitat that the Governor in Council may, on the recommendation of the Minister, by order, specify. ...

(4) The Minister must make a recommendation if he or she is of the opinion, after consultation with the appropriate provincial or territorial minister, that

(a) there are no provisions in, or other measures under, this or any other Act of Parliament that protect the particular portion of the critical habitat ... ; and

(b) the laws of the province or territory do not effectively protect the critical habitat.

. . .

64(1) The Minister may, in accordance with the regulations, provide fair and reasonable compensation to any person for losses suffered as a result of any extraordinary impact of the application of

(a) section 58, 60 or 61; or

(b) an emergency order in respect of habitat identified in the emergency order that is necessary for the survival or recovery of a wildlife species. ...

Management of Species of Special Concern

65. If a wildlife species is listed as a species of special concern, the competent minister must prepare a management plan for the species and its habitat. The plan

must include measures for the conservation of the species that the competent minister considers appropriate and it may apply with respect to more than one wildlife species.

. . .

Agreements and Permits

73(1) The competent minister may make an agreement with a person, or issue a permit to a person, authorizing the person to engage in an activity affecting a listed wildlife species, any part of its critical habitat, or the residences of its individuals.

(2) The agreement may be entered into, or the permit issued, only if the competent minister is of the opinion that

(a) the activity is scientific research relating to the conservation of the species ... ;

(b) the activity benefits the species or is required to enhance its chance of survival in the wild; or

(c) affecting the species is incidental to the carrying out of the activity.

(3) The agreement may be entered into, or the permit issued, only if the competent minister is of the opinion that

(a) all reasonable alternatives to the activity that would reduce the impact on the species have been considered and the best solution has been adopted;

(b) all feasible measures will be taken to minimize the impact of the activity on the species or its critical habitat or the residences of its individuals; and

(c) the activity will not jeopardize the survival or recovery of the species.

. . .

77(1) Despite any other Act of Parliament, any person or body, other than a competent minister, authorized under any Act of Parliament other than this Act, to issue or approve a licence, a permit or any other authorization that authorizes an activity that may result in the destruction of any part of the critical habitat of a listed wildlife species may enter into, issue, approve or make the authorization only if the person or body has consulted with the competent minister, has considered the impact on the species' critical habitat and is of the opinion that

(a) all reasonable alternatives to the activity that would reduce the impact on the species' critical habitat have been considered and the best solution has been adopted; and

(b) all feasible measures will be taken to minimize the impact of the activity on the species' critical habitat.

. . .

Emergency Orders

80(1) The Governor in Council may, on the recommendation of the competent minister, make an emergency order to provide for the protection of a listed wildlife species.

(2) The competent minister must make the recommendation if he or she is of the opinion that the species faces imminent threats to its survival or recovery. ...

(4) The emergency order may ...
   (ii) include provisions ... prohibiting activities that may adversely affect
the species and [its] habitat; ... .

NOTES AND QUESTIONS

1. The SARA provides different degrees of protection for so-called federal and non-federal species. What are the main differences in the types of protection afforded these two categories (see ss. 34, 58, and 61)? Why do you think the drafters of the Act chose to treat aquatic species, migratory birds, and species on federal lands as "federal," and all other species as "non-federal" (that is, primarily a provincial responsibility)? Is this bifurcated approach required for constitutional reasons? Under the constitution, what is the source of the federal government's power to enact s. 61 (the Alberta government has threatened to bring a constitutional challenge to this section)?

2. Habitat protection is the key to saving endangered species. Parliament's environment committee wanted to make habitat protection mandatory ("shall"), and the government wanted it to be discretionary ("may"). The end result was the current negotiated wording. Is critical habitat protection now mandatory under s. 58? How is a species' critical habitat determined? How long does it take (after listing) before critical habitat is (a) identified and (b) protected? What happens in the meantime?

3. Section 58(5.1) treats migratory birds differently from other "federal" species in terms of habitat protection. What are the main differences, and why do you think that the drafters did this? Read the *Migratory Birds Convention Act, 1994*, SC 1994, c. 22; what is the "habitat to which that Act applies"?

4. Parliament's environment committee made two key amendments to s. 61: (a) adding *criteria* for determining when a province's laws provide "effective protection," and (b) making it *mandatory* (not discretionary) that Cabinet apply federal protection where a province's laws do not provide "effective protection." These changes were removed by the government on the bill's third reading. Why do you think that the government was opposed to these changes?

5. The Act automatically prohibits the destruction of a listed species' "residence" (s. 33). What is a "residence"? How does it differ from "habitat"?

6. Almost all scientists and environmental groups wanted species listing decisions to be made by COSEWIC, whereas the government wanted Cabinet to make this decision. During final debate on the bill, a compromise was reached. Under s. 27, how is the ultimate listing decision made? Does the decision have to be based on science (as is required under the US Act)?

7. There also was debate over what to do with the existing COSEWIC list of species at risk—should it be the initial list under the Act, or should the Act start with no listed species? Through an amendment by Parliament's environment committee, 233 of COSEWIC's 415 species were inserted as the initial list under the Act (schedule 1). "Special concern" species were left off, along with dozens of species that the government wanted COSEWIC to reassess.

8. Section 64 allows the government to provide compensation for losses resulting from "any extraordinary impact" of SARA's habitat protection requirements? Does this

go further than the usual rule (under common law and statute) that compensation is only available for "expropriation" (see *Tener* and *Mariner*, above)? Do you think that governments should compensate when compliance with environmental regulations imposes substantial costs on companies or individuals (short of expropriation)? See chapter 13.

9. The US *Endangered Species Act* (and most US environmental laws) specifically permits citizens to bring a civil enforcement action against anyone who violates the Act. Only one jurisdiction in Canada (Ontario) allows such "citizen suits," and then only in limited circumstances. The *Species At Risk Act* does not provide for "citizen suits"; they were included in an earlier version of the bill, but were removed because of the objections of industry and landowner groups.

3. Provincial Legislation

In October 1996, the federal government and all provinces and territories signed the National Accord for the Protection of Species At Risk, summarized online at http://www.ec.gc.ca/press/wild_b_e.htm. The accord commits each jurisdiction to pass endangered species legislation containing 15 specific minimum requirements (such as habitat protection, recovery plans, etc.). Only 6 of 13 provinces and territories have passed endangered species legislation (Ontario, New Brunswick, Quebec, Manitoba, PEI, and Nova Scotia), and none has yet to come close to fulfilling the requirements of the accord.

Listing. Five of the provinces' acts (all except Nova Scotia) take a similar approach to listing: Cabinet makes the decision at its discretion. Ontario's *Endangered Species Act*, RSO 1990, c. E. 15, provides:

3(1) The Lieutenant Governor in Council may make regulations declaring any species of flora and fauna to be threatened with extinction ... .

Under this section, would it be possible to bring a lawsuit against Cabinet for failing to list a species when there was clear scientific evidence it was endangered (as in the *Spotted Owl* case)? Ontario has listed less than 30 percent of the species that COSEWIC has found to be endangered or threatened in the province—meaning over 70 percent of Ontario's endangered species are left unprotected. The track record of Manitoba, Quebec, and New Brunswick, which also leave listing decisions up to Cabinet, is not much better (which is why there was debate under SARA about whether COSEWIC or Cabinet would make listing decisions). The Nova Scotia *Endangered Species Act*, SN 1988, c. 11, takes a different approach: it stipulates that all species listed by COSEWIC that are found in Nova Scotia *must* be listed under the provincial Act.

Habitat. Four of the six provincial acts include automatic prohibitions against destroying the habitat of a listed endangered species. For example, the Manitoba *Endangered Species Act*, SM 1989-90, c. 39; CCSM, c. E111 provides that

10(1) No person shall ...
(b) destroy, disturb or interfere with the habitat of an endangered or threatened species; or
(c) damage, destroy, obstruct or remove a natural resource on which a threatened or endangered species depends for its life and propagation.

This strong prohibition is somewhat undermined by a provision allowing the minister to exempt any development, "if the Minister is satisfied that (a) protection or preservation of the species or the habitat is assured; *or* (b) appropriate measures ... will be established to reduce the impact of a development on an endangered or threatened species or [its] habitat" (s. 12(1)). The latter clause gives the minister broad discretion to authorize habitat destruction. Quebec's *Threatened and Vulnerable Species Act*, RSQ, c. E-12.01 also contains a fairly broad exemption provision. The New Brunswick *Endangered Species Act*, SNB 1996, c. E-9.101 and the Ontario Act also prohibit habitat destruction and do not allow for exemptions (except for scientific reasons). Compare the approach in these provincial laws (which automatically prohibit habitat destruction from the time of listing) with the approach in SARA.

Several other provinces have added provisions to their wildlife acts allowing Cabinet or the minister, if he or she so chooses, to designate endangered species of wildlife. These acts typically prohibit hunting or taking of an endangered species, but leave habitat protection up to the discretion of Cabinet. See, for example, Saskatchewan's *Wildlife Act*, SS 1998, c. W-13.12.

The spotted owl provides a graphic illustration of the relative strength of the Canadian and US endangered species programs. Efforts to protect the owl are controversial because doing so involves setting aside large tracts of coastal old growth forests, a valuable commodity to powerful timber companies. In the United States, as a result of litigation, the owl was listed in 1990, and vast areas of its critical habitat were identified and set aside. In Canada, the owl was listed by COSEWIC as endangered in 1986. Despite this listing, no recovery plan has been adopted yet, and no new critical habitat areas have been legally protected (outside of parks). The owl is now close to extinction in British Columbia.

Under the US Act, a political decision has been made that preserving species is of paramount importance. Once science indicates that a species is endangered, it must be listed and its habitat must be protected. Exceptions to this rule can be made in individual cases, but doing so requires a tremendous political campaign by those opposed to species protection. Under the Canadian system, a firm political commitment has yet to be made to protect species. Scientists indicate whether a species is endangered, but it is left to politicians to decide on a case-by-case basis whether to list a species and protect its habitat. In many ways, Canadian protection of endangered species has yet to catch up to where the United States was thirty years ago.

For further information, see J.A. Burnett et al., *On the Brink: Endangered Species in Canada* (Saskatoon: W. Producers Prairie Books, 1989) and I. Attridge, ed., *Biodiversity Law and Policy in Canada* (Toronto: CIELAP, 1996).

D. Other Approaches

Many people have criticized the "endangered species" approach to protecting species. These criticisms come from a number of angles.

Some have argued that the goal of saving every species is impossible. Recovery efforts are expensive. The overall price tag for saving all of Canada's 240 threatened and endangered species could easily run over $100 million per year. Some argue that this is an unreasonable cost. Others point out that this is less than the cost of 10 miles of new highway. If we decide that we cannot save every species, we face difficult decisions. Which ones do we sacrifice? On what basis? Politicians' natural inclination is to save large mammals and "warm and fuzzy" species because they evoke the most emotional response in people. But scientists point out that cuteness is not always an accurate measure of ecological value. No one has yet come up with a satisfactory solution to the problem of deciding which species to save.

Others have recommended that rather than trying to save individual species, we should focus on saving endangered ecosystems. Saving the ecosystem would also save its resident species. The problem with this approach is how to identify an endangered ecosystem. One of the best ways to identify an ecosystem, and to measure its health, is to examine the species that depend on it. Thus, we are back to protecting species again.

Some maintain that we should focus on protecting biological diversity. This argument begs the question. How much biological diversity should we save? Which species can we let go? One promising approach is to identify "hot spots" of biological diversity. By conserving the areas of greatest biological diversity, we can put our limited species preservation dollars to their best use.

Almost everyone agrees that species protection needs to shift from its present "critical care" focus toward a more "preventative" approach. Saving species is much more expensive once they are on the brink of extinction.

For more information, see W. J. Snappe, ed., *Biodiversity and the Law* (Washington, DC: Island Press, 1996) and "Playing God: Why We Shouldn't Try to Save Every Endangered Species," [1992] vol. 269, no. 1 *Atlantic Monthly* 47-88.

FURTHER READINGS

K. Beazley and R. Boardman, *Politics of the Wild: Canada and Endangered Species* (Don Mills, ON: Oxford University Press, 2001).

J. Benedickson, "Protecting Spaces and Species: Parks, Wilderness, Habitat and Wildlife," in J. Benedickson, *Environmental Law*, 2d ed. (Toronto: Irwin Law, 2002), chapter 14.

R. Boardman, "Canada's Threatened Wildlife: Civil Society, Intergovernmental Relations, and the Art of the Possible," in D. Van Nijnatten and R. Boardman, eds., *Canadian Environmental Policy*, 2d ed. (Don Mills, ON: Oxford University Press, 2002).

CHAPTER THIRTEEN

Municipal and
Land-Use Planning

Arlene J. Kwasniak

I. INTRODUCTION

Every province in Canada has legislation empowering the creation of local governments, here called "municipalities." Although authorizing legislation varies from jurisdiction to jurisdiction, core elements remain constant. Relevant to this chapter, all Canadian provinces delegate to municipalities specified planning and regulatory powers over land uses.

In exercising these powers, municipalities play key and critical roles in affecting environment quality—for better or worse. Through their land-use plans and policies and authority over zoning and subdivision, municipalities control and regulate many private land development and uses that affect environmental quality. Through zoning powers, municipalities prescribe how private land may be developed in an area. One land-use zone may permit intense industrial development, which could negatively affect environmental quality, while another may be structured to enhance environmental quality and maintain green spaces. Through subdivision powers, municipalities may affect environmental quality by either allowing or limiting fragmentation of green spaces. As well, legislation might authorize municipalities to require a subdivision applicant to dedicate undevelopable or other land, which in effect, could protect green spaces. Also, through their land-use and development powers, municipalities regulate facets of roads, sewers, and other infrastructure, all which could affect environmental quality. For example, a municipality might carry out its role in locating a road so that it truncates a wetland, thereby destroying something with environmental value, or so that the road goes around the wetland, thereby preserving an environmental amenity.

This chapter explores legal aspects of some of the ways in which municipalities affect environmental quality, including green spaces, through exercising land-use planning and subdivision and development functions. The first section considers sources of and limitations on municipal planning and subdivision and development powers to regulate environmental quality. It offers case excerpts that address the issue of how far municipalities may engage in environmental regulation through their legislative authority over the land-use

521

aspects of so-called undesirable facilities such as landfills or potentially polluting industries. The second section focuses on how far municipalities may go to protect green
spaces without engaging in a "taking" or without exceeding jurisdiction, including protections through the use of conservation easements. The third section looks at conservation
easements and their potential use by municipalities in exercising their land-use planning
and development authority.

II. SOURCE OF AND LIMITATIONS ON POWERS

A. Authorizing Legislation

As statutory creations, municipalities have no authority beyond the powers expressly
granted by legislation, or which are necessarily or fairly implied by an express grant. In
interpreting the scope of legislative authority, courts have strictly limited municipal
powers in accordance with what has been known as Dillon's Rule. The rule derives from
a 1906 case (12 OR 290, at 299 (CA)) that states:

> It is a general and undisputed proposition of law that a municipal corporation possesses and
> can exercise the following powers and no others, first, those granted in express words;
> second, those necessarily or fairly implied in or incident to the powers expressly granted;
> third, those essential to the declared objects and purposes of the corporation, not simply
> convenient, but indispensable. Any fair reasonable doubt concerning the existence of power
> is resolved by the courts against the corporation, and the power is denied.

In 1993, the Supreme Court of Canada reaffirmed this rule. In *R v. Greenbaum*, [1993] 1
SCR 674, it stated "[m]unicipalities are entirely the creatures of provincial statutes.
Accordingly, they can exercise only those powers which are explicitly conferred upon
them by a provincial statute."

Dillon's Rule remains good law in Canada; however, its harness can be and has been
somewhat loosened. One way of relaxing its effects is by enacting legislative changes to
avoid its application. For example, in revamping the Alberta *Municipal Government Act*,
RSA 2000, c. M-26, in the mid-1990s, the legislature plainly aimed at weakening the
effect of the rule. One notable change in the new Act was the granting of *natural person*
powers to a municipality (s. 6). Under natural person powers, a municipality enjoys the
same capacity, rights, powers, and privileges accorded to a natural person. Recent research claims that this power is unique to Alberta. (See D. Manderscheid, "The Alberta
Municipality: The New Person on the Block" (1998) vol. 36, no. 3 *Alberta Law Review*
692.) Any limitation on these rights must be set out in the *Municipal Government Act* or
in other legislation. The powers enable municipalities to conduct business as a natural
person would, even though specific authorization is not given by legislation. For example, a municipality may barter, sell, negotiate contracts, and carry on businesses, even
where not specifically authorized.

Another way to use legislation to avoid application of Dillon's Rule is to couch
statements of municipal purposes and grants of authority in broad general terms rather
than explicit, express terms and by legislatively requiring that purposes and general
grants be liberally interpreted. Such legislative language should provide a municipality

with more flexibility than it would a province, whose municipal legislation contains only explicit, detailed purposes and grants. See F. Hoehn, *Municipalities and Canadian Law* (Saskatoon: Purich, 1996).

The breadth of permissible decisions of an administrative body acting pursuant to municipal laws depends in part on the standard of review that a court employs when reviewing municipal actions. In 2000, the Supreme Court of Canada confirmed that courts should apply a pragmatic and functional approach when interpreting broad discretionary municipal powers to determine the appropriate standard of review. If the approach shows that the administrative body's impugned decision involved questions of law or jurisdiction, such as requiring council to apply principles of statutory interpretation in order to determine legal scope of authority, then the appropriate standard of review is correctness. Where the court reviews an *intra vires* municipal decision, then the standard of review is one of patent unreasonableness and not unreasonableness alone. See *City of Namaimo v. Rascal Trucking*, [2001] 1 SCR 342.

A recent Supreme Court of Canada decision, *114957 Canada Ltée (Spraytech, Société d'arrosage) v. Hudson (Town)*, [2001] 2 SCR 241, considering a matter going to jurisdiction, supports much of the view that courts should liberally interpret legislated statements of municipal purposes and general or omnibus grants of power. The court said (para. 53):

> It appears to be sound legislative and administrative policy, under such provisions, to grant local governments a residual authority to deal with the unforeseen or changing circumstances, and to address emerging or changing issues concerning the welfare of the local community living within their territory. Nevertheless, such a provision cannot be construed as an open and unlimited grant of provincial powers. It is not enough that a particular issue has become a pressing concern in the opinion of a local community. This concern must be closely related to problems that engage the community as a local entity, not a member of the broader polity. It must be closely related to the immediate interests of the community within the territorial limits defined by the legislature in a matter where local governments may usefully intervene.

The reader must be cautioned, however, when interpreting the effect of the *Spraytech* case because it applies to legislative grants relating to planning, zoning, subdivision, and development. Often provincial legislation will couch these grants in explicit, express terms and not in broad general ones. Consequently, the case may have limited application. The following case demonstrates just how closely a court will look at legislation when interpreting municipal legislative powers—even in the wake of *Spraytech*. The case concerns the municipal powers of regulating land uses, in this case, regulating forestry practices within certain land-use zones on private land.

Denman Island Local Trust Committee v. 4064 Investments Ltd.
2001 BCCA 736

SAUNDERS JA: I have had the privilege of reading in draft the reasons for judgment of my colleague Madam Justice Rowles, but would reach, with respect, a different result. In my view ss. 879 and 920 of the *Local Government Act*, RSBC 1996, c. 323, when read in context, do not empower local government, in a broad way, to regulate forestry practices in an area designated under s. 879. ... The Denman Island Local Trust Committee is constituted under the *Islands Trust Act*, RSBC 1996, c. 239 to exercise most of the powers and authority of a regional district board under the *Local Government Act*. The *Islands Trust Act* provides:

> The object of the trust is to preserve and protect the trust area and its unique amenities and environment for the benefit of the residents of the trust area and of British Columbia generally, in cooperation with municipalities, regional districts, improvement districts, other persons and organizations and the government of British Columbia.

The *Local Government Act*, formerly the *Municipal Act*, is the statute under which all local government in British Columbia, excepting the City of Vancouver which has its own special Act, derives statutory authority. The Act covers incorporated municipalities that are largely urban in nature, and regional districts that include within their boundaries both incorporated municipalities and unorganized territory. By virtue of s. 29 of the *Islands Trust Act* certain provisions of the *Local Government Act*, including ss. 879 and 920, apply to local trust committees. ...

The story of the relevant sections of the *Local Government Act* starts in 1985 when the then *Municipal Act* was amended:

(1) to allow municipalities and regional districts to designate areas "for the protection of the natural environment" in an official Community Plan, where land could not be altered without a permit:

> 945(4) A community plan may for the purposes of s. 976, designate areas for the protection of the natural environment, ...

and

(2) to provide municipalities and regional districts the power to pass specific by-laws that restrict or regulate tree cutting in areas of land subject to flooding, erosion, land slip or avalanche.

What is now s. 923 provides:

> 923(1) A board may, by bylaw, designate areas of land that it considers may be subject to flooding erosion, land slip or avalanche as tree cutting permit areas.
>
> (2) A bylaw may, in respect of an area designated under subsection (1),
>
> (a) regulate or prohibit the cutting down of trees, and
>
> (b) require an owner to obtain, on payment of a fee set by the bylaw, a permit before cutting down a tree.

In 1992 the Act was amended again by the addition of what is now Division 2 of Part 22 of the *Local Government Act*, applicable only to municipalities, giving broad powers to prohibit and regulate the cutting of trees. ... These tree cutting provisions in Division 2 of Part 22 of the *Local Government Act* do not apply to regional districts or the Local Trust Committee.

Finally, in 1997 ss. 945 and 976 were amended and renumbered. To what was s. 945 and became s. 879(1)(a) (now s. 919.1(a)) were added the words "its ecosystems and biological diversity":

879(1) For the purposes of section 920, a community plan may designate areas for one or more of the following:

(a) protection of the natural environment, its ecosystems and biological diversity;

To what was s. 976 and became s. 920, a provision was added permitting protection of natural features or areas: ...

920(7) For land designated under section 879(1)(a), a development permit may do one or more of the following: ...

(b) require specified natural features or areas to be preserved, protected, restored or enhanced in accordance with the permit. ...

(e) require protection measures, including that vegetation or trees be planted or retained in order to

(i) preserve, protect, restore or enhance fish habitat or riparian areas,

(ii) control drainage, or

(iii) control erosion or protect banks.

The issue in this case is whether s. 879(1)(a) and s. 920(7), together, give the Local Trust Committee the power to enact bylaws restricting and regulating the felling of trees on the respondent's land.

• • •

Are the impugned bylaws within the legislative authority conferred by ss. 879 and 920 of the *Local Government Act*?

• • •

What is the consequence of the power advocated by the appellant? In the absence of regulation under the *Forest Land Reserve Act* or other legislative provisions, the respondent possessed the common law right to harvest the trees upon its land, or to clear the land for other purposes. It is well known that trees, like gravel and sand, have commercial value that may be harnessed by an owner, itself or by sale to another. For this reason they are included within the general definition of a "*profit à prendre.*"

• • •

Considering that the bylaws in question impinge upon this common law right incidental to ownership of the property, without compensation, this is a case, in my view, appropriate for a somewhat stricter construction of the enabling legislation ... .

I have reviewed the language of s. 920(7) in the context of the specific tree cutting provisions in the Act and in other legislation, the significance generally in British Columbia of forest management issues both commercially and aesthetically, the breadth of application of these sections which ranges from the Local Trust Committee to the most rural and largest of regional districts, and the proprietary common law nature of the right curtailed by the bylaws. In this context, I consider that it is a more reasonable interpretation to see the words "specified natural features or areas" as referring to parts of property, for example geographical or topographical features such as bluffs, gullies and rock outcroppings, and discreet areas such as beaches, streams, glades and bogs, than to view them as referring to the forest cover of significant tracts of land (in the case of Bylaw 113, over one-half of the land area of the island) with assorted features and areas. I conclude, in the context of the legislative history of the Act and forestry practice regulations, that had the Legislature intended to give regional districts the authority to regulate generally forest practices on private land, which it clearly could do, it would have done so expressly. I would find it did not do so in these sections.

. . .

I turn now to the individual bylaws. The learned chambers judge held five bylaws, nos. 110, 111, 112, 113, and 114 *ultra vires* the Local Trust Committee based on his characterization of them as forest management regulation, saying:

> [118] However, this also underlines the fact that the Denman Island Local Trust Committee is, in Bylaw 113, purporting to fill the forest practices regulatory gap by extending regulation to private forest lands not otherwise touched by the provincial scheme.

The chambers judge discussed the details of bylaw 113 and then moved on to consider the other bylaws saying:

> [127] I will not refer to the other bylaws in any detail.
>
> [128] There is no doubt that they take a more focused approach to the regulation of logging in specific areas like streams and wetlands (Bylaw 112) and steep slopes (Bylaw 111).
>
> [129] And there is no doubt that aspects of these more focused bylaws are within the letter and spirit of the powers granted under s. 879 of the Act and, in particular, under s-ss.(1)(a) and (b).
>
> [130] However, it is clear that the Amending Bylaws are an integrated package and their primary thrust, their pith and substance, is the regulation of forest practices on private lands. ...

He concluded the bylaws are an integrated package and that the entire package is invalid.

> [141] I have also said that the Amending Bylaws are an integrated collection of regulations advanced by the Denman Island Local Trust Committee as a package, indeed staff have called them collectively the "Forest Bylaws."
>
> [142] They were passed at one time. They are closely interrelated. For example, Bylaw 110 contains the definitions for various terms in the other bylaws.
>
> [143] The Amending Bylaws are intended to create a regulatory scheme that is cumulative.

. . .

> [145] In my view, ... I should not sever off such bylaws or parts thereof that might be good from those that are bad.
>
> [146] To give but one example of the inappropriateness of leaving part of the Local Trust Committee's legislative package in place, I note that prior to the adoption of the Amending Bylaws, the DPA setback from streams and watercourses was set at 60 metres. The Amending Bylaws reduced that setback to 30 metres, presumably because, as a whole, the new regulations made a 30 metres setback appropriate. To strike down sig-

nificant portions of the new regulations while leaving this setback reduction in place, for example, would serve to totally frustrate the scheme which the Local Trust Committee members thought they were promulgating.

[147] There will be a declaration as to the invalidity of the entire package.

The Local Trust Committee contends that even in the event this Court finds that bylaw 113 is beyond the scope of its powers, the other bylaws in the package should not be declared invalid. I agree. Bylaws 110 to 114 were each passed separately, and in the manner of their enactment the Local Trust Committee has shown an intention to deal separately with the subject matter. This separation of subject matter is, in my respectful view, confirmed on a reading of the bylaws. Bylaws 110 and 114 deal with definitions and procedures respectively, and to the extent that any provisions are interrelated to and dependent upon bylaw 113 for substance, they can be severed. Bylaws 111 and 112 have substance, but independent of bylaw 113. Further, bylaws 111 and 112, as observed by the chambers judge, are more narrow in focus than bylaw 113. Bylaw 111 purports to protect land from erosion in a fashion that may bring the bylaw within s. 923 of the *Local Government Act*. Bylaw 112 purports to protect riparian and wetland areas in a fashion that may fit within the ambit of s. 920(7) as I have described it. Given the fashion in which the issues developed in the Supreme Court, these questions were not explored in the reasons of the chambers judge. Nor were they addressed fully, or at all, on appeal.

• • •

In conclusion, I would dismiss the appeal as it concerns bylaw 113. I would set aside the order appealed declaring bylaws 110, 111, 112 and 114 invalid and remit the issue of their validity to the Supreme Court of British Columbia for fresh determination.

NOTES AND QUESTIONS

1. Do you think that governmental regulation of forestry practices on private lands is a limitation on property rights? Does regulation of forestry practices on private lands differ from other environmental rules (for example, regulation of polluting uses) or planning legislation (for example, land-use restrictions through zoning) that society on the whole accepts? If so, how does it differ? Does this difference justify or explain why some environmental regulation is acceptable and some not?

2. The court puts considerable weight on the fact that "trees, like gravel and sand, have commercial value that may be harnessed by an owner, itself or by sale to another." The court states that for "this reason they are included within the general definition of a 'profit à prendre.'" The court then concluded that because of this it will very strictly interpret the legislative powers relating to cutting trees. In doing so the court is no doubt relying on the legal principle that in order to remove common law property rights, legislation must do it expressly or by necessary implication. As a matter of fact and law, technically, an owner of land in fee simple does not hold a profit à prendre to cut and remove trees since such lesser interest merges with the fee simple. Therefore, by regulating harvesting of trees, the impugned bylaws do not remove a profit à prendre. They do

not even remove a landowner's right to grant a profit à prendre to harvest trees. A landowner could still grant this interest although the exercise of any rights given under it would be subject to the bylaws. Do you think that the court was correct in applying the principle relating to removing common law property right? Do you think that the court was correct in strictly interpreting the bylaw because of this principle?

B. Jurisdictional Conflicts

Municipalities are created under provincial legislation. Accordingly, the powers delegated by a province to municipalities may not exceed the powers that a province may validly carry out under the *Constitution Act, 1867* ((UK), 30 & 31 Vict., c. 3). For example, since the constitution gives the federal government exclusive legislative authority over seacoast fisheries, (s. 91(12)), a municipality could not validly pass laws regulating them.

Municipal regulation or action also may be *ultra vires* other provincial laws or *ultra vires* federal laws. For example, suppose general environmental laws authorize a provincial environment department to regulate polluting emissions. Assuming that the province's legislation does not authorize municipalities to regulate air emissions per se, a court would likely find a municipal bylaw regulating exhaust emissions to be *ultra vires* if it directly conflicts with regulation under environmental legislation. To illustrate, in *Toronto (City) v. Toronto Transit Commission* (1992), 12 MPLR 190, the Ontario Divisional Court declared invalid such municipal bylaws on the ground that they directly conflicted with regulations under the Ontario *Environmental Protection Act*, RSO 1990, c. E. 19.

To complicate matters, just because a provincial department regulates a matter under specific provincial or federal legislation, it does not follow that municipalities may not also regulate some aspects of that matter. For example, in some situations a municipal body may consider environmental quality issues in exercising its planning and development authority even when specialized land-use or environmental legislation confers regulatory authority over these issues on other persons or bodies. In 2001, the Supreme Court of Canada in *Spraytech*, above, approved of the "dual compliance" test to determine whether a municipal bylaw and a federal or provincial law may coexist. Under the dual compliance test, a conflict is fatal to a municipal legislative provision only where it is impossible to follow the municipal provision at the same time as following an allegedly conflicting provincial or federal legislative provision.

The next two cases, both involving so-called undesirable facilities, shed light on when municipalities may engage in environmental regulation while carrying out land-use planning and development functions. The first case concerns a landfill, and the second, a propane facility.

Robertson et al. v. City of Edmonton
(1990), 104 AR 374 (QB)

FEEHAN J: Bruce Robertson, Linda Robertson and Sten Berg (the applicants) bring this application on their own behalf and as representatives of the members of the

407403 Alberta Society, also known as the Stop Aurum Dump Association (hereinafter called the "society"), to quash and declare *ultra vires* and void Edmonton by-laws 9239 and 9240. By-law 9239 adopted a new Aurum Industrial Area Structure Plan to reflect the changes which would occur as a result of the proposed landfill operation in the area. By-law 9240 redistricted the lands in question to DC5 (Site Specific Development Control) District and A (Metropolitan Recreation) District from their previous designations.

In preparation for the passage of these two by-laws, the city published notices of a public hearing to be held on 12th September 1989. The notices were published on 30th and 31st August in the Edmonton Journal. In addition, the city sent notice of the hearing to parties with an assessable interest in lands within 60 metres of the subject site and to those who had advised the city that they were interested in the by-laws in question.

On this basis, Mr. Berg addressed city council. He was advised that he had five minutes to speak and his request for an extension was denied. The transcript of the hearing shows that Mr. Berg initially spoke for approximately six minutes and then there were further discussions for approximately a further thirteen minutes. No other members of the society addressed council. The by-laws passed first and second readings on 12th September and third reading on 26th September 1989.

The applicants seek:

(a) an order quashing the by-laws for illegality pursuant to s. 414 of the *Municipal Government Act*, RSA 1980, c. M-26;
(b) judicial review in the nature of *certiorari* quashing the by-laws; and
(c) a declaration that the by-laws are *ultra vires* and void.

• • •

Hereunder is a partial transcript of what was said at the council meeting:

MAYOR CAVANAGH: You have five minutes, Mr. Berg.

MR. BERG: Your Worship, we became aware of the possibility of the making of the presentation to City Council about a month ago and we made some inquiries as to what the process was. We understood that, initially, there won't be a time limit, so first of all I would like to ask for the indulgence of Council with regard to the time limit because we are dealing here with a major issue with an application that cost you millions to put together which is highly technical and covers many, many areas. ...

MAYOR CAVANAGH: It's a five-minute regulation. That's what we have in Council, Mr. Berg. Unless Council at the end say go ahead then ... .

MR. BERG: Well, I am afraid it is impossible to deal with an $80 million project and rising with all of the information we have looked at in order to put this brief together in five minutes. It is an impossible situation so I would ask for the indulgence, I would plead for the indulgence of Council to allow us to present what we have worked so hard to do. ...

ALDERMAN WHITE: Mr. Mayor, might I just ask for a moment. We are dealing with land use items here. We are not dealing with the ... I read the titles here on the various paragraphs and there are a couple of … the rest are clean water and plastic liners and the environmental concerns. In fact, we have dealt with those by instructing our department to do the best they can to make application to the Board of Health. In fact, my understanding is that the Board of Health are the final adjudicators of those matters. Now if … I don't see any great need to go through those here and if Mr. Berg wishes to speak to the land use items and only the land use items, then I don't have any difficulty with extending his time to accommodate that. But I'm afraid I'm not prepared to extend the time in order to listen to items that I don't have jurisdictions over which is the … all the pollution control, plastic liners, clean water acts and things of that nature, so that if Mr. Berg wishes to inform Council that's what he intends to do is deal with specifically those items of land use, extraneous of those other issues, then I'm quite prepared to make that motion.

MAYOR CAVANAGH: Well, your presentation reads, Presentation City Council, City of Edmonton, in opposition to Bylaw 9239, so you are opposing us rezoning this. That's all we are talking about today.

MR. BERG: With due respect you can't separate them because the proposed land use bylaw is making the application possible.

MAYOR CAVANAGH: Correct. That is what is before us, that is what we are dealing with today, sir, and you have five minutes and you can start now. …

ALDERMAN WHITE: Mr. Berg, I assume that you'll make these representations at, which we believe is the appropriate location in most of the environmental considerations, at the hearings, will you not? …

MR. BERG: Alderman White, you cannot separate land use from this question. You cannot. … Because the purpose of the change is to accommodate the dump. It's there in black and white. Your expert there talked about it for a considerable length of time, about the dump and he gave you that information. …

ALDERMAN HAYTER: … There is a forum that is going to be provided for this, the environmental aspects are going to be covered. That will be before the Board of Health and you will have ample opportunity to make your presentation at that time. What we are talking here is about a rezoning application.

   Mr. Berg wanted to speak on environmental issues. The mayor, Alderman White and Alderman Hayter wanted him to restrict his statements to the land use by-law. Alderman Kinisky attempted to help Mr. Berg by asking an environmental question but was stopped by the mayor.

. . .

Failure To Take Into Account Relevant Considerations

The applicants submit that council failed to take into consideration relevant planning considerations in making their decision to adopt by-laws 9239 and 9240 and thereby committed a jurisdictional error. The key considerations which it is submitted that council failed to consider were the environmental implications of the by-laws, although there was some suggestion that council had ignored archaeological and historical considerations as well.

The respondents contend that council did not fail to consider these issues and that council members received information, asked questions and obtained answers to questions covering a large number of issues, including environmental and health issues.

The transcript of the 12th September hearing indicates that speakers addressing by-laws 9239 and 9240 did, in fact, talk about environmental issues. ...

The fact that the speakers were allowed to talk about environmental considerations does not end the matter. The issue is whether council took these considerations into account in deliberating on by-laws 9239 and 9240. In my opinion, they did not. The transcript of the hearing shows that council overwhelmingly indicated that it was not concerned with environmental issues.

It should be noted that the city conceded in oral argument that environmental issues were relevant to council's decision. The city argued from the standpoint that these issues had been considered by council in any event and so did not directly address the issue in written argument.

The consideration of environmental issues is not specifically imposed on council by the *Planning Act* in either the provisions dealing with land use by-laws or the provisions dealing with area structure plans. The applicants argue that the Act has set a broad framework for what is relevant to planning issues (I.M. Rogers, QC, *Canadian Law of Planning and Zoning* (1973), at p. 3):

> The prime objective of community planning is the evolution of the ideal environment for carrying on the various activities of living of the individuals who make up the community. There are two basic aspects of community planning. The first is concerned with the physical surroundings of the community: the organization of land use, streets, buildings, recreation areas and other public services. Both beauty and utility are essential. The second aspect of community planning emphasizes the social and economic relationships and characteristics of the community: family life, recreational, cultural, political and other group activities. Planning seeks to achieve that physical environment that will best promote the economic, social and moral welfare of the inhabitants of the community.
>
> The two fundamental concepts are to a great extent inter-related. Planning the physical organization of the community without consideration of its social and moral objectives will result in a plan of little functional value. At the same time, it is unlikely that the social and moral objectives will be attained without careful physical organization of the community.

It is also instructive to look to the terms of reference adopted in the proposed area structure plan by-law 9239. Area structure plans are dealt with in s. 64 of the *Planning Act*. That section provides:

> 64(1) For the purpose of providing a framework for subsequent subdivision and development of an area of land in a municipality, a council may, by by-law passed in accordance with Part 6, adopt a plan to be known as the (name) Area Structure Plan.

(2) An area structure plan shall

    (a) conform to any general municipal plan in existence and affecting the area that is the subject of the area structure plan; ...

    (c) contain any other matters the council considers necessary.

The area structure plan adopted by city council in by-law 9239, itself, deals with environmental conditions, stating, "[t]he terms of reference for area structure plan preparation require an assessment of environmental conditions within the plan area." The plan also states:

> As part of these studies an Environmental Impact Assessment (EIA) has been prepared ... . The main objective of this EIA is to assess whether construction of an operation of the proposed waste management facilities can be carried out in an environmentally acceptable manner. A complete hydrologic [sic] investigation has also been prepared ... . The resulting information will be considered by the local Board of Health, the Board's various referral agencies, including Alberta Environment, *and the city of Edmonton as part of the plan review process.* [Emphasis added.]

Whether or not the Act specifically required environmental considerations to be taken into account in the area structure plan, it appears that the plan encompassed these concerns as one of the "other matters that the council considers necessary" it should contain: s. 64(c). It makes little sense that the issue be included in the area structure plan and yet speakers addressing the by-law adopting the plan be discouraged from dealing with it.

Given the land use being proposed and the area structure plan being adopted in the impugned by-laws, it makes sense to conclude that environmental issues were relevant to the decision being made.

To be fair to council, the transcript of the hearing in no way indicates that the members thought that environmental issues were irrelevant altogether. Rather, the impression one gets is that council felt this issue was to be dealt with extensively by the public Board of Health. Furthermore, since before the waste management facilities could be developed on the site, approval had to be given by the local Board of Health, the decision by council to adopt the by-laws was, in effect, subject to the decision of the board about health and environmental issues.

. . .

In any event, the public Board of Health is charged with reviewing environmental issues as they impact on the public health. Council must also take into account environmental issues in the context of making their planning decision. A positive response from the local Board of Health with respect to environmental considerations does not necessarily mean that environmental factors are favourable to a decision to rezone. Thus, it would be incorrect for city council to ignore environmental issues altogether as they are relevant planning considerations in and of themselves.

I thought it interesting to note that at least one other speaker at the hearing felt that city council was ignoring relevant considerations. Mr. Sjolie, who spoke after Mr. Berg on behalf of the county of Strathcona, said:

> The County does find it difficult to deal with the land use issues at this time without the benefit of the analyses that will eventually be gone through at the public hearing before

the Board of Health because by the essence of a number of the land use criteria, the health and environmental impact that is determined under those studies and discoveries will have a large impact on the land use criteria that is ultimately implemented in these bylaws. And in fact the area structure plan itself, as well as the land use bylaw, makes a number of references to these impacts. So to a certain extent, we must agree with the previous speaker that they will have a real impact on the make-up of these bylaws and I would state, at the outset that it is the request of the County of Strathcona that these bylaws not be finally passed until that review. That thorough review can be gone through and that information considered by Council with respect to the final form of the area structure plan and the land use criteria contained within the redistricting application as well ... .

A failure to take into account relevant considerations is as erroneous as the improper consideration of an irrelevant one: *Oakwood Dev. Ltd. v. St. Francois Xavier*, [1985] 2 SCR 164 ... . Thus, the failure of a municipality to take into account relevant factors constitutes a jurisdictional error and provides a basis for judicial review.

I am of the opinion that council should have allowed Mr. Berg to speak for his five minutes on anything relevant. Environmental matters were relevant.

For that reason, but in the main for the reason that the society was misled on the five-minute issue, I quash these two by-laws.

NOTES AND QUESTIONS

1. Why did the court find environmental matters to be relevant planning considerations?

2. How much latitude do you think the legislation at the time, the *Planning Act*, RSA 1980, c. P-9, gives council when it states that an area structure plan may "contain any other matters the council considers necessary"? In answering, consider the jurisdictional limitations that may imposed by the constitution, other conflicting legislation, and the purposes of municipal planning legislation.

Superior Propane Inc. v. York (City)*
(1995), 23 OR (3d) 161 (CA)

MORDEN ACJO (orally): This is an appeal by the applicants, Superior Propane Inc. and Propane Gas Association of Canada Inc., from an order of the Divisional Court dismissing their application for a declaration that By-law 1116-87, passed by the respondent, City of York, is invalid. ...

In our view, the *Energy Act*, RSO 1980, c. 139, and the regulation enacted under it contain a comprehensive scheme to regulate propane dispensing, installation, handling and storage and that these matters are not subject to legislative authority by municipalities. In this regard we note that s. 29 of the *Energy Act* is worded more

---

*   Motion for leave to appeal to the Supreme Court of Canada dismissed with costs March 7, 1996 (La Forest, Cory, and Major JJ).

broadly than the similar provision in the *Environmental Protection Act, 1971*, SO 1971, c. 86, which was considered by this court in *Ontario (Attorney General) v. Mississauga (City)* (1981), 33 OR (2d) 395 ... . This latter provision expressly required "a conflict" as a condition of the *Environmental Protection Act, 1971* and the regulations under it prevailing over other legislation. We refer in this regard to *Union Gas Ltd. v. Dawn (Township)* (1977), 15 OR (2d) 722 ... (Div. Ct.), where a provision virtually identical to s. 29 (s. 57(2) of the Ontario *Energy Board Act*, RSO 1970, c. 312) was applied.

In any event, if the requirement of conflict is implicit in s. 29 of the *Energy Act*, we are satisfied that there is a conflict of such a nature as to nullify the by-law. In *Ontario (Attorney General) v. Mississauga (City)*, the majority of this court said at 410:

> [I]f the competing pieces of legislation are intended to advance the same policy and the provision in the statute covers the same ground as the by-law in a way to give rise to the interpretation that the statutory provision is intended "completely, exhaustively, or exclusively [to express] what [shall be] the law governing the particular conduct ... to which its attention is directed," then there is a case of conflict. ... If, in covering the same ground the subordinate legislation works at cross purposes to the provincial statute, then the case for conflict is reinforced.

At 413, 414 and 415 this principle was applied to the facts of that case as follows:

> I gather from the argument on behalf of the city that the certificate of approval aspect of s. 8 [of the *Environmental Protection Act, 1971*] is a factor which strongly favours a conclusion that there is no conflict because, if a certificate is granted, this reduces the otherwise absolute prohibition and leaves room for the operation of the then more stringent provisions of the by-law. With respect, I take a different view of the effect of the certificate of approval feature. In a case where no certificate of approval is issued the two laws practically duplicate each other and there is no room for municipal regulation. Where a certificate has been issued then, it appears to me, the absolute prohibition in the by-law clashes with the legislative scheme embodied in the statute and the proper implementation of this scheme. The two pieces of legislation, in this regard, are at cross purposes. They are repugnant to each other ... .
>
> I think that it is reasonable to conclude that the statutory provision in this relatively narrow field is of such a detailed and comprehensive nature that it leaves no practical room for the operation of the by-law. ... The basic issue does not turn on a conflict between a policy of a Minister of the Crown and the by-law, although such a conflict may be involved, but rather on a conflict between the policy of the Legislature as to the way matters covered by s. 8 should be dealt with and that reflected in the by-law. As I have said, these two policies are at cross purposes and, accordingly, the by-law should be declared to be inoperative.

These statements are applicable to the case before us. We agree with the conclusion of Mr. Justice Hollingworth that the provincial law and the by-law are at cross-purposes. We think that the by-law is at cross-purposes with the regulation because it negates the operating effect of the latter respecting tank size, height, setbacks, and protection.

We also agree with Hollingworth J that the basic and predominant purpose of the by-law is one of advancing safety concerns respecting the handling, etc., of propane and not land use planning. While the legislative history of the by-law may indicate recognition on the part of the municipality that safety was a matter for the province, it is clear that the genesis of the by-law was a concern to enact safeguards to protect the inhabitants with respect to the installation of propane tanks in the City of York. We refer to the minutes of the Legislation and Planning Committee held on September 5, 1984. The terms of the by-law are consistent with the intention to give effect to safety concerns.

We do not share the view of the majority of the Divisional Court that this is properly a case of the "by-law merely enhanc[ing] the statute." First, there is the operative conflict to which we have referred. Second, the authority of the municipality relates, generally, to land use planning and not safety respecting propane handling. This may be compared to the situation in Mississauga where the municipal power authorized by-laws relating to nuisances "of any kind," thereby putting municipalities into the field covered by the statute: see 408-09. Third, even if one were to assume that the by-law in this proceeding properly relates to land use planning, there then would be no reasonable basis for regarding it as enhancing a law enacted for a different purpose.

For these reasons the appeal is allowed, the order of the Divisional Court is set aside, and an order is made granting the relief sought by the applicants.

NOTES AND QUESTIONS

1. Which of the three reasons given by the court for striking the bylaw do you find the most persuasive? Why?

2. This case precedes *Spraytech v. Town of Hudson*, above. Do you think that the court in *Superior Propane* would have decided the case differently on the basis of the dual compliance test?

3. Can you think of any circumstances in which safety respecting the handling of dangerous substances could be a valid land-use planning concern?

4. Why did the *Superior Propane* court find that it was beyond municipal authority to regulate environmental safety matters whereas, the *Robertson* court found it within municipal authority to consider environmental consequences of a landfill?

III. PLANNING REGULATION AND TAKINGS; EXCEEDING JURISDICTION

A. Takings

US courts recognize "regulatory takings" on the basis of constitutionally protected property rights by virtue of the Fifth and Fourteenth Amendments to the American *Bill of Rights*. The Fifth Amendment reads:

> No person shall be ... deprived of life, liberty or property without due process of law; nor shall private property be taken for public use, without just compensation.

The Fourteenth Amendment states:

> No state shall make or enforce any law which shall abridge the privileges or immunities of the citizens of the United States; nor shall any State deprive any person of life, liberty or property, without due process of law; nor deny to any person within its jurisdiction the equal protection of its laws.

A critical difference between Canada and the United States is that property rights are not enshrined in the Canadian constitution or the *Charter of Rights and Freedoms*. Consequently, in Canada there are no individual rights comparable to the US Fifth or Fourteenth Amendment rights. Not surprisingly, then, although there is ample Canadian case law dealing with out-and-out expropriations, there is no body of jurisprudence dealing with alleged regulatory takings as there is in the United States. Nevertheless, occasionally Canadian litigants ask courts to order compensation where government action has restricted or prohibited land uses.

Before looking at cases, the reader should be clear on the distinction between true expropriations and regulatory takings. Under Canadian law, if a government takes an interest in land without the owner's consent, and the statute under which the taking occurred either explicitly or implicitly gives the owner the right to compensation, the government must compensate the owner. Normally a government will take an interest in land by an out-and-out expropriation—for example, to expand a highway. This section is not about the normal case. Instead, it considers what rights an affected landowner might have when government does not out-and-out expropriate land, but rather imposes substantial regulation on land use so that the landowner cannot develop it as he or she had hoped. The "regulatory takings" issue is critical when considering how far municipalities may go in regulating uses of land in order to protect environmental values. Although not concerning municipal land-use planning and development law, the *Queen in Right of British Columbia v. Tener*, [1985] 1 SCR 533 (reproduced, in part, in chapter 12) should be noted since it is one of the leading "takings" or, as it is often called in Canada, "de facto expropriation" cases.

The plaintiffs, David and Gertrude Tener, were the registered owners of sixteen mineral claims granted by the province of British Columbia. The underlying title to the minerals as well as the right to access them remained in the provincial Crown. The Teners paid $100,000 for their rights. Their mineral rights were in respect of an area that subsequent to their purchase was put under parks legislation. Statutory protection for the park was upgraded through the years and in 1973 a legislative amendment required anyone with a mineral claim within the park to obtain a permit from the lieutenant governor in council in order to develop. Each year, from 1973 to 1978, the Teners asked for a permit. Finally, in 1978 the government decisively denied the permit. The Teners sued for approximately $5.5 million dollars, claiming an expropriation. The trial court denied their claim but the appellate division allowed compensation. The Crown appealed to the Supreme Court of Canada.

The Supreme Court of Canada dismissed the appeal and let the compensation award stand. The case is important since it sets out what a plaintiff must prove to establish a de facto expropriation. According to the case, the plaintiff must establish

a. [t]he existence of a property interest that was obtained by virtue of government legislation;

b. [t]he deprivation of the interest by government action;

c. [t]he acquisition of the interest by the government; and

d. [t]hat legislation explicitly or implicitly provides for compensation for the taking of the right.

In *Alberta v. Nillson* (1999), 31 Alta. LR (3d) 353 (QB), this last requirement was liberally interpreted to mean that normally there is a right to compensation for expropriation unless legislation explicitly denies the right.

In *Tener*, the fact that the mineral interest was an interest in land was not contested. It was either a property interest in the nature of a *profit à prendre* that consisted of an access right and exploitation right, or a simple mineral title interest. Regarding the second factor, the Supreme Court found that the government's absolute refusal to issue a permit amounted to total extinction of the interest. The Teners were left with nothing.

Regarding the third criterion, the Supreme Court noted that once the Crown de facto extinguished the Teners' interest, the interest was, in effect, absorbed back into the Crown's fee title. (The court stated that the only way of extinguishing a *profit à prendre* is by its being absorbed in the fee title.) Finally, the Supreme Court found that there was an explicit right to compensation under the British Columbia *Parks Act*, SBC 1965, c. 31, ss. 6, 9, 11, and 18.

Since the *Tener* decision, Canadian courts have heard only a few "takings" cases. The following case demonstrates how courts apply the principles set out in *Tener* in the context of municipal regulation.

Steer Holdings Ltd. v. Manitoba
[1993] 2 WWR 146 (CA)

HUBAND JA: Where the legislature imposes some limitation on the use of property, but the legislation does not provide for compensation to the injuriously affected owner, the general rule is that no compensation is payable. That rule has been stated and restated countless times.

. . .

Halsbury makes reference to the case of *Rockingham Sisters of Charity v. R*, [1922] 2 AC 315. That case involved a claim for damages for injurious affection to land in Nova Scotia. Lord Parmoor, in delivering reasons for judgment for the Privy Council, makes this statement of principle (at p. 322):

> Compensation claims are statutory and depend on statutory provisions. No owner of lands expropriated by statute for public purposes is entitled to compensation, either for the value of land taken, or for damage, on the ground that his land is "injuriously affected," unless he can establish a statutory right. The claim, therefore, of the appellants, if any, must be found in a Canadian statute.

. . .

What was said by Lord Parmoor was adopted by Thorson P in his reasons for judgment in *The King v. Woods Manufacturing Co. Ltd.*, [1949] Ex. CR 9 (at p. 13):

> It is also important to remember that the owner of expropriated property has no inherent right to compensation for the property lawfully taken from him. Nor has he any constitutional right, such as an owner has in the United States, to "just" or "reasonable" or "adequate" compensation. He has only such right as is conferred upon him by statute and no right at all apart therefrom.

But the general rule smacks of unfairness, particularly where there is more than regulation or limitation of use, and so courts have strained to award compensation for a taking of property by compulsory acquisition. In *Attorney-General v. De Keyser's Royal Hotel*, [1920] AC 508, the Crown took over possession of a hotel during wartime for the purpose of housing the headquarters personnel of a branch of the military. Subsequently, the hotel owner sued for compensation. In the course of his reasons for judgment, Lord Atkinson made this statement (at p. 542):

> The recognized rule for the construction of statutes is that, unless the words of the statute clearly so demand, a statute is not to be construed so as to take away the property of a subject without compensation.

. . .

So, in *Manitoba Fisheries Limited v. R*, [1978] 6 WWR 496, the Supreme Court of Canada, in a judgment by Ritchie J, granted compensation to a plaintiff whose goodwill had been taken over by the Crown in a compulsory statutory acquisition, in spite of the fact that the statute did not contain specific provision for compensation.

. . .

A clear distinction has been made, however, between those cases where there is a compulsory taking, as opposed to those cases where some right or interest in the property has been restricted or affected. In *The Queen v. Tener* (1985), 32 LCR 340, Wilson J, in the course of her reasons for judgment, makes these observations (at p. 361):

> Where land has been taken the statute will be construed in light of a presumption in favour of compensation (see: Todd, *The Law of Expropriation and Compensation in Canada* (1976) at 32-3) but no such presumption exists in the case of injurious affection where no land has been taken (see: Todd, *supra* at 292 et seq.; Challies, *The Law of Expropriation*, 2nd ed. (1963) at 132 et seq.). In such a case the right to compensation has been severely circumscribed by the courts (see: *The Queen v. Loiselle* (1962), 35 DLR (3d) 274, [1962] SCR 624) ... .

Thus, zoning by-laws passed by municipalities do not give rise to claims for compensation, and this is so even where there is a "down zoning" by which the owner's use of the property is more restricted. The typical response of a landowner to a down zoning of property is to sue for a declaration that the by-law is *ultra vires*, rather than for compensation. The fact that the by-law has imposed greater limits on the use of the land is not, in itself, a ground for declaring the by-law invalid: *Regina Auto Court v. Regina (City)* (1958), 25 WWR 167 and *Barrett Lumber Co. Ltd. v. Halifax County* (1977), 19 NSR (2d) 594. However, where the by-law is merely a disguise for an attempted confiscation of the land without compensation, the by-law will be set aside: *Columbia Estate Company Limited v. Corporation of the District of Burnaby*, [1974] 5 WWR 735 (BCSC).

British Columbia v. Tener, supra, involved a somewhat similar situation. The respondents owned certain mineral rights which it [sic] wished to exploit. The provincial government created a park in the area where the mineral rights were located, and then some years later upgraded the status of the park to one where the exploitation of minerals would not be allowed except by way of a ministerial permit which could be granted only in very limited circumstances. The effect of the legislation was to prevent the respondents from the normal development of their interest in the property. Estey J, writing for five of seven members of a unanimous court, concluded that the impact of what the government had done went beyond regulation, and amounted to a taking, entitling the respondents to compensation. Not only had the right to develop the minerals been taken away, but the result was an enhancement to the amenities of the provincial park (at p. 351):

> Here, the action taken by the government was to enhance the value of the public park. The imposition of zoning regulation and the regulation of activities on lands, fire regulation limits and so on, add nothing to the value of public property. Here the government wished, for obvious reasons, to preserve the qualities perceived as being desirable for public parks, and saw the mineral operations of the respondents under their 1937 grant as a threat to the park. The notice of 1978 took value from the respondents and added value to the park. The taker, the government of the province, clearly did so in exercise of its valid authority to govern. It clearly enhanced the value of its asset, the park. The respondents are left with only the hope of some future reversal of park policy and the burden of paying taxes on their minerals. The notice of 1978 was an expropriation and, in my view, the rest is part of the compensation assessment process.

In a concurring judgment, Wilson J agreed that the actions of the government constituted an expropriation, and said that "it is quite unreal to characterize it as merely injurious affection."

• • •

This assessment of the law is of no comfort to the plaintiff in the present action.

Steer Holdings Ltd. is the owner of property located on the north side of Portage Avenue in Winnipeg. The land, with a restaurant building located upon it, was purchased by the plaintiff in 1975. It is a substantial property, consisting of about 4.3 acres. The restaurant building and a large parking area is on the east half of the property. The west half of the property is undeveloped, and is basically a ravine through which Omand's Creek passes.

The plaintiff had no plans to use or develop the ravine from the time the property was acquired until the late 1980's. It then came to the plaintiff's attention that a landowner further to the north and slightly to the west, through whose property Omand's Creek also passes, had contemplated a development within the applicable zoning tolerances which would span Omand's Creek. Rather than permit such a development the Province of Manitoba acquired the property by purchase so that area of the creek could be developed as a nature park.

The plaintiff began its own plans for a commercial development which would span the creek. The Province of Manitoba was not interested in the subject property, but the City of Winnipeg was concerned, and entered into negotiations to either purchase from or exchange properties with the plaintiff. Before any agreement could be concluded, legislation was introduced by way of a Private Member's Bill, and enacted by the legislature of Manitoba to amend *The City of Winnipeg Act*. Section 624.1 was added to the Act ... .

The legislation prohibits the plaintiff from proceeding with a commercial development which would span the creek. The law is general in nature, but there seems little doubt that it was designed to prevent the development being contemplated by the plaintiff. Since no building permit had been obtained, no compensation is payable under sec. 624.1(3). As a consequence of the legislation, the City of Winnipeg broke off further negotiations with the plaintiff.

Counsel for the plaintiff argues that there was a "taking away" of a property right which the plaintiff had enjoyed, and that there was a corresponding benefit or acquisition flowing to the Province of Manitoba.

I am inclined to agree that there was a "taking away" in the sense that the legislation limited the plaintiff in what it could do with the property. But in my opinion there was no corresponding benefit or acquisition by the Province of Manitoba. Title to the land remains with the plaintiff. The creek and the ravine are an amenity to the restaurant. That amenity remains just as it was before the plaintiff was struck with the idea that a development proposal would persuade one government level or the other to pay a healthy price for the property.

Argument was mounted that the legislation benefits the Province of Manitoba by enlarging a park system through linkage with the nature park to the north. What is known as the Blue Stem Nature Park is not an adjacent property. It is slightly to the north, and is also to the west of the subject property, separated from the subject property by an intersecting railway line. There is no suggestion that people will be encouraged in any way to move from the nature park to the subject property. Moreover, the subject property remains private for the exclusive use of the plaintiff and its invitees.

Counsel for the plaintiff also argues that compensation is payable even if there is no acquisition by the Province of Manitoba. But that is not my reading of the law. Before one can imply a right to compensation in the legislation, there must be more than a limitation on use. To qualify for compensation there must be an expropriation, if not in name, then in effect. The limitation on usage must be balanced by some corresponding acquisition by the authority.

The learned trial judge assessed damages, and there was an appeal and a cross-appeal as to damages. Since I would dismiss the plaintiff's appeal concerning liability, there is no need to consider the appeals as to damages. The Province of Manitoba is entitled to costs on the appeal.

NOTES AND QUESTIONS

1. What is the difference between a regulatory and a confiscatory taking? Can you think of any examples where planning and development regulation to protect green spaces would be confiscatory?

2. To be a compensable taking, there must be a taking away of something that the plaintiff had enjoyed, and a corresponding benefit or acquisition flowing to the government taker. The Court of Appeal in *Steer Holdings* could find no such corresponding benefit. Can you think of any situations in which planning or development regulation to protect green spaces might confer such benefit?

B. Exceeding Jurisdiction

This section concerns jurisdictional limitations on municipalities acting to protect green spaces under their authority over land uses and development. Case law indicates that a court will quash such municipal action where it is shown to be discriminatory, carried out in bad faith, made without factual basis, or beyond legitimate planning objectives or authorization.

Generally speaking, "discrimination" means that the statutory delegate acts in a way that is partial and unequal. "Bad faith" on the part of a municipality typically involves fraud, corruption, or acting for ulterior motives that are unrelated to planning processes relevant to the decision in question. "Without factual basis" means the municipality did not act on the basis of the facts and evidence. "Beyond legitimate planning objectives or authorization" indicates that the challenged municipal action exceeded the authority of the plans, bylaws, or other regulation the municipality relied on.

The next two cases illustrate some of these concepts.

MacMillan Bloedel Ltd. v. Galiano Island Trust Committee*
(1995), 28 MPLR (2d) 157, at 203 (BCCA)

[In 1951, the plaintiff logging company acquired 66 parcels of mainly forested land on Galiano Island, one of the Gulf Islands off mainland British Columbia. The parcels ranged from 20 to 220 acres and consisted of over half the island. The 1973 planning bylaws under the BC *Municipal Act* allowed one family dwelling per legal parcel. The subdivision bylaw allowed a minimum parcel size of 20 acres.

In 1990, the BC legislature passed the *Island Trust Act*, which set forth a new land-use planning and development scheme for designated islands, including Galiano. The Act provided for the establishment of a local trust committee with municipal-like powers related to land-use planning and development. The Galiano Trust Committee was established under this Act. Relevant provisions of the legislation governing the trustees are that they had jurisdiction to

> 3(2)(a) make recommendations to the Lieutenant-Governor in Council respecting the determination, implementation, and carrying out of policies for the preservation and protection of the trust area and its unique amenities and environment; ...
>
> (c) co-ordinate and assist in the determination, implementation, and carrying out of municipal and Provincial Government policies for the preservation and protection of the trust area and its unique amenities and environment;

---

*   Leave to appeal to the Supreme Court of Canada refused.

Over the next fifteen years, the *Islands Trust Act* was considerably amended, and in 1989 a new *Islands Trust Act*, SBC 1989, c. 68, which came into force on April 1, 1990, was promulgated.

The Islands Trust was continued under the Act, the object of which the Act states is

> 3. ... to preserve and protect the trust area and its unique amenities and environ-
> ment for the benefit of the residents of the trust area and of the Province generally, in
> cooperation with municipalities, regional districts, improvement districts, other per-
> sons and organizations and the government of the Province.

No comparable provision is to be found in any other BC legislation concerning municipal government.

Responding to growing opposition to its forestry practices, the plaintiff offered to sell its holdings to the local community, setting a November 30, 1990 deadline. A local conservation association could not raise the funds to buy the holdings at market value, which, according to the plaintiff, under the 1977 bylaws would be $20,000,000. The deadline passed. On January 3, 1991, the plaintiff advised the government that it would sell its holdings to the public. In late January, the trustees gave first reading to bylaws that would, in effect, change the zoning of the plaintiff's land by removing the permitted use of family dwellings and increasing the minimum parcel size to 50 acres. These bylaws frustrated the plaintiff's plans to sell lots to the public for residential purposes. The bylaws were adopted in January 1992.

The plaintiff applied to the trial court for a declaration that the bylaws were void for illegality. The trial judge granted the declaration finding the bylaws to be discriminatory and passed in bad faith. He found that the trustees' actual motive in passing the bylaws was to thwart the plaintiff's plan to subdivide and sell its holdings for residential purposes. The defendant appealed.]

SOUTHIN JA: With respect, in my opinion, the appellant, the respondent, and the learned trial judge, have all approached this case as if there were immutable principles of law restraining the exercise by a body such as the Galiano Trust Committee of powers conferred upon it by the Legislature. I consider that an erroneous approach.

It is not an immutable principle of law that a by-law may not discriminate or not be aimed at a particular land owner. It is not an immutable principle that a by-law may not have as its "objectives" one of the "facts" alleged [by the respondents] in paragraph 17. It is not an immutable principle of law, as was suggested in argument, that a body such as the committee must have for a by-law a "valid planning purpose," whatever that means. The *Islands Trust Act* and the *Municipal Act* require only (and they do so by necessary implication) that a by-law enacted under s. 963 be for the purpose of regulating land use. The only immutable principle of law is that a body with a power to enact subordinate legislation must act within the powers conferred. Sometimes a power expressly requires as a condition precedent to its exercise a certain purpose. Whether that purpose exists is a question of fact. Apart from the requirement that such a by-law be for the purpose of regulating land use, no purpose is to be found in the legislation. Thus, what is at issue here is an implication of purpose in the legislation.

I think it useful to recall and keep in mind certain fundamental principles. The first such principle is to be found in the *Constitution Acts*. It is indisputable that if the Legislature had itself put into a statute the provisions of these by-laws, that statute, by virtue of the eighth, thirteenth, and sixteenth heads of s. 92 would take effect according to its terms. Indeed, there is nothing to prevent the Legislature, even now, passing a by-law validation act, a practice frequently followed in the early years of this century (see, for instance, the *Municipal By-laws Confirmation Act, 1912*, SBC 1912, c. 27), and is even, from time to time, in use in what might be called modern times (see the *Municipalities Enabling and Validating Act*, RSBC 1960, c. 261, and the consolidation prepared for convenience only to be found immediately after the *Municipal Finance Authority Act*, RSBC 1979, c. 292, but only in the looseleaf edition).

The second such principle is that the Legislature is presumed not to confer certain powers or means of exercising power, unless the contrary clearly appears from the legislation. Thus, we presume that the Legislature does not intend to confer a power to act contrary to the rules of procedural fairness or to act corruptly. We also presume that the Legislature intends a power conferred to be used only for the purposes of the power as those powers are found in the legislation (see, for instance, *Roncarelli v. Duplessis*, [1959] SCR 121). We also presume that the Legislature does not intend to confer a power to expropriate without compensation (see, for instance, *Tener v. The Queen*, [1985] 1 SCR 533). But, by the combined effect of ss. 960 and 972, *supra* at p. 20, and s. 963, *supra* at p. 19, the Legislature of British Columbia authorizes a municipality to "downzone," an exercise of power many persons would consider equivalent to expropriation, and to do so without paying compensation. We also presume that the Legislature does not intend to confer a power to discriminate (see *Kruse v. Johnson*, [1898] 2 QB 91), although that is a somewhat vague proposition. For instance, by s. 963(1), the Legislature has conferred a power to do what at one time might well have been thought of as "discrimination."

But the Legislature, by the terms of the enactment, may oust any or all of these principles, so long as it itself does not contravene the *Constitution Acts*. The presumptions are not immutable. When, therefore, an attack is made on subordinate legislation, of which a by-law is but an example, as being outside the purposes of the legislation, that attack is no more than a different way of saying that the subordinate legislation is *ultra vires* or, to put it another way, that upon the true construction of the enactment under which the subordinate legislation was purportedly enacted, the Legislature had not conferred a power to enact it.

In considering such an issue, the nature of the body enacting the impugned subordinate legislation is a relevant consideration. The Legislature might well give powers to a body which is subject to control of the electors which it might well not grant to some other body. Municipal institutions have, for a very long time, been thought of as a third level of government, albeit such institutions may have their powers taken away by a stroke of the legislative pen. The Legislature of British Columbia has not only not taken away powers by strokes of the legislative pen but, over the last one hundred and fourteen years, has granted wider and wider powers to municipal institutions generally. Thus, for instance, in the first *Municipal Act*, SBC 1881, the general power section, then 104, had 90 subsections. By 1948 (see RSBC 1948, c. 232) the section had 301 sub-paragraphs. The present Act, indexed as RSBC 1979, c. 290, but enacted by SBC 1993, c. 54, is differently structured, but the powers conferred appear to be substantially greater than those conferred by the Act in force in 1948. Great though the powers are, a municipality, in the words of O'Halloran JA, "is not a state within a state. ... It is a creature and not a maker of statute law" (*Caponero v. Brakenbridge* (1944), 60 BCR 1, at 11 (CA)).

The cases cited and which in my opinion support the propositions to which I have adverted, fall, as I read them, into four categories:

1. where the power is given for an express purpose but is found as a fact to have been exercised for a different and unauthorized purpose;
2. where the power on its face authorizes the enactment but it is argued that some limitation of the power is to be implied in the statute and the exercise of power is contrary to that limitation;
3. where there is no express power to do the thing done but it is argued that the power sought is to be implied from a general power;
4. where the matter is essentially one of the interpretation of the power.

[A discussion follows exemplifying each category.]

In which of these niches do the allegations of the respondent belong?

I return to the statement of claim. Of the contested paragraphs, the respondent had failed to establish, as it had alleged in a reference to the Official Community Plan, that the amendments to the Official Community Plan did not have the broad support of the consensus of the citizens. (See s. 4(3) of the plan.) Indeed, the evidence showed the contrary.

For convenience I repeat the crucial allegations:

16. By-laws No. 81, 82, 84 and 85 are aimed at lands owned by the Plaintiff and unfairly discriminate against the Plaintiff as a landowner on Galiano Island. Furthermore, By-laws No. 81, 82, 84 and 85 are unreasonable in their ambit and effect.

17. By-laws No. 81, 82, 84 and 85 were proposed and adopted by the Defendant Trust Committee to reduce the value of the Plaintiff's lands and frustrate the Plaintiff's sales efforts, with a view to one or more of the following objectives:

(a) to permit a low-cost acquisition of the Plaintiff's lands by the Galiano Conservancy Association or a similar organization for the sole benefit of current landowners on Galiano Island other than the Plaintiff; or

(b) to appropriate the Plaintiff's lands for public purposes at a reduced cost;

(c) to place the Plaintiff's lands in a holding zone until the Defendant Trust Committee could develop some valid planning purpose.

18. The purpose or purposes for which these by-laws were proposed and adopted are improper, and constitute an illegal exercise of the Defendant Trust Committee and its statutory responsibilities.

The pleader would have, I think, brought this case into clearer focus if he or she, instead of paragraphs 16 to 18, had said something like this:

16. Upon the true construction of the *Municipal Act* and *Islands Trust Act*, it was beyond the powers of the Galiano Trust Committee to enact a by-law which:

(a) unfairly discriminated against the plaintiff as a landowner on Galiano Island;

(b) was unreasonable in ambit and effect;

(c) permitted a low-cost acquisition of the plaintiff's lands by the Galiano Conservancy Association for the sole benefit of current landowners on Galiano Island other than the plaintiff;

(d) appropriated the plaintiff's lands for public purposes at a reduced cost;

(e) placed the plaintiff's lands in a holding zone until the defendant trust committee could develop some valid plan and purpose.

17. Alternatively, upon the true construction of the said Acts, it was beyond the powers of the Galiano Trust Committee to enact by-laws which had such a purpose, whether or not such by-laws were effective for the purpose.

18. By-laws 81-85 have the effect and purpose alleged in paragraphs 16 and 17.

19. The purpose or purposes for which these by-laws were proposed and adopted are improper, and constitute an illegal exercise of the Defendant Trust Committee and its statutory responsibilities.

Sub-paragraphs (a) and (b), in my opinion, are really an assertion that the appellant has no power to pass a by-law which rezones half the land within its geographical authority if that half belongs to a single landowner. In my opinion, when one combines s. 3 of the *Islands Trust Act* and s. 963(1) of the *Municipal Act*, that assertion is unfounded.

What of assertion (c)?

On its face, it has an aspect of misfeasance. It resembles the assertion unsuccessfully made in *United Buildings Corporation, Ltd. v. City of Vancouver* [[1915] AC 345] ... that the purpose of the road closure was to benefit the Hudson's Bay Company. If members of a municipal council were to conspire together to downzone A's land so that B, an adjoining landowner who wanted it and to whom A had refused to sell, could buy it cheaply, the council could fairly be said to have acted in bad faith. From such an act, there would arise the stench of corruption.

I detect no stench of corruption in the sympathy of the members of the committee, especially Mrs. Griffiths, for the desire of the members of the Galiano Nature Conservancy to purchase these lands. There is today a very large segment of the citizenry, not only on Galiano Island but also in other parts of this Province, which considers the preservation of lands for wildlife of substantial public importance. Mrs. Griffiths, in her examination, said that in 1987, before she became a member of the committee, she was a member of the Galiano Naturalists, "I particularly was anxious about the cutting of trees right up to eagles' nests ... . There were others who did have concerns about strips beside streams and water." But that Mrs. Griffiths might be said not to be impartial between the eagles on the one hand and the respondent on the other, cannot in and of itself be condemned as "bad faith" in the sense in which that phrase is used in the cases. See by way of comparison *Jones v. Delta (Corp.)* (1992), 69 BCLR (2d) 239 (BCCA), in which the underlying dispute was between birds and golf. The council chose golf and its by-laws were upheld.

I doubt if, in 1991, there was a single municipal councillor in the whole of this Province who did not have some bent on questions of land use. Such questions have been, in recent years, the very stuff of municipal political life. Those who agree with a particular councillor's opinion consider him or her a person of sound conviction. Those who disagree say he or she has an axe to grind.

As to assertion (d), these by-laws did not appropriate the respondent's lands to public purposes at a reduced cost. Nothing in the by-laws prevented the respondent from logging every tree off its half of the island. What did prevent the respondent from doing so was that it wanted to sell the land as residential land, a course which I infer would be more profitable than logging it. Furthermore, I think it right to assume that the officials of the respondent, no less than the members of the committee, are honourable citizens who had no wish, even though the respondent had the right to do so, to denude the land of trees.

As to assertion (e), I see nothing in any provision of the *Islands Trust Act* or the *Municipal Act* which prevents this downzoning which is intended to prevent development while the governing authority gathers up all the advice and information it thinks helpful relating to the lands in issue and thereupon coming to a solution which it perceives to be in the long-term best interests of the community. Land use issues are difficult. Once land is developed, undoing the development, if it is harmful to the public interest or what some people perceive to be the public interest, is next to impossible. I have said "this downzoning" because it was implemented pursuant to both s. 963(1) of the *Municipal Act* and s. 3 of the *Islands Trust Act*. If there were no s. 3 of the *Islands Trust Act*, I might be of a different opinion but s. 3 is not a mere piety. To put it another way, these by-laws were enacted for the purposes or the objects of s. 3 as well as for the health and welfare of the inhabitants of Galiano Island. They therefore had a lawful purpose.

. . .

[Regarding allegations of bad faith …] In my opinion, a by-law which, upon its true construction, does not effect a purpose which would be illegal cannot be struck down because of the hopes or desires of the members of the council who enact it.

Thus, these by-laws were within and not beyond the powers conferred on these trustees under the legislation governing them. Since writing these reasons, I have had the privilege of reading in draft the reasons for judgment of Mr. Justice Finch. As I read his reasons, although he expresses himself in language more felicitous than my own, he is not saying anything different in substance.

Therefore, for his reasons as well as for my own, I would allow the appeal and dismiss the action.

FINCH JA: I have had the advantage of reading in draft, the reasons of Madam Justice Southin. I agree that the appeal should be allowed. However, I prefer to express my own reasons for reaching that conclusion.

. . .

The history of the *Islands Trust Act* indicates a legislative intent to increase the powers of local trust committees. It also shows an intent to give increased effect to the object statement now contained in s. 3 by setting out the object statement in a separate section of the Act. I think it a clear inference that local trust committees exercising the powers conferred under the Act, including the powers conferred in both s. 4(4) and s. 27(1)(a), have a legislative mandate to act in conformity with object statement in s. 3.

Moreover, all members of the Islands Trust Committees are now elected, either directly or indirectly. In my view courts should be slow to find bad faith in the conduct of democratically elected representatives acting under legislative authority, unless there is no other rational conclusion.

I return to the learned trial judge's conclusions in this case, measured against the powers conferred on the defendant by the *Islands Trust Act* and by the *Municipal Act*. He found the defendants true motives to be to prevent, or at least to delay residential subdivision, development and sale of the plaintiff's lands, and their long term intentions to be to obtain, in effect, park lands in several of the plaintiff's holdings by ensuring that no logging or only carefully controlled logging took place.

In my respectful view, both of these goals are clearly within the objects expressed in s. 3 of the Act "to preserve and protect the trust area and its unique amenities and environment."

Accepting the learned trial judge's conclusions that the trustees expressed motives did not conform with their real motives, that is to say that they acted for an ulterior purpose, does not lead me to conclude that the trustees exceeded their powers. Both the true and the expressed motives support the exercise of powers that are within the scope of the legislative grant. I think the learned trial judge erred because he did not have his mind directed to the effect of the *Islands Trust Act*, and to the powers conferred by sections 3, 4(4) and 27(1) when read together with the relevant provisions of the *Municipal Act*.

Once it is determined that the trustees acted within the scope of their legislative authority, I do not think it matters that they attempted to support their conduct on grounds other than those found to be the true basis for their actions. Both their expressed motives, and their true motives, were directed towards furtherance of the objects of the *Islands Trust Act*. An ulterior purpose that is within the ambit of the delegated power is not an improper purpose. To render the by-law illegal, the purpose of the by-law would have to extend beyond the powers of the delegated authority. In that event it would not matter whether the trustees acted for an ulterior purpose, because in that event the by-law would have been *ultra vires*.

In my respectful view in failing to direct his mind to the provisions of the *Islands Trust Act*, the learned trial judge applied the wrong legal test. It follows that the finding of bad faith can and should be set aside.

I too would allow the appeal.

NOTES AND QUESTIONS

1. What is the point of the discussion on real motives contrasted with expressed motives? Can you think of any instances where a court might determine a municipality to have acted in bad faith to protect environmental quality even where its ulterior purpose was within its powers?

2. Both of the judges' reasons heavily rely on the purposes set out in s. 3 of the *Islands Trust Act*, "to preserve and protect the trust area and its unique amenities and environment." Do you think that the result of the case would be different if the purposes were not so clearly stated; for example, if they simply read "to protect community amenities and environment"? In answering this question consider the *Spraytech* and *Denman Island Trust* cases, above.

IV. PROTECTING GREEN SPACES THROUGH PRIVATE CONSERVANCY

A. Introduction

During the last few decades, private individuals, non-government organizations (NGOs), and government agencies alike have recognized that certain areas of land, because of natural or cultural attributes such as their value as critical wildlife habitat, should be protected from development and other exploitation, and preserved in their natural state in perpetuity. A clear call to protect natural values of land was made in the Brundtland commission report, *Our Common Future* (Oxford: Oxford University Press, 1987). The World Wildlife Fund (WWF) Canada followed by proposing for the year 2000 that 12 percent of each province's land, whether publicly or privately owned, be set aside for conservation purposes. See WWF Canada, *Endangered Species: The Future for Canada's Wilderness* (1990). Many provinces' policies echoed WWF Canada's goal with similar land conservation programs.

Where land is owned by the federal or provincial Crown, it can be set aside and protected under protected areas legislation. Chapter 12, above, sets out many of the legislative mechanisms to effect such designation under public conservancy policies and programs. However, much of the land that has important natural values is privately owned, and, accordingly, protected areas legislation is usually inapplicable. There are some tools, however, at common law and, increasingly, under statutory law to assist private landowners to carry out their own conservancy objectives.

B. Common Law Tools

Common law tools include easements, restrictive covenants, and profits à prendre. An easement is a property interest that a landowner may grant to some other person, organization, or level of government. An easement generally gives the easement holder, the owner of one parcel of land (the grantee), a right to use the land of another (the grantor) for a specific purpose. Easements run with the land and bind subsequent owners in perpetuity. The common law requirements for an easement may be summarized as follows:

- There must be a *dominant tenement* and a *servient tenement*. The dominant tenement is the parcel of land that benefits from the easement. The servient tenement is the parcel of land that is subject to the easement and benefits the dominant tenement.
- The easement must benefit the dominant tenement in the sense of making it a better or more convenient property.
- The dominant and servient tenements must be separate parcels of land that are not owned and occupied by the same person.

- Although negative easements may be possible (S.G. Maurice, *Gale on Easements*, 15th ed. (London: Sweet & Maxwell, 1986), at 38), easements usually are positive in character in that they permit the owner of the dominant tenement to use the servient tenement for a purpose. For example, an easement might give the owner of the dominant tenement a right-of-way to pass over or put something on the servient tenement, or the right to discharge water onto the servient tenement.

See also A.J. McLean, "The Nature of an Easement" (1966) vol. 5 *Western Ontario Law Review* 32.

Alternatively, to constitute a valid common law restrictive covenant, the owner of one parcel of land, the dominant tenement, places restrictions on the uses of another parcel, the servient tenement. To be valid, the restrictions on the servient tenement must in some demonstrable way benefit the use and enjoyment of the dominant tenement. A restrictive covenant may only contain restrictions on use; any positive rights of the owner of the dominant tenement relating to the servient tenement may be unenforceable and could invalidate the entire restrictive covenant. Changes of use or circumstances also may invalidate a restrictive covenant. The common law rules require that the dominant and servient tenements be owned and occupied by separate persons.

A profit à prendre is a common law tool consisting of the right to enter the land of another person and to take some "profit" of the soil. The profit must be capable of being owned, such as minerals, oil, stones, trees, or grass, for the use of the owner of the right. Common law has recognized a variety of profits à prendre and there is no reason to think that the class of profits à prendre is closed; profits à prendre may exist in gross. This means that there is no need for a dominant and a servient tenement. A property owner may, for example, convey to another person the exclusive right to come on to his or her land and remove a profit such as timber without that other person owning any land to serve as a dominant tenement. As well, since the right may exist in gross, the person holding a profit à prendre may assign the right to someone else. A profit à prendre may be granted for a period of time or may be granted in perpetuity. A profit à prendre serves to protect the environment where the holder opts not to exercise it. For example, a profit à prendre that conveys the exclusive right to harvest a forest will protect the forest if the holder has obtained it to tie up harvest rights so that no one else may be granted a right to cut and remove trees.

These common law tools may be used separately or together to carry out private conservancy objectives. For example, a municipality and a landowner with adjacent land could enter into crisscross restrictive covenants to protect important environmental features. Either could grant an easement to the other for access to monitor compliance and to maintain environmental integrity. A profit à prendre carrying the exclusive right to harvest all trees in an area could be granted to a conservation organization. As long as the organization does not exercise the right, no one can harvest trees and they are thereby protected.

C. Statutory Tools—Conservation Easements

The single most important statutory legal tool to aid private conservancy is the conservation easement. Conservation easements are interests in land constituted through voluntary legal agreements that landowners may enter into to protect the natural values of all or a part of their land. The conservation easement agreement is then registered on title to property in accordance with authorizing legislation. The agreements forward private conservancy objectives by limiting uses that can be made of land and by imposing good stewardship obligations. For example, a conservation easement agreement aimed at protecting wildlife and habitat might prohibit subdivision (since it causes fragmentation), hunting, and activities that impair or destroy habitat such as use of harmful pesticides, timber harvesting, and intensive agricultural activities. It might also require that any permitted land-related activities be carried out in accordance with a land management plan designed to protect wildlife values.

A conservation easement is between the owner of land, the grantor, and the entity entitled by authorizing legislation to hold the easement, the grantee. There are two legislative approaches regarding who or what can be a grantee. First, authorizing legislation can set out criteria that a grantee must meet. If a grantee meets the criteria then it can hold a conservation easement. For example, in Alberta, only the minister of environment or "qualified organizations" may hold a conservation easement. A "qualified organization" can mean the provincial government, a provincial government agency, a local authority including a municipality, or a body corporate that is a registered charity under the *Income Tax Act*, RSC 1985, c. 1 (5th Supp.), as amended, and is constituted to hold conservation property interests and that meets other conditions set out in the legislation. (See *Environmental Protection and Enhancement Act*, RSA 2000, c. E-12, s. 22(1)(e).) In Alberta, there are a number of non-governmental qualified organizations, including the Nature Conservancy of Canada, the Alberta Fish and Game Association, Ducks Unlimited Canada, the Alberta Sports Recreation Parks and Wildlife Foundation, the Alberta Conservation Association, and the Southern Alberta Land Trust Society.

Second, authorizing legislation can name the entities that can hold conservation easements (for example, the appropriate minister) and give government the right to designate additional grantees. For example, the Nova Scotia *Conservation Easement Act*, SNS 2001, c. 28, s. 8 authorizes the provincial or federal crown, a municipality, and any organization designated by Cabinet or the regulations as qualified to be granted a conservation easement.

Conservation easements may be granted for a specific term of time or in perpetuity. Legislation normally will set out formal requirements, including how to register the interest against title. A conservation easement that is duly registered against title runs with title and binds future owners even though they were not party to the agreement. Legislation usually sets out how conservation easements may be amended or extinguished, should the need arise.

The legislation creating conservation easements typically removes many of the onerous conditions for restrictive covenants and easements. For example, legislation might state that conservation easement agreements are valid whether they are positive or negative and where there is no dominant tenement. Legislation also might say that a conservation easement will not lapse for non-enforcement and will remain valid even if there are changes in surrounding land use.

Conservation easements are attractive to entities that secure conservation interests because they do not require a purchase of an entire parcel of land. In almost every case, purchasing the rights to develop land will be less expensive than having to purchasing the entire fee. Also, with conservation easements, a grantee normally can encumber a part of a titled parcel of land without the need for subdivision. This further reduces costs. Conservation easements are also attractive to landowners since they can be assured that important environmental values of their property are protected without having to sell or donate the entire interest to a conservation-minded entity. With conservation-easements title stays in the name of the grantor.

Conservation easements are enforceable in accordance with their terms and as enabled by authorizing legislation. Common enforcement methods include the right to sue for infractions and the right to apply for an injunction to prevent or stop violations. Agreements may also allow for out of court dispute resolution methods such as mediation or arbitration.

D. Municipalities and Use of Common Law Tools and Conservation Easements

The preservation of natural environmental features is often the objective of municipalities' land-use plans and policies. However, legislation provides only limited tools to carry out such plans and policies; municipal legislation may give municipalities the right to require mandatory dedications where a landowner wishes to subdivide land, but the legislation will limit the purposes for dedications. For example, municipal legislation may authorize a municipality to require a landowner to dedicate land that is undevelopable because of features such as ravines, a high water table, or the presence of water bodies or watercourses. If a municipality wishes to protect important wildlife habitat within its boundaries, mandatory dedications will not help it achieve this goal in a subdivision context. A municipality might be able to negotiate voluntary conservation easements or use other private conservancy mechanisms to assist it in realizing its environmental policy objectives. However, as the following cases demonstrate, a municipality must be careful when using private conservancy mechanisms in carrying out its land-use planning and development functions.

Moore v. Saanich (District)
30 MPLR (2d) 132 (BCSC)

SPENCER J: This was an application brought under the *Judicial Review Procedure Act* to review a decision of Mr. Hopper as the Approving Officer for the District of Sanich. ... [T]he relief sought by the petitioners was narrowed to a declaration that Mr. Hopper's decision to require terms in a covenant as a condition of approval be set aside, with the result that the subdivision would be approved on the terms of the covenant proposed by the petitioners. The grounds for that relief were confined to paragraphs 3 (1) and (2), that Mr. Hopper acted in bad faith or that he proceeded on a specious and totally inadequate factual basis. ...

Mr. Hopper had been asked to approve the petitioners' proposed subdivision of four parcels of land they own between them and comprising some 38.65 acres, more or less. Parcel A and Lot 3 of the land are situated on prime undeveloped waterfront at Glencoe Cove. The whole acreage is for the most part undeveloped land in what is agreed to be a highly sensitive ecological area. It is agreed that the land is environmentally important.

The Topography

The dispute concerns only six lots out of 52 in the proposed subdivision. The six lots lie at the top of, and include, a steep bank which overlooks the North Beach. ... Inland from that, a broken line indicates where the horizontal distance measured back from the bottom of the bank achieves a distance equivalent to twice its height. I shall refer to it as the 2:1 line.

The History

The petitioners have been attempting to re-zone and subdivide their lands for a number of years. During that time, the District of Sanich, members of the general public including neighbours, and the Provincial Government, have expressed concern over the loss of wild sea-coast land which would result from its development. No government nor private authority was prepared to pay the price to secure the whole lands for the public, but in 1994 the Provincial Government and the District of Sanich agreed to buy 5.1 acres for park purposes. It was a condition of the purchase that the remaining lands be re-zoned by April 27, 1994 and that conditional approval for their subdivision be given by May 16, 1994. The purpose of those conditions precedent was to assure the petitioners that they need not sell the park area unless they were assured of the re-zoning and reasonably assured of the subdivision that would enable them to develop the rest of their lands.

Re-zoning and conditional approval were achieved and the 5.1 acres were sold. The conditional approval ... reserved [Mr. Hopper's] ... right to reject the subdivision on receipt of further information. It also stipulated this provision:

> "Before I can give final approval to the proposed subdivision, restrictive covenants containing terms and conditions satisfactory to me must be provided to my office. These covenants must be granted to the Municipality and be registered concurrently with the subdivision plan pursuant to Section 215 of the *Land Title Act*."

. . .

Certain covenants had already been proposed by the petitioners and discussed by both the District staff and council and seen by Mr. Hopper. They were required to protect the bank above the North Beach, a cormorant rookery and a rare plant area. The cormorant rookery and the rare plant area are not now in dispute. The parties agree that they have been protected. The present dispute concerns only the covenant to protect the bank above the North Beach.

. . .

The Scope of Judicial Review of an Approving Officer's Decision

It is convenient to remember here the principles to be applied on judicial review of an Approving Officer's decision. The court is not permitted to review the evidence and simply substitute its own conclusions for the Officer's; see: *Hlynsky v. West Vancouver (District) Approving Officer*, [1989] 37 BCLR 79 (BCCA). However, what the petitioners ask me to do here is to critically review the evidence to see if there is anything more than a totally inadequate factual basis for Mr. Hopper's decision or if it was made in bad faith. That is different from applying a critical analysis to the reasoning used by the Approving Officer which may not be done.

· · ·

The test I have already referred to, that of asking whether the decision was made on a specious or totally inadequate factual basis, comes from the Supreme Court of Canada decision in *City of Vancouver v. Simpson* (1976), 65 DLR (3d) 669. … In my respectful opinion, in the expression "a specious or totally inadequate factual basis," the Supreme Court of Canada was making a single reference to a basis that had no factual underpinning. That includes one which appears at first sight to have a factual underpinning but which on examination does not. … It is a single test to see whether there is an adequate factual underpinning.

· · ·

Mr. Hopper advances three main reasons for his requirements. The first is to preserve the bank overlooking the North Beach from the risk of erosion. The second is to preserve the bank and beach in its natural state for the benefit of the environment generally. The third is to preserve the viewscape presented by the bank for the benefit of neighbouring public lands. Pervading the last two reasons, is the concept of the public interest enjoined upon an Approving Officer by s. 85(3) of the *Land Title Act*.

In view of counsel's concession for Mr. Hopper, that if error is shown within the parameters of the *City of Vancouver v. Simpson* case, an order should go with the effect that the subdivision should be approved, I do not find it necessary to deal with each of the subject areas which both counsel canvassed in their careful and detailed submissions. Since the court's role is not to settle a negotiation but simply to say whether or not the decision was based on error, the finding of any error significant enough to vitiate part of the decision must vitiate the whole. I am not able to go through each of the terms of the covenant and impose or deny them piecemeal. With the greatest of respect to Mr. Hopper I think there were at least two errors of that magnitude.

Are Mr. Hopper's Reasons Specious and Totally Without
an Adequate Factual Basis?

It was because of the possibility of erosion that Mr. Hopper required terms preventing the installation of fences and stairs north of the 2:1 line, preventing the installation of garden facilities and landscaping north of that line and preventing the building of residences and services north of the 27 metre line. In effect, his requirements would prevent any use of the petitioners' lands north of the 2:1 line. The six lots in question contain land lying north of that line and reaching down the bank to the high water mark. They include small areas between the 2:1 line and the top of the bank which the petitioners wish to be able to landscape. The petitioners say all of their proposed lots north of the 2:1 line have been sterilized and that it amounts to expropriation without compensation. They say the expropriation is for the benefit of members of the public having access to the beach and to the 5.1 acres they sold to the Provincial Government as park. They point out that nothing was said to them about Mr. Hopper's presently proposed restrictions when that sale was negotiated. They say that because they were not told then about this restriction on the lots they have lost the opportunity to decide not to sell the park land.

· · ·

An examination of the evidence contained in the reports I have referred to shows that an engineer has recommended reduction of the 3:1 slope to a 2:1 slope as the appropriate set back in this case. Mr. Hopper's evidence on examination was that he construed the Coastal Procedures memorandum as not permitting reduction where that was recommended by an engineer. That interpretation is totally without factual foundation. His insertion of his own small margin of safety is contrary to the evidence in the Levelton and the Westland reports. In the *Noort* case [*Noort Holdings Ltd. v. Delta Approving Officer*, [1994] 26 MPLR (2d) 79 (SCBC)], Cohen J found the Approving Officer had acted on a specious and totally inadequate factual basis when he substituted his own inexpert opinion about the effects of electromagnetic fields for those of the experts who provided their opinions for him … . In my opinion, Mr. Hopper has fallen into the same error here with respect to his requirement that the building envelope on these six lots be restricted to 27 metres back from the front line to avoid the risk of erosion. The engineering and agronomy evidence is that it is safe to build to the 2:1 line provided there is no cutting and filling on the bank itself, that the vegetation on the bank is left undisturbed and the bank is monitored for stability.

Mr. Hopper's decision to refuse the building of fences and stairways on the bank and prohibit landscaping and garden structures north of the 2:1 line between it and the top of the bank stands on a different footing. The Westland report recommends limited stairways and no fences beyond a few feet set back from the top of the bank. The only changes to land between the 2:1 slope and the top of the bank, apart from limited trails and stairways, is the removal of the existing willow. It is not for the court to reach a different conclusion from the Approving Officer by re-weighing the evidence before him. There was evidence that he was entitled to accept. He was entitled to be wrong.

That does not end the matter of the stairs and access from the lots to the North Beach. There appears in Mr. Hopper's cross examination a reasoning that applies the wrong test of law to the facts that were before him with respect to Lot 17. At Questions 342 to 344 he said he refused the access trail from Lot 17 "because I feel it is unnecessary when they can access the public access as Lots 14 and 15 can." In paragraph 58 of his affidavit, Mr. Hopper gave the same lack of necessity as the reason for denying fences and staircases and trails to access the beach from the six lots. That is a ground not mentioned in ss. 85(3) and 86(1)(c)(i) and (vi) of the *Land Title Act*, which counsel agree are the sections in question here. With respect that is the wrong legal test to apply. For the purposes of this case, the subdivision is to be approved unless it fails the tests set out in those sections. In each case the burden was not on the petitioners but on the Approving Officer to show those tests were not met by the petitioners. The test is whether the proposed subdivision is against the public interest. With respect, Mr. Hopper has placed a burden of proving necessity on the petitioners. It is nowhere mentioned in the Act but Mr. Hopper says that is the test the petitioners failed. With respect that was a mistake of law on his part. It affects his decision with respect to access from all six lots to the North Beach.

. . .

The Bad Faith Argument

There are several aspects to this part of the petitioners' argument. The first is that Mr. Hopper has for several years been wedded to the concept that all 38.65 acres of the petitioners' lands should be dedicated to use as a public park. He previously supported its purchase by a level of government. The petitioners say that when the provincial and municipal governments proved financially unwilling to buy the whole, Mr. Hopper pursued his purpose and has espoused the demand by some members of the public for the preservation of a viewscape of these six lots by freezing development north of the 27 metre line as a means of enhancing the viewscape from the park and from the North Beach. They characterize it as an indirect expropriation of that part of their lands without compensation. They point out that in his examination he said he was still in favour of the preservation of the whole property for the public. The second aspect is that Mr. Hopper now insists on preserving the viewscape by keeping the lands north of the 2:1 line in a pristine state when neither he nor the Province nor the District raised that as a factor when the purchase of the 5.1 acres was consummated in 1994. At that stage, the petitioners were offering to keep that area in its natural state but subject to their right to build fences and staircases to the beach and to landscape the area between the 2:1 line and the top of the bank.

Mr. Hopper answers the first of those points in paragraphs 62 to 66 of his affidavit filed August 3, 1995. He denies being under any obligation to implement a greenways program and insists he rejected the petitioners' covenant solely on the statutory basis of a consideration of the public interest and its effect on the amenities of neighbouring properties. Mr. McDannold argued for him that his private opinion that the whole property should have been kept as park is his preference as a Planner and that he has divorced it from his role as Approving Officer. He answers the second by saying that it was too late to raise the issue of viewscape at the rezoning hearing because that might have prevented the sale of the park to government.

Mr. Hopper's evidence on this part of the matter is given in answer to Question 427 in his examination. It deals with the question why he did not tell the petitioners their proposed terms of the covenant were unacceptable before they finalized the sale of the 5.1 acres for park. It reads:

> Q. Mr. Hopper, if those are the circumstances why then did not you or the City
> Solicitor say to the developer while there was still a condition on the sale of the property

with the government, we are not going to accept the covenants in that form, we're not going to negotiate it, you either accept them as Mr. Nation has drawn them or you don't?

A. Because that would have negated the sale, as I understand it, of the land to the Province, because a condition of the zoning wouldn't have been met.

In my opinion that answer demonstrates that Mr. Hopper was anxious to procure the sale of the 5.1 acres and that to ensure it came about was less than frank with the petitioners about the changes he then intended to make to the covenant they were then proposing. In my opinion Mr. Hopper has failed to distinguish between his role as Planner and as Approving Officer in this case. The fact that he wrote his conditional acceptance letter of May 31, 1994 and his conditional rejection of May 29, 1995 as Planner, illustrate that failure. Further, in my opinion his failure to raise the issue of the viewscape at the re-zoning hearing and before the petitioners sold the 5.1 acres to the Provincial Government amounts to bad faith. He clearly had in mind the prospect of preserving the park viewscape but he said nothing for the specific purpose of enabling the sale to occur. Had he raised the issue at that time the petitioners would have had the choice of declining to sell. That would have given them a stronger bargaining position to obtain subdivision approval in exchange for the dedication of park land which both the District and Mr. Hopper were anxious to see acquired for the public.

Conclusion

My finding with respect to the two issues I have discussed must be decisive of the whole application. As I have already said, the concession made by Mr. McDannold precludes me from adjusting the terms of the covenant individually by deciding which was or was not rejected without an adequate factual basis or which was or was not coloured by bad faith. I think that was a concession properly made. I also doubt whether any part of the decision which was supported by adequate facts could in any event stand in the face of the bad faith I have found.

In the result, there will be an order setting aside the Approving Officer's decision to require a covenant in the terms he proposed, with the result that the subdivision will be approved on the terms of the covenant as submitted to him by the petitioners. There will be no third party to the covenant.

The petitioners are entitled to their costs.

NOTES AND QUESTIONS

1. Note that the court did not suggest that it was improper for the approving officer to require the applicant to enter into a restrictive covenant as a condition of subdivision in order to meet legitimate planning and development concerns. This accords with a statement of Professor Laux, who states that if a subdivision approving authority has the power to refuse an application "as a matter of discretion, it has the collateral right to approve the subdivision but subject to such conditions which will ameliorate the concerns that would have caused a refusal." (F. Laux, *Planning Law and Practice in Alberta*,

2d ed. (Scarborough, ON: Carswell, 1996), at 12-23). Applying Laux's view to *Moore v. Saanich*, we might say that although Mr. Hopper as approving officer had the right to impose a restrictive covenant as a condition of subdivision, his proposed terms went beyond what was required to ameliorate his *legitimate* concerns—that is, concerns that are explicitly or implicitly authorized by statute.

2. Do you think that Mr. Hopper's conditions would have constituted an "expropriation without compensation"? If so, following the reasoning in *Steer Holdings*, above, what was the "corresponding benefit" to the municipality? Does it matter that a restrictive covenant is an interest in land (as is a conservation easement)?

3. What advice would you give to a municipality that requested your opinion regarding legal limits on using conservation easements or restrictive covenants in land-use planning and development processes?

Stewart (Re)
[2001] AMGBO no. 128; board order MGB 121/01,
file no. SO1/STRA/CO-014

The proposal is to subdivide an 80.8-acre titled area into three parcels of 20.3 acres, 20.1 acres and 40.4 acres. The appellant intends to sell the smaller parcels for rural residential uses and continue residing on and grazing cattle on the larger remaining parcel.

. . .

The subject property is located approximately 12 miles northeast of Sherwood Park, adjacent to the western boundary of Elk Island National Park. The site is characterized by an undulating topography with low lying wetlands, a large water body and natural drainage courses. There is also heavy tree cover in the northern and south western portions of the titled area. According to the County, the subject site is considered a significant wildlife corridor for deer, moose and waterfowl due to the natural connections to the national park. However, the County concedes that suitable building sites are available on each proposed 20-acre parcel, located away from the environmentally sensitive areas.

The subject property is designated AR Rural District under the Strathcona County Land Use Bylaw (LUB) and is considered an Agricultural/Large Rural Residential Parcel Policy Area under the Municipal Development Plan (MDP). It has a Farmland Assessment Rating of 19.0%, which is generally considered to be poor agricultural land for the purposes of cereal crop production. The proposed 40-acre parcel encompasses a residence, barn, shed and garage while the area of the proposed 20-acre parcels is currently used for pasture.

The proposal complies with the 20-acre minimum parcel size provisions of the applicable portions of the MDP, however the current LUB districting of the subject land restricts the minimum parcel size to 80 acres.

The SA [Subdivision Authority] refused the proposed subdivision for three reasons. First, the SA was concerned that the proposal would result in the isolation of approximately 4.4 acres of land south of the drainage course on the proposed 40-acre parcel as well as the isolation of approximately 1.0 acre of land north of the drainage course on one of the proposed 20-acre parcels. Second, the SA was concerned that the proposal would result in the fragmentation of a natural water body into two separate titles of land, which the SA asserted could be more appropriately maintained by a single environmental reserve parcel. Lastly, the SA asserted that the proposal is not consistent with the minimum parcel size of 80.0 acres required by the LUB.

The SA Administration prepared an alternative subdivision design for consideration by the Appellant and the [Municipal Government Board] MGB. The SA asserted that the alternative plan of subdivision takes into consideration the natural features of the subject property and proposes to create a 20.3 acre parcel, a 17.8 acre parcel, 15.0 acres for environmental reserve, 2.5 acres for municipal reserve, with a remainder parcel of 25.2 acres encompassing the existing house and out buildings. The revised proposal was circulated to the affected utility companies, government agencies, and members of the County's Technical Advisory Committee and adjacent landowners. One adjacent landowner expressed concern for the environmental integrity of the property to the SA but did not attend the appeal hearing or make a submission to the MGB.

The Appellant does not accept the alternative plan, because of the large areas proposed for reserve land and the land that may become subject of a conservation easement. The Appellant maintains that the original subdivision proposal should be approved.

. . .

Municipal Government Act

617. The purpose of this Part and the regulations and bylaws under this Part is to provide means whereby plans and related matters may be prepared and adopted

    (a) to achieve the orderly, economical and beneficial development, use of land and patterns of human settlement, and

    (b) to maintain and improve the quality of the physical environment within which patterns of human settlement are situated in Alberta,

without infringing on the rights of individuals for any public interest except to the extent that is necessary for the overall greater public interest.

. . .

664(1) Subject to section 663, a subdivision authority may require the owner of a parcel of land that is the subject of a proposed subdivision to provide part of that parcel of land as environmental reserve if it consists of

    (a) a swamp, gully, ravine, coulee or natural drainage course,

    (b) land that is subject to flooding or is, in the opinion of the subdivision authority, unstable, or

    (c) a strip of land, not less than 6 metres in width, abutting the bed and shore of any lake, river, stream or other body of water for the purpose of

        (i) preventing pollution

        (ii) providing public access to and beside the bed and shore

    (2) If the owner of a parcel of land that is subject of a proposed subdivision and the municipality agree that any or all of the land that is to be taken as environmental reserve

is instead to be the subject of an environmental reserve easement for the protection and enhancement of the environment, an easement may be registered against the land in favour of the municipality at a land titles office.

. . .

Summary of the SA's position

The SA submitted that the proposal is consistent with the provisions outlined in the Agricultural/Large Rural Residential Parcel Policy Area of the MDP, however the land should be redesignated to reflect the MDP as a condition of subdivision approval. The SA also suggests that approval of the proposed subdivision should include provision for a joint access between proposed lots 1 and 2 (the two 20 acre parcels), road widening and other standard conditions normally applied to subdivision approvals.

According to the SA, the main issue respecting the proposed subdivision is the requirement for protection of the environment. The environment can be protected through several means including dedication of environmental reserve, environmental reserve easements and a conservation easement to protect the wetland habitat areas and bushland.

Summary of the Appellant's Position

The Appellant does not agree with the alternate subdivision plan prepared by the County due to the extensive amount of land that would be dedicated for reserve or restricted from normal use by environmental and conservation easements. For example, a conservation easement could be so restrictive that cattle may not be able to legally graze on the farm. The Appellant submitted that he is willing to enter into an environmental reserve in order to protect the unnamed water body and enter into a drainage easement to protect the drainage course on the property, both of which are significant portions of the wildlife corridor.

. . .

Reasons [for Decision]

With respect to the issues on the protection of the environment, the MGB finds that the better method of protecting the water body is by authorizing the dedication of a 6 metre wide environmental reserve surrounding the water body. This dedication will occur only for that area adjacent to the area claimed for ownership by the Crown, whether or not actual water covers the bed and shore of the slough, it is the ownership claim of the Crown that defines the location of the environmental reserve dedication. With respect to the environmental reserve easement for the drainage courses, the MGB finds such easement is authorized by the Act for this purpose. In the MGB's opinion, the easement option is better than dedicating the drainage areas as reserve because ownership of the land involved will remain with the owner of the parcel and will not result in the fragmentation of titled areas. Further, the easement allows continued access to and through the easement areas provided no development occurs and the natural state of the drainage course is respected. The MGB has also included a condition requiring the dedication of municipal reserve on the east side of the slough up to the Range Road. This type of reserve dedication is also authorized by the Act and the MGB agreed to the land dedication at the request of the County.

During the hearing there was discussion respecting a requirement for the Appellant to enter into a conservation easement. In the MGB's opinion, a conservation easement only works well when the landowner and the County are in agreement on the terms of the agreement and the areas of land subject to the agreement. In this case, the Appellant will not enter into a conservation easement because the land intended to be subject of the easement goes well beyond the type of land authorized by the Act for inclusion as environmental reserve. Further, the terms of the agreement may place restrictions on land use and accessibility that are not authorized by the Act and that do not enhance the landowner's enjoyment of his own property.

NOTES AND QUESTIONS

1. Alberta's Municipal Government Board (MGB) stated that "the Appellant will not enter into a conservation easement because the land intended to be subject of the easement goes well beyond the type of land authorized by the Act for inclusion as environmental reserve." Can a municipality require a landowner to dedicate land where the purposes for the dedication are not specifically authorized by legislation? Suppose that a landowner agrees to a dedication that goes beyond legislated purposes. Could a successor in title have the dedication set aside by a court? How would you advise a municipality in a situation where a landowner was agreeable to a dedication that went beyond statutory purposes? Are there alternate ways of securing land limitations?

2. Legislation that gives municipalities the right to hold conservation easements may be different from the legislation that gives municipalities authorities powers in respect of planning, subdivision, and development. For example, in Alberta, the *Environmental Protection and Enhancement Act*, RSA 2000, c. E-12 authorizes municipalities to hold conservation easements (s. 22.1(1)(e)), but part 17 of the *Municipal Government Act*, RSA 2000, c. M-26 gives municipalities authorities regarding planning, subdivision, and development processes. Do you think that there are arguments to challenge a municipality for using conservation easements in, for example, a subdivision context, instead of using legislated processes specifically authorized by legislation dealing with subdivisions? How could a municipality respond to the arguments?

FURTHER READINGS

I. Attridge, *Conservation Easement Valuation and Taxation in Canada* (Toronto: North American Wetlands Conservation Council, 1996).

A. Hillyer and B. Findlay, *Here Today, Here Tomorrow: Legal Tools for the Voluntary Protection of Private Land in British Columbia* (Vancouver: West Coast Environmental Law Association, 1994).

F. Hoehn, *Municipalities and Canadian Law* (Saskatoon: Purich, 1996).

A. Kwasniak, *Conservation Easement Guide for Alberta* (Edmondon: Environmental Law Centre, 1997).

H. Pock, *Corporate and Municipal Environmental Law* (Scarborough, ON: Carswell, 1989).

L. Reynolds, "Environmental Regulation and Management by Local Public Authorities in Canada" (1993) vol. 3 *Journal of Environmental Law and Practice* 41.

I. Rogers, *Canadian Law of Planning and Zoning* (Scarborough, ON: Carswell, 1973).

CHAPTER FOURTEEN

Alternative Dispute Resolution in Environmental Law: Uses, Limitations, and Potentials

H. Ian Rounthwaite

I. INTRODUCTION

Alternative dispute resolution (ADR) is the term that is used to distinguish innovative decision-making methods from the traditional decision-making processes of North American political and judicial institutions. ADR has a lengthy history of use in attempting to resolve "private" disputes and a somewhat shorter history in addressing disputes that involve broader questions of public interest and policy.

It is the level of public involvement that distinguishes alternative dispute resolution from traditional decision making methods. In conventional public policy processes, public involvement is generally limited, with public input simply taken into consideration by decision making authorities. In the ADR movement, the citizen's role is direct. The level of true collaboration and involvement of non-decision makers with the decision making authorities is what defines ADR as "alternative."

Dorcey and Reik identify three general "modes of decision-making," each of which involve an increasing degree of public participation. The first, "authoritative decision-making," involves the imposition of a decision by an individual or organization without consulting those who will be affected. Court-rendered decisions fall into this category. The second, "consultative decision-making," involves the consultation by the individual or organization of those affected before making the decision. Public hearings fall into this category. The third, "negotiative decision-making," involves individuals or organizations making trade-offs with those affected by the decision. (R.A. Kelly and D.K. Alper, *Transforming British Columbia's War in the Woods: An Assessment of the Vancouver Island Regional Negotiation Process of the Commission on Resources and Environment* (Victoria: University of Victoria Institute for Dispute Resolution, 1995), at 9.)

In the realm of environmental disputes, the ADR method that has received the most attention in the literature is environmental mediation. However, the applicability of ADR to environmental disputes is not limited to mediation. Negotiation toward settlement is a form of ADR well known to lawyers, civil servants, and business interests. ADR techniques such as conciliation, negotiated rule making, negotiated consent decrees under the US *Comprehensive Environmental Response, Compensation and Liability Act*, 42 USCA (1980) (CERCLA), mediation, arbitration, mini-trials, "rent-a-judge," and private contracts are some of the non-adjudicatory forms of dispute resolution that have been attempted during the past two decades.

One commentator has summarized the history of environmental ADR in the United States this way:

> ADR has been used with varying degrees of success in many areas of environmental policy-making, standard setting, the determination of development choices, and in the enforcement of environmental standards. It has been recognized and given a formal role by way of federal policy guidelines or regulations in the area of negotiated rule-making, and in the area of settlement of disputes primarily affecting the disposal of solid and hazardous waste, under CERCLA and RCRA [*Resource Conservation and Recovery Act*]. The formal documents that reflect federal acceptance of dispute resolution approaches include the interim CERCLA settlement policy, the Department of Justice policy on consent judgments in actions to enjoin discharges of pollutants, the interim guidance document on streamlining the CERCLA settlement decision process, and guidance on the use of alternative dispute resolution techniques in enforcement actions. (F.P. Grad, "Alternative Dispute Resolution in Environmental Law" (1989) vol. 14 *Columbia Journal of Environmental Law* 157, at 161.)

Many of these forms of ADR have also been used in Canada. This chapter is intended to introduce and analyze the three forms of public ADR that have received the most attention so far: mediation, contract negotiation (including negotiated regulation or *reg-neg*), and CORE, the BC attempt to introduce systematic ADR techniques for resolving land-use and resource conflicts. It will also consider the recent introduction of legislative requirements for collaborative decision making in federal environmental statutes that are designed, in part, to acknowledge the shared constitutional responsibilities for environmental law and policy (discussed in chapter 2).

Each of these forms of ADR as practised in Canada has involved, to a greater or lesser extent, the intervention of a third party to assist the parties to resolve their differences. The results achieved through ADR may be non-binding, binding, voluntary, or non-voluntary depending on the legal and regulatory regime under which the technique takes place. It is essential that sufficient attention is paid to the institutional and legal setting in which ADR may occur when considering ADR as an option to traditional civil litigation or administrative adjudication. Legislation and the environmental policies of governments may place significant constraints on ADR options available to the parties and will certainly affect the implementation of the results that ADR may achieve. See J. McKenzie, "Conflict Assessment: A Critical Element of Public Dispute ADR Practice" (1995) vol. 7 *Canadian Journal of Dispute Resolution* 5. Throughout this chapter, you will be reminded to consider the institutional and legal setting in which the environmental controversy may arise.

II. THE JUSTIFICATION FOR ADR IN ENVIRONMENTAL DISPUTES

The ability of the courts and judicial or quasi-judicial administrative agencies to deal effectively with environmental controversies has been severely criticized for more than 20 years. It has been argued that judges have neither the inclination nor the expertise to adequately address disputes that raise complex scientific and technical issues that are often beset by the problem of inadequate or uncertain empirical data. Many of the critiques of the "role of the courts in environmental protection" see the limited scope of judicial review of administrative activities as a barrier to the effectiveness of adjudication as a dispute resolution process. Judicial review of administrative decision making in Canada has tended to focus strongly on the procedural aspects of the decision-making process rather than on the substantive merits of a particular administrative decision. Administrative law doctrines such as *ultra vires*, natural justice, and fairness all emphasize the common law tradition of the courts' supervisory role in judicial review.

A further criticism lies in the nature of litigation itself. Litigation is an adversarial process. Canadian legal procedures are designed to ensure that the parties to a dispute identify the *legal* issues to be decided by the court. Judicial decision making, through legal doctrines such as *stare decisis*, encourage the parties to frame the issues specifically and as narrowly as possible. Consequently, the court may be unlikely to address the underlying political, economic, social, or environmental values that may have motivated the parties to manifest their dispute by resorting to litigation. Procedural and substantive limitations of the legal decision-making process have contributed to widespread dissatisfaction with a process of resolving environmental controversy that relies on an adversarial decision-making process and has led to a search for a more appropriate framework within which environmental conflicts may be managed or resolved.

During the 1970s, environmental advocates argued strongly that a greater emphasis on public participation in the decision-making processes of the federal government would lead to qualitatively better environmental decision making. See, for example, A.R. Lucas, "Legal Techniques for Pollution Control: The Role of the Public" (1971) vol. 6 *UBC Law Review* 167, and E. Gellhorn, "Public Participation in Administrative Proceedings" (1971) vol. 81 *Yale Law Journal* 359. The federal response was the introduction of environmental impact assessment guidelines in the early 1970s and a greater emphasis on public consultation in environmental legislation and administrative decision-making policies. By the 1980s, it had become evident that public participation itself did not necessarily lead to better (or more acceptable) environmental decision making. It was perceived that the cost and delay factors of widespread public consultation could not be justified in many environmental disputes and did not necessarily result in greater acceptance of the decisions made in particular cases. Rather than bringing public policy making "out from behind closed doors" and introducing previously underrepresented (or unrepresented) views into the decision-making process, public meetings, public hearings, and inquiries became isolated from the established decision-making processes of government. See R.J. Anthony, "Comment," in N. Bankes and J.O. Saunders, eds., *Public Disposition of Natural Resources: Essays from the First Banff Conference on Natural Resources* (Calgary: Canadian Institute of Resources Law, 1984), at 231-34.

Since the release of the Brundtland Report (World Commission on Environment and Development, *Our Common Future* (Oxford: Oxford University Press, 1987), government techniques to provide public participation in the environmental decision-making process have become more refined. At both the federal and provincial levels of government, workshops and "roundtables" have been used in an attempt to broaden the debate over environmental legislative and policy options. Neither, however, is a form of ADR since "the level of true collaboration and involvement of non-decision makers with the decision making authorities" is strictly limited to providing citizen input into the final decisions, which ultimately continue to rest with governments. Although these "public participation" techniques may not be ADR methods discussed in this chapter, they are some of the many different forms of collaborative decision making that have become increasingly popular in recent years.

III. COLLABORATIVE DECISION MAKING AND ADR

Collaborative decision making in Canada takes many different forms. Collaborative decision-making processes include private individuals working together to preserve a particular natural resource, community-based conservation groups, and facilitated or mediated negotiations mandated by federal or provincial legislation. Each involves the coming together of individuals with diverse interests to work collaboratively toward a solution to an environmental or natural resource dispute. Often, collaborative decision making will require individual interests to make *compromises* in order to reach a greater benefit than could be reached without compromise. Compromise in the context of collaborative decision making is simply part of the negotiating process, although the implications of each proposed compromise must be carefully weighed and assessed; what individual goals are being compromised for what ultimate benefits?

Collaborative decision making is a *consensus*-driven process. Consensus has been defined as follows:

> In a general sense, people refer to *building consensus* as a process of developing sufficient support among competing interests to pass a piece of legislation, to create a new program, or otherwise make a decision or change that is seen as legitimate and able to be implemented successfully. A more narrow definition, and one that is used in many collaborative processes, is that of a decision that has been developed cooperatively by a group of some fixed membership. In this circumstance, a *consensus agreement* or *consensus decision* is one that is acceptable to, and supported by *all* group members. A consensus decision may include portions that are less than desired for any particular group but that are acceptable in the context of the overall agreement. (*Collaboration: A Guide for Environmental Advocates*, below, at 6.)

E.F. Dukes and K. Firehock
Collaboration: A Guide for Environmental Advocates
(Charlottesville, VA: University of Virginia, Wilderness Society, and National Audubon Society, 2001), at 9-10

The increasing number and influence of collaborative processes has profound implications for natural resource management. It can impact on how decisions get made, who makes them, and the relative influence of various groups among many other things. The extent, role, and positive and negative implications of these changes are hotly debated. This Guide focuses primarily on how environmental advocates respond to individual collaborative processes, proposals, or opportunities. However, an understanding of the issues surrounding the collective impact of collaborative processes will give a helpful perspective on any single collaborative effort. It may also influence decisions about when and how to participate. This Section summarizes the broader discussion surrounding the collective impact of resource management by collaborative processes.

The Promise of Collaboration

Potential Benefits

Proponents of collaborative processes argue that collaboration has the potential to achieve benefits that may be more difficult for other forms of public involvement or natural resource management decision processes to produce. These benefits include:

- Bridging what were formerly viewed as insurmountable differences to achieve gains in relationships, to craft agreements that are creative and stable, and to develop on-the-ground improvements for the environment;
- Bringing together sufficient resources to accomplish what cannot be accomplished by any one single party or smaller coalition;
- Engaging former adversaries in respecting the views and values of others so as to *enlarge* what had been a narrow self-interest to encompass a broader interest combining environmental, social, and economic goals;
- Developing citizens who practice the art of active citizenship;
- Providing a positive public relations alternative for corporations and public officials;
- Engaging citizens in ways that promote mutual education, including development of an environmental ethic;
- Making decisions in ways that are faster and cheaper, by avoiding costly and time-consuming administrative, legislative, or judicial public processes; and
- Creating environmental gains beyond the minimum standards required by laws or policies.

Philosophical Foundations

There is no single philosophy driving the increased use of collaborative processes. The best known early collaborative efforts emerged from circumstances unique to each particular community. A collaborative process is usually seen as an *alternative* to some less acceptable option, such as a stalemate that blocks environmental improvement and economic development. An example would be a private collaborative effort to reintroduce an endangered species into a particular area when the public agencies responsible for such introduction have been ineffective in doing so by traditional regulatory means alone.

As word spread of collaborative efforts that brought agreements between traditional adversaries, observers began linking these with the philosophy and theory of participatory democracy. One such argument for collaborative processes is that they provide an essential forum for the development of "small d" democracy—the networks of reciprocity and exchange, mutual obligation, understanding and caring—which are required for sustainable governance. ...

Concerns About Collaboration

Many criticisms and concerns have been raised about collaborative approaches for the management of natural resources. These criticisms fall into two categories:

1. On a large scale, there are significant concerns with how the cumulative impact of policymaking by collaborative processes threatens to displace traditional practices of democracy and constitutional governance and increase local (neighboring communities) influence over public resources, including federal lands; and

2. On a smaller scale, there are concerns with how and when individual processes are constituted and managed.

Examples abound of collaborative decision-making processes involving environmental and resource management issues in Canada. The Accelerated Reduction/Elimination of Toxics (ARET) process was a voluntary, collaborative pollution prevention initiative conducted by representatives of environmental, labour, industry, government, health, and professional associations. For an evaluation of the outcome of the ARET process, see D.L. VanNijnatten, "The ARET Challenge," and "The Day the NGO's Walked Out," in R. Gibson, ed., *Voluntary Initiatives: The New Politics of Corporate Greening* (Peterborough, ON: Broadview Press, 1999), at 93-100 and 101-10.

The recently enacted *Species At Risk Act*, SC 2002, c. 29 (SARA) has legislatively mandated collaborative decision making by embracing the concept of "stewardship," through the development of management strategies and action plans designed to protect and recover endangered and threatened species. Strategies and action plans will be developed and implemented under the Act with the collaboration of the provinces, territories, First Nations, and private landowners in recognition of the need for on-the-ground measures to ensure the survival of the nation's threatened and endangered species. Many of the substantive legislative policies enshrined in SARA were formulated through a collaborative decision-making process involving a consensus agreement reached by the Species At Risk Working Group, which involved representatives of governments, resource industry representatives, and environmental and aboriginal groups. Other examples of collaborative decision making include Ontario's recent review of provincial land-use policies and British Columbia's review of law and policies for the management of the province's fish, wildlife, and park recreation services. See *Natural Heritage Planning Policy in Ontario: A Review of County and Regional Official Plans*, a WWF-Canada initiative, in partnership with Ontario Professional Planners Institute, Ontario Ministry of the Environment, Ontario Ministry of Natural Resources, and Ontario

Ministry of Municipal Affairs and Housing (Community Development Group Ltd., August 1999) and the *Draft Report and Recommendations of the Recreation Stewardship Panel, September 15, 2002* (Victoria: Ministry of Water, Land and Air Protection). Collaborative decision-making processes have also been applied in the fisheries industry. In May 2000, the federal Department of Fisheries and Oceans (DFO) appointed the Institute of Dispute Resolution at the University of Victoria to facilitate an independent review of the department's discussion paper, "A Framework for Improved Decision-Making in the Pacific Salmon Industry." The independent review team instituted a collaborative decision-making process "to begin the public dialogue on key consultation issues with a wide range of government and stakeholder groups, including the provincial government, local governments, First Nations, commercial fishers and processors, recreational fishers, community associations, environmental organizations, and academics." (Institute for Dispute Resolution, available online at http://dispute.resolution.uvic.ca/ research/fishreview.htm). Consultations began in September 2000 and continued until March 2001, resulting in the review team submission of detailed recommendations to the DFO (*Independent Review of Improved Decision Making in the Pacific Salmon Fishery: Final Recommendations*, available from the DFO, Pacific Region, online at http://www-comm.pac.dfo-mpo.gc.ca/).

NOTES AND QUESTIONS

1. Law students and lawyers are trained to think in terms of legal rights and remedies. ADR and collaborative decision making, although cognizant of the legal process, are decision-making processes that attempt to address the concerns of all the stakeholders to an environmental dispute, including the so-called public interest. Should environmental legislation or regulation make ADR, collaboration, or consultation a mandatory element of the law of standing before a party can resort to litigation? In all environmental disputes? Consider these questions again after you have studied the provisions of the *Canadian Environmental Assessment Act* (CEAA), reproduced below.

2. Proponents of litigation as a dispute resolution technique often argue that it provides the litigants with a "level playing field." Do you agree? If not, why not?

3. Scientific uncertainty caused by rapid technological change is a common feature of much environmental litigation. The onus of proof "beyond a reasonable doubt" or "on the balance of probabilities" may often tip the decision in favour of a defendant because scientific uncertainty in the face of technological change makes it difficult, if not impossible, for the bearer of the burden of proof to meet the requisite onus; see *Palmer v. Nova Scotia Forest Industries* (1983), 2 DLR (4th) 397 (NSTD) in chapter 3. Are ADR techniques more attractive alternatives to litigation in these kinds of cases? Many participants in ADR processes identify the lack of scientific information by one or more of the parties as an impediment to reaching consensus. Notwithstanding this criticism, is scientific uncertainty less of a problem for ADR techniques than it is for litigation? *Collaboration: A Guide for Environmental Advocates*, above, emphasizes the importance of "good science" in collaborative decision-making processes. See *Collaboration*, above, chapter 7, The Role of Science: Addressing Information Needs, Monitoring and Adaptive Management, at 43-51.

IV. ENVIRONMENTAL MEDIATION IN CANADA*

Environmental mediation is a form of ADR that is a voluntary process of resolving environmental disputes that requires the intervention of a "neutral." It is distinguished from other forms of ADR that use the intervention of a "neutral" on the basis of two distinctions. First, unlike some forms of ADR such as arbitration and fact finding, environmental mediation is unfettered by procedural formality, other than those procedures negotiated and agreed to by the participants themselves. (It should be remembered that legislative requirements and institutional policy may create invisible procedural constraints.) Second, the "neutral" in environmental mediation plays a role that is unique from the role played by neutrals in other ADR processes. Essentially, environmental mediation is a dispute resolution process in which the participants attempt to resolve the dispute by reaching consensus through the voluntary assistance of the mediator, the "neutral."

Environmental mediation literature has identified a number of prerequisites that must exist for environmental mediation to be successful. It is a voluntary process and the parties are free to pursue any other legal remedies that may be available to them. Since it is a process intended to resolve the dispute through consensus, it is essential that the parties identify and determine the scope of the issues to be resolved through mediation and that all participants are prepared to negotiate in "good faith." The participants themselves must define the objectives of the process and agree when those objectives have been reached. Unlike adjudication, environmental mediation cannot impose a solution or settlement on the participants and can proceed through consensus only.

Environmental mediation is a non-binding process. Although a settlement of the dispute cannot be imposed upon the participants, the legislative and regulatory structures must be in place in order to implement a settlement achieved through mediation. Otherwise, there will be little inducement for the disputants to attempt to reach consensus through mediation.

Environmental mediation requires that the participants themselves choose a mediator who is to serve as an independent instrumentality of all of the participants. The selection of the mediator is perhaps the most crucial moment in the mediation process. The mediator may be appointed by a regulatory agency or selected through negotiations among the participants. If a mediator is appointed by a regulatory agency, the appointment should be made on the recommendation of the parties who have reached consensus on the identity of the mediator. Otherwise, the mediator may lack the trust of all parties. "Trust" is the *sine qua non* of successful ADR.

Once a mediator has been appointed, the participants attempt to reach a consensual settlement through the mediator. The role of the mediator may be described as largely passive because he or she does not normally participate actively in the resolution of the substantive issues. However, the mediator need not only be concerned with procedural issues, such as fairness and freedom from bias. The mediator is also likely to play some

---

*   Part IV of this chapter is based on research done by the author and Dr. Peter Mercer of the University of Western Ontario Faculty of Law for the Law Reform Commission of Canada, submitted on March 31, 1990. See P. Mercer and H.I. Rounthwaite, *Environmental Mediation Study, Draft Final Report*, March 31, 1990.

role in educating the participants by providing information relevant to the issues and by ensuring that each participant is sensitive to the position of the other participants. The mediator is also concerned with encouraging results that are fair, efficient, and capable of lasting. This last point, that the mediator's role should be "passive," is a contentious issue. Some mediators believe that it may be necessary for the mediator actively to attempt to advocate a particular compromise if it appears that the negotiations are reaching an impasse. Mediated negotiation is a dynamic process and the mediator must be sensitive to the ever-changing dynamics of the negotiations.

There have been an increasing number of attempts to settle environmental disputes through mediation in Canada. In most cases, environmental mediation has not succeeded, if the measure of success is whether the negotiations resulted in the parties reaching consensus. For example, mediation has failed in an attempt to site a hazardous waste treatment facility in Ontario. One of the few successful examples is the mediation of the Northern Flood Agreement in Manitoba. Consequently, there is very little practical experience to indicate the kinds of legal issues and problems that can arise as a result of the environmental mediation process. Some of these issues and problems, however, are evident given the nature of the process itself. Many of the legal issues relating to environmental mediation are discussed in E. Swanson, *Environmental Conflict and ADR: Resolution Through Law Reform* (Edmonton: Environmental Law Centre, 1995) and L. Boule and K.J. Kelly, *Mediation: Principles, Process, Practice* (Markham, ON: Butterworths, 1998), at chapter 9, Legal Issues in Mediation.

A. Essential Criteria of Viability for Environmental Mediation

1. Issues Relating to the Participants

Identification of the participants in the mediation may often be a difficult task given the nature of many environmental disputes. Since mediation is dependent on reaching consensus, it is essential that all parties that may have an interest in the dispute or that may be affected by the outcome are identified and invited to participate in the mediation. Given that environmental disputes may involve complex technical, scientific, and social issues, identification of all the relevant participants may be extremely difficult. Further, the broadening of standing rules and increased willingness of special interest groups to participate in administrative and adversarial proceedings further complicates the task of ensuring that all affected interests are invited to participate.

A good example of attempted environmental mediation that failed to identify and include all of the affected parties of the dispute was the Dona Lake Agreement mediation and negotiation. Although the negotiations resulted in a concluded agreement between the proponent, the aboriginal bands affected by the development, and the Ontario regulatory departments, the mediated negotiations failed to include non-aboriginal residents and environmentalists, which detracted from the agreement being accepted by the excluded parties. The framework under which the negotiations took place also failed to include the trade unions that would be involved in the development, with the result that the provisions of the agreement relating to aboriginal employment have been challenged under Ontario's labour legislation. For a rather optimistic analysis of the Dona Lake Agreement, see M. Doelle, "Regulating the Environment by Mediation and Contract

Negotiation: A Case Study of the Dona Lake Agreement" (1992) vol. 2, *Journal of Environmental Law and Practice* 189. Doelle concludes that, at the time of writing, it was premature to measure the success of the negotiations. However, newspaper reports since 1992 report that the Dona Lake mine has proven to be uneconomic and has been plagued by labour and regulatory problems. The Dona Lake Agreement is a good example of participants in ADR failing to address adequately the institutional restraints under which development takes place. A significant issue in the negotiations involved aboriginal employment guarantees in the start up and operation of the mine. Under the master agreement, the parties agreed to negotiate a series of subagreements, one of which was the subagreement on human resource development. The human resource development subagreement provided for a range of human resource issues, including native employment, training, and apprenticeship programs. The parties to the subagreement failed to consider the existing legislative framework governing labour relations in Ontario and failed to develop a native employment policy consistent with it. Representatives of trade unions whose members would be employed at the mine were not parties to the negotiations.

Identification of the participants also requires the selection of an experienced professional mediator to help the parties decide whether to pursue mediation. The selection of the mediator is considered by many to be the most important factor contributing to the success of the mediation. See, for example, G. Bingham et al., *Environmental Conflict Resolution: Annotated Bibliography* (Washington, DC: Conservation Foundation, 1981).

The willingness of all the participants to negotiate in good faith is absolutely essential if the mediation is to succeed in arriving at a consensual solution. Whether this is the case will depend in most cases on the nature of the environmental controversy. The importance of "good faith" and the development of "trust" in successful mediation is considered in an excellent article by J. Keeping, "Environmental Protection Through the Land Claims Processes: The Importance of Trust," in S.A. Kennett, ed., *Law and Process in Environmental Management: Essays from the Sixth CIRL Conference on Natural Resources Law* (Calgary: Canadian Institute of Resources Law, 1993), at 383-96. See also S.A. Moore, "The Role of Trust in Social Networks: Formation, Function and Fragility," in S.A. Saunders, J. Craig, and E.M. Mattiske, eds., *Nature Conservation 4: The Role of Networks* (Chipping Norton, NSW: Surrey Beatty and Sons, 1995).

2. The Nature of the Environmental Dispute

One of the virtues of environmental mediation is that it permits the participants to examine the nature of the problem at hand, unencumbered by the straightjacket of substantive and procedural rules that bind the adjudicative process. Rather than ask "what is the rule?" or "what is the best rule?" participants engaged in mediation are able to ask "what is the nature of the basic problem and how shall we choose among the various procedures of social ordering that might be applied to it?" (L. Fuller, "Mediation— Its Forms and Functions" (1971) vol. 44 *Southern California Law Review* 305, at 307).

The environmental mediation literature is almost uniformly of the opinion that there must be a relative balance of power among the participants. Balancing of power, however, is inherent in the life cycle of conflict. Conflict may be seen as consisting of five phases: (1) latent conflict, (2) the initiation of conflict, (3) the balancing of power, (4) the balance of power, and (5) the disruption of equilibrium. See J. Folberg and A. Taylor, *Mediation: A Comprehensive Guide to Resolving Conflicts Without Litigation* (San Francisco: Jossey-Bass, 1984). Mediation is a form of ADR that, if successful, has the effect of achieving a balance of power among the participants.

Power is also relevant to environmental mediation on an entirely different level. While the outcome of successful negotiations, with or without mediation, may be the balance of power among the participants, a balance can only be reached if the participants are willing to expend the resources necessary to reach a resolution of the dispute. Potential participants in environmental mediation are likely to invest in the process only if there is a relative balancing of power at the commencement of the negotiations.

The relative balancing of power among the potential participants is a further illustration of the interplay between the legal rights and remedies of each participant and the likelihood of resolving the environmental dispute through mediation. It is unlikely that a party to an environmental dispute will agree to attempt to reach a solution through mediation (or any other form of ADR) if it believes that its legal position will prevail through adjudication. Environmental legislation and regulation that promotes a balancing of legal power between parties to an environmental dispute should provide further impetus for attempting to resolve disputes through mediation. As it becomes increasingly unclear which interests may prevail through adjudication, the risk factor makes environmental mediation more attractive. This is a further illustration of the importance of assessing the institutional and policy setting under which the negotiations are to take place.

The notion of "balancing of power" should not be confused with the notion of "empowerment" as the latter is currently being used in the environmental mediation literature. The "balancing of power" among the participants in environmental mediation is a consideration relating to issues such as whether any party may or may not enter into the process, and is a factor in evaluating whether the process has been successful in reaching a resolution to the environmental dispute. It is of particular importance if environmental mediation is viewed as a problem-solving technique; if so, whether consensus has been reached through a balancing of power between the participants becomes an important measure of success for the process. "Empowerment" proponents, on the other hand, view the mediation process not as a problem-solving process primarily, but as part of a process of participatory democracy. "Empowerment" is a process of transformation whereby the success of the mediation is measured by the extent to which the process has resulted in transformation of the decision-making process from one of reaching a consensus outcome as the only measure of success to one in which success is measured through empowerment leading to an appreciation and respect for the other parties' viewpoints and problems. See R.A. Bush and J. Folger, *The Promise of Mediation: Responding to Conflict Through Empowerment and Recognition* (San Francisco: Jossey-Bass, 1994).

3. Other Factors

The mediation literature has identified a series of other relevant factors that should be considered when a potential participant is contemplating participation in environmental mediation. One checklist of relevant considerations is given by G.W. Cormick, "Where, When and How To Use Mediated Negotiations: A Checklist for the Potential Participant"

(1988) vol. 3, no. 1 *Canadian Environmental Mediation Newsletter* 7. A very useful checklist is also provided by B. Sadler, "Mediation Provisions and Options in Canadian Environmental Assessment" (1993) vol. 13 *Environmental Impact Assessment Review* 375, at 380, table 1. Factors that most commentators consider to be essential include:

1. Has the dispute reached an impasse such that the issues have been defined and the parties at interest can be identified? It should be noted, however, that mediation has also had a measure of success in assisting the participants to identify and define the issues in dispute among them. Mediation may have some utility even in cases where a consensual resolution cannot be reached through its empowerment and transformative functions.

2. Has the dispute reached a point of providing for a zero-sum solution such that each participant believes that it must compromise its initial position?

3. Will a solution achieved through mediated compromise jeopardize fundamental values or priorities firmly held by any of the participants? No form of ADR that relies on resolution of conflict through voluntary consensus of the participants will succeed if consensus can only be achieved if one or more of the participants must sacrifice a fundamental value choice. The proposal of Eldorado Nuclear to build a uranium hexa-fluoride plant at Corman Park, Saskatchewan is an example of such a dispute. Opponents of the project held fundamental moral and religious beliefs that could not be compromised through negotiation. It is essential that the nature of the dispute be considered carefully to determine whether the underlying values of the participants would be compromised in reaching a settlement through mediation. When one or more of the parties to an environmental dispute orders its priorities on the basis of deeply held moral, ethical, religious, cultural, or ecological values, the conflict may not be a suitable candidate for environmental mediation. These disputes are likely to be settled only through adjudication which imposes a solution on all of the parties, although mediation may serve important educational and sensitizing functions.

An unwillingness to compromise fundamental values (and legal rights) may also account for the reluctance of Canadian aboriginal groups to embrace mediation as a means of resolving resource use conflicts. See C. Darling, *In Search of Consensus: An Evaluation of the Clayoquot Sound Sustainable Development Task Force Process* (Victoria: University of Victoria Institute for Dispute Resolution, 1991).

B. The Institutional and Legal Framework of the Dispute

Environmental disputes do not arise in a vacuum; rather, existing law and policy will have a profound effect on the range of ADR options that may or may not be available to resolve the dispute. Legislation may be such that the dispute *must* be resolved by resort to adjudicatory procedures. Government policy may dictate that the dispute *must* be determined by a decision maker who imposes a result on the affected parties. Regardless of whether ADR provides a viable alternative to traditional decision-making processes, a conflict assessment must be undertaken. James McKenzie, a mediator and instructor in environmental mediation and negotiation, defines a conflict assessment as "a methodical collection of information about a dispute, designed to: *Learn about the dispute and the parties. ... Test the parties' ability to recognize that they may not achieve their ultimate goal; ... [and] Ascertain whether the institutional setting in which the dispute is embedded will accommodate and support a negotiated settlement, assisted or otherwise."* (J. McKenzie, "Conflict Assessment: A Critical Element of Public Dispute ADR Practice" (October 1995) *ADR Forum*, at 5-6.) McKenzie stresses that much of ADR practice focuses too much on the first two of these criteria of conflict assessment and too little on the third criteria. It may be thought that the exercise of discretion, inherent in environmental decision making, provides opportunities for ADR intervention. However, institutional practices and procedures may be such that ADR is impossible. McKenzie uses the class environmental assessment (EA) procedures under Ontario's *Environmental Assessment Act*, RSO 1990, c. E.18, to argue that the screening criteria employed by the EA branch of the ministry to evaluate "bump-up" requests for an individualized EA operate to effectively preclude ADR intervention. The onus is on the requestor to demonstrate that the class EA planning process was not followed properly or that a proposed undertaking will have a deleterious effect on the environment (McKenzie, above, at 6, col. 2). Since the EA branch requires expert analysis to meet this burden and most requesters lack the resources to hire the necessary experts, there is no incentive for proponents of projects covered by the class EA to negotiate "because they may safely assume that the EA Branch will not recommend a 'bump-up' request." The point for the lawyer advising a client on ADR as an alternative is that he or she must conduct a conflict assessment and pay due consideration to the institutional context of the dispute, the conventional approval process, and the professional norms and procedures for addressing the dispute (McKenzie, above, at 5, col. 2).

Particular attention should be paid to drafting the terms of the agreement reached by the participants. At a minimum, it must clearly and comprehensively state all of the terms of settlement. The primary purpose of the agreement is to preserve the balance of power achieved through the mediation process. It must be enforceable and it is essential that the appropriate federal and provincial agencies are bound by its terms. A well-drafted agreement should also attempt to forestall a disruption of equilibrium by including a process for resolving future disputes that may arise. For example, the Northern Flood Agreement attempted to anticipate and forestall the natural life cycle of conflict by including a continuing arbitration process as part of the agreement. Many of the items discussed by Barton et al., *A Contract Model for Pollution Control*, below, have direct relevance to an agreement reached through mediation and should be considered carefully.

The National Round Table on the Environment and the Economy (NRTEE) has developed a series of "principles" to "inform and guide the use" of a consensus-building process.

G. Cormick et al.
Building Consensus for a Sustainable Future:
Putting Principles into Practice
(Ottawa: National Round Table on the Environment and Economy, 1996), at 7

Principle 1. Purpose-driven. People need a reason to participate in the process.
Principle 2. Inclusive, not exclusive. All parties with a significant interest in the issues should be involved in the consensus process.

Principle 3. Voluntary participation. The parties who are affected or interested participate voluntarily.

Principle 4. Self-design. The parties design the consensus process.

Principle 5. Flexibility. Flexibility should be designed into the process.

Principle 6. Equal opportunity. All parties have equal access to relevant information and the opportunity to participate effectively throughout the process.

Principle 7. Respect for diverse interests. Acceptance of the diverse values, interests, and knowledge of the parties involved in the consensus process is essential.

Principle 8. Accountability. The participants are accountable both to their constituencies and to the process that they have agreed to establish.

Principle 9. Time limits. Realistic deadlines are necessary throughout the process.

Principle 10. Implementation. Commitments to implementation and effective monitoring are essential parts of any agreement.

NOTES AND QUESTIONS

1. What, if any, guidelines should be developed to ensure that all affected interests are represented in the mediation? In the event that it subsequently appears that an affected interest has been passed over during the identification stage of the mediation, what are the legal consequences for mediation stages that may already have taken place?

2. What should a participants' agreement look like? The example that follows is the Agreement used by the Alberta Environmental Appeal Board.

Environmental Appeal Board
Participants' Agreement To Mediate

In the matter of the mediation of the appeal of the decision of the Director, (REGION), Regional Services, Alberta Environment, to issue (APPROVAL/ETC.) under the (*Water Act*, RSA 2000, c.W-3, OR the *Environmental Protection and Enhancement Act*, RSA 2000, c. E-12) to (INSERT).

Between: (APPELLANT)   }
                and   }
                (DIRECTOR)   } the "Parties"
                and   }
                (APPROVAL HOLDER)   }

The Parties agree as follows:

1. The purpose of this agreement is to indicate the intention of the undersigned to participate in mediation in an effort to resolve this appeal.

2. The Parties have been advised to seek independent legal advice, to ensure that they are fully informed of their legal rights and obligations.

3. The mediator has been appointed by the Environmental Appeal Board to assist the Parties in reaching a mutually agreeable resolution of the appeal, based on full and frank disclosure between them.

4. All communications made to or through the Mediator and Board staff who attend the mediation shall be confidential and without prejudice to the position of a Party in any

further proceedings. This means that communications during this mediation can only be raised in subsequent hearings or court proceedings with the written consent of all Parties. Confidentiality dos not apply to the documents, records, materials or other correspondence provided to the Environmental Appeal Board with respect to the main part of the appeal even if they are used in the context of the mediation.

5. The Mediator and Board staff who attend the mediation are not compellable as a witnesses and shall not be called as witnesses by any of the Parties in any subsequent hearings or court proceedings.

6. The mediator will not take part in any subsequent deliberations, discussions or hearings of the Environmental Appeal Board pertaining to the matters of this appeal.

7. In accordance with section 12 of the Environmental Appeal Board Regulation, AR 114/93, if a resolution of the appeal is reached, either a Report and Recommendations reflecting the agreed upon resolution will be submitted by the Environmental Appeal Board to the Minister of Environment, or the Environmental Appeal Board will issue a Decision reflecting the resolution.

8. The Parties acknowledge that the Board does not generally award costs relating to the preparation for or attendance at a mediation. The Parties agree they shall not submit a request to the Environmental Appeal Board for costs respecting the mediation after the conclusion of the mediation. This does not preclude costs between the Parties being addressed in an agreement between the Parties.

9. The Parties will abide by the terms of this agreement and at all times negotiate in good faith.

10. By signing this Agreement, the Parties agreed to abide by the Environmental Appeal Board Ground Rules for Mediation Meetings.

[The ground rules for mediation meetings deal with issues of confidentiality, communication among parties, observers, media statements, the mediator's role, and whether the agreement will include regulatory or contractual clauses.]

Dated at (CITY), Alberta on (DATE).

_____

(INSERT APPELLANT NAME)

_____

(INSERT DIRECTOR NAME AND REGION)

_____

(INSERT APPROVAL HOLDER NAME)

3. The identification of affected interests is a different issue from the question of how such interests should be represented in the mediation exercises. The mediator must be constantly on guard for internal divisions within each interest participant group. For example, in the unsuccessful attempt to mediate the siting of a landfill operation in Perkinsville, Ontario, the participants included six municipalities, two ministries, a number of ratepayer groups and residents, and two individuals. The failure of this mediation can be attributed, not to the large number of participants, but to the lack of

communication within individual negotiating participant groups and the inability of negotiating representatives to make decisions binding on their constituents. See M. Picher, "Mediating the Siting of Waste Disposal Facilities—Two Views: The Mediator's Perspective" (1986) vol. 1 *Canadian Environmental Mediation Newsletter* 1. A similar conclusion has also been advanced in an analysis of the Clayoquot Sound Sustainable Development Task Force Process. Among other problems that plagued the attempt to reach consensus among participants to the task force, representation and accountability of negotiators to their constituents have been identified as two of the primary factors leading to the failure of the task force to reach a consensus agreement. See Darling, above.

4. Information exchange is an important part of most forms of ADR. One of the major roles of the environmental mediator is to provide information to the participants so that they can accurately assess the strengths and weaknesses of their positions. Many of the legal issues that arise with respect to confidentiality, solicitor–client privilege, and the like may also arise in the context of attempting environmental mediation. See E. Swanson, *Environmental Conflict and ADR: Resolution Through Law Reform* (Edmonton: Environmental Law Centre, 1995). In the Sandspit Small Craft Harbour Mediation, discussed below, independent technical expertise was retained by the mediator to provide the parties with technical and process support. Question how these issues are dealt with when considering the following provisions of the *Canadian Environmental Assessment Act.*

Canadian Environmental Assessment Act
SC 1992, c. 37

2(1) In this Act,

"interested party" means, in respect of an environmental assessment, any person or body having an interest in the outcome of the environmental assessment for a purpose that is neither frivolous nor vexatious;

"mediation" means an environmental assessment that is conducted with the assistance of a mediator appointed pursuant to section 30 and that includes a consideration of the factors required to be considered under subsections 16(1) and (2);

· · ·

4. The purposes of this Act are ...

(d) to ensure that there be an opportunity for public participation in the environmental assessment process.

· · ·

12(3) Every federal authority that is in possession of specialist or expert information or knowledge with respect to a project shall, on request, make available that information or knowledge to the responsible authority or to a mediator or review panel. ...

13. Where a project is described in the comprehensive study list or is referred to a mediator or a review panel, notwithstanding any other Act of Parliament, no power, duty or function conferred by or under that Act or any regulation made thereunder shall be exercised or performed that would permit the project to be carried out in whole or in part unless an environmental assessment of the project has been completed

and a course of action has been taken in relation to the project in accordance with paragraph 37(l)(a) ... .

14. The environmental assessment process includes, where applicable, ...

(b) a mediation or assessment by a review panel as provided in section 29 and the preparation of a report; ... .

15(1) The scope of the project in relation to which an environmental assessment is to be conducted shall be determined by ...

(b) where the project is referred to a mediator or a review panel, the Minister, after consulting with the responsible authority.

(2) For the purposes of conducting an environmental assessment in respect of two or more projects, ...

(b) where at least one of the projects is referred to a mediator or a review panel, the Minister, after consulting with the responsible authority, may determine that the projects are so closely related that they can be considered to form a single project.

(3) Where a project is in relation to a physical work, an environmental assessment shall be conducted in respect of every construction, operation, modification, decommissioning, abandonment or other undertaking in relation to that physical work that is proposed by the proponent or that is, in the opinion of

(a) the responsible authority, or

(b) where the project is referred to a mediator or a review panel, the Minister, after consulting with the responsible authority, likely to be carried out in relation to that physical work.

[Chapter 6, Environmental Impact Assessment, considers the importance of scoping in environmental assessment processes. Under the CEAA, the minister determines the "scope of the project in relation to which an environmental assessment is to be conducted." Case studies of environmental ADR in both Canada and the United States demonstrate that the parties must play a significant role in scoping decisions if a consensus solution to the dispute is to be reached.]

16(1) Every screening or comprehensive study of a project and every mediation or assessment by a review panel shall include a consideration of the following factors:

(a) the environmental effects of the project, including the environmental effects of malfunctions or accidents that may occur in connection with the project and any cumulative environmental effects that are likely to result from the project in combination with other projects or activities that have been or will be carried out;

(b) the significance of the effects referred to in paragraph (a);

(c) comments from the public that are received in accordance with this Act and the regulations;

(d) measures that are technically and economically feasible and that would mitigate any significant adverse environmental effects of the project; and

(e) any other matter relevant to the screening, comprehensive study, mediation or assessment by a review panel, such as the need for the project and alternatives to the project, that the responsible authority or, except in the case of a screening, the Minister after consulting with the responsible authority, may require to be considered.

(2) In addition to the factors set out in subsection (1), every comprehensive study of a project and every mediation or assessment by a review panel shall include a consideration of the following factors:

(a) the purpose of the project;

(b) alternative means of carrying out the project that are technically and economically feasible and the environmental effects of any such alternative means;

(c) the need for, and the requirements of, any follow up program in respect of the project; and

(d) the capacity of renewable resources that are likely to be significantly affected by the project to meet the needs of the present and those of the future.

(3) The scope of the factors to be taken into consideration pursuant to paragraphs (1)(a),(b) and (d) and (2)(b), (c) and (d) shall be determined ...

(b) where a project is referred to a mediator or a review panel, by the Minister, after consulting the responsible authority, when fixing the terms of reference of the mediation or review panel.

[Like the scoping process, the setting of the terms of reference of the mediation are to be determined by the minister, after consultation with the responsible authority. The terms of reference are often vigorously debated by the proponent, the responsible authority, and the Canadian Environmental Assessment Agency. Although it is the practice of the agency to seek public input into the terms of reference, they are ultimately imposed by the minister.]

20(1) The responsible authority shall take one of the following courses of action in respect of a project after taking into consideration the screening report and any comments filed pursuant to subsection 18(3): ...

(c) where

(i) it is uncertain whether the project, taking into account the implementation of any mitigation measures that the responsible authority considers appropriate, is likely to cause significant adverse environmental effects,

(ii) the project, taking into account the implementation of any mitigation measures that the responsible authority considers appropriate, is likely to cause significant environmental effects and paragraph (b) does not apply, or

(iii) public concerns warrant a reference to a mediator or a review panel,

the responsible authority shall reer the project to the Minister for a referral to a mediator or a review panel in accordance with section 29 ... .

21. Where a project is described in the comprehensive study list, the responsible authority shall

(a) ensure that a comprehensive study is conducted, and a comprehensive study report is prepared and provided to the Minister and the Agency; or

(b) refer the project to the Minister for a referral to a mediator or a review panel in accordance with section 29 ... .

[Bill C-9, *An Act To Amend the Canadian Environmental Assessment Act*, 37th Parl., 2nd sess. (September 2002), if enacted, amends s. 21 requiring the responsible authority to report certain matters to the minister and to *recommend* that the project be referred to a mediator or review panel. Section 21.1 is added directing the minister to continue the comprehensive study or refer the project to a mediator or review panel. Section 21.1(2) adds "Despite any other provision of this Act, if the Minister refers the project to a responsible authority under paragraph (1)(a), it may not be referred to a mediator or review panel in accordance with section 29."]

23. The Minister shall take one of the following courses of action in respect of a project after taking into consideration the comprehensive study report and any comments filed pursuant to subsection 22(2): ...
    (b) where,
        (i) it is uncertain whether the project, taking into account the implementation of any appropriate mitigation measures, is likely to cause significant adverse environmental effects,
        (ii) the project, taking into account the implementation of any appropriate mitigation measures, is likely to cause significant adverse environmental effects and subparagraph (a)(ii) does not apply, or
        (iii) public concerns warrant a reference to a mediator or a review panel,
    the Minister shall refer the project to a mediator or a review panel in accordance with section 29 ... .
25. Subject to paragraphs 20(1)(b) and (c), where at any time a responsible authority is of the opinion that
    (a) a project, taking into account the implementation of any mitigation measures that the responsible authority considers appropriate, may cause significant adverse environmental effects, or
    (b) public concerns warrant a reference to a mediator or a review panel, the responsible authority may request the Minister to refer the project to a mediator or a review panel in accordance with section 29 ... .
26. Where at any time a responsible authority decides not to exercise any power or perform any duty or function referred to in section 5 in relation to a project that has not been referred to a mediator or a review panel, it may terminate the environmental assessment of the project.
27. Where at any time a responsible authority decides not to exercise any power or perform any duty or function referred to in section 5 in relation to a project that has been referred to a mediator or a review panel, the Minister may terminate the environmental assessment of the project.
28. Where at any time the Minister is of the opinion that
    (a) a project for which an environmental assessment may be required under section 5, taking into account the implementation of any appropriate mitigation measures, may cause significant adverse environmental effects, or
    (b) public concerns warrant a reference to a mediator or a review panel, the Minister may, after offering to consult with the jurisdiction, within the meaning of

subsection 12(5), where the project is to be carried out and after consulting with the responsible authority or, where there is no responsible authority in relation to the project, the appropriate federal authority, refer the project to a mediator or a review panel in accordance with section 29 ... .

29(1) Subject to subsection (2), where a project is to be referred to a mediator or a review panel, the Minister shall

    (a) refer the environmental assessment relating to the project to

        (i) a mediator, or

        (ii) a review panel; or

    (b) refer part of the environmental assessment relating to the project to a mediator and part of that assessment to a review panel.

(2) An environmental assessment or a part thereof shall not be referred to a mediator unless the interested parties have been identified and are willing to participate in the mediation.

(3) The Minister may, at any time, refer any issue relating to an assessment by a review panel to a mediator where the Minister is of the opinion, after consulting with the review panel, that mediation is appropriate in respect of that issue.

(4) Where at any time after an environmental assessment or part of an environmental assessment of a project has been referred to a mediator, the Minister or the mediator determines that the mediation is not likely to produce a result that is satisfactory to all the participants to the mediation, the Minister shall terminate the mediation of the issue and refer the issue to a review panel.

[Bill C-9, above, amends s. (4) by deleting *terminate* and substituting *order the conclusion of*. Sections 20, 21, 23, 25, and 28 determine the circumstances under which a project may be referred to a mediator or review panel in accordance with s. 29. Consider the wording of s. 29 carefully, particularly ss. 2, 3, and 4. A project may only be referred to a mediator if "the interested parties have been identified and are willing to participate in the mediation." Is it likely that interested parties will be willing to participate in mediation if they have not participated in the scoping process or in setting the terms of reference of the environmental assessment? Are interested parties likely to invest scarce resources in a mediation process that can be terminated if "the Minister or the mediator determines that the mediation is not likely to produce a result that is satisfactory to all the participants to the mediation"?]

30(1) Where a reference is made under subparagraph 29(1)(a)(i) in relation to a project, the Minister shall, after consulting with the responsible authority and all parties who are to participate in the mediation,

    (a) appoint as mediator any person who

        (i) is unbiased and free from any conflict of interest relative to the project and who has knowledge or experience in acting as a mediator, and

        (ii) may have been selected from a roster established pursuant to subsection (2); and

    (b) fix the terms of reference of the mediation.

[Although the minister must "consult" with the parties to the mediation, it is the minister who will appoint the mediator and set the terms of reference for the mediation.]

31. The mediator may, at any time, allow an additional interested party to participate in a mediation.

32(1) A mediator shall, at the conclusion of the mediation, prepare and submit a report to the Minister and to the responsible authority.

(2) No evidence of or relating to a statement made by a mediator or a participant to the mediation during the course of and for the purposes of the mediation is admissible without the consent of the mediator or participant, in any proceeding before a review panel, court, tribunal, body or person with jurisdiction to compel the production of evidence.

[There is unanimous agreement among ADR theorists and practitioners that mediation discussions must be privileged and inadmissible in subsequent proceedings. Otherwise, the give and take necessary to develop trust and reach consensus could not take place.]

36. On receiving a report submitted by a mediator or a review panel, the Minister shall make the report available to the public in any manner the Minister considers appropriate to facilitate public access to the report, and shall advise the public that the report is available.

[Mediator's reports are posted on the public registry established by s. 55 of the Act and can be accessed through the agency's Web site at http://www.ceaa.gc.ca/.]

38(1) Where a responsible authority takes a course of action pursuant to paragraph 20(l)(a) or 37(l)(a), it shall, in accordance with the regulations made for that purpose, design any follow-up program that it considers appropriate for the project and arrange for the implementation of that program.

(2) A responsible authority referred to in subsection (1) shall, in accordance with any regulations made for that purpose, advise the public of ...

(c) the extent to which the recommendations set out in any report submitted by a mediator or a review panel have been adopted and the reasons for not having adopted any of those recommendations; ... .

[Note that the Act requires the "responsible authority" to design an appropriate followup program in accordance with the regulations. Should a followup program be part of the terms of reference for the mediation and is this possible in light of s. 38(1)? Bill C-9 significantly weakens mandatory design of a followup program by giving the responsible authority the discretion to "consider whether a follow-up program for the project is appropriate in the circumstances." If the responsible authority decides that a followup program is not appropriate, no such program will be designed. Bill C-9 replaces s. 47(1) and allows projects to be referred to a mediator or review panel where

the minister is of the opinion that a project may cause significant adverse environmental effects occurring outside Canada and outside federal lands. The bill also makes
extensive amendments to s. 55, the Canadian Environmental Assessment Registry.]

    58(1) For the purposes of this Act, the Minister may

        (a) issue guidelines and codes of practice respecting the application of this Act
and the regulations and, without limiting the generality of the foregoing, establish
criteria to determine whether a project, taking into account the implementation of
any appropriate mitigation measures, is likely to cause significant adverse environmental effects or whether such effects are justified in the circumstances; ...

        (f) establish criteria for the appointment of mediators and members of review
panels; ... .

    (1.1) For the purposes of this Act, the Minister shall establish a participant fund-
ing program to facilitate the participation of the public in mediations and assessments by review panels ... .

[Bill C-9 amendments will include public participation in comprehensive studies.]

    (3) The Minister shall provide reasonable public notice of and a reasonable op-
portunity for anyone to comment on draft guidelines, codes of practice, agreements,
arrangements, criteria or orders under this section.

    (4) Any guidelines, codes of practice, agreements, arrangements, criteria or order
shall be made available to the public.

NOTES AND QUESTIONS

    1. Several other sections of the Act refer to mediation but have not been reproduced.
Projects that may have transboundary effects on another province or internationally and
that do not require the exercise of a s. 5 power, duty, or function by a federal authority
may be referred to a mediator if the minister is of the opinion that the project may cause
significant adverse environmental effects. See ss. 46 (provinces), 47 (international), and
48 (other federal lands including Indian lands). Subsection (2) of each of these sections
prohibits the minister from referring the project to a mediator unless the minister is
satisfied that specified conditions have been met. When such a project is referred to
mediation, however, ss. 50(1) and (2) authorize the minister to issue a ministerial order
prohibiting the proponent of the project from taking any step in carrying out the project
until the minister is satisfied that the project is not likely to cause significant adverse
environmental effects or that such effects can be justified. Ministerial orders may be
enforced by injunction at the suit of the attorney general (s. 51).

    2. The Act also contains detailed provisions concerning access to information and
information disclosure in s. 55.

    3. It is difficult to assess the extent to which mediation will play a meaningful role in
the federal environmental assessment process, though it has largely been ignored to date.
Assuming that a "project" is subject to an environmental assessment, can you identify the
situations in which it may be referred to mediation as part of the environmental assessment process? The recently published Regulations Respecting the Coordination by Federal

Authorities of Environmental Assessment Procedures and Requirements, SOR/97-181, part II, vol. 9, 1168 and the Draft Criteria for Substitution of a Panel Review Under Section 43 may have a significant effect on the future of mediation under the CEAA. The draft Substitution Regulations provide the basis on which the minister will make a decision to substitute a panel review under the CEAA for review under the environmental assessment provisions of another jurisdiction. The Federal Coordination Regulations, above, outline the procedures that the CEAA will follow in processing a project submitted under the Act. Bill C-9, *An Act To Amend the Canadian Environmental Assessment Act*, above, will establish a Federal Environmental Assessment Coordinator who will have significant powers affecting the federal role in environmental assessment and mediation. (See the proposed amendments at ss. 12.1, 12.2, 12.3, 12.4, and 12.5.)

4. Most provincial jurisdictions do not expressly contemplate mediation or other forms of ADR in their environmental assessment or other environmental legislation. Notable exceptions can be found in British Columbia's *Environmental Assessment Act*, RSBC 1996, c. 119, s. 66; Nova Scotia's new *Environment Act*, SNS 1994-95, c. 1, provisions respecting the cost of cleaning up contaminated sites that require ADR attempts before a cleanup order can be made by the minister; and settlement negotiations using ADR techniques that have been made part of the appeal process by the Environmental Appeal Board (EAB) established under Alberta's *Environmental Enhancement and Protection Act*, RSA 2000, c. E-12. That Act authorizes publication of the Alberta Environmental Appeal Board's Rules of Practice, which are available online at http://www3.gov.ab.ca/eab/97Rules.html. In s. 2 of the rules, the board states that it "has all of the powers necessary to conduct the fair, expeditious and impartial hearing of an appeal, including ... where appropriate, to inform the parties as to the availability of one or more alternative means of dispute resolution, and encourage the use of such methods" and "to hold conferences for the settlement or simplification of the issues including, where appropriate, the use of preliminary meetings and alternative means of dispute resolution." See also EAB regulation 114/93. The EAB has made extensive use of ADR and currently mediates the majority of appeals it receives. See W. Tilleman, *Environmental Appeal Boards: A Comparative Look at the US, Canada and England* (1996) vol. 21 *Columbia Journal of Environmental Law* 1.

5. Consider the definition of "interested party." The rules of court for most provinces provide for the striking out of a statement of claim on the grounds that the claim is "frivolous or vexatious." Should the Canadian Environmental Assessment Agency or the minister be guided by the jurisprudence that has considered this term in deciding whether all of the "interested parties" have been identified for the purposes of s. 29(2)? Who should be entitled to participate as an interested party in the mediation of a project to double the capacity of a ski resort located in a national park?

6. Does the Act provide sufficient incentive for an interested party to participate in the mediation of a project? If a mediation is conducted and the participants reach a consensual agreement, how will the agreement be enforced? Must it be enforced? If not, why participate? Review the comments to the provisions of the Act, reproduced above.

7. Consider the situations in which mediation will rely on the discretion of the minister. In most instances, the minister must consult the responsible authority before exercising the discretion to refer the project to mediation. Pursuant to s. 29(4), the minister shall terminate (Bill C-9, "order the conclusion") a mediation if the minister or

the mediator is of the opinion that the mediation is not likely to reach a result that is satisfactory to all of the participants. At what stage in a mediation should this determination be made? Does this provision underestimate the educative feature of environmental mediation? Since the minister "shall" terminate the mediation, does this place undue pressure on the participants to compromise their positions? Should the CEAA be amended to recognize the transformative aspects of environmental mediation?

8. Since the CEAA is a procedural law, what is there to mediate? The environmental impact assessment process?

9. Environmental mediation may be a useful means of assisting the participants to a dispute to identify and define the issues that underlie the dispute, though mediation may have no chance of reaching an ultimate consensual solution. Does the Act contemplate mediation in these types of conflicts? Consider the requirements of s. 16. Does this section provide a disincentive to participate in mediation of some environmental disputes? Contrast the approach to mediation taken in the CEAA, above, with the approach to mediation under British Columbia's *Environmental Assessment Act*:

> 66(1) The board [Environmental Assessment Board] or the executive director may make the services of a mediator available to parties interested in the outcome of an application for a project approval certificate.
>
> (2) If satisfied that mediation will be conducive to the settlement of one or more issues related to the review of the application, the board or the executive director may
>
> > (a) invite the proponent, and any parties interested in the outcome of the application, to participate in mediation of an issue or issues.
> >
> > (b) refer the issue or issues to a mediator for mediation, and
> >
> > (c) require the mediator to report the results of the mediation to the board or the executive director by a time to be specified in the referral.

10. The Canadian Environmental Assessment Agency Web site, http://www.ceaa.gc.ca/, notes that "to date the formal provision for mediation contained in the Act has not been used" but that "informal mediation and other alternative dispute resolution (ADR) methods" have been used on "a number of environmental assessments." The major trial mediation to date dealt with Canada-British Columbia South Moresby Agreement, which provided for the construction of a small craft harbour near Sandspit, British Columbia. An initial environmental evaluation of the proposed harbour site identified potentially significant adverse environmental impacts at the site preferred by the Sandspit community and the matter was referred to mediation as part of the initial environmental assessment of the project. In April 1992, Glenn Sigurdson, a Vancouver-based mediator, was appointed by the minister to mediate the Sandspit Small Craft Harbour Project. Initial terms of reference for the mediation process were developed by the Federal Environmental Assessment Review Office (FEARO, now the Canadian Environmental Assessment Agency) in consultation with potential participants identified by FEARO. At the mediation table, the participants agreed upon a set of "ground rules" that would guide the mediation process.

The objective of the mediation process as defined in the "ground rules" was "to define a commonly acceptable way to provide the community of Sandspit, British Columbia with a small craft harbour pursuant to the provisions of part II of the Canada-British

Columbia South Moresby Agreement and consistent with the principles of sustainable development and the Federal Environmental Assessment [and] Review Process." See J. Mathers, *Sandspit Small Craft Harbour Mediation Process: A Review and Evaluation* (Canadian Environmental Assessment Agency, March 1995), 1.

The Agency points to the Sandspit Small Craft Harbour Project as the first full-scale use of mediation within the federal environmental assessment process. Although a consensus agreement was reached over the course of 14 months of mediation, it is difficult to conclude that the mediation was successful. The Agency's internal evaluation judges the exercise as a success based on the "Guiding Principles of Consensus Processes" developed by the Canadian Round Tables' 1993 *Building Consensus for a Sustainable Future: Guiding Principles: An Initiative Undertaken by the Canadian Round Tables*, August 1993. Mathers, above, also concludes that the mediation was successful based on post-mediation interviews with the participants. However, it can be noted that difficulties arose both during and after the mediation with clearly identifying a proponent for the project, that the costs of the mediation were $248,000 (similar to the costs of a review panel assessment of a small project), and there is some debate whether the site of the harbour agreed upon through the mediation is indeed the best site. It should also be noted that a second mediation was required in order to establish a fund for the operation and maintenance of the harbour and that several affected interests had been excluded from the initial mediation sessions.

V. NEGOTIATION-BASED APPROACHES

A. The Contract Model of Alternative Dispute Resolution

B.J. Barton, R.T. Franson, and A.R. Thompson
A Contract Model for Pollution Control
(Vancouver: Westwater Research Centre, 1984), c. V

In this chapter we will explain how we envisage that contracts can be used as an alternative to conventional means of pollution control. We will develop our ideas on the use of contracts in specific detail, first outlining the form the contracts could take, then discussing the place of the contracts in the waste management legislation, and finally considering how to incorporate public participation.

The contract model is best suited for "process pollution," by which we mean pollution that is a normal by-product of a desirable human activity. The model is also intended for persons or companies who desire to avoid pollution and intend to comply with the law. A properly drafted agreement would deal firmly with deliberate or reckless acts of pollution, but would do so in part by turning the matter over to the criminal law. An agreement would not be contemplated where such acts were likely.

The Form and Content of the Agreement

The basis of a contractual mode of pollution control as an alternative to a criminal law mode is a contract made between the Waste Management Branch and the company as willing parties and forming the entire framework for the relationship between them. The basic framework would not be the statutory structure of permits, orders and prosecutions, although the relationships of those mechanisms with contracts will have to be considered in detail in the next section.

In appearance and content the contract would be governed by the functions which the parties desire it to carry out.

The Negotiating of Agreements

A contract would be negotiated on the same occasions and in the same manner as the de facto agreements which are so frequently negotiated under the permit system. We have concentrated on the agreements which would be concluded at the time when the parties have reached a consensus on discharge levels and control equipment, since this is the time when permits are usually issued. There are of course other possibilities, such as an agreement at an early stage to explore technical options and to gather baseline data, or a multi-stage agreement to cope with different phases of a development. Another possibility is an agreement made when a previous agreement is overtaken by events and needs to be renegotiated, perhaps even in cases where a default has occurred.

The business of negotiating agreements draws attention to the vital factor of voluntariness. To be separate and distinct from the permit system and to be truly based on agreement, the contract model must be voluntary. A system which leaves the company no choice but to sign the contract offered to it would not be based on agreement; it would be no different in substance from a permit system. Both the company and the Branch must have some other avenue open if it seems that negotiating an agreement will not produce acceptable results. Either party should have the choice of using the permit system instead of the contract system, whether from the outset or by calling off negotiations on an agreement. Even though a company must continue to deal with the Branch if it wishes to obtain a right to discharge pollutants, the permit system with its appeal rights offers a real alternative to an agreement.

The process of negotiating a waste management agreement is likely to take more expertise, time and effort than reaching agreement on the terms of a permit. As well as the engineering skills which must always be drawn on, negotiations will probably demand increased legal and financial expertise. When a company negotiates for a permit, it makes its case as well as it can, and then waits to see what the Branch will allow and what it will impose. On the other hand, if a contract is involved, a company is much more likely to negotiate towards a regime that it believes it can comply with even under the adverse possibilities that it can foresee. Most people in commercial or technical pursuits try to plan not only for the optimum outcome but also for the setbacks, failures and inadequacies that may occur.

This extra time and effort put into negotiation is in fact one of the main advantages of the contract model. It naturally induces both the Branch and the company to look ahead and prepare for a variety of future contingencies. It obliges the parties to consider together how they are going to deal with unpredictable future events. This contingency planning is invaluable.

Basic Contents of the Contract

The negotiating position of each party would give the first indication of what would be included in the contract. Most of the conditions now imposed in permits would be relevant; the quality and quantity of the discharge, precise location, term, monitoring, reporting and so forth. In addition, three other elements would be present. The first is the elimination of statutory offences, orders and penalties except in extreme instances. The second is the provision and clarification of contractual remedies for defaults, bringing the sanctions within the terms of the agreement. The third element, not related to enforcement matters, is the exploitation of the enormous flexibility that contracting allows in order to create incentives, to resolve disputes and to provide for consequences to fit each different case.

Agreement Not To Prosecute or To Make Statutory Orders

If a real departure from the criminal law mode is to be made, it will have to be spelled out that criminal sanctions will not apply. If the Branch could launch a prosecution at any time for the breach of a term of an agreement, no advance would have been made on the permit system. Similarly, the power to issue orders would have to be removed. Consequently a waste management agreement must contain a clause in which the Branch agrees not to prosecute or make statutory orders except in limited and clearly defined circumstances.

Such a clause could be controversial. An outcry could develop if it was thought that the Branch was surrendering its rights to take pollution offenders to court. It would have to be carefully explained to the public that prosecutions had by no means been abandoned, and that the contract included penalty and enforcement provisions under the law of contract that, in real terms, are likely to be more effective than the sanctions under the criminal law.

Contractual Remedies

All of the remedies usually made available by law and equity, including damages and injunctions, could apply to breaches of waste management contracts.

Damages are the primary redress for breach of contract, and financial liability would indeed seem to be a useful and logical sanction to encourage compliance. However there are problems in this particular application; damages are normally compensatory and are only rarely awarded to punish or coerce the defendant. The Branch would have to show that the Crown had suffered loss in consequence of the breach, and at best could only recover damages sufficient to restore it, as far as money can do so, to the position it would have had if there had been no breach. These general principles raise specific obstacles. The Branch would have to prove the loss that it had suffered; it would have to prove that the breach caused the loss. Its case would fail if it could not prove any adverse effect on the property or financial position of the Crown. If the physical damage from pollution only affected the property of third parties, or substances or qualities not capable of ownership, or intangible values such as the quality of the environment, no damages would be payable. (Third parties would be blocked from contractual recovery by a lack of privity.) The Branch's case would be immensely complicated by difficulties in proving which particular discharge in a busy area was the cause of environmental degradation, or what was the exact damage caused by a delay in constructing pollution abatement facilities. Even if damages are recovered, they may bear little relation to the cost which the polluter has avoided by being in breach.

The usual solution for these problems in building contracts is a liquidated damage clause which provides for the payment of a fixed sum on the occasion of specified breach without proof of actual loss. Delay is often dealt with in this fashion. A liquidated damages clause might be sufficient here to deal with questions of causation and quantification, but it might not overcome some of the other obstacles which we have pointed out. It must be kept in mind that the courts will only award liquidated damages if the fixed sum bears some relation to the realities of liability, and is a genuine pre-estimate of loss. A sum fixed with the simple intention of forcing a party to perform the contract, without relation to estimated loss, may be struck down for being a penalty. A further problem is that agreed liquidated damages bind both parties. In a case where the Crown's losses are in fact much greater than the sum fixed as liquidated damages, the recoverable damages would be limited to that fixed sum. An alternative approach is to measure damages by the cost of replacing defective works.

Even with these difficulties, liquidated damages present a beneficial remedy for non-performance of a contract. Each party knows in advance where it stands, problems of proof are avoided, and the losses which a breach could cause to a wider range of persons than the Branch can be taken into account. Financial sanctions are flexible and could be adapted to implement a system of economic incentives inducing compliance. In light of these advantages of financial sanctions, it may be worthwhile to circumvent the rule of equity that penalties are unenforceable.

Bonds are frequently used (both in pollution control permits and in commercial contracts) to ensure satisfactory performance and to safeguard the payment of compensation for breach. Their enforcement is also prone to attack as a penalty rather than liquidated damages.

Specific performance and injunctions should also be considered in the drafting of a waste management contract. With the difficulties that at times complicate the damages remedy, the equitable remedies have definite attractions. Specific performance is becoming more readily available with the erosion of the rule against granting it where constant supervision by the court would be necessary.

In some ways, the equitable remedies are similar to the powers of the Branch under the existing permit system to issue orders, but there is a difference in the forum before which they are enforced and in their amenability to the conditions of the contract.

Damages and equitable remedies may often be the best way of dealing with breaches of contracts, but in some cases the best sanction may be to deprive the company of some advantage or privilege which is conferred by the contract. For example it could be stated, in each clause of a contract in which one of these privileges is granted, that default in performance will result in loss of the privilege.

The ultimate withdrawal of a privilege would be withdrawal of the right to discharge pollutants. This should occur only on a breach sufficiently serious to warrant termination of the contract. It is a simple matter to state in the contract what acts or omissions would entitle the Branch to terminate the contract. Indeed it is common practice in contracts to specify which breaches entitle the injured party to rescind. A complete withdrawal of the right to discharge pollutants is perhaps the most effective remedy open to the Branch. However we have previously noted the difficulty of employing it where, for instance, it would force the closure of a locally important industry.

Rescission also raises the question of what rules are to govern the relationship between the parties after the termination of the contract. If the company continues to discharge pollutants, the discharge is an unauthorized one, and could soon attract a prosecution. On termination the company would be obliged to apply for a permit or negotiate a new contract without delay. The situation would be the same as if a conventional permit had been invoked or breached. It becomes obvious, though, that the circumstances in which a contract is to terminate must be considered with much care. In many cases it may be preferable to keep the contract in force without termination for as long as possible, through all but the worst breaches of its terms, resorting instead to financial and other sanctions to bring about due performance.

Incentives

The flexibility that a regulatory contract allows can be used to offer incentives to encourage compliance with the contract and fulfilment of the regulatory goals. In the pollution control context, we can assume that the main incentives for the Branch to enter into a contract are that higher standards can be achieved and enforced. Several possibilities may be suggested to illustrate how the contract model could be used to offer incentives to a company.

A right of renewal—on compliance with the terms of the contract—could be an effective incentive. Another incentive which could be negotiated is a right to adjust the standards of effluent downward if, for example, it is proven that the adjustment would cause no harm to the environment. In some circumstances, release of a duty to post a bond may be a fitting incentive; in others there could be clauses insisting on the Branch or the company making public announcements, or commitments by the Branch to undertake certain studies, or to make financial grants to the firm; or performance of the contract could be linked to the assistance being offered (on Crown land grants, for instance) by other agencies of the government. Finally, it may be suggested that the very flexibility that the contract mode offers is itself an incentive for a company to keep itself outside the conventional permit mode.

Procedures

Contractual flexibility could also be used to create procedures and mechanisms which would facilitate the parties' dealings with each other.

An engineer could be appointed to oversee the works or operations to be carried out by the company and to make decisions called for by the contract.

It may also be necessary to include procedures to deal with emergencies. One would expect the Branch, mindful of its duties to the public, to reserve the right to

take immediate unilateral action in urgent cases. It would insist that where an immediate threat to the health of any persons was posed a clause would allow the Branch
to override all other provisions of the contract and prohibit all discharges into the
environment. Similarly, the contract should not exclude the province's statutory powers to deal with pollution emergencies under section 5 of the *Environmental Management Act*. These are examples of methods that the Branch, as one of the negotiating
parties could use to secure the interests of the public at large.

Adaptability

Some of the devices which we suggest as terms of a waste management contract
could equally be implemented as terms of a permit; but it will be apparent that many
could not, and that negotiations on permit conditions usually result in informal
understandings rather than in adaptations in the permit itself. In our view the flexibility of a contract allows negotiations to cover a much broader range of subjects. Every
aspect of the relationship between the Branch and the company can be scrutinized for
its appropriateness. For example, a proposed right of renewal "on full compliance
with each term of this contract" might be renegotiated to allow renewal "on substantial compliance."

Agreements could be adapted for the special difficulties of a particular site, to deal
with a staged development, or to cope with changes in circumstances such as the
economic picture. An agreement could be signed between a number of different agencies or companies if a number of different interests were involved.

How Agreements Fit Under Legislation

Waste management contracts must have a foundation in a regulatory system which is
based upon legislative authority. Consequently the introduction of waste management contracts would require an amendment to the legislation. The general prohibition
against polluting conduct which is the first step usually taken by a waste management statute would be retained; but the permit system and the criminal sanctions
which normally follow would be constrained.

At an earlier stage we pointed out that in order to be truly consensual, a contract
system requires some alternative to entering into the agreement, and that the most
obvious alternative is to revert to the permit system. This is certainly a workable
route to take under waste management legislation.

Legislation establishing a contract model would need to provide procedural rules
for the making of applications (or invitations to treat), public notice, lodging appeals,
and the like, either in the statute or in the regulations. In order to be generally
acceptable, a contract system would undoubtedly have to provide levels of public
notification, openness and involvement which are equivalent to the levels presently
available under the permit system.

We previously pointed out that an agreement under the contract system must contain a clause in which the Branch agrees not to prosecute or make statutory orders
except in limited and clearly defined circumstances. Statutory authority for these key

conditions is imperative. The wording most in accordance with the spirit of the contract model may be that a person who discharges waste into the environment while an agreement is in effect does not commit an offence under this or any other legislation, except in the case of wilful or reckless misconduct or in other cases specified in the agreement. Alternatively, the legislation could simply authorize the making of an agreement not to bring criminal proceedings, but in that case interventions by private prosecution would also have to be ruled out in order to eliminate notions of criminality from the contract system.

Public Participation

Any model comes with a certain amount of intellectual baggage. Like the criminal law model, the contract model causes expectations that are not appropriate for the task of environmental regulation. One of the principal expectations of the contract model is privacy. The contracts that one enters with another are usually no one else's business. Contracts between government and regulated firms would normally be treated as private matters between them. The public would not be seen as having any role to play.

This expectation of privacy is not appropriate to environmental regulation. It is clear that the public expects to play a role and is increasingly granted a role in the form of public hearings and so on. Moreover, it is appropriate for the public to be involved. Environmental standards embody society's goals with respect to environmental quality. Exclusion of the public from the standard-setting process would deny the democratic right of all to participate in the establishing of important societal objectives.

We propose that the public should have an opportunity of objecting to any proposed waste management contract. This could be accomplished by requiring that any proposed agreement be made public after negotiations are complete. A waiting period could be established, during which time anyone who wished could file objections to the agreement. At the end of this period the contracting parties could choose to redraw the agreement to respond to the criticisms. If they did not, and chose to proceed with the agreement, the objectors would have the right to appeal to the Environmental Appeal Board, which would be empowered to decide whether or not the public interest required that the objection be sustained. The Board would have no power to rewrite the agreement. For our model to work, waste management agreements must truly be the agreements of the parties. However, if the Board sustained the objection, the government would be prevented from entering into the proposed waste management agreement. At that point, the agreement could be renegotiated, or the company could simply pursue its right to seek a waste management permit under the existing scheme. It is likely that most companies would try to negotiate a new agreement, probably including the objectors in the negotiations.

NOTES AND QUESTIONS

1. The authors of the "contract model" argue that it should be considered as an alternative to the existing waste management legislation in British Columbia because of

its flexibility and ease of enforcement. At this point, you should recall some of the limitations of the regulatory approach raised in chapter 5 and the discussion of the administrative compliance versus criminal sanctions dichotomy in chapter 9. The basic content of a pollution control contract should include not only what would be required under the regulatory legislation, but would substitute contractual remedies for statutory quasi-criminal offences and penalties and permit the parties to fashion creative techniques to resolve disputes. Presumably, such dispute resolution mechanisms could include arbitration, mediation, conciliation, or any other alternative to litigation.

2. The "contract model" of pollution control would result in a private contract between the regulator and the company. As a contract, the law of contracts would be applied to the same extent as it applies to any other commercial agreement. It seems likely that these "contracts" would lead to much litigation in the absence of a comprehensive alternative dispute resolution mechanism being included in the contract. Even if such a mechanism was included, litigation may be required to determine the extent to which common law principles of the law of contract should govern the agreement between the parties. Would a non-contracting party lack standing to challenge the agreement by virtue of the doctrine of privity of contract or can the contracting parties confer benefits (the right to sue) on parties who do not have privity of contract with the contracting parties? In the event of a breach of the pollution contract, would the principles of *Hadley v. Baxendale* (1854), 156 ER 145 (the two-pronged foreseeability test of remoteness) apply to determine the extent of the defendant's liability in damages? Consider again the shortcoming of the common law approach to environmental protection discussed in chapter 3 and the efforts taking place in the United States to broaden the concept of damages in situations where the polluter's conduct has placed the plaintiff in a position of facing an enhanced risk of personal injury. Is it possible that a pollution contract regime would shift the focus of attention from the inadequacies of tort law to a consideration of the adequacy (or inadequacies) of the law of contract?

3. The principal reading recognizes that the "contract model" of pollution control cannot be implemented without legislative authority that, at present, does not generally exist in Canadian environmental regulatory legislation (although legislative authority does exist for intergovernmental environmental agreements under numerous federal and provincial statutes). Consider, however, ss. 295-309 of CEPA 1999, which provide for "environmental protection alternative measures" as a substitute for a traditional sentence after conviction for an offence under the Act. These "alternative measures" seem to contemplate the negotiation of an agreement by the offender to implement an environmental protection program. How does the CEPA 1999 model compare to the "contract model" described above?

B. Negotiation of Private Agreements Through Consensus: The ARET Process

Although no Canadian legislation for government–industry pollution control contracts yet exists, headway is being made through the federal government's policies encouraging voluntary compliance by industry in lieu of more stringent regulation. In late 1991, the federal minister of the environment in conjunction with industry and environmental leaders proposed a cooperative approach to eliminating and reducing toxic substances. The ARET Stakeholders Committee was formed in 1992 consisting of representatives from industry, government, health and professional associations, academia, and environmental groups. From the outset, ARET agreed that all decisions would be arrived at through consensus on the basis of scientific information and common sense. Participation in ARET was voluntary, and decision making by participants was to be open, nonprescriptive, and consensus driven. See *Environmental Leaders 2* (Ottawa: Environment Canada, ARET Secretariat, 1997), chapter 1, 1. By 1993, ARET had arrived at a list of substances for action consisting of 117 substances divided into 5 categories based on toxicity, bioaccumulation, and persistence of the substance. Consensus was reached for 4 of the 5 categories; the stakeholders committee did not reach consensus on category A-2 substances on whether they meet persistence, bioaccumulation, and toxicity criteria. The long-term goal of ARET was to reduce emissions of 30 A-1 and A-2 substances by 90 percent and emissions of 87 B-1, B-2, and B-3 substances by 50 percent by the year 2000. Although ARET officially ended in 2000, Environment Canada is negotiating a successor program, ARET 2 (more details are available online at http://www.ec.gc.ca/aret/).

After consensus was reached on the ARET list of substances but before any action plans were submitted by industry, a division arose within the members of the stakeholders committee representing environmental labour groups and the industry representatives over the issue of elimination of toxic substance use as opposed to reduction of use. By 1994, it had become clear that consensus could not be reached on this issue and Pollution Probe, the Canadian Labour Congress, the Toxics Watch Society of Alberta, the West Coast Environmental Law Association, Great Lakes United, and Union québécoise pour la conservation de la nature resigned from the stakeholders committee. Notwithstanding these resignations, ARET issued a challenge to Canadian companies to voluntarily reduce or eliminate their emissions of substances on the ARET list of substances. Between 1994 and 2000, 171 companies or government departments submitted action plans to reduce emissions of ARET-listed substances, achieving a reported total reduction in releases of 28,000 tonnes. Of these, a large number come from the chemical industry.

In another industry-sponsored initiative, pursuant to a "Memorandum of Understanding for Environmental Protection Through Action Under the Canadian Chemical Producer's Association Responsible Care," Environment Canada and the Canadian Chemical Producer's Association (CCPA) have negotiated a voluntary agreement to reduce emissions of benzene, a class 1 carcinogen. Benzene is classed as a B-3, Toxic and Persistent substance on the ARET list of substances. The Draft Agreement Between the Government of Canada and the Canadian Chemical Producers Association (CCPA) on Reducing Benzene Emissions (benzene agreement) was signed and released in May 1997. The benzene agreement commits the CCPA and 10 named producers of benzene emissions to work to achieve projected emission reductions of 70 percent by 2001 from a 1994 base year. This will meet the benzene phase 1 Canada-wide standard negotiated by the CCME. The CCPA agreed to take "reasonable measures" to reach this target and it was expressly understood that "reasonable measure" requires that technological and economic factors must be fully factored into what constitutes a reasonable measure. "CCPA believes that environmental protection is best addressed through a mix of instruments with regulation to be used only where no appropriate voluntary or other non-regulatory alternatives can achieve the desired result" (benzene agreement, background clause, paragraph 2). For an overview of the responsible care initiative of the CCPA, see J.A. O'Connor, "Responsible Care: Doing the Right Thing," available online at http://www.ccpa.ca/english/library/document/index.html (under "History of Responsible Care"). As of early 2003, the outcome of the benzene agreement has not been reported.

NOTE

Does the responsible care benzene agreement provide some evidence of industries' willingness to enter into contractual relations with government as an alternative to regulatory control? The agreement states that public involvement will take place through an advisory committee established by the memorandum of understanding (MOU) and through the community processes established by the MOU. One should question whether an industry-established citizens advisory body is truly democratic and participatory. It should also be noted that the negotiated, voluntary agreement between the government of Canada and the CCPA does not legally bind the CCPA member companies to achieve the proposed benzene reduction targets but only to "work to achieve projected emission reductions." Recall the consideration of CEPA 1999 in chapter 5. Are voluntary government–industry agreements compatible with the goal of CEPA 1999 to virtually eliminate toxic substances through regulation? Are they objectionable in principle? See also D.L. Van Nijnatten, "The Day the NGO's Walked Out," above.

VI. PUTTING COLLABORATIVE DECISION MAKING AND ADR INTO PRACTICE: THE BRITISH COLUMBIA CORE PROCESS

In July 1992, British Columbia enacted the *Commissioner on Resources and Environment Act*, SBC 1992, c. 34, a process for land-use planning that would last for 10 years. The Act authorized the lieutenant governor in council to appoint a commissioner on resources and environment (s. 2(1)) for the purpose of advising the executive council on land-use and related environmental issues in an independent manner and to recommend legislation, policies, and practices respecting these issues. The commissioner was also empowered to make a report to the public on the need for legislation, policies, or practices respecting land-use or resource and environmental issues if he or she was of the opinion that such a report would serve the public interest. The mandate of the commissioner was to "develop for public and government consideration a British Columbia wide strategy for land use and related resource and environmental management" (s. 4(1)). In addition, the commissioner was to facilitate the development and implementation of, *inter alia,* a dispute resolution system to resolve land-use and related resource and environmental conflicts in British Columbia.

In August 1992 the commission released its *Report on a Land Use Strategy for British Columbia* (Victoria: Commission on Resources and Environment [CORE], 1992) for public discussion. The commissioner recognized that "the traditional approach to land and resource allocation, based primarily on the responsibility of statutory decision-makers, is no longer accepted in British Columbia as necessarily the best way to make decisions" (at 8). As a result of public alienation from the decision-making process, the

Commission on Resources and Environment suggested a "shared decision-making" process whereby decision making would shift for a specified period of time to negotiating teams consisting of government participants and representatives of interests that may be directly affected by the decisions to be made (at 8). Central to the commission carrying out its mandate was the Draft Land Use Charter, published at 14-18 of the report, above. The Land Use Charter sets out the principles that guided the commissioner in developing a new dispute resolution system. The Charter principle covering decision-making processes provides (at 16):

> These environmental, economic and social principles shall be implemented and reconciled in neutrally administered decision-making processes that we open to the participation of all interests. The processes shall promote decision-making through the building of consensus amongst diverse perspectives and stakeholders.

Implementation of the Charter principle was to be achieved through negotiation processes at the regional level and shared decision making at the community level. There is no doubt that the commission envisioned extensive use of environmental mediation techniques to resolve resource-use conflicts. The Framework for Process recommended in the Report sets out a mediation process designed to provide recommendations to the public and Cabinet that have been arrived at through negotiations leading to consensus with the assistance of an independent mediator acceptable to all participants in the mediation. The Report designed a new approach to resolving environmental conflicts that, if successful, would have served to legitimize creative ADR mechanisms as a more appropriate means of resolving environmental conflicts. See S.A. Kennett, "Is British Columbia Leading the Way in Natural Resources Management? Part 1: The Commission on Resources and Environment" (1992) vol. 40 *Resources* 1.

The CORE process was implemented in three regions of British Columbia: Cariboo, Kootenay Boundary, and Vancouver Island. Preliminary assessments of the process were largely, although not completely, positive.

R.A. Kelly and D.K. Alper
Transforming British Columbia's War in the Woods: An Assessment of the Vancouver Island Regional Negotiation Process of the Commission on Resources and Environment
(Victoria: University of Victoria Institute for Dispute Resolution, 1995), at 6-32

A Brief Overview of the Development of CORE

The British Columbia government created the Commission on Resources and Environment (CORE) in January 1992 to provide Cabinet with independent advice on land use and related resource and environmental issues. CORE drew upon the strategies of the BC Round Table in drafting principles to guide its land use planning process. However, CORE's mandate is broader than that of the BC Round Table; it goes beyond simply offering advice to government. Its purpose, according to CORE Commissioner Stephen Owen (1993), is to "develop and implement a world-leading strategy for land use planning and management as part of a larger commitment to sustainability."

The CORE mandate set out in the *Commissioner on Resources and Environment Act* of 1992 includes the following:

> The Commissioner shall facilitate the development and implementation, and shall monitor the operation of:
>
> a) Regional planning processes to define the uses to which areas of British Columbia may be put,
>
> b) [subregional] community based participatory processes to consider land use and related resource and environmental management issues, and
>
> c) a dispute resolution system for land use and related resource and environmental issues in British Columbia.

The first section on regional planning processes is the focus of this study. It should be noted that, whereas this study analyzes the dispute resolution aspect of the Vancouver Island regional planning process, this is not the "dispute resolution system" referred to in c). This is a separate system currently being developed to address the overall provincial land use planning system.

The first three regions in which CORE planning processes took place were Vancouver Island, Cariboo-Chilcotin, and Kootenay-Boundary. Negotiation processes were initiated in each of these regions shortly after CORE was formed. Vancouver Island was the first to convene a regional table, using a consensus-based, shared decision making process. According to CORE, shared decision making is "an integrative management tool designed to support, rather than replace, the traditional public decision making processes. It is an open and inclusive means of transcending political, bureaucratic, sectoral and jurisdictional boundaries to help resolve public conflicts and bring about broadly supported action."

Public Participation and CORE

The public participates in the regional negotiation processes through constituencies called sectors. Owen defines a sector as "a coalition of groups and organizations who share common concerns and values." Owen claims that "CORE has attempted to ensure that the processes are inclusive by making no prior assumptions about which interests will be represented." He claims this is accomplished by "facilitating discussion among interested parties, leading to the development 'from the bottom up' of broad but cohesive sectors of interest." The result is that representation at the table includes "not only sectors which may comprise traditional interest groups, but also new coalitions of subgroups which may never before have come together."

The tool for bringing these sectors together is what CORE refers to as the "sector representation model." The sector representation model focusses on representation of "sector-wide public perspectives," not special interest groups. The intent is for interest groups that have a common "stake" to form into coalitions. According to the sector representation model, the formation of sectors and the way they would interact is largely self-defining; participants directly contribute to the design of the decision making process. The questions asked of prospective participants to determine this, according to CORE, are: "What would the process have to look like in order for you to participate effectively? How can you, with others of like mind, sharing similar values on land use, coalesce into a sector-a community of interests-that can be represented at the table?" CORE facilitates sector formation by organizing meetings with interested parties. A unique feature of CORE's sector representation model is the way government is represented. At the Vancouver Island CORE table, government had one seat, representing government as a singular "corporate" entity. Similar tables, including the BC Round Table, were overwhelmed with government representation— up to seventeen government representatives in some cases. Also unique is the fact that CORE operates as an independent commission, maintaining an "arm's length" from government in developing land use recommendations.

The legitimacy of sector representation is largely tied to accountability to the constituency being represented. To address the issue of accountability within the sector representation model, each sector developed a "statement of accountability and responsibility" to be signed by all sectors. In this statement, each sector was asked to give a rationale as to what qualified it as a sector; the table as a whole then had the option to either accept or reject its rationale. The objective was to enable the table itself to determine representation.

Participation in the context of CORE refers to the participation of "stakeholder groups." The definition of interest groups offered by Pross applies to stakeholder groups: "organizations whose members act together to influence public policy in order to promote their common interest." When interest groups—or in this case stakeholder groups—attempt to influence public policy, they are exhibiting a "communication function" as a means of accessing their government. Access alone, however, will not ensure that a group will be successful in influencing government. The communication of the group's concerns is of little impact unless decision makers can be induced to accept the group's recommendations and support for them.

The following excerpts from a CORE document elucidate its intentions with respect to public participation:

> Meaningful public participation is an essential component of good representative government. The CORE process is designed to help reconcile the demand for greater local control and democratic choice from the community of interests affected by land use decisions with the need for a broader perspective, administrative efficiency and decisive policy making in the tradition of representative government. A shared decision making forum permits local aspiration and experience to interplay with broader public policy making, creating an opportunity for information-sharing, greater understanding and collaborative outcomes. Shared decision-making at the regional tables is one stage along a spectrum of increased public participation. It begins with broad consultation and constituency building, and proceeds to interest-based negotiations involving accountable representatives of all government and non-government interests. The process represents the most direct public participation in land use decision-making ever offered to British Columbians (CORE 1994, 3).

The CORE process has been thus legitimized on the grounds that the public has access to, and is empowered in, the public policy decision making process. This is consistent with the principles inherent in what has become known as alternative dispute resolution (ADR) ... .

[Kelly and Alper proceed to analyze the extent to which the Vancouver Island Regional Negotiation Process was a success, pointing out that the table did not reach consensus on all issues in the time frame allotted to it. Success is measured in terms of a transformative approach emphasizing inclusiveness and effectiveness as well as on the basis of the empowerment perceptions of the participants determined by a questionnaire and telephone interviews with sector representatives. They report the following findings and conclusion.]

Findings and Conclusion

A major goal of the Vancouver Island CORE regional negotiating process was to generate a consensus set of recommendations to present to the Commissioner. While consensus was reached in some areas, only a partial set of land use recommendations was presented to the Commissioner. The other three regional processes—Cariboo-Chilcotin, and East and West Kootenay—also generated only partial recommendations. It has thus been the task of the Commissioner to generate land use recommendations for each of these regions built upon the partial recommendations generated by the tables. As a result, there is concern from the public that these regional processes "failed" because the land use recommendations have come from the Commissioner himself and not the regional table. While this study does not directly address this issue, a comparative analysis of the tables' reports to the Commissioner, the Commissioner's reports to Cabinet, and land use plans adopted by Cabinet would be one way to approach this concern.

The specific purpose of this study is to assess CORE in terms of whether and to what degree it met the stated goals inherent in its sector representation model and shared decision making framework. We also examined the implications of this framework for policy processes which follow the ADR model.

The data analysis revealed that the participants perceived some strong and some weak points in achieving these stated goals. From the perceptions of the sector representatives, CORE essentially achieved its stated goals of facilitating access. The fourteen sector representatives believed that, although some assumptions were made about who should be included, and although inclusion was "hard fought" for some, CORE largely succeeded at including interested parties. The complex issue of inclusion of First Nations was discussed earlier. These findings suggest that the sector representation model essentially served its purpose in facilitating access.

The sector representatives' perceptions of CORE's performance at facilitating empowerment were more mixed. First, many expressed frustration at their inability to effectively communicate with their sector because of financial constraints. This led to problems of accountability to their constituencies, which called into question the legitimacy of the sectors altogether. Second, many representatives perceived an imbalance of influence among sectors of influence at the table. Third, most were disappointed with the effectiveness of the participant assistance policy over all.

Shared Decision Making: A Transformative Approach

Those involved in ADR processes like CORE have tended to work from the premise that their job, and the goal of the process, is to reach a consensus outcome in the most efficient manner possible. One important consequence of this is that, in the name of efficiency, facilitators often become directive, exerting strong influence over the substantive outcome. Sometimes this means directing parties toward a specific settlement. For the Vancouver Island process, CORE staff expressed that, in retrospect, they might have offered a stronger leadership role in facilitating a settlement. But as Darling noted at 5, "A question that remains unanswered is whether the process would have accepted more direction at the time ... . The very people who criticized us most for spending months on process and procedure were the ones who wanted to negotiate every issue of procedure, and who regularly told us to stand back." As discussed earlier, this "problem-solving" approach of being more directive to ensure a consensus outcome can potentially have a negative impact on the "transformative" approach of ensuring the empowerment of the participants.

It is apparent from the statements from CORE used in our survey that the Commission has embraced the transformative approach. Clearly, an emphasis on empowerment exists as the very foundation of the sector representation model and the shared decision making framework. This study shows that CORE has obtained a degree of success in the meeting these "transformative" goals. Participants perceived themselves as empowered within the decision making process and some felt they gained legitimacy in the eyes of government as a result of participation.

CORE now has a difficult task. If success is viewed strictly from a "problem-solving" approach and consensus outcome is pegged as the measure of success, the Commission in the future might be inclined to be more directive to assure consensus outcomes. However, this may come at the expense of other measures of success inherent in the transformative approach discussed above. It may become difficult to maintain the integrity of the sector representation model and shared decision making framework if the Commission is under pressure to ensure the tables reach consensus outcomes. However, by not reaching consensus, the Commissioner's recommendations are less a product of the "table's work" than would otherwise be the case. This situation raises serious questions about empowerment in the process. If the participants are to perceive that they genuinely have access to, and are empowered in, the decision making process, CORE must balance these factors in order to deliver on its promise that "those with the authority to make a decision and those who will be affected by that decision are empowered jointly to seek an outcome." This is clearly not an "either/or" situation for CORE; it involves striking a tenuous balance in the overall process.

NOTES AND QUESTIONS

1. The principal article notes that the decision-making process employed in the Vancouver Island Regional Negotiation Process did not represent CORE's statutory mandate to develop and implement a dispute resolution system for land-use and related resource and environmental issues in British Columbia. In February 1995, CORE released the four-volume *Provincial Land Use Strategy* (Victoria: Commission on Resources and Environment, 1994). Volume 4 is entitled "Dispute Resolution—Developing a Comprehensive System—Ensuring Fairness and Effectiveness."

CORE proposed that a comprehensive dispute resolution system, ensuring fairness and effectiveness, needed to combine "preventive dispute resolution" strategies with "adjudicative dispute resolution"strategies. Both preventive and adjudicative strategies would include interest-based negotiation as part of the dispute resolution process. The following are among the recommendations made by CORE:

- government should integrate public participation by recognizing in law the general right of members of the public to participate meaningfully, and by setting out the responsibilities of participants in a code of conduct
- government should encourage and support appropriate and consistent levels of public participation in decision-making processes
- government should modify the institutional framework to support and respond to the requirement for public participation more effectively
- ensure that persons significantly affected should have the opportunity for a timely internal review [of administrative decisions] as a first opportunity for dispute resolution
- ensure that internal reviews are structured as informal and cost-effective processes with a problem-solving orientation
- authorize external appeal bodies [such as the Environmental Appeal Board] to apply negotiated-approaches where appropriate
- responsibility for the organization, administration and delivery of mediation services should be consolidated in a neutral office of mediation to ensure accountability, coordination and efficiency. This could be part of a coordinating secretariat or ministry within government, an independent commission or the sustainability appeal board [CORE recommends establishing a sustainability appeal board under a proposed *Sustainability Act* in volume 1 of the *Provincial Land Use Strategy*]
- opportunities for negotiation and mediation should be formalized in legislation as part of the review and appeal process
- a professional development program should be established to build negotiation and mediation skills in the public service through formal training and field experience opportunities

2. The province has not, as yet, enacted a *Sustainability Act* as recommended by CORE although steps have been taken to implement some of the recommendations designed to improve adjudicatory dispute resolution. See *Environment, Lands and Parks Statutes Amendment Act, 1997*, SBC 1997, c. 18. As of late 2002, regional plans were no longer being initiated in British Columbia and had been replaced by subregional land and resource management planning (LRMP). This smaller scale planning is said to "provide a

better fit for the public involvement and shared decision-making model now applied in the province" (Ministry of Sustainable Resource Management, available online at http://srmwww.gov.bc.ca/rmd/regional/index.htm). However, the development and implementation of land and resource management plans in British Columbia remains incomplete. Of the 21 subregions, planning remains incomplete in 12. For example, the Ministry of Sustainable Resource Development reports that after five years of extensive discussions and negotiations, the Lillooet LRMP table was unable to reach consensus on a single set of recommendations and, as a result, submitted two phase 1 framework proposals for Cabinet consideration. See Ministry of Sustainable Resource Management, available online at http://srmwww.gov.bc.ca/rmd/lrmp/lrmpstat.htm.

3. Other CORE publications of interest include D.W. Brown, *Strategic Land Use Planning Source Book* (Victoria: Commission on Resources and Environment, 1996); CORE, *On the Road to Sustainability: A Synopsis of Provincial Sustainability Initiatives, Dunsmuir III* (Victoria: CORE, 1996); CORE, *British Columbia's Strategy for Sustainability: Report, 1994-95* (Victoria: CORE, 1996); NRTEE, *Local Round Tables, Realizing Their Full Potential: A Report on the Canadian Experience with Multi-Stakeholder Processes* (Ottawa: NRTEE, 1994); and CORE, *Finding Common Ground: A Shared Vision for Land Use in British Columbia* (Victoria: CORE, 1994).

VII. THE FUTURE OF ENVIRONMENTAL ADR AND COLLABORATIVE CONSULTATION

It is tempting to argue that ADR processes have become a permanent part of the decision-making structures of Canadian environmental law and policy. Mediation is legislatively sanctioned as part of the federal environmental assessment review process and is finding its way into provincial environmental impact assessment legislation as well. Several experiments have taken place using contract negotiation techniques as a means of resolving environmental conflicts and environmental appeal boards are turning to ADR as a means of settling disputes prior to adjudication by the board. For example, Alberta's EAB uses ADR extensively. Consensus-building mechanisms such as round tables and workshops are becoming increasingly popular with governments wishing to obtain public participation and input into environmental policy formation and implementation.

Notwithstanding these efforts, it is difficult to predict the future for ADR in resolving environmental conflicts. How is the "success" of ADR processes measured? Is a negotiation successful even when consensus agreement cannot be reached? Is a mediated settlement successful simply because consensus has been reached or is it necessary to conduct continuing studies into the implementation of the agreement? Are we spending too much time focused on the decision reached, while neglecting upfront processes such as interviewing the parties? Ultimately, is ADR reaching the kinds of decisions and results that government finds helpful in determining resource allocation and environmental policy decisions? Research is only beginning to come to grips with these difficult questions.

On the theoretical level, agreement has not been reached on how to measure success in environmental ADR cases. Two common measurements involve whether a consensus settlement was reached and the evaluation of participants' satisfaction. In British Columbia, CORE appeared to be moving to a "transformative" test of success for its negotiation-based regional land-use planning processes. Recently, Susan Moore argued that success must be measured based on the participants' definitions of success, which involves a multifaceted and sequential assessment of success:

> Participants described dispute resolution as unconditionally successful, conditionally successful, or not successful. I labeled this group of descriptions "the first dimension of success." Participants also referred to different types or categories of success, including product-oriented success, which is the usual definition associated with getting a written agreement. They also described four other categories of success: politically-oriented, interest-oriented, responsibility-oriented, and relationship-oriented success. Successful resolution generally included more than one of these categories, with one category preceding another. I labeled this group of categories "the second dimension of success." (S.A. Moore, "Defining Successful Environmental Dispute Resolution: Case Studies from Public Land Planning in the United States and Australia" (1996) vol. 16 *Environmental Impact Assessment Review* 151, at 153.)

Defining successful ADR in environmental conflicts is important for practical reasons. If ADR does not "result in quicker, cheaper, and better settlements than those achieved using traditional legal or administrative remedies," it is likely to lose the support of legislators and agency officials. (N.G. Sipe and B. Stiftel, "Mediating Environmental, Enforcement Disputes: How Well Does It Work?" (1995) vol. 15 *Environmental Impact Assessment Review* 139, at 140) One area in which ADR has achieved its highest level of success in the United States is in the area of negotiated rule making and in mediation of environmental enforcement disputes. Unfortunately, few attempts at negotiated rule making have been made in Canada, likely due to our legal tradition of enacting regulations by ministerial or cabinet order. In a previous edition of this chapter, it was suggested that opportunities existed for introducing or making greater use of creative ADR techniques in the mandatory five-year review of the 1988 CEPA or the proposed legislation to protect and restore viable populations of endangered and threatened species. In 1999, Parliament enacted the CEPA 1999. However, the Act failed to incorporate ADR measures, instead relying on ministerial consultation with stakeholders that may be affected or interested in decisions made under the Act. Although CEPA 1999 establishes a review board to consider notices of objection filed under the Act, the board simply makes a report to the minister and publishes the report for public information. The recently enacted *Species at Risk Act*, SC 2002, c. 29 is also silent with respect to ADR, relying on consultation and collaboration in the formulation and implementation of recovery strategies and action plans. An additional opportunity to experiment with ADR techniques and processes was available when the new *Pest Control Products Act*, SC 2002, c. 28 was before Parliament. Again, the legislation was enacted without incorporating forms of ADR, relying on consultation and collaborative requirements similar to those required under CEPA 1999.

The enthusiasm for ADR found in the 1980s and 1990s seems to have dissipated somewhat in the new millennium. Governments, both federal and provincial, have primarily relied upon forms of consultation and collaborative decision in legislating public participation in the decision-making process rather than empowering the citizen by legislating compulsory ADR processes where consensus-based decisions must be given serious consideration by authorities empowered to make a final decision. Perhaps the most telling example for the future of ADR can be found in the use of mediation under the CEAA, the only piece of federal environmental legislation to explicitly recognize mediation as possibility for resolving disputes under the Act. Although the Canadian Environmental Assessment Agency continues to cite the Sandspit Small Craft Harbour Mediation Process as a successful exercise in ADR under the earlier EA law (the EARP Guidelines), no project requiring assessment under the CEAA has been referred to mediation since the Act was passed in 1995. Further, the proposed amendments to the CEAA in Bill C-9, above, do not alter or modify the mediation provisions of the CEAA in any significant or substantive way. While ADR has become part of the mainstream process of resolving private disputes, governments have demonstrated considerable reluctance in requiring ADR techniques for resolving, or attempting to resolve, environmental problems and disputes about the use of natural resources.

FURTHER READINGS

J. Benedickson, *Environmental Law*, 2d ed. (Toronto: Irwin Law, 2002), chapter 16.

L. Boule and K. Kelly, *Mediation: Principles, Process, Practice* (Markham, ON: Butterworths, 1998).

D. Brach, P. Field, L. Susskind, and W. Tilleman, "Overcoming the Barriers to Environmental Dispute Resolution in Canada" (2002) vol. 81 *Canadian Bar Review* 396.

E.F. Dukes and K. Firehock, *Collaboration: A Guide for Environmental Advocates* (Charlottesville, VA: University of Virginia, Wilderness Society, and National Audubon Society, 2001).

C. Morris, *Conflict Resolution and Peacebuilding: A Selected Bibliography*, 4th ed. rev. (University of Victoria Institute for Dispute Resolution, 2001), available online at http://www.peacemakers.ca/bibliography/bibintro99.html.

L. Susskind, P. Levy, and J. Thomas-Larmer, *Negotiating Environmental Agreements: How To Avoid Escalating Confrontation, Needless Costs, and Unnecessary Litigation* (Washington, DC: Island Press, 2000).

M. Taylor, P. Field, L. Susskind, and W. Tilleman, "Using Mediation in Canadian Environmental Tribunals: Opportunities and Best Practices" (1999) vol. 22 *Dalhousie Law Journal* 51.

CHAPTER FIFTEEN

Bilateral and Multilateral Dimensions of International Environmental Law*

Paul Muldoon

I. INTRODUCTION

This chapter examines agreements, treaties, and other arrangements between Canada and other countries pertaining to environmental protection and natural resource use. Needless to say, space dictates that the review of the international dimensions of environmental law and policy can only be undertaken in the most cursory fashion. This chapter attempts to provide an overview of how international law works with particular emphasis on environmental rights and duties of states.

The first part of the chapter introduces the nature, sources, and character of international law. With this general framework in place, the chapter then introduces the reader to the multilateral dimensions of international environmental law. After a general review of international principles, the chapter reviews a number of customary law principles and international conventions governing some part of the environment. The chapter also examines the bilateral relationship between Canada and the United States and the emerging trilateral relationship between Canada, the United States, and Mexico. These relationships may well illustrate both the potential and the limits of international law to protect the environment and to appropriately manage shared natural resources. Included is a review of bilateral arrangements pertaining to the Great Lakes basin, since they represent perhaps one of the most advanced attempts to manage a shared international resource.

II. THE NATURE OF INTERNATIONAL LAW

What is the nature and what are the sources of international law? This section provides a response to this question. It should be recognized that although international law is neither created nor enforced like domestic law, it is nevertheless "law" that governs state

---

* I would like to thank Andrew Wray for his research assistance on this chapter.

behaviour. Even though there is no effective central enforcement authority, breach of international law may result in a variety of sanctions, including collective sanctions under the UN Charter and state action such as recourse to the International Court of Justice (ICJ), arbitration, economic sanctions, and diplomatic protests. Moreover, there are more intangible enforcement mechanisms, such as the political consequences for a state alleged to be in breach of an international duty.

A. What Is International Law?

Although there are numerous definitions of international law, the most common is that it is a system of principles and rules to govern relationships between states and other internationally recognized persons. At first glance, some may question whether international law is "law" at all. For instance, there is no legislature for the enactment of new laws. There is no court system to which states are required to submit for the purpose of settling disputes. Also, of course, there are only limited means of enforcing international law.

Although international law is different from national law, it still can be considered law because states regard it as law. In many ways, states treat international law as law since it is in their self-interest. Even though they have to respect it, they can also claim the protection afforded by it. It is commonly noted that, when a state does not live by the rules of international law, there is seldom a denial of the existence of international law. Instead, states argue the inapplicability of that rule to the situation at hand.

Nevertheless, international law has evolved over the centuries and, in many ways, it may be more important today than ever before, especially with respect to environmental matters. It is fair to say that environmental issues have played an important role in forcing the development of a more comprehensive and enhanced framework of law to govern states.

B. What Are the Sources of International Law?

If there is no legislature, how does one know what the applicable rules are to guide state behaviour? In many instances, this is not an easy task. However, article 38 of the Statute of the International Court of Justice (1977 ICJ Acts and Docs. 77) is thought to be the definitive statement on the sources of international law. When there is a dispute before the court, resort is made to this article to identify the applicable law. Article 38 reads as follows:

> The Court, whose function is to decide in accordance with international law such disputes as are submitted to it, shall apply:
>
>   (a) international conventions, whether general or particular, establishing rules expressly recognized by the contesting states;
>
>   (b) international custom as evidence of a general practice accepted as law;
>
>   (c) the general principles of law recognized in civilized nations;
>
>   (d) ... judicial decisions and the teachings of the most highly qualified publicists of the various nations, as subsidiary means for the determination of rules of law.

In this context, the court must examine whether a treaty has been enacted to bind the states in question, whether there are applicable international customs, and so on down the list.

These sources of international law reveal the important distinction between "conventional" international law and "customary" international law. Conventional law is created when a state binds itself with obligations and duties with one or more states by way of a treaty, convention, protocol, or some other instrument that they have ratified.

Customary law is law that has been established over time without any formally concluded international instrument. It is established by consistent compliance (state practice) and by the acceptance of states that they are practicing these rules because they believe that they are bound by them (*opinio juris*). Although at one time it was thought that customary international law could only evolve over a very long period of time, it is now fairly clear that it can evolve quite rapidly, especially with respect to environmental matters.

C. The Notion of "Soft Law"

The trend to recognize "soft law" as a source of law is based on the assumption that non-binding policy instruments are quicker to negotiate, less expensive, and more responsive to the needs of the day. Professors Birnie and Boyle note the following about soft law as a non-traditional source of international law.

P.W. Birnie and A.E. Boyle
International Law and the Environment, 2d ed.
(Oxford: Oxford University Press, 2002), at 24-26

So-called "soft law" is a highly controversial subject. Some lawyers harbour such strong dislike of the appellation that they refuse even to mention it, especially in connection with sources. Generally, what distinguishes law from other social rules is that it is both authoritative and prescriptive and in that sense binding. In this strict sense law is necessarily "hard": to describe it as "soft" may appear to be a contradiction in terms.

Nonetheless, in the case of international law, in the absence of any supreme authoritative body with law-making powers, and given the political, cultural, and religious diversity of contemporary international society, the point has already been made that it is not always easy to secure widespread consent to new rules, whether by treaty or custom.

. . .

Increasing use has been made, therefore, of half-way stages in the law-making process, especially on environmental and economic matters, in the form of codes of practice, recommendations, guidelines, resolutions, declarations of principles and standards, often within the context of so-called "framework" or "umbrella" treaties, in a way that does not fit neatly into the categories of legal sources referred to in Article 38(1) of the ICJ Statute. These instruments are not law in the sense used by that article but nonetheless they do not lack all authority. It is characteristic of all of them that they are carefully negotiated, and often carefully drafted statements, which are in many cases intended to have some normative significance despite their non-binding, non-treaty form. There is at least an element of good faith commitment, an expectation that they will be adhered to if possible, and in many cases, a desire to influence the state practice and an element of law-making intention and progressive development. Thus they may provide good evidence of *opinio juris*, or constitute authoritative guidance on the interpretation of more general treaty provisions or rules of customary law.

· · ·

Several international bodies have made special use of soft law, most notably the UN Environmental Programme (UNEP), many of whose non-binding principles and codes have served as a starting point for the evolution of new regulatory treaties.

A classic set of soft law principles is the Rio Declaration on Environment and Development (1992) vol. 31 *International Legal Materials* 876 ("Rio Declaration"), concluded at the 1992 UN Conference on Environment and Development (UNCED). UNCED, also known as the Earth Summit, raised expectations about the role of international law to address environmental problems. The Rio Declaration, with excerpts given below, includes some 27 principles directed toward achieving sustainable development as endorsed by the United Nations. At the Earth Summit, a number of other important documents were also concluded including Agenda 21, available online at http://www.un.org/esa/sustdev/agenda21text.htm (which was intended to be a comprehensive workplan for national and international cooperation concerning the environment); the UN Framework Convention on Climate Change (1992) vol. 31 *International Legal Materials* 848; the Convention of Biological Diversity (1992) vol. 32 *International Legal Materials* 818 (excerpts of which are given below); and the Statement of Principles on the Management, Conservation and Sustainable Development of All Types of Forests (1992) vol. 31 *International Legal Materials* 881. Despite the ambition of the international instruments, there is considerable debate as to the long-term impact and success of the Earth Summit. This debate continued at the 10th anniversary of the UNCED conference, the World Summit on Sustainable Development (WSSD), in South Africa in September 2002. At the WSSD, soft law documents outlining key outcomes, a political declaration, and a plan of implementation were developed. They are available online at the stakeholder's forum Earth Summit 2002, http://www.earthsummit2002.org/ and at the official WSSD Web site, http://www.un.org/events/wssd/.

United Nations Conference on Environment and Development
Rio Declaration on Environment and Development
(1992) vol. 31 *International Legal Materials* 876

Principle 1 Human beings are at the centre of concerns for sustainable development. They are entitled to a healthy and productive life in harmony with nature.

Principle 2 States have, in accordance with the Charter of the United Nations and the principles of international law, the sovereign right to exploit their own resources pursuant to their own environmental and developmental policies, and the responsibilities to ensure that the activities within their jurisdiction or control do not cause damage to the environment of other States or of areas beyond the limits of national jurisdiction.

Principle 3 The right to development must be fulfilled so as to equitably meet developmental and environmental needs of present and future generations.

. . .

Principle 20 Women have a vital role in environmental management and development. Their full participation is therefore essential to achieve sustainable development.

Principle 21 The creativity, ideals and courage of the youth of the world should be mobilized to forge a global partnership in order to achieve sustainable development and ensure a better future for all.

Principle 22 Indigenous people and their communities, and other local communities, have a vital role in environmental management and development because of their knowledge and traditional practices. States should recognize and duly support their identity, culture and interests and enable their effective participation in the achievement of sustainable development.

QUESTIONS

1. Do you consider international law to be "law"? If not, what would you call it? If so, how is it enforced?

2. How effective, in your mind, is international law in addressing global environmental problems? What are its strengths and weaknesses? Are there alternatives?

3. Does soft law have any utility? Are there examples to support your point of view?

FURTHER READINGS

E. Brown Weiss, "International Environmental Law: Contemporary Issues and the Emergence of a New World Order" (1993) vol. 81 *Georgetown Law Journal* 675.

A. Daniel, "Environmental Threats to International Peace and Security: Combatting Common Security Threats Through Promotion of Compliance with International Environmental Agreements," in Canadian Council on International Law, *International Peace and Security, Proceedings of the 1994 Conference of the Canadian Council on International Law* (Ottawa: CICL, 1994), 134-46.

T. Homer-Dixon, "Environmental Scarcities and Violent Conflict: Evidence from Cases" (1994) vol. 19 *International Security* 5.

III. AN OVERVIEW OF CUSTOMARY AND CONVENTIONAL LAW

A. Customary International Law

Even though there are many important customary international law duties relating to the environment, the following customs represent some of the best recognized principles, as well as some of the emerging ones. The excerpts quoted below are often used as evidence of the international custom for the following principles.

1. "Good Neighbour" Principle as a Custom

The *Trail Smelter Arbitration* (1941), 3 UN Rep. Int. Arb. Awards 1908, involved a dispute between Canada and the United States that led to the articulation of the "good neighbour" principle. It is interesting to note that the dispute did go before the International Joint Commission for investigation and report (without invoking the commission's arbitral powers, which are outlined below in the excerpt from the Boundary Waters Treaty). When the United States rejected the commission's report, a bilateral convention was signed that created a three-member arbitration board. That tribunal enunciated the following principle (at 1965):

> under the principles of international law, as well as the law of the United States, no State has the right to use or permit the use of its territory in such a manner as to cause injury by fumes in or to the territory of another or the properties of persons therein, when the case is of serious consequence and the injury is established by clear and convincing evidence.

Apart from this case, see also principle 2 of the Rio Declaration, above, and

Stockholm Declaration on the Human Environment
(1972), 21 UN Doc. A/Conf. 48/14, reprinted in (1972) vol. 11
International Legal Materials 1416

Principle 21: States have, in accordance with the Charter of the United Nations and the principles of international law, the sovereign right to exploit their own resources pursuant to their own environmental policies, and the responsibility to ensure that activities within their jurisdiction or control do not cause damage to the environment of other States or of areas beyond the limits of national jurisdictions.

2. Principle of Equitable Utilization of Shared Natural Resources

Where two or more states share a common resource, the customary rule of equitable utilization dictates that each state has a right to reasonable use and an equitable share of that resource. This principle is codified in the Helsinki Rules of 1966, below, which deal with the use of shared watercourses. Article IV outlines the basic principle. What is a reasonable or equitable share of the resource is to be determined in light of "all relevant factors in each particular case." Article V then sets out a non-exhaustive list of factors that can be considered.

International Law Association
Helsinki Rules on the Uses of the Waters of International Rivers
(August 1966) *Report of the 52nd Conference*

Article IV

[E]ach basin state is entitled within its territory to a reasonable and equitable share in the beneficial uses of the waters of an international drainage basin.

Article V

Relevant factors to be considered include, but are not limited to: ...

· · ·

(a) the geography of the basin, including in particular the extent of the drainage basin in the territory of each basin State;

(b) the hydrology of the basin, including in particular the contribution of water by each basin State;

(c) the climate affecting the basin;

(d) the past utilization of the waters of the basin, including in particular existing utilization;

(e) the economic and social needs of each basin State;

(f) the population dependent on the waters of the basin in each basin State;

(g) the comparative costs of alternative means of satisfying the economic and social needs of each basin state;

(i) the avoidance of unnecessary waste in the utilization of waters of the basin;

(j) the practicality of compensation to one or more of the co-basin States as a means of adjusting conflict among uses; and

(k) the degree to which the needs of the basin State may be satisfied without causing injury to a co-basin State.

NOTE

Similar principles have now been codified in the 1997 UN Convention on the Law of the Non-navigational Uses of International Watercourses (1997) vol. 36 *International Legal Materials* 703, arts. 5 and 6.

3. Duty To Ensure Equal Access

Another international customary law duty provides that countries undertaking activities that may have adverse impacts should ensure that those in the affected countries have access to the legal and administrative regimes within the country to seek redress for those adverse impacts. One example where this duty is made clear is article 235(2) of the UN Convention on the Law of the Sea (1982) vol. 21 *International Legal Materials* 1261 ("Law of the Sea Treaty"), which provides that

> [s]tates shall ensure that recourse is available in accordance with legal systems for prompt and adequate compensation or other relief in respect of damage caused by pollution of the marine environment by natural or judicial persons under their jurisdiction.

Two other examples of the furtherance of this obligation can be found in article II of the Boundary Waters Treaty, below, and article 6 of the North American Agreement on Environmental Cooperation, below.

4. Duty To Inform and Negotiate

Finally, another customary duty is that countries undertaking activities that may have transboundary impacts are under an obligation to inform neighbouring countries and attempt to resolve any differences. The following is an example.

International Law Association
Montreal Rules on Water Pollution in an International Drainage Basin
(August 1982) *Report of the 60th Conference*

Article 5

Basin states shall: ...

(b) notify other states concerned in due time of any activities in their own territories that may involve a significant threat, or increase in, water pollution in the territories of those other states; and

(c) promptly inform states that might be affected, of any sudden change of circumstances that may cause or increase water pollution in the territories of those other states.

Also see Convention on the Protection of the Environment ("Nordic Convention"), reprinted in (1974) vol. 13 *International Legal Materials* 591.

5. The Precautionary Principle

As noted above, the good neighbour principle deals with the duty of a state not to cause unreasonable harm to other states. States may also have duties to further the "precautionary principle." Although its recent international roots can be traced to the 1984 North Sea Conference, the 1992 Rio Declaration, above, provides clear evidence of an emerging international custom:

Principle 15: In order to protect the environment, the precautionary approach shall be widely applied by states according to their capabilities. Where there are threats of serious or irreversible damage, lack of full scientific certainty shall not be used as a reason for postponing cost-effective measures to prevent environmental degradation.

Since the early 1990s, the precautionary principle has been incorporated in a wide variety of international instruments. For example, reference is made to the principle in both the Convention on Climate Change, above, and the Convention of Biological Diversity, above. More recently, the Cartagena Protocol on Biosafety ("Protocol on Biosafety"), adopted in January 2000 (vol. 39 *International Legal Materials* 1027), expressly recognized and incorporated the precautionary principle in its rules concerning the safe transfer, handling, and use of living modified organisms resulting from biotechnology. The Stockholm Convention on Persistent Organic Pollutants ("Stockholm Convention"), below, adopted in May 2001, also expressly recognizes the principle in its regime, which deals with the phase-out of the most dangerous toxic substances.

While the precautionary principle may be recognized as an emerging or accepted custom of international law, there remains a wide-ranging debate on its scope and implications. Issues with respect to when it should be triggered, who has the onus, and what measures must be taken, among many others, suggest that it may be some time before the dimensions of the principle are fully understood.

T.A. Berwick
"Responsibility and Liability for Environmental Damage: A Roadmap for International Environmental Regimes"
(1998) vol. 10 *Georgetown International Environmental Law Review* 257, at 262

Despite these optimistic signs, the precautionary approach is vulnerable because some balancing of environmental concerns with other interests is inevitable. The primary conflicts are likely to occur with respect to international trade and economic development. International environmental regimes are already aware that "the concept of significant negative impacts is not an absolute one, for ... one person's 'unacceptable consequence' is another person's 'regrettable necessity." To uphold the effectiveness of the precautionary approach, the principle could be used to reevaluate or reinterpret existing instruments and regimes. For instance, under the Law of the Sea Convention, when states determine the allowable catch for a particular area on the high seas, they must act "on the best scientific evidence available." Under a traditional interpretation, fishing would be allowable absent proof of overfishing, but a precautionary interpretation would require scientific evidence of the sustainability of fish stocks before fishing activity could begin. Accordingly, for regimes attempting to implement the precautionary principle, the challenge is one of changing perceptions as much as changing institutions or technical mechanisms. It is a challenge to our way of viewing the world as much as to our views of the role of science, or the burden of proof.

NOTE

In terms of its application to domestic law, Canada has now recognized the precautionary principle in various legislative initiatives. For instance, it is recognized in the *Oceans Act*, SC 1996, c. 31, and perhaps more fully in CEPA 1999. While it may be too early to fully understand the implications of this principle as applied to domestic law, Professor VanderZwaag regards these legislative attempts as "hesitant acceptance" of the principle. Time will tell whether this hesitancy will be removed. For a more in-depth discussion, read D. VanderZwaag, "The Precautionary Principle in Environmental Law and Policy: Elusive Rhetoric and First Embraces" (1999) vol. 9 *Journal of Environmental Law and Practice* 355; Poul Harremoës et al., eds., *The Precautionary Principle in the 20th Century: Late Lessons from Early Warning* (London: Earthscan, 2002); and J. Abarchar, "The Precautionary Principle in Canada: The First Decade" (2002) vol. 32 *Environmental Law Reporter* 11407.

B. Conventional International Law

While customary international environmental law continues to evolve, it is apparent that conventional or treaty law is accelerating while attempting to deal with some of the difficult environmental challenges. It is simply not possible to review, or even provide a fair appreciation of, the nature, extent, and breadth of international conventional law affecting the environment. The excerpts below, however, should give some insight into the evolution and trends in this area. They start with general commentary on the evolution of conventional international environmental law and then specific examples of international conventions follow.

1. General

A. D'Amato and K. Engel, eds.
International Environmental Law Anthology
(Cincinnati: Anderson, 1996), at 1-3

In 1972, international environmental law was a fledgling field with less than three dozen multilateral agreements. Today international environmental law is arguably setting the pace for cooperation in the international community in the development of international law. There are nearly nine hundred international legal instruments that are either primarily directed to international environmental issues or contain important provisions on them. This proliferation of legal instruments is likely to continue.

· · ·

The scope of international agreements has expanded significantly since 1972: from transboundary pollution agreements to global pollution agreements; from control of direct emissions into lakes to comprehensive river basin regimes; from preservation of certain species to conservation of ecosystems; from agreements that take effect only at national borders to ones that restrain resource use and control activities within national borders, such as for world heritages, wetlands, and biologically diverse areas. The duties of the parties to these agreements have also become more comprehensive; from undertaking research and monitoring to preventing pollution and reducing certain pollutants to specific levels. Notably, there is no example in which the provisions of earlier conventions have been weakened; rather they have been strengthened or their scope has been expanded.

· · ·

The last seven years, from 1985 to 1992, illustrate the increasingly rapid development of international environmental law. During this period, countries have negotiated a surprisingly large number of global agreements. These include the Vienna Convention on the Protection of the Ozone Layer; the Montreal Protocol on Substances that Deplete the Ozone Layer with London Adjustments and Amendments; the Protocol on Environmental Protection (with annexes) to the Antarctic Treaty, the Basel Convention on Transboundary Movement of Hazardous Wastes and their Disposal; the two International Atomic Energy Agency (IAEA) Conventions on Early Notification of a Nuclear Accident or Radiological Emergency; the International Convention on Oil Pollution Preparedness, Response and Co-operation; the Framework Convention on Climate Change; the Convention on Biological Diversity; the principles on forests; the non-binding legal instrument of the Arctic Environmental Protection Strategy; and the London Guidelines for the Exchange of Information on Chemicals in International Trade.

———————————

As noted above, recent times have witnessed considerable activity in the negotiation of international environmental agreements. The treaties and agreements range from resource protection (such as biodiversity), to protection of specific geographical areas (such as the Great Lakes, discussed in the next section), to eliminating toxic substances. The Montreal Protocol on Substances that Deplete the Ozone Layer (1987) vol. 26 *International Legal Materials* 1541 and the Stockholm Convention (discussed below) are perhaps the best known conventions of the latter type. See also L. Nolan and C. Rolfe, *Kyoto, POPs, and Straddling Stocks: Understanding Environmental Treaties* (Vancouver: West Coast Environmental Law, 2003).

2. Specific Regimes

Below are excerpts or commentary with respect to three areas—biological diversity, toxic substances, and climate change—where there are well-known international agreements in place.

a. Biological Diversity

A new regime is developing that pertains to biological diversity. As noted above, a convention was formally adopted at the Earth Summit in Brazil in June 1992.

Convention on Biological Diversity
(1992) vol. 32 *International Legal Materials* 818
(available online at http://www.biodiv.org/)

Article 1—Objectives

The objectives of this Convention, to be pursued in accordance with its relevant provisions, are the conservation of biological diversity, the sustainable use of its components and the fair and equitable sharing of the benefits arising out of the utilitization of genetic resources, including appropriate access to genetic resources and by appropriate transfer of relevant technologies, taking into account all rights over those resources and to technologies, and by appropriate funding.

. . .

Article 6—General Measures for Conservation and Sustainable Use

Each Contracting Party shall, in accordance with its particular conditions and capabilities:

(a) Develop national strategies, plans or programmes for the conservation and sustainable use of biological diversity or adopt for this purpose, existing strategies, plans or programmes which shall reflect, *inter alia*, the measures set out in this Convention relevant to the Contracting Party concerned; and

(b) Integrate, as far as possible and as appropriate, the conservation and sustainable use of biological diversity into relevant sectoral or cross-sectoral plans, programmes and policies.

. . .

Article 8—In-Situ Conservation

Each Contracting Party shall, as far as possible and as appropriate:

(a) Establish a system of protected areas or areas where special measures need to be taken to conserve biological diversity; …

(c) Regulate or manage biological resources important for the conservation of biological resources important for the conservation of biological diversity whether within or outside protected areas, with a view to ensuring their conservation and sustainable use; …

(g) Establish or maintain means to regulate, manage or control the risks associated with the use and release of living modified organisms resulting from biotechnology which are likely to have adverse environmental impacts that could affect the conservation and sustainable use of biological diversity, taking also into account the risks to human health; …

(h) Prevent the introduction of, control or eradicate those alien species which threaten ecosystems, habitats or species; …

(k) Develop or maintain necessary legislation and/or other regulatory provisions for the protection of threatened species and populations.

. . .

Article 19—Handling of Biotechnology and Distribution of Its Benefits

1. Each Contracting Party shall take legislative, administrative or policy measures, as appropriate, to provide for the effective participation in biotechnological research activities by those Contracting Parties, especially developing countries, which provide the genetic resources for such research, and where feasible in such Contracting Parties.

2. Each Contracting Party shall take all practicable measures to promote and advance priority access on a fair and equitable basis by Contracting Parties, especially developing countries, to the results and benefits arising from biotechnologies based upon genetic resources provided by those Contracting Parties. Such access shall be on mutually agreed terms.

3. The Parties shall consider the need for and modalities of a protocol setting out appropriate procedures, including, in particular, advance informed agreement, in the field of the safe transfer, handling and use of any living modified organism resulting from biotechnology that may have adverse effect on the conservation and sustainable use of biological diversity.

In January 2000, the conference of the parties to the Convention on Biological Diversity adopted a protocol to the convention, the Cartagena Protocol on Biosafety, below. The protocol's primary focus pertains to the safe transfer, handling, and use of biotechnology products (usually referred to as living modified organisms or genetically modified organisms). The protocol includes a number of features, including an advanced informed agreement process. Under this process, a country exporting biotechnology products intended for environmental release (such as genetically modified seeds) must first provide notice to the importing country. The importing country may then regulate whether those products can be imported and under what conditions. A biosafety clearing house is also established to facilitate information exchange. Obligations are created relating to the management of risk associated with living modified organisms, handling and transboundary movement, assistance with respect to capacity building, enhancing public awareness, and issues pertaining to the prevention of illegal movement of living modified organisms.

An innovation of the protocol, one that was subject to intense debate and controversy during and after the negotiations, was the express recognition of the precautionary principle. This inclusion can be viewed as further evidence that the principle is becoming, or is, an internationally accepted principle of customary law.

Cartagena Protocol on Biosafety
(2000) vol. 39 *International Legal Materials* 1027 (available online at
http://www.biodiv.org/)

Article 1—Objective

In accordance with the precautionary approach contained in Principle 15 of the Rio Declaration on Environment and Development, the objective of this Protocol is to contribute to ensuring an adequate level of protection in the field of the safe transfer, handling and use of living modified organisms resulting from modern biotechnology that may have adverse effects on the conservation and sustainable use of biological diversity, taking into account risks to human health, and specifically focusing on transboundary movements.

Article 2—General Provisions

1. Each Party shall take necessary and appropriate legal, administrative and other measures to implement its obligations under the Protocol.

2. The Parties shall ensure that the development, handling, transport, use, transfer and release of any living modified organism are undertaken in a manner that prevents or reduces the risks to biological diversity, taking also into account risks to human health.

. . .

Article 4—Scope

This Protocol shall apply to the transboundary movement, transit, handling and use of all living modified organisms that may have adverse effects on the conservation and sustainable use of biological diversity, taking into account risks to human health.

For more in-depth discussion, see:

J.H. Adler, "More Sorry Than Safe: Assessing the Precautionary Principle and the Proposed International Biosafety Protocol" (2001) vol. 35 *Texas International Law Journal* 173.

P.E. Hagen and J. Barlow Weiner, "The Cartagena Protocol on Biosafety: New Rules for International Trade in Living Modified Organism" (2000) vol. 12 *Georgetown International Environmental Law Review* 697.

b. Toxic Substances

Negotiations for a new global initiative to control and eliminate the most dangerous toxic substances began under the auspices of the UNEP in June 1998 and were concluded in Stockholm in May 2001. Even though Rachel Carson brought the dangers of DDT to public attention in her seminal 1962 book, *Silent Spring*, it was almost 40 years later that the Stockholm Convention finally put in place a regime for the global phase-out of the substance (in annex B). The convention also aims to phase out aldrin, chlordane, dieldrin, endrin, hephachlor, hexachlorobenzene (HCB), mirex, toxaphene, and PCBs (in annex A) and dioxins and furans (in annex C, along with unintentionally produced HCB and PCBs), with provisions to add more substances later.

Stockholm Convention on Persistent Organic Pollutants
(2001) UN Doc. no. UNEP/POPS/ CONF2 (available online at
http://www.pops.int/)

Article 1—Objective

Mindful of the precautionary approach as set forth in Principle 15 of the Rio Declaration on Environment and Development, the objective of this Convention is to protect human health and the environment from persistent organic pollutants.

. . .

Article 3—Measures To Reduce or Eliminate Releases from
Intentional Production and Use

1. Each Party shall:

(a) Prohibit and/or take the legal and administrative measures necessary to eliminate:

(i) Its production and use of the chemicals listed in Annex A subject to the provisions of that Annex; and

(ii) Its import and export of the chemicals listed in Annex A in accordance with the provisions of paragraph 2; and

(b) Restrict its production and use of the chemicals listed in Annex B in accordance with the provisions of that Annex.

2. Each Party shall take measures to ensure:

(a) That a chemical listed in Annex A or Annex B is imported only:

(i) For the purpose of environmentally sound disposal as set forth in paragraph 1 (d) of Article 6; or

(ii) For a use or purpose which is permitted for that Party under Annex A or Annex B; …

3. Each Party that has one or more regulatory and assessment schemes for new pesticides or new industrial chemicals shall take measures to regulate with the aim of preventing the production and use of new pesticides or new industrial chemicals which, taking into consideration the criteria in paragraph 1 of Annex D, exhibit the characteristics of persistent organic pollutants.

. . .

Article 5—Measures To Reduce or Eliminate Releases from
Unintentional Production

Each Party shall at a minimum take the following measures to reduce the total releases derived from anthropogenic sources of each of the chemicals listed in Annex C, with the goal of their continuing minimization and, where feasible, ultimate elimination:

(a) Develop an action plan or, where appropriate, a regional or subregional action plan within two years of the date of entry into force of this Convention for it, and subsequently implement it as part of its implementation plan specified in Article 7, designed to identify, characterize and address the release of the chemicals listed in Annex C and to facilitate implementation of subparagraphs (b) to (e). The action plan shall include the following elements:

(i) An evaluation of current and projected releases, including the development and maintenance of source inventories and release estimates, taking into consideration the source categories identified in Annex C;

(ii) An evaluation of the efficacy of the laws and policies of the Party relating to the management of such releases;

(iii) Strategies to meet the obligations of this paragraph, taking into account the evaluations in (i) and (ii);

(iv) Steps to promote education and training with regard to, and awareness of, those strategies;

(v) A review every five years of those strategies and of their success in meeting the obligations of this paragraph; such reviews shall be included in reports submitted pursuant to Article 15;

(vi) A schedule for implementation of the action plan, including for the strategies and measures identified therein;

(b) Promote the application of available, feasible and practical measures that can expeditiously achieve a realistic and meaningful level of release reduction or source elimination;

(c) Promote the development and, where it deems appropriate, require the use of substitute or modified materials, products and processes to prevent the formation and release of the chemicals listed in Annex C, taking into consideration the general guidance on prevention and release reduction measures in Annex C and guidelines to be adopted by decision of the Conference of the Parties.

. . .

Article 7—Implementation Plans

1. Each Party shall:

(a) Develop and endeavour to implement a plan for the implementation of its obligations under this Convention;

(b) Transmit its implementation plan to the Conference of the Parties within two years of the date on which this Convention enters into force for it; and

(c) Review and update, as appropriate, its implementation plan on a periodic basis and in a manner to be specified by a decision of the Conference of the Parties.

J.A. Mintz
**"Two Cheers for Global POPs: A Summary and Assessment of the
Stockholm Convention on Persistent Organic Pollutants"**
(2001) vol. 14 *Georgetown International Environmental
Law Review* 319, at 330-32

How likely is the Stockholm Convention to be an effective mechanism for redressing the global dangers posed by the POPs? The answer may well depend on how promptly, thoroughly, and faithfully the parties carry out their obligations under this important new agreement.

The Stockholm Convention is clearly a major step forward in the world community's collective efforts to combat pollution. It represents the first international agreement to eliminate or significantly restrict a particularly pernicious set of chemical compounds that pose very real threats to public health and ecological integrity. Although limited by modest exemptions and exceptions, the Convention's action-forcing provisions do seem likely to reduce the production and use of POP-laden products, as well as the haphazard stockpiling and disposal of POP waste by-products. Moreover, the

Convention's drafters acted wisely in affirming the "precautionary approach" incorporated in the Rio Declaration, and in the creating a working mechanism by which the treaty annexes may be amended to refer to POPs in addition to the handful of compounds addressed in the Convention's original version.

The Convention is farsighted in its approach to intergovernmental assistance and technology transfer. Its explicit recognition of the social and economic difficulties facing developing nations—together with institutional mechanisms it creates to co-ordinate new and additional financial and technical assistance—reflect a progressive, realistic approach to problems that might otherwise seriously undermine the treaty's effectiveness.

The Convention's provisions regarding information exchange and public education are also significant and laudable, as is the agreement's sensible emphasis on the development and use of substitute or modified chemical products and processes as means of preventing the formation and release of POP waste by-products. Moreover, the treaty's negotiators acted prudently in rejecting proposals that would have permitted states to challenge the implementation of POP-related trade sanctions under existing treaties at the World Trade Organization.

Notwithstanding these significant strengths, however, the Stockholm Convention also has several shortcomings. One area of weakness is with respect to the Convention's timing. As noted above, the Convention requires that at least fifty states ratify, accept, approve, or accede to its terms before it will enter into force. This is likely to cause a delay of at least several years, while numerous national governments consider and debate the treaty's language and requirements, before the action-forcing portions of the agreement begin to have their intended, beneficial effects. Additionally, States have until 2025 to eliminate PCBs from electrical equipment, and until 2028 to manage PCB-containing liquids in an environmentally sound manner. While the creation of some reasonable "phase out period" for this industrially useful compound may well make good sense, in view of the extraordinary durability and toxicity of PCBs those long lead times appear dilatory and inconsistent with the Convention's sound preamble and objective.

Beyond this, the Convention's language in Annex C (with respect to the establishment of best available techniques for unintentionally released POPs) directs that "costs" be among the factors to be considered when such techniques are prescribed. As a general matter, cost-effectiveness is a worthy objective in the selection of pollution control equipment. Moreover, Annex C also requires that the "benefits" of potential best available techniques be considered, along with costs and a range of other pertinent factors, when these techniques are defined. Nonetheless, the inclusion of an express reference to costs in this portion of the agreement creates a troubling possibility that environmentally needed approaches to reducing the release of listed POPs will be set aside and that less costly and less effective technical solutions may be employed instead when best available techniques are given specific meanings as Convention provisions are carried out with respect to particular chemicals.

· · ·

Similarly, the Convention's declaration that "this Convention and other international agreements in the field of trade and the environment are mutually supportive," while not the wholesale accession to the WTO supremacy that had been sought by chemical industry trade associations and their allies, seems nonetheless to represent a missed opportunity to make it abundantly clear that legitimate, environmentally-based trade sanctions are not to be subject to WTO jurisdiction and remedies.

However, these unfortunate caveats do not outweigh the Convention's necessary and important potential benefits. Notwithstanding the Convention's miscellaneous shortcomings it is, in the main, a realistic, progressive and fundamentally sound agreement. If faithfully implemented, the Convention holds great promise for reducing the numerous risks to human health and environmental values currently posed by POPs.

c. Climate Change

Global climate change has been, perhaps, one of the most controversial international environmental issues. The excerpt that follows outlines the background and essentials of the Convention on Climate Change, above, and the Kyoto Protocol (1998) vol. 37 *International Legal Materials* 22, and the international legal effort to address this important, albeit highly contentious, issue.

G.M. Bankobeza et al.
"Environmental Law"
(2001) vol. 35 *International Lawyer* 659, at 667-68

1. Update on the Kyoto Protocol Negotiations

a. Background

The United Nations Framework Convention on Climate Change (UNFCCC), an outgrowth of the 1992 Earth Summit, entered into force in 1994. In 1995, at the first Conference of Parties to the Convention, Parties recognized that commitments would be insufficient to achieve the Convention's objective to stabilize atmospheric concentrations of greenhouse gas (GHG) concentrations, and agreed to negotiate additional commitments for developing countries. The "Berlin Mandate" called for establishment of "quantified emission limitation and reduction objectives" for industrialized countries listed in Annex I of the Convention.

These negotiations led to the adoption of the Kyoto Protocol in 1997. Upon entry into force, the Kyoto Protocol would establish legally binding emission targets for Annex I countries covering the "commitment period" 2008-2012. These targets range from 10 percent above 1990 levels for Iceland, to 8 percent below 1990 levels for the European Union. The United States has a target of 7 percent below 1990 levels.

The Kyoto Protocol contains several other important elements, which have been the focus of negotiations since 1997. Most important are several market-based mechanisms to provide Parties with flexibility in how they achieve emission reductions. These include: (1) emissions trading, which allows developed countries to trade portions of their emission targets (called assigned amount in the Protocol's parlance); (2) joint implementation, which allows a developed country to invest in and take credit for projects to reduce GHG emission in another developed country; (3) the Clean Development Mechanism (CDM), under which emission reduction projects must occur in a developing country.

In addition, the Protocol provides that carbon sequestration from certain specific land-use change and forestry activities (carbon "sink") count toward a Party's target, and leave open the possibility of including additional sink activities. The Protocol further calls for the establishment of compliance procedures and the development of methodologies and infrastructure for reporting and review of Parties' implementation.

. . .

b. Developments in 2000

(i) Key Mechanisms

The issues that plagued discussions of the Kyoto Mechanisms in previous years continued in 2000.

Parties continued to disagree about the desirability of limiting use of the market-based mechanisms (such as emissions trading) on the basis of "supplementarity," a concept derived from language in Article 17 of the Protocol stating that emissions trading must be supplemental to domestic action. The Umbrella Group [United States, Australia, Japan, Canada, Norway, New Zealand, Ukraine, and Russia] vehemently opposed restrictions arguing that the Protocol did not provide for quantification or other elaboration of "supplementarity" and that such limitations would raise implementation costs by undermining the efficiency of the market, without providing any additional environmental benefit. The European Union, supported by the Alliance of Small Island States (AOSIS), just as vigorously supported limitations in order to force Parties to take more domestic action to reduce emissions. In the late hours of COP6 (the Sixth Conference of the Parties), the EU agreed to, but then re-thought, a compromise in the form of nonbinding qualitative language.

A linked and equally contentious issue was the question of which Party to an emissions trade should be held responsible in the event that the selling Party exceeds its emissions target at the end of the commitment period. Environmentalists and some countries initially advocated a "buyer liability" approach, under which, if a Party exceeds its emissions target, any transfers in excess of the amount needed for compliance would be retroactively invalidated and could not be used by the acquiring Party. This approach was opposed by the Umbrella Group, on the grounds that the uncertainty and risk it created would be detrimental to the functioning of the system. An alternative proposal by Switzerland, which would have prevented any trades until a Party demonstrated that it had assigned amounts in excess of its emissions, was also criticized for unduly inhibiting the emissions trading market. Finally, during COP6, it appeared that support was growing around the concept of a "compliance reserve." Under this model, a Party would be required to hold a specific quantity of assigned amounts at all times to prevent significant overselling. Trading would be permitted above this threshold, and could not be retroactively invalidated. Various levels (from 70 percent to 98 percent of a Party's target) were proposed, but negotiators did not reach agreement on this issue.

A particular concern of developing countries in 2000 was the issue of "fungibility." Most Annex I Parties consider units attained under any of the Kyoto Mechanisms to be fundamentally interchangeable and equal for purposes of meeting emissions targets. In contrast, the developing countries, led by India, China, and Brazil, argued that units were not equal and must be treated differently. This alternative proposal is driven by the concern of many developing countries that the Protocol's "assigned amounts" for developed countries imply an entitlement to pollution rights, and a view that any additions to assigned amounts (i.e., through gains achieved through Kyoto Mechanisms) should be used as a reason for reducing emissions targets in a subseqent commitment period. Parties debated over the terminology used in accounting for use of the mechanisms, whether Parties could retransfer units acquired through the mechanisms, and whether any unused units could be carried over ("banked") for use in the next commitment periods. No signficant progress toward resolving these issues were made at COP6.

NOTES

1. A second session of the Sixth Conference of the Parties (COP6) resumed in Bonn in July 2001, where consensus was finally reached on a number of key issues, including financial assistance, technology transfers, Kyoto flexibility mechanisms, carbon sinks, and compliance. See the Bonn Agreements on the Implementation of the Buenos Aires Plan of Action (July 2001), Decision 5/CP.6 FCCC/CP/2001/5, available online at http://unfcc.int/. At the Seventh Conference of the Parties (COP7) in Marrakesh, the underlying legal texts for the Bonn Agreements were finalized. See the Marrakesh Accords (October 2001), Decision 2/CP.7-14/CP.7FCCC/CP/2001/13/Add.1, also available online at http://unfcc.int/.

2. Not surprisingly, the international controversy concerning climate change echoes very loudly in Canada. Under the protocol, Canada is to reduce greenhouse gas emissions by 6 percent relative to 1990 levels. Some have suggested, however, that the actual reduction is over 20 percent from 2003 levels. In the summer of 2002, Canadian Prime Minister Jean Chrétien announced that Canada would ratify the protocol, over the protests of many provinces. Like in many situations, while the federal government has the authority to negotiate an international instrument, it is the provinces that often have the constitutional authority to actually implement portions of it.

To give some exposure to this debate, one only has to read the headlines in media reports. For example, the headline of a September 25, 2002 *Globe and Mail* front-page article reads: "Ottawa Pegs Kyoto Job Risk at 200,000." The article states:

> [The] Kyoto Protocol could cost Canada 200,000 jobs and as much as $16.5 billion in lost economic growth, according to new draft documents prepared for cabinet officials. Although private-sector estimates of Kyoto job losses and economic damage have been higher, the new numbers are based on internal government analysis of Ottawa's recent Kyoto strategies, senior officials say."

The article went on to state that the federal analysis warns that consumers may also face higher tax bills if Kyoto is implemented and that industries could face a cost of up to $550 million per year to reduce their emissions under Kyoto.

A short time later, a group of non-governmental organizations (NGOs) released a report with various claims concerning the impact of the Kyoto Protocol. The news release, in part, reads:

> Canadians will pocket $200 billion in energy savings by 2030 if Ottawa meets and exceeds the Kyoto Protocol's greenhouse gas emission reduction targets, says a new study from the David Suzuki Foundation and the Climate Action Network.
>
> Released in Ottawa today, the report is in stark contrast to claims from powerful business interest that the Kyoto targets are unrealistic and too expensive. *Kyoto and Beyond* sets out how Canada can dramatically cut its greenhouse gas emissions by 50 per cent by 2030, while creating jobs and cutting energy costs at the same time.
>
> . . .
>
> "It's a straightforward approach that is based on existing technologies and practical, proven energy efficiency techniques," said Ralph Torrie, the report's author and one of Canada's leading sustainable energy experts. "It includes retrofitting buildings, using alternative forms of energy and improving public transportation. Taking these steps would move Canada beyond the modest Kyoto target of reducing emission six per cent below 1990 levels. In fact, it puts us on a path to cutting our emissions in half."

The news release and the report, *Kyoto and Beyond: The Low-Emission Path to Innovation and Efficiency*, can be found at http://ww.davidsuzuki.org/Publications/Climate_Change_Reports/default.asp#Kyoto. See, generally, "The Kyoto Protocol to the United Nations Framework Convention on Climate Change" (1998) vol. 92 *American Journal of International Law* 91. The protocol was ratified by Canada on December 10, 2002.

3. In addition to biodiversity, POPs, and climate change, multilateral treaty law exists on a wide variety of issues, including acid rain, the ozone layer, marine pollution, hazardous waste, whaling and fisheries, endangered species, and nuclear energy. See, generally, Birnie and Boyle, above.

C. Enforcement and Dispute Settlement

Enforcement of international law is a complex but interesting topic. The next excerpt provides a summary of some of the issues that this topic gives rise to in an environmental context. The remainder of this section outlines some specific examples of dispute settlement mechanisms.

1. General

D.S. Ardia
"Does the Emperor Have No Clothes? Enforcement of International Laws Protecting the Marine Environment"
(1998) *Michigan Journal of International Law* 497, at 508-13

It is an axiomatic principle of international law that sovereign states may bind themselves through international agreements. Furthermore, the central precept of *pacta sunt servanda* requires that States obey their international commitments in good faith. However, by committing to an international regulatory regime a State necessarily relinquishes some of its inherent sovereignty. As expected, sovereignty is often an agonizing possession for a State to give up. "States often vigorously defend their sovereignty because they consider their physical integrity and political identity as important elements in their foreign policies."

...

The tension between state sovereignty and the need for international environmental initiatives is often a significant barrier to both environmental enforcement and to the creation of international environmental agreements in the first place. Although the capacity to unilaterally withdraw, either legally or clandestinely, may increase the likelihood that a State will agree to an international norm, this power can seriously undermine the enforcement and effectiveness of environmental initiatives. In addition, States will often require as a condition of their ratification that the collective action of multiple parties be required to implement and enforce the agreement. Inevitably, these "international bureaucracies" further increase the opportunities for unilateral withdrawal. It should thus not be surprising that there is a growing number of unenforced, uncoordinated international environmental agreements.

Because most multilateral environmental agreements are only morally binding, the success of each agreement depends upon the willingness of countries to abide by the provisions they have agreed to and to enforce compliance among their citizens. Thus, the effectiveness of international environmental initiatives hinges on voluntary compliance; governments determine for themselves whether they are in compliance. Whether as a result of changing domestic politics or economic conditions, treaty commitments can become burdensome on party states. Inevitably, when a particular commitment becomes contrary to a State's interest—either sociopolitical or economic—it is less likely that the commitment will be honored.

In light of such compelling reasons to strengthen international monitoring and enforcement regimes, why has the international community failed to act? The failure can be attributed to a number of factors. First, "positivist notions of international law require that states be bound only when they have given their express or tacit consent to be the subject of an international right or obligation." As previously noted, state sovereignty must necessarily prevail over the needs of the international community even where that sovereignty puts the world community at risk or is contrary to a clear majority of the world's citizens.

Second, international agreements ordinarily go through demanding domestic ratification processes and, because many are not self-executing, require domestic implementing legislation before they can be enforced. Even treaties that are considered self-executing often require tacit domestic approval in order to obtain the funding required for implementation. Furthermore, the act of signing a treaty entails little actual obligation on the signatory state; not only does signing a treaty fail to obligate the State, in many instances it does not even require a signatory state to undertake its own ratification process or to deposit a ratified treaty with the appropriate international body. Many States that sign international environmental agreements either fail to enact any implementing legislation or "draft ill-conceived and poorly structured domestic legislation," leaving the agreements as virtual "dead letters."

Third, most international environmental regimes are structurally incapable of providing the necessary monitoring and enforcement mechanisms. Indeed, "international environmental treaties often lack domestic enforcement mechanisms precisely because environmental agreements are put into effect by secretariats, international organizations, and other international bodies that lack "international jurisdiction." Most environmental agreements establish an organizational structure consisting of a plenary body of representatives from each signatory country, a smaller body that meets in order to perform treaty functions, and a secretariat. The majority of the monitoring and enforcement work logically falls on the treaty secretariat who is typically responsible for implementation. However, "[i]mplementing and enforcing international environmental treaties is especially burdensome for secretariats because their duties are not always precisely defined, budgets are limited, and many treaties are not self executing." Consequently, many secretariats cannot effectively implement their own treaties without substantial assistance from other international organizations and from party states themselves.

Finally, many countries, particularly developing countries, lack the financial and technological capacity to meaningfully enforce environmental regulations.

E. McWhinney
"The New International Environmental Protection Law: The Enforcement Role of the International Court of Justice"
in Canadian Bar Association Committee Report, *Sustainable Development in Canada: Options for Law Reform* (Ottawa: Canadian Bar Association, 1990), 303, at 303-5

There is no *a priori* basis for distinguishing the institutions and procedures for dispute settlement in the special area of international environmental law from those in general international law. International environmental law is a relatively new area that relies, for its progressive development, on the imaginative induction of new principles from customary international law and from old doctrines or, increasingly, on the negotiation and conclusion of new treaties. It is quite common to include in new treaties express provisions as to conflicts resolution, usually by listing in extenso the alternative, historically recognized modes such as diplomatic negotiation, good offices, conciliation, arbitration and judicial settlement and without attempting to rank these hierarchically or to establish any preferred sequence as to their uses.

. . .

The International Court has not yet developed any significant jurisprudence in the area of international environmental law. This is because, as already noted, it is a new branch of law and states party to the Court's Statute hardly seem to have envisaged the Court, as yet, as a convenient and easy forum for elaborating and refining its principles or for resolving conflicts. The French Nuclear Tests cases of the early 1970s ...

turned essentially on procedural, adjectival law points and not on substantive law issues. The Court's eschewing of a seemingly ready-made opportunity to break new international legal ground seemed dictated by the practical political difficulties in building a firm majority coalition within the Court's ranks in favour of the immediate cessation of nuclear tests in the instant case.

NOTE

More recently, the ICJ revisited the topic of nuclear weapons in its 1996 Advisory Opinion on the Legality of the Threat or Use of Nuclear Weapons (1996) vol. 35 *International Legal Materials* 814, where the court reaffirmed the customary law principle to be a good neighbour and to not cause transboundary harm.

2. Dispute Settlement

Dispute settlement institutions can be either *ad hoc* or permanent. It may be recalled that the *Trail Smelter* case, above, was resolved by an *ad hoc* arbitration board. There are, though, a number of ongoing institutions whose task is to resolve disputes. Some of these have a general mandate, while others relate to a specific issue. Other dispute resolution methods include transborder litigation.

a. International Joint Commission

The International Joint Commission is an institution established under the *Boundary Waters Treaty*, excerpts of which are outlined below. It does have an arbitral power. It has never been employed, probably because of the very difficult conditions precedent needed to invoke it.

Treaty Between the United States and Great Britain Relating to Boundary Waters, and Questions Arising Between the United States and Canada
(1909) 36 Stat. 2448; (1910) TS no. 548

Article X

Any questions or matters of difference arising between the High Contracting Parties involving the rights, obligations, or interests of the United States or of the Dominion of Canada either in relation to each other or to their respective inhabitants, may be referred for decision to the International Joint Commission by the consent of the two Parties, it being understood that on the part of the United States any such action will be by and with the advice and consent of the Senate, and on the part of His Majesty's Government with the consent of the Governor General in Council. In each case so referred, the said Commission is authorized to examine into and report upon, the facts and circumstances of the particular questions any matters referred, together with such conclusions and recommendations as may be appropriate, subject, however, to any restrictions or exceptions which may be imposed with respect thereto by the terms of the reference.

A majority of the said Commission shall have power to render a decision or finding upon any of the questions or matters so referred.

Agreement Between the Government of Canada and the Government of the United States of America on Air Quality
(1991) vol. 30 *International Legal Materials* 676

Article XIII—Settlement of Disputes

1. If, after consultations in accordance with Article I, a dispute remains between the Parties over the interpretation or the implementation of this Agreement, they shall seek to resolve such dispute by negotiations between them. Such negotiations shall commence as soon as practicable, but in any event not later than ninety days from the date of receipt of the request for negotiation, unless otherwise agreed by the Parties.

2. If a dispute is not resolved through negotiation, the Parties shall consider whether to submit that dispute to the International Joint Commission in accordance with either Article I or Article X of the Boundary Waters Treaty. If, after such consideration, the Parties do not elect either of these options, they shall, at the request of either Party, submit the dispute to another agreed form of dispute resolution.

b. Commission on Environmental Cooperation

When reviewing the mandate and role of the Commission on Environmental Cooperation (CEC), the agency established under the North American Agreement on Environmental Cooperation (North American Free Trade Agreement [NAFTA] Side Agreement) (1993) vol. 32 *International Legal Materials* 1480, it is probably fair to state that the commission has a general dispute settlement mechanism through articles 10 and 13, excerpts of which are below. Article 14 of the side agreement provides the opportunity for an NGO to make a submission to the CEC with respect to an allegation that a party is failing to effectively enforce its environmental law. The commission's Web site (http://www.cec.org/) gives an inventory of the article 14 submissions and the status of those submissions.

In addition, any party—that is, Canada, the United States, or Mexico—may request consultations with any other party regarding whether there has been a persistent pattern of failure by that other party to effectively enforce its environmental law pursuant to article 22. Where the consultation fails to resolve the matter, any party may request in writing a special session of the CEC governing body, its council. If the matter is still not resolved within 60 days after the council has convened, the council shall, upon a written request by a consulting party and by a two-thirds vote, convene an arbitral panel to consider the matter. The panel is then to present an initial report within 180 days and a final report within 60 days after the presentation of the initial report. If the panel agrees that there has been a persistent pattern of failure by the party, the disputing parties may agree on a mutually satisfactory action plan. If an action plan cannot be agreed upon, the panel can be reconvened and establish a plan consistent with the law of the party complained against and, where warranted, impose a monetary enforcement assessment according to an annex appended to the agreement.

c. Domestic Mechanisms for Control of Transboundary Pollution

There are also other mechanisms within a jurisdiction that may assist in resolving international problems. For example, domestic provisions may be enacted to allow residents of another country access to the courts and tribunals of the country causing an environmental problem. For instance, article 6(2) of the NAFTA Side Agreement, above, states that

> Each Party shall ensure that persons with a legally recognized interest under its law in a particular matter have appropriate access to administrative, quasi-judicial or judicial proceedings for the enforcement of the Party's environmental laws and regulations.

Also see the discussion under the heading "Duty To Ensure Equal Access," above, where such mechanisms were discussed in the context of the principles of international customary law.

IV. TRENDS AND ISSUES

One of the clear trends in recent years relates to the participation of NGOs both in the negotiation and implementation of international law.

J. Cameron
"Future Directions in International Environmental Law:
Precaution, Integration and Non-State Actors"
(1996) vol. 19 *Dalhousie Law Journal* 122, at 138

Although most early developments in international environmental law were reactive to specific incidents or new scientific evidence, recent advances in the field have begun to reflect a measure of maturity as underlying policy objectives increasingly embrace more comprehensive methods. Specifically, environmental problem solvers no longer feel they have the luxury to wait for conclusive scientific evidence of environmental degradation before designing regulatory programs. They are building into their decision making systems an element of precaution, which is gradually emerging as a principle of customary international law. Similarly, environmental media are no longer seen as closed independent systems, nor are economic and environmental problems viewed as solvable separately. Here an integrated approach is recognized as crucial to achieving sustainable development. Finally, the players themselves, the problem solvers engaging in this evolving enterprise, are no longer affiliated only with the states of their birth, but represent wider and more diverse interests than those which attach to citizenship. They need to be formally incorporated into the decision making process.

P.L. Lallas
"The Role of Process and Participation in the Development of Effective International Environmental Agreements: A Study of the Global Treaty on Persistent Organic Pollutants (POPs)"
(2000/2002) vol. 19 *UCLA Journal of Environmental Law and Policy* 83, at 86-89

An underlying consideration of this discussion is that the ground rules, and practical realities, relevant to issues such as public and government participation in treaty negotiations not only are changing, but are perhaps not well known to many outside the negotiating circles. These (evolving) rules and realities yield many benefits, but also raise important questions.

For example, members of the public representing a wide variety of non-governmental organizations (NGOs), indigenous communities, industry and other interests were directly involved in POPs treaty negotiation process, and played a significant and often catalyzing role in the events leading up to this process.

. . .

The discussion of these questions of process and participation is framed within the larger context of an ongoing evolution of the basic ground rules over who participates in the making and implementation of international law. In past years, for example, members of the public—and not just states—have begun to obtain rights and obligations in certain fields of international law, notably in the human rights field and under international investment agreements.

As illustrated by the POPs treaty process, the field of international *environmental* law is in some respects situated at or near the forefront of this evolution, at least with respect to how treaties in this field are negotiated. Many of the basic principles on environment and development adopted by the international community at the 1992 Rio Earth Summit (the Summit), and important sections of the Summit's agenda for the 21st century (Agenda 21), focus upon the need to promote public participation in the policy making process. Rules of procedure for individual treaty negotiations in the environmental field often authorize members of the public, business, and non-profit organizations to become directly involved in meetings and discussions to develop and implement treaties. Increasingly (though slowly), there is also some tendency for greater public involvement in the process of implementing these treaties, and there is a growing set of experiences of how this actually occurs.

The internet is also having its effect. It has given the public and policymakers access to information not even remotely available ten years ago. It and other factors have facilitated the creation of new "networks" of organizations, individuals and experts devoted to finding new ways to do work in the field—whether in conjunction with or wholly apart from work by government officials. This new capability helps bring to the international setting the possibility of decentralized, grass-roots style communication and action that has been such an important part of environmental policy in the domestic context.

P.W. Birnie and A.E. Boyle
International Law and the Environment, 2d ed.
(Oxford: Oxford University Press, 2002), at 9-10

Does Existing International Law Adequately Protect the Environment?

This is an important question to which there is no easy or single answer. International environmental law has evolved at a time when the heterogencity of the international community has rapidly intensified and when, simultaneously, the economic problems and development needs and aspirations of the less developed states have become urgent. Given these problems, the progress made in developing a body of international law with an environmental focus is, in our view, a remarkable achievement, given the strains imposed on the international legislative process. It has been pointed out, however, that the Rio Conference's endorsement of sustainable development evinces a strictly utilitarian, anthropocentric, non-preservationist, view of environmental protection, which, because it entails negotiating balanced solutions taking account of environmental and developmental concerns, is likely to inhibit the scope for further development of a more truly "environmental" perspective to the international legal system. Ultimately, whether the protection offered to the environment by international law is "adequate" in scope and stringency is of course a value judgment, which will depend on the weight given to the whole range of competing social, economic, and political considerations.

. . .

As far as measuring the effectiveness of international environmental law is concerned, much depends on the criteria used. Effectiveness has multiple meanings: it may mean solving the problem for which the regime was established (for example, avoiding further depletion of the ozone layer); achievement of goals set out in the constitutive instrument (for example, attaining a set percentage of sulphur emissions); altering behaviour patterns (for example, moving from use of fossil fuels to solar or wind energy production); enhancing national compliance with rules in international agreements, such as those restricting trade in endangered species. As we shall see in subsequent chapters, the effectiveness of different regulatory and enforcement techniques is largely determined by the nature of the problem. What works in one case may not work in others. In this respect considerable advantage has been taken of the flexibility of international law processes, and their ability to incorporate new concepts and techniques.

QUESTIONS

1. Do customary international law principles provide a suitable framework for environmental protection? What are the relative benefits or weaknesses of conventional law?

2. How does one establish that an international custom is being broken?

3. How should the success or failure of the Earth Summit be judged? Compare its outcome to the results of the 2002 WSSD.

FURTHER READINGS

E. Duruigbo, "International Relations, Economics and Compliance with International Law: Harnessing Common Resources To Protect the Environment and Solve Global Problems" (2001) vol. 31 *California Western International Journal* 177.

C. Giorgetti, "From Rio to Kyoto: A Study of the Involvement of Non-Governmental Organizations in the Negotiations on Climate Change" (1999) vol. 7 *NYU Environmental Law Journal* 201.

J. Manno, "Advocacy and Diplomacy in the Great Lakes: A Case History of Non-Governmental-Organization Participation in Negotiating the Great Lakes Water Quality Agreement" (1993) vol. 1 *Buffalo Environmental Law Journal* 1.

P. Muldoon, *Cross Border Litigation: Environmental Rights in the Great Lakes Ecosystem* (Toronto: Carswell, 1986).

World Commission on Environment and Development, Experts Groups on Environmental Law, *Environmental Protection and Sustainable Development: Legal Principles and Recommendations* (London: Graham & Trotman/Martinus Nijhoff, 1987).

V. NORTH AMERICAN ENVIRONMENTAL RELATIONS

With the general introduction provided above, the remainder of this chapter is intended to give the reader a more specific application of some of the above principles with respect to the North American context. The focus of this chapter is on the robust Canada–US environmental relationship, with emphasis on the Great Lakes ecosystem regime and the emerging trinational relationship of Canada–United States–Mexico. It may be some time before one can state whether the continental relationship will become as sophisticated as either the Canada–US or US–Mexico bilateral relationships pertaining to environmental protection and natural resource use.

A. The Historical Context

1. The Canada–US Relationship

The Canada–US relationship has had a long history in environmental protection and natural resource use. In most contexts, the relationship has been, at least historically, described as a "special relationship," a "partnership" or "good neighbours."

Perhaps one of the most divisive issues throughout the 1970s, 1980s, and now into the 1990s, that has driven a wedge in that "special relationship," has been an array of environmental problems and resource management conflicts. Hence, the relationship can probably be best described as one of extremes—on one hand, a relationship with a legacy of successful bilateralism and with a considerable degree of institution building, while, on the other hand, a relationship plagued by a continuing list of seemingly intractable environmental problems along the "common frontier."

J.E. Carroll
Environmental Diplomacy—An Examination and a Prospective of
Canadian–US Transboundary Relations
(Ann Arbor, MI: University of Michigan Press, 1983), at 1-2

Yet there have always been certain philosophical and institutional differences between the two peoples and the relationship has not always been a warm, familial one. The history of Canadian–US relations has been viewed as being divided into nine historical periods: a relationship of enmity and rather poor relations prior to 1910; a decade of pulling together for the Great War; a decade of revelling in the prosperity of the 1920s; a decade of sharing the misery of the 1930s; a decade of meeting the global wartime and postwar challenge (1940s); a decade of passivity and joint development, both planning and carrying out megascale projects together (1950s); a decade of coming apart on large and small issues (1960s); a decade of serious problems and the end of the "special relationship" in diplomacy (1970s); and a continuation of those serious problems today (1980s).

. . .

In the past, bilateral frictions usually arose from political, military, or economic issues. The possibility of disagreement in these fields has not been eliminated, but while some of the traditional issues lie dormant, a whole new sphere of interaction has recently come to the fore. Of the many issues inhibiting a harmonious relationship, the environment is rapidly becoming prominent. Bilateral environmental disagreements are becoming more numerous, more serious, and less tractable and are beginning to represent greater stakes than ever before. They now constitute a substantial portion of all of the bilateral difficulties between the two nations and are strongly represented on any list of the top five or ten most serious diplomatic differences outstanding at any one time.

2. The Emerging Trilateral Relationship

The continental relationship that considers North America as an ecological unit is a fairly new concept. One commentator has asked why the trilateral relationship of Canada–United States–Mexico was so long in establishing a more formal relationship to protect the continent's ecology.

A. Szekely
"Transboundary Issues in North America"
in First North American Conference on Environmental Law, Proceedings,
CIELAP, ELI, FUNDEA, Tepotzotlan, Mexico (1992), 79, at 79
(English translation)

It is surprising that all three countries in the North American region, in spite of its impressive geographic dimensions, the incredible biological diversity and natural richness in their land and seas, and the numberless natural links relating its varied ecosystems, an environmental regional cooperation system has yet to be created. It is more surprising when comparing the region with the advanced status of almost all others in the planet, in spite of many being of significantly more modest dimensions, but with agreements on cooperation to solve common environmental problems and to handle and preserve their national and international natural resources, even to establish important mechanisms to implement such agreements.

An inventory on this biological diversity and natural richness in the region, especially because of the ecological links joining them, shows there is a significant agenda of environmental cooperation to be negotiated among all three countries making the region. The various isolated attempts conducted so far in the regions, translated into entering some bilateral and some trilateral agreements, are but the precedents for a great challenge presented today more clearly but increasingly urgently to be unavoidably faced as soon as possible. Especially, atmospheric interferences in our time are an unavoidable challenge for the region. Simply with the potential heating of the climate, for instance, the threat to the North American hydrographic basin reserves is of such extent, it is necessary to have timely and foresighted planning and coordination of joint actions by all three countries. The concern for environmental impacts in North America due to extraregional activities is no less significant.

B. The Legal Context of the Relationships

As noted above, international law can evolve through convention (that is, where two or more countries agree by treaty do or not to do something) or custom (that is, where countries follow certain rules and follow them because they believe they are required to). In the Canada–US context, there is a substantial body of conventional international law in addition to the evolving customary international environmental law. The next excerpt is from the 1909 Boundary Waters Treaty; the treaty persists as the framework for governing, or at least providing a foundation for, bilateral resource management. The treaty finds its importance in the principles it enunciates, the institution it establishes, and the powers it gives to that institution. Other agreements and arrangements are acknowledged throughout the remainder of the chapter.

As noted above, the emerging trinational relationship is only in its very early stages of development and as such has not had the advantage of the long legal history of the Canada–US relationship. Hence, the legal ties that bind this trinational relationship include the trade relationship under the NAFTA (1993) vol. 32 *International Legal Materials* 298 and 605, and the NAFTA Side Agreement to that initiative, above. As mentioned previously, excerpts from this side agreement are included as it does establish a new institution, the Commission for Environmental Cooperation, along with a number of duties and powers for this institution.

1. Canada–United States

Treaty Between the United States and Great Britain Relating to Boundary Waters, and Questions Arising Between the United States and Canada
(1909) 36 Stat. 2448; (1910) TS no. 548

Article I

The High Contracting Parties agree that the navigation of all navigable boundary waters shall forever continue free and open for the purposes of commerce to the inhabitants and to the ships, vessels, and boats of both countries equally, subject, however, to any laws and regulations of either country, within its own territory, not inconsistent with such privilege of free navigation and applying equally and without discrimination to the inhabitants, ships, vessels, and boats of both countries. ...

Article II

Each of the High Contracting Parties reserves to itself or to the several State Governments on the one side and the Dominion or Provincial Governments on the other as the case may be, subject to any treaty provisions now existing with respect thereto, the exclusive jurisdiction and control over the use and diversion, whether temporary or permanent, of all waters on its own side of the line which in their natural channels would flow across the boundary or into boundary waters; but it is agreed that any interference with or diversion from their natural channel of such waters on either side of the boundary, resulting in any injury on the other side of the boundary, shall give rise to the same rights and entitle the injured parties to the same legal remedies as if such injury took place in the country where such diversion or interference occurs; but this provision shall not apply to cases already existing or to cases expressly covered by special agreement between the parties hereto.

Article III

It is agreed that, in addition to the uses, obstructions, and diversions heretofore permitted or hereafter provided for by special agreement between the Parties hereto, no further or other uses or obstructions or diversions, whether temporary or permanent, of boundary waters on either side of the line, affecting the natural level or flow of boundary waters on the other side of the line shall be made except by authority of the United States or the Dominion of Canada within their respective jurisdictions and with the approval, as hereinafter provided, of a joint commission, to be known as the International Joint Commission.

Article IV

The High Contracting Parties agree that, except in cases provided for by special agreement between them, they will not permit the construction or maintenance on their respective sides of the boundary of any remedial or protective works or any dams or other obstructions in waters flowing from boundary waters or in waters at a lower level than the boundary in rivers flowing across the boundary, the effect of which is to raise the natural level of waters on the other side of the boundary unless the construction or maintenance thereof is approved by the aforesaid International Joint Commission.

It is further agreed that the waters herein defined as boundary waters and waters flowing across the boundary shall not be polluted on either side to the injury of health or property on the other.

. . .

Article VII

The High Contracting Parties agree to establish and maintain an International Joint Commission of the United States and Canada composed of six commissioners, three on the part of the United States appointed by the President thereof, and three on the part of the United Kingdom appointed by His Majesty on the recommendation of the Governor in Council of the Dominion of Canada.

Article VIII

This International Joint Commission shall have jurisdiction over and shall pass upon all cases involving the use or obstruction or diversion of the waters with respect to which under Articles III and IV of this Treaty the approval of this Commission is required, and in passing upon such cases the Commission shall be governed by the following rules or principles which are adopted by the High Contracting Parties for this purpose:

The High Contracting Parties shall have, each on its own side of the boundary, equal and similar rights in the use of the waters hereinbefore defined as boundary waters.

The following order of precedence shall be observed among the various uses enumerated hereinafter for these waters, and no use shall be permitted which tends materially to conflict with or restrain any other use which is given preference over it in this order of precedence:

(1) Uses for domestic and sanitary purposes;
(2) Uses for navigation, including the service of canals for the purposes of navigation;
(3) Uses for power and for irrigation purposes.

The foregoing provisions shall not apply to disturb any existing uses of boundary waters on either side of the boundary. …

The majority of the Commissioners shall have power to render a decision. …

Article IX

The High Contracting Parties further agree that any other questions or matters of difference arising between them involving the rights, obligations, or interests of either in relation to the other or to the inhabitants of the other, along the common frontier between the United States and the Dominion of Canada, shall be referred from time to time to the International Joint Commission for examination and report, whenever either the Government of the United States or the Government of the Dominion of Canada shall request that such questions or matters of difference be so referred.

The International Joint Commission is authorized in each case so referred to examine into the report upon the facts and circumstances of the particular questions and matters referred, together with such conclusions and recommendations as may be appropriate, subject, however, to any restrictions or exceptions which may be imposed with respect thereto by the terms of the reference.

Such reports of the Commission shall not be regarded as decisions of the questions or matters so submitted either on the facts or the law, and shall in no way have the character of an arbitral award.

NOTE

While the IJC was established under the Boundary Waters Treaty, above, in 1909, the International Boundary and Water Commission to address concerns related to the US–Mexico border was formed originally in 1889, with its modern mandate given by the 1944 US–Mexico Water Treaty. See Treaty Regarding Utilization of Waters of Colorado and Tijuana Rivers and of the Rio Grande, February 3, 1994, US–Mexico, 59 Stat. 1219.

2. Canada–United States–Mexico

North American Agreement on Environmental Cooperation Between the Government of Canada, the Government of the United Mexican States and the Government of the United States of America
(NAFTA Side Agreement) reprinted in (1993) vol. 32
International Legal Materials 1480

Article 1: Objectives

The objectives of this Agreement are to:

(a) foster the protection and improvement of the environment in the territories of the Parties for the well-being of present and future generations;

(b) promote sustainable development based on cooperation and mutually supportive environmental and economic policies;

(c) increase cooperation between the Parties to better conserve, protect, and enhance the environment, including the flora and fauna; ...

(f) strengthen cooperation on the development and improvement of environmental laws, regulations, procedures, policies and practices;

(g) enhance compliance with, and enforcement of, environmental laws and regulations; ...

(j) promote pollution prevention policies and practices.

. . .

Article 3: Levels of Protection

Recognizing the right of each Party to establish its own levels of domestic environmental protection and environmental development policies and priorities, and to adopt or modify accordingly its environmental laws and regulations, each Party shall ensure that its laws and regulations provide for high levels of environmental protection and shall strive to continue to improve those laws and regulations.

. . .

Article 8: The Commission

1. The Parties hereby establish the Commission for Environmental Cooperation.

2. The Commission shall comprise a Council, a Secretariat and a Joint Public Advisory Committee.

Section A: The Council

Article 9: Council Structure and Procedures

1. The Council shall comprise cabinet-level or equivalent representatives of the Parties, or their designees. ...

6. All decisions and recommendations of the Council shall be taken by consensus, except as the Council may otherwise decide or as otherwise provided by this Agreement.

Article 10: Council Functions

1. The Council shall be the governing body of the Commission and shall:

(a) serve as a forum for the discussion of environmental matters within the scope of this Agreement; ...

(c) oversee the Secretariat;

(d) address questions and differences that may arise between the Parties regarding the interpretation or application of this Agreement; ... .

2. The Council may consider, and develop recommendations regarding: ...

(b) pollution prevention techniques and strategies; ...

(g) transboundary and border environmental issues, such as the long-range transport of air and marine pollutants; ...

(i) the conservation and protection of wild flora and fauna and their habitat, and specially protected natural areas; ...

(j) the protection of endangered and threatened species; ... .

3. The Council shall strengthen cooperation on the development and continuing improvement of environmental laws and regulations, including by: ...

(b) without reducing levels of environmental protection, establishing a process for developing recommendations on greater compatibility of environmental technical regulations, standards and conformity assessment procedures in a manner consistent with the NAFTA.

Section B: The Secretariat

Article 11: Secretariat Structure and Procedures

1. The Secretariat shall be headed by an Executive Director, who shall be chosen by the Council for a three-year term, which may be renewed by the Council for one additional three-year term. The position of Executive Director shall rotate consecutively between nationals of each Party. The Council may remove the Executive Director solely for cause.

[Article 13: Secretariat Reports outlines the ability of the secretariat to gather information and prepare reports for the council.]

Article 14: Submissions on Enforcement Matters

1. The Secretariat may consider a submission from any non-governmental organization or person asserting that a Party is failing to effectively enforce its environmental law, if the Secretariat finds that the submission: ...

(c) provides sufficient information to allow the Secretariat to review the submission, including any documentary evidence on which the submission may be based. ...

Article 15: Factual Record

1. If the Secretariat considers that the submission, in light of any response provided by the Party, warrants developing a factual record, the Secretariat shall so inform the Council and provide its reasons.

2. The Secretariat shall prepare a factual record if the Council, by a two-thirds vote, instructs it do so.

C. Canada–US Environmental Relations: The Water Example

It is not possible to provide a full catalogue of the international treaties, agreements, and other instruments governing the Canada–US environmental relationship. These treaties, agreements, and such cover issues ranging from fisheries, to hazardous waste exports, acid rain, and migratory birds. What is included is a sampling of instruments that govern the management of the shared resource of water. Both water quality and water quantity issues are reviewed.

1. Water Quality

If the Boundary Waters Treaty, above, is the foundation for bilateral water issues, the primary operational agreement between Canada and the United States pertaining to water quality is the Great Lakes Water Quality Agreement, below. Excerpts of the agreement are provided in order to give the reader an appreciation of its scope and comprehensiveness. The subsequent excerpt describes one of the key conceptual components of the agreement—"the ecosystem approach" to resource management.

Great Lakes Water Quality Agreement of 1978 Between the United States and Canada signed at Ottawa, November 22, 1978
(1978) Canada Treaty Series 20, as amended by Protocol signed
November 18, 1987; (1987) Canada Treaty Series 32

Article I—Definitions

As used in this Agreement: ...
  (g) "Great Lakes Basin Ecosystem" means the interacting components of air, land, water and living organisms, including humans, within the drainage basin of the St. Lawrence River at or upstream from the point at which this river becomes the international boundary between Canada and the United States; ... .

Article II—Purpose

The purpose of the Parties is to restore and maintain the chemical, physical, and biological integrity of the waters of the Great Lakes Basin Ecosystem. In order to achieve this purpose, the Parties agree to make a maximum effort to develop programs, practices and technology necessary for a better understanding of the Great Lakes Basin Ecosystem and to eliminate or reduce to the maximum extent practicable the discharge of pollutants into the Great Lakes System.
  Consistent with the provisions of this Agreement, it is the policy of the Parties that:
    (a) The discharge of toxic substances in toxic amounts be prohibited and the discharge of any or all persistent toxic substances be virtually eliminated; ... .

Annex 12—Persistent Toxic Substances

General Principles

  (a) Regulatory strategies for controlling or preventing the input of persistent toxic substances to the Great Lakes System shall be adopted in accordance with the following principles:

(i) The intent of the programs specified in this Annex is to virtually eliminate the input of persistent toxic substances in order to protect human health and to ensure the continued health and productivity of living aquatic resources and human use thereof;

(ii) The philosophy adopted for control of inputs of persistent toxic substances shall be zero discharge.

L.K. Caldwell
"Introduction: Implementing an Ecological Systems Approach to
Basinwide Management"
in L.K. Caldwell, ed., *Perspectives on Ecosystem Management for the Great Lakes—A Reader* (Albany, NY: State University of New York Press, 1988), at 3-6

By formal agreement between Canada and the United States of America, policies directed toward the restoration and enhancement of water quality in the Great Lakes are to be based upon a basinwide ecosystemic view of the field of action. ... An ecosystem approach means, therefore, that action affecting the lakes, taken or authorized by the governments, shall proceed on the understanding that the bounded field of policy is no less than the basinwide watershed of the Great Lakes and the multifarious relationships interacting within and intruding from without. ...

The adoption of a basinwide ecosystem approach to management for the lakes is a decision of major international importance. In its *Second Biennial Report* (December 31, 1984), the IJC, charged with special responsibilities and functions relating to the 1979 Great Lakes Water Quality Agreement made the following statement regarding ecosystem approaches and their implications. Because it is the most complete official interpretation of the concept by the IJC, the statement is cited here in full.

> The Great Lakes Water Quality Agreement is a milestone document, one of the first international statements that technical, diplomatic, and administrative approaches to resource management need to be considered in terms of holistic ecological concepts. Land, water, air and biota interact and are mutually influenced. Existing resource management approaches which partition the environment into separate components of land, water and air with associated biota are recognized as inadequate since management of a resource component in isolation from adjacent or interacting components would likely produce short-sighted strategies to protect one component of the environment at the expense of another. Because existing environmental and resource programs are separated, compartmentalized and spread throughout various bureaus, agencies, ministries and departments, the new approach requiring a holistic overview entails, at the very least, a reorganization of thinking, and perhaps a reorganization of institutional arrangements. ...

Viewed retrospectively from the future, this binational commitment reiterated and reinforced, may be seen as not less significant than the Boundary Waters Treaty of 1909 upon which it has been based. In the perspective of international law, the agreement of 1978 may be of even greater significance. The treaty of 1909 was largely within the customary and conventional arrangements of international law. Many binational and multinational treaties establishing rights and obligations in boundary waters have been consummated before and since. The mutual obligations in the treaty of 1909 to prevent water pollution that could impair health or property across the international boundary reaffirmed a principle already asserted by authorities on international law— that no state should permit the use of its territory in ways harmful to its neighbors.

NOTE

It is interesting to reread the Stockholm Convention, above, after reading the Great Lakes Water Quality Agreement (GLWQA). It is no coincidence that the Stockholm Convention, concluded well over two decades after the signing of the GLWQA, has similar principles and approaches on the elimination of toxic substances. Many NGOs, government bureaucrats, academics, and other stakeholders that were familiar with the Great Lakes regime played important roles in the development of the new international treaty.

Eighth Biennial Report Under the Great Lakes Water Quality Agreement of 1978 to the Governments of the United States and Canada and the State and Provincial Governments of the Great Lakes Basin
(Washington, DC/Ottawa: IJC, 1996), at 8-9

The Governments committed themselves to this far-sighted provision to protect human and ecological health in the Great Lakes basin. Canadians and Americans should take comfort in this commitment, and must be assured that it will be accomplished. The elimination of persistent toxic substances is the cornerstone of the Agreement, and must remain an important focus of programs to restore and protect the Great Lakes Ecosystem.

The Agreement's principles of virtual elimination and zero discharge are neither impossible nor impractical as long-term goals. In its past three Biennial Reports, the Commission provided over 50 recommendations that involved toxic and persistent toxic substances. Governments have accepted most of the recommendations in principle and have begun to implement a number of them. Progress has been made in addressing virtual elimination as a concept, as in Lake Superior, and governments and industry are vigorously addressing particular chemicals and processes. Continued efforts by all parties are needed to focus on *eliminating* rather than *reducing* input in order to make virtual elimination a reality in the basin.

FURTHER READINGS

S. Billups et al., "Treading Water: A Review of Government Progress Under the Great Lakes Water Quality Agreement" (1998) *Toledo Journal of Great Lakes' Law, Science and Policy*, part I at 91 and part II at 245.

2. Water Quantity/ Diversions/ Export

Historically, one of the most controversial issues in North America is the apportionment or diversion of water. Some of the most ambitious proposals have proposed to transfer water resources from the northern part of the continent to the southern portions. Perhaps the best known is the Great Recycling and Northern Development (GRAND) Canal Project, which proposed to build a dyke across James Bay in order to turn the southern part of this saltwater body into a freshwater body. Through a series of pumping stations and rerouted waterways, the Great Lakes would be turned into a reservoir for further diversion to the US Midwest and Southwest.

The issue of water diversions continues to be topical in the Great Lakes, in part due to the growing list of proposals for interbasin and intrabasin diversions, and will be the focus of the excerpts below. A study by Farid et al., *The Fate of the Great Lakes— Sustaining or Draining the Sweetwater Seas?* (Toronto: Canadian Environmental Law Association and Great Lakes United, 1997), listed (at 28) some of the other major proposals as follows (although the study also outlines serious concerns about the smaller, potentially more numerous proposals):

- A plan by the North American Water and Power Alliance and the Mexico–United States Hydroelectric Commission to drain Great Lakes water into the Mississippi River and ultimately to Mexico (1964-68);
- A plan to build a slurry pipe using water to transport coal from Lake Superior to Wyoming (1981);
- A project to pipe Great Lakes water to the High Plains states and the Southwest (1984);
- A project to blast a four-hundred-mile-long paved canal from Lake Superior to the Missouri River in South Dakota (1983);
- Legislation to blast a canal from Lake Erie to the Ohio River (1986-91);
- A federally funded plan to punch a hole in the bottom of Lake Michigan to drain water through bedrock layers for use in southern Illinois (1987).

To address the diversion issue, the Great Lakes states and provinces developed a Great Lakes Charter. According to Farid et al., above, at 37, between the years 1985 and 1997, only one consumptive use or diversion was above the "trigger point" for the notification requirements. Nevertheless, there have been attempts to use the Charter for a number of diversions below the trigger.

Great Lakes Charter
reprinted in *Final Report and Recommendations: Great Lakes Governors Task Force on Water Diversion and Great Lakes Institutions*, A Report to the Governors and Premiers of the Great Lakes States and Provinces prepared at the Request of the Council of Great Lakes Governors (January 1985), at 23

Principles for the Management of Great Lakes Water Resources

In order to achieve the purposes of this Charter, the Governors and Premiers of the Great Lakes States and Provinces agree to the following principles:

· · ·

Principle III: Protection of Water Resources of the Great Lakes

The signatory States and Provinces agree that new or increased diversions and consumptive uses of Great Lakes Basin water resources are of serious concern. In recognition of their shared responsibility to conserve and protect the water resources of the Great Lakes Basin for the use, benefit, and enjoyment of all their citizens, the States and Provinces agree to seek (where necessary) and to implement legislation establishing programs to manage and regulate the diversion and consumptive use of Basin water resources. It is the intent of the signatory States and Provinces that diversions of Basin Water resources will not be allowed if individually or cumulatively they would have any significant adverse impacts on lake levels, in-basin uses, and the Great Lakes Ecosystem.

Principle IV: Prior Notice and Consultation

It is the intent of the signatory States and Provinces that no Great Lakes State or Province will approve or permit any major new or increased diversion or consumptive use of the water resources of the Great Lakes Basin without notifying and consulting with and seeking the consent and concurrence of all affected Great Lakes States and Provinces.

On June 18, 2001, the Great Lakes governors and the premiers of Ontario and Quebec signed the Great Lakes Annex 2001, an amendment to the 1985 Great Lakes Charter. Under directive no. 1 of the Charter, the parties agreed to prepare binding basin-wide agreements for the purpose of protecting and managing the use of Great Lakes water. Directive no. 3 commits the parties to establish a decision-making standard that the states and provinces will use to review new proposals to withdraw water from the Great Lakes. For more information about the annex, see http://www.cglg.org/.

Related to diversions are plans, sometimes ambitious, to export Canadian water in bulk. In 1998, a proposal by the Nova Group to export Lake Superior water by tanker set off an international debate. The company was issued a provincial permit to export the water, which, after much outcry, was eventually rescinded. Much of the outcry related to the fear that once water export was allowed, the NAFTA, above, would be triggered, thus diminishing Canadian sovereignty over its resources.

The event also outlined the lack of protections in this regard and was a major factor when Parliament amended the *International Boundary Waters Treaty Act*, RSC 1985, c. I-17 in 2001. This statute incorporates the Boundary Waters Treaty, above, into the domestic law of Canada. The purposes of the amendments are to prohibit the removal of boundary waters out of the water basin in which they are located and to require that parties must obtain a licence from the minister of foreign affairs for any activity in boundary or transboundary waters that would have the effect of altering the natural level or flow of the water on the US side of the border.

The federal government made it clear when the amendments were introduced that the amendments were not a ban on exports of water (which might raise NAFTA issues), but instead a prohibition of bulk removal of boundary waters out of their water basin (which could be justified on environmental grounds). The regulations define which water basins are subject to the Act. Moreover, the prohibition only applies to boundary waters. It is for this reason that the federal government attempted to secure an accord with all of the provinces to mirror the protections in the amendments. Those attempts failed. However, virtually all the provinces now have put in place or are developing legislation, regulations, or policies, the effect of which would be to achieve the same goal.

For water quantity regimes in other areas of Canada, see the Columbia River Treaty, Treaty Relating to Cooperative Development of the Water Resources of the Columbia River Basin, January 17, 1961, with related agreements effected by exchange of notes at Washington, DC, January 22, 1964, and at Ottawa, September 16, 1964, [1964] CTS no. 2; 542 UNTS 244; 15 UST 1555.

Water quantity issues have also had a long history along the US–Mexican border; for an overview, see A. Szekely, "Emerging Boundary Environmental Challenges and Institutional Issues: Mexico and the United States" (1993) vol. 33 *Natural Resources Journal* 33. For a review of Canada–US and US–Mexican water management frameworks, see Commission for Environmental Cooperation, *North American Boundary and Transboundary Inland Water Management Report* (Cowansville, QC: Éditions Yvon Blais, 2001), chapters 4 and 5.

3. Trade

Even a few years ago, few would have suggested that trade should be considered an environmental issue. Space in this text does not permit an appropriate treatment of this very complex and large topic. However, an excerpt has been included of a recent report that provides a critical analysis of trade and environment issues. Notably, at least one major conflict involves bulk water exports.

M. Swenarchuk
Civilizing Globalization: Trade and Environment, Thirteen Years On
Canadian Environmental Law Association Report no. 399, March 2001,
at 2-6 and 9-11 (available online at CELA, http://www.cela.ca/)

The fundamental goal of the current international trade regime is to promote deregulated trade in goods, services, and investment through the removal of "barriers" to trade, both tariffs and "non-tariff barriers." Standards and regulations for all sectors of public protection, including environmental ones, (regarding pesticides, food and water safety, resource management) are frequently seen as non-tariff barriers to trade. Trade negotiators deliberately established "disciplines" on countries' scope to establish domestic standards. In both the WTO agreements and NAFTA, standard-setting is limited by the provisions of two chapters: Technical Barriers to Trade (TBT) and Sanitary and Phytosanitary Standards (SPS).

The TBT provides an entire scheme for the setting of regulations and standards. It requires that they not have the effect of creating unnecessary obstacles to international trade, although they are permitted in order to meet legitimate objectives including "protection of human health or safety, animal or plant life or health, or the environment." With an emphasis on international harmonization of measures, the chapter requires that they should be based on science; and comply with international standards where such exist. Further, domestic standardizing bodies, both governmental and non-governmental, are to comply with the TBT and related Code of Good Practice (TBT 4). The TBT recognizes the ISO, the International Organization for Standardization, as an international standard-setter.

· · ·

The SPS agreement establishes a comprehensive set of rules to govern countries' domestic setting of SPS measures, which concern plant and animal health, such as food safety and pesticide regulations. The chapter also names international bodies, including the Codex Alimentarius, a Rome-based UN agency, as the international standard-setters.

Environmentalists are concerned about the problems inherent in the requirements for risk assessment in these chapters, the power of corporate lobbyists over government regulators, and the limitations of so-called science-based standard-setting. They also emphasize the loss of potential influence for local public interest groups seeking to improve local and national standards, given the dominance of trade law in domestic discussions, and the removal of standard-setting to remote, international standard-setting bodies including the International Standardization Organization and the Codex Alimentarius Commission.

· · ·

WTO Cases on Environment and Health: The Necessity Test

It is instructive to consider the WTO's treatment of two areas of public interest standards, those pertaining to environmental protection and health, since an "environmental and health clause" has existed in the GATT since 1948 and could have been the basis of reconciling environmental, health, and sovereignty concerns.

· · ·

Five WTO cases (post-1994) are relevant:

- 1996: US Regulations under the *Clean Air Act* regarding composition of gasoline auto emissions designed to reduce air pollution were found contrary to GATT III by both the Panel and Appellate Body. The Panel found the regulations could not be justified under GATT XX (b), (d) or (g). The Appellate Body held that the regulations fell under XX (g) but did not satisfy the chapeau of the article (the introductory wording) prohibiting "disguised restriction(s) on trade."
- 1998: EC measures to ban certain hormones in beef were challenged by both the US and Canada. The case was decided under the SPS chapter, and both the WTO Panel and Appellate Body found the EC's ban on certain hormone-treated beef was inconsistent with the EC's obligations under the SPS. Although the Panel and Appellate Body decisions differed in some respects, the Appellate Body upheld the Panel's ruling that the EC measure was unjustifiable as it was not "based on" a risk assessment. (Despite the decision, the EC has not revoked the ban, and is currently subject to trade sanctions from the US).

- 1998: US prohibitions under the *Endangered Species Act* on shrimp imports caught without turtle excluder devices could not be justified under GATT XX, either because it did not satisfy XX (g) (in the Panel's opinion) or because it did not satisfy the chapeau of GATT XX (the Appellate Body's decision). This is the case that provoked the "turtle" protestors in Seattle at the WTO Ministerial debacle of December 1999.
- 1998: ... Australia's quarantine restrictions on certain salmon imports were found inconsistent with the SPS on the basis of available scientific evidence.
- 2000: EC: In the only case to uphold a defence based on the necessity test, the panel found that a French directive banning chrysotile asbestos, challenged by Canada, is justifiable under GATT XX(b) and the chapeau of the article. However, the Panel also found that asbestos products are "like" products to those substitutes which are less carcinogenic. The decision has been appealed to the Appellate Body.

Of [a total of] eleven cases, ten held that the challenged measure could not be maintained. The last case, the Asbestos case, is not yet concluded, having been appealed by Canada to the Appellate Body. It appears to turn on the existence of international standards for asbestos, rather than affirming the right of France and the EC to legislate for public health. Further, in holding that products containing asbestos are "like products" to alternatives selected because they are less carcinogenic, the Panel has set back moves to clean technologies and set the stage for further challenges against measures to phase out environmentally-damaging products.

NAFTA Chapter 11—Investor-State Cases to Date

The most notorious source of conflict between environmental laws and trade and investment agreements has resulted from NAFTA Chapter 11, the investment chapter, whose potential effects were not foreseen by environmentalists when NAFTA was implemented in 1994.

• • •

The chapter also allows investors to sue national governments directly for virtually any action which decreases its expected profits, alleging expropriation or "measures tantamount" to expropriation. [NAFTA article 1110] Countries are permitted to take such measures for public purposes, on a non-discriminatory basis, after due process of law, but only if they pay compensation to the foreign investor.

• • •

There are now 12 investment cases, based on arguments that would not give rise to expropriation claims in Canadian domestic law, six of which concern environmental measures. Since they are conducted in confidential arbitral processes, inaccessible to public scrutiny and participation, (in contrast to proceedings in domestic courts which are open) information on ongoing cases is sketchy. However, the available information is summarized below.

Ethyl Corporation

In this first and best-known investor-state case, Ethyl Corporation of the US sued the Canadian government for US \$250 million and obtained, in 1998, a settlement of US \$13 million for the Canadian ban on the gasoline additive, MMT, a nerve toxin. The ban was reversed. The proceedings were conducted in secret, in accordance with the NAFTA Investment chapter provisions, were widely criticized in Canada, and provided a rude awakening to other governments regarding the impacts of the NAFTA expropriation provision. They also resulted in a direct reduction of Canadian health and environmental protections.

[Officially, the federal legislation banning MMT was withdrawn because it contravened the federal–provincial domestic Agreement on Internal Trade.]

Sun Belt Water Inc.

This California-based company is suing Canada for the decision of the provincial government of British Columbia to refuse consent for the company to export bulk water from BC. The government subsequently enacted the *Water Protection Act* which bans bulk water exports and inter-basin diversions by domestic and foreign investors alike. In a "colourful" claim which alleges a decade of "smelly" actions by successive BC governments, Sun Belt Water expounds on the growing world-wide demand for water, assumes that water export must be a positive benefit (ignoring environmental and conservation requirements) and makes extravagant claims of improprieties by the BC government and BC courts. In a BC court action, Sun Belt did not achieve its desired result. It is therefore using NAFTA Chapter 11 to seek damages of "between 1 and 10.5 billion" US dollars. Besides using the investment chapter for very dubious business practices, the case raises the fundamental issues of the uses of the investment chapter to evade the result of an action in a domestic court, and to challenge a non-discriminatory policy and legislation by a subnational (provincial) government. The BC government is deeply concerned about this threat to its resource management and conservation laws.

D. Bilateral Institutional/ Governance Arrangements

The IJC is the primary institution in the Canada–US environmental relationship. Its basic purposes were outlined in articles I, VI, VIII, IX, X, and XII of the Boundary Waters Treaty, above. The commission's role is also enhanced through various provisions of the GLWQA, some of which are provided below. Following these excerpts, a recent report by the IJC outlines a proposal for its expanded role.

Great Lakes Water Quality Agreement of 1978 Between the United States and Canada signed at Ottawa, November 22, 1978
(1978) Canada Treaty Series 20, as amended by Protocol signed
November 18, 1987; (1987) Canada Treaty Series 32

Article VIA—Powers, Responsibilities and Functions of the
International Joint Commission

1. The International Joint Commission shall assist in the implementation of this Agreement. Accordingly, the Commission is hereby given, by a Reference pursuant to Article IX of the Boundary Waters Treaty, the following responsibilities:

(a) Collation, analysis and dissemination of data and information supplied by the Parties and State and Provincial Governments relating to the quality of the boundary waters of the Great Lakes System and to pollution that enters boundary waters from tributary waters and other sources; ...

(c) Tendering of advice and recommendations to the Parties and to the State and Provincial Governments on problems of and matters related to the quality of boundary waters of the Great Lakes System ... ;

(d) Tendering of advice and recommendations to the Parties in connection with matters covered under the Annexes to this Agreement; ...

(f) Provision of assistance in and advice on matters related to research in the Great Lakes Basin Ecosystem, ... ;

(g) Investigations of such subjects related to the Great Lakes Basin Ecosystem as the Parties may from time to time refer to it.

. . .

3. The Commission shall make a full report to the Parties and to the State and Provincial Governments no less frequently than biennially concerning progress toward the achievement of the General and Specific Objectives including, as appropriate, matters related to Annexes to this Agreement. ...

4. The Commission may in its discretion publish any report, statement or other document prepared by it in the discharge of its functions under this Reference.

5. The Commission shall have authority to verify independently the data and other information submitted by the Parties and by the State and Provincial Governments through such tests or other means as appear appropriate to it, consistent with the Boundary Waters Treaty and with applicable legislation.

NOTES AND QUESTIONS

1. When the protocol was added to the GLWQA in 1987, one of the annexes provided for Remedial Action Plans (RAPs). Essentially, a RAP is a process to deal with the 42 most contaminated areas within the Great Lakes (one has been delisted) by involving a wide variety of interests—government, industry, the public—to identify the problems and propose remedial options. In effect, it is an experiment for both the implementation of the ecosystem approach and local decision processes.

**Great Lakes Water Quality Agreement of 1978 Between the United States and
Canada signed at Ottawa, November 22, 1978**
(1978) Canada Treaty Series 20, as amended by Protocol signed
November 18, 1987; (1987) Canada Treaty Series 32

Annex 2—Remedial Action Plans and Lakewide Management Plans

2. General Principles

(a) Remedial Action Plans and Lakewide Management Plans shall embody a systematic and comprehensive ecosystem approach to restoring and protecting beneficial uses in Areas of Concern or in open lake waters.

(b) Such Plans shall provide a continuing historical record of the assessment of Areas of Concern or Critical Pollutants, proposed remedial actions and their method of implementation, as well as changes in environmental conditions that result from such actions, including significant milestones in restoring beneficial uses to Areas of Concern or open lake waters. They are to serve as an important step toward virtual elimination of persistent toxic substances and toward restoring and maintaining the chemical, physical and biological integrity of the Great Lakes Basin Ecosystem. ...

(e) The Parties, in cooperation with State and Provincial Governments, shall ensure that the public is consulted in all actions undertaken pursuant to this Annex.

---

2. There are a wide variety of institutions pertaining to some aspect of the Canada–US environmental relationship. The table provided below is an indication of the nature and range of those institutions. There are also a number of bilateral institutions between the United States and Mexico, although there are relatively few from a continental point view, apart from the Commission on Environmental Cooperation.

3. Should the powers of the International Joint Commission be expanded or enhanced? What is the relationship between the International Joint Commission and the Commission on Environmental Cooperation? Are new institutions needed? Why?

Table 1 Binational Governance Arrangements Outside the Great Lakes Agreement

Institution	Purpose	Members	Activities/History
Great Lakes Fishery Commission	Coordinate maintenance of fisheries	4 from each side, named by Privy Council and President	Control sea lamprey, coordinate and advise on other fishery matters
Council of Great Lakes Governors	Provide a forum on mutual interests	Governors, with premiers as associate members	Developed Great Lakes Charter and seek to promote economic development in region
GL/St. Lawrence Maritime Forum agenda	Promote trade and commerce	Include govt. and nongovt. organizations	Promote use of Seaway but has no formal
Internatl. Assoc. of GL Ports	Promote GL shipping	4 US, 5 Canadian port authorities	Lobby on impediments to use of Seaway
Niagara River Toxics Committee	Investigate toxic chemical problems	2 each EPA, NY, Ontario, and Environment Canada	Formed by agencies to recommend actions on Niagara toxics
Upper GL Connecting Channels	Assess toxics in rivers and Lake St. Clair	Fisheries and Environment agencies, with IJC observer	Formed in 1984, with study to be completed in 1988
Coordinating Committee on Hydraulic and Hydrologic Data	Coordinate methodology for data collection	Environment Canada, Fisheries and Oceans Corps, and NOAA	Formed in 1953 to assure compatibility of data
Michigan–Ontario Transboundary Air Pollution Committee	Develop cooperative program for air pollution	Wayne County, Michigan DNR, and 2 from Ontario Ministry of Environment	Initiated by governors and premiers; worked closely with IJC air board to 1983
Memorandum of Intent on Transboundary Air Pollution	Develop basis for negotiating agreement especially on acid rain	Govt. scientists organized in 4 technical working groups	Committee work stalled, with negotiations now by formal diplomatic procedures
Migratory Birds Convention	Control killing of migratory birds	No formal body for implementation	Signed 1916
Internatl. Migratory Birds Committee	Foster cooperation under 1916 convention	Resource ministers and cabinet secretaries	Established 1960s, has not met since 1970s
Canada–US Programme Review Committee	Advise govts. on protection of migratory birds	3 each from federal govt.	Developing North American Waterfowl Management Plan
Mississippi Flyway Council	Recommend hunt regulations	1 from each state and province	Recommend regulations to federal governments
St. Lawrence Seaway Authority and Development Corp.	Coordinate construction, operation of seaway	Administrators appointed by federal govts.	Determine policies jointly for separate implementation
Seaway Internatl. Bridge Corp.	Operate bridge at Cornwall	8 members, most from Canada	Maintain bridges and collects tolls
4 Internatl. Boards of Control	Assist IJC decision on levels and flows	Equal members from each side named by IJC commissioners	Develop and implement regulations plans, since 1909
Internatl. GL Levels Advisory Board	Advise IJC on levels and public information	16 members, 8 per side, with half members from public	Carry out studies, reports twice a year
Internatl. GL Technical Info Network	Study adequacy of levels and flows measurements	Environment Canada, Fisheries and Oceans Corps, and NOAA	Reported to IJC 1984 on user needs and adequacy of data
Internatl. Air Pollution Board	To advise govts. about air quality	EPA, 1 NY, and 3 Environment Canada	Report twice yearly on transboundary pollution
Joint Response Team for Great Lakes	Spills clean up of oil/hazardous materials	Canada and US Coast Guards and other agencies	Maintain Joint Contingency Plan invoked 9 times since 1971

Source: H.A. Regier, "Progress with Remediation, Rehabilitation and the Ecosystem Approach" (September/October 1986) vol. 13, no. 3 *Alternatives* 47, at 51.

FURTHER READINGS

L.M. Bloomfield and G.F. Fitzgerald, *Boundary Water Problems of Canada and the United States* (Toronto: Carswell, 1958), 1-13

L. Botts and P. Muldoon, *The Great Lakes Water Quality Agreement: Past Successes and Uncertain Future*, a project sponsored by the Institute on International Environmental Governance (Dartmouth, NS: Dartmouth College, 1997).

Commission for Environmental Commission, *North American Boundary and Transboundary Inland Water Management Report* (Cowansville, QC: Éditons Yvon Blais, 2001).

H. Ingram and D. White, "International Boundary and Water Commission: An Institutional Mismatch for Resolving Transboundary Water Problems" (1993) vol. 33 *Natural Resources Journal* 153.

A. Szekely, "Establishing a Region for Ecological Cooperation in North America" (1992) vol. 32 *Natural Resources Journal* 563.

CHAPTER SIXTEEN

The Future of Environmental Law

Marcia Valiante

Environmental law is here to stay. A growing population on a finite Earth guarantees that environmental problems will persist and that governments, corporations, special interests, and individuals will turn to the law for solutions.

> L. Huffman, "The Past and Future of Environmental Law" (2000) vol. 30
> *Environmental Law* 23

[T]he world has been converted in an instant of time from a wild natural one to one in which humans, one of an estimated 10 million or more species, are consuming, wasting, or diverting an estimated 45% of the total net biological productivity on land and using more than half of the renewable fresh water. The scale of changes in Earth's systems, ... is so different from before that we cannot predict the future, much less chart a course of action, on the basis of what has happened in the past.

> P.H. Raven, "Presidential Address: Science, Sustainability, and the Human Prospect"
> (2002) vol. 297, no. 5583 *Science* 954

I. INTRODUCTION

Modern environmental law in Canada began to evolve more than 30 years ago as governments responded to several "crises" threatening environmental quality. In responding to public concern, Canadian governments took on the role of regulators of industry, constructing increasingly complex standards and administrative machinery to ensure compliance. Enormous efforts and financial resources have been expended by government and industry in implementing these rules. The result of these efforts has been marked improvements in air and water quality in many areas, as well as a shift of environmental awareness into mainstream political discourse. However, even as environmental concern is recognized by central institutions as a "fundamental value in Canadian society" and of "superordinate importance" (Laforest J, in *R v. Hydro Quebec* (1997), 217 NR 241 (SCC)), it is clear that ever-more difficult and challenging threats to the environment continue to demand the attention of Canadian society and its institutions.

Thus, despite much progress, we are nowhere near the end of the demand for environmental law. Predicting how environmental law will develop in the future is fraught with risk: there is too much uncertainty to make any useful predictions, especially in the long term. Since its inception, Canadian environmental law has undergone several waves of change, adapting to new understandings; new challenges; and shifting economic, political, and legal trends. In the short term, Canadian environmental law will likely develop much as it has in the past, through evolution rather than revolution, through trial and error and experimentation, and through efforts at all levels of government and society.

The nature of Canadian environmental law reflects the dominant world view and values of our society with respect to the earth, other species, coming generations, and the place of humans in relation to nature. Because these values influence one's perception of the problems and the appropriate solutions, they will continue to influence the shape of environmental law and policy; as they change, so, too, will the legal response.

There are other factors that will influence the future direction of environmental law. A universal frustration with the existing regime has led to a wide range of experiments with alternative ways of achieving environmental goals, such as decentralization, "voluntary" initiatives, economic instruments, and ADR, and these experiments will likely continue. At the same time, there are increasing pressures for greater openness and accountability, for more democratic processes, and for justice, all of which require accommodation in the design and implementation of environmental law. The economy (and particularly the process of globalization), the developments in information technology, and the shift to a service economy will have a significant impact; legal developments at the international level will increasingly affect Canadian environmental law.

While many of the trends in environmental law are resulting in more responsive, efficient, and integrated design, there still exists the usual inertia of existing institutions resistant to change and the perennial challenge of federal–provincial politics that influence the appetite of governments for change. As well, there are significant counter-pressures evidencing a resistance to support for environmental values and against a strong government role in directing environmental protection. These factors will also help shape the debate about the future directions of Canadian environmental policy and law.

The other chapters of this book examine specific reforms to policy, legislation, and regulations. The purpose of this chapter is to explore more generally the underlying conceptual bases for these reforms and to explore a number of critical perspectives that challenge the dominant approach to the goals, design, and methods of Canadian environmental law and policy. Understanding these perspectives could strengthen the quality of the debate over the appropriate societal response to a number of interlocking problems. At the very least, they help broaden the debate about the future of environmental law and its capacity to incorporate principles of sustainability, diversity, equity, respect, and democracy.

NOTES AND QUESTIONS

1. A debate has surfaced in recent years over whether environmental problems continue to deserve priority attention from governments and society. This view is exemplified in the book *The Skeptical Environmentalist: Measuring the Real State of the World* by B. Lomborg (Cambridge: Cambridge University Press, 2001). He assembles a great deal of evidence to show that environmental quality and the quality of human existence

are improving and not getting worse, as is usually suggested by what he calls "the Litany" of pessimistic environmentalists. This conclusion is echoed in other works, such as G. Easterbrook's *A Moment on the Earth: The Coming Age of Environmental Optimism* (New York: Viking, 1995). However, Lomborg also argues that evidence that environmental policy and law were irrelevant in achieving these improvements, most current environmental problems are exaggerated, and technology will respond to those problems that do arise. A good example of the rebuttal to these conclusions is presented in a book review by M. Grubb, "Relying on Manna from Heaven?" (2001) vol. 294, no. 5545 *Science* at 1285. Do you agree that contemporary environmental problems can be solved in the absence of public policy and legal initiatives?

2. Lomborg is but one example of the "backlash" against environmentalists and environmental law. For discussion of different aspects of this backlash, see Z.J.B. Plater, "Environmental Law as a Mirror of the Future: Civic Values Confronting Market Force Dynamics in a Time of Counter Revolution" (1996) vol. 23 *Environmental Affairs* 733; Canadian Environmental Law Association, *Trashing Environmental Protection: Ontario's Four Part Strategy*, available online at http://www.cela.ca/; C. Tollefson, "Strategic Lawsuits Against Public Participation: Developing a Canadian Response" (1994) vol. 73 *Canadian Bar Review* 200; D. Helvarg, *The War Against the Greens: The "Wise Use" Movement, the New Right and Anti-Environmental Violence* (San Francisco: Sierra Club Books, 1997); J. Vaughn Switzer, *Green Backlash: The History and Politics of Environmental Opposition in the US* (Boulder, CO: Lynne Rienner Publishers, 1997); and S. Beder, *Global Spin: The Corporate Assault on Environmentalism* (Totnes, UK: Green Books, 1997).

II. UP AGAINST THE LIMITS OF THE EXISTING FRAMEWORK

The only thing about environmental law on which there seems to be universal agreement is that its "first generation" design has reached the limits of effectiveness and change is now needed. The traditional "command and control" approach is credited by most commentators with making significant improvements in air and water quality by targeting large point sources and media-specific discharges, but as a stand-alone approach it is unable to address the complexity of contemporary environmental problems. The following excerpts address the limits of this approach from different perspectives.

World Commission on Environment and Development
Mandate for Change: Key Issues, Strategy and Workplan
(Geneva: WCED, 1985), at 22-26

Limitations of the Standard Agenda

When considered globally against the test of results ... and against the Commission's mandate, the standard agenda appears to have several limitations. Four stand out as worthy of mention. *First*, with few exceptions, the standard agenda tends to focus action on the effects of environmental problems rather than on their sources. This may be a natural evolution. Awareness of the health effects of polluted water, or air, for example, gives rise to concern about the pollution, and then to action to identify the polluting activities. Further action or, more correctly, re-action, leads to the development of curative measures, including add-on technologies, to the assessment of the benefits and costs of those measures and, eventually, to decisions to require additional investment or not.

As noted, this react-and-cure approach has led to significant achievements on certain issues and it will remain an essential part of public policy. Given future trends however, react-and-cure measures are clearly not sufficient. Unless they are rapidly reinforced by anticipate-and-prevent measures, it is doubtful that even the richer industrial nations will be able to catch up with the environment and development effects of past activities, let alone keep up with those of future activities. And, even if some could, they would do so at an unnecessarily high cost. As far as the poorer nations are concerned, experience to date suggests that there is little prospect that they will be able to afford the cost of after-the-fact, react-and-cure strategies in many areas. They must instead look to before-the-fact, anticipate-and-prevent strategies that are, almost invariably, more effective, more economic and, in the medium to longer term, more affordable. ...

Second, much of the work to date has tended to examine the key issues as environmental issues alone, or as resource, conservation or management issues, rather than as development issues, or as joint environment-and-development issues. Yet the consequences of many of the issues for development (and vice versa) are enormous.

Third, most of the work to date has tended to examine each of the critical issues in isolation. Thus, for example, one report deals with acid rain, another with climatic change induced by higher levels of CO_2, still another with air pollutants in general, or with lead in petrol, or with other heavy metals. ...

But it has become abundantly clear that these problems are all tightly linked to one or two common causes: energy policies that favour fossil fuel combustion; or transportation, tax and trade policies that favour large vehicles.

Similarly, considerable work has been done on the eutrophication of surface waters, on nitrate pollution of groundwater, and on the degradation of soils. But it has become clear that in many jurisdictions these problems, too, all share a common cause: agricultural policies which promote and induce an excessive use of chemical fertilizers and pesticides.

Fourth, most of the work to date, with its focus on effects and on ways and means to ameliorate effects, reflects a very narrow view of environmental policy and, indeed, of broader policy needs and obligations. Whatever the intentions of a decade ago, with few exceptions, environmental policy has come through as a limited policy field, essentially an "add-on" to other policy fields, whose mission is to react to damage done and to cure it after the fact.

There is clearly a need now to shift the focus from the effects of environmental problems to their policy sources. ... Environmental policy needs to become a comprehensive, horizontal policy field and an integral component of economic and social policy, whose mission is, at least, to anticipate damage and reduce the negative external effects of human activity and, at best, to propose and promote economic and social policies that expand the basis for sustainable development. In doing so, it should also allow for the diversity and uniqueness of specific regional and local situations.

**National Wildlife Federation and Canadian Institute for
Environmental Law and Policy**
*A Prescription for Healthy Great Lakes:
Report of the Program for Zero Discharge*
(Toronto: CIELAP and NWF, 1991), at 9-10

The Failure of the Pollution Control Approach

[D]espite all our laws, all our efforts and all our expenditures, massive amounts of toxic pollutants continue to be dumped into the environment every day. The current regulatory approach is not working.

The current regulatory approach focusses on the discharge of toxic substances. On a case-by-case basis, government agencies issue permits that, at best, require modest, incremental reductions in the concentration of a limited number of toxics being dumped into the environment.

This pollution control approach has several flaws:

1. *The burden of proof is on the person trying to prevent the pollution*: In the pollution control approach, community residents, or government agencies trying to protect the environment, or workers trying to protect their health must prove that the contaminants will cause serious harm. If they cannot, the polluter is allowed to proceed.

This assumption that chemicals and discharges are innocent until proven guilty puts citizens, workers and the environment at considerable risk. It means that chemicals may be in use for many years before their dangerous impacts are known. By then it may be too late. Massive quantities of toxics have irretrievably contaminated the environment.

2. *Reductions in total discharges are not required*: Attention is focussed on assessing each individual source of pollution in isolation, rather than determining the combined impacts of pollutants discharged into all parts of the environment from all sources.

In focussing on each discharge, government agencies fail to adequately assess:

(i) the current condition of the environment and society's goals for protecting or improving the overall environment;
(ii) the combined impact of discharges from other polluters, including other discharges from the same factory into the air or water; and
(iii) pollution from other kinds of sources, such as past dumping, leaking landfills, contaminated sediments and toxic fallout from the air.

As a result, total discharges of contaminants into the environment may increase, even though an individual discharge may appear insignificant.

3. *Dilution is not the solution to pollution*: The pollution control approach still accepts the outdated dilution solution to meet environmental standards for toxics.

Discharge permit limits are based on the *concentration* of pollutants instead of on the total amount of pollutants being discharged … . The dilution approach is myopic: while it may ensure that discharges won't immediately kill fish near the end of a pipe, it fails to consider the long-term build-up of contaminants in the environment.

4. *Pollution control focuses on end-of-the-pipe solutions*: The pollution control approach tries to trap contaminants after they are produced in the factory, but before they are released into the environment. This end-of-the-pipe approach has two fatal flaws:

(i) Inevitably, some of the contaminants are released into the environment through the stack or pipe. … This approach assumes that there is a safe or acceptable level for chemicals in the environment. Even if this were true, there is inadequate information to determine acceptable levels for all chemicals being discharged, let alone acceptable levels of multiple contaminants.

(ii) *The end-of-the-pipe approach amounts to a "toxic shell game."* End-of-pipe technologies often prevent pollutants from getting into one part of the environment by putting them into another. For example, wastewater treatment systems collect and concentrate pollutants into a sludge. This sludge is incinerated, buried in a landfill or spread on land. Sludge disposal by these means causes pollution of the air or of ground or surface water. This transfer from one environmental medium to another is a self-defeating effort; overall pollution is not necessarily reduced.

Because most government environmental agencies have different branches controlling air, water, waste disposal, pesticides and toxic substances, requirements may vary substantially. This promotes a "toxic shell game."

Executive Resource Group for the Ontario Ministry of the Environment
***Managing the Environment: A Review of Best Practices*, vol. 1**
(Ontario: Ministry of the Environment, 2001), at 14-15

Limitations of the Traditional Model

Leading jurisdictions acknowledge the inadequacy of this traditional model—often described as *command and control*—as the *primary* or *stand-alone* approach in terms of dealing with the changing and increasingly complex environmental challenges of today and the future. These jurisdictions point to the following:

The emphasis to date on large point source pollution has been pushed as far as possible. In many cases, new *end of pipe* technology is yielding decreasing/marginal environmental benefits at increasingly high costs.

Today's issues—for example, smog, global climate change, increased respiratory illnesses—are much more complex in terms of causes, interactions, and their impact on human health, quality of life, and/or the environment. As such, they require more complex, partnership-based solutions in addition to simply *set the rules, follow the rules*, based on minimum standards.

Developments in scientific and risk analysis indicate more clearly than ever that the effects of pollution on land, water, and air, and ultimately human beings are not separate and discrete. Large, small, and non-point source pollution cuts across all media (air, land, and water), is cumulative in nature, and needs to be viewed and dealt with as such.

There is a growing acceptance that government cannot *do it all*. There are simply not enough resources in any jurisdiction to regulate everything, assuming that traditional regulation could even be an effective strategy for dealing with smaller point and non-point source pollution and addressing today's more complex and cumulative health and environmental problems.

Governments have a better understanding that the *single department* approach does not level all of the energies and resources of government in dealing with complex problems. This is particularly true where ministries or departments have real or perceived conflicting mandates or advocacy roles on behalf of client groups, i.e., agriculture, industry, forestry, fisheries.

There is increasing awareness that an informed public, with access to environmental information, including performance information, can be an effective tool in achieving environmental goals.

J.B. Ruhl
"Thinking of Environmental Law as a Complex Adaptive System: How To Clean Up the Environment by Making a Mess of Environmental Law"
(1997) vol. 34 *Houston Law Review* 933, at 940, 942-43, 967-68, and 1002

Complex adaptive systems, because of their highly collectivized, nonlinear, dynamic behavior, defy prediction through classical reductionist method, or any other known method for that matter. Yet we have not designed our environmental law system with this underlying property in mind. Rather, it is mired in a reductionist, linear, predictivist mentality ignorant of underlying complex system behaviors. We find ourselves as a result constantly befuddled when the intended benefits of environmental regulation fail to materialize or, worse, when consequences contrary to the intended effects materialize. To be sure, the coercive, regulatory, command-and-control state has produced some admirable results in terms of environmental protection, but the underlying reductionist premises of that approach have exhausted their usefulness and will never allow us to tackle the significant environmental challenges ahead.

Complex adaptive systems combine qualities of coherent stability and disordered change to produce sustaining, adaptive performance over the long run. Five important features of complex adaptive systems explain how they are able to balance stability and change to produce this outcome. First, they perform according to complex, large-scale behaviors that emerge from the aggregate interactions of less complex agents, such as how the trends of macroeconomic scale represent the aggregate behavior of many individual firms or investors. Second, the interactions of the system exhibit unpredictable, nonlinear relationships incapable of being neatly plotted as straight line formulae, as revealed in the complex dynamics of many predator-prey populations. Third, the complex adaptive system can be described through the varied flows of its mediums—fluids, money, energy, information and so on—just as the weather reporter traces the jet stream to describe storm patterns. Fourth, complex adaptive systems are defined by their diverse ingredients and context, as in how a biologist might describe the diverse species in an ecosystem. Fifth, all four of these properties combine into self-organizing critical state behavior through which change is transformed into a stabilizing rather than disrupting force.

Although all fields of law regulate human behavior, environmental law is different. Environmental law regulates human behavior toward the environment. This quality presents a two-fold challenge for environmental law, for both the target of environmental regulation, humans, and the purported beneficiary of regulation, the environment, display the discontinuities and synergies characteristic of complex adaptive systems. Thus, it is not surprising to find few issues of environmental policy that can be described as easy, uncomplicated, or well-defined. Rather, environmental policy issues usually are multidimensional and multidisciplinary; they involve monetary and nonmonetary aspects; they involve scarce resources upon which the effects of policy decisions may be irreversible; their impacts are multisectoral and felt over broad scales of time and space; and they carry with them high levels of uncertainty of causation and outcome.

By and large, unfortunately, modern American environmental law is not designed based on that fundamental reality. Rather, both the present structure of the law as well as the most touted proposed reforms display an amazing degree of ignorance of complex adaptive system dynamics. The underlying tradition of environmental law— a tradition that is hardly abandoned in current reform frameworks—is based on a conception of nature as uniformitarian, a nature in which change takes place, but in the form of trends that are capable of extrapolation and prediction which lead toward an ordered state of equilibrium. We know that this paradigm is a fiction; so why does our legal framework cling to it? ...

The last three decades of environmental law, the command-and-control era of so-called "cooperative federalism," made great strides by taking shortcuts around the reality that the subject matter of environmental law is a set of complex adaptive systems. But shortcuts can only work for so long. We find ourselves staring into the reality of environmental policy as never before, asking questions like: "Will we be able to sustain the planet, and for how long?" There are no simple answers to those questions; rather, we will have to resign ourselves to having to answer and reanswer those questions over and over, taking risks along the way through experimentation, though with the benefit of as much information as we can collect. The process will be a mess! It will not be easy, or inexpensive, or something we can leave to only a few "experts" in centralized administrative agencies to carry out. We will never be able to rest from the task, but if we are right in asking questions of that magnitude, then we should demand nothing less of ourselves.

The single greatest obstacle to getting there, to even beginning to talk about how to get there, is trust, specifically overcoming the complete lack of trust that personifies today's environmental law and policy.

NOTES AND QUESTIONS

1. Environmental law evolved in a piecemeal fashion, addressing separate problems as they arose by adding another law for each category of problems, such as water, air, waste, and toxics, and by adding another branch of administration. (This development is addressed in chapter 1.) Can this approach to environmental law be transformed into a more holistic approach? How? What are some of the obstacles to changing this system of law now that it seems to be at the end of its usefulness?

2. A good summary of the limitations of the existing regulatory approach (which the authors refer to as "permissive regulation") and of the need to respond to inherent uncertainty is found in R.M. M'Gonigle et al., "Taking Uncertainty Seriously: From Permissive Regulation to Preventive Design in Environmental Decision Making" (1994) vol. 32 *Osgoode Hall Law Journal* 99.

3. The economic case against the traditional approach is found extensively in the US literature. As summarized by one US commentator: "(1) it is inefficient; (2) it is static; (3) it produces a proliferation of regulations that are difficult to keep abreast of, much less comply with; and (4) it discourages creative approaches that may actually result in less pollution than occurs under the present regime." (M.A. Stach, "The Gradual Reform of Environmental Law in the Twenty-First Century: Opportunities Within a Familiar Framework" (1997) vol. 22 *Journal of Corporation Law* 621.) See also J.D. Fraiberg and M.J. Trebilcock, "Risk Regulation: Technocratic and Democratic Tools for Regulatory Reform" (1998) vol. 43 *McGill Law Journal* 835.

4. Numerous views on the limits and potential of environmental law and various reform proposals (in a US context) are found in "Symposium: Twenty-Five Years of Environmental Regulation" (1994) *Loyola of Los Angeles Law Review* 779; "Symposium: Environment 2000—New Issues for a New Century" (2001) vol. 27 *Ecology Law Quarterly* 909; "Symposium: Innovations in Environmental Policy" (2000) *University of Illinois Law Review* 1; and "The National Symposium on Second Generation Environmental Policy and the Law" (2001) vol. 29 *Capital University Law Review* 1. To what extent is the critique of the US regulatory approach relevant to Canada?

5. For further reading on adaptive management see G. Andrews Emison, "The Potential for Unconventional Progress: Complex Adaptive Systems and Environmental Quality Policy" (1996) vol. 7 *Duke Environmental Law and Policy Forum* 167 and K.N. Lee, *Compass and Gyroscope: Integrating Science and Politics for the Environment* (Washington, DC: Island Press, 1993).

III. REFORM OF ENVIRONMENTAL LAW WITHIN THE EXISTING FRAMEWORK

Numerous efforts are underway across Canada to reform environmental law, including experiments with deregulation, "voluntary" initiatives, economic instruments, harmonization, citizen participation, and the like. Examples of many of these are discussed in the other chapters of the book. This approach to reform in Canada has been largely ad hoc, with little apparent coherent motivation, direction, or theoretical basis other than a desire to reduce the burden regulation places on government and industry. In this section, several excerpts suggest a more structured approach to reform.

D.P. Emond
"The Greening of Environmental Law"
(1991) vol. 36 *McGill Law Journal* 742, at 759 and 761-63

Not much has worked very well in the environmental protection field up to this point. Granted there have been some notable successes, but the general consensus seems to be that we are slipping further and further behind. The problem is that the approach has generally been wrong. It has proceeded from an adversarial, competitive, rights-oriented model that was destined to siphon off creative energies in a contest of rights regulated only by the logic of justice and due process. The focus has been on defining rights and fine-tuning the dispute resolution process, rather than on solving environmental problems. What is needed is a new model that will redirect these energies toward practical solutions to real environmental problems. This model must be based on principles that emphasize interdependence, connectedness, respect, obligation, and co-operative approaches to problem-solving. ... Competitive, adversarial approaches tend to divert creative energies away from potential solutions. Co-operative, problem-solving approaches, on the other hand, tend to show that all parties have a community of interest in solving environmental problems, and that the public interest groups must play a key role in finding and implementing those solutions.

· · ·

The process that will extricate us from this dilemma is one that is sometimes described as alternative dispute resolution but is more accurately labelled co-operative or creative problem-solving. It is a multifaceted process. It starts with a basic redistribution of rights, principally through legislative recognition of basic environmental rights. Rights define power, and without the power that derives from judicially enforceable rights, the public is not likely to be an effective participant in any form of co-operative problem-solving. The problem-solving must, therefore, take place in the shadow of the law and the courts.

The principal approach to resolving environmental problems must be negotiation. Roger Fisher and William Ury (with B. Patton, ed.), in the book *Getting to Yes: Negotiating Agreement Without Giving In* (NY: Penguin Books, 1991), emphasize that co-operative problem-solving or "win/win" solutions demand a principled approach to negotiation. By this they mean negotiation that separates the people and personalities from the problem at hand; focuses on interests, not on positions; invents options for mutual gain; and employs objective criteria.

Because not all negotiations can generate agreement, the process must also include mechanisms to enable the parties to employ the assistance of a facilitator or mediator.

· · ·

This process is multifaceted. It recognizes a policy or rule-making component, a rule-implementation component, and an enforcement dimension. It recognizes that no one process is appropriate for all tasks. Nor is it a process that naively suggests that the public can be a full participant in solving environmental problems without a fundamental redistribution of rights. It recognizes an important role for the process designer. Just as adjudication will not solve all problems, so too negotiation and mediation cannot be expected to solve all problems. The trick is to know when and how to use each process and then to sell that approach to the parties.

N. Gunningham and P. Grabosky, with D. Sinclair
Smart Regulation: Designing Environmental Policy
(Oxford: Clarendon Press, 1998), at 8-10 and 15-16

Even in the unlikely event that ... the pendulum were to swing back towards more regulation ("bigger and better" regulatory agencies, more standards, tougher enforcement, etc.) this would raise as many problems as it would solve. First, there is little evidence that policy-makers have overcome many of the serious limitations of this approach which became evident during the "first phase" of regulation. Secondly, government resources are necessarily limited ... as a result, it may well be that, in many circumstances, traditional regulation is neither the most efficient nor the most effective strategy. If so, then it is, at best, only a partial solution, which should be used selectively rather than "across the board."

Were the pendulum to swing to the opposite extreme, with free-market and property-rights approaches substantially replacing regulation, there is little reason to believe that environmental outcomes would be any better ... . [T]heir capacity to deliver optimal environmental outcomes is, in most cases, even more limited than that of command and control regulation. The crucial question thus becomes: where should one go next in terms of regulatory policy?

In our view, the challenge for regulatory strategy is to transcend this ideological divide by finding ways to overcome the inefficiencies of traditional regulation on the one hand, and the pitfalls of deregulation on the other. That is, to move beyond the market-state dichotomy to devise better ways of achieving environmental protection at an acceptable economic and social cost. This will involve a "third phase" of regulation: one which still involves government intervention, but selectively and in combination with a range of market and non-market solutions, and of public and private orderings.

The central thesis of this book is that recruiting a range of regulatory actors to implement complementary combinations of policy instruments, tailored to specific environmental goals and circumstances, will produce more effective and efficient policy outcomes. Further, that this approach will reduce the regulatory burden on government, thus freeing up scarce public resources to be allocated to situations where government intervention or assistance is most required.

We place particular emphasis on the potential for second and third parties (business or commercial or non-commercial third parties) to act as surrogate or quasi-regulators, complementing or replacing government regulation in certain circumstances. We do not do so to fulfil the ideological agenda of deregulation, but because we consider that it will build a more robust and comprehensive policy mix than traditional approaches, at the same time as achieving more cost-effective outcomes for business ... .

We do not, however, advocate a "smorgasbord" approach, where the greater the number of different instruments and actors the better. There are limits to government and private sector resources which necessitate a careful selection of the most cost-effective regulatory combinations. There are also limits to the administrative burden that can reasonably be placed on regulatees in satisfying a multiplicity of regulations. Excessive administrative burdens may well divert internal firm resources away from more productive pollution prevention activities. Finally, appropriate mixes of instruments and actors will vary depending on the nature of the environmental problem and industry sectors being addressed, making it difficult if not impossible to generalize concerning optimal combinations. ... What is needed, then, is not simply the introduction of a broad range of policy instruments, but the matching of instruments with the imperatives of the environmental issue being addressed, with the availability of different regulatory actors, and with the intrinsic qualities of each other.

National Wildlife Federation and Canadian Institute for
Environmental Law and Policy
A Prescription for Healthy Great Lakes: Report of
the Program for Zero Discharge
(Toronto: CIELAP and NWF, 1991), at 15 and 18

The Call for Zero Discharge

A zero discharge strategy must be based on five fundamental principles:

1. *Eliminate the Use of Toxics*: Instead of focussing on reducing and treating wastes, polluters must eliminate the use of toxics to avoid creating the wastes in the first place.

2. *Decrease Total Quantities of Toxics in the Environment*: The *total amounts* of toxics entering the Great Lakes ecosystem must be substantially reduced according to a strict timetable.

3. *Address All Sources of Pollution*: All sources of toxics must be controlled, including discharges from municipal sewage treatment plants and industries, and agricultural and urban run-off. These sources must be addressed regardless of whether the initial release of toxics is into water, air or on to land.

4. *Enforce the "No Right to Pollute" Principle*: No one has the right to pollute. Permits that have been granted that allow pollution are only temporary concessions and must be phased out as quickly as possible.

5. *Institute a Reverse Onus Requirement*: The user or discharger of a possibly toxic substance must prove that the substance will not harm the environment. A chemical should be assumed to be harmful unless proven otherwise.

A zero discharge strategy means making society less dependent on the *use* of toxic chemicals. "Zero discharge" means maximum use of all of the following techniques:

> Replacing toxic products or activities with non-toxic products and methods; for example, using environmentally benign pest control methods instead of chemical pesticides, and using chemicals other than chloroflorocarbons for coolants;
>
> Using raw materials in production processes that are less hazardous; for example, replacing lead or mercury in paint with less toxic constituents, and substituting water-based inks for solvent-based ones;
>
> Redesigning products so they don't require the use of hazardous materials in their production; for example, using unbleached paper so that chlorine does not have to be used in pulp and paper mills;

Changing production processes; for example, replacing organic solvents for cleaning machinery with mechanical processes;

Reusing toxic raw materials instead of throwing them away; for example, recycling
and reusing inks in a printing shop; and

Instituting better operating practices; for example, using more efficient equipment,
preventive maintenance, employee training or good housekeeping to ensure optimal
process conditions and minimal leakage.

Executive Resource Group for the Ontario Ministry of the Environment
Managing the Environment: A Review of Best Practices, **vol. 1**
(Ontario: Ministry of the Environment, 2001), at 14-17, 20, 23, 28, and 33

In light of these inadequacies [in the traditional approach], leading jurisdictions are
actively engaged in trying to move to the next level of dealing with the environment,
sometimes referred to as a new vision of *environmental management*. This new vision
clearly builds on the strengths of traditional regulation and the command and control
model, but also integrates it with a broader, more comprehensive approach.

This broader approach builds on and steps beyond minimum standards to emphasize continuous improvement for all sources of pollution, cross-media and cumulative
impacts, and broader public participation and access to information. It typically
includes less overall emphasis on the role of government as *doer*, i.e., protecting
human health and the environment by traditional regulation and enforcement, and a
greater emphasis on the role of government to provide overall *system management*
through a range of partnerships, processes, structures, and tools ... .

Consistent with the overarching *strategic shift* towards *Environmental Management*,
we have isolated a number of these approaches, or *strategic shifts*, that are being
pursued by leading jurisdictions.

Strategic Shift #1 Towards a high-level, government-wide vision and goals with
implementation shared across different departments. ...

Strategic Shift #2 Towards a new and broader emphasis on strategies to promote
continuous improvement in environmental performance and accountability across all
sources of pollution. ...

Strategic Shift #3 Towards a place-based approach with boundaries that make
environmental sense and facilitate a cross-media, cumulative approach (such as watershed management). ...

Strategic Shift #4 Towards a comprehensive, more flexible set of regulatory and
non-regulatory tools and incentives. ... This new approach is often referred to as an
integrated compliance assurance strategy. ...

Strategic Shift #5 Towards an approach based on shared responsibility with the
regulated community, NGOs, the public, and the scientific/technical community.

NOTES AND QUESTIONS

1. Discussions of the next generation of environmental policy and law often focus on increased reliance on economic instruments and incentives, voluntary initiatives, flexible regulation, information strategies, and other non-regulatory programs. A good overview of the implications of these policy initiatives is found in the many contributions to M.R. Chertow and D.C. Esty, *Thinking Ecologically: The Next Generation of Environmental Policy* (New Haven, CT: Yale University Press, 1997). A Canadian perspective is provided in another collection: E.A. Parson, ed., *Governing the Environment: Persistent Challenges, Uncertain Innovations* (Toronto: University of Toronto Press, 2001). The work of Professor Richard Stewart of NYU has been central to this debate; for a comprehensive review of the tools for this second generation of environmental law, see R.B. Stewart, "A New Generation of Environmental Regulation?" (2001) vol. 29 *Capital University Law Review* 21. What is the appropriate role of government in these "alternative" programs? The authors of *Smart Regulation*, above, suggest that there is an ideal, efficient, and effective response to each type of environmental problem. What criteria should guide the application of these programs?

2. Reducing or eliminating the use of toxic substances is commonly known as "pollution prevention" or "toxics use reduction." Governments in Europe and North America are promoting pollution prevention as the key strategy for dealing with the toxics problem now that it is obvious that the "pollution control" approach has not been useful with respect to persistent, bioaccumulative toxic substances. Several states in the United States have adopted toxic use reduction laws. The Massachusetts law, *An Act To Promote Reduced Use of Toxic and Hazardous Substances in the Commonwealth*, no. 6161 (1989), for example, requires major toxics users and generators to audit their processes and develop and implement a plan for reducing their use or generation of toxics by a specified percentage by a specified date. Most other pollution prevention initiatives are voluntary, using different types of incentives to encourage the adoption of reduction techniques. In what circumstances might a voluntary approach be appropriate?

3. In 1999, CEPA was amended to provide authority for the federal minister of the environment to require the development of pollution prevention plans with respect to substances on the toxic substances list (SC 1999, c. 33, part 4). These provisions are designed to serve as an alternative to regulation and to operate with minimal administrative oversight; how can public scrutiny be assured with such a system? CEPA 1999 also included a new regulatory track for the virtual elimination of persistent, bioaccumulative toxic substances (SC 1999, c. 33, part 5). Where the requisite criteria are met, this track is required to be implemented by the mechanism of individual facilities preparing virtual elimination plans. Public input will be sought for the general requirements but not with respect to individual plans. How is this track an improvement over the previous regulatory scheme?

4. Emond, above, goes on to discuss how the roles that lawyers play for the government, for corporations, and for public interest groups must change under his model. He contends that public interest counsel have difficulty in adapting to this new model for several reasons: that resources are inadequate to participate effectively; that counsel who are skilled at cross-examination are not necessarily skilled at negotiation; that no one else can be blamed for an unacceptable outcome; that public interest groups are not structured

in a way that counsel can effectively negotiate on the members' behalf; and that many environmentalists are not willing to compromise on many issues. Do you agree?

5. How pervasive should Emond's approach be? Are there situations where it is *not* appropriate? How does one ensure that those negotiating represent all of the affected interests? What if compromise does prove impossible? Who is accountable to the public for the outcomes of negotiation? See chapter 14.

6. A number of experiments that bypass the existing regulatory approach are being undertaken, both within and outside of government. See, for example, Accelerated Reduction/Elimination of Toxics, *Environmental Leaders 3 Update: Voluntary Action on Toxic Substances* (Quebec: ARET Secretariat, 2000) and Environment Canada, "Policy Framework for Environmental Performance Agreements," available online at http://www.ec.gc.ca/epa-epe/pol/en/framewktoc.cfm. The US Environmental Protection Agency has been redesigned (or "reinvented") to allow for more flexible approaches and more experimentation. Examples of new initiatives include Project XL and the Common Sense Initiative: see http://www.epa.gov/. Unfortunately, few studies have objectively evaluated the effectiveness of these programs and many inflated claims of their success are promoted. A serious criticism of such initiatives is their impact on democratic accountability; see, for example, K. Harrison, "Voluntarism and Environmental Governance," in E.A. Parson, ed., *Governing the Environment: Persistent Challenges, Uncertain Innovations* (Toronto: University of Toronto Press, 2001). How can accountability to the public be assured in these programs?

7. An excellent effort to structure the debate over the use of "voluntary" programs as an alternative to regulation is found in R.B. Gibson, ed., *Voluntary Initiatives and the New Politics of Corporate Greening* (Peterborough, ON: Broadview Press, 1999).

8. Proponents of "adaptive management" argue that the lessons of complex adaptive systems theory should be applied to the development and implementation of environmental law. To do so would require the following changes, as suggested by G. Andrews Emison, "The Potential for Unconventional Progress: Complex Adaptive Systems and Environmental Quality Policy" (1996) vol. 7 *Duke Environmental Law and Policy Forum* 167, at 187:

> give priority to generating detailed environmental data, in order to be able to adapt to inevitable, continuous change;
>
> establish clear goals for all stakeholders, requiring them to "consistently perform slightly better than they do currently. As the system achieves these goals, the goals can be adjusted to provide for an ever-improving environment";
>
> use all tools available for environmental management, in the most effective combinations for the particular circumstances, to "increase the chance of success";
>
> use positive rewards and incentives for responsible behaviour;
>
> focus implementation at the lowest "component" level and focus less attention on policy design and more on actual implementation;
>
> emphasis in policy should consciously shift from "control and stability" to "innovation and improvement";
>
> not mere dabbling but support for purposeful innovation and creativity to achieve continuous improvement in environmental quality; and
>
> "adopt flexibility as a specific policy objective."

How would you modify existing environmental laws to accommodate the insights of complex adaptive systems theory? Would one need to throw out the existing regulations and start over, or can these shifts be accomplished through incremental reform of the existing system? What would be the role of lawyers under such a system? If "there can never be a final decision in science-based management," how can the traditional concerns of the legal system, such as procedural fairness, be ensured? See A.D. Tarlock, "The Nonequilibrium Paradigm in Ecology and the Partial Unraveling of Environmental Law" (1994) vol. 27 *Loyola of Los Angeles Law Review* 1121.

9. In Europe, the notion of "ecological modernization" has been influential in the reform of environmental law. It is a means of operationalizing the precautionary principle through the use of technological innovation, green accounting, tax reform, and environmental management. Unlike traditional environmental economics, however, it seeks structural change toward environmental health and innovative production rather than simply greater "efficiency." See M. Skou Andersen and I. Massa, "Ecological Modernization— Origins, Dilemmas and Future Directions" (2000) vol. 2 *Journal of Environmental Policy and Planning* 337. However, it is criticized by some as being at odds with the aims of the environmental movement: M.A. Hajer, "Ecological Modernisation as Cultural Politics," in S. Lash, B. Szerszynski, and B. Wynne, *Risk, Environment and Modernity: Towards a New Ecology* (London: Sage Publications, 1996).

IV. SHIFTING PARADIGMS: "OTHER" PERSPECTIVES AND RADICAL CRITIQUE IN THE FUTURE OF ENVIRONMENTAL POLICY AND LAW

Mainstream environmentalism has come under heavy criticism from many quarters for supporting policies that reflect elite values of educated, white, middle-class North American society and for failing to take into account the effects of those policies on people of colour, the poor, workers, and others. Environmental groups, governments, and private sector decision makers are being challenged to respond with policies and practices that reflect a more comprehensive understanding of "environmental" issues. In addition, many writers critique environmental policy from outside a traditional liberal perspective, seeking to replace existing structures with radically different approaches. These perspectives lend much insight into current approaches to environmental issues and offer alternative visions of a holistic future. However, because many of these alternative paradigms are seen by some as irreconcilable and competing, they have not had a significant impact on environmental policy. One suggestion is to leave theorizing behind and focus instead on a pragmatic agenda—on the things in common between radical theorists—rather than on the differences. See B.G. Norton, *Toward Unity Among Environmentalists* (Oxford: Oxford University Press, 1991) and K. Hirokawa, "Some Pragmatic Observations About Radical Critique in Environmental Law" (2002) vol. 21 *Stanford Environmental Law Journal* 225. As you read through the following sections, consider the potential impact of each vision on the future of Canadian environmental law and policy and consider whether there is or could be a common agenda among environmentalists that could serve as the catalyst for success on policy direction.

A. Aboriginal Values and Environmental Protection

T. Alcoze
"Our Common Future: Native Land Use and Sustainable Development"
in *The Guelph Seminars on Sustainable Development*
(Guelph, ON: University of Guelph, 1990), at 21-24

One of the ideas that is central to this whole forum has to do with the new buzz words, "sustainable development." Is this going to be another cliche like "ecology" or "holistic," that may be bantered about in all sorts of different ways or will this "new" concept be taken seriously? The answer to this is "yes, we must take it seriously." Because it has to do with our survival and it's very clear on a wide variety of fronts that if we don't carefully consider this issue of resource use and sustainability, we jeopardize our future in a very real way. Certainly we jeopardize future generations.

The way in which native traditions have always dealt with this problem is to consider seven generations into the future. What we do today, we do with the understanding that it will have some kind of impact. That changes our perspective a bit.

Another question is: How can we understand sustainable development as an idea? My answer to that is really very simple. At least the principle is simple enough. Consider this place as our home, that's the answer. Believe it, accept that we live here, that this is our home. We must realize that we don't have any other "new" lands to explore, or infinite resources to exploit. To do this, we simply have to live it. Live with this land, this issue, live with these resources, because they are ours and we are theirs. We live that connection.

We have lived with the understanding that it's simply not possible, it's simply not feasible for us to use up our resources, to eat all our food and walk next door and ask our neighbours, "Well, we ate all ours up, may we have yours now, please?" Because that's not the way the world works. So it's a fiction to believe that we can simply pull up stakes and move somewhere else and engage in another era of cataclysmic conquest, cataclysmic exploration. Resource management for native nations has always, not only implied, but it has always meant sustainability. For us it has always been taken for granted that the way you must use your resources is to do so in such a way that you sustain the availability of those resources.

Native Nations have always maintained an integrated relationship with the land. An intimate relationship with nature's resources, with nature, with the earth. That relationship is one of respect. When we have harvested resources, harvested medicine, harvested food, harvested a piece of dry wood, harvested a beauty, harvested a feeling, there was always relationship and a thanksgiving. It's possible to give thanks in a moment, a sunrise, a sunset, a beautiful cloud, a wonderful animal, a moment in time. To say "meegwetch," which is Ojibwa for giving thanks to life for life, being thankful about life. Because life is something that it is possible to rejoice with all the time, and not wait for only the good moments. Make all your life good moments and sustain that.

Well trees are alive, animals are alive, forests are alive, clouds and water, these things are a part of our life because we are a part of the same planet, the same biosphere. The same, one. We are part of the same circle, all of us, all of mainstream society, all of non-mainstream society, the lunatic fringe, everything. We must (certainly we can) begin to recognize this, what I'll call a fundamental fact, that we are a part of that circle. There is only one earth. There is only one community, the community of the earth.

Now, how do we do this? People sometimes ask me, "Well, it sounds great for you Indians to have done, your people did that, that's great, but how can we? We're talking about the modern world here!" Native people have no monopoly on being able to relate to the earth, to creation. All people and cultures have an ability to live as bonded communities with the earth. Traditional native practices for maintaining a relationship with the earth, with resources developed over centuries, over thousands of generations of our time, of our life, as members of a community within a community. As a modern society, we must begin to see the land and resources as vital to our life, and incorporate a land ethic into our modern culture. ...

Well, how to incorporate such a concept into modern resource use practices is another issue altogether. To say we have to live it, is easier said than done, but certainly it's possible. We have the ability, we have all had the ability. We have all used that ability to sustain our historic cultures. Wherever we are on this planet there has been that kind of relationship. What has happened for all of us in some way or another, is that we've lost that, we've lost that connection. We've lost that belief that a tree can be a living thing. A tree can hurt. ...

The earth that we all depend on for our survival, to sustain us, is still there waiting for us to come home. It only requires that we ask a question, that we ask her. She has the medicine, she has the knowledge, she has the food, she has the way to do this. She can teach us, we can learn from her. We can learn from each other. All we have to do is ask. And we will find ourselves sustaining our life into a future. A good future for our grandchildren.

R. Kapashesit and M. Klippenstein
"Aboriginal Group Rights and Environmental Protection"
(1991) vol. 36 *McGill Law Journal* 925, at 929-32

There is increasing interest in Aboriginal environmental perspectives ... . Care must be taken when attempting to generalize about the belief systems of hundreds of distinct Aboriginal groups in North America. However, Aboriginal environmental belief systems share a number of features which can be identified and considered. These include a lack of division between humans and the rest of the environment, a spiritual relationship with nature, concern about sustainability, attention to reciprocity and balance, and the idiom of respect and duty (rather than rights).

Aboriginal ethics do not share the European tendency to pose "nature" in distinct opposition to humans. There is no gulf between these two components of the world. ... Aboriginal belief systems have no counterpart to the admonition in Genesis to "fill the earth and subdue it, and have dominion over ... every living thing." In a world in which humans are seamlessly related to other animals and things, such an injunction would seem almost incomprehensible.

Aboriginal environmental values, unlike Western values, ascribe an important spiritual role to nature. In addition, since Aboriginal people rarely distinguish between their religious and secular life, every aspect of life includes a spiritual dimension. There is never a sense of disconnectedness from the earth as its sacredness is lived consciously and completely at all times.

A long term view of ecological stability, or what might be called a concern for sustainability, is to native communities an obviously central and necessary part of any attitude toward their surroundings. Emigration and technological "fixes" have not been viable alternatives. ... The need for reciprocity and balance is also a common feature of Aboriginal environmental ethics. ...

Finally, an Aboriginal's relationship to others is considered in a context of respect and duty, rather than in a model of claims and rights. ... For Aboriginal peoples, the clash of opposing rights misses the subtleties that the principles of respect and duty bring, whether speaking of humans or animals. Respect and duty are flexible principles that situate the "right" in a context of a relationship or many relationships, and cannot be abstracted from the nature of those relationships. The context of respect and duty will also foster a sense of humility, rather than assertiveness, in recognition of the fact that the individual occupies a part of a large and supportive web.

We believe that the principles that characterize Aboriginal environmental ethics are fundamentally conducive to protection of the environment. It is for that reason that the central aspect of our argument is that acknowledging and reinforcing the practice of these environmental ethics by Aboriginal communities is in itself desirable.

It is not feasible to borrow Aboriginal environmental ethics and graft these onto non-Aboriginal cultures because Aboriginal cultures are embedded in a particular context where the impact and meaning of a tradition stems from life-long conditioning, preparation, and participation. Aboriginal cultures are built into language, into the way day-to-day life is lived, and it is found within a specific physical/social context. However, while non-Aboriginals cannot adopt an Aboriginal world view, they can look to this world view for inspiration, and for a reminder that positive relationships with the environment can and do exist.

NOTES AND QUESTIONS

1. Do you agree with Kapashesit and Klippenstein, above, that recognition of aboriginal rights as "group rights" will make a substantial difference in ecological management? A number of First Nations have entered into comprehensive land claims and self-government agreements with Canadian governments that require direct community participation in managing resources and environmental protection. Is self-government the most effective means for integrating traditional values and knowledge into decisions affecting health and the environment? What mechanisms are available for communities without such agreements?

2. Alcoze, above, and Kapashesit and Klippenstein, above, disagree that aboriginal environmental values can be adopted by non-aboriginal societies as a means to ecological management. Are there lessons from the aboriginal world view that can be brought into non-aboriginal systems? Could "ecosystemic integrity" be incorporated into non-aboriginal

environmental impact assessments schemes? See *Nunavut Land Claims Agreement* (Ottawa: Indian and Northern Affairs Canada, 1993), article 12.

3. For a discussion of resource development projects that attempt to bridge the gap between aboriginal and eurocentric culture in Canada, see P. Charest, "Aboriginal Alternatives to Megaprojects and Their Environmental and Social Impacts" (1995) vol. 13 *Impact Assessment* 371. Also see "Aboriginal Peoples and Resource Development: Conflict or Cooperation?" (1991) vol. 18, no. 2 *Alternatives* 1; H. Bombay, "Many Things to Many People: Aboriginal Forestry in Canada Is Looking Toward Balanced Solutions" (Spring 1993) *Cultural Survival Quarterly* 15. A review of co-management efforts in different parts of Canada and a discussion of their role in the future is found in Canada, Royal Commission on Aboriginal Peoples, *Report: Restructuring the Relationship*, vol. 2 (Ottawa: Supply and Services Canada, 1996), chapter 4 and appendix 4B. Also see G. Poelzer, "Aboriginal Peoples and Environmental Policy in Canada: No Longer at the Margins," in D.L. VanNijnatten and R. Boardman, *Canadian Environmental Policy: Context and Cases*, 2d ed. (Don Mills, ON: Oxford University Press, 2002).

4. The Report of the Royal Commission on Aboriginal Peoples takes note of many environmental problems and their effects on Canada's aboriginal communities: "What we heard in public hearings regarding environmental degradation was like an extended lament, a refrain of loss and fear" (Canada, Royal Commission on Aboriginal Peoples, *Report: Gathering Strength*, vol. 3 (Ottawa: Supply and Services Canada, 1996), at 18). They describe three types of effects of environmental degradation on the health and well-being of aboriginal peoples: negative physical health consequences, reduction in the amount and quality of traditional foods and medicines, and an "assault" on mental and spiritual health from the "erosion of ways of life dependent on the purity of the land, water, flora and fauna" (ibid). The commission also makes extensive recommendations regarding changes to land and resource management; see vol. 2, chapters 3 and 4 and vol. 4, chapter 6.

B. Ecocentrism: Deep Ecology

Deep ecology is a movement that both critiques the approach and philosophical underpinnings of mainstream or "shallow" environmentalism and proposes an alternative. The term originated with Arne Naess in an article written in 1973 where he set out a "deeper, more spiritual approach to nature." Deep ecology challenges the dominant world view whose elements include human separation from and domination of nature, the superiority of humans over other species, economic growth as the appropriate measure of well-being, consumerism, centralized control, and a belief in high-tech solutions. The deep ecology world view emphasizes the equality of species and the inherent value of all life, simple means, quality of life, appropriate technology, limits on resources, and decentralized (community or bioregional) control and governance.

A shift in world view is necessary to bring about profound change in human destruction of nature. Thus, deep ecology emphasizes this shift in individual consciousness and direct personal actions as the instruments of change. Such an approach largely excludes legal "solutions" to environmental problems as well as traditional political actions of, for example, lobbying or participation in elections.

C. Giagnocavo and H. Goldstein
"Law Reform or World Re-form: The Problem of Environmental Rights"
(1990) vol. 35 *McGill Law Journal* 345, at 375-76, 378, and 381

Deep Ecology: Re-forming the Roots

The teleological and ontological impoverishment of legislative approaches to our world crisis underlines the important role which a fundamental reconsideration of being and value must play in any attempt to realize significant world reform. The enactment of legislation creating *rights* for the natural environment can at best do very little, and even then at a very high cost. One has to consider the institutional backdrop against which such rights are created, in order to gauge the efficacy of a rights regime. Only after we have uncovered and analyzed the larger world view upon which such rights are created, will we be in a position to evaluate the soundness of environmental rights.

According to Paul Emond a development oriented world-view is the source of legal attempts at environmental protection. As Emond states, environmental protection laws are premised on the "[assumption] that society has the *right* to develop, exploit and control the environment, subject only to the *restrictions* and *regulations* that are imposed on the most unacceptable activity." If, as Emond suggests, the telos behind legislative attempts at environmental protection is one whose primary concern is still material prosperity, the ability of environmental rights to protect our battered planet will be severely hampered.

One of the most disheartening turn of events in regard to the growth and development of the modern environmental movement has been the extent to which its adherents have remained faithful to technocratic approaches (such as environmental rights) to our world crisis. These so-called "shallow ecologists," who make up the bulk of the environmental movement, are not so much concerned with changing the ends which we as a culture pursue, as with changing the environmentally insensitive means by which we intend to attain those ends. Given their basically uncritical acceptance of our existing institutional framework and its accompanying values, such mainstream environmentalists primarily focus on technological solutions rather than on defining and addressing the underlying problem.

By virtue of their failure to address the teleological dimensions of our environmental crisis, mainstream environmentalists remain implicitly supportive of the status quo. Instead of becoming involved in a "process of ever-deeper questioning of ourselves, the assumptions of the dominant world-view in our culture, and the meaning and truth of our reality," shallow environmentalists prefer to labour in their laboratories and legislatures in the hope they will discover a new miracle cure. But miracle cures are impossible when it is precisely this kind of belief in fantastic techniques that produces the disease. What is needed is not a new potion or elixir that would merely mask the symptoms of our ailment, but a therapy designed to deal with the *causes* of our imminent demise. Deep ecology grew out of a desire to deal with the roots of our environmental crisis rather than with its rotting fruit.

Deep ecology, when it speaks of the rights of all living things, is not envisioning a courtroom full of advocates litigating on behalf of beavers, trees, and other mistreated forms of life. Neither is it attempting to formulate an ethic(s) which would allow us to ascertain in each "hard-case" conflict whose interest (between the human and non-human) is more vital. Instead, deep ecology offers us an alternative picture of ontology, one which emphasizes the constitutive role which other beings have for our being. This, coupled with the principles of biospherical egalitarianism, forms a different kind of environmental philosophy unlike the "vapid environmentalism" alluded to earlier. Deep ecology does not look to technological or legal innovation as the antidote to environmental degradation. Its focus is not outward, but inward, in the belief that only by changing ourselves (and our notion of "us"), can we hope to change the world.

Deep ecology does not lend itself to blueprints for action, instead it invites us to reconsider ourselves and the world and how the two are inter-related, and then to act in a manner faithful to those personal insights. This may result in starting an organic garden, or it may lead to heavily insulating one's home, shunning factory farmed products or participating in grassroots political protest and action; no party line has to be followed. What is shared, however, is a metaphysic which sees all of life, not just persons, as having import and a goal of creating a world in which that life can flourish. In addition, more pragmatically, deep ecologists also share an aversion to legislative or technological panaceas. Since they see the roots of the "environmental problem" as running very deep, they are averse to any attempt to merely doctor the visible blight. Significant activism for the ecologist requires actions that not only temporarily maximize environmental utility, but that also contribute to changing our cultural consciousness and the forms of life (of lifestyles) we practice.

Deep ecology's critique of shallow ecological incrementalism is centered upon the insight that superficial institutional reform cannot re-form the world. Environmental rights legislation might buy technocrats some time, or win politicians an election, but it cannot sufficiently change our consciousness. As a result a new approach to re-forming our world is needed. Deep ecology claims to be that approach, an approach to world re-form that begins at our metaphysical roots.

NOTES AND QUESTIONS

1. Deep ecologists are deeply critical of present environmental politics and urge instead a transformation of individual consciousness. How can this transformation be catalyzed throughout society? Presumably this will take time to occur; if one believes that we are in an environmental crisis, can we afford to wait? What actions that are consistent with deep ecological consciousness should be taken in the interim?

2. For a discussion of the principles of deep ecology, see B. Devall and G. Sessions, *Deep Ecology: Living as if Nature Mattered* (Salt Lake City: Gibbs M. Smith, 1985) and B. Devall, *Simple in Means, Rich in Ends* (Salt Lake City: Gibbs M. Smith, 1989).

3. Even though most deep ecology theorists are not concerned with law reform, it has been argued that their vision has influenced the direction of environmental law. For a detailed account of the impact deep ecological thinking has had on US environmental

policy, see P.F. Cramer, *Deep Environmental Politics: The Role of Radical Environmentalism in Crafting American Environmental Policy* (Westport, CT: Praeger, 1998).

4. Deep ecology has been criticized as being, among other things, naive, puritanical, reactionary, anti-democratic, intolerant, and tending toward "eco-fascism." Although it is one of a number of theories that critique modernism, because deep ecology makes claims to universal truths about human relationships with nature, it is not in line with much postmodern thinking. Some of the strongest criticism of deep ecology comes from the "social ecologists" who attribute environmental problems not to anthropocentrism per se but to the hierarchical social structures that allow some humans to dominate other humans and destroy nature. For a comprehensive discussion of the complex literature, see M.E. Zimmerman, *Contesting Earth's Future: Radical Ecology and Postmodernity* (Berkeley, CA: University of California Press, 1994).

5. Another branch of ecocentric philosophy that shares the critique of anthropocentrism is that of animal rights. Within this branch, there are divergent views on how best to improve the status of non-human animals. Some argue for the recognition of legal rights equivalent to personhood for animals, and for the abolition of animals as objects of property. Others argue for the legal protection of animals from mistreatment without necessarily supporting "rights" for them or a particular type of legal status. See S.M. Wise, *Rattling the Cage: Toward Legal Rights for Animals* (Cambridge, MA: Perseus Books, 2000) and T. Regan, *The Case for Animal Rights* (Berkeley, CA: University of California Press, 1983). What characteristic, if any, do non-human animals lack that humans possess? See also the discussion in chapter 11.

6. There has been a schism between the animal rights and environmental movements, because "one believes in the inherent value and equality of the individual [animal], while the other believes in the superiority of the whole": H. Guither, *Animal Rights: History and Scope of a Radical Social Movement* (Carbondale, IL: Southern Illinois University Press, 1998), at 131. However, some writers do not see them as inherently incompatible because they share a common belief in the ethical standing of non-human life; see G.E. Varner, *In Nature's Interests? Interests, Animal Rights and Environmental Ethics* (New York: Oxford University Press, 1998). What are the implications of animal rights for specific policy decisions such as endangered species protection or biotechnology?

C. Ecofeminism

Y. King
"The Ecology of Feminism and the Feminism of Ecology"
in J. Plant, ed., *Healing the Wounds: The Promise of Ecofeminism*
(Toronto: Between the Lines, 1989), at 20-25

In the project of building Western industrial civilization, nature became something to be dominated, overcome, made to serve the needs of men. She was stripped of her magical powers and properties and was reduced to "natural resources" to be exploited by human beings to fulfill human needs and purposes which were defined in opposition to nature. ... A dualistic Christianity had become ascendant with the earlier demise of old goddess religions, paganism, and animistic belief systems. With the disen-chantment of nature came the conditions for unchecked scientific exploration and technological exploitation. We bear the consequences today of beliefs in unlimited control over nature and in science's ability to solve any problem, as nuclear power plants are built without provisions for waste disposal, and satellites are sent into space without provision for retrieval.

In this way, nature became "other," something essentially different from the domi-nant, to be objectified and subordinated. Women, who are identified with nature, have been similarly objectified and subordinated in patriarchal society. Women and nature, in this sense, are the original "others." The recognition of the connections between women and nature and of woman's bridge-like position between nature and culture poses three possible directions for feminism. One direction is the integration of women into the world of culture and production by severing the woman-nature connection. This position does not question nature-culture dualism itself, and it is the position taken by most socialist-feminists. ...

Other feminists have reinforced the woman-nature connection: woman and nature, the spiritual and intuitive, versus man and the culture of patriarchal rationality. This position also does not necessarily question nature-culture dualism or recognize that women's ecological sensitivity and life orientation is a socialized perspective that could be socialized right out of us depending on our day-to-day lives. There is no reason to believe that women placed in positions of patriarchal power will act any differently from men, or that we can bring about a feminist revolution without con-sciously understanding history and without confronting the existing economic and political power structures.

Ecofeminism suggests a third direction: a recognition that although the nature-culture dualism is a product of culture, we can nonetheless *consciously choose* not to sever the woman-nature connection by joining male culture. Rather, we can use it as a vantage point for creating a different kind of culture and politics that would inte-grate intuitive, spiritual, and rational forms of knowledge, embracing both science and magic insofar as they enable us to transform the nature-culture distinction and to envision and create a free, ecological society.

The goals of harmonizing humanity and nonhuman nature, at both the experiential and theoretical levels, cannot be attained without the radical vision and understand-ing available from feminism. The twin concerns of ecofeminism—human liberation and our relationship to nonhuman nature—open the way to developing a set of ethics required for decision-making about technology. Technology signifies the tools that human beings use to interact with nature, including everything from the digging stick to nuclear bombs.

Few peoples of the earth have not had their lives touched and changed to some degree by the technology of industrialization. Ecofeminism as a social movement resists this social simplification through supporting the rich diversity of women the world over, and seeking a oneness in that diversity. Politically, ecofeminism opposes the ways that differences can separate women from each other, through the oppres-sions of class, privilege, sexuality, and race.

The special message of ecofeminism is that when women suffer through both social domination and the domination of nature, most of life on this planet suffers and is threatened as well. It is significant that feminism and ecology as social movements have emerged now, as nature's revolt against domination plays itself out in human history and in nonhuman nature at the same time. As we face slow environmental poisoning and the resulting environmental simplification, or the possible unleashing of our nuclear arsenals, we can hope that the prospect of the extinction of life on the planet will provide a universal impetus to social change. Ecofeminism supports utopian visions of harmonious, diverse, decentralized communities, using only those technologies based on ecological principles, as the only practical solution for the continuation of life on earth.

S. Prentice
"Taking Sides: What's Wrong with Eco-Feminism?"
(Spring 1988) *Women and Environments* 9

My criticism of eco-feminism is three-fold. It is flawed because it is idealist, not in the sense of "visionary" or "utopian," because I think those are fine and sustaining characteristics, but "idealist" in the sense that it assumes women and men to have an essential human nature that transcends culture and socialization. And further, that in that transcendence, women have a privileged position. The epistemological assumption of eco-feminism, based on its analysis of human nature, is that men "think wrong" and make women and the planet suffer accordingly.

In simple terms, this is a feminist assertion that "biology is destiny." This means that domination (and its attendant dualism and oppression) is basic to men, and can never be overcome—making men, in an ultimate sense, toxic to all living things. A corollary assumption to the biology-is-destiny argument is that women are always attuned to the planet, and always good for it. In strategic terms, this would seem to mean that whatever women initiate is healthy and good. Men may be tainted by biology, but women are blessed by it.

Eco-feminism trivializes several centuries of history, economics and politics by simply glancing over the formidable obstacles of social structures. Eco-feminism's idealism allows it to wish social structures away. By locating the origin of the domination of women and nature in male consciousness, eco-feminism makes political and economic systems simply derivative of male thinking, a by-product of idealism. There is an internal logic to capitalism—for example, its relations and forces of production, commodity fetishism, exploitation, domination, alienation, etc.—that makes exploiting nature a *sensible* thing for capitalism as a world-system to do. This is no mere failure or stunting of consciousness: it is consciousness directed and organized for a different end.

The trivialization of the socio-political in eco-feminism is a major weakness. Capitalism is never seriously tackled by eco-feminists as a process with its own particular history, logic and struggle. Because eco-feminism lacks this analysis, it cannot develop an effective strategy for change.

A completely unintended, but not altogether surprising, consequence of eco-feminism is that it is reactionary. I believe it actually sets the feminist movement back a good 15 years. ...

Eco-feminism is also reactionary because its standpoint is very privileged. For the millions of women who feel their oppression directly as survivors of imperialism, racism, and poverty, an analysis which first wants to "change male thinking" and reflect upon "women's special relationship to nature" is completely useless—even if, in the longest run, they might reap some benefit from it.

As a distinct epistemology, ontology and (sometimes) praxis, eco-feminism should disappear. No effort should be put into "improving," "refining" or "exploring" it.

Instead, the truly useful insight of eco-feminism should be saved. The awareness of the inter-connectedness of human, global, and planetary life should be incorporated into a politic and practice that can challenge multiple systems of domination and oppression, in an analysis that tackles (among others) class, gender and racism alongside environmental destruction.

E.L. Hughes
"Fishwives and Other Tails: Ecofeminism and Environmental Law"
(1995) vol. 8, no. 2 *Canadian Journal of Women and the Law* 502, at 516

I have a strong sense that what feminists have learned about violence against women (and the laws' response to it) is reflected in our societal attitudes toward nature. Why don't police always pursue an aggressive charging policy against batterers? Why don't government officials always prosecute polluters? Why is rape without physical injury not as bad (legally) as rape with it? Why is a sub-lethal dosage of a toxic chemical licensed and an acutely lethal concentration banned? Why is it "worse" when a little girl gets physically or sexually abused than when a prostitute does? Why is it worse when baby seals die than when mosquitoes do?

Every ecosystem that has violence visited upon it, regardless of the "type" of violence, has similar responses. Whether the ecosystem is the victim of toxic contamination, resource removal, or climate change, the impacts on it are similar: loss of biodiversity, loss of (re)productive capacity, ecosystem instability, altered microclimates. Yet our laws regulate, rather than prohibit, this environmental damage, just as they engage in the social regulation (not prohibition) of the degree of violence against women. Meanwhile, both environmentalism and feminism are trivialized; we're just a bunch of crazy radicals! Who is threatened by the environmental and women's movements? Who won't take it seriously? Who benefits? Is it an accident?

Even more importantly, we need to ask how we can change all this, and what we can change it into … .

How can we use ecofeminist principles to re-envision the framework of laws like this? My approach has been to try to imagine a law in which nature is of central importance. Using the fisheries example, I have tried to put fish into a social position of substantive equality, where their interests are accorded no less importance than human interests (while recognizing that their well-being *is* in our best interests). While there is a danger of anthropomorphism here, I have tried to avoid this by framing the law on the basis of human *responsibility* to nature, not by looking at nature's "rights." In other words, I have tried to draft a model law in which we are required to realize that fish *do* count, and which makes people both individually and collectively responsible for behaviour that treats fish as a "lesser other." ...

I have also tried, ... to incorporate into law some of the ecofeminist principles of kinship, interconnection, cyclic patterns, use of emotion, and responsibility. To do this, I found it necessary to build in a great deal more participatory democracy, risk-aversiveness, environmental reclamation, and accountability than one ever finds in existing environmental law.

NOTES AND QUESTIONS

1. Ecofeminism is explored in a number of collections. These include J. Plant, ed., *Healing the Wounds: The Promise of Ecofeminism* (Toronto: Between the Lines, 1989); K.J. Warren, ed., *Ecological Feminism: Special Issue of Hypatia* (Bloomington, IN: Indiana University Press, 1991); I. Diamond and G. Feman Orenstein, eds., *Re-Weaving the World: The Emergence of Ecofeminism* (San Francisco: Sierra Club Books, 1990); J. Biehl, *Finding Our Way: Rethinking Ecofeminist Politics* (Montreal: Black Rose Books, 1991); J. Seager, *Earth Follies: Coming to Terms with the Global Environmental Crisis* (New York: Routledge, 1993); M. Mies and V. Shiva, *Ecofeminism* (Halifax: Fernwood Publishing, 1993); and M. Wyman, *Sweeping the Earth: Women Taking Action for a Healthy Planet* (Charlottetown: Gynergy Books, 1999).

2. As ecofeminism has evolved, several different strands have become evident, sometimes divided into "spiritual" or "cultural" ecofeminism and "political" or "socialist" ecofeminism. One significant difference between these strands is how social change is effected. Cultural or spiritual ecofeminists tend to focus on the need for personal, spiritual transformation, while socialist or political ecofeminists tend to focus on the need for changes in social structures and material circumstances. M. Mellor explores these differences and the potential for common ground in detail in her book *Feminism and Ecology* (New York: New York University Press, 1997).

3. How can the insights of ecofeminism be harnessed in the political effort to transform the environment? Do you agree with Hughes, above, that ecofeminism can form the foundation for environmental law?

4. For a discussion of a number of intersecting perspectives, see A. Salleh, "Class, Race and Gender Discourse in the Ecofeminism/Deep Ecology Debate" (1993) vol. 14 *Environmental Ethics* 227.

D. Environmental Justice

R.D. Bullard
"Anatomy of Environmental Racism and the Environmental Justice Movement"
in R.D. Bullard, ed., *Confronting Environmental Racism: Voices from the Grassroots* (Boston: South End Press, 1993), 15, at 21-23

Whether at home or abroad, the question of who *pays* and who *benefits* from current industrial and development policies is central to any analysis of environmental racism.

In the United States, race interacts with class to create special environmental and health vulnerabilities. People of color, however, face elevated toxic exposure levels even when social class variables (income, education, and occupational status) are held constant. Race has been found to be an independent factor, not reducible to class, in predicting the distribution of: 1) air pollution in our society; 2) contaminated fish consumption; 3) the location of municipal landfills and incinerators; 4) the location of abandoned toxic waste dumps; and 5) lead poisoning in children. ...

One reason for this is that African Americans and whites do not have the same opportunities to "vote with their feet" by leaving unhealthy physical environments. The ability of an individual to escape a health-threatening environment is usually correlated with income. However, racial barriers make it even harder for millions of African Americans, Latinos, Asians, Pacific Islanders, and Native Americans to relocate. ... White racism helped create our current separate and unequal communities. It defines the boundaries of the urban ghetto, *barrio*, and reservation, and influences the provision of environmental protection and other public services. Apartheid-type housing and development policies reduce neighborhood options, limit mobility, diminish job opportunities, and decrease environmental choices for millions of Americans. It is unlikely that this nation will ever achieve lasting solutions to its environmental problems unless it also addresses the system of racial injustice that helps sustain the existence of powerless communities forced to bear disproportionate environmental costs.

· · ·

Not surprisingly, mainstream [environmental] groups were slow in broadening their base to include poor and working-class whites, let alone African Americans and other people of color. Moreover, they were ill-equipped to deal with the environmental, economic, and social concerns of these communities. During the 1960s and 1970s, while the "Big Ten" environmental groups focused on wilderness preservation and conservation through litigation, political lobbying, and technical evaluation, activists of color were engaged in mass direct action mobilizations for basic civil rights in the areas of employment, housing, education, and health care. Thus, two parallel and sometimes conflicting movements emerged, and it has taken nearly two decades for any significant convergence to occur between these two efforts. In fact, conflicts still remain over how the two groups should balance economic development, social justice, and environmental protection. ...

The crux of the problem is that the mainstream environmental movement has not sufficiently addressed the fact that social inequality and imbalances of social power are at the heart of environmental degradation, resource depletion, pollution, and even overpopulation. The environmental crisis can simply not be solved effectively without social justice.

L.W. Cole
"Foreword: A Jeremiad on Environmental Justice and the Law"
(1995) vol. 14 *Stanford Environmental Law Journal* ix, at ix-xi and xviii

The concept of environmental justice has finally taken hold of the legal profession; whether this is a positive development has yet to be seen. The signs of the interest and involvement of the legal profession are many: lawyers and law students have produced an ever-growing number of lawsuits, administrative complaints, symposia, classes, and articles on environmental justice during the past three years. Even the American Bar Association has weighed in, passing a resolution on environmental justice at its 1993 annual meeting.

Community groups, environmental and civil rights organizations, and private attorneys have filed dozens of lawsuits in community struggles for environmental justice in the last five years. ... The legal struggle has moved beyond the courtroom as well. In the past fifteen months, more than twenty administrative complaints alleging environmental racism have been filed with the US Environmental Protection Agency under Title VI of the *Civil Rights Act of 1964*, with more being filed each month. ... The interest in environmental justice is not limited to practitioners; in fact, there may be greater interest in law schools than anywhere else. ... Legal scholars were prominently silent on the topic of environmental justice for some two decades while activists, journalists, and social scientists documented and fostered the movement. Now, though, that silence has ended and a veritable blizzard of articles has resulted. ...

Amidst all this activity, however, exist some significant pitfalls. The environmental justice movement is in danger of being overwhelmed by the attention of its "friends." Legal strategies themselves can be dangerous for community groups, and the rise of legal institution-building in the environmental justice arena threatens to displace ongoing community organizing efforts and to prevent new ones from beginning.

· · ·

The law is dangerous to social movements because it is a cocooning and self-referential game in which its players believe they are important simply because they are playing—whether or not they are losing or winning. Certainly there is a role for law and lawyers in any social movement, and one measure of a movement's success is the codification of its goals ... . But without a broad social movement to back up those laws, to insist on their enforcement, to push for their strengthening, to defend against the evisceration, the laws mean little. As we have learned by watching the traditional environmental movement do its work in Washington, we who live by the pen can die by the pen: if our "victories" are won in back room deals in Congress, or in court, then so can they be lost in the next back room bargaining session, or in the next lawsuit.

· · ·

Too much of the focus of the traditional environmental movement has been on the law and legal tools; this misapplication of resources threatens to infect the environmental justice movement as well. All of the jumping on the environmental justice bandwagon by legal groups and academics threatens to break the wagon's wheels—

or redirect the wagon in the wrong direction. For the environmental justice movement to stay vibrant, oppositional, creative, and strong, it must reject the self-reinforcing tendency to use a legal strategy as its primary strategy. Instead of looking to the law, traditional environmental groups should use the grassroots, community-based and community-led environmental justice movement—which is broader in its goals and healthier as a *movement* than the traditional environmental movement—as a model.

As the Gulf Coast Tenants Organization reminds us, "lawyers are no better or worse than any other member of the movement, and should be judged by the same standards." We must always remember the slogan of the 1960s, that the movement needs "lawyers on tap, not lawyers on top."

NOTES AND QUESTIONS

1. What is the Canadian context for environmental justice? Is there evidence that people of colour, immigrants, or the poor bear a greater burden of environmental risk than the white middle class? What obstacles to empowerment exist?

2. Aboriginal communities in Canada have been disproportionately affected by many polluting activities and development projects. Health in communities dependent on fish or game for food has been in some cases severely affected. Examples include communities in the Great Lakes Basin, the Grassy Narrows, and White Dog communities in Ontario; the communities along the Churchill and Nelson Rivers in Manitoba; and Cree communities near James Bay. Many of these cases are documented in the work of the Royal Commission on Aboriginal Peoples, *Report of the Royal Commission on Aboriginal Peoples* (Ottawa: Supply and Services Canada, 1996), especially vol. 3, chapter 3. What opportunities and techniques are available to change this tragic legacy?

3. In the United States, President Clinton responded to the evidence of environmental racism by issuing an executive order that requires every federal agency to "make achieving environmental justice part of its mission by identifying and addressing, as appropriate, disproportionately high and adverse human health or environmental effects of its programs, policies, and activities on minority populations and low-income populations" (Executive Order 12898, February 11, 1994, s. 1-101) and by ensuring that their activities do not exclude persons from participation or discriminate against them on the basis of race, colour, or national origin. Agencies were also required to develop environmental justice strategies and a National Environmental Justice Advisory Council was established to oversee progress on the issue. Is such a national approach to environmental justice compatible with Cole's view, of the preferred approach, above?

4. There has been an explosion of academic writing on the issue of environmental justice in the United States in the last few years, but very little has been written in Canada. Several books are useful in providing a foundation: R.D. Bullard, ed., *Confronting Environmental Racism: Voices from the Grassroots* (Boston: South End Press, 1993); L. Westra and P.S. Wenz, *Facing Environmental Racism: Confronting Issues of Global Justice* (Lanham, MD: Rowman & Littlefield Publishers, 1995); D.E. Camacho, ed., *Environmental Injustices, Political Struggles: Race, Class and the Environment* (Durham, NC: Duke University Press, 1998); and L.W. Cole and S.R. Foster, *From the Ground Up: Environmental Racism and the Rise of the Environmental Justice Movement* (New York:

New York University Press, 2001). A good guide to the research and sources of information on environmental justice is found in C. Shanklin, "Pathfinder: Environmental Justice" (1997) vol. 24 *Ecology Law Quarterly* 333.

FURTHER READINGS

M.R. Chertow and D.C. Esty, eds., *Thinking Ecologically: The Next Generation of Environmental Policy* (New Haven, CT: Yale University Press, 1997).

E.A. Parson, ed., *Governing the Environment: Persistent Challenges, Uncertain Innovations* (Toronto: University of Toronto Press, 2001).